ATHENAZE

Oxford University Press

Oxford   New York   Toronto
Delhi   Bombay   Calcutta   Madras   Karachi
Petaling Jaya   Singapore   Hong Kong   Tokyo
Nairobi   Dar es Salaam   Cape Town
Melbourne   Auckland

and associated companies in
Berlin   Ibadan

Copyright © 1991 by Oxford University Press, Inc.

Published by Oxford University Press, Inc.,
198 Madison Avenue, New York, New York 10016-4314

Oxford is a registered trademark of Oxford University Press

Library of Congress Cataloging-in-Publication Data
(Revised for volume 2)
Balme, M. G.
Athenaze.
English and Ancient Greek. Includes index.
1. Greek language—Grammar—1950– .
2. Greek language—Readers. I. Lawall, Gilbert.
PA258.B325 1990   488.82′421   89-22967
ISBN 0-19-505621-3 (v. 1 : pbk.)
ISBN 0-19-506384-8 (teacher's handbook, v. 1)
ISBN 0-19-505622-1 (v. 2)
ISBN 0-19-506930-7 (teacher's handbook, v. 2)

9

Printed in the United States of America
on acid-free paper

ATHENAZE

An Introduction to Ancient Greek

Revised Edition
Book II

Maurice Balme
and
Gilbert Lawall

New York   Oxford
OXFORD UNIVERSITY PRESS
1991

CONTENTS

ATHENAZE

OVERVIEW OF THE GREEK VERB

This Overview of the Greek Verb will expand on the Preview of New Verb Forms in Book I, page 123. It will provide additional information that will help you begin to find your way around the chart on the following pages and give you a firm structure within which you can situate the new tenses, voices, and moods that you will study in the second half of this course.

You are not expected to learn all of the forms in the chart on the following pages right away. You might begin by locating the forms that were formally presented in Book I. In the upper left-hand box these are: (1) the present active indicative, (2) the imperfect active indicative, (3) the second person singular and plural present active imperatives, (4) the present active infinitive, and (5) the present active participle. In the middle left-hand box you will find the middle voice forms that you have learned that correspond to the active voice forms above: (1) the present middle indicative, (2) the imperfect middle indicative, (3) the second person singular and plural present middle imperatives, (4) the present middle infinitive, and (5) the present middle participle. In the third box from the left at the top you will find the first aorist active forms that you have learned: (1) the aorist active indicative, (2) the second person singular and plural aorist active imperatives, (3) the aorist active infinitive, and (4) the aorist active participle. In the box below you will find the corresponding middle voice forms that you have learned: (1) the aorist middle indicative, (2) the second person singular and plural aorist middle imperatives, (3) the aorist middle infinitive, and (4) the aorist middle participle.

In the Preview of New Verb Forms in Book I you learned that the letter σ is usually the sign of the future tense, and you will note in the first two boxes of the second column from the left that the future forms are exactly like the present forms except that they all have a σ before the ending.

You should be pleased to note that you have already learned approximately half of the verb forms on the chart!

You were introduced to the perfect active in the Preview of New Verb Forms, and you can locate it in the upper right-hand box in the chart on the following pages. It is easily recognized by reduplication at the beginning and the -κα suffix: λέ-λυ-κα. The forms and uses of the perfect and the kindred pluperfect will be formally presented in Chapters 27 and 28.

The chart on the following pages is divided into three horizontal registers: active voice (upper register), middle voice (middle register), and passive voice (lower register). A verb is said to be in the active voice if it fits into a sentence pattern such as "the Minotaur *eats* men" or "the Minotaur *runs*." In the middle voice, as you learned in Chapter 6, Grammar 1, the subject of the verb is thought of as acting *upon* itself, e.g., ἐγείρομαι "I wake (myself) up," or as acting *for* itself or *in its own interests*, e.g., λύομαι τὸν αἰχμάλωτον "I ransom the captive," i.e., I secure the release of the captive *for myself* or *in my own interests*. The passive voice, where the verb fits into a sentence pattern such as "Men *are eaten* by the Minotaur," will be treated in Chapters 23 and 24. You will find that in the present, imperfect, perfect, and pluperfect verbs have exactly the same forms for the middle and the passive and are distinguishable only by the context in which they are used. In the aorist and the future, however, there are distinct forms for the passive; these are given in the lower register on the following chart.

In the readings you have seen many verbs in the *indicative mood*, the form used to express statements and questions about reality or fact. You have also seen many verbs in the *imperative mood*, the form used to express commands. So far you have seen only second person imperatives, e.g., "Xanthias, (you) lift the stone!" or "Oxen, drag the plow!" Greek also has third person imperative forms, not addressed directly to the person who is to do the action but to someone else, e.g., "Let Xanthias do it!" "Let the oxen drag the plow!" You will find these forms on the chart on the following pages, and they will be formally presented in Chapter 31. In addition, you have seen *infinitives*, verb forms that are not limited (*-fin-* is from the Latin word *fīnis* that means "end" or "limit") by person or number and that fit into a sentence pattern such as "I am not able *to work*." You have also seen many participles or verbal adjectives that fit into sentence patterns such as the following: "The man *working* in the field lifted the stone." In Book II you will learn two new moods, the *subjunctive* and the *optative*. In main clauses these do not express simple statements or questions about reality or fact but instead fit into sentence patterns such as "What are we to do?" or "I wish I had my sight restored!" They are also used in various types of subordinate clauses. Subordinate clauses that require these moods will generally use the subjunctive if the verb of the main clause is in a primary tense (present, future, or perfect) and the optative if the verb of the main clause is in a secondary tense (imperfect, aorist, or pluperfect).

At first sight the chart on the following pages may seem overwhelming in its complexity. If, however, you have located the forms that you have already studied and seen where the forms you are yet to learn fit into the chart, you may have begun to realize that there are large and simple patterns of organization that are made clear by the chart. Once you learn the rules for the formation of the various blocks of verb forms, you will be able to recognize or make up any and all of the forms on the chart yourself if you know six basic forms of any given verb. These six forms are called the *principal parts,* and they are as follows:

present active	future active	aorist active
λύω	λύσω	ἔλῡσα
perfect active	perfect middle/passive	aorist passive
λέλυκα	λέλυμαι	ἐλύθην

The other forms are constructed as follows:

> The imperfect is constructed from the present stem: ἔ-λῡ-ον.
>
> The present, future, and aorist middle are constructed from the corre-
> sponding active stems: λῡ́-ομαι, λῡ́σ-ομαι, ἐ-λῡσ-άμην.
>
> The future passive is constructed from the aorist passive stem: λυθή-σομαι.

The principal parts of many verbs follow simple patterns, so that if you
know the first principal part (the present active indicative) you can construct
the remaining principal parts according to rules that are easy to learn.
Many verbs, however, follow complex linguistic patterns, so that their principal parts cannot all be predicted on the basis of easy rules. In some verbs the
stem appears in different forms in the different tenses; for example, in the
forms of the verb λῡ́ω given above you can see two slightly different stems, λῡ-
and λυ-. A knowledge of stems is useful, and where helpful they are given in
parentheses in the lists of principal parts that follow the reading passages in
this book. A few common verbs use linguistically unrelated stems to supply
missing forms, e.g., the verb αἱρέω does not have an aorist related to the stem
αἱρε- but instead uses the unrelated stem ἑλ- to supply the missing aorist.
The other principal parts of this verb are regular (except for ε instead of η in
the aorist passive):

αἱρέω   αἱρήσω   εἷλον   ᾕρηκα   ᾕρημαι   ᾑρέθην

For convenience grammarians say that the stems of this verb are αἱρε- and
ἑλ-. (Note that verbs such as this that begin with a vowel or diphthong have a
temporal augment instead of reduplication in the perfect tense. Verbs that begin with certain consonants or consonant clusters will also have temporal
augment instead of reduplication, e.g., σπεύδω, *perfect* ἔσπευσμαι.)

In Book I from Chapter 11 on we gave both the present and the aorist of
most verbs, and we included the aorist participle to show the unaugmented
aorist stem. In Book II we will give in the chapter vocabulary lists full sets of
principal parts for most verbs. (We will not give the principal parts of regular contract verbs that follow the patterns of the model contract verbs φιλέω,
τῑμάω, and δηλόω; for the principal parts of these model verbs and of simple
verbs that appear in the vocabulary lists compounded with prefixes, see the
Greek to English vocabulary list at the end of this book.) We will stop giving
the participles, but we will occasionally include other forms when they de-
serve special attention. Also, after the reading passages we will give full sets
of principal parts of important verbs, most of which you met in Book I. These
sets are arranged according to certain linguistic principles (see Reference
Grammar, paragraph 35) to help you see similarities among verbs and orga-
nize them into helpful groupings in your own mind. Seeing the similarities
and shared patterns will make it easier for you to learn the principal parts.

The chart on the following pages should be studied carefully with all the
points mentioned above in mind, and it should be consulted regularly in the
course of your reading and further study of verb forms in Book II.

THE CONJUGATION OF λύω, I LOOSEN

ACTIVE VOICE

	PRESENT	IMPERFECT	FUTURE	AORIST	PERFECT	PLUPERFECT
Indicative	λύω λύομεν	ἔλυον ἐλύομεν	λύσω λύσομεν	ἔλυσα ἐλύσαμεν	λέλυκα λελύκαμεν	ἐλελύκη ἐλελύκεμεν
	λύεις λύετε	ἔλυες ἐλύετε	λύσεις λύσετε	ἔλυσας ἐλύσατε	λέλυκας λελύκατε	ἐλελύκης ἐλελύκετε
	λύει λύουσι	ἔλυε ἔλυον	λύσει λύσουσι	ἔλυσε ἔλυσαν	λέλυκε λελύκασι	ἐλελύκει ἐλελύκεσαν
Subjunctive	λύω λύωμεν			λύσω λύσωμεν	λελυκὼς ὦ* λελυκότες ὦμεν	
	λύῃς λύητε			λύσῃς λύσητε	λελυκὼς ᾖς λελυκότες ἦτε	
	λύῃ λύωσι			λύσῃ λύσωσι	λελυκὼς ᾖ λελυκότες ὦσι	
Optative	λύοιμι λύοιμεν		λύσοιμι λύσοιμεν	λύσαιμι λύσαιμεν	λελυκὼς εἴην* λελυκότες εἴημεν	
	λύοις λύοιτε		λύσοις λύσοιτε	λύσαις* λύσαιτε	λελυκὼς εἴης λελυκότες εἴητε	
	λύοι λύοιεν		λύσοι λύσοιεν	λύσαι* λύσαιεν*	λελυκὼς εἴη λελυκότες εἴησαν	
Imperative	λῦε λύετε			λῦσον λύσατε	λελυκὼς ἴσθι λελυκότες ἔστε	
	λυέτω λυόντων			λυσάτω λυσάντων	λελυκὼς ἔστω λελυκότες ὄντων	
Infinitive	λύειν		λύσειν	λῦσαι	λελυκέναι	
Participle	λύων, λύουσα, λῦον		λύσων, λύσουσα, λῦσον	λύσᾱς, λύσᾱσα, λῦσαν	λελυκώς, -υῖα, -ός	

*See pages 162–163.   *See page 117.

(Middle/Passive)

	PRESENT	IMPERFECT	FUTURE	AORIST	PERFECT	PLUPERFECT
Indicative	λύομαι λῡόμεθα	ἐλῡόμην ἐλῡόμεθα	λύσομαι λῡσόμεθα	ἐλυσάμην ἐλῡσάμεθα	λέλυμαι λελύμεθα	ἐλελύμην ἐλελύμεθα
	λύῃ* λύεσθε	ἐλύου ἐλύεσθε	λύσῃ* λύσεσθε	ἐλύσω ἐλύσασθε	λέλυσαι λέλυσθε	ἐλέλυσο ἐλέλυσθε
	λύεται λύονται	ἐλύετο ἐλύοντο	λύσεται λύσονται	ἐλύσατο ἐλύσαντο	λέλυται λέλυνται	ἐλέλυτο ἐλέλυντο
Subjunctive	λύωμαι λῡώμεθα			λύσωμαι λῡσώμεθα	λελυμένος ὦ λελυμένοι ὦμεν	
	λύῃ λύησθε			λύσῃ λύσησθε	λελυμένος ᾖς λελυμένοι ἦτε	
	λύηται λύωνται			λύσηται λύσωνται	λελυμένος ᾖ λελυμένοι ὦσι	

*or λύει   *or λύσει

MIDDLE VOICE

	Present	Future	Aorist	Perfect
Optative	λῡοίμην λῡοίμεθα λύοιο λύοισθε λύοιτο λύοιντο	λῡσοίμην λῡσοίμεθα λύσοιο λύσοισθε λύσοιτο λύσοιντο	λῡσαίμην λῡσαίμεθα λύσαιο λύσαισθε λύσαιτο λύσαιντο	λελυμένος εἴην λελυμένοι εἴημεν λελυμένος εἴης λελυμένοι εἴητε λελυμένος εἴη λελυμένοι εἴησαν
Imperative	λύου λύεσθε λῡέσθω λῡέσθων		λῦσαι λύσασθε λῡσάσθω λῡσάσθων	λέλυσο λέλυσθε λελύσθω λελύσθων
Infinitive	λύεσθαι	λύσεσθαι	λύσασθαι	λελύσθαι
Participle	λῡόμενος, -η, -ον	λῡσόμενος, -η, -ον	λῡσάμενος, -η, -ον	λελυμένος, -η, -ον

PASSIVE VOICE

Present passive same as middle above

Imperfect passive same as middle above

	Future	Aorist
Indicative	λυθήσομαι λυθησόμεθα λυθήσῃ λυθήσεσθε λυθήσεται λυθήσονται	ἐλύθην ἐλύθημεν ἐλύθης ἐλύθητε ἐλύθη ἐλύθησαν
Subjunctive		λυθῶ λυθῶμεν λυθῇς λυθῆτε λυθῇ λυθῶσι
Optative	λυθησοίμην λυθησοίμεθα λυθήσοιο λυθήσοισθε λυθήσοιτο λυθήσοιντο	λυθείην λυθεῖμεν λυθείης λυθεῖτε λυθείη λυθεῖεν
Imperative		λύθητι λύθητε λυθήτω λυθέντων
Infinitive	λυθήσεσθαι	λυθῆναι
Participle	λυθησόμενος, -η, -ον	λυθείς, λυθεῖσα, λυθέν

Perfect passive same as middle above

Pluperfect passive same as middle above

17
Η ΕΠΙΔΑΥΡΟΣ (α)

"οἱ ἰᾱτροὶ κελεύουσί με παρὰ τὸν Ἀσκλήπιον ἰέναι· ἴσως γὰρ ὠφελήσει με ὁ θεός."

Vocabulary

Verbs

ἀπέχω, (*imperfect*) ἀπεῖχον,
ἀφέξω, ἀπέσχον,
ἀπέσχηκα, ἀπέσχημαι I am
distant (from + *gen.*); (*middle*)
I abstain from (+ *gen.*)

ἀφικνέομαι, ἀφίξομαι,
ἀφῑκόμην, ἀφῖγμαι I arrive,
arrive at (+ εἰς + *acc.*)

γιγνώσκω, γνώσομαι,
ἔγνων, ἔγνωκα, ἔγνωσμαι,
ἐγνώσθην I get to know,
learn

ἕπομαι, (*imperfect*) εἱπόμην,
ἕψομαι, ἑσπόμην (+ *dat.*) I
follow

οἶδα I know

πλέω, πλεύσομαι, ἔπλευσα,
πέπλευκα I sail

τυγχάνω, τεύξομαι, ἔτυχον,
τετύχηκα (+ *gen.*) I hit, hit
upon, get; (+ *participle*) I
happen to

Pronoun

ἔγωγε (*an emphatic* ἐγώ) I

Preposition

σύν (+ *dat.*) with

Adverbs

ἴσως perhaps

ποῖ; to what place? where to?

πρότερον formerly, before,
earlier, first

Conjunction

πότερον . . . ἤ (whether . . .) or

Expression

σὺν θεοῖς God willing, with
luck

ἐν δὲ τούτῳ ὁ Δικαιόπολις τῷ Φιλίππῳ ἡγούμενος ἐκ τῆς νεὼς
ἐξέβη καί, "ἄγε δή, ὦ παῖ," ἔφη, "τί δεῖ ποιεῖν; ἆρα βούλῃ οἰνοπώλιον
ζητῆσαι καὶ δεῖπνον ἑλέσθαι;" ὁ δέ, "μάλιστά γε, ὦ πάτερ. σὺ μὲν
οὖν ἡγοῦ, ἐγὼ δ' ἕψομαι." οἰνοπώλιον οὖν εὑρόντες ἐγγὺς τοῦ
λιμένος ἐκαθίζοντο οἶνόν τε πίνοντες καὶ τοῖς παροῦσι διαλεγόμενοι.   5
τῶν δὲ παρόντων γυνή τις τὸν Δικαιόπολιν ἤρετο ποῖ πορεύεται καὶ
μαθοῦσα ὅτι πρὸς τὴν Ἐπίδαυρον πορεύεται, "καὶ ἐγώ," ἔφη, "πρὸς
τὴν Ἐπίδαυρον πορεύομαι. νοσῶ γὰρ τὴν γαστέρα καὶ οὐδὲν
δύνανται ὠφελεῖν με οἱ ἰατροί· κελεύουσί μ' οὖν παρὰ τὸν
Ἀσκλήπιον ἰέναι· ἴσως γὰρ ὠφελήσει με ὁ θεός. ἀλλ' εἰπέ μοι, πότε   10
δὴ ἀποπλεύσεται ἡ ναῦς; πότερον τήμερον εἰς τὴν Ἐπίδαυρον
ἀφιξόμεθα ἢ οὔ;" ὁ δὲ Δικαιόπολις, "οὐκ οἶδα ἔγωγε· λέγουσι δὲ ὅτι
οὐ πολὺ ἀπέχει ἡ Ἐπίδαυρος. ἴσως οὖν ἀφιξόμεθα πρὸ τῆς νυκτὸς ἢ
καὶ πρότερον. ἀλλ' ἄκουε δή· δι' ὀλίγου γὰρ γνωσόμεθα· τοῦ γὰρ
ναυκλήρου ἀκούω ἡμᾶς καλοῦντος. ἆρ' οὐ ταχέως ἐπάνιμεν πρὸς   15
τὴν ναῦν;"

[οἰνοπώλιον wine-shop, inn   τὴν γαστέρα with respect to my stomach
τήμερον today   ἐπάνιμεν shall we return?]

ἀναστάντες οὖν πρὸς τὴν ναῦν ἔσπευδον. ὁ δὲ ναύκληρος ἰδὼν
αὐτοὺς προσιόντας, βοήσας, "εἴσβητε ταχέως," ἔφη, "εὐθὺς γὰρ
ὁρμησόμεθα· δεῖ γὰρ πρὸ τῆς νυκτὸς εἰς τὴν Ἐπίδαυρον ἀφικέσθαι."
ὁ δὲ Δικαιόπολις, "πότε δή," ἔφη, "ἐκεῖσε ἀφιξόμεθα;" ὁ δὲ   20
ναύκληρος, "οὐρίου γε ἀνέμου τυχόντες σὺν θεοῖς ταχέως
πλευσόμεθα καὶ πρὸς ἑσπέραν παρεσόμεθα. ἀλλὰ σπεύδετε· εὐθὺς
γὰρ λύσομεν τὴν ναῦν."

[προσιόντας approaching   οὐρίου favorable   παρεσόμεθα we will be there]

οἱ μὲν οὖν ταχέως εἰσέβησαν, οἱ δὲ ναῦται τὴν ναῦν λύσαντες καὶ
πρὸς τὴν θάλατταν προερέσαντες τὰ ἱστία ἦραν. ἄνεμος δὲ οὔριος   25
τὰ ἱστία ἔπλησεν ὥστε ἡ ναῦς ταχέως διὰ τῶν κυμάτων ἔτρεχεν.

[προερέσαντες rowing forward   ἦραν (from αἴρω) raised   ἔπλησεν filled]

Principal Parts: Stems in -υ- and -αυ-

λύω (λῡ-/λυ-), λύσω, ἔλῡσα, λέλυκα, λέλυμαι, ἐλύθην I loosen
δακρύω, δακρύσω, ἐδάκρυσα, δεδάκρῡκα, δεδάκρῡμαι (I am in tears)
   I cry, weep
παύω, παύσω, ἔπαυσα, πέπαυκα, πέπαυμαι, ἐπαύθην I stop; (middle,
   intransitive) I stop (+ participle), cease from (+ gen.)

Word Study

Explain the following English words with reference to their Greek roots, making clear the difference in meaning between 1, 2, and 4:

1. psychologist (ἡ ψῡχή = soul)   4. psychoanalyst
2. psychiatrist   5. psychic phenomena
3. analysis

Grammar

1. The Future Tense

Most verbs form the future tense by adding the infix -σ- and adding the same endings as in the present tense, e.g.:

Indicative	*Infinitive*	*Participle*
λΰ-σ-ω	λΰ-σ-ειν	λΰ-σ-ων,
λΰ-σ-εις		λΰ-σ-ουσα,
λΰ-σ-ει		λΰ-σ-ον
λΰ-σ-ομεν		
λΰ-σ-ετε		
λΰ-σ-ουσι(ν)		
λΰ-σ-ομαι	λΰ-σ-εσθαι	λῦ-σ-όμενος, -η, -ον
λΰ-σ-ῃ (-ει)		
λΰ-σ-εται		
λῦ-σ-όμεθα		
λΰ-σ-εσθε		
λΰ-σ-ονται		

There is no future imperative.

Note what happens when the stem of the verb ends in a consonant instead of a vowel (compare the similar formations of the first aorist of such verbs; see Book I, page 141):

a. If the stem ends in a *labial* (β, π, φ), the labial + σ coalesce to form ψ, e.g.:

βλάπτω (stem βλαβ-), (future) βλάψω, (aorist) ἔβλαψα
πέμπ-ω, (future) πέμψω, (aorist) ἔπεμψα
γράφ-ω, (future) γράψω, (aorist) ἔγραψα

b. If the stem ends in a *guttural* (γ, κ, χ), the combination with the σ of the future produces ξ, e.g.:

πρᾱ́ττω (stem πρᾱγ-), (future) πρᾱ́ξω, (aorist) ἔπρᾱξα
φυλάττω (stem φυλακ-), (future) φυλάξω, (aorist) ἐφύλαξα
δέχ-ομαι, (future) δέξομαι (aorist) ἐδεξάμην

c. If the stem ends in a *dental* (δ, ζ, θ, τ), the last consonant of the stem drops out before the σ of the future, e.g.:

δείδ-ω (I fear), (future) δείσω, (aorist) ἔδεισα
παρασκευάζ-ω, (future) παρασκευάσω, (aorist) παρεσκεύασα
πείθ-ω, (future) πείσω, (aorist) ἔπεισα
πάττω (I sprinkle; stem πατ-), (future) πάσω, (aorist) ἔπασα

Note, however, that if the stem ends in -ίζω, the future ends in -ιέ-ω (with the ε contracting with the personal endings as in the verb φιλέω), e.g.:

κομίζ-ω, (future) κομιῶ, (aorist) ἐκόμισα
ἐλπίζ-ω, (future) ἐλπιῶ, (aorist) ἤλπισα

d. If the stem ends in a *liquid* (λ, μ, ν, ρ), do not insert σ but add -ε to the stem and contract this with the personal endings. In other words, verbs with stems ending in a liquid have *contract futures* in which the endings are the same as those of φιλέω in the present tense, e.g.:

μέν-ω, (future) μενέ-ω > μενῶ, (aorist) ἔμεινα

For the aorist of liquid verbs, see Book I, page 149.

The present and future of liquid verbs are often distinguished only by the circumflex accent in the future. In some liquid verbs, however, the stem is shortened in the future, e.g.:

ἀγγέλλω, (future) ἀγγελῶ, (aorist) ἤγγειλα
φαίνομαι, (future) φανοῦμαι, (aorist) ἐφηνάμην
αἴρω, (future) ἀρῶ, (aorist) ἦρα

The verb μάχομαι also has a contract future:

μάχομαι, (future) μαχοῦμαι, (aorist) ἐμαχεσάμην

Contract verbs, with stems ending in -ε-, -α-, or -ο-, lengthen this final stem vowel and then add the σ for the future, e.g.:

φιλέ-ω, (future) φιλήσω, (aorist) ἐφίλησα
τῑμά-ω, (future) τῑμήσω, (aorist) ἐτῑμησα
δηλό-ω, (future) δηλώσω, (aorist) ἐδήλωσα

Some verbs, active in the present tense, have futures that are middle in form but active in meaning (i.e., deponent), e.g.:

ἀκούω, (future) ἀκούσομαι, (aorist) ἤκουσα
βαίνω, (future) βήσομαι, (second aorist) ἔβην
γιγνώσκω, (future) γνώσομαι, (second aorist) ἔγνων
κάμνω, (future) καμοῦμαι, (second aorist) ἔκαμον
πάσχω, (future) πείσομαι, (second aorist) ἔπαθον
πλέω, (future) πλεύσομαι, (first aorist) ἔπλευσα
τρέχω, (future) δραμοῦμαι, (second aorist) ἔδραμον
φεύγω, (future) φεύξομαι, (second aorist) ἔφυγον

A few verbs lengthen the ε of one form of their stem and add σ, e.g.:

μανθάνω (stems μαθ-, μαθε-), (future) μαθήσομαι, (second aorist)
    ἔμαθον
ἐθέλω (stems ἐθελ-, ἐθελε-), (future) ἐθελήσω, (first aorist) ἠθέλησα
γίγνομαι (stems γεν-, γενε-), (future) γενήσομαι, (second aorist)
    ἐγενόμην

The verb δύναμαι has future δυνήσομαι.

The future of εἰμί (ἐσ-) "I am" is deponent:

Indicative	Infinitive	Participle
ἔσομαι	ἔσεσθαι	ἐσόμενος, -η, -ον
ἔσῃ/ἔσει		
ἔσται		
ἐσόμεθα		
ἔσεσθε		
ἔσονται		

Exercise 17a

Give the first person singular future and aorist of the following verbs:

1. αἰτέω	6. νομίζω (I think)	11. σῴζω*
2. ἀναγκάζω	7. ὠφελέω	12. φυλάττω
3. ἄρχω (I begin, rule)	8. δουλόω (I enslave)	13. ἀποκρίνομαι
4. βλέπω	9. ζητέω	14. πιστεύω
5. νῑκάω	10. γράφω	15. νέμω (I distribute)

*no iota subscript in future

Exercise 17b

Give the corresponding future and aorist forms of the following:

1. πέμπει	6. ἀποκρίνεται	11. πράττουσι
2. λῡόμενοι	7. δηλοῦν	12. κομίζει
3. τῑμῶμεν	8. βοῶσι(ν)	13. βαίνειν
4. φιλεῖτε	9. γιγνώσκει	14. μανθάνετε
5. μένομεν	10. πλέομεν	15. βοᾷς

Exercise 17c

Read aloud and translate:

1. τί ποιήσεις, ὦ παῖ; πότερον οἴκαδε ἐπάνει (will you return) ἢ ἐνταῦθα
   μενεῖς;
2. πότε ἀφιξόμεθα εἰς τὸν λιμένα; ἆρα ταχέως ἐκεῖσε πλευσόμεθα;
3. οὗτος ὁ νεᾱνίᾱς ἐν τῷ ἀγῶνι νῑκήσει καὶ στέφανον (wreath) δέξεται.
4. πότερον ἐν τῷ ἄστει πᾶσαν τὴν ἡμέρᾱν μενεῖς ἢ οἴκαδε σπεύσεις;
5. δι' ὀλίγου μαθησόμεθα τί ἐγένετο.

6.   εἰς τὸ ἄστυ σπεύσομεν καὶ ἐν τῇ ἀγορᾷ ὑμᾶς μενοῦμεν.
7.   ὁ ἰατρὸς τὸν παῖδα πρὸς τὴν Ἐπίδαυρον πέμψει· ἴσως γὰρ ὠφελήσει αὐτὸν
      ὁ Ἀσκλήπιος.
8.   ταῦτα μαθὼν ὁ στρατηγὸς βοήθειαν (*help*) ἡμῖν εὐθὺς πέμψει.
9.   δύο ἡμέρᾱς ἐν τῇ νήσῳ σε μενοῦμεν.
10. οἴκαδε ἐπελθόντες γνώσεσθε τί πάσχουσιν αἱ γυναῖκες.

Exercise 17d

Translate into Greek:

1.   Stand up and work; for the master will soon be here.
2.   Will you not be silent, young man, and listen to the general?
3.   The merchants, who are sailing in that ship, will arrive at Corinth
      within three days.
4.   Perhaps we will arrive home before night.
5.   The doctor will not be able to help you but will tell you to go to
      Epidaurus.

Healing Sanctuaries: Asclepius and Epidaurus

Epidaurus; the fourth-century theater

According to legend, Asclepius was the son of Apollo, god of healing, and
a mortal girl, Coronis, who was unfaithful to him. Apollo sent his sister
Artemis to punish her with death, but, as she lay on the pyre and the flames
flickered around her body, Apollo snatched from her womb the unborn baby,
his son. He gave him to the wise old centaur Cheiron to bring up and told him
to teach the child to heal men of their sicknesses.

And all who came to him suffering from sores caused by nature, or whose
limbs were wounded by gray bronze or the far-flung stone, or whose
bodies were wasting from summer's heat or winter's cold, he freed from
their various pains and cured. Some he treated with soft incantations,
some with soothing medicines, on the limbs of others he put healing
ointments, and yet others he made straight with the surgeon's knife.

                                                   (Pindar, *Pythian* 3.82–93).

In the end Asclepius attempted to restore the dead to life, and Zeus in anger
struck him down with a thunderbolt.

In time the status of the mortal hero rose to reach that of a god, and shrines
were dedicated to him throughout Greece as the preserver of health and healer
of sickness, a god who loved mankind, their savior. Of all the sanctuaries of
Asclepius, the greatest was at Epidaurus. Here, in an undulating valley, sur-
rounded by mountains, was a site that had been holy from times
immemorial, sacred first to a local hero, then to Apollo, and finally to Apollo
and Asclepius. The cult of Asclepius seems to have arrived there early in the
fifth century, and by the end of the century the sanctuary was visited by
pilgrims from all over the Greek world.

Pilgrims arriving at the port and city of Epidaurus had a walk of five
miles to reach the sanctuary, through a deep ravine, cut by a stream, where
wild olive and plane trees and laurel abounded. They arrived at last at a
splendid entrance building resembling a temple, on the gates of which they
saw this inscription:

ἁγνὸν χρὴ νᾱοῖο θυώδεος ἐντὸς ἰόντα
ἔμμεναι· ἁγνείᾱ δ᾽ ἐστὶ φρονεῖν ὅσια.

He must be pure who enters the fragrant
    shrine; purity is thinking holy thoughts.

Most of the buildings of which the remains can be seen today were built in
the fourth century when the cult of Asclepius was at its height, but there would
have been humbler versions of the most important buildings there when
Philip visited the sanctuary. In the center stood the temple of Asclepius himself and close to it the ἄβατον, a long, narrow building in which patients seeking a cure had to sleep the night; opposite this was the θόλος, a round building
that was probably the home of the sacred serpents. To the west of the main
sanctuary lay the stadium, to the southeast the καταγώγιον, a large square
building, where the pilgrims stayed, and beyond this on the hillside the great
theater, for which Epidaurus is now most famous. Procession, choral dance,
and sacrifice took place throughout the year, and every four years there was a
great festival with athletic, dramatic, and musical competitions.

The procedure for consulting Asclepius was simple: patients first had to
purify themselves by ritual washing and to make an offering (often a honey-
cake). When night came they were conducted to the ἄβατον and waited for the
god to appear while they slept. A patient who had a visitation from Asclepius
described his experience as follows:

It was like seeming to touch him, a kind of awareness that he was there in person; one was between sleep and waking, one wanted to open one's eyes, and yet was anxious lest he should withdraw too soon; one listened and heard things, sometimes as in a dream, sometimes as in waking life; one's hair stood on end; one cried, and felt happy; one's heart swelled, but not with vainglory. What human being could put that experience into words? But anyone who has been through it will share my knowledge and recognize the state of mind. (Aelius Aristides, *Oration* 48.31ff., quoted by Dodds, *The Greeks and the Irrational,* page 113).

The walls of the temple were covered with tablets set up by grateful patients; the cure we ascribe to Philip is taken from one of these. Here is the record of another cure of blindness, set up by a patient who had been a sceptic:

Ambrosia of Athens, blind in one eye. She came as a suppliant to the god, but walking around the sanctuary, she scoffed at some of the cures as incredible and impossible, that the lame and blind should be made whole, merely by seeing a vision in their sleep. But she, in her sleep, saw a vision. It seemed to her that the god stood over her and announced that he would cure her but that, in payment, he would ask her to present to the sanctuary a pig made of silver as a reminder of her ignorance. After saying this, he cut open her diseased eye and poured in some drug. When day dawned, she went out cured. (Stele 1.33–41).

Many were sceptical of the whole business, like Cicero, who said: "Few patients owe their lives to Asclepius rather than Hippocrates." The reputation of the sanctuary, however, continued to attract pilgrims for hundreds of years, and it is impossible to believe that all the cures recorded by grateful patients were mere fictions.

The inscription
reads:

ΑΣΚΛΗ
ΠΙΩ
ΚΑΙ
ΥΓΕΙΑ
ΤΥΧΗ
ΕΥΧΑΡΙΣ
ΤΗΡΙΟΝ

To Ascle-
pius
and
Health
Tyche (dedicates this)
(as a) thank
offering

Votive offering for the cure of a leg

Η ΕΠΙΔΑΥΡΟΣ (β)

Vocabulary

Verbs

ἀκέομαι, ἀκοῦμαι, ἠκεσάμην
  I heal
ἐπιτρέπω, ἐπιτρέψω,
  ἐπέτρεψα, ἐπιτέτροφα,
  ἐπιτέτραμμαι, ἐπετράπην
  (+ dat.) I entrust
ἔρχομαι, εἶμι, (infinitive) ἰέναι,
  ἦλθον, ἐλήλυθα I go, come
  ἀπέρχομαι I go away
  εἰσέρχομαι (+ εἰς + acc.)
    I go in, come in
  ἐξέρχομαι (+ ἐκ + gen.)
    I go out of, come out of
  ἐπανέρχομαι I come
    back, return, return to
    (+ εἰς or πρός + acc.)
  παρέρχομαι I go past,
    come forward (to speak)
  προσέρχομαι (+ dat. or πρός
    + acc.) I approach
θαρρέω I am confident
  θάρρει. Cheer up! Don't be
  afraid!
φρονέω I think, am minded
χρή, (imperfect) ἔχρην it is
  necessary, one ought, must
  (+ infinitive or acc. and
  infinitive)

Nouns

ὁ ἱκέτης, τοῦ ἱκέτου
  suppliant
ὁ νόμος, τοῦ νόμου law, custom
τὸ τέμενος, τοῦ τεμένους
  sacred precinct
ὁ ὑπηρέτης, τοῦ ὑπηρέτου
  servant, attendant
ἡ ψυχή, τῆς ψυχῆς soul

Adjectives

ἱερός, -ά, -όν holy, sacred
καθαρός, -ά, -όν clean, pure
ὅσιος, -ᾱ, -ον holy, pious

Preposition

κατά (+ acc.) down, on,
  according to

Adverbs

ὀψέ late
πως (enclitic) somehow, in any
  way

Conjunction

ὡς (+ future participle) to . . .
  (expressing purpose)

Expression

οὐ διὰ πολλοῦ not much later,
  soon

Proper Name

τὸ Ἀσκληπιεῖον, τοῦ
  Ἀσκληπιείου the sanctuary
  of Asclepius

πλεύσαντες οὖν πᾶσαν τὴν ἡμέρᾱν, ὡς ἐγίγνετο ἡ ἑσπέρᾱ, εἰς τὴν
Ἐπίδαυρον ἀφίκοντο, οὐδὲν κακὸν παθόντες. ὡς δ' ἐξέβησαν εἰς τὴν
γῆν τῷ μὲν Δικαιοπόλει ἔδοξεν εὐθὺς πρὸς τὸ Ἀσκληπιεῖον ἰέναι· οὐ
γὰρ πολὺ ἀπεῖχεν· ἡ δὲ γυνὴ ἡ τὴν γαστέρα νοσοῦσα οὕτως ἔκαμνεν
ὥστε οὐκ ἤθελεν ἰέναι ἐκείνῃ τῇ ἡμέρᾳ ἀλλ' ἔμεινεν ἐν καταγωγίῳ τινὶ   5
ἐγγὺς τοῦ λιμένος. οἱ δὲ ὥρμησαν καὶ δι' ὀλίγου ἀφικόμενοι ηὗρον
τὰς πύλᾱς κεκλεισμένᾱς. ὁ οὖν Δικαιόπολις, "κεκλεισμέναι εἰσὶν αἱ
πύλαι," ἔφη, "τί οὖν δεῖ ποιεῖν; πότερον κόψω τὰς πύλᾱς ἢ εἰς τὸν

λιμένα ἐπάνιμεν; ὀψὲ γάρ ἐστιν." ὁ δὲ Φίλιππος, "ἀλλὰ κόψον, ὦ
πάτερ, εἰ δοκεῖ. ἴσως γὰρ ἀκούσεταί τις καὶ ἡγήσεται ἡμῖν παρὰ τὸν   10
ἱερέᾱ." ὁ μὲν οὖν Δικαιόπολις ἔκοψεν, ἐξελθὼν δὲ ὑπηρέτης τις οὐ
διὰ πολλοῦ, "τίς ὢν σύ," ἔφη, "κόπτεις τᾱς πύλᾱς τηνικαῦτα τῆς
ἡμέρᾱς; πόθεν ἤλθετε καὶ τί βουλόμενοι πάρεστε;" ὁ δὲ Δικαιόπολις,
"ἐγὼ μέν εἰμι Δικαιόπολις Ἀθηναῖος ὤν, τὸν δὲ παῖδα κομίζω, ἐάν πως
ὁ θεὸς ἐθέλῃ τοὺς ὀφθαλμοὺς αὐτῷ ἀκεῖσθαι. τυφλὸς γὰρ γέγονεν.   15
ἆρ' οὐχ ἡγήσῃ ἡμῖν παρὰ τὸν σὸν δεσπότην;"

[καταγωγίῳ inn   κεκλεισμένᾱς shut   τηνικαῦτα τῆς ἡμέρᾱς at this time of
day   ἐάν πως . . . ἐθέλῃ in the hope that . . . may be willing   γέγονεν has
become, is]

ὁ δὲ ὑπηρέτης, "ὀψέ ἐστιν, ἀλλ' ὅμως μείνατε ἐνταῦθα. ἐγὼ γὰρ
εἰμι ὡς ζητήσων τὸν δεσπότην καὶ ἐρωτήσω εἰ ἐθέλει ῡμᾱς δέξασθαι."
οἱ μὲν οὖν ἔμενον ἐπὶ ταῖς πύλαις· οὐ πολλῷ δ' ὕστερον ἐπανελθὼν ὁ
ὑπηρέτης, "εἴσιτε," ἔφη, "ὁ γὰρ δεσπότης ῡμᾱς δέξεται." ταῦτα δ'   20
εἰπὼν ἡγεῖτο αὐτοῖς εἰς τὸ τέμενος.

[πολλῷ by much   εἴσιτε come in!]

ἀμειψάμενοι οὖν τᾱς πύλᾱς εἰς αὐλὴν μεγάλην εἰσῆλθον· ἐκεῖ δὲ
ἐγγὺς τοῦ ἱεροῦ ἐκαθίζετο ἀνήρ τις γεραιός, ὃς ἰδὼν αὐτοὺς
προσιόντας, "χαίρετε, ὦ φίλοι," ἔφη. "τί βουλόμενοι ἥκετε;" ὁ μὲν οὖν
Δικαιόπολις πάντα ἐξηγήσατο, ὁ δὲ ἱερεὺς πρὸς τὸν παῖδα εὐμενῶς   25
βλέψᾱς, "εἰπέ μοι, ὦ παῖ," ἔφη, "ἆρα σεαυτὸν τῷ Ἀσκληπίῳ ἐπιτρέψεις;
ἆρα τοῦτο πιστεύεις, ὅτι ὁ θεὸς δυνήσεταί σε ὠφελεῖν;" ὁ δὲ Φίλιππος,
"μάλιστά γε· πάντα γὰρ τοῖς θεοῖς δυνατά· τῷ θεῷ πιστεύω καὶ
ἐμαυτὸν αὐτῷ ἐπιτρέψω." ὁ δὲ γέρων, "εὖ γε, ὦ παῖ. νῦν μὲν ἄπιτε εἰς
τὸ καταγώγιον, αὔριον δὲ ὁ ὑπηρέτης ῡμῖν πάρεσται ὡς ἡγησόμενος   30
τῷ παιδὶ παρά με." ἀπελθόντες οὖν ὅ τε πατὴρ καὶ ὁ παῖς τὴν νύκτα
ἔμενον ἐν τῷ καταγωγίῳ.

[ἀμειψάμενοι having passed through   αὐλήν courtyard   προσιόντας
approaching   εὐμενῶς kindly   ἄπιτε go away!]

τῇ δὲ ὑστεραίᾳ ἐπεὶ πρῶτον ἐγένετο ἡ ἡμέρᾱ, παρελθὼν ὁ
ὑπηρέτης τὸν Φίλιππον ἤγαγε παρὰ τὸν ἱερέᾱ. ὁ δὲ εὐμενῶς
δεξάμενος τὸν παῖδα, "ἄγε δή, ὦ παῖ," ἔφη, "νῦν χρή σε   35
παρασκευάζεσθαι· δεῖ γὰρ ὅσιά τε φρονεῖν καὶ καθαρὸν εἶναι τὴν
ψῡχήν. ἀλλὰ μηδὲν φοβοῦ· φιλανθρωπότατος γάρ ἐστιν ὁ
Ἀσκλήπιος τῶν θεῶν καὶ τοῖς καθαροῖς οὖσι τὴν ψῡχὴν αἰεὶ ἵλαός

ἐστιν. θάρρει οὖν." οὕτω δ' εἰπὼν τὸν παῖδα εἰς τὸ ἱερὸν ἤγαγεν. ἐκεῖ
δὲ πρῶτον μὲν ὁ Φίλιππος ἐκαθήρατο, ἔπειτα δὲ πᾶσαν τὴν ἡμέρᾱν   40
ἐν τῷ ἱερῷ ἔμενεν, ὅσιά τε φρονῶν καὶ τὸν θεὸν εὐχόμενος ἐν τῷ ὕπνῳ
ἐπιφανῆναι.

[ὅσια . . . φρονεῖν to have holy thoughts   τὴν ψῡχήν with respect to your soul
φιλανθρωπότατος   most benevolent   ἐκαθήρατο   purified himself
ἐπιφανῆναι to appear, manifest himself]

τέλος δὲ ἐπεὶ ἐγίγνετο ἡ ἑσπέρᾱ, ἐπανελθὼν ὁ ἱερεύς, "ἄγε δή, ὦ
παῖ," ἔφη, "πάντα γὰρ ἕτοιμά ἐστιν. ἕπου μοι." τὸν δὲ παῖδα ἐκ τοῦ
ἱεροῦ ἀγαγὼν πρὸς τὸν βωμόν, ἐκέλευσεν αὐτὸν σπονδὴν κατὰ   45
νόμον ποιεῖσθαι. ὁ δὲ τὴν φιάλην ταῖς χερσὶ λαβὼν σπονδὴν
ἐποιήσατο καὶ τὰς χεῖρας πρὸς τὸν οὐρανὸν ἄρᾱς, "'Ασκλήπιε," ἔφη,
"σῶτερ, φιλανθρωπότατε τῶν θεῶν, ἄκουέ μου εὐχομένου, ὃς ὅσιά τε
φρονῶν καὶ καθαρὸς ὢν τὴν ψῡχὴν ἱκέτης σοῦ πάρειμι. ἵλαος ἴσθι
μοι τυφλῷ γεγονότι καί, εἴ σοι δοκεῖ, τοὺς ὀφθαλμούς μοι ἀκοῦ."   50

[τὴν φιάλην the cup   ταῖς χερσί in his hands   ἄρᾱς (from αἴρω) raising
σῶτερ savior   γεγονότι who has become]

ἐνταῦθα δὴ ὁ ἱερεὺς τῷ παιδὶ εἰς τὸ ἄβατον ἡγησάμενος
ἐκέλευσεν αὐτὸν ἐπὶ τῇ γῇ κείμενον καθεύδειν. ὁ οὖν Φίλιππος
κατέκειτο ἀλλὰ πολὺν δὴ χρόνον οὐκ ἐδύνατο καθεύδειν· μόνος
γὰρ ὢν ἐν τῷ ἀβάτῳ μάλα ἐφοβεῖτο· νὺξ γὰρ ἦν καὶ πανταχοῦ
σκότος καὶ σῑγή, εἰ μὴ σπανίως ἤκουε τῶν ἱερῶν ὄφεων ἠρέμα   55
συρῑζόντων.

[τὸ ἄβατον the holy place   σκότος darkness   σῑγή silence   εἰ μή except
σπανίως occasionally   ὄφεων ἠρέμα συρῑζόντων snakes hissing gently]

Principal Parts: Stems in -ευ-

πιστεύω, πιστεύσω, ἐπίστευσα, πεπίστευκα, πεπίστευμαι, ἐπιστεύθην
    (+ dat.) I trust, am confident (in), believe
κελεύω, κελεύσω, ἐκέλευσα, κεκέλευκα, κεκέλευσμαι, ἐκελεύσθην I
    order, tell (someone to do something)
πορεύομαι, πορεύσομαι, πεπόρευμαι, ἐπορεύθην I go, walk, march,
    journey

Word Building

Deduce the meanings of the words in the following sets (δυσ- = "bad"):

1. τυγχάνω (τυχ-)   ἡ τύχη   εὐτυχής, -ές   δυστυχής, -ές ἀτυχής, -ές
2. πιστεύω   ἡ πίστις   πιστός, -ή, -όν ἄπιστος, -ον ἀπιστέω
3. δύναμαι   ἡ δύναμις δυνατός, -ή, -όν ἀδύνατος, -ον

4.   γιγνώσκω   (γνω-)   ἡ γνώμη   γνωστός, -ή, -όν   ἄγνωστος, -ον
5.   γράφω   ἡ γραφή   γραπτός, -ή, -όν   ἄγραπτος, -ον

Grammar

2. The Irregular Verb εἶμι

The verb εἶμι in the *indicative* refers to future time and means "I will go." In Attic Greek it is used as the future of ἔρχομαι. However, the imperative, infinitive, and participle of εἶμι usually refer to present time and are used instead of the corresponding forms of ἔρχομαι. The imperfect describes continuing action in past time. The verb has two grades of stem: short vowel stem ἰ- and long vowel stem εἰ- (compare Latin *īre*).

Indicative	*Imperative*	*Infinitive*	*Participle*
εἶμι		ἰέναι	ἰών, ἰοῦσα, ἰόν
εἶ	ἴθι		
εἶσι(ν)			
ἴμεν			
ἴτε	ἴτε		
ἴᾶσι(ν)			

Imperfect

ἦα	ἦμεν	Note that in the imperfect the ε of the
ᾔεισθα	ἦτε	long vowel stem is augmented to η
ᾔει	ἦσαν	and that the ι becomes subscript.

3. Purpose: ὡς + Future Participle

Look at the following sentences:

ἐγὼ εἶμι **ὡς ζητήσων** τὸν δεσπότην.
I will go *to seek* the master.

αὔριον δὲ ὁ ὑπηρέτης ὑμῖν πάρεσται **ὡς ἡγησόμενος** τῷ παιδὶ παρά με.
Tomorrow the attendant will be with you *to lead* the child to me.

In Greek, ὡς + the future participle may be used to express purpose, where English uses a simple infinitive.

4. Article + Participle

You have already seen that the article and a participle form a noun phrase, which may be translated by a noun or a relative clause in English (see Book I, page 110). Here are some further examples:

οἱ θεώμενοι the watching people = the spectators
οἱ τοὺς χοροὺς θεώμενοι the watching the dances people = those who are
   watching the dances
οἱ τρέχοντες the running people = the runners
ἡ γυνὴ ἡ τὴν γαστέρα νοσοῦσα = the woman who was sick in the
   stomach (17β:4)

οἱ παρόντες the being present people = those who are present (examples
are τοῖς παροῦσι and τῶν . . . παρόντων, 17α:5, 6)

Exercise 17e

Read aloud and translate:

1. ἴθι δή, ὦ παῖ, καὶ τῇ μητρὶ εἰπὲ ὅτι πρὸς τῇ θύρᾳ μενῶ.
2. ἆρ' οὐκ ἴτε εἰς τὴν ἀγορὰν ὡς μαθησόμενοι τὰ γενόμενα;
3. ὁ δοῦλος ἐξῄει ὡς τὸν δεσπότην ζητήσων.
4. δεῖ σε ἄγγελον πέμψαι ὡς τῷ βασιλεῖ πάντα λέξοντα.
5. ὁ Ξέρξης ναυτικὸν μέγιστον παρεσκεύαζεν ὡς τοὺς Ἕλληνας δουλώσων.
6. οἵ Ἕλληνες παρεσκευάζοντο ὡς ἀνδρείως μαχούμενοι.
7. τοὺς ἐν ταύτῃ τῇ μάχῃ ἀποθανόντας αἰεὶ τῑμήσομεν.
8. τὰς παρθένους κελεύσω οἴκαδε εὐθὺς ἰέναι.
9. οἱ πάντα κατὰ νόμον πράττοντες φίλοι τοῖς θεοῖς γενήσονται.
10. οἱ παῖδες οἴκαδε ἐπανῇσαν ὡς τῇ μητρὶ τὰ γενόμενα ἐξηγησόμενοι.

Exercise 17f

Translate into Greek:

1. We will go to the city to learn what happened.
2. The general will send a messenger to tell the citizens (*dative*) what
   they ought to do.
3. The men are taking the women to the city to watch the dances.
4. The priest will return to the temple to make a libation.
5. Those staying in the agora wish to hear the messenger.

*   *   *

ΟΙ ΠΕΡΣΑΙ ΤΑΣ ΑΘΗΝΑΣ
ΔΕΥΤΕΡΟΝ ΑΙΡΟΥΣΙΝ

*Read the following passage (adapted from Herodotus 9.1–10) and answer the
comprehension questions below:*

When Xerxes returned to Asia after Salamis, he left Mardonius with a large
army to subdue Greece the following year.

ἅμα δὲ ἦρι ἀρχομένῳ ὁ Μαρδόνιος ὁρμώμενος ἐκ Θεσσαλίᾱς ἦγε τὸν στρατὸν
σπουδῇ ἐπὶ τὰς Ἀθήνας. προϊόντι δὲ αὐτῷ οὐδεὶς τῶν Βοιωτῶν ἀντεῖχεν, οὐδὲ
ἐβοήθουν τοῖς Ἀθηναίοις οἱ Λακεδαιμόνιοι. ἀφικόμενος δὲ εἰς τὴν Ἀττικὴν οὐχ ηὗρε
τοὺς Ἀθηναίους ἀλλὰ ἔμαθεν ὅτι ἔν τε Σαλαμῖνι οἱ πλεῖστοί εἰσι καὶ ἐν ταῖς
ναυσίν· αἱρεῖ τε ἔρημον τὸ ἄστυ. ἐπεὶ δὲ ἐν ταῖς Ἀθήναις ἐγένετο, ἄγγελον   5
ἔπεμψεν εἰς τὴν Σαλαμῖνα, λόγους φέροντα ἐπιτηδείους· εἶπε γὰρ ὅτι ὁ βασιλεὺς
τήν τε Ἀττικὴν τοῖς Ἀθηναίοις ἀποδώσει καὶ συμμαχίᾱν ποιήσεται, ἐᾱν τοῦ
πολέμου παύσωνται. οἱ δὲ Ἀθηναῖοι τοὺς λόγους οὐκ ἐδέξαντο ἀλλὰ τὸν ἄγγελον
ἀπέπεμψαν.

[ἅμα . . . ἦρι ἀρχομένῳ with the beginning of spring   ὁ Μαρδόνιος
Mardonius   Θεσσαλίας Thessaly   προϊόντι going forward, advancing   τῶν
Βοιωτῶν of the Boeotians   ἔρημον deserted   ἐπιτηδείους friendly   ἀποδώσει
will give back   συμμαχίᾱν alliance   ἐὰν . . . παύσωνται if they cease]

1. What did Mardonius do at the coming of spring?
2. What was the response of the Boeotians and the Spartans?
3. What did Mardonius find when he reached Athens?
4. What were the terms of the proposal that Mardonius sent to the Athenians?
5. What was the response of the Athenians?

εἰς δὲ τὴν Σαλαμῖνα διέβησαν οἱ Ἀθηναῖοι ὧδε· ἕως μὲν ἤλπιζον στρατὸν   10
πέμψειν τοὺς Λακεδαιμονίους ὡς βοηθήσοντα, ἔμενον ἐν τῇ Ἀττικῇ· ἐπεὶ δὲ οἱ μὲν
Λακεδαιμόνιοι οὐκ ἐβοήθουν, ὁ δὲ Μαρδόνιος προϊὼν εἰς τὴν Βοιωτίᾱν ἀφίκετο, οὕτω
δὴ ἐξεκόμισαν πάντα ἐκ τῆς Ἀττικῆς καὶ αὐτοὶ διέβησαν εἰς τὴν Σαλαμῖνα. καὶ
εἰς Λακεδαίμονα ἔπεμπον ἀγγέλους ὡς μεμψόμενοι τοῖς Λακεδαιμονίοις, διότι οὐκ
ἐβοήθουν. ὡς δὲ ἀφίκοντο εἰς τὴν Λακεδαίμονα οἱ ἄγγελοι, εἶπον τάδε, "ἔπεμψαν   15
ἡμᾶς οἱ Ἀθηναῖοι ὡς λέξοντας ὅτι ὁ βασιλεὺς τῶν Περσῶν ἐθέλει τήν τε Ἀττικὴν
ἀποδοῦναι καὶ συμμαχίᾱν ποιεῖσθαι· ἡμεῖς δέ, καίπερ ἀδικούμενοι ὑφ᾽ ὑμῶν,
ἐκείνους τοὺς λόγους οὐκ ἐδεξάμεθα. νῦν δὲ κελεύομεν ὑμᾶς ὡς τάχιστα στρατιὰν
πέμψαι ὡς τοὺς βαρβάρους ἀμυνοῦσαν τῇ Ἀττικῇ."

[διέβησαν crossed   ὧδε thus   ἕως as long as   στρατὸν . . .
Λακεδαιμονίους that the Spartans would send an army   προϊὼν advancing
τὴν Βοιωτίᾱν Boeotia   ἐξεκόμισαν they took out, removed   διέβησαν they
crossed over   Λακεδαίμονα Lacedaemon, Sparta   ὡς μεμψόμενοι to blame,
criticize (+ dat.)   διότι because   ἀποδοῦναι to give back   ἀδικούμενοι ὑφ᾽
ὑμῶν wronged by you   στρατιάν an army]

6. What had the Athenians done as long as they hoped for help?
7. When did they cross to Salamis?
8. What message did they send to Sparta?

Exercise 17g

Translate into Greek:

1. The Spartans, who were holding a festival at this time, were not
   willing (refused) to go out against (ἐπεξιέναι ἐπί + acc.) the
   Persians but still delayed (ἔμελλον).
2. Finally the messengers of the Athenians said: "You Spartans are
   betraying (προδίδοτε) your allies, and the Athenians, wronged by
   you, will make a peace treaty with (πρός + acc.) the Persians.
3. "Having made a peace treaty and having become allies of the
   Persians (dat.), we will wage war with them against (ἐπί + acc.) the
   Peloponnesus."
4. "Then you will learn by suffering (having suffered) that you ought
   not betray (προδοῦναι) your allies."
5. Finally, fearing these words, the Spartans sent their army to Attica.

18
Ο ΑΣΚΛΗΠΙΟΣ (α)

ὁ Ἀσκλήπιος σεμνός τ' ἦν καὶ μέγας.

Vocabulary

Verbs

γελάω, γελάσομαι, ἐγέλασα, ἐγελάσθην I laugh

δίδωμι, (*imperfect*) ἐδίδουν, δώσω, ἔδωκα, (*infinitive*) δοῦναι, (*participle*) δούς, δέδωκα, δέδομαι, ἐδόθην I give

 ἀποδίδωμι I give back, return, pay

κῑνέω I move

τίθημι, (*imperfect*) ἐτίθην, θήσω, ἔθηκα, (*infinitive*) θεῖναι, (*participle*) θείς, τέθηκα, τέθειμαι, ἐτέθην I put, place

 ἐπιτίθημι I put X (*acc.*) on Y (*dat.*)

Nouns

ὁ ὕπνος, τοῦ ὕπνου sleep

ἡ χάρις, τῆς χάριτος (*acc.* τὴν χάριν) thanks, gratitude

Adjectives

δῆλος, -η, -ον clear

εὐμενής, -ές kindly

σεμνός, -ή, -όν holy, august

Prepositions

περί (+ *gen.*) around; (+ *acc.*) around

ὑπέρ (+ *gen.*) on behalf of, for, above; (+ *acc.*) over, above

Expressions

δῆλόν ἐστι(ν) it is clear

χάριν ἀποδίδωμι (+ *dat.*) I render thanks, thank

τέλος δὲ οὕτως ἔκαμνεν ὁ Φίλιππος ὥστε εἰς βαθὺν ὕπνον ἔπεσεν.
καθεύδοντι δ' αὐτῷ ἐφάνη ὁ θεός· σεμνός τ' ἦν καὶ μέγας καὶ τῇ
δεξιᾷ βάκτρον ἔφερε, περὶ οὗ εἰλίττετο ὁ ἱερὸς ὄφις. ἔστη δὲ παρὰ τῷ
παιδὶ καὶ εὐμενῶς βλέψας τάδε εἶπεν, "τί πάσχεις, ὦ παῖ; διὰ τί
καθεύδεις ἐν τῷ ἐμῷ ἀβάτῳ;" ὁ δὲ οὐδὲν φοβούμενος—εὐμενὴς γὰρ   5
ἐφαίνετο ὁ θεός—"τυφλός εἰμι, ὦ Ἀσκλήπιε," ἔφη, "ἥκω οὖν ὡς
αἰτήσων σε τοὺς ὀφθαλμούς μοι ἀκεῖσθαι." ὁ δὲ θεός, "ἐὰν δ' ἐγὼ
ἀκέσωμαί σοι τοὺς ὀφθαλμούς, τί σύ μοι δώσεις;" ὁ δὲ παῖς πολὺν δὴ
χρόνον ἠπόρει τί χρὴ λέγειν, τέλος δέ, "πολλὰ μὲν οὐκ ἔχω," ἔφη,
"δώσω δέ σοι τοὺς ἐμοὺς ἀστραγάλους." ὁ δὲ θεὸς γελάσας   10
προσεχώρησε καὶ τὰς χεῖρας ἐπέθηκε τοῖς ὀφθαλμοῖς αὐτοῦ. ταῦτα
δὲ ποιήσας ἀπέβη.

[βαθύν deep   ἐφάνη appeared   βάκτρον staff   εἰλίττετο curled   ὄφις
serpent   ἀβάτῳ holy place   ἐὰν . . . ἀκέσωμαι if I heal   ἀστραγάλους
knucklebones (used as dice in gaming)]

τῇ δ' ὑστεραίᾳ ἐπεὶ πρῶτον ἐγένετο ἡ ἡμέρᾱ, ἠγέρθη ὁ Φίλιππος
καί—ἰδού—βλέπειν ἐδύνατο· τόν τε γὰρ οὐρανὸν εἶδε καὶ τὸν ἥλιον
ὑπὲρ τοὺς λόφους ἀνίσχοντα καὶ τὰ δένδρα τῷ ἀνέμῳ κῑνούμενα·   15
καὶ ἐτέρπετο θεώμενος· πάντα γὰρ αὐτῷ κάλλιστα δὴ ἐφαίνετο.
ἔσπευδεν οὖν ὡς τὸν ἱερέᾱ ζητήσων. ὁ δὲ ἰδὼν αὐτὸν προσιόντα,
"χαῖρε, ὦ παῖ," ἔφη, "δῆλόν ἐστιν ὅτι ὁ θεὸς εὐμενὴς προσῆλθέ σοι.
χάριν οὖν τῷ θεῷ ἀπόδος. ἀλλ' ἴθι ὡς τὸν πατέρα ζητήσων."

[ἠγέρθη (from ἐγείρω) woke up   ἀνίσχοντα (from ἀνίσχω, a variant of ἀνέχω)
rising   ἀπόδος = aorist imperative of ἀποδίδωμι]

Principal Parts: -ε- and -α- Contract Verbs

φιλέω, φιλήσω, ἐφίλησα, πεφίληκα, πεφίλημαι, ἐφιλήθην I love
καλέω (καλε-/κλη-), καλῶ, ἐκάλεσα, κέκληκα, κέκλημαι (I am called),
   ἐκλήθην I call
τῑμάω, τῑμήσω, ἐτίμησα, τετίμηκα, τετίμημαι, ἐτῑμήθην I honor

Word Study

*Explain the meaning of the following English
words with reference to their Greek roots:*

1. autobiography
2. autograph
3. automatic
4. autonomous
5. autistic

Women
playing
knucklebones

Grammar

1. The Verbs δίδωμι and τίθημι

The stems of these verbs have both long and short vowel grades:

δίδωμι: long vowel grade stem δω-; short vowel grade stem δο-
τίθημι: long vowel grade stem θη-; short vowel grade stem θε-

In the present and imperfect the stems are reduplicated, i.e., the first consonant + ι is put before the stem. The personal endings are then added straight to the stem. Note that in the present and aorist active the long vowel stem is used in the singular forms; in the imperfect some of the forms in the singular show contractions with the short stem vowel. The future tense of these verbs (δώσω and θήσω) is completely regular (like λύσω) and therefore not included in these charts.

δίδωμι: Active Voice

Present Tense

Indicative	Imperative	Infinitive	Participle
δί-δω-μι		δι-δό-ναι	δι-δούς, δι-δοῦσα, δι-δόν
δί-δω-ς	δί-δο-ε > δίδου		
δί-δω-σι(ν)			
δί-δο-μεν			
δί-δο-τε	δί-δο-τε		
δι-δό-ᾱσι(ν)			

Imperfect Tense

ἐ-δί-δο-ον > ἐδίδουν
ἐ-δί-δο-ες > ἐδίδους
ἐ-δί-δο-ε > ἐδίδου
ἐ-δί-δο-μεν
ἐ-δί-δο-τε
ἐ-δί-δο-σαν

Aorist

ἔ-δω-κα		δοῦ-ναι	δούς, δοῦσα, δόν
ἔ-δω-κας	δό-ς		
ἔ-δω-κε(ν)			
ἔ-δο-μεν			
ἔ-δο-τε	δό-τε		
ἔ-δο-σαν			

Note that the singular of the aorist indicative is a first aorist formation, with κα instead of σα.

δίδωμι: Middle Voice

Present Tense

δί-δο-μαι   δί-δο-σθαι   δι-δό-μενος, -η, -ον
δί-δο-σαι   δί-δο-σο
δί-δο-ται
δι-δό-μεθα
δί-δο-σθε   δί-δο-σθε
δί-δο-νται

Imperfect Tense

ἐ-δι-δό-μην
ἐ-δί-δο-σο
ἐ-δί-δο-το
ἐ-δι-δό-μεθα
ἐ-δί-δο-σθε
ἐ-δί-δο-ντο

Compare the forms of δύναμαι and κεῖμαι (Reference Grammar, charts 52 and 53).

Aorist

ἐ-δό-μην   δό-σθαι   δό-μενος, -η, -ον
ἔ-δο-σο > ἔδου   δοῦ
ἔ-δο-το
ἐ-δό-μεθα
ἔ-δο-σθε   δό-σθε
ἔ-δο-ντο

τίθημι: Active Voice

Present Tense

τί-θη-μι   τι-θέ-ναι   τι-θείς, τι-θεῖσα, τι-θέν
τί-θη-ς   τί-θε-ε > τίθει
τί-θη-σι(ν)
τί-θε-μεν
τί-θε-τε   τί-θε-τε
τι-θέ-ᾱσι(ν)

Imperfect Tense

ἐ-τί-θη-ν
ἐ-τί-θε-ες > ἐτίθεις
ἐ-τί-θε-ε > ἐτίθει
ἐ-τί-θε-μεν
ἐ-τί-θε-τε
ἐ-τί-θε-σαν

Aorist

ἔ-θη-κα   θεῖ-ναι   θείς, θεῖσα, θέν
ἔ-θη-κας   θέ-ς
ἔ-θη-κε(ν)
ἔ-θε-μεν
ἔ-θε-τε   θέ-τε
ἔ-θε-σαν

Note again that the singular of the aorist indicative is a first aorist
formation, with κα instead of σα.

τίθημι: **Middle Voice**

Present Tense

τί-θε-μαι   τί-θε-σθαι   τι-θέ-μενος, -η, -ον
τί-θε-σαι   τί-θε-σο
τί-θε-ται
τι-θέ-μεθα
τί-θε-σθε   τί-θε-σθε
τί-θε-νται

Imperfect Tense

ἐ-τι-θέ-μην
ἐ-τί-θε-σο
ἐ-τί-θε-το
ἐ-τι-θέ-μεθα
ἐ-τί-θε-σθε
ἐ-τί-θε-ντο

Again, compare the forms of δύναμαι and κεῖμαι.

Aorist

ἐ-θέ-μην   θέ-σθαι   θέ-μενος, -η, -ον
ἔ-θε-σο > ἔθου   θοῦ
ἔ-θε-το
ἐ-θέ-μεθα
ἔ-θε-σθε   θέ-σθε
ἔ-θε-ντο

Exercise 18a

*In the reading passage at the beginning of this chapter, locate four instances
of the verbs δίδωμι and τίθημι or their compounds, and identify the form of
each.*

Exercise 18b

Identify and translate the following forms:

1. ἐδίδου	6. δίδως	11. ἐτίθεντο
2. τίθεται	7. ἐδίδοτε	12. δοῦ
3. δίδοσθαι	8. τιθείς	13. διδόᾱσι
4. θεῖναι	9. ἔδωκας	14. τίθης
5. διδοῦσα	10. ἔθεσαν	15. ἐδίδοντο

Exercise 18c

Put into the aorist: Put into the present: Put into the middle:

1. δίδου	6. ἔθεσαν	11. διδόᾱσι(ν)
2. τίθεσο	7. θεῖναι	12. ἔδοσαν
3. δίδοντα	8. δόσθαι	13. θές
4. τιθέμενος	9. δούς	14. δόντες
5. διδόναι	10. ἔθεντο	15. ἔθηκε(ν)

Exercise 18d

Read aloud and translate:

1. ὁ γέρων οὐκ ἠθέλησε τὸ ἀργύριον τῷ ξένῳ δοῦναι.
2. οἱ παῖδες, τῆς μητρὸς σῖτον δούσης, εὐθὺς ἤσθιον.
3. ὁ δεσπότης τὸν δοῦλον ἔπεμψεν ὡς τὸ ἀργύριον ἡμῖν ἀποδώσοντα.
4. ἴμεν ὡς αἰτήσοντες τὸν βασιλέᾱ ὑμῖν βοηθεῖν.
5. χάριν τῷ θεῷ ἀπόδος· ἔσωσε γὰρ ἡμᾶς.
6. ὁ αὐτουργὸς τὸν φίλον ᾔτησε τὸν κύνα ἀποδοῦναι.
7. σὺ μὲν δός μοι τὸν οἶνον, ἐγὼ δὲ δώσω σοι τὸν σῖτον.
8. ὁ πατὴρ εὐμενῶς γελάσᾱς τῷ παιδὶ τὸν κύνα ἔδωκεν.
9. οἱ ἱκέται παρὰ τῷ βωμῷ καθιζόμενοι χάριν τῷ θεῷ ἀπέδοσαν.
10. ὁ θεὸς τὰς χεῖρας τοῖς τοῦ παιδὸς ὀφθαλμοῖς ἐπιθεὶς ἀπέβη.

Exercise 18e

Translate into Greek:

1. The captain gave the money to the sailor.
2. Having thanked the god, the women went home.
3. I told you to put the plow in the field and give food to the oxen.
4. You put (εἰστίθημι) the sails into the ship, and I will put in the oars (ἡ κώπη).
5. It is clear that these women gave no money to this old man.
6. After paying the captain three drachmas, the foreigners boarded the ship.

Sparta and Corinth

In the chaos following the breakdown of Bronze Age civilization in the Eastern Mediterranean (ca. 1200 B.C.), there were widespread migrations. New peoples entered Greece and Asia Minor from north of the civilized world and either pushed out or merged with the previous population. In Greece the newcomers were Greeks who spoke a different dialect, Doric, and this movement is traditionally called the Dorian invasion, although it probably took the form of sporadic raids over a long period of time rather than an organized invasion. When the dust settled, the whole of the Peloponnesus except the central plateau of Arcadia was occupied by Doric speakers.

Dorians calling themselves Lacedaemonians were settled in the fertile valley of the Eurotas by 1,000 B.C. and by about 850 four or five villages united to form the *polis* of Sparta. As its population increased, Sparta gradually conquered her neighbors to the north and east, reducing them to dependent status; the conquered were called περίοικοι. They had local autonomy but were obliged to serve in the Spartan army. About 735 B.C., when other states were about to solve their population problem by sending out colonies, Sparta crossed the mountain range of Taygetus and in a war lasting twenty years conquered Messenia. The inhabitants were reduced to the status of serfs, called helots, who worked the land for their Spartan masters.

This conquest determined the future history of Sparta. Up to this time her development had been not unlike that of other Greek states, except that she had retained a monarchy, or rather a dyarchy, since she had two hereditary kings coming from two separate royal families. Within fifty years of the conquest of Messenia she had developed into a totalitarian military state quite different from any other in Greece. The reason for this was the absolute necessity of dominating the helots, who outnumbered the Spartans by seven to one and revolted whenever the opportunity occurred.

Sometime in the seventh century there was a revolution in Sparta caused partly by economic factors (the new wealth produced by the conquest of Messenia) and partly by military reorganization (the introduction of the hoplite phalanx). Both developments gave more importance to the ordinary Spartan and challenged the authority of kings and nobles. The outcome was a revised constitution, ascribed to a lawgiver called Lycurgus. The kings were advised by a council of elders, all aged over sixty, the Gerousia. The ancient assembly of all the Spartans, the Apella, was given the final authority, i.e., the right to accept or reject proposals put by the Gerousia. In addition there were five officials called *ephors* (overseers), elected by the whole citizen body, whose function was to guard the rights of the people in its relation with the kings.

The other feature of the Lycurgan reforms was the ἀγωγή (training); this was the system by which every male Spartan was trained to devote his life to service in the army. At birth the child was inspected by the heads of his tribe, and, if the child was weak or unhealthy, it was exposed on Taygetus and left to die. At seven the boy began his education in the state school, where the whole training was aimed at discipline, endurance, and patriotism. At twenty he joined the army and might marry but continued to live in barracks. At thirty he became a man and joined the ranks of the ὅμοιοι (equals) but continued to dine in the public mess with his fellow soldiers. Every Spartan was supported by a κλῆρος (farm) worked by helots, and so they could devote their whole life to achieving military excellence; it is not surprising that Sparta became the greatest power in Greece, though the numbers of Spartans were always small. While childbearing was a high priority for Spartan women, they enjoyed considerable freedom and received training in gymnastics and music.

In 660 B.C. Sparta, still trying to extend her territory northward, suffered a severe defeat at the hands of her northern neighbor, Argos. Soon after this the helots rose in revolt, no doubt supported by Argos. There followed a long and bitter war from which Sparta eventually emerged victorious. By the end of the century Argive power had declined. Sparta became the dominant power in the Peloponnesus and enrolled all the states except Argos in a loose confederacy called the Peloponnesian League.

The other Greeks either admired Sparta for her stability (εὐνομίᾱ) or hated her for her oppressive and xenophobic regime. Nevertheless, Sparta was recognized as the most powerful state in Greece.

The *polis* of Corinth was formed from a union of seven villages perhaps about 800 B.C., and, when she emerges into the light of history, we find her ruled by a Dorian clan, the Bacchiadae. Her position on the Isthmus, at the very center of Greece with ports on both seas, assured her future as a commercial city. Under the Bacchiadae she founded the earliest colonies in the West (except for Ischia) at Corcyra and Syracuse (734 B.C.); she led the way in improvements in the design of ships and in the manufacture of pottery. The distinctive Corinthian ware was exported all over the Greek world and beyond in the eighth and seventh centuries.

About 650 B.C. the Bacchiadae were overthrown and driven out by Cypselus. He was the first of many Greek tyrants, a word which did not have its present connotations but simply meant one who seized power unconstitutionally. The tyrants often won power as champions of the people against the oppression of the nobles and were the product of economic and military developments similar to those that occasioned the revolution at Sparta. Under Cypselus and his son Periander, Corinth flourished and became the leading maritime and commercial state. His regime became bloody and oppressive, as conspiracies drove him to suspect all citizens of wealth and influence. He died in 585 B.C., and his successor was assassinated within a few years. From then on Corinth was ruled by an oligarchy (which means rule by the few: in Corinth's case, the wealthy merchants).

Corinth remained one of the most prosperous states of Greece, achieving by the fifth century a near monopoly of western trade. When Athens began to rival Corinth in the West, Corinth had every reason to fear her ambitions.

Ο ΑΣΚΛΗΠΙΟΣ (β)

Vocabulary

Verbs

ἁμαρτάνω, ἁμαρτήσομαι,
  ἥμαρτον, ἡμάρτηκα,
  ἡμάρτημαι, ἡμαρτήθην I
  miss (+ gen.); I make a
  mistake, am mistaken
ἀνατίθημι (see τίθημι for
  principal parts) I set up,
  dedicate
ἐπιστρατεύω (see στρατεύω for
  principal parts) (+ dat. or ἐπί +
  acc.) I march against, attack
κάθημαι I sit
κρατέω (+ gen.) I rule, have
  power over, control, prevail
παραδίδωμι (see δίδωμι for
  principal parts) I hand over,
  give
προστρέχω, προσδραμοῦμαι,
  προσέδραμον,
  προσδεδράμηκα I run toward
τολμάω I dare

Nouns

ἡ γνώμη, τῆς γνώμης
  opinion, judgment, intention
ὁ ἐχθρός, τοῦ ἐχθροῦ enemy
ἡ θυσία, τῆς θυσίας sacrifice
τὸ κράτος, τοῦ κράτους
  power
τὸ πρᾶγμα, τοῦ πράγματος
  matter, trouble
τὰ χρήματα, τῶν χρημάτων
  money

Adjectives

ἐχθρός, -ά, -όν hostile
ὑγιής, -ές healthy
φιλαίτερος, -ᾱ, -ον and
  φίλτατος, -η, -ον (irregular
  comparative and superlative of
  φίλος) dearer, dearest

Prepositions

διά (+ gen.) through; (+ acc.)
  because of
ἐπί (+ dat.) at, upon, on, for (of
  price or purpose); (+ acc.) at,
  against, onto

Adverbs

ἡδέως sweetly, pleasantly,
  gladly
μᾶλλον more, rather
  μᾶλλον ἤ rather than
πάλαι long ago
  πάλαι εἰσίν they have been
  for a long time now

Conjunctions

διότι because
μέντοι however
οὔκουν and so . . . not

Expressions

ὀρθῶς γιγνώσκω I am right
πῶς ἔχει τὰ πράγματα;
  How are things?
τίνα γνώμην ἔχεις; What do
  you think?

τὸν δὲ Δικαιόπολιν ηὗρον πρὸ τοῦ καταγωγίου καθήμενον. ὁ δὲ
ὡς εἶδε τὸν παῖδα βεβαίως βαδίζοντα καὶ βλέποντα, ἀνέστη καὶ
προσδραμὼν ἠσπάζετο αὐτὸν καί, "ὦ φίλτατε παῖ," ἔφη, "ἆρα
ἀληθῶς ὁρῶ σε ὑγιῆ ὄντα; ἆρα ἀληθῶς ἠκέσατό σοι τοὺς
ὀφθαλμοὺς ὁ θεός; δεῖ πλείστην χάριν τῷ Ἀσκληπίῳ ἀποδοῦναι." 5
καὶ πρὸς τὸν ἱερέα τρεψάμενος, "ἆρ' ἔξεστι θυσίᾱν ποιεῖσθαι; ἆρ'

ἔξεστι καὶ ἄγαλμα ἀναθεῖναι τῷ θεῷ;" ὁ δὲ ἱερεύς, "πῶς γὰρ οὔ;
ἔξεστί σοι. ἆρα βούλῃ καὶ μνημεῖον τῆς ἀκέσεως ἀναθεῖναι ἐν τῷ
ἱερῷ; σὺ μὲν γὰρ τρεῖς δραχμάς μοι παράδος, ἐγὼ δὲ θυσίᾱν
ποιήσομαι καὶ μνημεῖον ἀναθήσω ὑπὲρ σοῦ." ὁ δὲ Δικαιόπολις   10
οἰμώξᾱς, "τρεῖς δραχμὰς λέγεις; φεῦ τῆς δαπάνης." ὁ δὲ ἱερεύς, "οὐδὲν
λέγεις, ὦ ἄνθρωπε· οὐ γὰρ μεγάλη ἡ δαπάνη. τὴν γὰρ θυσίᾱν
ποιήσομαι ἐπὶ μιᾷ δραχμῇ, τὸ δὲ μνημεῖον ἀναθήσω ἐπὶ δυοῖν. δός
μοι οὖν τρεῖς δραχμάς, εἰ βούλῃ με ταῦτα ποιῆσαι." ὁ δὲ
Δικαιόπολις, "ἀλλὰ τρεῖς δραχμὰς οὐκ ἔχω· ἀνὴρ γὰρ πένης εἰμί.   15
ἆρα δύο σοι ἀρκοῦσιν;" ὁ δὲ ἱερεύς, "ἔστω· δύο ἀρκοῦσιν, εἰ μὴ
πλέον ἔχεις." ὁ μὲν οὖν Δικαιόπολις δύο δραχμὰς παρέδωκεν, ὁ δὲ
ἱερεὺς τὸν ὑπηρέτην καλέσᾱς ἐκέλευσεν ἀλεκτρυόνα ἐνεγκεῖν καὶ
ἡγησάμενος αὐτοῖς πρὸς τὸν βωμὸν τὴν θυσίᾱν ἐποιήσατο.

[τοῦ **καταγωγίου** the inn   **ἠσπάζετο** greeted, embraced   **ἄγαλμα** gift,
offering (often a dedicatory statuette)   **πῶς γὰρ οὔ;** why not? of course
μνημεῖον τῆς ἀκέσεως memorial (tablet) of the cure   **οἰμώξᾱς** groaning   **φεῦ
τῆς δαπάνης** alas for the expense!   **πένης** poor   **ἀρκοῦσιν** are sufficient
ἔστω let it be so! all right!   **ἀλεκτρυόνα** a cock   **ἐνεγκεῖν** (*from* φέρω) to bring]

ὁ δὲ Φίλιππος, "ἀλλὰ δεῖ καὶ ἐμέ," ἔφη, "δοῦναί τι. τῷ γὰρ θεῷ   20
εἶπον ὅτι τοὺς ἐμοὺς ἀστραγάλους δώσω. ἰδού—τούτους λαβὼν
ἀνάθες τῷ θεῷ καὶ γράψον ἐν τῷ μνημείῳ, εἴ σοι δοκεῖ, ὅτι ὁ Φίλιππος
τούτους τοὺς ἀστραγάλους τῷ Ἀσκληπίῳ ἀνέθηκε μεγίστην χάριν
ἔχων." ὁ δὲ ἱερεύς, "ἀλλὰ ἡδέως ταῦτα ποιήσω· χαιρήσει γὰρ ὁ θεὸς
τούτους δεξάμενος. ἀλλὰ νῦν γε δεῖ ῡ̔μᾶς οἴκαδε πορεύεσθαι. ἄγε   25
δή, ἀκολουθήσω ῡ̔μῖν πρὸς τὰς πύλᾱς."

[**ἀκολουθήσω** (+ *dat.*) I will follow, accompany]

ἐν ᾧ δὲ πρὸς τὰς πύλᾱς ἐβάδιζον, ὁ ἱερεὺς τῷ Δικαιοπόλει, "σὺ
μέν," ἔφη, "ἐν ταῖς Ἀθήναις νεωστὶ παρῆσθα· εἰπέ μοι οὖν, πῶς ἔχει τὰ
πρᾱ́γματα; πότερον πόλεμος ἔσται πρὸς τοὺς Λακεδαιμονίους ἢ
εἰρήνην δυνήσεσθε σῴζειν; δῆλον γάρ ἐστιν ὅτι οἱ Κορίνθιοι τοὺς   30
Λακεδαιμονίους εἰς πόλεμον ὀτρῡ́νουσιν, ἐχθροὶ ὄντες τοῖς
Ἀθηναίοις. τίνα οὖν γνώμην ἔχεις; ἆρα δίκην τῶν διαφορῶν
ἐθελήσουσι διδόναι ἢ πολέμῳ τὰς διαφορὰς διαλῡ́σονται μᾶλλον ἢ
λόγοις;"

[**νεωστὶ** lately   **ὀτρῡ́νουσιν** are urging on   **δίκην τῶν διαφορῶν** . . .
διδόναι to give (allow) arbitration of their differences   **τὰς διαφορὰς**
διαλῡ́σονται will resolve their differences]

ὁ δὲ Δικαιόπολις, "πάλαι μὲν ἐχθροί εἰσιν οἱ Κορίνθιοι καὶ ἡμῖν 35
ἐπιβουλεύουσιν, ὅμως δὲ πόλεμον οὐ ποιήσονται οἱ Λακεδαιμόνιοι·
αἰεὶ γὰρ ἡσυχάζουσι, τὸ τῶν Ἀθηναίων κράτος φοβούμενοι." ὁ δὲ
ἱερεύς, "ἀλλ' οὐ δήπου φοβοῦνται τοὺς Ἀθηναίους οἱ
Λακεδαιμόνιοι· ἔστι γὰρ στρατὸς αὐτοῖς τε καὶ τοῖς συμμάχοις
μέγιστος δή, ᾧπερ οὐ τολμήσουσιν οἱ Ἀθηναῖοι ἀντέχειν κατὰ γῆν." 40
ὁ δὲ Δικαιόπολις ἀποκρινάμενος εἶπεν· "ἀλλ' ἡμεῖς τῆς γε θαλάττης
κρατοῦμεν, ὥστε πλέονα ἔχομεν τὰ τοῦ πολέμου· πλεῖστα μὲν γὰρ
χρήματά ἐστιν ἡμῖν, πλεῖσται δὲ νῆες· οὔκουν δυνήσονται ἡμᾶς
βλάπτειν οὐδὲ μακρὸν πόλεμον νικῆσαι, οὐδ' οὖν τολμήσουσιν ἡμῖν
ἐπιστρατεῦσαι." ὁ δὲ γέρων, "σὺ μὲν δῆλος εἶ τῇ τε σῇ πόλει μάλα 45
πιστεύων καὶ τῷ κράτει αὐτῆς. διὰ τοῦτο μέντοι, ὡς ἔμοιγε δοκεῖ,
πόλεμον ποιήσονται οἱ Λακεδαιμόνιοι, διότι τὸ τῶν Ἀθηναίων
κράτος φοβούμενοι οὐκ ἐθελήσουσι περιορᾶν αὐτὸ αὐξανόμενον.
ὅμως δὲ χαιρήσω, ἐὰν σὺ μὲν ὀρθῶς γιγνώσκων φανῇς, ἐγὼ δὲ
ἁμαρτάνων."   50

[ἐπιβουλεύουσιν plot against (+ *dat.*)   δήπου surely   τὰ τοῦ πολέμου
resources for war   οὐδ' οὖν nor indeed   ἔμοιγε (*emphatic form*) to me
περιορᾶν to overlook, disregard   ἐὰν ... φανῇς if you are proved]

ἤδη δὲ εἰς τὰς πύλᾱς παρῆσαν. χαίρειν οὖν τὸν γέροντα
κελεύσαντες ὅ τε Δικαιόπολις καὶ ὁ παῖς ἐπορεύοντο.
[ἐπορεύοντο began their journey]

Principal Parts: -α- and -ο- Contract Verbs

πειράω, πειρᾱσω, ἐπείρᾱσα, πεπείρᾱκα, πεπείρᾱμαι, ἐπειρᾱθην (active or
   middle) I attempt, try
χράομαι, χρήσομαι, ἐχρησάμην, κέχρημαι, ἐχρήσθην (+ *dat.*) I use,
   enjoy, consult (an oracle)
δηλόω, δηλώσω, ἐδήλωσα, δεδήλωκα, δεδήλωμαι, ἐδηλώθην I show

Word Building

*From the meaning of the words at the left, deduce the meaning of those to the
right:*

1. δίδωμι (δω-/δο-)   ἡ δόσις   ἀποδίδωμι   ἐνδίδωμι   παραδίδωμι
2. προδίδωμι (I betray) ὁ προδότης ἡ προδοσίᾱ
3. τίθημι   ἀνατίθημι   ἐπιτίθημι   συντίθημι

Grammar

2. Uses of αὐτός, αὐτή, αὐτό

a. As we saw in Chapter 5 (Grammar 4, pages 50–52), the genitive,
   dative, and accusative cases of the word αὐτός, αὐτή, αὐτό when they

stand by themselves are used as pronouns meaning "him," her,"
"it," "them," and so forth. The genitive = "his," "her," "its," "their,"
e.g.:

> εἶδον **αὐτάς**. I saw *them*.
>
> εἶδον τὸν παῖδα **αὐτῆς** I saw *her* child (literally, the child *of her*).

b. In Chapter 5 we also saw that the nominative forms αὐτός, αὐτή, αὐτό
and their plurals αὐτοί, αὐταί, αὐτά can be used as *intensive adjectives*
to emphasize the understood pronominal subject of the sentence, e.g.:

> **αὐτὸς** αἴρει τὸν λίθον.
> He *himself* lifts the stone.

The word may also be used as an intensive adjective modifying a
noun in any of its cases, e.g.:

> ἡ παρθένος **αὐτὴ** προσῆλθε πρὸς τὴν κρήνην.
> The girl *herself* approached the spring.

> εἶδον **αὐτὴν** τὴν παρθένον προσιοῦσαν πρὸς τὴν κρήνην.
> I saw the girl *herself* approaching the spring.

Note that when used this way the adjective stands in the predicate
position either before or after the article-noun group but never between
the article and the noun.

c. When αὐτός stands in the attributive position between the article and
the noun, it means "same," e.g.:

> ἡ **αὐτὴ** παρθένος προσῆλθε πρὸς τὸν οἶκον.
> The *same* girl approached the house.

3. Another Type of Adjective: ταχύς, ταχεῖα, ταχύ

A small group of adjectives has forms like those of ταχύς, ταχεῖα, ταχύ
"quick," "swift." The masculine and neuter are third declension, while
the feminine is first declension (with α, because the stem ends in ι;
compare the declension of μάχαιρα, Reference Grammar, paragraph 2,
page 229):

	SINGULAR			**PLURAL**		
	Masc.	*Fem.*	*Neut.*	*Masc.*	*Fem.*	*Neut.*
Nom.	ταχύς	ταχεῖα	ταχύ	ταχεῖς	ταχεῖαι	ταχέα
Gen.	ταχέος	ταχείας	ταχέος	ταχέων	ταχειῶν	ταχέων
Dat.	ταχεῖ	ταχείᾳ	ταχεῖ	ταχέσι(ν)	ταχείαις	ταχέσι(ν)
Acc.	ταχύν	ταχεῖαν	ταχύ	ταχεῖς	ταχείας	ταχέα
Voc.	ταχύ	ταχεῖα	ταχύ	ταχεῖς	ταχεῖαι	ταχέα

The following adjectives are declined like ταχύς:

βραδύς, βραδεῖα, βραδύ slow   βαθύς, βαθεῖα, βαθύ deep
ἡδύς, ἡδεῖα, ἡδύ sweet   τραχύς, τραχεῖα, τραχύ rough

Exercise 18f

Read aloud and translate:

1. οἱ πολέμιοι οὐ τολμήσουσι τὰ αὐτὰ αὖθις πρᾶξαι.
2. ἡ γυνὴ τὰ χρήματα τῷ ἰατρῷ παραδοῦσα οἴκαδε ἐπανῆλθε τῇ αὐτῇ ὁδῷ.
3. αὐτὸς ὁ βασιλεὺς εἰς τὴν ἀγορὰν εἴσιν ὡς ταῦτα τῷ δήμῳ ἀγγελῶν.
4. χρή σε τῷ θεῷ αὐτῷ χάριν δοῦναι.

Exercise 18g

Translate into Greek:

1. The sailors themselves were afraid of the storm.
2. We sailed home in the same ship, which was swift and big.
3. The farmer is driving the same oxen up the rough road.
4. I will send you (**παρά σε**) the messenger himself to tell you what you ought to do.

*   *   *

Η ΕΝ ΤΑΙΣ ΠΛΑΤΑΙΑΙΣ ΝΙΚΗ

Read the following passage (adapted from Herodotus 11.13, 19, 20, 50–51, and 63–65), describing the Plataea campaign of spring, 479 B.C., and answer the comprehension questions below:

ὁ δὲ Μαρδόνιος μαθὼν ὅτι οἱ Λακεδαιμόνιοι ἤδη στρατεύονται, τὰς Ἀθήνᾱς ἐμπρήσᾱς καὶ πάντα τά τε οἰκήματα καὶ τὰ ἱερὰ διαφθείρᾱς, εἰς τὴν Βοιωτίᾱν ὑπεξεχώρει. οἱ μὲν οὖν Λακεδαιμόνιοι προϊόντες εἰς τὴν Ἀττικὴν ἀφίκοντο, οἱ δὲ Ἀθηναῖοι διαβάντες ἐκ τῆς Σαλαμῖνος τοῖς Πελοποννησίοις συνεμίγησαν.

[ὁ . . . **Μαρδόνιος** Mardonius   **ἐμπρήσᾱς** (*from* ἐμπίμπρημι) having set fire to
τὰ . . . **οἰκήματα** the dwellings   **ὑπεξεχώρει** withdrew   **προϊόντες**
advancing   **διαβάντες** having crossed over   **συνεμίγησαν** (*from* συμμείγνῡμι)
joined with (+ *dat.*)

1. What did Mardonius learn?
2. What three things did he then do in Athens? What did he do next?
3. What did the Lacedaemonians and Athenians do?

ἐπεὶ δὲ εἰς τὴν Βοιωτίᾱν ἀφίκοντο, ἔγνωσαν ὅτι οἱ βάρβαροι ἐπὶ τῷ Ἀσώπῳ   5
ποταμῷ στρατοπεδεύονται· ἀντετάσσοντο οὖν ἐπὶ λόφῳ τινί. ὁ δὲ Μαρδόνιος, ὡς οὐ
κατέβαινον εἰς τὸ πεδίον οἱ Ἕλληνες, πᾶν τὸ ἱππικὸν ἐξέπεμψεν ἐπ' αὐτούς. οἱ δὲ
Ἕλληνες τό τε ἱππικὸν ὤσαντο καὶ αὐτὸν τὸν στρατηγὸν ἀπέκτειναν, ὥστε
ἐθάρρησαν πολλῷ μᾶλλον. μετὰ δὲ ταῦτα ἔδοξεν αὐτοῖς καταβῆναι πρὸς τὰς
Πλαταιάς. οἱ δὲ βάρβαροι, μαθόντες ὅτι οἱ Ἕλληνές εἰσιν ἐν Πλαταιαῖς, καὶ αὐτοὶ   10
ἐκεῖσε ἐπορεύοντο. ὁ δὲ Μαρδόνιος τὸν στρατὸν ἔταξεν ὡς μαχούμενος.

[τῷ **Ἀσώπῳ ποταμῷ** the Asopus River   **στρατοπεδεύονται** are pitching camp
ἀντετάσσοντο they positioned themselves opposite (them)   τὸ **πεδίον** the plain

τὸ ἱππικόν their cavalry   ὦσαντο pushed back   τὰς Πλαταιάς Plataea
ἔταξεν (from τάττω) drew up in battle array   μαχούμενος (future participle)]

4. When the Lacedaemonians and Athenians arrived in Boeotia, what did
   they learn? What did they do then?
5. What did Mardonius do when the Greeks did not come down onto the
   plain?
6. What happened to Mardonius' cavalry and its general?
7. What did the Greeks then decide to do? What did the barbarians do?

ἕνδεκα μὲν οὖν ἡμέρᾱς ἔμενον, οὐδέτεροι βουλόμενοι μάχης ἄρξαι· τῇ δὲ
δωδεκάτῃ τῷ Παυσανίᾳ ἔδοξεν αὖθις μεταστῆναι· ἅμα μὲν γὰρ σῑ́του ἐδέοντο καὶ
ὕδατος, ἅμα δὲ κακὰ ἔπασχον ὑπὸ τοῦ ἱππικοῦ αἰεὶ προσβάλλοντος. νύκτα οὖν
μείναντες ἐπορεύοντο. ἐπεὶ δὲ ἐγένετο ἡ ἡμέρᾱ, ὁ Μαρδόνιος εἶδεν τὸ τῶν   15
Ἑλλήνων στρατόπεδον ἔρημον ὄν· τοὺς οὖν Ἕλληνας δρόμῳ ἐδίωκεν. καὶ πρῶτον
μὲν οἱ βάρβαροι τοὺς Ἀθηναίους κατέλαβον, οἳ ἀνδρειότατα μαχόμενοι τὸ ἱππικὸν
ὦσαντο. ἔπειτα δὲ ὁ Μαρδόνιος τοῖς Λακεδαιμονίοις ἐνέπεσεν, καὶ καρτερὰ
ἐγένετο μάχη. ἐπεὶ δὲ αὐτὸς ὁ Μαρδόνιος ἀπέθανεν, οἱ βάρβαροι τρεψάμενοι εἰς τὸ
στρατόπεδον οὐδενὶ κόσμῳ ἔφυγον.   20

[οὐδέτεροι neither side   ἄρξαι (from ἄρχω) to begin (+ gen.)   τῇ . . .
δωδεκάτῃ on the twelfth day   τῷ Παυσανίᾳ to Pausanias   μεταστῆναι to
change his position   ἐδέοντο they needed, lacked (+ gen.)   ὑπὸ τοῦ ἱππικοῦ by
or at the hands of the cavalry   τὸ στρατόπεδον the camp   ἔρημον deserted
δρόμῳ at a run, at full speed   ὦσαντο pushed back   καρτερά mighty]

8. What did Pausanias finally decide to do? Why? Cite three reasons.
9. What did Mardonius discover the next day? What did he do?
10. When the barbarians and Athenians engaged in combat, who fought
    most bravely and with what result?
11. What happened when Mardonius attacked the Lacedaemonians?
12. What did the barbarians do when Mardonius was killed?

Exercise 18h

Translate into Greek:

1. The Spartans, pursuing the barbarians to their camp, attacked the
   wall but could not take it.
2. When the Athenians came to help (use βοηθέω for the whole verbal
   idea here), the barbarians did not flee but fought bravely.
3. Finally the Greeks climbed (went up onto) the wall, and the
   barbarians fled in disorder.
4. After the battle, Pausanias, the general of the Spartans, himself set up
   a memorial (μνημεῖον) at Delphi (Δελφοῖς):
   Ἑλλήνων ἀρχηγὸς (leader) ἐπεὶ στρατὸν ὤλεσε (destroyed) Μήδων,
   Παυσανίᾱς Φοίβῳ (to Phoebus Apollo) μνῆμ' ἀνέθηκε τόδε.

19
Ο ΝΟΣΤΟΣ (α)

τῶν ἀνθρώπων ἐλάᾱς συλλεγόντων, παῖς τις εἰς τὸ δένδρον ἀναβαίνει.

Vocabulary

Verbs

ἐσθίω, ἔδομαι, ἔφαγον,
  ἐδήδοκα I eat
νοστέω I return home
συλλέγω, συλλέξω,
  συνέλεξα, συνείλοχα,
  συνείλεγμαι, συνελέγην
  I collect, gather

Nouns

ἡ ἐλάᾱ, τῆς ἐλάᾱς olive,
  olive tree
ὁ νόστος, τοῦ νόστου return
  (home)
τὸ πεδίον, τοῦ πεδίου plain

Expression

μὰ Δία by Zeus

ὡς δὲ εἰς τὸν λιμένα ἀφίκοντο μάλα ἔκαμνον καί, ἤδη θάλποντος
τοῦ ἡλίου, ὑπὸ ἐλάᾳ καθιζόμενοι οἶνόν τε ἔπιον καὶ σῖτον ἔφαγον.
δι' ὀλίγου δὲ ὁ Δικαιόπολις εἶπεν· "τί δεῖ ποιεῖν, ὦ παῖ; οὐδενὸς γὰρ
ὄντος ἡμῖν ἀργυρίου, οὐκ ἔξεστιν ἡμῖν κατὰ θάλατταν οἴκαδε
νοστεῖν. δεῖ οὖν πεζοὺς ἰέναι." ὁ δὲ Φίλιππος, "μὴ περὶ τούτου   5
φρόντιζε, ὦ πάτερ· ἐγὼ γὰρ χαιρήσω πεζὸς ἰὼν καὶ τὰ ἔργα θεώμενος
καὶ τὰ ὄρη. ἀλλὰ πῶς εὑρήσομεν τὴν ὁδὸν τὴν πρὸς τὰς Ἀθήνᾱς
φέρουσαν;" ὁ δέ, "μὴ περὶ τούτου γε φρόντιζε, ὦ παῖ· ῥᾳδίως γὰρ
εὑρήσομεν αὐτήν. ἀνάστηθι οὖν· εἰ γὰρ δοκεῖ, καιρός ἐστιν
ὁρμῆσαι."   10

[θάλποντος being hot   τὰ ἔργα tilled fields]

ἀναστάντες οὖν ἐπορεύοντο, καὶ πρῶτον μὲν διὰ πεδίου ἦσαν, ἐν
ᾧ πολλὰ ἦν ἔργα ἀνθρώπων· πολλοὺς δὲ ἀνθρώπους ἑώρων ἐν τοῖς
ἀγροῖς ἐργαζομένους, ὧν οἱ μὲν τοὺς βοῦς ἤλαυνον ἀροτρεύοντες
τὴν ἄρουραν, οἱ δὲ τὰς ἐλάᾱς συνέλεγον εἰς τὰ δένδρα ἀναβαίνοντες.
ὡς δὲ τοῖς ὄρεσι προσεχώρουν, ἀλώᾱς ἑώρων, ἐν αἷς οἱ ἄνθρωποι   15
τοὺς βότρυας συνέλεγον· καὶ τῶν βοτρύων τοὺς μὲν οἴκαδε ἔφερον
ὄνοι ἐν μεγάλοις κανθηλίοις, τοὺς δὲ αἱ γυναῖκες ἐπὶ τῇ γῇ ἐτίθεσαν
ὥστε τῷ ἡλίῳ τέρσεσθαι.

[ἑώρων (*imperfect of* ὁράω) they saw   **τὴν ἄρουραν** the plowland   **ἀλώᾱς**
vineyards   **τοὺς βότρυας** bunches of grapes   **ὄνοι** donkeys   **κανθηλίοις**
baskets   **τέρσεσθαι** to dry]

Principal Parts: Labial Stems (-β-, -π-)

βλάπ-τω (βλαβ-), βλάψω, ἔβλαψα, βέβλαφα, βέβλαμμαι, ἐβλάφθην *o r*
    ἐβλάβην I harm
λείπω (λειπ-/λοιπ-/λιπ-), λείψω, ἔλιπον, λέλοιπα, λέλειμμαι (I am left
    behind, am inferior), ἐλείφθην I leave
πέμπω (πεμπ-/πομπ-), πέμψω, ἔπεμψα, πέπομφα, πέπεμμαι, ἐπέμφθην
    I send

Word Study

*Explain the meaning of the following English words with reference to their
Greek roots:*

1. aristocracy
2. autocracy
3. plutocracy (ὁ πλοῦτος = wealth)
4. theocracy
5. bureaucracy
6. technocracy (ἡ τέχνη = art, skill)

Grammar

1. The Genitive Absolute

Examine the following sentence:

θάλποντος τοῦ ἡλίου, ὑπὸ ἐλάᾳ ἐκαθίζοντο.
Since the sun was hot, they were sitting under the olive tree.

The words in boldface consist of a participle and a noun in the genitive
case. They have no grammatical relationship to the rest of the sentence.
This use of a participle with a noun or pronoun in the genitive case is
called a *genitive absolute*. The term *absolute* comes from a Latin word
meaning "separated" or "independent." Here are other examples:

οὐδενὸς ὄντος ἡμῖν **ἀργυρίου**, οὐκ ἔξεστιν ἡμῖν κατὰ θάλατταν
οἴκαδε νοστεῖν.
There being no money for us (= since we have no money), we cannot
return home by sea.

ἡμέρᾱς γενομένης, ὁ πατὴρ τὸν παῖδα καλέσᾱς ἔπεμψε ὡς ζητήσοντα
τὰ μῆλα.
At daybreak, the father, upon calling his son, sent him to seek the
flocks.

In this sentence, ἡμέρᾱς γενομένης is absolute, i.e., not part of the structure
of the rest of the sentence, whereas the participle καλέσᾱς agrees with
πατήρ, the subject in the main clause, and the participle ζητήσοντα agrees
with παῖδα, the direct object in the main clause.

Genitive absolutes can often best be translated into English with
clauses beginning with "since," "as," "when," or "although." The
choice of which introductory word to use will usually be clear from the
meaning of the sentence as a whole, but sometimes a word such as καίπερ
"although" will provide a helpful clue.

Exercise 19a

*Read aloud and translate the following sentences. Pay particular attention
to aspect in the Greek and to tense in English when translating participles:*

1. ἑσπέρᾱς γιγνομένης, οἱ ξένοι εἰς τὸ ἄστυ ἀφίκοντο.
2. τοῦ γέροντος ὀργιζομένου, ὁ παῖς ἐφοβεῖτο.
3. πάντων ἑτοίμων ὄντων, ὁ ἱερεὺς τὴν θυσίᾱν ἐποιήσατο.
4. τοῦ ἀνέμου μείζονος γενομένου, ἡ ναῦς, ὀλίγη οὖσα, ἐν κινδύνῳ ἦν.
5. καίπερ τῆς πόλεως πολὺ ἀπεχούσης, οὐκ ἐσπεύδομεν.
6. νυκτὸς γενομένης, ἔδοξεν ἡμῖν ἐν τῷ ἄστει μένειν.
7. τῶν αὐτουργῶν ἐχθρῶν γενομένων, οἱ νεᾱνίαι τὸ πεδίον καταλιπόντες
   ἐπὶ τὸ ὄρος ἀνέβησαν.
8. καίπερ καμνούσης τῆς γυναικός, ὁ ἀνὴρ ταχέως κατὰ τὸ ὄρος κατῄει.
9. τῆς θυγατρὸς αἰτούσης, βραδύτερον ἐβάδιζεν ὁ πατήρ.
10. τοῦ ἱερέως αἰτήσαντος, οἱ ἱκέται ἄγαλμα (*offering*) ἀνέθεσαν.
11. τῶν ἱκετῶν πολὺ ἀργύριον ἀποδόντων, ὁ ἱερεὺς ἄγαλμα ἀνέθηκεν.
12. τοῦ ἡλίου ἀνατέλλοντος (*rising*), ὁ παῖς ἤδη πρὸς τὸν ἀγρὸν ᾔει.
13. τοῦ ἡλίου καταδύντος (*having set*), πᾶσαν τὴν ἡμέρᾱν ἐργασάμενος ὁ
    παῖς οἴκαδε ἐπανιέναι ἐβούλετο.

Exercise 19b

Translate into Greek:

1. At daybreak, we went on foot to the harbor.
2. At the sailor's request (= the sailor having asked), we decided (= it
   seemed good to us) to board the ship immediately.
3. On the captain's order (= the captain ordering), the sailors cast off
   (*use form of* λύω) the ship.
4. Although the wind was strong (*use form of* μέγας) and the waves
   were big, no one was afraid.
5. Since the ship was in danger, the captain ordered the sailors to lower
   (στεῖλαι) the sails.

Mycenae

On their return journey overland, Philip and his father visit the famous ruins of Mycenae, which were not far off their route. The lion gate to the citadel is shown here.

Mycenae stands on a hill skirted by two deep ravines. The site is a natural strong point, dominating the plain of Argos. It was first occupied about 3,000 B.C., and a new settlement was made about 2,000 B.C., which is generally believed to be the time when Greek speakers arrived in Greece. There is clear evidence for a sudden increase in the importance and prosperity of this settlement about 1,600 B.C.; two grave circles have been found, one inside the later walls and containing six shaft graves, excavated by Schliemann in the 1870s, the other rather earlier in date, outside the walls, discovered in 1950. These graves contained a mass of gold and other precious objects of great beauty, including imports from Minoan Crete and Egypt.

The power and wealth of Mycenae increased rapidly. There was soon a uniform culture in mainland Greece, stretching from Thessaly in the north to the south of the Peloponnesus, with palaces at Thebes, Athens, Mycenae, Tiryns, and Pylos and probably at other sites not yet discovered. Although the palaces were the administrative centers of separate kingdoms, it seems likely that Mycenae was the leading, if not the dominant, kingdom. From 1500 B.C. the kings of Mycenae were buried in massive stone tombs outside the walls, of which the largest, the so-called Treasury of Atreus, is a magnificent architectural achievement.

About 1450 B.C. the Achaeans, as the Greeks of the Mycenaen period were called, invaded Crete and destroyed all the Minoan palaces except Knossos, which they occupied. Succeeding to Minoan control of the seas, the Achaeans now traded widely throughout the Eastern Mediterranean and made settlements on the islands and in Asia Minor. The zenith of Mycenaean power and prosperity was in the early thirteenth century; in this period were built the walls, some of which still stand, and the lion gate. By about 1250 B.C., when the defenses were renewed and improved, there is evidence of destruction outside the walls. Trade declined; a period of upheaval and deterioration had begun. The Trojan War is thought to have occurred about this time. The traditional date for the fall of Troy is 1184 B.C., but the American archaeologist Blegen, who made the most complete recent excavations and found clear evidence of a prolonged siege, dates the destruction of Troy to about 1240 B.C. It looks as though the Trojan expedition was the last united effort of the Achaeans.

Mycenae was subjected to three successive attacks in the following years. In the first, the houses outside the walls were destroyed; in the second, the citadel was sacked; in the third, it was finally destroyed and not reoccupied. The other mainland palaces were all sacked around 1200 B.C., presumably by bands of invading Dorians.

The entrance to the Treasury of Atreus

During the Dark Ages a new settlement was made on the site of Mycenae, which developed into a miniature *polis;* this sent a small contingent to fight at Plataea, but in 468 B.C. it was attacked and destroyed by Argos. When Philip visited it in our story, the site was abandoned; the massive walls and the lion gate still stood, but the rest was overgrown and undisturbed until Schliemann arrived in 1876.

Around Mycenae centered one of the most important cycles of Greek myth. The royal house of Mycenae was doomed. Its founder had been Pelops. His father Tantalus wanted to find out whether the gods were really omniscient. He killed his own child Pelops and served him up to the gods at a feast; none of the gods would touch the meat except for Demeter, who was distracted by grief and ate part of his shoulder. The gods restored him to life and replaced his missing shoulder with one of ivory. When he had grown up, he wooed Hippodamia, daughter of Oenomaus. In order to win her hand, he had to beat her father in a chariot race. He bribed Oenomaus' charioteer to remove the linchpin of the axle. In the race, Oenomaus was thrown and killed, but as he lay dying he cursed Pelops.

Pelops carried off the dead king's daughter to Mycenae and founded a dynasty that was unremittingly haunted by the curse. His sons were Atreus and Thyestes. Thyestes seduced Atreus' wife, and Atreus banished him. Atreus then pretended to be reconciled and invited his brother to a banquet; at this feast he served up Thyestes' own children. Thyestes found a human finger in his portion and, realizing what Atreus had done, kicked over the table and fled, cursing Atreus and all his family. Thyestes had a son, Aegisthus, by his own daughter; together they murdered Atreus.

Agamemnon succeeded Atreus as king, and when he led the Greeks to Troy, he left the kingdom in the care of his wife, Clytemnestra. The Greek fleet, however, en route for Troy was held up by unceasing contrary winds. The prophet said that these winds would only cease if Agamemnon sacrificed his daughter to Artemis. Agamemnon sent for his daughter Iphigenia on the pretext that she was to wed Achilles, and with his own hand he cut her throat over the altar.

During Agamemnon's absence, Clytemnestra took Aegisthus as her lover and planned vengeance. When, after ten years, Agamemnon returned, the lovers murdered him, entrapping him in a net while he was in the bath. Orestes, the young son of Agamemnon and Clytemnestra, escaped into exile, saved by his nurse; the daughters, Chrysothemis and Electra, remained in the palace. When Orestes grew to manhood, he consulted Apollo's oracle at Delphi and was ordered to avenge his father's murder. He returned to Mycenae secretly and with Electra's help murdered both Aegisthus and his own mother. He was then pursued by the Furies and took refuge at Apollo's altar. The curse, which had haunted the family through four generations, was finally laid to rest when Athena acquitted Orestes of bloodguilt on the grounds that he had been ordered by Apollo to perform the murders.

Ο ΝΟΣΤΟΣ (β)

Vocabulary

Verbs
ἀγνοέω I do not know
ἀναπαύομαι, ἀναπαύσομαι,
  ἀνεπαυσάμην,
  ἀναπέπαυμαι I rest
ἐντυγχάνω (see τυγχάνω for
  principal parts) (+ dat.) I meet
παραινέω, παραινέσω,
  παρῄνεσα, παρῄνεκα,
  παρῄνημαι, παρῃνέθην
  (+ dat. and infinitive) I advise
  (someone to do something)
σημαίνω, σημανῶ, ἐσήμηνα,
  σεσήμασμαι, ἐσημάνθην I
  signal, sign, show

Nouns
ὁ ποιμήν, τοῦ ποιμένος
  shepherd
ἡ ὕλη, τῆς ὕλης woods, forest
ὁ φόβος, τοῦ φόβου fear, panic
ὁ ὦμος, τοῦ ὤμου shoulder

Adjectives
βαθύς, -εῖα, -ύ deep
ἔρημος, -ον deserted
τραχύς, -εῖα, -ύ rough

Adverbs
ἥδιστα (superlative of ἡδέως)
  most sweetly, most pleasantly,
  most gladly

Proper Name
ἡ Ἄργη, τῆς Ἄργης Arge
  (name of a dog)

οὐ μέντοι διὰ πολλοῦ τὰ τῶν ἀνθρώπων ἔργα καταλιπόντες,
ἀνέβησαν ἐπὶ τὰ ὄρη· καὶ σπανίως ἤδη ἐνετύγχανον ἀνθρώποις,
ποιμένας δὲ ὀλίγους ἑώρων οἳ τὰ μῆλα ἔνεμον. ἦσαν δὲ διὰ μεγάλων
ὑλῶν, ἐν αἷς πολλαί τε δρύες ἦσαν καὶ πολλαὶ ἐλάται. τραχείᾱς δὲ
γενομένης τῆς ὁδοῦ καὶ οὐ ῥᾱδίᾱς εὑρεῖν, ὁ μὲν Δικαιόπολις εἰς   5
ἀπορίᾱν κατέστη ἀγνοῶν τὴν ὁδόν· ὁ δὲ Φίλιππος ἄνθρωπον ἰδὼν
προσιόντα, "ἰδού, ὦ πάτερ," ἔφη, "ἆρα ὁρᾷς ἐκεῖνον τὸν ἄνδρα
κατιόντα πρὸς ἡμᾶς;" ὁ δὲ Δικαιόπολις, "ἀλλὰ ποῦ ἐστιν; οὐ γὰρ
ὁρῶ." ὁ δὲ Φίλιππος, "ἐκεῖ, ἐγγὺς ἐκείνης τῆς δρυός. φαίνεται δὲ
κυνηγέτης ὤν· κύων γὰρ Λάκαινα ἕπεται αὐτῷ."   10

[σπανίως rarely   ἔνεμον were grazing   δρύες oaks   ἐλάται pines
κατέστη got into   κυνηγέτης hunter   Λάκαινα Laconian, Spartan]

προσχωροῦντος δὲ τοῦ νεᾱνίου, ἡ κύων ἀγρίως ὑλακτεῖ καὶ
ὁρμᾶται ἐπ' αὐτούς· ὁ δὲ νεᾱνίᾱς ἔστη καὶ βοήσᾱς, "στῆθι, Ἄργη,"
ἔφη, "καὶ σίγησον." ὁ οὖν Δικαιόπολις προσιών, "χαῖρε, ὦ νεᾱνίᾱ,"
ἔφη, "ἆρ' οἶσθά σὺ εἰ αὕτη ἡ ὁδὸς πρὸς τὴν Κόρινθον φέρει;" ὁ δέ,
"μάλιστά γε, ἐκεῖσε φέρει· ἰδού—ἔξεστιν αὐτὴν ἰδεῖν ὑπὲρ τὸ ὄρος   15
φέρουσαν. ῥᾳδίως δὲ γνώσεσθε αὐτήν, τῶν γε ἑρμάτων σημαινόντων.

ἀλλὰ πολὺ ἀπέχει ἡ Κόρινθος καὶ δι' ὀλίγου ἡ νὺξ γενήσεται· ἴσως δὲ
εἰς κίνδῡνον καταστήσεσθε μόνοι ἐν τοῖς ὄρεσι νυκτερεύοντες.
ἐρήμων γὰρ ὄντων τῶν ὀρῶν οὐδενὶ ἐντεύξεσθε ἀνθρώπων εἰ μὴ
ποιμένι τινί. ἀλλ' ἄγε, πῶς ἔχετε τοῦ σίτου; ἀλλὰ μείνατε· δώσω γὰρ   20
ὑμῖν λαγών. ἰδού." καὶ ταῦτα εἰπὼν τὸ ῥόπαλον, ὃ ἐπὶ τοῖς ὤμοις
ἔφερε, κατέθηκεν· δύο γὰρ θηρία ἐκ τοῦ ῥοπάλου ἐκρέματο, ὧν ἕνα
λύσᾱς τῷ Δικαιοπόλιδι παρέδωκεν. ὁ δὲ δεξάμενος πλείστην χάριν
ἀπέδωκεν. ὁ δὲ νεᾱνίᾱς, "οὐδέν ἐστιν," ἔφη, "πλεῖστοι γὰρ λαγὼ
γίγνονται ἐν τοῖς ὄρεσιν, ἐγὼ δὲ ῥᾳδίως αἱρῶ αὐτούς· δεινότατος γάρ   25
εἰμι κυνηγετεῖν. χαίρετε οὖν καὶ εὐτυχοῖτε." ταῦτα δ' εἰπὼν
ἐπορεύετο κατὰ τὴν ἀτραπόν, οἱ δὲ βραδέως ἀνῇσαν.

[ὑλακτεῖ barks   ἆρ' οἶσθα do you know?   τῶν . . . ἑρμάτων the stone heaps,
cairns   καταστήσεσθε you will get into   νυκτερεύοντες spending the night
πῶς ἔχετε τοῦ σίτου how are you off for food?   λαγών hare   ῥόπαλον
hunter's staff   θηρία beasts, animals   ἐκρέματο (from κρεμάννῡμι) were
hanging   δεινότατος very skilled at (+ infinitive)   κυνηγετεῖν to hunt
εὐτυχοῖτε good luck to you!   τὴν ἀτραπόν the path]

ἑσπέρᾱς δὲ γιγνομένης ποιμένι τινὶ ἐνέτυχον, ὃς τὰ μῆλα κατὰ τὴν
ὁδὸν ἤλαυνεν. ὁ δὲ ἰδὼν αὐτοὺς προσιόντας εἰς φόβον κατέστη καὶ
βοήσᾱς, "τίνες ἐστέ," ἔφη, "οἳ διὰ τῆς νυκτὸς πορεύεσθε; πόθεν ἤλθετε   30
καὶ ποῖ ἴτε;" ὁ δὲ Δικαιόπολις προσιὼν πάντα ἐξηγήσατο, ὁ δὲ ποιμὴν
εὐμενῶς δεξάμενος αὐτούς, "ἀλλὰ πάντες," ἔφη, "πρὸς Διός εἰσι
πτωχοί τε ξεῖνοί τε. ἀλλὰ νυκτὸς ἤδη γιγνομένης παραινῶ ὑμῖν
μόνοις οὖσι μὴ νυκτερεύειν ἐν τοῖς ὄρεσιν. ἄγετε δή, ἔλθετε μετ' ἐμοῦ
εἰς τὴν καλύβην, ἐν ᾗ ἔξεστιν ὑμῖν μένειν τὴν νύκτα." οἱ δ' οὖν τοὺς   35
τοῦ ποιμένος λόγους ἀσμένως δεξάμενοι εἵποντο αὐτῷ εἰς ὀλίγην τινὰ
καλύβην. ὁ δὲ ποιμήν, "ἰδού· εἴσιτε. ἐγὼ μὲν τάς τ' αἶγας ἀμέλξω καὶ
τὰς οἶς, ὑμεῖς δὲ τὰ σκεύη καταθέντες πῦρ καύσατε καὶ καθίζεσθε."

[πρὸς Διός under the protection of Zeus   πτωχοί τε ξεῖνοί τε beggars and
strangers   τὴν καλύβην my hut   ἀσμένως gladly   εἵποντο (imperfect of
ἕπομαι) were following   τάς . . . αἶγας my goats   ἀμέλξω I will milk   τὰς
οἶς my ewes   τὰ σκεύη baggage   καύσατε (aorist imperative of καίω)]

ὁ μὲν οὖν Φίλιππος πῦρ ἔκαυσεν, ὁ δὲ πατὴρ καθιζόμενος
ἀνεπαύετο ἐκ μακρᾶς ὁδοῦ. ὁ δὲ ποιμὴν τὰ μῆλα ἀμέλξᾱς, ἐπανιὼν   40
δεῖπνον παρεσκεύαζε—σῖτόν τε καὶ τῡρὸν καὶ γάλα. ὁ δὲ
Δικαιόπολις, "ἰδού, ὦ φίλε," ἔφη, "κυνηγέτης τις, ᾧ κατὰ τὴν ὁδὸν
ἐνετύχομεν, τόνδε τὸν λαγὼν ἡμῖν ἔδωκεν. ἆρ' οὖν βούλῃ ὀπτᾶν
αὐτὸν ἐπὶ δείπνῳ;" ὁ δέ, "μάλιστά γε· οὕτω γὰρ ἥδιστα δειπνήσομεν·

μετὰ δὲ τὸ δεῖπνον ὁ παῖς μέλη ᾄσεται." τὸν οὖν λαγὼν ὀπτήσαντες   45
ἡδέως ἐδείπνησαν· ἔπειτα δὲ ὁ μὲν Φίλιππος μέλη ᾖδεν, ὁ δὲ ποιμὴν
μύθους ἔλεγεν, ἕως πάντες οὕτως ἔκαμνον ὥστε εἰς βαθὺν ὕπνον
ἔπεσον.

[τῡρόν cheese   γάλα milk   ὀπτᾶν to roast   μέλη ᾄσεται will sing songs
ᾖδεν he sang]

Principal Parts: More Labial Stems (-π-, -φ-)

κόπ-τω, κόψω, ἔκοψα, κέκοφα, κέκομμαι, ἐκόπην I strike, knock on (a
    door)
τύπ-τω (τυπ-/τυπτε-), τυπτήσω I strike
γράφω, γράψω, ἔγραψα, γέγραφα, γέγραμμαι, ἐγράφην   I write

Word Building

*From your knowledge of the prepositions at the left, deduce the meaning of the
adverbs at the right:*

1. ἀνά   ἄνω   3. ἐκ, ἐξ   ἔξω   5. κατά   κάτω
2. εἰς   εἴσω   4. ἐν   ἔνδον   6. πρός   πρόσω

Grammar

2. Attributive and Predicate Position of Adjectives

As we have seen, adjectives may stand in either an attributive or a
predicate position with respect to the article-noun group that they modify
(see Book I, page 52), e.g.:

Attributive Position: Predicate Position:

ἡ **καλὴ** παρθένος   **καλὴ** ἡ παρθένος.
ἡ παρθένος ἡ **καλή**   ἡ παρθένος **καλή**.
the *beautiful* girl   The girl is *beautiful*.

The demonstrative adjectives always occupy the predicate position
(see Book I, page 179), e.g.:

ἐκείνη ἡ παρθένος
that girl

Note the following examples:

οἱ Πέρσαι αἱροῦσιν τὸ **ἔρημον** ἄστυ.
    The Persians take the *deserted* city. (attributive)
οἱ Πέρσαι αἱροῦσιν **ἔρημον** τὸ ἄστυ.
    The Persians take the city *deserted*. (predicate)

In the first example above the adjective in the attributive position tells
which city the Persians took: they took the *deserted* city. In the second
example the adjective in the predicate position adds a comment about
the city that the Persians took: it was *deserted*.

3. Other Attributives

Genitives of nouns, prepositional phrases, and adverbs may occupy the same position as attributive adjectives, e.g.:

αἱ **τῶν βαρβάρων** νῆες or αἱ νῆες αἱ **τῶν βαρβάρων**
the *barbarians'* ships

οἱ **ἐν τῷ ἀγρῷ** δοῦλοι or οἱ δοῦλοι οἱ **ἐν τῷ ἀγρῷ**
the slaves *in the field*

οἱ **νῦν** παῖδες or οἱ παῖδες οἱ **νῦν**
the children *of today*

(Note, however, that the possessive genitive of αὐτός takes the predicate position, e.g., ἡ μάχαιρα **αὐτοῦ** or **αὐτοῦ** ἡ μάχαιρα = *his* knife.)

4. Further Uses of the Article

Genitives of nouns, prepositional phrases, and adverbs may be attached to the article as attributives without a noun, e.g.:

ὁ βασιλέως = the (son) of the king, the king's son
οἱ ἐν τῇ ἀγορᾷ = the men in the market place
αἱ πρὸς τῇ κρήνῃ = the women at the spring
οἱ πάλαι = the men of long ago
οἱ νῦν = the present generation

Note especially the use of τά + the genitive case in phrases such as the following:

τὰ τῆς πόλεως = the things (e.g., the affairs) of the city
τὰ τοῦ πολέμου = the things (e.g., the resources) of *or* for war
τὰ τῆς τύχης = the things (e.g., the ways) of fortune

Article + Adjective = Noun Phrase. Note the following:

οἱ ἀνδρεῖοι = brave men
αἱ σώφρονες = sensible women
τὰ κακά = evils, troubles

The neuter of the adjective + the article is often used as an abstract noun, e.g., τὸ καλόν = beauty, virtue, honor; τὸ αἰσχρόν = dishonor, disgrace, vice; τὸ ἀληθές or τὰ ἀληθῆ = truth; and τὸ δίκαιον = justice.

Exercise 19c

Read aloud and translate:

1. οἱ ἐν τῇ νήσῳ πολλὰ καὶ κακὰ ἔπασχον.
2. οὐ σώφρων ὁ γέρων· οὐ γὰρ ἐπίσταται τὰ τῆς τύχης.
3. οἱ νῦν οὐδὲν κακίονές εἰσι τῶν προγόνων.

4. πάντες οἱ σώφρονες ἐτίμων τοὺς ἐν ἐκείνῃ τῇ μάχῃ ἀποθανόντας.
5. οἱ Ἕλληνες τὰ τῆς θαλάττης ἐπιστάμενοι ἐδύναντο τοὺς βαρβάρους
   νῑκῆσαι, καίπερ ἐλάττονας ἔχοντες ναῦς.
6. τὰ τοῦ πολέμου οὐκ ἔχοντες μόλις δυνάμεθα πολεμίοις ἀντέχειν.
7. αἱ τῶν βαρβάρων νῆες μείζονες ἦσαν καὶ βραδύτεραι ἢ αἱ τῶν Ἑλλήνων.
8. οἱ ναῦται οἱ ἐν ἐκείνῃ τῇ νηῒ ἀγνοοῦσι πόσος χειμὼν γενήσεται.
9. ἆρα ἐνέτυχες τῷ ποιμένι τῷ τὰ μῆλα ἀνὰ τὴν ὁδὸν ἐλαύνοντι;
10. χαλεπὸν τὸ καλόν· οὕτω λέγουσιν οἱ σοφοὶ καὶ οὐχ ἁμαρτάνουσιν.

Exercise 19d

Translate into Greek:

1. This girl is beautiful; don't you admire beauty?
2. Good men help (their) friends and harm (their) enemies.
3. Are you speaking the truth, boy? Those who tell lies fare badly.
4. The king's son did not know the ways of fortune.
5. We found the city deserted and corpses lying in the roads.

*   *   *

ΟΙ ΕΛΛΗΝΕΣ ΤΟΥΣ ΠΕΡΣΑΣ ΚΑΤΑ ΘΑΛΑΣΣΑΝ ΔΕΥΤΕΡΟΝ ΝΙΚΩΣΙΝ

Read the following passages and answer the comprehension questions:

The battle of Mycale took place, according to tradition, on the same day as the battle of Plataea, in spring 479 B.C. The Greek victory eliminated the Persian fleet in the Aegean and was followed by a second revolt of the Ionians from Persia. The following passage is adapted from Herodotus 9.90–104.

ἅμα ἦρι ἀρχομένῳ τὸ τῶν Ἑλλήνων ναυτικὸν εἰς τὴν Αἴγῑναν συνελέγετο, νῆες ἀριθμὸν δέκα καὶ ἑκατόν. ἐντεῦθεν δὲ εἰς τὴν Δῆλον ἔπλευσαν, βουλόμενοι τοὺς Ἴωνας ἐλευθερῶσαι. παρόντος δὲ τοῦ ναυτικοῦ ἐν τῇ Δήλῳ, ἦλθον ἄγγελοι ἀπὸ τῆς Σάμου, οἳ ᾔτησαν αὐτοὺς πρὸς Σάμον πλεύσαντας τοῖς βαρβάροις ἐπιστρατεῦσαι· "οἱ γὰρ βάρβαροι," ἔφασαν, "οὐ πολλὰς ναῦς ἔχουσιν, οἱ δὲ Ἴωνες   5
ὑμᾶς ἰδόντες εὐθὺς ἀποστήσονται ἀπὸ τῶν Περσῶν. οὕτως οὖν ἔξεστιν ὑμῖν καὶ ἄνδρας Ἕλληνας ἐλευθερῶσαι καὶ ἀμῦναι τοὺς βαρβάρους." ὁ οὖν στρατηγὸς ὁ τῶν Ἑλλήνων τούτους τοὺς λόγους δεξάμενος ταῖς ναυσὶ πρὸς Σάμον ἡγεῖτο.

[ἅμα ἦρι ἀρχομένῳ with the beginning of spring   τὴν Αἴγῑναν Aegina ἀριθμόν in number   ἐντεῦθεν from there   τὴν Δῆλον Delos   ἀποστήσονται will revolt from]

1. Where did the Greek fleet assemble, and how many ships were there?
2. Why did the fleet sail to Delos?
3. What did messengers from Samos ask the Greeks at Delos to do?
4. What two facts did the messengers cite in urging the Greeks to act?
5. What two things do the messengers claim that the Greeks could do?

6. What was the response of the Greek general?

ὡς δὲ εἰς Σάμον ἀφικόμενοι παρεσκευάζοντο εἰς ναυμαχίᾱν, οἱ Πέρσαι εὐθὺς
ἀπέπλευσαν πρὸς τὴν ἤπειρον· ἔδοξε γὰρ αὐτοῖς μὴ ναυμαχίᾱν ποιεῖσθαι· οὐ γὰρ   10
ἀξιόμαχοι ἦσαν αἱ νῆες αὐτῶν. ἀποπλεύσαντες οὖν πρὸς τὴν Μυκάλην τὰς ναῦς
ἀνείρυσαν καὶ τεῖχος ἐποίησαν περὶ αὐτάς. οἱ δὲ Ἕλληνες ταῦτα γνόντες ἐδίωκον
αὐτοὺς εἰς τὴν Μυκάλην. ὡς δὲ ἐγγὺς ἐγένοντο τοῦ τῶν πολεμίων στρατοπέδου
καὶ οὐδεὶς ἐφαίνετο ἀναγόμενος ἀλλὰ ναῦς εἶδον ἀνειλκυσμένᾱς ἔσω τοῦ τείχους,
πρῶτον μὲν παραπλέοντες τοὺς Ἴωνας ἐκάλεσαν, κελεύοντες αὐτοὺς ἀποστῆναι   15
ἀπὸ τῶν Περσῶν, ἔπειτα δὲ εἰς τὴν γῆν ἐκβάντες τῷ τείχει προσέβαλλον.
[εἰς ναυμαχίᾱν for a battle at sea   τὴν ἤπειρον the mainland   ἀξιόμαχοι
battle-worthy   τὴν Μυκάλην Mycale   ἀνείρυσαν (from ἀνερύω) they beached
τοῦ . . . στρατοπέδου the camp   ἀναγόμενος putting out to sea
ἀνειλκυσμένᾱς (from ἀνέλκω) beached, drawn up on the shore   ἔσω inside (+
gen.) παραπλέοντες sailing past   ἀποστῆναι to revolt from]

7. What did the Persians do when the Greeks arrived at Samos? Why?
8. How did the Persians protect their fleet?
9. How did the Greeks respond to this maneuver of the Persians?
10. When the Greeks saw that the Persians were not putting to sea and were
     continuing to protect their beached fleet, what two things did they do?

πρῶτον μὲν οὖν ἀνδρείως ἐμάχοντο οἱ βάρβαροι, ἐπεὶ δὲ οἱ Ἕλληνες μιᾷ ὁρμῇ
προσφερόμενοι τὸ τεῖχος εἷλον, τρεψάμενοι ἔφυγον. οἱ δὲ Ἴωνες, ὡς εἶδον τοὺς
Ἕλληνας νῑκῶντας, πρὸς αὐτοὺς αὐτομολήσαντες τοῖς βαρβάροις ἐνέπεσον. οὕτως
οὖν τὸ δεύτερον ἀπέστησαν οἱ Ἴωνες ἀπὸ τῶν Περσῶν.   20
[ὁρμῇ rush, onset   προσφερόμενοι charging   αὐτομολήσαντες deserting
ἀπέστησαν revolted]

11. What action of the Greeks put the Persians to flight?
12. At what moment did the Ionians desert the Persians?
13. When the Ionians deserted the Persians, what did they do?

Exercise 19e

Translate into Greek:

1. At the Ionians' request (*use genitive absolute with* αἰτέω), the general
    decided to lead the fleet to Samos.
2. The messengers said, "We will not betray (προδώσομεν) you but will
    revolt (ἀποστησόμεθα) from the Persians."
3. When the barbarians saw (*use participle*) the ships of the Greeks
    approaching, they fled to the mainland.
4. The Greeks disembarked from their ships and attacked the wall and
    took it. (*Use participles for "disembarked" and "attacked."*)
5. When the Ionians saw (*use participle*) the Greeks winning, they
    revolted from the Persians and helped the Greeks.

20
Ο ΝΟΣΤΟΣ (γ)

ἐν αὐτοῖς τοῖς δώμασι τοῦ Ἀγαμέμνονος ἵσταντο.

Vocabulary

Verbs

ἀρέσκει, ἀρέσει, ἤρεσε (+ *dat.*) it is pleasing

ἵστημι, (*imperfect*) **ἵστην, στήσω,** (*first aorist*) **ἔστησα,** (*second aorist*) **ἔστην, ἔστηκα, ἐστάθην** I make to stand, stop, set up; (*second aorist, intransitive*) I stood, stood still, stopped; (*perfect, intransitive*) I stand

    καθίστημι I set up, appoint, put into a certain state; (*middle and intransitive tenses of active*) I am appointed, established, get into a certain state (+ εἰς + *acc.*), I become

καθοράω (*see* ὁράω *for principal parts*) I look down on

Nouns

τὸ αἷμα, τοῦ αἵματος blood

ὁ λέων, τοῦ λέοντος lion

τὸ μέγεθος, τοῦ μεγέθους size

τὸ τέκνον, τοῦ τέκνου child

ὁ τόπος, τοῦ τόπου place

Adjectives

ἀσφαλής, -ές safe

λίθινος, -η, -ον made of stone

Preposition

ἐντός (*adverb or preposition + gen.*) within

Adverbs

ἄνω up, above

ἐξαίφνης suddenly

κάτω down, below

Particle

δήπου I suppose

Proper Names

αἱ Ἐρῑνυες, τῶν Ἐρῑνυῶν the Furies, avenging spirits

οἱ Κύκλωπες, τῶν Κυκλώπων the Cyclopes

αἱ Μυκῆναι, τῶν Μυκηνῶν Mycenae

γενομένης δὲ τῆς ἡμέρας τὸν ποιμένα χαίρειν κελεύσαντες
ἐπορεύοντο καὶ τέλος ἀφίκοντο εἰς ἄκρα τὰ ὄρη, ἀφ' ὧν κατεῖδον τό
τε πεδίον κάτω κείμενον καὶ τείχη τινὰ ἐπὶ λόφου ἑστηκότα. ὁ δὲ
Φίλιππος τὸν πατέρα στήσας, "πάππα," ἔφη, "τείχη τινὰ μεγάλα ὁρῶ
ἐπ' ἐκείνου τοῦ λόφου ἑστηκότα. ἀλλ' εἰπέ μοι, τίνα ἐστίν;" ὁ δὲ   5
Δικαιόπολις πολύν τινα χρόνον πρὸς τὰ τείχη βλέπων, "ἐκεῖνά ἐστιν,
ὦ παῖ," ἔφη, "ὡς ἐμοὶ δοκεῖ, τὰ τῶν Μυκηνῶν τείχη." ὁ δὲ Φίλιππος,
"ἆρα ἀληθῆ λέγεις;" ἔφη. "ἆρα ἐκεῖ ᾤκησεν ὁ Ἀγαμέμνων; ἆρα
ἔξεστιν ἡμῖν ἐκεῖσε καταβῆναι καὶ τὰ τοῦ Ἀγαμέμνονος δώματα
θεωρεῖν;" ὁ δὲ Δικαιόπολις, "ἔξεστι καταβῆναι, εἴ σοι δοκεῖ. οὐ γὰρ   10
μάλα πολὺ ἀπέχει τὰ τείχη τῆς ὁδοῦ, καί—ὀψὲ γάρ ἐστιν—τὴν
νύκτα ἐντὸς τῶν τειχῶν ἀσφαλεῖς μενοῦμεν."

[ἑστηκότα standing   τὰ . . . δώματα the palace]

οὕτως εἰπών, τῷ παιδὶ κατὰ τὸ ὄρος ἡγήσατο. δι' ὀλίγου οὖν τοῖς
τείχεσι ἐπλησίαζον καὶ ἐπὶ τὸν λόφον ἀναβάντες εἰς τὰς πύλας
ἀφίκοντο. ὁ δὲ Φίλιππος τὰ τείχη θεώμενος τὸ μέγεθος ἐθαύμαζε   15
καί, "ὦ πάτερ," ἔφη, "γίγαντες δήπου ταῦτα τὰ τείχη ᾠκοδόμησαν·
ἄνθρωποι γὰρ τοσούτους λίθους αἴρειν οὐκ ἐδύναντο." ὁ δὲ
Δικαιόπολις, "ἀληθῆ λέγεις, ὦ τέκνον," ἔφη· "οἱ γὰρ Κύκλωπες, ὡς
φασιν, ταῦτα ἐποίησαν. ἀλλ' ἰδού, βλέπε ἄνω." ὁ δὲ Φίλιππος
ἀναβλέπων δύο λέοντας λιθίνους εἶδε τὰς πύλας φυλάττοντας.   20
τούτους δὲ θεασάμενοι προὐχώρουν καὶ εἰς ἄκρον τὸν λόφον
ἀφικόμενοι ἐν αὐτοῖς τοῖς δώμασι τοῦ Ἀγαμέμνονος ἵσταντο, τό τε
πεδίον καθορῶντες καὶ τὴν θάλατταν τῷ ἡλίῳ λαμπομένην.

[ἐπλησίαζον they approached (+ dat.)   γίγαντες giants   ᾠκοδόμησαν built
λαμπομένην shining]

ἐξαίφνης δὲ ἔφριξεν ὁ Φίλιππος καὶ εἰς φόβον κρυερὸν κατέστη.
"ὦ πάτερ," ἔφη, "οὐκ ἀρέσκει μοι οὗτος ὁ τόπος. αἵματος γὰρ ὄζει." ὁ   25
δὲ Δικαιόπολις, "μηδὲν φοβοῦ, ὦ τέκνον," ἔφη· "ἴσως αἱ Ἐρίνυες
Ἀγαμέμνονός τε καὶ τῆς παγκάκης γυναικὸς ἔτι καὶ νῦν περιφοιτῶσιν.
ἀλλ' οὐ βλάψουσί σε, τέκνον. ἐλθέ. δός μοι τὴν χεῖρα. ἐγώ σοι
ἡγήσομαι." καὶ οὕτως εἰπών, τῷ παιδὶ ὡς τάχιστα κάτω ἡγήσατο.

[ἔφριξεν (from φρίττω) shuddered   κρυερόν icy   ὄζει it smells of (+ gen.)
παγκάκης completely evil   περιφοιτῶσιν wander about]

Principal Parts: Guttural Stems (-γ-)

πράττω (πρᾱγ-), πρᾱξω, ἔπρᾱξα, πέπρᾱγα, πέπρᾱγμαι, ἐπράχθην I do, fare
ἄγω, ἄξω, ἤγαγον, ἦχα, ἦγμαι, ἤχθην I lead, take
φεύγω (φευγ-/φυγ-), φεύξομαι, ἔφυγον, πέφευγα I flee, escape

Word Study

Deduce the meaning of the Greek word from which the first part of each of the following words is derived. Then give a definition of the English word:

1. photograph (τὸ φῶς, τοῦ φωτός = ?)   4. paleography (παλαιός, -ά, -όν = ?)
2. seismograph (ὁ σεισμός = ?)   5. cryptography (κρύπτω = ?)
3. telegraph (τῆλε = ?)

Give two other English words beginning with tele- *and explain their meanings and Greek roots.*

Grammar

1. The Verb ἵστημι

Stems: long vowel grade στη-; short vowel grade στα- (set up, stand)

You have already studied the second aorist of this verb (ἔστην = "I stood") in Chapter 15, and you have studied other -μι verbs (δίδωμι and τίθημι) in Chapter 18.

Formation of the Active:

The present and imperfect are formed by putting ἱ- (reduplication: = σι-, cf. Latin *sistō*) before the stem and adding the personal endings, e.g., ἵ-στη-μι. In the imperfect the ἱ- augments to ῑ-. In the singular the long vowel grade stem is used, and in the plural, the short, in both present and imperfect. Compare δί-δω-μι and τί-θη-μι.

The future στή-σω is formed regularly, as is the first aorist ἔ-στη-σα.

Formation of the Middle:

Present: ἵ-στα-μαι
Future: στή-σ-ο-μαι
Aorist: ἐ-στη-σά-μην

Meaning of the Active:

Forms in the active voice in the present, future, imperfect, and first aorist are *transitive* and take direct objects. They mean "make to stand," "stop," or "set up," e.g.:

ὁ ποίμην τὸν κύνα ἵστησιν.	The shepherd is stopping his dog.
ὁ ποίμην τὸν κύνα στήσει.	The shepherd will stop his dog.
ὁ ποίμην τὸν κύνα ἔστησεν.	The shepherd stopped his dog.
ὁ ναυτὴς τὸν ἱστὸν ἔστησεν.	The sailor set up the mast.

The second aorist, ἔστην, means "I stood, stood still, stopped," and the perfect, ἔστηκα, to be studied later, means "I stand." These forms are *intransitive* and do not take direct objects.

Meaning of the Middle:

The present, imperfect, future, and first aorist middle may be used *transitively*, e.g.:

φύλακας ἱστάμεθα/ἱστάμεθα.   φύλακας στησόμεθα.
We are/were setting up (posting) guards.   We will post guards.
(for ourselves = for our own protection)

The present, imperfect, and future middle may be used *intransitively*, e.g.:

ἐν αὐτοῖς τοῖς δώμασι τοῦ Ἀγαμέμνονος ἵσταντο.
They were standing in the actual palace of Agamemnon.

N.B.: The first aorist middle is not used intransitively; the second aorist active ἔστην is used instead = I stood, stood still, stopped.

The present and future middle are *intransitive* in the compound form ἀφίσταμαι = I set myself away from, revolt from, e.g.:

οἱ Ἴωνες ἀπὸ τῶν Περσῶν ἀφίστανται/ἀποστήσονται.
The Ionians are revolting/will revolt from the Persians.

Also *intransitive* is the second aorist active, e.g.:

οἱ Ἴωνες ἀπὸ τῶν Περσῶν ἀπέστησαν.
The Ionians revolted from the Persians.

The forms of ἵστημι are as follows:

ἵστημι: Active Voice

Indicative Present Tense	Imperative	Infinitive	Participle
ἵ-στη-μι		ἱ-στά-ναι	ἱ-στάς, ἱ-στᾶσα, ἱ-στάν
ἵ-στη-ς	ἵ-στη		
ἵ-στη-σι(ν)			
ἵ-στα-μεν			
ἵ-στα-τε	ἵ-στα-τε		
ἱ-στᾶ-σι(ν)			

Imperfect Tense

ἵ-στη-ν
ἵ-στη-ς
ἵ-στη
ἵ-στα-μεν
ἵ-στα-τε
ἵ-στα-σαν

Indicative	*Imperative*	*Infinitive*	*Participle*
First Aorist			
ἔ-στη-σα		στῆσαι	στήσᾱς, στήσᾱσα, στῆσαν
ἔ-στη-σας	στῆσον		
ἔ-στη-σε(ν)			
ἐ-στή-σαμεν			
ἐ-στή-σατε	στήσατε		
ἔ-στη-σαν			

Second Aorist

ἔστην		στῆναι	στάς, στᾶσα, στάν
ἔστης	στῆθι		
ἔστη			
ἔστημεν			
ἔστητε	στῆτε		
ἔστησαν			

ἵστημι: **Middle Voice**

Present Tense

ἵ-στα-μαι		ἵ-στα-σθαι	ἱ-στά-μενος, -η, -ον
ἵ-στα-σαι	ἵ-στα-σο		
ἵ-στα-ται			
ἱ-στά-μεθα			
ἵ-στα-σθε	ἵ-στα-σθε		
ἵ-στα-νται			

Imperfect Tense

ἱ-στά-μην
ἵ-στα-σο
ἵ-στα-το
ἱ-στά-μεθα
ἵ-στα-σθε
ἵ-στα-ντο

First Aorist

ἐ-στη-σάμην		στήσασθαι	στησάμενος, -η, -ον
ἐ-στή-σω	στῆσαι		
ἐ-στή-σατο			
ἐ-στη-σάμεθα			
ἐ-στή-σασθε	στήσασθε		
ἐ-στή-σαντο			

The future tense is formed regularly, e.g., active στήσω, στήσεις, στήσει, etc., middle στήσομαι, στήσῃ, στήσεται, etc.

2. The Verb καθίστημι

The commonest compound of ἵστημι is καθίστημι = I set up, appoint, put into a certain state. In its intransitive forms this verb = I am appointed, established, get into a certain state, become.

Study the following examples carefully and translate them:

ὁ κύων τὸν ξένον εἰς φόβον κατέστησεν. (*transitive*)
ὁ ξένος εἰς φόβον κατέστη. (*intransitive*)
ὁ δῆμος τὸν Περικλῆ στρατηγὸν κατέστησεν. (*transitive*)
ὁ Περικλῆς στρατηγὸς κατέστη. (*intransitive*)
οἱ Ἀθηναῖοι νόμους κατεστήσαντο. (*transitive*)

Exercise 20a

Identify and translate the following forms of ἵστημι *and* ἀφίστημι:

1. στῆθι
2. ἱστάναι
3. στῆναι
4. ἵστασθε
5. στήσασθαι

6. ἔστησαν (two ways)
7. ἵστη
8. στῆσον
9. στάς
10. στησάμενος

11. ἀφίσταται
12. ἀφίσταντο
13. ἀποστήσονται
14. στήσᾱς
15. ἀφίστασο

Exercise 20b

Read aloud and translate:

1. ὁ ποιμὴν τὸν κύνα ἔστησεν.
2. ὁ αὐτουργὸς ἐξαίφνης ἐν τῇ ἀγορᾷ ἔστη.
3. ὁ παῖς ἀνέστη.
4. ὁ πατὴρ τὸν παῖδα ἀνέστησεν.
5. οἱ Ἀθηναῖοι εἰς πόλεμον κατέστησαν.
6. οἱ πολέμιοι ῡ̔μᾶς εἰς φυγὴν καταστήσουσιν.
7. τίς σὲ κριτὴν (*judge*) ἡμῶν κατέστησεν;
8. ὁ Θησεὺς βασιλεὺς τῶν Ἀθηναίων κατέστη.
9. οἱ Ἀθηναῖοι νόμους κατεστήσαντο.
10. οἱ ναῦται τὸν λιμένα καταλιπόντες τὸν ἱστὸν (*mast*) ἔστησαν.
11. οἱ Ἕλληνες τοὺς Λακεδαιμονίους ἡγεμόνας (*leaders*) κατεστήσαντο.
12. οἱ στρατηγοὶ εἰς φόβον καταστάντες ἀποφεύγειν ἐβούλοντο.
13. τοὺς Πέρσᾱς νῑκήσᾱς ὁ Παυσανίᾱς τροπαῖον (*a trophy*) ἐστήσατο.
14. μὴ φύγετε, ὦ φίλοι, ἀλλὰ στῆτε καὶ ἀνδρείως μάχεσθε.
15. τοσαῦτα παθόντες οὐδέποτε (*never*) εἰς πόλεμον αὖθις καταστησόμεθα.

Exercise 20c

Translate into Greek:

1. When we saw the foreigner, we stopped and asked where he was going.
2. The young man stopped (his) horse and showed us the road that led to the city.
3. The people appointed this (man) general again.
4. When this (man) was appointed general, he advised the people not to fight.
5. He told us to cease from war and gave the city peace (= put the city into a state of peace).

War Clouds

The alliance formed between Sparta and Athens during Xerxes' invasion did not last. When the allies rejected the general whom the Spartans sent to command the fleet in 478 B.C. and formed the Delian League under Athenian leadership, Sparta did not demur. However, she watched the successes of the League and the growth of Athenian power with increasing anxiety. In 464 B.C. there was an earthquake at Sparta, and in the ensuing chaos the helots revolted. The Spartans asked their allies, including Athens, to send help, and the Assembly was persuaded by Cimon to send a force under his command. When this force failed to take the helot stronghold, the Spartans dismissed them.

This rebuff resulted in a volte-face in Athenian policy. As soon as Cimon returned (461 B.C.), an ostracism was held, and Cimon was sent into exile for ten years. Pericles emerged as the dominant statesman, a position he held until his death in 429 B.C. Under his leadership, Athens broke with Sparta, made an alliance with Argos, and soon became involved in a sporadic war with Sparta and her allies, which lasted intermittently for fifteen years.

On the whole, Athens was successful, and at one time her empire extended to include Boeotia and Megara, but she was overextended. In 446 B.C. when Euboea and Megara revolted and a Lacedaemonian army advanced to the borders of Attica, she was glad to make peace. The Thirty Years' Peace stipulated that each side should respect the other's sphere of influence and not admit into her alliance an ally of the other.

There followed a period of peace and retrenchment, during which Pericles eschewed imperialistic adventures, observed the terms of the peace, and built up Athenian resources. Sparta and her allies, however, especially Corinth, continued to distrust Athens and to fear her ambitions. The Aegean and Black Sea were already Athenian preserves; when she began to extend her influence in the west, Corinthian fears increased.

In 433/432 B.C. the Corinthian colony of Corcyra (Corfu) was embroiled in a quarrel with her mother city and asked Athens for help. Athens agreed to make a defensive alliance, and when Corinth attacked Corcyra an Athenian squadron, which had been sent to "observe," joined in the battle and routed the Corinthian fleet. Shortly after this, Potidaea, which was both a colony of Corinth and a member of the Athenian Empire, revolted from Athens and asked Corinth for help. The Corinthians sent "volunteers," and Athens laid siege to the city.

In late summer 432 B.C., representatives of the Peloponnesian League voted that Athens had broken the terms of the peace and that war should be declared. Both sides tried to make the other appear the aggressor. Finally, the Spartans sent an ultimatum: "The Lacedaemonians desire peace, and there would be peace, if you let the Greeks be independent." Pericles advised the Athenians to reject this ultimatum and to call on the Spartans to submit their differences to arbitration under the terms of the peace. By now the Peloponnesian army was mustered, and in early summer 431 B.C. it invaded Attica.

Ο ΝΟΣΤΟΣ (δ)

Vocabulary

Verbs

κρύπτω, κρύψω, ἔκρυψα,
κέκρυμμαι, ἐκρύφθην I hide
λανθάνω, λήσω, ἔλαθον,
λέληθα (+ acc. and/or
participle) I escape notice,
escape the notice of
οἰκτίρω, οἰκτιρῶ, ᾤκτῑρα I
pity
προέρχομαι (see ἔρχομαι for
principal parts) I go forward,
advance

Noun

ἡ ὀργή, τῆς ὀργῆς anger

Adjective

ἔνιοι, -αι, -α some

Preposition

ἔξω (adverb or preposition
+ gen.) outside
ἐπί (+ gen.) toward, in the
direction of; (+ dat.) at, upon,
on, for; (+ acc.) at, against,
onto

Adverbs

μή (with infinitive) not
πολύ far, by far
τήμερον today

ἔδοξεν οὖν αὐτοῖς μὴ ἐγγὺς τῶν Μυκηνῶν νυκτερεύειν ἀλλὰ τὰ
τείχη καταλιπόντες προῇσαν ἐπὶ τῆς Κορίνθου. δι᾽ ὀλίγου, ἤδη
καταδύντος τοῦ ἡλίου, εἰς κώμην τινὰ ἀφίκοντο. ἐκεῖ δὲ αὐτουργός
τις αὐτοῖς πρὸς τῇ ὁδῷ ἀναπαυομένοις ἐντυχὼν ᾤκτῑρε καὶ οἴκαδε
ἤγαγεν. ἡ μὲν οὖν γυνὴ αὐτοῦ σῖτον παρέσχε, ὁ δὲ αὐτουργὸς   5
ἐκέλευσεν αὐτοὺς ἐγγὺς τοῦ πυρὸς καθίζεσθαι. ἐπεὶ δὲ ἐδείπνησαν, ὁ
αὐτουργὸς ἤρετο αὐτοὺς ποῖ πορεύονται καὶ ἀκούσας ὅτι πρὸς τὴν
Κόρινθον πορεύονται, "ἡ Κόρινθος," ἔφη, "πολὺ ἀπέχει. οὔκουν
δύνασθε ἐκεῖσε ἀφικέσθαι τήμερον. ἀλλ᾽ εἰ δοκεῖ, ἔξεστιν ὑμῖν
ἐνθάδε νυκτερεύειν." οἱ δὲ χάριν μεγίστην αὐτῷ ἀπέδοσαν καὶ ἐγγὺς   10
τοῦ πυρὸς κατέκειντο. τῇ δὲ ὑστεραίᾳ, ἀνατέλλοντος τοῦ ἡλίου, τὸν
αὐτουργὸν χαίρειν κελεύσαντες ἐπὶ τῆς Κορίνθου ἔσπευδον. ἀλλὰ
μακρὰ ἦν ἡ ὁδὸς καὶ ἑσπέρᾱς ἤδη γιγνομένης εἰς τὴν πόλιν ἀφίκοντο
καὶ καταγώγιον ἐζήτουν.

[νυκτερεύειν to spend the night   καταδύντος setting, having set   κώμην
village   οὔκουν and so . . . not   ἀνατέλλοντος rising   καταγώγιον inn]

προσιόντες οὖν πρὸς ἄνδρα τινὰ ὃς διὰ τῆς ὁδοῦ παρῄει, ἤροντο   15
ποῦ ἐστι καταγώγιόν τι. ὁ δὲ δεινὸν βλέψᾱς καὶ εἰς ὀργὴν καταστάς,
"πρὸς τῶν σιῶν," ἔφη, "Ἀθηναῖοι φαίνεσθε ἐόντες. τί βούλεσθε; τί δὰ
πρᾱττετε ἐν τᾷ Κορίνθῳ;" τοῖς δὲ παροῦσι βοήσᾱς, "δεῦρο ἕρπετε,
φίλοι. Ἀθηναῖοί τινες πάρεντιν· κατάσκοποι δᾱπου ἐντίν, οἳ ἦνθον

τὰ νεώρια κατασκεψόμενοι." ὁ δὲ Δικαιόπολις, "τί λέγεις, ὦ ἄνθρωπε; 20
οὐκ ἐσμεν κατάσκοποι ἀλλὰ αὐτουργοί, οἵπερ ἀπὸ τῆς Ἐπιδαύρου
Ἀθήναζε ἐπανερχόμεθα." ἀλλ' ἤδη συνῆλθεν ὅμῑλος Κορινθίων οἳ
ἀγρίως ἐβόων· ἔνιοι δὲ καὶ λίθους ἐλάμβανον ὡς αὐτοὺς βαλοῦντες.

[καταγώγιον inn   πρὸς τῶν σιῶν = *Doric Greek for the Attic* πρὸς τῶν θεῶν by
the gods!   ἔοντες = *Doric for* ὄντες   δά = *Doric for* δή   τᾷ = *Doric for* τῇ
ἔρπετε = *Doric for* ἐλθέτε   πάρεντιν = *Doric for* πάρεισιν   κατάσκοποι spies
δάπου = *Doric for* δήπου surely   ἐντίν = *Doric for* εἰσίν   ἦνθον = *Doric for*
ἦλθον   τὰ νεώρια the docks   κατασκεψόμενοι about to spy on, to spy on
βαλοῦντες about to pelt, to pelt]

ὁ οὖν Δικαιόπολις εἰς φόβον καταστάς, "φύγε, Φίλιππε," ἔφη, "ὡς
τάχιστα."   οἱ μὲν οὖν ἔφυγον πρὸς τὰς πύλᾱς, οἱ δὲ Κορίνθιοι 25
διώκοντες λίθους ἔβαλλον. τρέχοντες δὲ ὅ τε Φίλιππος καὶ ὁ πατὴρ
τοὺς διώκοντας ἔφυγον καὶ ἔλαθον ἐν τάφρῳ τινὶ κρυψάμενοι, ἐν ᾗ
ἅπᾱσαν τὴν νύκτα ἔμενον. γενομένης δὲ τῆς ἡμέρᾱς εὐθὺς ἐπορεύοντο καὶ πάντας ἀνθρώπους ἔλαθον ταχέως σπεύδοντες. ὡς δὲ τοῖς
Μεγάροις προσεχώρουν, οὐκ εἰσῆλθον εἰς τὴν πόλιν ἀλλὰ 30
παρῆλθον ἔξω τῶν τειχῶν. οὕτως οὖν τέλος ἔλαθον εἰς τὴν Ἀττικὴν
εἰσελθόντες καὶ ἐπεὶ πρῶτον ἀφίκοντο εἰς τὴν Ἐλευσῖνα, κείμενοι
πρὸς τῇ ὁδῷ ἀνεπαύοντο· πολλὰ γὰρ καὶ δεινὰ παθόντες μάλα
ἔκαμνον, ὥστε οὐκ ἐδύναντο προιέναι.

[τοῖς Μεγάροις Megara   τάφρῳ ditch]

Principal Parts: More Guttural Stems (-κ-, -χ-)

διώκω, διώξομαι *or* διώξω, ἐδίωξα, δεδίωχα, ἐδιώχθην I pursue
φυλάττω (φυλακ-), φυλάξω, ἐφύλαξα, πεφύλαχα, πεφύλαγμαι (I am on
   my guard), ἐφυλάχθην I guard
δοκέω (δοκ-/δοκε-), δόξω, ἔδοξα, δέδογμαι, ἐδόχθην I seem, think
εὔχομαι, εὔξομαι, ηὐξάμην, ηὖγμαι I pray, pray to (+ *dat.*)

Word Building

*The following table illustrates some ways in which nouns and verbs can be
formed from a single stem. Define each word:*

Stem

1. τῑμα-	ἡ τῑμή	τῑμάω			
2. ἀναγκα-	ἡ ἀνάγκη	ἀναγκάζω			
3. ὀργα-	ἡ ὀργή	ὀργίζομαι			
4. οἰκο/ε-	ὁ οἶκος	οἰκέω	ἡ οἴκησις	ὁ οἰκητής	τὸ οἴκημα
5. δουλο-	ὁ δοῦλος	δουλόω	ἡ δούλωσις		
6. κηρῡκ-	ὁ κῆρυξ	κηρύττω			τὸ κήρῡγμα

Grammar

3. Verbs That Take Supplementary Participles: λανθάνω, τυγχάνω, φθάνω, and φαίνομαι

In the last paragraph of the second reading passage in this chapter you saw the following sentences:

ἔλαθον ἐν τάφρῳ τινὶ **κρυψάμενοι**.
They escaped notice, hiding themselves in a ditch.

πάντας ἀνθρώπους **ἔλαθον** ταχέως **σπεύδοντες**.
Hurrying quickly, they escaped the notice of <u>everyone</u>.

The verb λανθάνω, λήσω, ἔλαθον, λέληθα, meaning "I escape notice," "I escape the notice of," is regularly used with a supplementary participle, as in the examples above. It may also take an object in the accusative case, as it does with πάντς ἀνθρώπους in the second example above.

Other Greek verbs may also be used with supplementary participles:

a.   τυγχάνω, τεύξομαι, ἔτυχον, τετύχηκα   I happen to (of a coincidence)

ἔτυχον παρόντες οἱ πρέσβεις.
The ambassadors happened to be present.

b.   φθάνω, φθήσομαι, ἔφθασα *or* ἔφθην   I anticipate, do something before someone else

ἐφθάσαμεν ὑμᾶς **ἀφικόμενοι**.
We anticipated you arriving. = We arrived before you.

c.   φαίνομαι, φανήσομαι *or* φανοῦμαι, πέφηνα, ἐφάνην   I appear, seem

You have seen this verb meaning "I appear," "I seem," and used with an infinitive, e.g.:

ἡ γυνὴ **φαίνεται** σώφρων **εἶναι**.
The woman appears to be sensible.

With a participle instead of an infinitive, it means "I am shown to be," "I am proved to be," "I am clearly," e.g.:

ἡ γυνὴ σώφρων **οὖσα φαίνεται**.
The woman is shown to be sensible/is clearly sensible.

Exercise 20d

Read aloud and translate:

1.   οἱ Κορίνθιοι ἐχθροὶ γίγνεσθαι ἐφαίνοντο.
2.   οἱ Κορίνθιοι ἐχθροὶ ὄντες φαίνονται.
3.   ἄγε, Φίλιππε, τοὺς διώκοντας λάθε ἐν ταύτῃ τῇ τάφρῳ κρυψάμενος.
4.   ὁ Φίλιππος τὸν πατέρα ἔφθασε τὸν λόφον καταβάς.

5. προσιόντος τοῦ ἀνδρὸς ἡ γυνὴ ἔτυχε καθιζομένη ἐν τῇ αὐλῇ (courtyard).
6. "φαίνη ἀργὸς (idle) οὖσα, ὦ γύναι," ἔφη· "διὰ τί οὐκ ἐργάζῃ;"
7. οἱ Πέρσαι τοὺς Ἕλληνας ἔφθασαν ἀποπλεύσαντες πρὸς τὴν ἤπειρον (mainland).
8. οἱ Πέρσαι ἐφαίνοντο οὐ βουλόμενοι ναυμαχεῖν.
9. ὁ δεσπότης τυγχάνει καθεύδων.
10. ἔφθασαν τὸν χειμῶνα εἰς τὸν λιμένα εἰσπλέοντες.

*   *   *

ΟΙ ΑΘΗΝΑΙΟΙ ΤΟΥΣ ΛΑΚΕΔΑΙΜΟΝΙΟΥΣ ΑΝΑΜΙΜΝΗΙΣΚΟΥΣΙΝ

Read the following passage (adapted from Thucydides 1.73–75) and answer the comprehension questions below:

Nearly fifty years after the battle of Salamis, the Corinthians were urging the Spartans to make war on Athens. Athenian ambassadors, who happened to be in Sparta on other business, took the opportunity to remind the Spartans of what they owed to Athens.

λέγομεν ὅτι ἔν τε τῷ Μαραθῶνι μόνοι ἐκινδῡνεύσαμεν τοῖς βαρβάροις μαχόμενοι, καὶ ἐπεὶ τὸ δεύτερον ἦλθον, οὐ δυνάμενοι κατὰ γῆν ἀμύνεσθαι, εἰσβάντες εἰς τὰς ναῦς πανδημεὶ ἐν Σαλαμῖνι ἐναυμαχήσαμεν, ὥστε οὐκ ἐδύναντο οἱ βάρβαροι κατὰ πόλιν ἐπιπλέοντες τὴν Πελοπόννησον διαφθείρειν. τεκμήριον δὲ μέγιστον τούτων αὐτοὶ οἱ βάρβαροι ἐποίησαν· ἐπεὶ γὰρ ταῖς ναυσὶν ἐνῑκήσαμεν,   5 ἐκεῖνοι ὡς τάχιστα τῷ πλέονι τοῦ στρατοῦ ἀνεχώρησαν.

[τῷ **Μαραθῶνι** Marathon   **ἐκινδῡνεύσαμεν** we ran risks   **πανδημεί** all of us together   **κατὰ πόλιν** city by city   **τεκμήριον** proof   **τῷ πλέονι τοῦ στρατοῦ** with the greater part of their army]

1. Who were the only ones to risk fighting the barbarians at Marathon?
2. When the barbarians came a second time how did the Athenians prevent them from destroying the Peloponnesus?
3. What proof did the barbarians give of the point that the Athenians are making here?

οἱ δὲ Ἀθηναῖοι ἐν τούτοις τρία τὰ ὠφελιμώτατα παρέσχομεν, ἀριθμόν τε νεῶν πλεῖστον, καὶ ἄνδρα στρατηγὸν σοφώτατον, καὶ προθῡμίᾱν ἀοκνοτάτην. νεῶν μὲν γὰρ τὰ δύο μέρη τῶν πᾱσῶν παρέσχομεν, Θεμιστοκλέᾱ δὲ στρατηγόν, ὃς ἔπεισε τοὺς ἄλλους στρατηγοὺς ἐν τοῖς στενοῖς ναυμαχῆσαι, προθῡμίᾱν δὲ τοσαύτην   10 ἐδηλώσαμεν ὥστε ἐπεὶ ἡμῖν κατὰ γῆν οὐδεὶς ἐβοήθει, ἐκλιπόντες τὴν πόλιν καὶ τὰ οἰκεῖα διαφθείραντες, εἰσβάντες εἰς τὰς ναῦς ἐκινδῡνεύσαμεν. ὑμεῖς μὲν γὰρ ἐπεὶ ἐφοβεῖσθε ὑπὲρ ὑμῶν καὶ οὐχ ἡμῶν, ἐβοηθήσατε (ὅτε γὰρ ἦμεν ἔτι σῷοι, οὐ παρεγένεσθε)· ἡμεῖς δὲ κινδῡνεύοντες ἐσώσαμεν ὑμᾶς τε καὶ ἡμᾶς αὐτούς.

[τὰ ὠφελιμώτατα the most useful things   ἀριθμόν number   προθῡμίᾱν
eagerness   ἀοκνοτάτην most unhesitating, resolute   τὰ δύο μέρη two-thirds
ἐκλιπόντες having left behind   τὰ οἰκεῖα our property, belongings   ἔτι still
σῶοι safe]

4. What three most useful things did the Athenians offer in the struggle
    against the barbarians?
5. What percentage of the ships did they supply?
6. What was Themistocles responsible for?
7. By what four actions did the Athenians show their προθῡμίᾱ?
8. What was it that finally prompted the Spartans to send aid?
9. Whom do the Athenians claim to have saved?

   τοσαύτην τε προθῡμίᾱν τότε δηλώσαντες καὶ τοσαύτην γνώμην, ἆρ' ἄξιοί   15
ἐσμεν, ὦ Λακεδαιμόνιοι, τοσαύτης ἔχθρᾱς τῶν Ἑλλήνων διὰ τὴν ἀρχὴν ἣν ἔχομεν;
καὶ γὰρ αὐτὴν τήνδε ἀρχὴν ἐλάβομεν οὐ βιασάμενοι, ἀλλὰ ὑμῶν οὐκ
ἐθελησάντων παραμεῖναι πρὸς τὰ ὑπόλοιπα τῶν βαρβάρων, ἡμῖν δὲ προσελθόντων
τῶν συμμάχων καὶ αὐτῶν αἰτησάντων ἡμᾶς ἡγεμόνας καταστῆναι.
[ἔχθρᾱς hatred   τὴν ἀρχήν the empire   βιασάμενοι using force
παραμεῖναι to stand fast, stand your ground   τὰ ὑπόλοιπα the remnants, those
remaining   ἡγεμόνας leaders]

10. What do the Athenians ask the Spartans?
11. How do the Athenians claim to have secured their empire?
12. Why did the allies of the Athenians choose the Athenians to be their
    leaders rather than the Spartans?

Exercise 20e

Translate into Greek:

1. The Spartans, having heard both the accusations (τὰ ἐγκλήματα) of
    (their) allies and the words of the Athenians, debated (βουλεύομαι
    περί) the matter alone.
2. Many said that the Athenians were acting wrongly (*use present tense
    of* ἀδικέω) and (that) they must (it is necessary to) wage war
    immediately.
3. But Archidamus, being king, advised them not to get into war.
4. "For," he said, "they have (*use possessive dative*) very much money
    and very many ships. We cannot defeat them by sea. And so we will
    suffer (κακὰ πάσχω) ourselves more than we will harm them.
5. But he could not persuade the Spartans, who decided to wage war.

21

Η ΕΚΚΛΗΣΙΑ (α)

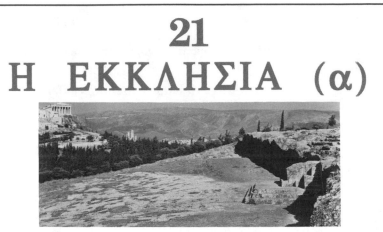

πρὸς τὴν Πύκνα σπεύδουσιν ἵνα εἰς τὴν ἐκκλησίᾱν ἐν καιρῷ πάρωσιν.

Vocabulary

Verbs

ἀγορεύω I speak in the Assembly; (*more generally*) I speak, say

ἀναγιγνώσκω (*see* γιγνώσκω *for principal parts*) I read

ἵημι, (*infinitive*) ἱέναι, (*participle*) ἱείς, **ἥσω, ἧκα,** (*infinitive*) εἷναι, (*participle*) εἵς, **εἷκα, εἷμαι, εἵθην** I send, release, let go; (*middle*) I hasten, go

    ἀφίημι I send away, let go, give up

βουλεύω, βουλεύσω, ἐβούλευσα, βεβούλευκα, βεβούλευμαι, ἐβουλεύθην (*active or middle*) I deliberate, plan

θύω, θύσω, ἔθῡσα, τέθυκα, τέθυμαι, ἐτύθην I sacrifice

πολεμέω I make war, go to war

πρόκειμαι, προκείσομαι (+ *dat.*) I lie before

ψηφίζομαι, ψηφιοῦμαι, ἐψηφισάμην, ἐψήφισμαι I vote

Nouns

ἡ ἀρχή, τῆς ἀρχῆς beginning, rule, empire

ἡ ἐκκλησίᾱ, τῆς ἐκκλησίᾱς assembly

ὁ πρέσβυς, τοῦ πρέσβεως old man, ambassador; (*usually plural*) **οἱ πρέσβεις, τῶν πρέσβεων** ambassadors

ὁ ῥήτωρ, τοῦ ῥήτορος speaker, politician

Adjectives

μύριοι, -αι, -α ten thousand, numberless

νέος, -ᾱ, -ον young, new

Prepositions

ἕνεκα (+ *preceding gen.*) for the sake of, because of

περί (+ *gen.*) around, about, concerning; (+ *acc.*) around

Conjunctions

ἐάν (+ *subjunctive*) if

ἵνα (+ *subjunctive*) so that, in order to (*expressing purpose*)

Proper Names

οἱ Πελοποννήσιοι, τῶν Πελοποννησίων Peloponnesians

ἡ Πνύξ, τῆς Πυκνός the Pnyx, the hill in Athens on which the Assemblies were held

οὐ πολλῷ δ' ὕστερον ἀναστὰς ὁ Δικαιόπολις τῷ Φιλίππῳ,
"ἀνάστηθι, ὦ παῖ," ἔφη· "καιρὸς γάρ ἐστι πορεύεσθαι. εὐθὺς οὖν
σπεύδωμεν πρὸς τὴν πόλιν." ὁρμήσαντες οὖν δι' ὀλίγου πολλοῖς
ἐνετύγχανον αὐτουργοῖς Ἀθήναζε πορευομένοις. ὁ οὖν Δικαιόπολις
γέροντί τινι προσχωρήσᾱς, ὃς ἐγγὺς αὐτοῦ ἐβάδιζεν, ἤρετο τίνος   5
ἕνεκα τοσοῦτοι Ἀθήναζε σπεύδουσιν. ὁ δέ, "τί λέγεις, ὦ ἄνθρωπε;"
ἔφη· "ἆρα τοῦτο ἀγνοεῖς, ὅτι τήμερον ἐκκλησίᾱ γενήσεται; πάντες
οὖν πρὸς τὸ ἄστυ σπεύδομεν τούτου ἕνεκα, ἵνα ἐν τῇ ἐκκλησίᾳ τῶν
ῥητόρων ἀκούωμεν. πράγματα γὰρ μέγιστα τῷ δήμῳ πρόκειται περὶ
ὧν χρὴ βουλεύεσθαι." ὁ δὲ Δικαιόπολις, "ἀλλὰ τίνα δὴ πρόκειται τῷ   10
δήμῳ, ὦ γέρον;" ὁ δέ, "ἀλλὰ τίς τοῦτο ἀγνοεῖ, ὅτι χρὴ βουλεύεσθαι
πότερον πόλεμον ποιησώμεθα πρὸς τοὺς Πελοποννησίους ἢ εἰρήνην
σώσωμεν;"

[**σπεύδωμεν** let us hurry   **ἀκούωμεν** we may hear   **ποιησώμεθα** we should
make]

ὁ δὲ Δικαιόπολις, "ἀλλὰ τί νέον ἐγένετο; πάλαι γὰρ ἐχθροί εἰσιν
οἱ Πελοποννήσιοι ἀλλ' οὐκ εἰς πόλεμον κατέστημεν ἀλλὰ μένουσιν   15
αἱ σπονδαί. διὰ τί οὖν νῦν γε δεῖ περὶ τοῦ πολέμου διακρίνειν;" ὁ δὲ
γέρων, "ἀλλὰ καὶ τοῦτο ἀγνοεῖς, ὅτι πρέσβεις νεωστὶ ἔπεμψαν οἱ
Λακεδαιμόνιοι οἳ ταῦτα εἶπον· Λακεδαιμόνιοι βούλονται τὴν
εἰρήνην εἶναι· εἰρήνη δ' ἔσται, ἐὰν τοὺς Ἕλληνας αὐτονόμους
ἀφῆτε.' κελεύουσιν οὖν ἡμᾶς τὴν ἀρχὴν ἀφιέναι. τοῦτο οὖν   20
βουλεύεσθαι δεῖ, πότερον τὴν ἀρχὴν ἀφῶμεν ἢ πόλεμον πρὸς τοὺς
Πελοποννησίους ποιησώμεθα." ὁ δὲ Δικαιόπολις, "ὦ Ζεῦ," ἔφη· "τοῦτ'
ἔστιν ἐκεῖνο. νῦν γὰρ ἐπίσταμαι διὰ τί οἱ Κορίνθιοι εἰς ὀργὴν
καταστάντες προσέβαλλον ἡμῖν, γνόντες ὅτι Ἀθηναῖοί ἐσμεν. ἀλλὰ
σπεύδωμεν, ὦ παῖ, ἵνα ἐν καιρῷ πάρωμεν."   25

[**διακρίνειν** to decide   **νεωστί** recently   **ἐάν** if   **ἀφῆτε** (*from* ἀφίημι) you
let ... go   **αὐτονόμους** independent, free   **ἀφιέναι** (*from* ἀφίημι) to let go, give
up   **ἀφῶμεν** (*from* ἀφίημι) we should let go, give up   **πάρωμεν** (*from* πάρειμι) we
may be present]

εὐθὺς οὖν ὥρμησαν καὶ εἰς τὰς πύλᾱς ἀφικόμενοι πρὸς τὴν
Πυκνὰ ἔτρεχον. ἐκεῖ δὲ ἤδη συνηγείρετο ὁ δῆμος καὶ μύριοι
παρῆσαν, τοὺς πρυτάνεις μένοντες. δι' ὀλίγου δ' εἰσιόντες οἵ τε
πρυτάνεις καὶ ὁ ἐπιστάτης καὶ οἱ ἄλλοι βουλευταὶ ἐκάθηντο. ἔπειτα
δὲ ἐσίγησαν μὲν οἱ παρόντες, ὁ δὲ ἱερεὺς πρὸς τὸν βωμὸν προσελθὼν   30

τό τε ἱερεῖον ἔθῡσε καὶ τοῖς θεοῖς ηὔξατο, ἵνα τῷ δήμῳ εὐμενεῖς ὦσιν.
ἐνταῦθα δὴ ὁ μὲν ἐπιστάτης τὸν κήρῡκα ἐκέλευσε τὸ προβούλευμα
ἀναγνῶναι. ὁ δὲ κῆρυξ τὸ προβούλευμα ἀναγνοὺς τὸν δῆμον ἤρετο
πότερον δοκεῖ εὐθὺς ψηφίζεσθαι ἢ χρὴ πρότερον βουλεύεσθαι περὶ
τοῦ πράγματος. ὁ δὲ δῆμος ἐχειροτόνησε, δηλῶν ὅτι πάντες βού-   35
λονται περὶ τοῦ πράγματος βουλεύεσθαι τοσούτου ὄντος. ἐνταῦθα
δὴ ὁ κῆρυξ εἶπεν· "τίς ἀγορεύειν βούλεται;" τῶν οὖν ῥητόρων πολλοὶ
πρὸς τὸ βῆμα παριόντες ἠγόρευον, ἄλλοι μὲν λέγοντες ὅτι χρὴ
πολεμεῖν, ἄλλοι δὲ ὅτι οὐδὲν χρὴ ἐμπόδιον εἶναι τῆς εἰρήνης.

[τοὺς πρυτάνεις the presidents of the tribes of citizens   ὁ ἐπιστάτης the
chairman   βουλευταί councilors   ὦσιν (from εἰμί) they might be   τὸ
προβούλευμα the motion for debate   ἐχειροτόνησε voted (by show of hands)
τὸ βῆμα the speakers' platform   ἐμπόδιον (+ gen.) in the way of]

Principal Parts: Dental Stems (-δ-, -ζ-)

σπεύδω, σπεύσω, ἔσπευσα, ἔσπευκα, ἔσπευσμαι I hurry
φράζω, φράσω, ἔφρασα, πέφρακα, πέφρασμαι, ἐφράσθην I tell of, show,
    explain; (middle and aorist passive in middle sense) I think about, consider
θαυμάζω, θαυμάσομαι, ἐθαύμασα, τεθαύμακα, τεθαύμασμαι,
    ἐθαυμάσθην I wonder at, am amazed, admire

Word Study

Explain the meaning of the following English words with reference to their
Greek roots:

1. anthropology   4. anthropophagous (φαγ- = ?)
2. philanthropy   5. misanthrope (μῑσέω = ?)
3. anthropomorphous (ἡ μορφή = ?)   6. pithecanthropus (ὁ πίθηκος = ?)

Grammar

1. Verb Forms: The Subjunctive Mood

Up until this chapter, most of the verbs you have encountered in the
reading passages were in the indicative or imperative mood or were
infinitives or participles. In this chapter, in order to express different
ranges of ideas, some of the clauses and sentences have their verbs in the
subjunctive mood, e.g.:

a. εὐθὺς οὖν **σπεύδωμεν** πρὸς τὴν πόλιν.
    Let us hurry immediately to the city.

b. σπεύδομεν τούτου ἕνεκα, ἵνα ἐν τῇ ἐκκλησίᾳ τῶν ῥητόρων **ἀκούωμεν**.
    We are hurrying for this reason, so that *we may hear* the speakers in
    the Assembly.

c. πότερον πόλεμον **ποιησώμεθα** πρὸς τοὺς Πελοποννησίους ἢ εἰρήνην **σώσωμεν**;
Should we make war against the Peloponnesians or *should we keep*
peace?

Note that each of the subjunctive verb forms above has an ω immediately
before the personal ending. An η or ω appears in all forms of the
subjunctive, except when it is obscured in some forms of the contract
verbs, and when present it allows you to identify this mood with ease.

2. Forms of the Subjunctive

Present Active Subjunctive

λύ- ω		φιλέ-ω >	φιλῶ
λύ-ῃς		φιλέ-ῃς >	φιλῇς
λύ-ῃ		φιλέ-ῃ >	φιλῇ
λύ-ωμεν		φιλέ-ωμεν >	φιλῶμεν
λύ-ητε		φιλέ-ητε >	φιλῆτε
λύ-ωσι(ν)		φιλέ-ωσι(ν) >	φιλῶσι(ν)
τῑμά-ω >	τῑμῶ	δηλό-ω >	δηλῶ
τῑμά-ῃς >	τῑμᾷς	δηλό-ῃς >	δηλοῖς
τῑμά-ῃ >	τῑμᾷ	δηλό-ῃ >	δηλοῖ
τῑμά-ωμεν >	τῑμῶμεν	δηλό-ωμεν >	δηλῶμεν
τῑμά-ητε >	τῑμᾶτε	δηλό-ητε >	δηλῶτε
τῑμά-ωσι(ν) >	τῑμῶσι(ν)	δηλό-ωσι(ν) >	δηλῶσι(ν)

Note that the usual contractions take place.

Present Middle Subjunctive

λύ-ωμαι	φιλῶμαι	τῑμῶμαι	δηλῶμαι
λύ-ῃ	φιλῇ	τῑμᾷ	δηλοῖ
λύ-ηται	φιλῆται	τῑμᾶται	δηλῶται
λυ-ώμεθα	φιλώμεθα	τῑμώμεθα	δηλώμεθα
λύ-ησθε	φιλῆσθε	τῑμᾶσθε	δηλῶσθε
λύ-ωνται	φιλῶνται	τῑμῶνται	δηλῶνται

Aorist Active and Middle Subjunctives

The aorist active and middle subjunctives are formed by adding to the
aorist stem the same endings as for the present subjunctive; note that
there is no augment in the subjunctive mood. The middle voice uses
primary endings in the subjunctive.

Regular First Aorist (λύω, ἔλῡσ-α):

λύσ-ω, λύσ-ῃς, λύσ-ῃ, λύσ-ωμεν, λύσ-ητε, λύσ-ωσι(ν)

λύσ-ωμαι, λύσ-ῃ, λύσ-ηται, λυσ-ώμεθα, λύσ-ησθε, λύσ-ωνται

First Aorist of Liquid Verbs (αἴρω, ἦρ-α):

ἄρ-ω, ἄρ-ῃς, ἄρ-ῃ, ἄρ-ωμεν, ἄρ-ητε, ἄρ-ωσι(ν)

ἄρ-ωμαι, ἄρ-ῃ, ἄρ-ηται, ἀρ-ώμεθα, ἄρ-ησθε, ἄρ-ωνται

Second Aorist (λείπω, ἔλιπ-ον):

λίπ-ω, λίπ-ῃς, λίπ-ῃ, λίπ-ωμεν, λίπ-ητε, λίπ-ωσι(ν)

λίπ-ωμαι, λίπ-ῃ, λίπ-ηται, λιπ-ώμεθα, λίπ-ησθε, λίπ-ωνται

The subjunctives of εἰμί "I am" and εἶμι "I will go" are:

εἰμί: ὦ, ᾖς, ᾖ, ὦμεν, ἦτε, ὦσι(ν)

εἶμι: ἴω, ἴῃς, ἴῃ, ἴωμεν, ἴητε, ἴωσι(ν)

3. Uses of the Subjunctive Mood:

a. The subjunctive (usually first person plural) is used in exhortations, as in the example from the reading above (1a). This is called the *hortatory subjunctive*, and its negative is μή, e.g.:

ἀνδρείως **μαχώμεθα**. *Let us fight* bravely.
μὴ εὐθὺς **ἴωμεν**. *Let us* not *go* immediately.
μὴ τοιοῦτο **ποιήσωμεν**. *Let us* not *do* such a thing.

Note that the difference between the present and aorist subjunctive is in aspect, not in time; i.e., the present subjunctive is used when the action is viewed as a process, and the aorist is used when the action is viewed as an event. This applies to the other uses below as well.

b. The present or aorist subjunctive (usually first person) may be used in *deliberative questions*, as in example 1c above and in the following:

τί **ποιῶμεν**; πότερον **μένωμεν** ἢ οἴκαδε **ἐπανίωμεν**;
What *are we to do*? *Are we to stay* or *return* home?

Note that the double question is introduced by πότερον, "whether," which is not translated.

c. The *aorist* subjunctive is used with μή in *prohibitions* or *negative commands* (as with all commands or prohibitions, the reference is to present or future time), e.g.:

μὴ τοῦτο **ποιήσῃς**. *Do not do* this.

d. The subjunctive is used in subordinate clauses introduced by ἵνα, ὅπως, or ὡς to express *purpose*, as in example 1b above. A negative purpose clause is introduced by ἵνα μή, ὅπως μή, ὡς μή, or simply μή. The following are examples:

ἀνδρείως μαχόμεθα **ἵνα** τὴν πατρίδα **σώσωμεν**.
We are fighting bravely *so that we may save* our fatherland (= *to save* our fatherland).

σπεύδουσιν **ὅπως μὴ** ὀψὲ **ἀφίκωνται.**
They are hurrying *so that they may not arrive* late (= *so that they won't arrive* late = *so as not to arrive* late).

Note that several different translations are possible in English. Note also, however, that Attic Greek prose does not use a simple infinitive to express purpose as we most commonly do in English.

e. The subjunctive is used in some types of *conditional clauses*, e.g.:

εἰρήνη δ' ἔσται, **ἐὰν** τοὺς Ἕλληνας αὐτονόμους **ἀφῆτε.**
There will be peace, *if you let* the Greeks *go* free.

This and other uses of the subjunctive in subordinate clauses will be discussed later, pages 74–76 and 192–194. Note the use of ἐάν (= εἰ + ἄν).

Exercise 21a

Change the following to the subjunctive:

1. λύομεν	6. ἔλαβον	11. μαχόμεθα
2. ἔλῡσεν	7. εἰσί	12. ἐστί
3. τῑμᾷ	8. ἵμεν	13. εἴδετε
4. δηλοῦμεν	9. ἐγένετο	14. ἐβουλεύσατο
5. λύονται	10. ἐφίλησας	15. ηὔξατο

Exercise 21b

Read aloud and translate into English; identify each use of the subjunctive:

1. στῆτε, ὦ φίλοι· σκοπῶμεν τί ποιήσωμεν;
2. πότερον οἴκαδε ἐπανέλθωμεν ἢ προΐωμεν;
3. ἑσπέρᾱς γιγνομένης, μὴ μένωμεν ἐν τοῖς ὄρεσιν ἀλλὰ οἴκαδε σπεύδωμεν.
4. πῶς οἴκαδε ἀφικώμεθα; τὴν γὰρ ὁδὸν ἀγνοοῦμεν.
5. ἰδού, ἔξεστιν ἐκεῖνον τὸν ποιμένα ἐρέσθαι τίνα ὁδὸν ἑλώμεθα.
6. μὴ ἀποφύγῃς, ὦ γέρον, ἀλλ' εἰπὲ ἡμῖν τίς ὁδὸς πρὸς τὸ ἄστυ φέρει.
7. μὴ ἐκεῖσε νῦν γε ὁρμήσητε· οὐ γὰρ ἀφίξεσθε πρὸ νυκτός.
8. τί ποιῶμεν, ὦ φίλοι; ὁ γὰρ ποιμὴν λέγει ὅτι οὐ δυνάμεθα ἀφικέσθαι πρὸ νυκτός.
9. εἰς τὸ πεδίον καταβάντες οἰκίαν τινὰ ζητῶμεν ἵνα ἀναπαυώμεθα.
10. ἡμέρᾱς δὲ γενομένης, εὐθὺς ὁρμήσωμεν.

Exercise 21c

Translate into Greek:

1. The Athenians are deliberating whether they are to make war against the Peloponnesians.
2. Let us hurry to the city and listen to the speakers.
3. Are we to yield to the enemy or save the city?
4. Don't listen to the ambassadors; they are not telling the truth.
5. Let us send them away immediately.

The Athenian Democracy

This photograph shows the Acropolis from the west with the Areopagus (the hill of Ares, god of war) in the foreground; here the ancient Council of the Areopagus met.

The radical democracy of Pericles' time had evolved over many years. Solon, in his reforms of 594/593 B.C. (see essay, Chapter 8, page 87), had broken the old aristocratic (*eupatrid*) monopoly of power by making wealth, not birth, the criterion for political privilege. He also gave the Assembly a more important role in decision making; it elected the nine magistrates (archons) from the top two property classes and was supported by a new Council of 400, which prepared business for debate in the Assembly and which also formed a counterweight to the old Council of the Areopagus, which before Solon's reforms had been the governing body of Athens. The most democratic feature of Solon's constitution was the Heliaea; this was the Assembly sitting as a court of appeals from the decisions of magistrates.

Solon's constitution continued to function throughout the following period of strife between factions of the nobility and throughout the ensuing tyranny of Pisistratus and his son Hippias. When Hippias was driven out in 510 B.C., the noble families began to compete for power once more. Herodotus (5.66) says, "Two men were preeminent, Cleisthenes the Alcmeonid and Isagoras. These were involved in a struggle for power, and Cleisthenes, being worsted, took the people into partnership." In 508 Isagoras was driven into exile, and Cleisthenes put through a program of reforms, which established a moderate democracy.

First, he probably extended the citizenship, so that every free man, landless or not, had the right to vote. Secondly, to prevent the recurrence of dynastic rivalry, he instituted an elaborate system that destroyed the territorial basis of the nobles' power. He divided Attica into about 170 demes (see essay, Chapter 3, pages 24–25), each with its own assembly and demarch; he abolished the four old Athenian tribes, based on kinship, and replaced them with ten new tribes, which were artificial political units, so constituted that the political influence of clan and locality was ended.

The new tribes formed the basic administrative and military units of the state. Each tribe provided fifty members (a prytany) to the Council of 500, which now replaced Solon's Council of 400; every deme elected a fixed number of councilors in proportion to its size. The new Council had a key role; it prepared business for the Assembly in its probouleutic function and was also responsible as an executive committee of the Assembly for seeing that decisions of the people were carried out. In the military sphere, each tribe provided one brigade, which was commanded by one of the ten generals elected by the Assembly.

The Assembly of all adult male citizens was sovereign. It elected the nine archons, whose functions were largely judicial, and the ten generals; it met regularly to debate issues brought before the people by the Council, and it continued to function as a court of appeals as the Heliaea. The ancient Council of the Areopagus still had important but vague powers, especially in judicial matters and as guardian of the constitution.

To Cleisthenes, probably, should also be ascribed the institution of ostracism. Once a year the Assembly was asked whether it wished to send one of the citizens into exile. If the people voted in favor of an ostracism, a meeting was held at which every citizens scratched on a fragment of pottery (ὄστρακον) the name of the politician he would like to see banished. The man against whom most ostraca were cast was sent off into honorable exile for ten years.

In 487 B.C. a change was introduced by which the nine archons were selected by lot (from the top two property classes) instead of by election. It followed that the importance of the archons declined while that of the generals, who were still elected, increased. In 462 B.C. a statesman named Ephialtes, supported by the young Pericles, put through measures that stripped the Areopagus of its powers and transferred them to the Assembly, Council, or popular courts, which now became courts of first instance instead of courts of appeal.

Ephialtes was assassinated soon after his reforms, and his place as leader of the people was taken by Pericles, who dominated the Assembly until his death in 429 B.C., thirty-two years later. The key principles of democracy that had long been recognized were the rule of law and the equality of all citizens before the law (ἰσονομία). To these Pericles added two further principles, which the Greeks considered characteristic of radical democracy, namely, selection for office by lot and payment of all officials. Lot had been used for selecting the archons since 487 B.C., but now it was extended to the selection of councilors. At the same time the archonship was opened to the third property class, the ζευγῖται. Now that any citizen, rich or poor, might be selected for office, it became essential that officials should be paid. Soon pay was instituted not only for the archons and councilors but also for the 10,000 members of the jury panel, who received a small wage for each day they sat in one of the courts into which the Heliaea was now divided.

Η ΕΚΚΛΗΣΙΑ (β)

Vocabulary

Verbs

ἄρχω, ἄρξω, ἦρξα, ἦργμαι,
ἤρχθην (+ gen.) (active or
middle) I begin; (active) I rule

ἐπιβουλεύω (see βουλεύω for
principal parts) (+ dat.) I plot
against

νομίζω, νομιῶ, ἐνόμισα,
νενόμικα, νενόμισμαι,
ἐνομίσθην I think

πληρόω I fill

προάγω (see ἄγω for principal
parts) I lead forward

Nouns

ἡ ἀνάγκη, τῆς ἀνάγκης
necessity

ἡ δίκη, τῆς δίκης custom,
justice, right, lawsuit, penalty

ἡ δύναμις, τῆς δυνάμεως
power, strength, (military)
forces

ὁ ἰδιώτης, τοῦ ἰδιώτου
private person

ἡ στρατιά, τῆς στρατιᾶς
army

ἡ τῑμή, τῆς τῑμῆς honor

ὁ τρόπος, τοῦ τρόπου manner,
way

ἡ χώρᾱ, τῆς χώρᾱς land

Adjectives

ἀδύνατος, -ον impossible,
incapable

δυνατός, -ή, -όν possible,
capable

ἑκάτερος, -ᾱ, -ον each (of
two)

ὅμοιος, -ᾱ, -ον (+ dat.) like

τελευταῖος, -ᾱ, -ον last

τοιόσδε, τοιάδε, τοιόνδε such
(as the following)

τοιοῦτος, τοιαύτη, τοιοῦτο
such

χρόνιος, -ᾱ, -ον lengthy

Preposition

κατά (+ acc.) down, on,
according to, at (of time)

Adverbs

ἰδίᾳ privately

πεζῇ on foot

Expression

ἀνάγκη ἐστί(ν)   it is
necessary

Spelling

The following passage and the passage at the end of this chapter are
adapted from the historian Thucydides. He used the Ionic spelling -σσ- in
words that in Attic have -ττ-, e.g., πράσσειν for πράττειν; he used the Homeric
and early Attic spelling ξύν (ξυν-) for σύν (συν-); and he used ἐς (ἐσ-) instead
of εἰς (εἰσ-). We have preserved these spellings in the passages from
Thucydides in this and the following chapters and in the exercises associated
with them. In Chapter 22 when the narrative returns to Dicaeopolis and his
family, we use the Attic forms. Chapter 23, based on Thucydides, again uses
his spellings. Chapter 24 on the education of Philip, which includes a passage
adapted from Plato, uses the Attic forms. In chapters 25–28 the readings are
based on Herodotus, and some features of his Ionic Greek are preserved, as
they have been in earlier readings based on Herodotus (e.g., ἐς for εἰς and
πράσσω for πράττω).

τέλος δὲ παρελθὼν Περικλῆς ὁ Ξανθίππου, ἀνὴρ κατ' ἐκεῖνον τὸν χρόνον πρῶτος Ἀθηναίων, λέγειν τε καὶ πράσσειν δυνατώτατος, παρήνει τοιάδε· "τῆς μὲν γνώμης, ὦ Ἀθηναῖοι, αἰεὶ τῆς αὐτῆς ἔχομαι, μὴ εἴκειν Πελοποννησίοις. δῆλον γάρ ἐστιν ὅτι οἱ Λακεδαιμόνιοι καὶ πρότερον καὶ νῦν ἡμῖν ἐπιβουλεύουσιν. ἐν μὲν γὰρ ταῖς ξυνθήκαις 5 εἴρητο ὅτι χρὴ δίκας μὲν τῶν διαφορῶν ἀλλήλοις διδόναι καὶ δέχεσθαι, ἔχειν δὲ ἑκατέρους ἃ ἔχομεν· νῦν δὲ οὔτε δίκας αὐτοὶ ᾔτησαν οὔτε ἡμῶν διδόντων δέχονται ἀλλὰ βούλονται πολέμῳ μᾶλλον ἢ λόγοις τὰ ἐγκλήματα διαλύεσθαι. πολλά τε γὰρ ἄλλα ἡμῖν ἐπιτάσσουσι, καὶ οἱ τελευταῖοι οἵδε ἥκοντες ἡμᾶς κελεύουσι 10 τοὺς Ἕλληνας αὐτονόμους ἀφιέναι. ἐγὼ οὖν ὑμῖν παραινῶ μηδὲν εἴκειν ἀλλὰ τὴν ἀρχὴν σῴζειν καὶ πολεμεῖν παρασκευάζεσθαι.

[ἔχομαι I cling to (+ *gen.*) ταῖς ξυνθήκαις the treaty εἴρητο (*from* εἴρω) it was (*literally*, had been) stated δίκᾱς ... τῶν διαφορῶν ... διδόναι καὶ δέχεσθαι to give and accept arbitration of (our) differences τὰ ἐγκλήματα διαλύεσθαι to settle their complaints ἐπιτάσσουσι they impose, dictate ἀφῑέναι (*from* ἀφίημι) to let go]

"ἐὰν δὲ ἐς πόλεμον καταστῶμεν, τὰ τοῦ πολέμου οὐκ ἀσθενέστερα ἕξομεν· γνῶτε γὰρ ἀκούοντες· αὐτουργοὶ γάρ εἰσιν οἱ Πελοποννήσιοι καὶ οὔτε ἰδίᾳ οὔτ' ἐν κοινῷ χρήματά ἐστιν αὐτοῖς. 15 καὶ οἱ τοιοῦτοι οὔτε ναῦς πληροῦν οὔτε πεζὰς στρατιὰς πολλάκις ἐκπέμπειν δύνανται· οὐ γὰρ ἐθέλουσιν ἀπὸ τῶν κλήρων πολὺν χρόνον ἀπεῖναι καὶ τὰ χρήματα δεῖ ἀπὸ τῶν ἑαυτῶν ἐσφέρειν. μάχῃ οὖν μιᾷ πρὸς ἅπαντας Ἕλληνας δυνατοί εἰσιν οἱ Πελοποννήσιοι καὶ οἱ ξύμμαχοι ἀντέχειν, πόλεμον δὲ χρόνιον ποιεῖσθαι πρὸς ἡμᾶς 20 ἀδύνατοι.

[ἀσθενέστερα weaker ἕξομεν we will have ἐν κοινῷ in the treasury τῶν κλήρων their farms ἀπὸ τῶν ἑαυτῶν from their own (private property)]

"ἡμεῖς γὰρ τῆς θαλάσσης κρατοῦμεν. καὶ ἐὰν ἐπὶ τὴν χώραν ἡμῶν πεζῇ ἴωσιν, ἡμεῖς ἐπὶ τὴν ἐκείνων πλευσόμεθα. μέγα γάρ ἐστι τὸ τῆς θαλάσσης κράτος. πόλιν γὰρ οἰκοῦμεν νήσῳ ὁμοίᾱν ἣν οὐδεὶς πολέμιος δύναται λαβεῖν. χρὴ οὖν τὴν μὲν γῆν καὶ τὰς οἰκίᾱς 25 ἀφεῖναι, τὴν δὲ θάλασσαν καὶ τὴν πόλιν φυλάσσειν.

[ἀφεῖναι (*from* ἀφίημι) to let go, give up]

"νῦν δὲ τούτοις ἀποκρῑνάμενοι ἀποπέμπωμεν, ὅτι τὰς πόλεις αὐτονόμους ἀφήσομεν, ἐὰν καὶ ἐκεῖνοι ἀφῶσι τὰς πόλεις ἃς

ὑπηκόους ἔχουσιν, δίκᾱς τε ὅτι ἐθέλομεν δοῦναι κατὰ τὰς ξυνθήκᾱς,
πολέμου δὲ οὐκ ἄρξομεν, εἰ δὲ ἄρξουσιν ἐκεῖνοι, ἀμῡνούμεθα.   30

[ἀφήσομεν (*from* ἀφίημι) we will let go, give up   ἀφῶσι (*from* ἀφίημι) they let go,
give up   ὑπηκόους subjected, obedient   δίκᾱς . . . δοῦναι to submit to
arbitration   τὰς ξυνθήκᾱς the treaty]

"ταῦτα δὲ ἐπίστασθαι χρή, ὅτι ἀνάγκη ἐστὶ πολεμεῖν, καὶ ὅτι ἐκ
τῶν μεγίστων κινδύνων καὶ πόλει καὶ ἰδιώτῃ μέγισται τῑμαὶ
περιγίγνονται. οἱ μὲν πατέρες ὑμῶν τούς τε βαρβάρους ἀπεώσαντο
καὶ ἐς τὴν νῦν δύναμιν προήγαγον τὴν πόλιν, ὑμᾶς δὲ οὐ χρὴ αὐτῶν
κακῑ́ονας γίγνεσθαι ἀλλὰ τούς τε ἐχθροὺς παντὶ τρόπῳ ἀμύνεσθαι   35
καὶ τοῖς ἐπιγιγνομένοις τὴν πόλιν μὴ ἐλάσσονα παραδοῦναι."

[περιγίγνονται result from   ἀπεώσαντο (*from* ἀπωθέω) they pushed back, drove
off   τοῖς ἐπιγιγνομένοις those coming after, our descendants]

ὁ μὲν οὖν Περικλῆς τοιαῦτα εἶπεν, οἱ δὲ Ἀθηναῖοι νομίσαντες ὅτι
ἄριστα παρῄνεσεν, ἐψηφίσαντο ἃ ἐκέλευε καὶ τοῖς Λακεδαιμονίοις
ἀπεκρῑ́ναντο κατὰ πάντα ὡς ἔφρασεν. οἱ δὲ πρέσβεις ἀπεχώρησαν
ἐπ᾽ οἴκου καὶ οὐκέτι ὕστερον ἐπρεσβεύοντο.   40

[κατὰ πάντα point by point   ἐπρεσβεύοντο came as ambassadors]

—adapted from Thucydides 1.140–146

Principal Parts: More Dental Stems (-ιζ-, -θ-)

κομίζω, κομιῶ, ἐκόμισα, κεκόμικα, κεκόμισμαι, ἐκομίσθην I bring,
   take
ὀργίζομαι, ὀργιοῦμαι *or* ὀργισθήσομαι, ὤργισμαι, ὠργίσθην I grow
   angry (at + *dat.*), am angry
πείθω (πειθ-/ποιθ-), πείσω, ἔπεισα, πέπεικα (I have persuaded) *or* πέποιθα
   (I trust + *dat.*), πέπεισμαι, ἐπείσθην I persuade; (*middle, present and future*
   + *dat.*) I obey

Word Building

Deduce or find the meanings of the words in the following sets:

1. ἡ δίκη δίκαιος, -ᾱ, -ον ἡ δικαιοσύνη ἄδικος, -ον ἀδικέω τὸ ἀδίκημα
2. ἡ βουλή βουλεύω ὁ βουλευτής τὸ βούλευμα προβουλεύω τὸ προβούλευμα

Grammar

4. The Verb ἵημι

Stems: long vowel grade ἡ-; short vowel grade ἑ- (send)
Principal Parts: ἵημι, ἥσω, ἧκα, εἷκα, εἷμαι, εἵθην

This verb is particularly common in compounds, and some of its forms are found only in compounds in Attic Greek. In the present and imperfect the stems (ἡ-, ἑ-) are preceded by an aspirated iota, giving ἱη-, ἱε-. (originally σι-ση-, σι-σε-).

In the active voice, ἵημι means "I send, release, let go"; in the middle, "I send myself, hasten, go" (present and imperfect only).

The compound ἀπο- + ἵημι > ἀφίημι "I send away, let go, give up" is common.

ἵημι: Active Voice

Indicative	*Subjunctive*	*Imperative*	*Infinitive*	*Participle*
Present Tense				
ἵημι	ἱῶ		ἱέναι	ἱείς, ἱεῖσα, ἱέν
ἵης	ἱῇς	ἵει		
ἵησι	ἱῇ			
ἵεμεν	ἱῶμεν			
ἵετε	ἱῆτε	ἵετε		
ἱᾶσι	ἱῶσι			
Imperfect Tense				
ἵην				
ἵεις				
ἵει				
ἵεμεν				
ἵετε				
ἵεσαν				
Aorist				
ἧκα	ὧ		εἶναι	εἵς, εἶσα, ἕν
ἧκας	ἧς	ἕς		
ἧκε	ἧ			
εἷμεν	ὧμεν			
εἷτε	ἧτε	ἕτε		
εἷσαν	ὧσι			

ἵημι: Middle Voice

Present Tense				
ἵεμαι	ἱῶμαι		ἵεσθαι	ἱέμενος, -η, -ον
ἵεσαι	ἱῇ	ἵεσο		
ἵεται	ἱῆται			
ἱέμεθα	ἱώμεθα			
ἵεσθε	ἱῆσθε	ἵεσθε		
ἵενται	ἱῶνται			

Imperfect Tense

ἱέμην
ἵεσο
ἵετο
ἱέμεθα
ἵεσθε
ἵεντο

Aorist

εἵμην	ὧμαι		ἕσθαι	ἕμενος, -η, -ον
εἷσο	ἧ	οὗ		
εἷτο	ἧται			
εἵμεθα	ὥμεθα			
εἷσθε	ἧσθε	ἕσθε		
εἷντο	ὧνται			

Exercise 21d

Identify the following forms of ἵημι, ἀφίημι, εἰμί, *and* εἶμι:

1. ἵεσθαι
2. ἱᾶσι(ν)
3. ἱέμενος
4. ἀφῆκε(ν)
5. ἀφείς

6. ἀφεῖσαν
7. ἄφες
8. ἀφεῖσθε
9. ἵεντο
10. ἀφῶμεν

11. ἄφου
12. ἰέναι
13. ἱέναι
14. εἶναι
15. εἶναι

Exercise 21e

Read aloud and translate into English:

1. οἱ ἔμποροι πρὸς τὸν λιμένα ἱέμενοι ναῦν ἐζήτουν μέλλουσαν πρὸς τὰς Ἀθήνᾱς πλεύσεσθαι.
2. οἱ μὲν πρέσβεις εἶπον· "τὴν ἀρχὴν ἄφετε ἐλευθέρᾱν, ὦ Ἀθηναῖοι, εἰ βούλεσθε τὴν εἰρήνην εἶναι."
3. ὁ δὲ Περικλῆς τοῖς Ἀθηναίοις παρήνεσε τὴν ἀρχὴν μὴ ἀφεῖναι.
4. τῶν Πελοποννησίων τῇ Ἀττικῇ προσχωρούντων ἔδει τοὺς αὐτουργοὺς τὰς οἰκίᾱς ἀφέντας ἐς τὸ ἄστυ ξυνελθεῖν.
5. οὗτος ὁ δοῦλος δεῦρο ἱέμενος ἦλθεν ὅπως ἡμᾶς ἐκ κινδύνου σώσῃ.
6. οἴκαδε οὖν ἱέμενοι τὸν πατέρα αἰτῶμεν αὐτὸν ἐλεύθερον ἀφεῖναι.
7. ἡ μὲν γυνή, "μὴ ἀφῇς τὸν δοῦλον, ὦ ἄνερ," ἔφη.
8. ὁ δὲ ἀνὴρ τὸν δοῦλον ἀφεὶς Ἀθήναζε ἵετο ἵνα ἄλλον δοῦλον ὠνῆται (*might buy*).

Exercise 21f

Translate into Greek:

1. Pericles advised the Athenians not to give up the empire.
2. The Athenians did not give up the empire but prepared to go to war.

3. The farmer, hastening (*use form of* ἵημι), returned home in order to tell his wife what had happened.
4. We will let the slaves go free, if (ἐάν + *subjunctive*) they say that they are willing to help us.

* * *

ΟΙ ΑΥΤΟΥΡΓΟΙ ΑΝΙΣΤΑΝΤΑΙ

Read the following passage (adapted from Thucydides 2.14 and 16–17) and answer the comprehension questions:

οἱ δὲ Ἀθηναῖοι ἐπείθοντό τε τῷ Περικλεῖ καὶ ἐσεκομίζοντο ἐκ τῶν ἀγρῶν παῖδας καὶ γυναῖκας καὶ τὴν ἄλλην κατασκευὴν ᾗ κατ' οἶκον ἐχρῶντο· πρόβατα δὲ καὶ ὑποζύγια ἐς τὴν Εὔβοιαν ἔπεμψαν καὶ τὰς νήσους τὰς ἐπικειμένας. χαλεπὴ δὲ αὐτοῖς ἐγίγνετο ἡ ἀνάστασις, διότι αἰεὶ εἰώθεσαν οἱ πολλοὶ ἐν τοῖς ἀγροῖς οἰκεῖν. ἐβαρύνοντό τε οἰκίας τε καταλείποντες καὶ ἱερά, δίαιταν τε μέλλοντες μετα- 5 βάλλειν. ἐπειδὴ δὲ ἀφίκοντο ἐς τὸ ἄστυ, ὀλίγοις μέν τισιν ὑπῆρχον οἰκήσεις· οἱ δὲ πολλοὶ τά τε ἐρῆμα τῆς πόλεως ᾤκησαν καὶ τὰ ἱερά. καὶ κατεσκευάσαντο καὶ ἐν τοῖς πύργοις τῶν τειχῶν πολλοὶ καὶ ὡς ἕκαστός που ἐδύνατο. οὐ γὰρ ἐχώρησε ξυνελθόντας αὐτοὺς ἡ πόλις, ἀλλ' ὕστερον δὴ τά τε μακρὰ τείχη ᾤκησαν καὶ τοῦ Πειραιῶς τὰ πολλά. 10

[ἐσεκομίζοντο they brought in   κατασκευήν equipment   πρόβατα flocks ὑποζύγια beasts of burden (yoked)   ἐπικειμένᾱς nearby   ἡ ἀνάστασις the removal   εἰώθεσαν (*from* ἔθω; *pluperfect with imperfect sense*) were accustomed οἱ πολλοί the majority   ἐβαρύνοντο they were distressed   δίαιταν way of life   μεταβάλλειν to change   ἐπειδή when   ὑπῆρχον were (ready) οἰκήσεις dwellings   κατεσκευάσαντο they set up house   καί even   τοῖς πύργοις the towers   ἕκαστος each   που anywhere   ἐχώρησε accommodated, was large enough for   τὰ πολλά the greater part]

1. What did the Athenians bring with them from the country?
2. Why was the removal from the countryside difficult and distressing?
3. What problem confronted them when they arrived at the city?
4. Where did most of them settle?
5. In what other places did some of them set up their households?

Exercise 21g

Translate into Greek

1. As the enemy was advancing into Attica (*use genitive absolute*), obeying Pericles we all went to the city.
2. We were very distressed (at) leaving (our) homes behind.
3. When (ἐπεί) we arrived at the city, no house was ready (ὑπάρχω) for us.
4. And so at first we lived in a tower, but later we set up house near the long walls.
5. When (ἐπεί) the enemy withdrew, we returned to (our) homes.

22
Η ΑΝΑΣΤΑΣΙΣ (α)

φοβοῦμαι μὴ δι' ὀλίγου εἰς πόλεμον καταστῶμεν· ὁ γὰρ νεᾱνίᾱς τόν τε πατέρα καὶ τὴν γυναῖκα χαίρειν κελεύει.

Vocabulary

Verbs

ἀνθίσταμαι, ἀντιστήσομαι, ἀντέστην, ἀνθέστηκα (+ *dat.*) I stand up against, withstand

ἀνίσταμαι, ἀναστήσομαι, ἀνέστην, ἀνέστηκα I stand up, am forced to move, remove

εἰσβάλλω (*see* βάλλω *for principal parts*) (+ εἰς + *acc.*) I invade

λούω, (*imperfect*) ἔλουν, λούσομαι, ἔλουσα, λέλουμαι I wash; (*middle, reflexive*) I wash myself, bathe

ὑπάρχω (*see* ἄρχω *for principal parts*) I am, exist, am ready

Nouns

ἡ ἀνάστασις, τῆς ἀναστάσεως removal

ἡ οἴκησις, τῆς οἰκήσεως dwelling

ἡ φυλακή, τῆς φυλακῆς guard, garrison

Relative and Interrogative Adjective

ὅσος, -η, -ον as great as, as much as; (*plural*) as many as

πάντα ὅσα all that, whatever

Preposition

ὑπό (+ *gen.*) by (of agent); (+ *dat.*) under

Conjunctions

ἐπειδή when, since

ἐπειδάν (+ *subjunctive*) when(ever)

τελευτησάσης δὲ τῆς ἐκκλησίᾱς καὶ τῶν πολῑτῶν ἀπιόντων, ὁ Δικαιόπολις, "ἄγε δή, ὦ παῖ," ἔφη· "οἴκαδε σπεύδωμεν ἵνα τῇ μητρὶ

ἅπαντα τὰ γενόμενα ἐξηγώμεθα." τάχιστα οὖν ἐπορεύοντο καὶ ἤδη
γενομένης τῆς νυκτὸς εἰς τὴν οἰκίαν ἀφίκοντο. τοῦ δὲ Δικαιοπόλιδος
κόψαντος τὴν θύρᾱν, ἐξῆλθεν ἡ Μυρρίνη καὶ τὸν Φίλιππον ἰδοῦσα   5
ὑγιῆ τ᾽ ὄντα καὶ βλέποντα ἠσπάζετο καὶ χαίρουσα ἐδάκρῡσεν. ὡς δ᾽
εἰσελθόντες ἐλούσαντό τε καὶ ἐδείπνησαν, ὁ μὲν Φίλιππος πάντα
ἐξηγεῖτο ὅσα ἐγένετο ἐν τῇ ὁδῷ καὶ ἐν τῷ Ἀσκληπιείῳ· ἡ δὲ ἐτέρπετο
ἀκούουσα.

[ἠσπάζετο embraced]

ὁ δὲ Δικαιόπολις ἅπαντα ἐξηγεῖτο ὅσα ἤκουσαν τῶν ῥητόρων ἐν   10
τῇ ἐκκλησίᾳ ἀγορευόντων. "οὕτως οὖν," ἔφη, "φοβοῦμαι μὴ δι᾽
ὀλίγου εἰς πόλεμον καταστῶμεν. χρὴ δὲ ἡμᾶς τῷ Περικλεῖ
πειθομένους ἅπαντα παρασκευάζεσθαι ὡς εἰς τὸ ἄστυ
ἀναστησομένους· ἐπειδὰν γὰρ οἱ Πελοποννήσιοι εἰς τὴν Ἀττικὴν
εἰσβάλωσιν, ἀνάγκη ἔσται τὴν οἰκίᾱν καταλιπόντας Ἀθήναζε   15
ἀναστῆναι." ἡ δὲ Μυρρίνη, "οἴμοι," ἔφη· "τί λέγεις, ὦ ἄνερ; πῶς γὰρ
δυνησόμεθα τήν τε οἰκίᾱν καταλιπεῖν καὶ τὰ πρόβατα καὶ τοὺς βοῦς;
καὶ εἰς τὰς Ἀθήνᾱς ἀναστάντες ποῦ δὴ οἰκήσομεν; οὐδεμία γὰρ ἡμῖν
ὑπάρχει οἴκησις ἐν τῷ ἄστει. ἀλλ᾽ οὐ δυνατόν ἐστι ταῦτα πρᾶξαι."

[τὰ πρόβατα the flocks]

ὁ δὲ Δικαιόπολις, "ἀλλ᾽ ἀνάγκη ἔσται, ὦ γύναι, ταῦτα πρᾶξαι   20
τούτων ἕνεκα· ἐπειδὰν γὰρ οἱ Πελοποννήσιοι εἰς τὴν γῆν εἰσβάλωσι,
ἡμεῖς οὐ δυνησόμεθα αὐτοῖς μάχῃ ἀντιστῆναι τοσούτοις οὖσιν· ὥστε
ὅστις ἂν ἔξω τῶν τειχῶν μένῃ, ἀποθανεῖται ὑπὸ τῶν πολεμίων·
ξυνελθόντες δὲ εἰς τὴν πόλιν, πάντες ἀσφαλεῖς ἐσόμεθα καὶ οὐδεὶς
κίνδῡνος ἔσται μὴ οἱ πολέμιοι ἡμᾶς βλάπτωσιν, τὴν μὲν γῆν ἀφέντας   25
καὶ τὰς οἰκίᾱς, τῆς δὲ θαλάσσης καὶ πόλεως φυλακὴν ἔχοντας.

[ὅστις ἂν . . . μένῃ whoever remains   ἀποθανεῖται will die, i.e., be killed
οὐδεὶς κίνδῡνος . . . μὴ οἱ πολέμιοι ἡμᾶς βλάπτωσιν no danger that the
enemy will harm us]

Principal Parts: Liquid Stems (-λ-, -ν-)

ἀγγέλλω (ἀγγελ-), ἀγγελῶ, ἤγγειλα, ἤγγελκα, ἤγγελμαι, ἠγγέλθην I
   announce
βάλλω (βαλ-/βλη-), βαλῶ, ἔβαλον, βέβληκα, βέβλημαι, ἐβλήθην I
   throw, put, pelt, strike
φαίνω (φαν-), φανῶ, ἔφηνα I show
   φαίνομαι, φανήσομαι or φανοῦμαι, πέφηνα, ἐφάνην (+ infinitive) I
   appear, seem; (+ participle) I am shown to be, proved to be, am clearly

Word Study

Give the Greek words from which the following English words for subjects of academic study are derived (check the Greek to English Vocabulary if necessary):

1. mathematics   3. geometry   5. biology
2. arithmetic   4. physics   6. zoology

Grammar

1. Clauses of Fearing

Examine these sentences from the reading passage above:

φοβοῦμαι μὴ δι᾽ ὀλίγου εἰς πόλεμον καταστῶμεν.
I am afraid *that we will (may) soon get into war.*

οὐδεὶς κίνδῡνος ἔσται μὴ οἱ πολέμιοι ἡμᾶς βλάπτωσιν.
There will be no danger *that the enemy will (may) harm us.*

Subordinate clauses introduced by μή state what is feared; such clauses of fearing may be introduced by verbs such as φοβοῦμαι or expressions such as κίνδῡνός ἐστιν, and the verb of the clause of fearing is in the subjunctive (present or aorist, differing in aspect only).

When the clause of fearing is negative, the introductory μή is accompanied somewhere in the clause by οὐ, e.g.:

ἐφοβούμην μὴ ἐν καιρῷ οὐκ ἀφίκωμαι.
I was afraid *that I would (might) not arrive in time.*

Where English uses the infinitive, so does Greek, e.g.:

φοβοῦμαι τοῦτο ποιῆσαι.
I am afraid *to do* this.

Exercise 22α

Read aloud and translate into English:

1. ἆρ᾽ οὐ φοβεῖσθε μὴ κακόν τι πάθωμεν;
2. κίνδῡνός ἐστι μὴ χειμὼν δι᾽ ὀλίγου γένηται.
3. καίπερ φοβουμένη μὴ χαλεπὴ γένηται ἡ ἀνάστασις, ἡ γυνὴ τῷ ἀνδρὶ πείθεται.
4. ὁ γέρων ἐλῡπεῖτο, φοβούμενος μὴ οὐδέποτε (*never*) ἐπανίῃ.
5. φοβοῦμαι μὴ οἱ φύλακες (*guards*) οὐκ ἐθέλωσιν ἀνοῖξαι (*to open*) τὰς πύλᾱς.
6. οἱ δοῦλοι ἐφοβοῦντο μὴ ὁ δεσπότης σφίσιν (*at them*) ὀργίζηται.
7. οὐ φοβούμεθα ἔξω τῶν τειχῶν μένειν.
8. οἱ παῖδες ἐφοβοῦντο τὰ ἀληθῆ λέγειν.
9. φοβούμενοι νυκτὸς ἐπανιέναι οἱ αὐτουργοὶ ἐν τῷ ἄστει ἔμενον.
10. ὁ ναύκληρος ἐφοβεῖτο μὴ ὁ χειμὼν τὴν ναῦν διαφθείρῃ.

Exercise 22b

Translate into Greek:

1. I fear we will (may) not arrive at the city in time.
2. There is a danger that the enemy will (may) soon come into the land.
3. We set out toward the city immediately, being afraid to stay in the country.
4. The farmers feared that the enemy would (might) destroy their homes.
5. Are you not more afraid (Don't you fear rather) to sail home than to go by land?

2. Indefinite or General Clauses

In relative, temporal, and conditional clauses, the indicative mood is used if the clauses are *definite*, i.e., specific in reference or in time, e.g.:

πάντες ἐκείνους τῑμῶσιν **οἳ ἐν Σαλαμῖνι ἐμαχέσαντο**.
All honor the men who fought at Salamis.

ἐπεὶ εἰς τὸ ἄστυ ἀφῑκόμεθα, πρὸς τὴν ἀγορὰν ἐσπεύσαμεν.
When we arrived at the city, we hurried to the agora.

οἱ Σπαρτιᾶται ἐμάχοντο **ἕως ἅπαντες ἔπεσον**.
The Spartans fought *until all fell.*

εἰ τῷ Περικλεῖ πιστεύεις, μῶρος εἶ.
If you believe Pericles (now), you are foolish.

If the reference or time is *indefinite* or *general*, ἄν + the subjunctive (present or aorist) is used; ἄν is placed after the relative pronoun or combined with some temporal conjunctions and with the conditional conjunction εἰ, e.g.:

ὅστις ἂν ἔξω τῶν τειχῶν μένῃ, ἀποθανεῖται ὑπὸ τῶν πολεμίων.
Whoever remains outside the walls will be killed by the enemy.

ὅστις ἂν τοῦτο ποιήσῃ, τῑμῆς ἄξιός ἐστιν.
Whoever does this is worthy of honor.

ἐπειδάν (= ἐπειδή + ἄν) **εἰς τὸ ἄστυ ἴωμεν**, πρὸς τὴν ἀγορὰν σπεύδομεν.
Whenever we go to the city, we hurry to the agora.

μείνατε **ἕως ἂν ἐπανέλθῃ ὁ πατήρ**.
Wait *until father returns.*

ἐὰν (= εἰ + ἄν) **τῷ Περικλεῖ πιστεύωμεν**, μῶροί ἐσμεν.
If we ever believe Pericles, we are (always) foolish.

The last example above is also called a *present general condition*.

Note that ὅστις ("anyone who," "whoever," "anything that," "whatever," *plural*, "all who," "all that") is commonly used in indefinite relative clauses. Both halves of the word decline as follows:

	Masculine	*Feminine*	*Neuter*
Nom.	ὅστις	ἥτις	ὅ τι
Gen.	οὗτινος	ἧστινος	οὗτινος
Dat.	ᾧτινι	ᾗτινι	ᾧτινι
Acc.	ὅντινα	ἥντινα	ὅ τι
Nom.	οἵτινες	αἵτινες	ἅτινα
Gen.	ὧντινων	ὧντινων	ὧντινων
Dat.	οἷστισι(ν)	αἷστισι(ν)	οἷστισι(ν)
Acc.	οὕστινας	ἅστινας	ἅτινα

The word ὅσοι, ὅσαι, ὅσα (often reinforced by πάντες, "as many as," "all who") is also used with ἄν and the subjunctive to mean "whoever" or "whatever," e.g.:

ὁ πατὴρ τῷ παιδὶ δίδωσιν (πάντα) ὅσ' ἂν αἰτῇ.
The father gives the child *whatever he asks for.*

Note the following words that may introduce indefinite temporal clauses. They all mean "whenever" and are used with verbs in the subjunctive:

ἐπειδάν = ἐπειδή + ἄν
ὅταν = ὅτε + ἄν
ὁπόταν = ὁπότε + ἄν

The difference between the present and aorist subjunctive in indefinite clauses is in aspect, not in time, i.e., the present subjunctive is used when the action is viewed as a process, and the aorist subjunctive is used when the action is viewed as an event (you will find this contrast illustrated in the first two sentences below).

Note that relative, temporal, and conditional clauses referring to *future* time are usually treated as indefinite in Greek, although sometimes we do not translate with an indefinite in English, e.g.:

ὅστις ἂν ἔξω τῶν τειχῶν μένῃ, ἀποθανεῖται ὑπὸ τῶν πολεμίων.
Whoever remains outside the walls will be killed by the enemy.

ἐπειδὰν ἐπανέλθῃ ὁ πατήρ, πάντα μαθησόμεθα.
When father returns, we will learn everything.

μείνατε **ἕως ἂν ἐπανέλθῃ ὁ πατήρ**.
Wait *until father returns.*

ἐὰν οἴκαδε ἐπανέλθωμεν, πάντα μαθησόμεθα.
If we return home, we will learn everything.

The last example above is also called a *future more vivid condition.*

Greek may also use εἰ + the future indicative in conditional clauses referring to future time, but this is a less common alternative and is usually reserved for threats and warnings, e.g.:

εἰ τοῦτο **ποιήσεις, ἀποθανῇ**.
If *you do* this, *you will die*.

Note that in this kind of condition we translate the future ποιήσεις as present in English.

Exercise 22c

Translate the following pairs of sentences:

1. ὅστις ἂν ἔξω τῶν τειχῶν μένῃ, ἐν κινδύνῳ ἔσται.
   Whoever arrives first will receive the money.
2. ἐπειδὰν γένηται ἡ ἐκκλησία, οἱ πολῖται εἰς τὴν Πύκνα σπεύδουσιν.
   Whenever the enemy invades the land, we all come together into the city.
3. μενοῦμεν ἐν τῇ ἀγορᾷ ἕως ἂν ἐπανέλθῃ ὁ ἄγγελος.
   We will not return home until day breaks (γίγνομαι).
4. μὴ εἴσβητε εἰς τὴν ναῦν ἕως ἂν κελεύσῃ ὁ ναύκληρος.
   Don't climb that mountain until spring (τὸ ἔαρ) begins (γίγνομαι).
5. ἐὰν οἱ Πελοποννήσιοι ἐπὶ γῆν ἡμῶν πεζῇ ἴωσιν, ἡμεῖς ἐπὶ τὴν ἐκείνων ναυσὶ πλευσόμεθα.
   If the farmers hurry into the city, they will all be safe.
6. ὅσ' ἂν ἔχωσιν οἱ παῖδες, πάντα ἡμῖν διδόναι ἐθέλουσιν.
   We must do whatever the king orders.
7. ἐπειδὴ ὁ αὐτουργὸς τοὺς βοῦς εἰς τὸν ἀγρὸν εἰσήλασεν, δι' ὀλίγου ἀροτρεύειν ἤρξατο.
   When the boy (had) gone into the field, he immediately called (his) father.
8. οἱ ποιμένες τὰ πρόβατα (*flocks*) ἐν τοῖς ὄρεσι νεμοῦσιν (*will pasture*) ἕως ἂν γένηται ὁ χειμών.
   We will not set out for home until the shepherd shows us the way.
9. ὅταν ἄπῃ ὁ δεσπότης, οἱ δοῦλοι παύονται ἐργαζόμενοι.
   Whenever the master approaches, the slaves get up and work.
10. εἰς κίνδυνον καταστήσεσθε, ὦ παῖδες, εἰ μὴ ποιήσετε ὅσ' ἂν παραινέσωμεν.
    Unless you listen to me, you will suffer terribly (terrible things).
11. οὗτοι οἱ παῖδες, οἳ τοῖς πατράσιν ἐβοήθουν, εἰργάζοντο ἕως ἐγένετο νύξ.
    Those women, who were sitting in the field, waited until their husbands stopped working.
12. ἐὰν τις τούτου πίῃ, ἀποθνῄσκει.
    If anyone (ever) does such a thing, we (always) become angry with him.

Athenian Democracy in Action

The Assembly (ἡ ἐκκλησία) was sovereign. Consisting of all adult male citizens, it had forty regular meetings each year, four in each prytany (one-tenth of a year). It met on the Pnyx (ἡ Πνύξ), the slope of a hill opposite the Acropolis. All eligible citizens were expected and required to attend, but in fact an attendance of 6,000 (the legal quorum for an ostracism) out of a citizen body of about 50,000 was probably a respectable number for a routine meeting. It must be remembered that the majority of the people lived in the country and could not possibly have come into the city for every meeting. The Assembly decided all issues by direct vote, by a show of hands.

The Council of 500 (ἡ βουλή) formed the steering committee of the Assembly. No matter could come before the Assembly that had not first been discussed in the Council. It presented motions to the Assembly in the form of "preliminary decrees" (προβουλεύματα), which were debated in the Assembly and passed, rejected, or amended by the people. If passed, the motion became a decree (ψήφισμα), which was recorded, usually on stone, and set up in public for all to read. Hundreds of fragments of such decrees survive, some fairly complete, which show the democracy in action. All begin ἔδοξε τῇ βουλῇ καὶ τῷ δήμῳ and then give the name of the prytany and chairman.

When the Assembly met, proceedings were opened by prayer and libation. Then the herald read out the motion for debate (τό προβούλευμα) and asked whether it should be accepted without debate or debated. If the people voted for a debate, the herald then asked "τίς ἀγορεύειν βούλεται;" and any citizen could come forward to the platform (τὸ βῆμα) and address the people. The Assembly did not tolerate the foolish or ill-informed, and in practice the speakers were usually drawn from a limited number of politicians (οἱ ῥήτορες). The regular meetings of the Assembly had a fairly standard agenda. At the first meeting of each prytany a vote was taken on whether to continue the magistrates in office or to depose any of them. Then the grain supply and security (especially the state of the navy) were discussed. At the second meeting of the prytany any citizen could bring up any topic of public or private interest (provided he had first introduced his proposal to the Council). At the third and fourth meetings current problems were dealt with under the headings of sacred affairs, foreign policy, and secular affairs. Besides the regular meetings, extraordinary meetings could be called by the Council in any emergency.

The 500 councilors (βουλευταί) were selected by lot in the demes from citizens over thirty years old. They served for one year only and might not serve more than twice in a lifetime. It follows statistically that most citizens would sooner or later have to serve their turn on the Council. Each of the ten tribes provided 50 councilors and these served in rotation for one-tenth of the year as "presidents" (πρυτάνεις). Every day a chairman (ὁ ἐπιστάτης) was selected by lot from the prytaneis, and for twenty-four hours he held the seal of state and the keys to the temples where the public moneys and archives were stored.

The chairman and one-third of the prytaneis were on twenty-four hour duty and slept and ate in the Tholos (Θόλος), the round building next to the Council House (Βουλευτήριον). The Council had a secretary (ὁ γραμματεύς), who was responsible for recording all business. The Council met daily, and the public could attend as observers. Any citizen could ask for leave to introduce business, and, possibly, the generals could attend *ex officio*.

The Council was divided into committees, usually of ten, each responsible for a different sphere of business. One was in charge of shipbuilding, another was responsible for the dockyards, a third for the upkeep of public buildings, and so forth. The audit committee checked the accounts of all magistrates who handled public moneys. All magistrates on entering office were scrutinized by the Council to see that they were fit and proper persons, and on resigning office they had to submit to a public examination of their record by the Council. The Council was in fact the linchpin that held the whole constitution together, and it is worth reflecting on the fact that at any given time there may have been 15,000 citizens in the Assembly who had served on the Council with all the political and administrative experience that this entailed. This gives substance to Pericles' claim that "we are all concerned alike with our personal affairs and the affairs of the city, and, despite our various occupations, we are adequately informed on politics."

It is remarkable that the Athenian democracy worked so well, considering that all offices, except for military commands and offices entailing technical expertise, were filled by lot and that all important decisions were taken by direct vote in a large and emotional assembly. Its success in the Periclean period may be ascribed to the dominance of one outstanding statesman, who could control and guide the Assembly by his eloquence and his known integrity: "it was (in Pericles' time) in theory a democracy but in practice rule by the leading man" (Thucydides 2.65). Thucydides, however, overstates his case. Pericles could have been dropped at any time (he was in fact deposed for a short time in 430 B.C.), and credit must be paid to the average Athenians, who had the political acumen to follow a great leader. Thucydides says that Pericles' successors as leaders of the people, because they did not have his influence and powers of persuasion and were motivated by personal ambition and the pursuit of private gain, gave the people what they wanted and made a series of political blunders that led to the downfall of Athens. Failures in the war certainly did result in the growth of an anti-democratic party (οἱ ὀλίγοι) and eventually to revolution and counterrevolution. After the war, however, the restored democracy continued to function throughout the fourth century without any outstanding leaders and with good success on the whole.

Η ΑΝΑΣΤΑΣΙΣ (β)

Vocabulary

Verbs

δείκνῡμι, δείξω, ἔδειξα,
δέδειχα, δέδειγμαι,
ἐδείχθην I show

ἐνδίδωμι (*see* δίδωμι *for
principal parts*) I give in,
yield

ζεύγνῡμι, ζεύξω, ἔζευξα,
ἔζευγμαι, ἐζεύχθην I yoke

ὀδῡ́ρομαι (*rare in tenses other
than present*) I grieve

προσδέχομαι (*see* δέχομαι *for
principal parts*) I receive,
admit, await, expect

Nouns

ἡ ἄμαξα, τῆς ἁμάξης wagon

ἡ βουλή, τῆς βουλῆς plan,
advice, Council

τὸ ἔαρ, τοῦ ἦρος spring

οἱ οἰκεῖοι, τῶν οἰκείων the
members of the house, family,
relations

ὁ πύργος, τοῦ πύργου tower

τὸ στρατόπεδον, τοῦ
στρατοπέδου camp, army

Adjectives

τοσόσδε, τοσήδε, τοσόνδε so
great; (*plural*) so many

Preposition

ἐκτός (+ *gen.*) outside

Adverb

οὐδέποτε never

Conjunctions and Particles

ὅπως (+ *subjunctive*) so that, in
order to

πρίν (+ *infinitive*) before

ταῦτα οὖν ἀκούσᾱσα ἡ Μυρρίνη σῑγήσᾱσα τῷ ἀνδρὶ ἐπείθετο,
καίπερ φοβουμένη μὴ χαλεπὴ γένηται ἡ ἀνάστασις. πάντα οὖν τὸν
χειμῶνα παρεσκευάζοντο ὡς Ἀθήναζε ἀναστησόμενοι ἐπειδὰν
εἰσβάλωσιν οἱ Πελοποννήσιοι. ἅμα δ' ἦρι ἀρχομένῳ ἄγγελος ἀπὸ
τῶν Ἀθηνῶν ἀφίκετο λέγων ὅτι ἤδη συλλέγονται οἵ τε Λακεδαιμόνιοι   5
καὶ οἱ σύμμαχοι εἰς τὸν Ἴσθμον· ὁ οὖν Δικαιόπολις τὸν Φίλιππον
καὶ τὸν Ξανθίᾱν ἔπεμψεν ὡς τὰ μῆλα εἰς τὴν Εὔβοιαν κομιοῦντας.
ἔπειτα δὲ αὐτός τε καὶ ἡ Μυρρίνη τὴν ἄμαξαν ἐξαγαγόντες πάνθ'
ὅσα φέρειν ἐδύναντο εἰσέθεσαν. πάντων δ' ἑτοίμων ὄντων ὁ
Δικαιόπολις τοὺς βοῦς ζεύξᾱς τὸν πάππον πολλὰ ὀδῡρόμενον   10
ἀνεβίβασεν. τέλος δὲ ἥ τε Μυρρίνη καὶ ἡ Μέλιττα αὐταὶ ἀνέβησαν.
οὕτως οὖν ἐπορεύοντο δακρῡ́οντες καὶ ὀδῡρόμενοι, φοβούμενοι μὴ
οὐδέποτε ἐπανίωσιν.

[ἀνεβίβασεν (*from* ἀναβιβάζω) put (him) onto the wagon]

μακρὰ δ' ἦν ἡ ὁδὸς καὶ χαλεπή. ἔδει γὰρ κατὰ τὴν ἁμάξιτον
ἰέναι, πολλοῖς δ' ἐνετύγχανον αὐτουργοῖς οἵπερ πρὸς τὴν πόλιν   15
σπεύδοντες ἄλλοι ἄλλοις ἐνεπόδιζον. τέλος δὲ ἑσπέρᾱς ἤδη

γιγνομένης ἐς τὰς πύλᾱς ἀφίκοντο καὶ μόλις εἰσελθόντες τὴν νύκτα ἐν
ἡρῴῳ τινὶ ἔμειναν. τῇ δ' ὑστεραίᾳ ὁ Δικαιόπολις παρὰ τὸν ἀδελφὸν
ἦλθεν ἵνα αἰτῇ αὐτὸν εἴ πως βοηθεῖν δύναται. ὁ δ' ἀδελφὸς οὐκ
ἐδύνατο αὐτοὺς εἰς τὴν οἰκίᾱν δέχεσθαι τοσούτους ὄντας ἀλλὰ   20
πύργον τινὰ αὐτῷ ἔδειξεν ὃς πάντας χωρήσει. ὁ οὖν Δικαιόπολις
πρὸς τοὺς οἰκείους ἐπανελθὼν ἡγήσατο αὐτοῖς πρὸς τὸν πύργον, ἐν
ᾧ ἔμελλον διὰ παντὸς οἰκήσειν, ἕως ἂν οἱ μὲν Πελοποννήσιοι
ἀπίωσιν, αὐτοὶ δὲ πρὸς τοὺς ἀγροὺς ἐπανίωσιν.

[τὴν ἁμάξιτον the wagon road   ἄλλοι ἄλλους ἐνεπόδιζον were getting in
one another's way   ἡρῴῳ shrine of a hero   χωρήσει would (literally, will) hold]

ἐν δὲ τούτῳ κῆρυξ ἀφίκετο ἐς τὰς Ἀθήνᾱς, πέμψαντος τοῦ   25
Ἀρχιδᾱμου τῶν Λακεδαιμονίων βασιλέως· οἱ δὲ Ἀθηναῖοι οὐ
προσεδέξαντο αὐτὸν ἐς τὴν πόλιν οὐδ' ἐπὶ τὴν βουλήν· ἦν γὰρ
Περικλέους γνώμη κήρῡκα καὶ πρεσβείᾱν μὴ δέχεσθαι Λακεδαιμονίων ἤδη στρατευομένων· ἀποπέμπουσιν οὖν αὐτὸν πρὶν
ἀκοῦσαι καὶ ἐκέλευον ἐκτὸς ὁρίων εἶναι αὐθήμερον, ξυμπέμπουσί τε   30
αὐτῷ ἀγωγούς, ὅπως μηδενὶ ξυγγένηται. ὁ δ' ἐπειδὴ ἐπὶ τοῖς ὁρίοις
ἐγένετο καὶ ἔμελλε διαλύσεσθαι, τοσόνδε εἰπὼν ἐπορεύετο ὅτι, "ἥδε ἡ
ἡμέρᾱ τοῖς Ἕλλησι μεγάλων κακῶν ἄρξει." ὡς δὲ ἀφίκετο ἐς τὸ
στρατόπεδον καὶ ἔγνω ὁ Ἀρχίδᾱμος ὅτι οἱ Ἀθηναῖοι οὐδέν πω
ἐνδώσουσιν, οὕτω δὴ ἄρᾱς τῷ στρατῷ προὐχώρει ἐς τὴν γῆν αὐτῶν.   35

[πρεσβείᾱν embassy   ὁρίων boundaries   αὐθήμερον that very day
ξυμπέμπουσι they send X (acc.) with Y (dat.)   ἀγωγούς escorts   ξυγγένηται he
would meet (+ dat.)   διαλύσεσθαι to part (from the escort)   πω at all   ἄρᾱς
(from αἴρω,ἀρῶ, ἦρα, here intransitive) τῷ στρατῷ setting out with his army]

—adapted from Thucydides 2.12

Principal Parts: More Liquid Stems (-ν-)

ἀποκτείνω (κτεν-/κτον-), ἀποκτενῶ, ἀπέκτεινα, ἀπέκτονα I kill
μένω (μεν-/μενε-), μενῶ, ἔμεινα, μεμένηκα I stay, wait; (transitive) I wait
    for
ἀποκρῑνομαι (κριν-), ἀποκρινοῦμαι, ἀπεκρῑνάμην, ἀποκέκριμαι I answer

Word Building

Verbs with present stems ending in -ττ- are formed from stems ending in gutturals (γ, κ, χ), e.g., πρᾱγ- > πρᾱττω; ταγ- > τάττω I arrange, draw up; φυλακ- > φυλάττω; and ταραχ- > ταράττω I confuse.

Give the meanings of the words in the following sets:

1. πρᾱττω   ἡ πρᾶξις   τὸ πρᾶγμα   πρᾱκτικός, -ή, -όν
2. τάττω   ἡ τάξις   τὸ τάγμα   τακτός, -ή, -όν   ἄτακτος, -ον
3. ταράττω   ἡ ταραχή   ἡ ἀταραξίᾱ   ἀτάρακτος, -ον
4. φυλάττω   ὁ φύλαξ   ἡ φυλακή

Grammar

3. The Verb δείκνῡμι

Stem: δεικ- (show)
Principal Parts: δείκ-νῡ-μι, δείξω, ἔδειξα, δέδειχα, δέδειγμαι, ἐδείχθην

In the present and imperfect tenses of this verb, endings are added directly to the extended present stem δεικ-νῡ-/-νυ-. Note the nasal infix -νῡ-/-νυ-. The other principal parts are formed regularly from the stem δεικ-. The following verbs are conjugated in the same way in the present:

ζεύγ-νῡ-μι, ζεύξω, ἔζευξα, ἔζευγμαι, ἐζεύχθην I yoke
ἀνοίγ-νῡ-μι, (*imperfect*) ἀνέῳγον, ἀνοίξω, ἀνέῳξα, ἀνέῳχα, ἀνέῳγμαι (I stand open), ἀνεῴχθην I open
ῥήγ-νῡ-μι, ῥήξω, ἔρρηξα, ἔρρωγα (I am broken), ἐρράγην I break

δείκνῡμι: Active Voice

Indicative	*Subjunctive*	*Imper.*	*Infin.*	*Participle*
Present Tense				
δείκνῡμι	δεικνύω		δεικνύναι	δεικνύς, δεικνῦσα,
δείκνῡς	δεικνύῃς	δείκνῡ		δεικνύν
δείκνῡσι	δεικνύῃ			
δείκνυμεν	δεικνύωμεν			
δείκνυτε	δεικνύητε	δείκνυτε		
δεικνύᾱσι	δεικνύωσι			

Imperfect Tense

ἐδείκνῡν
ἐδείκνῡς
ἐδείκνῡ
ἐδείκνυμεν
ἐδείκνυτε
ἐδείκνυσαν

δείκνῡμι: Middle Voice

Present Tense

δείκνυμαι	δεικνύωμαι		δείκνυσθαι	δεικνύμενος, -η, -ον
δείκνυσαι	δεικνύῃ	δείκνυσο		
δείκνυται	δεικνύηται			
δεικνύμεθα	δεικνυώμεθα			
δείκνυσθε	δεικνύησθε	δείκνυσθε		
δείκνυνται	δεικνύωνται			

Imperfect Tense

ἐδεικνύμην
ἐδείκνυσο
ἐδείκνυτο
ἐδεικνύμεθα
ἐδείκνυσθε
ἐδείκνυντο

4. Indirect Statements and Questions

Indirect statements and indirect questions have been used in the sentences of the stories from nearly the beginning of this course. Indirect statements may be introduced by ὅτι or ὡς "that" and have had their verbs in the indicative. Indirect questions may be introduced by any interrogative word ("when?" "why?" "who?") and have also had their verbs in the indicative.

You may have noticed that in these indirect statements and indirect questions, Greek, unlike English, always retains the tense of the original statement or question. Study the following examples:

ἡ παρθένος εἶπεν **ὅτι ἡ μήτηρ πρὸς τὴν κρήνην ἔρχεται.**
The girl said *that her mother was going to the spring.*
(She said: "Mother is going [ἔρχεται] to the spring.")
    (The present tense is retained in the indirect statement in Greek but is changed to the past in English.)

ὁ πατὴρ ἤρετο **πότε ἐπάνεισιν.**
The father asked *when she would return.*
(He asked: "When will she return [ἐπάνεισιν]?")
    (The future indicative is retained in the indirect question in Greek but is changed to "would return" in English.)

ἡ παρθένος ἀπεκρίνατο **ὡς οὐκ εἶπεν ἡ μήτηρ ὅσον χρόνον ἀπέσται.**
The girl answered *that mother had not said how long she would be away.*
(She said: "Mother did not say [οὐκ εἶπεν] how long she would be away [ἀπέσται].")
    Note here that the aorist (εἶπεν) in the original, direct statement is retained in the indirect statement in Greek but is translated by the

pluperfect ("had . . . said") in English when the main verb of the sentence (ἀπεκρίνατο) is in a past tense. Note also that the future tense in the original, direct statement (ἀπέσται) is retained in the indirect statement in Greek but is translated by "would be away."

Exercise 22d

Identify and translate the following forms of δείκνῡμι, ἀνοίγνῡμι, ζεύγνῡμι, *and* ῥήγνῡμι:

1. δεικνύᾱσι
2. δείκνυσθαι
3. ἐδείκνῡ
4. δεικνῦσα
5. ἐδείκνυσο

6. δεῖξαι
7. ἀνοίγνυτε
8. ἔρρηξαν
9. ζεύξᾱς
10. ἀνέῳξε

11. ῥήξουσι
12. δείκνυσο
13. ἀνοίξαντες
14. ῥηγνύναι
15. ζευγνύωμεν

Exercise 22e

Read aloud and translate:

1. ὁ πατὴρ τὴν παρθένον ἤρετο πόθεν ἦλθεν.
2. ἡ δὲ ἀποκρῑναμένη εἶπεν ὅτι ἦλθεν ἀπὸ τῆς οἰκίᾱς καὶ δι’ ὀλίγου ἐκεῖσε ἐπάνεισιν.
3. ὁ ἄγγελος εἶπεν ὅτι οἱ πρέσβεις ἤδη προσχωροῦσι καὶ δι’ ὀλίγου παρέσονται.
4. ὁ στρατηγὸς τὸν ἄγγελον ἐκέλευσε τὰς πύλᾱς ἀνοῖξαι καὶ τοὺς πρέσβεις δέχεσθαι.
5. ὁ ἄγγελος τοὺς φύλακας ἤρετο διὰ τί οὐκ ἀνοιγνύᾱσι τὰς πύλᾱς.
6. ὁ αὐτουργὸς τοὺς βοῦς ζεύξᾱς ἀροτρεύειν ἤρξατο.
7. τὸν δοῦλον καλέσᾱς λίθον μέγιστον ἔδειξεν αὐτῷ καὶ ἐκέλευσεν ἐκφέρειν ἐκ τοῦ ἀγροῦ.
8. ὁ δοῦλος εἶπεν ὅτι οὐ δυνατόν ἐστι λίθον τοσοῦτον αἴρειν.
9. ὁ δὲ δεσπότης ἀπεκρίνατο ὅτι λίθος τοσοῦτος τὸ ἄροτρον ῥήξει· ἀνάγκη οὖν ἐστι τὸν λίθον αἴρειν.
10. ὁ δὲ δοῦλος εἶπεν ὅτι ἐὰν μὴ βοηθῇ ὁ δεσπότης, οὐ δυνήσεται αἴρειν τὸν λίθον.

*   *   *

Η ΝΟΣΟΣ

Read the following passages (adapted from Thucydides 2.47–48) and answer the comprehension questions:

In early summer of 430 B.C., when the Peloponnesians invaded Attica for the second time, plague struck Athens. The city was crowded with refugees from the country, and living conditions were not healthy.

τοῦ δὲ θέρους εὐθὺς ἀρχομένου Πελοποννήσιοι καὶ οἱ ξύμμαχοι ἐσέβαλον ἐς τὴν Ἀττικήν· καὶ ὄντων αὐτῶν ἐν τῇ Ἀττικῇ οὐ πολλὰς ἡμέρᾱς, ἡ νόσος πρῶτον ἤρξατο

γενέσθαι τοῖς Ἀθηναίοις· λέγουσιν ὅτι πρότερον πολλαχόσε ἐγκατέσκηψεν, οὐ
μέντοι τοσοῦτός γε λοιμὸς ἐγένετο οὐδὲ τοσοῦτοι ἄνθρωποι ἀπέθανον.

[τοῦ . . . θέρους the summer   ἡ νόσος the disease, plague   πολλαχόσε onto
many places   ἐγκατέσκηψεν (from ἐγκατασκήπτω) it fell/had fallen (upon)
λοιμός plague]

1   What did the Peloponnesians do at the beginning of summer?
2. When did the plague begin in Athens?
3. How were the plague and its effects different in Athens from elsewhere?

οὔτε γὰρ ἰατροὶ ὠφέλουν τὸ πρῶτον ἀγνοοῦντες τὴν νόσον, ἀλλ' αὐτοὶ μάλιστα   5
ἔθνησκον ὅσῳ καὶ μάλιστα προσῇσαν τοῖς νοσοῦσιν, οὔτε ἄλλη ἀνθρωπεία τέχνη
ὠφέλει οὐδεμία. ἤρξατο δὲ ἡ νόσος τὸ μὲν πρῶτον, ὡς λέγουσιν, ἐξ Αἰθιοπίας τῆς
ὑπὲρ Αἰγύπτου, ἔπειτα δὲ καὶ ἐς Αἴγυπτον κατέβη καὶ ἐς βασιλέως γῆν τὴν
πολλήν.

[ἔθνησκον they died   ὅσῳ in as much as   προσῇσαν were near, consorted with
ἀνθρωπείᾱ human   τέχνη skill, art   Αἰθιοπίᾱς Ethiopia   ὑπέρ (+ gen.)
above, (here) south of   βασιλέως the king of Persia   γῆν τὴν πολλήν the greater
part of the land]

4. Why were doctors of no help? Why did they, especially, perish?
5. To what avail were other human efforts?
6. Where is the plague said to have originated?
7. What countries had it already ravaged?

ἐς δὲ τὴν Ἀθηναίων πόλιν ἐξαίφνης ἐσέπεσε, καὶ τὸ πρῶτον ἐν τῷ Πειραιεῖ   10
ἥψατο τῶν ἀνθρώπων· ὕστερον δὲ ἐς τὴν ἄνω πόλιν ἀφίκετο, καὶ ἔθνησκον πολλῷ
πλέονες ἤδη ἄνθρωποι. ἐγὼ δὲ οἷον ἐγίγνετο λέξω, αὐτός τε νοσήσᾱς καὶ αὐτὸς
ἰδὼν ἄλλους πάσχοντας.

[ἥψατο (from ἅπτω I fasten) it took hold of (+ gen.)   οἷον ἐγίγνετο what it was
like]

9.   Where did the plague begin to ravage the Athenians?
10. What happened when the plague reached the upper city of Athens?
11. What two reasons does Thucydides give for why he is a reliable source of
     information about the plague?

Exercise 22f

Translate into Greek:

1.   The doctors are afraid to approach the sick (*use participle*).
2.   For whoever touches (ἅπτομαι + *gen.*) a sick man (*use participle*),
     himself catches (falls into—*use participle of* ἐμπίπτω) the plague and
     dies.
3.   The doctors said that they could not help, not knowing the disease.
4.   Although we are afraid that we may become sick (fall into the
     sickness), we must stay in the city until the enemy goes away.
5.   If they go away soon, we will hurry to the country to escape the plague.

23

Η ΕΣΒΟΛΗ (α)

ἡ Ἀττικὴ γῆ τέμνεται ὑπὸ τῶν πολεμίων.

Vocabulary

Verbs

ἐπεξέρχομαι (*see* ἔρχομαι *for principal parts*) (+ *dat.*) I go out against, attack

καθέζομαι, καθεδοῦμαι I sit down, encamp

περιοράω (*see* ὁράω *for principal parts*) I overlook, disregard

τάττω (τάσσω), τάξω, ἔταξα, τέταχα, τέταγμαι, ἐτάχθην I marshal, draw up in battle array

τέμνω, τεμῶ, ἔτεμον, τέτμηκα, τέτμημαι, ἐτμήθην I cut, ravage

Nouns

ἡ αἰτίᾱ, τῆς αἰτίᾱς blame, responsibility, cause

ὁ δῆμος, τοῦ δήμου the people, township, deme

ἡ εἰσβολή (ἐσ-), τῆς εἰσβολῆς invasion

ἡ πεῖρα, τῆς πείρᾱς trial, attempt

ἡ προσβολή, τῆς προσβολῆς attack

τὸ φρούριον, τοῦ φρουρίου garrison

τὸ χωρίον, τοῦ χωρίου place, district

ὁ χῶρος, τοῦ χώρου place

Adjective

ἐπιτήδειος, -ᾱ, -ον friendly, suitable for (+ *infinitive*)

Adverb

ᾗπερ where

Conjunctions

ὁπόταν (+ *subjunctive*) when(ever)

ὁπότε when

Proper Names and Adjectives

αἱ Ἀχαρναί, τῶν Ἀχαρνῶν Acharnae

οἱ Ἀχαρνῆς, τῶν Ἀχαρνῶν inhabitants of Acharnae, the Acharnians

ὁ δὲ στρατὸς τῶν Πελοποννησίων προϊὼν ἀφίκετο τῆς Ἀττικῆς ἐς Οἰνόην πρῶτον, ᾗπερ ἔμελλον ἐσβαλεῖν. καὶ ὡς ἐκαθέζοντο, προσβολὰς παρεσκευάζοντο τῷ τείχει ποιησόμενοι μηχαναῖς τε καὶ ἄλλῳ τρόπῳ· ἡ γὰρ Οἰνόη οὖσα ἐν μεθορίοις τῆς Ἀττικῆς καὶ Βοιωτίας ἐτετείχιστο, καὶ αὐτῷ φρουρίῳ οἱ Ἀθηναῖοι ἐχρῶντο ὁπότε 5 πόλεμος γένοιτο. τάς τε οὖν προσβολὰς παρεσκευάζοντο καὶ ἄλλως ἐνδιέτριψαν χρόνον περὶ αὐτήν. αἰτίαν τε οὐκ ὀλίγην Ἀρχίδαμος ἔλαβεν ἀπ’ αὐτοῦ· οἱ γὰρ Ἀθηναῖοι πάντα ἐσεκομίζοντο ἐν τῷ χρόνῳ τούτῳ.

[μηχαναῖς siege engines   μεθορίοις borders   ἐτετείχιστο (from τειχίζω) had been fortified   ὁπότε πόλεμος γένοιτο whenever war occurred   ἄλλως in vain, fruitlessly   ἐνδιέτριψαν they spent, wasted]

ἐπειδὴ μέντοι προσβαλόντες τῇ Οἰνόῃ καὶ πᾶσαν ἰδέαν 10 πειράσαντες οὐκ ἐδύναντο ἑλεῖν, οἵ τε Ἀθηναῖοι οὐδὲν ἐπεκη- ρυκεύοντο, οὕτω δὴ ὁρμήσαντες ἀπ’ αὐτῆς ἐσέβαλον ἐς τὴν Ἀττικήν· ἡγεῖτο δὲ Ἀρχίδαμος Λακεδαιμονίων βασιλεύς.

[ἰδέαν sort, form (of attack)   ἐπεκηρῡκεύοντο made peace proposals]

καὶ καθεζόμενοι ἔτεμνον πρῶτον μὲν Ἐλευσῖνα καὶ τὸ Θριάσιον πεδίον. ἔπειτα δὲ προὐχώρουν ἕως ἀφίκοντο ἐς Ἀχαρνάς, χωρίον 15 μέγιστον τῆς Ἀττικῆς τῶν δήμων καλουμένων, καὶ καθεζόμενοι ἐς αὐτὸ στρατόπεδόν τε ἐποιήσαντο χρόνον τε πολὺν ἐμμείναντες ἔτεμνον. λέγεται δὲ ὅτι γνώμῃ τοιᾷδε ὁ Ἀρχίδαμος περί τε τὰς Ἀχαρνᾶς ὡς ἐς μάχην ταξάμενος ἔμεινε καὶ ἐς τὸ πεδίον ἐκείνῃ τῇ ἐσβολῇ οὐ κατέβη· ἤλπιζε γὰρ τοὺς Ἀθηναίους ἐπεξιέναι καὶ τὴν γῆν 20 οὐ περιόψεσθαι τεμνομένην.

[καλουμένων so-called   ἐμμείναντες remaining there   λέγεται it is said   ὡς ἐς μάχην as for battle   τεμνομένην being ravaged]

ἐπειδὴ οὖν αὐτῷ ἐς Ἐλευσῖνα καὶ τὸ Θριάσιον πεδίον οὐκ ἀπήντησαν, πεῖραν ἐποιεῖτο περὶ Ἀχαρνᾶς καθήμενος εἰ ἐπεξίασιν· ἅμα μὲν γὰρ αὐτῷ ὁ χῶρος ἐπιτήδειος ἐφαίνετο ἐνστρατοπεδεῦσαι, ἅμα δὲ ἐνόμιζε τοὺς Ἀχαρνέας μέγα μέρος ὄντας τῆς πόλεως 25 (τρισχίλιοι γὰρ ὁπλῖται ἐγένοντο) οὐ περιόψεσθαι τὰ σφέτερα διαφθειρόμενα ἀλλὰ ὁρμήσειν καὶ τοὺς πάντας ἐς μάχην.

[ἀπήντησαν (from ἀπαντάω) they went to meet (+ dat.)   ἅμα μὲν ... ἅμα δέ at the same time   ἐνστρατοπεδεῦσαι to encamp in   τρισχίλιοι three thousand τὰ σφέτερα διαφθειρόμενα their own things (property) being destroyed ὁρμήσειν would urge on, rouse]   —adapted from Thucydides 2.18–20

Principal Parts: More Liquid Stems (-ρ-)

αἴρω (ἀρ-), ἀρῶ, ἦρα, ἦρκα, ἦρμαι, ἤρθην I lift, raise up; (with reflexive
   pronoun) I get up; (intransitive) I get under way, set out
διαφθείρω (φθερ-/φθορ-/φθαρ-), διαφθερῶ, διέφθειρα, διέφθαρκα,
   διέφθορα (I am ruined), διέφθαρμαι, διεφθάρην I destroy
ἐγείρω (ἐγερ-/ἐγορ-/ἐγρ-), ἐγερῶ, ἤγειρα, ἐγρήγορα (I am awake),
   ἐγήγερμαι, ἠγέρθην I wake (someone) up; (middle and passive,
   intransitive) I wake up

Word Study

*Give the Greek words from which the following English political terms are
derived:*

1. politics
2. demagogue
3. rhetoric
4. democracy
5. monarchy
6. tyranny
7. ochlocracy (ὁ ὄχλος = mob)
8. autonomy

Grammar

1. The Passive Voice: Present and Imperfect Tenses

   In the present and imperfect tenses the passive forms of verbs are the
same as the middle forms. The context will make clear whether the verb
is middle or passive in meaning. Study the following sentences with
passive verbs taken from the reading passage above:

λέγεται δε ὅτι γνώμῃ τοιᾷδε ὁ Ἀρχίδαμος ... ἔμεινε. ...
It is said that Archidamus remained for some such reason as this. ...

οἱ Ἀθηναῖοι τὴν γῆν οὐ περιόψονται **τεμνομένην**.
The Athenians will not disregard their land *being ravaged* (= the fact
that their land *is being ravaged*).

οὐ περιόψονται τὰ σφέτερα **διαφθειρόμενα**.
They will not disregard their property *being destroyed* (= the fact that
their property *is being destroyed*).

   The agent by whom the action of the passive verb is carried out is
usually named in a prepositional phrase with ὑπό and the genitive case,
e.g.:

ἡ γῆ **ὑπὸ τῶν πολεμίων** τέμνεται.
The land is being ravaged *by the enemy*.

Exercise 23a

Read aloud and translate into English:

1. οἱ ὁπλῖται ὡς ἐς μάχην ὑπὸ τοῦ στρατηγοῦ ἐτάσσοντο.
2. ὁ παῖς ὑπὸ τοῦ ταύρου (bull) διωκόμενος βοῇ μεγίστῃ ἐχρῆτο.

3. οἱ αὐτουργοὶ ἐφοβοῦντο μὴ οἱ ἀγροὶ ὑπὸ τῶν πολεμίων τέμνωνται.
4. αἱ γυναῖκες ἐπὶ τῇ ἀμάξῃ φερόμεναι ταχέως ἐς τὸ ἱερὸν ἐκομίζοντο.
5. οἱ ἐν ἐκείνῃ τῇ μάχῃ μαχεσάμενοι αἰεὶ ὑπὸ τοῦ δήμου ἐτῑμῶντο.
6. οὐδεὶς κίνδῡνός ἐστι μὴ νῑκώμεθα ὑπὸ τῶν πολεμίων καίπερ τοσούτων ὄντων.
7. λέγεται ὅτι ὀργίζονται οἱ πολῖται ὁρῶντες τὰ σφέτερα διαφθειρόμενα.
8. ἐς τὸ ἄστυ σπεύδωμεν ὅπως μὴ ὑπὸ τῶν ἐσβαλλόντων βλαπτώμεθα.
9. ἅμ' ἦρι ἀρχομένῳ αἰεὶ ἠλαύνετο τὰ μῆλα πρὸς τὰ ὄρη.
10. ὅστις ἂν ἔξω τῶν τειχῶν λαμβάνηται ἐν μεγίστῳ κινδύνῳ ἔσται.

Exercise 23b

Translate into Greek:

1. When(ever) evening comes, the oxen are driven home by the farmer.
2. The men who were being chased (*use present participle*) by that dog scarcely escaped into the house.
3. The flocks, chased by these boys, got into a panic (**φόβος**).
4. I fear we may be defeated by the enemy.
5. All who (as many as) fight bravely for (their) fatherland are honored by the people.

2. Prepositional Prefixes and Euphony

Certain changes in spelling take place when prefixes are attached to verbs, e.g.:

a. ν before consonants:

> ν before β, π, φ, and ψ becomes μ, e.g., ἐν- + πίπτω > ἐμπίπτω (cf. ἐνέπεσον, ἐμπεσών).
> ν before γ, κ, ξ, and χ becomes γ, e.g., ἐν- + καλέω > ἐγκαλέω and συν- + γράφω > συγγράφω.
> ν before μ becomes μ, e.g., ἐν- + μένω > ἐμμένω.
> ν before λ or ρ is fully assimilated, e.g., συν- + λέγω > συλλέγω.

b. All prepositional prefixes ending in a vowel elide when followed by another vowel, except for πρό and περί, e.g., ἀνα- + ἔρχομαι > ἀνέρχομαι; ἀπο- + ἔρχομαι > ἀπέρχομαι; ἐπι- + ἔρχομαι > ἐπέρχομαι; but προέρχομαι and περιέρχομαι.

c. Prepositional prefixes compounded with a verb beginning with an aspirated vowel aspirate their final consonant if it is π or τ, e.g., ἀπο- + ὁρμάω > ἀφορμάω; ἐπι- + ἵστημι > ἐφίστημι; κατα- + ὁράω > καθοράω; μετα- + ἵημι > μεθίημι; ἀντι- + ἵστημι > ἀνθίστημι; and ὑπο- + αἱρέω > ὑφαιρέω.

The Peloponnesian War—First Phase (431–421 B.C.)

The events that led up to the war are briefly outlined in Chapter 20, page 52. Pericles was convinced that war was inevitable and, while observing the terms of the Thirty Years' Peace to the letter, he was not prepared to make any concessions to the Peloponnesians. He believed firmly that Athenian naval and financial superiority would bring victory in a war of attrition and that the war had better be fought now than later.

He had a clearly conceived strategy, which he outlined to the people in the speech from which you read extracts in Chapter 21β. The Athenian army could not risk battle in the field against the Peloponnesians, whose army outnumbered theirs by two to one and included the best hoplites in Greece. But the Athenians with a fleet of 300 triremes controlled the seas and the empire, so that Athens was invulnerable, provided that she was prepared to abandon Attica: "You must make up your minds to abandon your land and houses and keep guard over the sea and the city." At the same time, he intended to use the navy to make landings on enemy territory in the Peloponnesus and would attempt to regain control of Megara and its ports and to win over northwest Greece, so that a blockade of the Corinthian Gulf would bring Corinth to her knees.

Whether this Periclean strategy of a war of attrition, undermining the determination of the enemy, would have been successful, we cannot tell; for Pericles' calculations were upset by unforeseen factors, in particular by the plague that swept the city in 430–429 B.C. and by the cost of the war, which proved far higher than Pericles had calculated, so that by 422 B.C. the huge financial reserves on which he had relied were exhausted.

The war lasted from 431 to 404 B.C. with an intermission from 421 to 416. In this essay we will outline the events of the first half only, the Archidamian War, as it is called. In early summer 431 B.C. the Peloponnesian army under the Spartan king Archidamus invaded Attica, staying for about a month, while the Athenians withdrew behind the walls of Athens and saw their land devastated. As soon as the Peloponnesian army withdrew, Pericles led the Athenian army out and devastated Megara. At the same time a fleet of 100 triremes together with allied contingents sailed around the Peloponnesus, landing at various points and causing havoc. In the autumn this force joined up with the Athenian army for a second attack on Megara.

The operations of the next few years followed a similar pattern with the northwest of Greece seeing more activity. Both sides had allies in this area and sent expeditions to help them win control of the approaches to the Corinthian Gulf. The outcome was inconclusive except in the Gulf itself, where the brilliant victories of the Athenian admiral Phormio over a much larger Peloponnesian fleet finally established Athenian naval supremacy beyond all doubt (see Chapters 29–30).

In 425 B.C. a minor operation nearly brought the war to an end. An Athenian fleet sailing around the Peloponnesus was forced by bad weather to land at Pylos, on the west coast of the Peloponnesus. When the fleet continued on its way, it left behind a small force that fortified the promontory of Pylos and held it against Spartan attacks until reinforcements arrived. In the course of this operation, 420 Spartans were cut off on the island of Sphacteria. Eventually, the surviving 292 Spartans surrendered and were taken to Athens. The Spartan authorities in their eagerness to recover the prisoners sent an embassy to Athens to negotiate peace; the generous terms offered were rejected by the Assembly on the advice of Cleon, who had succeeded Pericles as the most influential speaker in the Assembly.

The following year the war took a new turn when a Spartan officer named Brasidas led a small force overland through northern Greece to Thrace. There he fomented revolt among the cities of Chalcidice, which belonged to the Athenian Empire, and succeeded in taking Amphipolis, a city of great strategic importance on the river Strymon. The historian Thucydides was one of the generals commanding in this area. He arrived with a fleet just too late to save the city, and for this failure he was brought to trial and exiled.

The Spartans were still eager for peace, and the Athenians were weary of the war. There was now a strong peace party, led by Nicias. In 423 B.C. a one year truce was agreed upon, during which time negotiations for a permanent settlement were to go forward. When the truce ended, however, Cleon persuaded the Assembly to send him in command of an expedition to recover Amphipolis. He scored some initial successes, but then Brasidas attacked him outside the walls of Amphipolis. In the ensuing battle both he and Brasidas were killed.

With their deaths, the chief obstacles to peace were removed, and in 421 B.C. a treaty was negotiated between Athens and Sparta, which is known as the Peace of Nicias. Each side agreed to abandon nearly all the gains they had made in the war and to observe the peace for fifty years. The outcome of these ten years of costly and bitter struggle was thus a return to the position that had obtained before the war. It proved to be a stalemate, nor were the prospects for long-term peace good. Nothing had been resolved. The basic reason for the war, the Peloponnesian fears of Athenian power, was still valid, nor, as events showed, was Athenian ambition quenched. Eight years later the war was to start again, this time with consequences disastrous for Athens.

Η ΕΣΒΟΛΗ (β)

Vocabulary

Verbs

διαλύω (*see* λύω *for principal
  parts*) I disband (an army),
  disperse (a fleet)
ἐάω, ἐάσω, εἴᾱσα, εἴᾱκα,
  εἴᾱμαι, εἰάθην I allow, let be
ἐμμένω (*see* μένω *for principal
  parts*) I remain in
ἐξαμαρτάνω (*see* ἁμαρτάνω
  for principal parts) I miss,
  fail, make a mistake
οἴομαι *or* οἶμαι, (*imperfect*)
  ᾤμην *or* ᾠόμην, οἰήσομαι,
  ᾠήθην I think

Nouns

ἡ ἐλπίς, ἐλπίδος hope,
  expectation
ἡ ἔξοδος, τῆς ἐξόδου going
  out, marching forth, military
  expedition
τὸ στάδιον, τοῦ σταδίου;
  (*plural*) τὰ στάδια *or* οἱ
  στάδιοι stade (8.7 stades = 1
  mile)
Adjective
ἕκαστος, -η, -ον each
Proper Name
οἱ Βοιωτοί, τῶν Βοιωτῶν
  Boeotians

Ἀθηναῖοι δὲ μεχρὶ μὲν οὗ περὶ Ἐλευσῖνα καὶ τὸ Θριάσιον πεδίον
ὁ στρατὸς ἦν, ἐλπίδα τινὰ εἶχον αὐτοὺς ἐς τὸ ἐγγυτέρω μὴ προϊέναι·
ἐπειδὴ δὲ περὶ τὰς Ἀχαρνὰς εἶδον τὸν στρατὸν ἑξήκοντα σταδίους
τῆς πόλεως ἀπέχοντα, οὐκέτι ἀνασχετὸν ἐποιοῦντο, ἀλλά, τῆς γῆς
τεμνομένης ἐν τῷ ἐμφανεῖ, δεινὸν αὐτοῖς ἐφαίνετο καὶ ἐδόκει τοῖς τε   5
ἄλλοις καὶ μάλιστα τοῖς νεανίαις ἐπεξιέναι καὶ μὴ περιορᾶν. κατὰ
ξυστάσεις τε γιγνόμενοι ἐν πολλῇ ἔριδι ἦσαν, οἱ μὲν κελεύοντες
ἐπεξιέναι, οἱ δέ τινες οὐκ ἐῶντες. οἵ τε Ἀχαρνῆς οἰόμενοι αὐτοὶ
μέγιστον μέρος εἶναι τῶν Ἀθηναίων, ὡς αὐτῶν ἡ γῆ ἐτέμνετο, ἐνῆγον
τὴν ἔξοδον μάλιστα.   10

[μεχρὶ . . . οὗ as long as   ἐς τὸ ἐγγυτέρω closer   ἀνασχετόν   tolerable
ἐποιοῦντο they considered   ἐν τῷ ἐμφανεῖ visibly, within eyesight   κατὰ
ξυστάσεις . . . γιγνόμενοι assembling into groups   ἔριδι contention, strife
ἐνῆγον (*from* ἐν- + ἄγω) were urging]

παντί τε τρόπῳ ἀνηρέθιστο ἡ πόλις καὶ τὸν Περικλέᾱ ἐν ὀργῇ
εἶχον, καὶ ἐκείνων ὧν παρῄνεσε πρότερον ἐμέμνηντο οὐδέν, ἀλλ'
ἐκάκιζον αὐτὸν ὅτι στρατηγὸς ὢν οὐκ ἐπεξάγει, αἴτιόν τε ἐνόμιζον
αὐτὸν εἶναι πάντων ὧν ἔπασχον. Περικλῆς δὲ ὁρῶν μὲν αὐτοὺς πρὸς
τὸ παρὸν ὀργιζομένους καὶ οὐ τὰ ἄριστα φρονοῦντας, πιστεύων δὲ   15

ὀρθῶς γιγνώσκειν περὶ τοῦ μὴ ἐπεξιέναι, ἐκκλησίαν οὐκ ἐποίει οὐδὲ
ξύλλογον οὐδένα, ἵνα μὴ ὀργῇ μᾶλλον ἢ γνώμῃ ξυνελθόντες
ἐξαμάρτωσί τι, ἀλλὰ τήν τε πόλιν ἐφύλασσε καὶ δι᾽ ἡσυχίας μάλιστα
ὅσον ἐδύνατο εἶχεν.

[ἀνηρέθιστο (from ἀνερεθίζω) had been stirred up, was excited   ἐμέμνηντο they
remembered   ἐκάκιζον they were abusing   ὅτι because   ἐπεξάγει he was (not)
leading (them) out against (the enemy)   πρὸς τὸ παρόν regarding the present
state of affairs   περὶ τοῦ μὴ ἐπεξιέναι about not going out to attack   ξύλλογον
gathering, meeting   δι᾽ ἡσυχίας . . . εἶχεν he kept them quiet]

οἱ δὲ Πελοποννήσιοι, ἐπειδὴ οὐκ ἐπεξῇσαν αὐτοῖς οἱ Ἀθηναῖοι ἐς   20
μάχην, ἄραντες ἐκ τῶν Ἀχαρνῶν ἐδῄουν τῶν δήμων τινὰς ἄλλους
καὶ ἐμμείναντες ἐν τῇ Ἀττικῇ πολύν τινα χρόνον, ἀνεχώρησαν διὰ
Βοιωτῶν, οὐχ ᾗπερ ἐσέβαλον.   ἀφικόμενοι δὲ ἐς Πελοπόννησον
διέλῡσαν τὸν στρατὸν καὶ ἕκαστοι ἐς τὴν ἑαυτῶν πόλιν ἐπανῆλθον.

[ἐδῄουν (from δῃόω) were laying waste, ravaging   διέλῡσαν they disbanded]

—adapted from Thucydides 2.21–23

Principal Parts: Verbs with Nasal Infix (-αν-)

αὐξ-άν-ω (αὐξ-/αὐξε-), αὐξήσω, ηὔξησα, ηὔξηκα, ηὔξημαι,
    ηὐξήθην I increase
λαμβ-άν-ω (λαβ-/ληβ-), λήψομαι, ἔλαβον, εἴληφα, εἴλημμαι,
    ἐλήφθην I take; (middle + gen.) I seize, take hold of
μανθ-άν-ω (μαθ-/μαθε-), μαθήσομαι, ἔμαθον, μεμάθηκα   I learn,
    understand

Word Building

Verbs and nouns are formed by adding suffixes to a root. Give the meaning of
the verbs and nouns in the following sets:

	Root	Verb	Noun
1.	λεγ-	λέγ-ω	ὁ λόγ-ος
	τρεπ-	τρέπ-ω	ὁ τρόπ-ος
	γραφ-	γράφ-ω	ἡ γραφ-ή
	μαχ-	μάχ-ομαι	ἡ μάχ-η

2. The following noun suffixes denote *agent*:

-τα (nominative -της)	ποιε-	ποιέ-ω	ὁ ποιη-τής
	κρῑ-/κρι-	κρῑ́-νω	ὁ κρι-τής
-ευ (nominative -ευς)	γραφ-	γράφ-ω	ὁ γραφ-εύς
	γεν-/γον-/γν-	γί-γν-ομαι	ὁ γον-εύς
-τηρ (nominative -τηρ)	σω-	σῴ-ζω	ὁ σω-τήρ
	δω-/δο-	δί-δω-μι	ὁ δο-τήρ
-τρο (nominative -τρος)	ῑᾱ-	ῑᾱ́-ομαι	ὁ ῑᾱ-τρός

3. The following noun suffixes denote *action*:

-σι (nominative -σις)	λῡ-/λυ-	λύω	ἡ λύσις
	ποιε-	ποιέ-ω	ἡ ποίη-σις
	κρῑ-/κρι-	κρῑ-νω	ἡ κρί-σις
-μα (nominative -μη)	φη-/φα-	φη-μί	ἡ φή-μη
	γνω-/γνο-	γι-γνώ-σκω	ἡ γνώ-μη

4. The suffix -ματ (nominative -μα) denotes *result of action*:

ποιε-	ποιέ-ω	τὸ ποίη-μα
πρᾱγ-	πρᾱττω	τὸ πρᾱγ-μα
γραφ-	γράφ-ω	τὸ γράμ-μα

The suffixes illustrated above are the most common ones, but there are many others.

Grammar

3. Indirect Statements with Infinitives

Indirect statements may be expressed with the infinitive instead of with ὅτι or ὡς and the indicative (see Chapter 22, Grammar 4, pages 83–84), e.g.,

ὁ νεᾱνίᾱς μοι ἔφη **τῷ γέροντι βοηθήσειν**.
The young man said to me *that he would help the old man*.

The tense of the infinitive in Greek is the same as the tense of the original or direct statement. In the example above the direct statement would have been τῷ γέροντι βοηθήσω "I will help the old man."

The infinitive construction for indirect statement is always used with φημί "I say," (imperfect) ἔφην "I said" (see summary in Grammar 4, page 96).

With λέγω "I say," both constructions are used; with εἶπον "I said," the construction with ὅτι or ὡς and the indicative is usually used.

Indirect statements with the infinitive may be introduced by other verbs as well, especially verbs of *thinking* and *believing*, e.g.:

ὁ Περικλῆς ἐπίστευεν **ὀρθῶς γιγνώσκειν** περὶ τοῦ μὴ ἐπεξιέναι.
Pericles was confident *that he was right* about not going out to attack.

Note that in the sentence above the subject of the indirect statement is the same as that of the leading verb; in this case it is usually not expressed in Greek, but it must be expressed in the English translation.

Sometimes the adjective αὐτός, αὐτή, αὐτό is used to emphasize or intensify the subject of the indirect statement in Greek; when so used it is in the nominative case, e.g.:

ἐνόμιζεν **αὐτὸς** ὀρθῶς γιγνώσκειν.
He thought that he *himself* was right.

οἱ Ἀχαρνῆς ᾤοντο **αὐτοὶ** μέγιστον μέρος εἶναι τῶν Ἀθηναίων.
The Acharnians thought that they *themselves* were the greatest part of
the Athenians.

If the subject of the infinitive is different from that of the leading verb,
it is in the accusative case, e.g.:

ἐπίστευεν αὐτὸς μὲν ὀρθῶς γιγνώσκειν, **ἐκείνους** δὲ ἁμαρτάνειν.
He was confident that he himself was right but that *they* were wrong.

αἴτιον ἐνόμιζον **αὐτὸν** εἶναι πάντων ὧν ἔπασχον.
They thought that *he* was responsible for everything they were
suffering.

The negative is the same in the indirect statement as it was in the
direct statement, e.g.:

ᾤετο τὸν πατέρα **οὐ** παρεῖναι.
He thought that his father was *not* present.
    (The original thought was: ὁ πατὴρ οὐ πάρεστιν).

οὐκ ἔφη βοηθήσειν.
He said that he would *not* help. = He denied that he would help.
    (The original statement was: οὐ βοηθήσω.)

Note the position of the negative in the indirect statement; it is placed
before φησί or ἔφη = he/she says/said that . . . not = he/she denies/denied.

Verbs of *hoping*, *threatening*, and *promising* and equivalent phrases
are often followed by the negative μή in indirect statements, e.g.:

οἱ πολῖται ἤλπιζον τοὺς πολεμίους τῇ πόλει **μὴ** προσβαλεῖν.
The citizens hoped that the enemy would *not* attack the city.

οἱ Ἀθηναῖοι ἐλπίδα τινὰ εἶχον αὐτοὺς **μὴ** ἐς τὸ ἐγγυτέρω προϊέναι.
The Athenians had some hope that they (i.e., the enemy) would *not*
come closer.

4. Indirect Statements with Participles

After verbs of *knowing*, *seeing*, and *hearing* indirect statements are
expressed with a participle instead of an infinitive, e.g.:

εἶδον **τὸν στρατὸν ἑξήκοντα σταδίους τῆς πόλεως ἀπέχοντα.**
They saw *that the army was sixty stades away from the city.*

Περικλῆς ὁρῶν **αὐτοὺς πρὸς τὸ παρὸν ὀργιζομένους καὶ οὐ τὰ
ἄριστα φρονοῦντας,** ἐκκλησίαν οὐκ ἐποίει.
Pericles, seeing *that they were angry at present and not thinking the
best (thoughts),* did not hold an assembly.

Again, as with the infinitive construction, the subject of the indirect statement is not expressed if it is the same as that of the leading verb. Note that in this case the participle is in the nominative case. Also, αὐτός, αὐτή, αὐτό may be used in the nominative case to emphasize the subject of the indirect statement. Note the following:

ἐπίστανται εἰς μέγιστον κίνδῡνον καταστάντες.
They know *that they have gotten into the greatest danger.*

οἶδα **αὐτὸς μὲν ὀρθῶς γιγνώσκων**, ἐκείνους δὲ ἁμαρτάνοντας.
I know *that I myself am right* and they are wrong.

All of the rules for the tenses, cases, and negatives are the same for the participle construction as for the infinitive construction.

Summary:

After	*Expect usually*
φημί/ἔφην	infinitive
λέγω and other verbs of saying, e.g., ἀποκρίνομαι	infinitive or ὅτι/ὡς
εἶπον	ὅτι/ὡς
verbs of thinking and believing	infinitive or occasionally ὅτι/ὡς
verbs of hoping, threatening, and promising	infinitive (negative usually μή)
verbs of knowing	participle or ὅτι/ὡς
verbs of perceiving (hearing, seeing, etc.)	participle or, of intellectual perception, ὅτι/ὡς

5. The Verb φημί

This verb shows a long vowel grade stem φη- and a short vowel grade stem φα-. Learn its forms from the chart in the Reference Grammar, paragraph 49, page 258. The future and first aorist are regular: φήσω, ἔφησα (rare).

Exercise 23c

Translate the following pairs of sentences:

1. ὁ ἄγγελος ἔφη τοὺς πρέσβεις ἤδη ἀφικέσθαι ἐς τὰς πύλᾱς.
   The old man said that the boy had already returned home.
2. οἱ νεᾱνίαι νομίζουσι τοὺς πολεμίους ῥᾳδίως νῑκήσειν.
   We think that we will easily take the city.
3. οἱ παῖδες οὐκ ἔφασαν τὸν πατέρα ἐν τῇ ἀγορᾷ ἰδεῖν.

The foreigners said that they had not found (denied that they had found) the money.

4. ὁρῶ ὑμᾶς πολλὰ καὶ κακὰ πάσχοντας.
   We see that they are mistaken.

5. χειμῶνος γιγνομένου οἱ ναῦται ἔγνωσαν μόλις ἐς τὸν λιμένα ἀφιξόμενοι.
   The women realized (γιγνώσκω) that they would get into big danger.

6. ἡ παρθένος ᾤετο τὴν μητέρα πρὸς τῇ κρήνῃ ὄψεσθαι.
   The shepherd thought that he would find (his) dog by the river.

7. οἱ δοῦλοι ἤλπιζον τὸν δεσπότην σφίσι (with them) μὴ ὀργιεῖσθαι.
   We hope the dog will not harm the flocks.

8. αἱ γυναῖκες ἠπίσταντο οὐδένα σῖτον ἐν τῷ οἴκῳ σφίσιν (for them) ὑπάρχοντα.
   The farmers knew that there was no house (ready–ὑπάρχω) for them in the city.

9. οἱ Ἀθηναῖοι ᾤοντο τοὺς ἐχθροὺς σφίσιν ἐπιβουλεύειν.
   We thought that the foreigner was leading us to the temple.

10. ἡ γυνὴ ἐπίστευεν αὐτὴ μὲν ὀρθῶς γιγνώσκειν, τὸν δὲ ἄνδρα ἁμαρτάνειν.
    Each (man) thought that he was safe and the others in danger.

6. Attraction of Relative Pronouns to Case of Antecedent

Examine the following from page 92 (lines 11–14):

τὸν Περικλέα ἐν ὀργῇ εἶχον, καὶ ἐκείνων **ὧν** παρῄνεσε πρότερον ἐμέμνηντο οὐδέν ... αἴτιόν τε ἐνόμιζον αὐτὸν εἶναι πάντων **ὧν** ἔπασχον.
They were angry with Pericles and remembered nothing of those things *that* he had formerly advised ... and they thought that he was responsible for all *that* they were suffering.

In this sentence the relative pronouns serve as direct objects of the verbs in their clauses, requiring the accusative case according to the usual rule. Here, however, they have been attracted into the case of their antecedents ἐκείνων and πάντων respectively.

Such attraction to the case of the antecedent often occurs when (1) the relative pronoun would normally be in the accusative case and (2) the antecedent is in the genitive or dative case. The attraction is optional.

Sometimes the relative pronoun precedes its antecedent, e.g.:

ὁ στρατηγὸς ἐπορεύετο σὺν ᾗ εἶχε δυνάμει (= σὺν δυνάμει ἥν/ᾗ εἶχε).
The general was marching with the (military) forces *that* he had.

Where the antecedent is a demonstrative pronoun, it is frequently omitted when attraction is used; for example, ἐπαινῶ σε ἐφ᾽ οἷς λέγεις "I praise you for what you say" would be more usual than the fuller expression ἐπὶ τούτοις ἃ λέγεις "for these things that you say."

Exercise 23d

Read aloud and translate. For each relative pronoun, give the form in which it would have been if attraction had not taken place, and give (where applicable) the omitted demonstrative pronoun antecedent.

1. μὴ πιστεύωμεν τοῖς πρέσβεσιν οἷς ἔπεμψαν οἱ Λακεδαιμόνιοι.
2. ἄξιοι ἔστε, ὦ ἄνδρες, τῆς ἐλευθρίας ἧς κέκτησθε (*you have won*).
3. δεῖ ὑμᾶς ἀφ' ὧν ἴστε (*you know*) αὐτοὶ τὰ πράγματα κρῖναι (*to judge*).
4. ὁ στρατηγὸς ἀφίκετο ἄγων ἀπὸ τῶν πόλεων ὧν ἔπεισε στρατιάν.
5. ἀμαθέστατοί (*most ignorant*) ἐστε ὧν ἐγὼ οἶδα Ἑλλήνων.

* * *

Ο ΠΕΡΙΚΛΗΣ

Read the following passages (adapted from Thucydides 2.65) and answer the comprehension questions:

The plague undermined Athenian morale. The people blamed Pericles for their sufferings and sent envoys to Sparta to discuss peace terms. Pericles made a speech to try to raise their spirits. Thucydides here summarizes the achievements of Pericles.

τοιαῦτα ὁ Περικλῆς λέγων ἐπειρᾶτο τοὺς Ἀθηναίους τῆς ἐς αὐτὸν ὀργῆς παραλύειν. οἱ δὲ δημοσίᾳ μὲν τοῖς λόγοις ἐπείθοντο καὶ οὔτε πρὸς τοὺς Λακεδαιμονίους πρέσβεις ἔτι ἔπεμπον ἔς τε τὸν πόλεμον μᾶλλον ὥρμηντο, ἰδίᾳ δὲ τοῖς παθήμασιν ἐλυποῦντο. οὐ μέντοι πρότερόν γε ἐπαύσαντο ἐν ὀργῇ ἔχοντες αὐτὸν πρὶν ἐζημίωσαν χρήμασιν. ὕστερον δὲ οὐ πολλῷ αὖθις στρατηγὸν αὐτὸν εἵλοντο   5
καὶ πάντα τὰ πράγματα ἐπέτρεψαν.

[ἐς (+ *acc.*) against   παραλύειν to rid X (*acc.*) of Y (*gen.*)   δημοσίᾳ publicly   οὔτε = οὐ   ὥρμηντο (*pluperfect passive of* ὁρμάω) they had been aroused, were in a state of eagerness   τοῖς παθήμασιν sufferings   πρίν until   ἐζημίωσαν they penalized, fined   χρήμασιν *dat. of* χρήματα "*money," with* ἐζημίωσαν   εἵλοντο they chose]

1. What was Pericles attempting to do?
2. What three things did the Athenians publicly do in response?
3. What did they do in private?
4. What did the Athenians have to do before they could stop being angry at Pericles?
5. What did they do shortly thereafter?

ὅσον τε γὰρ χρόνον προΰστη τῆς πόλεως ἐν τῇ εἰρήνῃ, μετρίως ἡγεῖτο καὶ ἀσφαλῶς ἐφύλαξεν αὐτήν, καὶ ἐγένετο ἐπ' ἐκείνου μεγίστη· ἐπειδή τε πόλεμος κατέστη, φαίνεται ὁ Περικλῆς καὶ ἐν τούτῳ προγνοὺς τὴν δύναμιν αὐτῆς. ἐπεβίω δὲ δύο ἔτη καὶ ἓξ μῆνας· καὶ ἐπειδὴ ἀπέθανεν, ἐπὶ πλέον ἐγνώσθη ἡ πρόνοια   10
αὐτοῦ ἡ ἐς τὸν πόλεμον.

[ὅσον . . . χρόνον as long as   προὔστη (*from* προΐστημι) he was at the head of,
in charge of (+ *gen.*)   μετρίως moderately   ἐπ' ἐκείνου in his time   κατέστη
began   προγνούς (*from* προγιγνώσκω) having foreknown   ἐπεβίω (*from* ἐπιβιόω)
he lived on, survived   μῆνας months   ἐπὶ πλέον more, further   ἐγνώσθη ἡ
πρόνοια αὐτοῦ his foresight was recognized]

6. How did the city fare with Pericles in charge of it during peacetime?
7. When war came did Pericles appear to be right or wrong in his thinking
    about the city?
8. What was recognized even more after Pericles' death?

ὁ μὲν γὰρ ἔφη ἡσυχάζοντάς τε καὶ τὸ ναυτικὸν φυλάσσοντας καὶ ἀρχὴν μὴ
ἐπικτωμένους ἐν τῷ πολέμῳ μηδὲ τῇ πόλει κινδῡνεύοντας αὐτοὺς νῑκήσειν. οἱ δὲ
ταῦτα πάντα ἐς τὸ ἐναντίον ἔπρᾱξαν καὶ κατὰ τὰς ἰδίᾱς φιλοτῑμίᾱς καὶ ἴδια
κέρδη κακῶς ἐπολίτευσαν. αἴτιον δὲ ἦν ὅτι ἐκεῖνος δυνατὸς ὢν οὐκ ἤγετο ὑπὸ τοῦ   15
δήμου μᾶλλον ἢ αὐτὸς ἦγε. ἐγίγνετό τε λόγῳ μὲν δημοκρατίᾱ, ἔργῳ δὲ ὑπὸ τοῦ
πρώτου ἀνδρὸς ἀρχή.

[ἐπικτωμένους increasing, adding to   τῇ πόλει κιδῡνεύοντας putting the city
at risk   οἱ δὲ but they (i.e., his successors)   ἐς τὸ ἐναντίον in the opposite way
τὰς ἰδίᾱς φιλοτῑμίᾱς their private ambitions   κέρδη profits   κακῶς
ἐπολίτευσαν pursued bad policies   αἴτιον the reason]

9. What four things had Pericles said the citizens should do if they were to
    be victorious?
10. Did the Athenians do as Pericles said they should?
11. What two things motivated the Athenians?
12. How did they conduct themselves as citizens?
13. What reasons does Thucydides give for Pericles' success as a leader?
14. How does Thucydides describe the system of government under
    Pericles?

Exercise 23e

Translate into Greek:

1. When Pericles died, his successors (οἱ ὕστερον) did not lead the
    citizens but were led by them.
2. For each wishing to be first said, "I will give the citizens all that
    (whatever) they want."
3. But they made many mistakes and sent away the expedition to Sicily
    (ἡ Σικελίᾱ), hoping that they would thus please (χαρίζομαι + *dat.*)
    the people.
4. But when they heard that the generals were being defeated by the
    enemy, they did not send help (ἡ βοήθεια).
5. For competing (ἀγωνίζομαι) against each other about the leadership
    (ἡ προστασίᾱ) of the people, they were being persuaded to neglect
    (ἀμελέω + *gen.*) the war.

24
ΕΝ ΔΙΔΑΣΚΑΛΩΝ (α)

ἐν διδασκάλων· ἐπ' ἀριστερᾷ μὲν ὁ παῖς κιθαρίζειν διδάσκεται ὑπὸ κιθαριστοῦ· ἐπὶ δὲ δεξιᾷ καθίζεται ὁ παιδαγωγός· μεταξὺ δὲ ὁ γραμματιστὴς τὰ γράμματα διδάσκει.

Vocabulary

Verbs

διδάσκω, διδάξω, ἐδίδαξα, δεδίδαχα, δεδίδαγμαι, ἐδιδάχθην I teach

ζάω (*infinitive*) **ζῆν,** (*imperfect*) **ἔζων, ζήσω** I live

μελετάω I study, practice

παιδεύω, παιδεύσω, ἐπαίδευσα, πεπαίδευκα, πεπαίδευμαι, ἐπαιδεύθην I educate

συνίημι (*see* ἵημι *for principal parts*) (+ *gen. of person, acc. of thing*) I understand

φοιτάω I go, visit

Nouns

τὸ γράμμα, τοῦ γράμματος letter (of the alphabet); (*plural*) writing

ὁ γραμματιστής, τοῦ γραμματιστοῦ schoolmaster

ἡ γυμναστική, τῆς γυμναστικῆς gymnastics

ὁ διδάσκαλος, τοῦ διδασκάλου teacher

ὁ κιθαριστής, τοῦ κιθαριστοῦ lyre player

ἡ μουσική, τῆς μουσικῆς music

ἡ παίδευσις, τῆς παιδεύσεως education

ὁ σοφιστής, τοῦ σοφιστοῦ wise man, sophist

ὁ τεκών, τοῦ τεκόντος parent

ὁ υἱός, τοῦ υἱοῦ son

Adjectives

ἄδικος, -ον unjust

αἰσχρός, -ά, -όν shameful

ἄσμενος, -η, -ον glad(ly)

δίκαιος, -ᾱ, -ον just

σμῑκρός, -ά, -όν small

Conjunction
ὅπως (+ *subjunctive*) so that, in
   order to; (+ *future indicative*)
   that
Expressions
καθ' ἡμέρᾱν every day

περὶ πολλοῦ ποιοῦμαι I
consider of great importance
περὶ πλείστου ποιοῦμαι I
consider of greatest
importance

μέχρι μὲν οὗ οἵ τε Πελοποννήσιοι ἐν τῇ Ἀττικῇ ἔμενον καὶ οἱ
Ἀθηναῖοι ἐπολιορκοῦντο, ὁ Φίλιππος καθ' ἡμέρᾱν ἤγετο ὑπὸ τῶν
ἀνεψιῶν εἰς διδασκάλων. τά τ' οὖν γράμματα ἐδιδάσκετο ὑπὸ τοῦ
γραμματιστοῦ καὶ ὑπὸ τοῦ κιθαριστοῦ τὴν μουσικήν· ἐφοίτᾱ δὲ καὶ
εἰς τοῦ παιδοτρίβου ὅπως τὴν γυμναστικὴν μελετᾷ. ἐπεὶ δ' ἠγγέλθη   5
ὅτι οἱ Πελοποννήσιοι ἀπῆλθον, ἅπαντες οἱ αὐτουργοὶ φόβου
λελυμένοι εἰς τοὺς ἀγροὺς ἐπανῇσαν. ὁ μὲν οὖν Δικαιόπολις τήν τε
γυναῖκα καὶ τοὺς παῖδας ἔμελλεν οἴκαδε κομιεῖν, ὁ δὲ ἀδελφὸς ἤρετο
αὐτὸν εἰ ἐθέλει τὸν Φίλιππον παρ' ἑαυτῷ λείπειν ἵνα μὴ παύηται
παιδευόμενος. ὁ μὲν οὖν Δικαιόπολις ταῦτα ἄσμενος δεξάμενος καὶ   10
τὸν υἱὸν τῷ ἀδελφῷ ἐπιτρέψᾱς ἐπορεύετο, ὁ δὲ Φίλιππος καταλειφθεὶς
ἔτι πλέονα ἐπαιδεύετο.

[**μέχρι . . . οὗ** as long as   **τῶν ἀνεψιῶν** his cousins   **τοῦ παιδοτρίβου**
trainer   **ἠγγέλθη** it was announced   **λελυμένοι** freed from (+ *gen.*)   **παρ'**
ἑαυτῷ at his house   **καταλειφθεὶς** left behind]

ὁποῖᾱ δ' ἦν αὕτη ἡ παίδευσις δύναταί τις γιγνώσκειν διάλογόν
τινα τοῦ Πλάτωνος σκοπῶν, ἐν ᾧ σοφιστής τις, Πρωταγόρᾱς ὀνόματι,
ἐνδείκνυσθαι πειρᾶται ὅτι διδακτόν ἐστιν ἡ ἀρετή. ὁ γὰρ   15
Πρωταγόρᾱς λέγει ὅτι ἅπαντες οἱ τεκόντες τοῦτο περὶ πλείστου
ποιοῦνται, ὅπως ἀγαθοὶ γενήσονται οἱ παῖδες.

[**ὁποῖᾱ** of what sort   **διάλογον** dialogue   **ἐνδείκνυσθαι** to show, prove
διδακτόν a teachable thing]

"ἐκ παίδων σμῑκρῶν," φησίν, "ἀρξάμενοι μέχρι οὗπερ ἂν ζῶσιν,
καὶ διδάσκουσι καὶ νουθετοῦσιν. ἐπειδὰν πρῶτον συνίῃ τις τὰ
λεγόμενα, καὶ τροφὸς καὶ μήτηρ καὶ παιδαγωγὸς καὶ αὐτὸς ὁ πατὴρ   20
περὶ τούτου διαμάχονται, ὅπως ὡς βέλτιστος ἔσται ὁ παῖς, παρ'
ἕκαστον ἔργον καὶ λόγον διδάσκοντες καὶ ἐνδεικνύμενοι ὅτι τὸ μὲν
δίκαιον, τὸ δὲ ἄδικον, καὶ τόδε μὲν καλόν, τόδε δὲ αἰσχρόν, καὶ τόδε
μὲν ὅσιον, τόδε δὲ ἀνόσιον, καὶ τὰ μὲν ποίει, τὰ δὲ μὴ ποίει. καὶ ἐὰν
μὲν πείθηται—, εἰ δὲ μή, εὐθύνουσιν ἀπειλαῖς καὶ πληγαῖς."   25

[νουθετοῦσιν warn, advise   τὰ λεγόμενα things being said, speech   τροφός nurse   διαμάχονται strive hard   ὡς βέλτιστος as good as possible   παρ' (+ acc.) in (respect of each)   ἐνδεικνύμενοι pointing out, showing   τὸ μὲν ... τὸ δέ ... this is ... but that is   ἀνόσιον unholy   εὐθύνουσιν they straighten (him) out   ἀπειλαῖς with threats   πληγαῖς with blows]

—The last paragraph above is adapted from Plato, *Protagoras* 325c5–d7.

Principal Parts: More Verbs with Nasal Infix (-ν-, -νε-, -ιν-, and -νῦ-/-νυ-)

κάμ-ν-ω (καμ-/κμη-), καμοῦμαι, ἔκαμον, κέκμηκα I am sick, tired
ἀφικ-νέ-ομαι (ἱκ-), ἀφίξομαι, ἀφῑκόμην, ἀφῖγμαι I arrive, arrive at (+ εἰς + acc.)
βα-ίν-ω (βα-), βήσομαι, ἔβην, βέβηκα I step, walk, go
δείκ-νῦ-μι (δεικ-), δείξω, ἔδειξα, δέδειχα, δέδειγμαι, ἐδείχθην I show

Grammar

1. The Passive Voice: First Aorist and First Future Passive

In Chapter 23 you learned that in the present and the imperfect tenses the middle and passive voices have identical forms. In the aorist and future tenses the passive voice has forms different from those of the middle. In the first paragraph of the reading passage above you met the following aorist passive forms, easily identified by the presence of the letter θ: ἠγγέλθη "it was announced" and καταλειφθείς "left behind."

To form the aorist passive, most verbs add -θη-/-θε- to the verb stem. The indicative is augmented, and the subjunctive shows contractions. The resulting forms are called first aorist passives.

Indicative	*Subjunctive*	*Imperative*	*Infinitive*	*Participle*
ἐ-λύ-θην	λυ-θῶ		λυ-θῆναι	λυ-θείς,
ἐ-λύ-θης	λυ-θῇς	λύ-θητι		λυ-θεῖσα,
ἐ-λύ-θη	λυ-θῇ			λυ-θέν
ἐ-λύ-θημεν	λυ-θῶμεν			
ἐ-λύ-θητε	λύ-θῆτε	λύ-θητε		
ἐ-λύ-θησαν	λυ-θῶσι(ν)			

The declension of the aorist passive participle is as follows:

	Masculine	*Feminine*	*Neuter*
Nom.	λυθείς	λυθεῖσα	λυθέν
Gen.	λυθέντος	λυθείσης	λυθέντος
Dat.	λυθέντι	λυθείσῃ	λυθέντι
Acc.	λυθέντα	λυθεῖσαν	λυθέν
Nom.	λυθέντες	λυθεῖσαι	λυθέντα
Gen.	λυθέντων	λυθεισῶν	λυθέντων
Dat.	λυθεῖσι	λυθείσαις	λυθεῖσι
Acc.	λυθέντας	λυθείσᾱς	λυθέντα

To form the first future passive, add -θη- to the verb stem and then add the same letters as for the future middle. Remember that there are no future subjunctives or imperatives, and of course there is no augment.

Indicative	*Infinitive*	*Participle*
λυ-θή-σ-ομαι	λυ-θή-σ-εσθαι	λυ-θη-σ-όμενος, -η, -ον
λυ-θή-σ-ῃ		
λυ-θή-σ-εται		
λυ-θη-σ-όμεθα		
λυ-θή-σ-εσθε		
λυ-θή-σ-ονται		

Contract verbs lengthen the stem vowel, e.g.:

φιλε-:	ἐ-φιλή-θην
	φιλη-θή-σ-ομαι
τῑμα-:	ἐ-τῑμή-θην
	τῑμη-θή-σ-ομαι
δηλο-:	ἐ-δηλώ-θην
	δηλω-θή-σ-ομαι

Stems ending in labials (β, π, and φ) and gutturals (γ, κ, and χ) aspirate the last consonant, e.g.:

πέμπ-ω:	ἐ-πέμφ-θην
	πεμφ-θή-σ-ομαι
πρᾱ́σσω (πρᾱγ-):	ἐ-πρᾱ́χ-θην
	πρᾱχ-θή-σ-ομαι

Stems ending in dentals (δ, ζ, θ, and τ) change the last consonant to σ, e.g.:

νομίζ-ω:	ἐ-νομίσ-θην
	νομισ-θή-σ-ομαι

Note the following:

βάλλω (βαλ-/βλη-)	ἐβλή-θην
	βλη-θή-σ-ομαι
ἐλαύνω (ἐλα-):	ἠλά-θην
	ἐλα-θή-σ-ομαι
κελεύω:	ἐ-κελεύσ-θην
	κελευσ-θή-σ-ομαι
λαμβάνω (λαβ-/ληβ-):	ἐ-λήφ-θην
	ληφ-θή-σ-ομαι
ὁράω (ὀπ-):	ὤφ-θην
	ὀφ-θή-σ-ομαι

2. Second Aorist Passive and Second Future Passive

Some verbs add -η-/-ε- instead of -θη-/-θε- to form their aorist
passives and -η- instead of -θη- to form their future passives; these are
called second aorist and second future passives, e.g.:

γράφω: ἐ-γράφ-η-ν
              γραφ-ή-σ-ομαι

φαίνω: ἐ-φάν-η-ν
              φαν-ή-σ-ομαι

3. Aorist of Deponent Verbs

A few deponent verbs have aorists that are passive instead of middle
in form, e.g.:

διαλέγομαι, διελέχθην "I talked"
ἥδομαι, ἥσθην "I enjoyed/was glad/was delighted"
ὀργίζομαι, ὠργίσθην "I grew angry"
πορεύομαι, ἐπορεύθην "I journeyed"

4. ὅπως + Future Indicative after Verbs Expressing Care or Effort

Note the use of ὅπως + future indicative in the following sentences:

διαμάχονται, **ὅπως ὡς βέλτιστος ἔσται ὁ παῖς.**
They strive hard (to see to it) *that the child will be as good as possible.*

The negative is ὅπως μή, e.g.:

οἱ διδάσκαλοι πάντα πράττουσιν, **ὅπως μηδὲν κακὸν ποιήσουσιν οἱ
παῖδες.**
The teachers do everything (to see to it) *that the children will do nothing
bad.*

Exercise 24a

Read aloud and translate into English:

1. ἐπειδὴ ἠγγέλθη τοὺς Πελοποννησίους εἰς τὴν Ἀττικὴν εἰσβάλλειν, τῶν
   αὐτουργῶν οἱ πολλοὶ (*the majority*) εὐθὺς πρὸς τὸ ἄστυ ἐπορεύθησαν.
2. ἔνιοι, οἳ οὐκ ἤθελον τὰς οἰκίᾱς καταλιπεῖν, ὑπὸ τῶν πολεμίων ἐλήφθησαν.
3. τῶν Πελοποννησίων ἀπελθόντων, πάντες φόβου λελυμένοι (*freed*)
   παρεσκευάζοντο οἴκαδε ἐπανιέναι.
4. ἆρ' οὐκ ἥσθης εἰς τοὺς ἀγροὺς ἐπανελθών;
5. πάντα πράττωμεν, ὦ φίλοι, ὅπως μὴ ὑπὸ τῶν πολεμίων ληφθησόμεθα.
6. ὁ πατὴρ πάντα ἔπραττεν ὅπως εὖ παιδευθήσεται ὁ υἱός (*son*).
7. ἐὰν ἀνδρείως μάχησθε, ὦ ἄνδρες, ἡ πατρὶς ἐλευθερωθήσεται, ὑμεῖς δὲ ὑπὸ
   πάντων τῑμηθήσεσθε.
8. ὁ ἀνὴρ ἰδὼν τὴν γυναῖκα ξένῳ τινὶ διαλεγομένην μάλιστα ὠργίσθη.
9. μὴ διαλεχθῇς τούτῳ τῷ νεανίᾳ, ὦ γύναι· ξένος γάρ ἐστιν.
10. ἡ γυνὴ ὑπὸ τοῦ ἀνδρὸς εἰσιέναι κελευσθεῖσα εἰς τὴν οἰκίᾱν ἔσπευσεν.

Exercise 24b

Translate into Greek:

1. The hoplites, defeated by the enemy, were driven into the city.
2. Messengers were sent by the people to ask for (*use* ὡς + *future participle*) a peace treaty.
3. Fearing that his master would grow angry, the slave fled.
4. He tried (*use finite verb*) to leave the city by night but was seen and caught (*use participle and finite verb*).
5. A hundred ships will be sent to help the allies.

Greek Education

At the trainer's: boys practice boxing, throwing
javelins and the discus, and running

The Greeks divided education into "music" and "gymnastics." Music meant everything concerned with the Muses, including literacy, literature, and music in our sense. Gymnastics meant physical training. It was commonly said that "music" educated the soul and "gymnastics" trained the body.

Girls did not, as far as we know, attend schools. Their education was at home and centered on the domestic arts but must have also included music and dancing. Boys went to school from about the age of seven and usually had three different teachers. The writing master (ὁ γραμματιστής) taught basic literacy, numbers, and literature, the latter consisting of the traditional poets, especially Homer. The music teacher (ὁ κιθαριστής) taught the lyre and sometimes also the double pipe, singing, and dancing. The trainer (ὁ παιδοτρίβης) taught exercises such as running, jumping, throwing the javelin and discus, and wrestling.

There were no state schools, though the state did pay for the education of some children, in particular the sons of those who had died fighting for the

city. Other parents had to pay the teachers a small fee. A boy was usually accompanied by a slave called a παιδαγωγός, who was responsible for his safety
on the way to and from school and for his good behavior.

It is impossible to say confidently how large a proportion of the citizens
received this education or how widespread literacy was. It seems likely that
the vast majority received schooling. The Athenian democracy functioned
on the assumption that all male citizens were literate. Officers of state were
selected by lot, and an illiterate could hardly have carried out the duties of a
councilor, let alone act as chairman of the Assembly. Moreover, laws and
decrees were displayed in public places for all to read, and at an ostracism it
was assumed that every citizen could at least write on an ostracon the name of
the politician he wished to see exiled.

The education we have described was elementary. There was no higher
education until the sophists arrived on the scene (see below), and, as
Protagoras says in the passages quoted in this chapter, the moral element in
education was considered quite as important as the intellectual. In fact, the
purpose of the educational system was not to train the intellect at all, but to im-
part basic skills that would be essential in adult life and, above all, to hand
down the traditional values of piety, morality, and patriotism, which were
enshrined in poetry, especially in Homer. Plato says of Homer: "This poet
has educated Greece." Boys learned extensive passages of the *Iliad* by heart
and in so doing imbibed Homeric values.

With the development of democracy there arose a demand for a new sort
of education. Birth was no longer the passport to political power. The aspir-
ing politician needed the ability to persuade others, especially in the law
courts and the Assembly. It was this ability that had given Pericles, for instance, his pre-eminence. This demand was met by the sophists, who were
itinerant teachers who began to appear on the scene in the second half of the
fifth century. They offered to the sons of the rich a form of higher education
in return for large fees. Different sophists included different topics in their
courses, but common to all was rhetoric, that is, the art of speaking persua-
sively, especially in public.

One of the earliest and greatest of the sophists was Protagoras, born in
Abdera on the coast of Macedonia about 485 B.C. He was extremely successful
and had such a reputation that wherever he went rich and clever young men
flocked to hear him. In Plato's *Protagoras*, Socrates takes the young Hippocrates to meet Protagoras. When they arrive at the house where he is staying, they find Protagoras walking around in a portico accompanied by some
of the richest and noblest young men of Athens, including two sons of Pericles. They see other famous sophists who have come to meet Protagoras, including one who is teaching astronomy. They then approach the great man,
and Socrates explains the purpose of their visit: "Hippocrates here wishes to
make a mark in the city and thinks he would be most likely to achieve this if
he became your pupil; and so he would like to know what he will gain if he
comes to you." "Young man," replies Protagoras, "this is what you will
gain, if you come to me; on the very day you join me you will go home a better

man, and on the next day the same will happen, and every day you will continually progress toward the better." Socrates answers that this may well be so, but in what particular sphere will he become better? Protagoras replies that anyone who comes to him will not learn irrelevant subjects such as arithmetic, astronomy, or geometry, but will learn precisely the subject for which he has come, namely good judgment in managing both his personal affairs and the affairs of the city, so that he may be most capable in political action and speech. Socrates asks: "Do I follow what you are saying? I think you mean the art of politics (ἡ πολῑτικὴ τέχνη) and profess to make men good citizens." "That," replies Protagoras, "is exactly what I do profess."

Protagoras accuses other sophists of teaching "irrelevant subjects," such as mathematics. Those who did teach such subjects would have said that they provided an intellectual training that was an essential preparation for further studies. The idea of training the intellect had come to stay.

The next century saw the foundation of institutes of higher education. Socrates' pupil Plato founded the Academy in 387 B.C. to train statesmen by teaching them philosophy; for only the philosopher knew what was really "good," and only one trained in philosophy could know what was good for the city. He believed in a rigorous intellectual training, based on the study of mathematics. Soon other schools were founded, such as Aristotle's Lyceum, which was a center for research in the sciences as well as a school of philosophy, and schools of rhetoric, such as that of Isocrates.

At school: (from left to right) a boy being taught to play the double pipe, a teacher examining a pupil's exercise, and a seated παιδαγωγός

ΕΝ ΔΙΔΑΣΚΑΛΩΝ (β)

Vocabulary

Verbs

ἐπιμελέομαι, ἐπιμελήσομαι,
ἐπιμεμέλημαι, ἐπεμελήθην
(+ gen.) I take care for; (+ ὅπως
+ future indicative) I take care
that

ἥδομαι, ἡσθήσομαι, ἥσθην (+
participle or dat.) I enjoy, am
glad, delighted

κιθαρίζω, κιθαριῶ,
ἐκιθάρισα I play the lyre

Nouns

ἡ ἁρμονίᾱ, τῆς ἁρμονίᾱς
harmony

τὸ βιβλίον, τοῦ βιβλίου book

ἡ διάνοια, τῆς διανοίᾱς
intention, intellect

ὁ ἔπαινος, τοῦ ἐπαίνου
praise

ὁ μαθητής, τοῦ μαθητοῦ pupil

ἡ πονηρίᾱ, τῆς πονηρίᾱς fault,
wickedness

ἡ πρᾶξις, τῆς πρᾱξεως deed

ὁ ῥυθμός, τοῦ ῥυθμοῦ rhythm

τὸ σῶμα, τοῦ σώματος body

ἡ σωφροσύνη, τῆς σωφροσύνης
moderation, self-discipline,
good sense

ἡ φωνή, τῆς φωνῆς voice,
speech

Adjectives

ὄλβιος, -ᾱ, -ον happy, blest,
prosperous

παλαιός, -ά, -όν old, of old

χρήσιμος, -η, -ον useful

χρηστός, -ή, -όν useful, good

Prepositions

ἐπί (+ gen.) toward, in the
direction of, on; (+ dat.) at,
upon, on, for; (+ acc.) at,
against, onto

πρός (+ dat.) at, near, by, in
addition to; (+ acc.) to, toward,
against, upon

Adverb

αὖ again

"μετὰ δὲ ταῦτα εἰς διδασκάλων πέμποντες πολὺ μᾶλλον τοὺς διδασκάλους κελεύουσιν ἐπιμελεῖσθαι εὐκοσμίᾱς τῶν παίδων ἢ γραμμάτων τε καὶ κιθαρίσεως· οἱ δὲ διδάσκαλοι τούτων τε ἐπιμελοῦνται, καὶ ἐπειδὰν αὖ γράμματα μάθωσιν καὶ μέλλωσιν συνήσειν τὰ γεγραμμένα ὥσπερ τότε τὴν φωνήν, παρατιθέᾱσιν αὐτοῖς   5 ἐπὶ τῶν βάθρων ἀναγιγνώσκειν ποιητῶν ἀγαθῶν ποιήματα καὶ ἐκμανθάνειν ἀναγκάζουσιν, ἐν οἷς πολλαὶ μὲν νουθετήσεις ἔνεισιν, πολλοὶ δὲ ἔπαινοι παλαιῶν ἀνδρῶν ἀγαθῶν, ἵνα ὁ παῖς μῑμῆται καὶ βούληται τοιοῦτος γενέσθαι.

[εὐκοσμίᾱς good behavior   κιθαρίσεως lyre-playing   τὰ γεγραμμένα things written, writing   παρατιθέᾱσιν they (i.e., the teachers) set X (acc., ποιήματα) in front of Y (dat., αὐτοῖς)   τῶν βάθρων the benches   ποιήματα poems   ἐκμανθάνειν to learn thoroughly   νουθετήσεις warnings, advice   μῑμῆται may imitate]

"οἵ τ' αὖ κιθαρισταὶ σωφροσύνης τε ἐπιμελοῦνται καὶ ὅπως μηδὲν 10
κακουργήσουσιν οἱ νέοι. πρὸς δὲ τούτοις, ἐπειδὰν κιθαρίζειν
μάθωσιν, ἄλλων αὖ ποιητῶν ἀγαθῶν ποιήματα διδάσκουσιν
μελοποιῶν, εἰς τὰ κιθαρίσματα ἐντείνοντες, καὶ τοὺς ῥυθμούς τε καὶ
τὰς ἁρμονίας ἀναγκάζουσιν οἰκειοῦσθαι ταῖς ψυχαῖς τῶν παίδων, ἵνα
ἡμερώτεροί τ' ὦσιν, καὶ εὐρυθμότεροι καὶ εὐαρμοστότεροι 15
γιγνόμενοι χρήσιμοι ὦσιν εἰς τὸ λέγειν τε καὶ πράττειν.

[κακουργήσουσιν (will) do wrong   μελοποιῶν of song writers (*the word here
stands in apposition to* ἄλλων . . . ποιητῶν ἀγαθῶν)   εἰς τὰ κιθαρίσματα
ἐντείνοντες (τείνω I stretch) setting them to the music of the lyre   οἰκειοῦσθαι to
be made familiar to (+ *dat.*)   ἡμερώτεροι gentler   εὐρυθμότεροι more
rhythmical, orderly, graceful   εὐαρμοστότεροι better joined, more harmonious
εἰς τὸ λέγειν τε καὶ πράττειν in/for both speech and action]

"ἔτι δὲ πρὸς τούτοις εἰς παιδοτρίβου πέμπουσιν, ἵνα τὰ σώματα
βελτίονα ἔχοντες ὑπηρετῶσι τῇ διανοίᾳ χρηστῇ οὔσῃ, καὶ μὴ
ἀναγκάζωνται ἀποδειλιᾶν διὰ τὴν πονηρίαν τῶν σωμάτων καὶ ἐν
πολέμοις καὶ ἐν ἄλλαις πράξεσιν." 20

[εἰς παιδοτρίβου to the trainer's   βελτίονα better   ὑπηρετῶσι they may
serve (+ *dat.*)   ἀποδειλιᾶν to play the coward]

—adapted from Plato, *Protagoras* 325d8–326c3

τοιαῦτα οὖν ἐπαιδεύετο ὁ Φίλιππος, καὶ ταύτῃ τῇ παιδεύσει
ἡδόμενος οὕτως ἀγαθὸς μαθητὴς ἐφαίνετο ὥστε ὁ διδάκαλος βιβλία
τινὰ αὐτῷ ἔδωκεν ἵνα αὐτὸς πρὸς ἑαυτὸν ἀναγιγνώσκῃ. τούτων δὲ
τῶν βιβλίων ἑνί τινι μάλιστα ἥσθη, τῇ τοῦ Ἡροδότου συγγραφῇ, ἐν ᾗ
ὁ Ἡρόδοτος τὰ Μηδικὰ ἐξηγεῖται· ὁ γὰρ Ἡρόδοτος οὐ μόνον τόν τε 25
πρὸς τοὺς Μήδους πόλεμον συγγράφει καὶ πάσας τὰς μάχας, ἀλλὰ
καὶ τὰς αἰτίας τοῦ πολέμου ἀποδείκνυσιν, δηλῶν τίνι τρόπῳ οἱ Μῆδοι
τὴν δύναμιν ηὔξησαν καὶ τίνα ἔθνη ἐφεξῆς ἐνίκησαν· ἐν οἷς πολλά τε
ἄλλα λέγεται καὶ ὁ περὶ Κροίσου λόγος· ὁ γὰρ Κροῖσος βασιλεὺς ἦν
τῶν Λυδῶν, ἀνὴρ ὀλβιώτατος γενόμενος καὶ δυνατώτατος, ὃς τοὺς 30
μὲν Ἕλληνας τοὺς ἐν Ἀσίᾳ κατεστρέψατο, αὐτὸς δὲ ὑπὸ τοῦ Κύρου,
βασιλέως ὄντος τῶν Μήδων, τέλος ἐνικήθη.

[συγγραφῇ history, book   τὰ Μηδικά Median affairs, i.e., the Persian Wars
συγγράφει writes about   ἀποδείκνυσιν reveals   ἔθνη nations, peoples
ἐφεξῆς in succession   κατεστρέψατο overthrew]

Principal Parts: Verbs in -(ί)σκω

ἀποθνῄ-σκω (θαν-/θνη-), ἀποθανοῦμαι, ἀπέθανον, τέθνηκα I die;
(*perfect*) I am dead

γιγνώ-σκω (γνω-/γνο-), γνώσομαι, ἔγνων (I learned, perceived), ἔγνωκα,
  ἔγνωσμαι, ἐγνώσθην I get to know, learn
εὑρ-ίσκω (εὑρ-/εὑρε-), εὑρήσω, ηὗρον or εὗρον, ηὕρηκα or εὕρηκα,
  ηὕρημαι or εὕρημαι, ηὑρέθην or εὑρέθην I find

Word Study

Give the Greek words from which the following English musical terms are derived:

1. music
2. harmony
3. rhythm
4. orchestra
5. chorus
6. symphony
7. melody
8. chord
9. diapason

Word Building

Many verbs are formed from the stems of nouns. They are called denominative verbs.

Note the following six different types of formation and give the meaning of each noun and verb:

1. ἡ τῑμή > τῑμάω
2. ὁ οἶκος > οἰκέω
3. ὁ δοῦλος > δουλόω
4. ὁ βασιλεύς > βασιλεύω
5. ἡ ἀνάγκη > ἀναγκάζω
6. ἡ ὀργή > ὀργίζομαι

Grammar

5. Comparison of Adjectives

Review Chapter 14, Grammar 1 and 2, and then study the following; remember that comparatives such as ἀμείνων can mean "rather good" in addition to the standard definition "better" and that superlatives such as ἄριστος can mean "very good" as well as "best."

Positive	Comparative	Superlative
ἀγαθός good	ἀμείνων better (stronger, braver, preferable, superior)	ἄριστος best
	βελτῑων better (more fitting, morally superior)	βέλτιστος best
	κρείττων better (stronger, more powerful)	κράτιστος best
κακός bad	κακῑων worse (morally inferior, more cowardly)	κάκιστος worst
	χείρων worse (inferior in strength, rank, or quality)	χείριστος worst
	ἥττων inferior, weaker, less	

Positive	Comparative	Superlative
καλός beautiful	καλλίων more beautiful	κάλλιστος most beautiful
αἰσχρός shameful	αἰσχίων more shameful	αἴσχιστος most shameful
ἐχθρός hostile	ἐχθίων more hostile	ἔχθιστος most hostile
ἡδύς sweet	ἡδίων sweeter	ἥδιστος sweetest
μέγας big	μείζων bigger	μέγιστος biggest
ὀλίγος small, (plural) few	ἐλάττων smaller, (plural) fewer	ὀλίγιστος smallest, least, (plural) fewest ἐλάχιστος smallest, least, (plural) fewest
πολύς much, (plural) many	πλείων or πλέων more	πλεῖστος most
ῥᾴδιος easy	ῥᾴων easier	ῥᾷστος easiest
ταχύς quick	θάττων quicker	τάχιστος quickest
φίλος dear	φιλαίτερος dearer	φίλτατος or φιλαίτατος dearest

Note that the comparatives have some alternative, contracted forms:

	Singular		Plural	
	M. & F.	N.	M. & F.	N.
Nom.	βελτίων	βέλτιον	βελτίονες (βελτίους)	βελτίονα (βελτίω)
Gen.	βελτίονος	βελτίονος	βελτιόνων	βελτιόνων
Dat.	βελτίονι	βελτίονι	βελτίοσι(ν)	βελτίοσι(ν)
Acc.	βελτίονα (βελτίω)	βέλτιον	βελτίονας (βελτίους)	βελτίονα (βελτίω)
Voc.	βέλτιον	βέλτιον	βελτίονες	βελτίονα

Exercise 24c

Read aloud and translate into English:

1. ἐπιμελοῦ, ὦ φίλε, ὅπως βέλτῑον κιθαριεῖς ἢ ὁ ἀδελφός.
2. οἱ χρηστοὶ οὐκ αἰεὶ ὀλβιώτεροι γίγνονται τῶν πονηρῶν (*the wicked*) οὐδὲ ῥᾷον ζῶσιν.
3. φοβοῦμαι μὴ αἱ τῶν πολεμίων νῆες θάττονες ὦσι τῶν ἡμετέρων.
4. ἐὰν τοῦτο ποιήσῃς, ἔχθιστός μοι γενήσῃ.
5. ὅστις ἂν τὰ τῶν ἀγαθῶν ποιητῶν ποιήματα ἀναγιγνώσκῃ, βελτίων γενήσεται.

*   *   *

Ο ΗΡΟΔΟΤΟΣ ΤΗΝ ΙΣΤΟΡΙΑΝ ΑΠΟΔΕΙΚΝΥΣΙΝ

Read the following passages (adapted from Herodotus' introduction to his history—1.1–6) and answer the comprehension questions:

Ἡροδότου Ἁλικαρνασσέος ἱστορίᾱς ἀπόδειξίς ἐστιν ἥδε, ὅπως μήτε τὰ γενόμενα ἐξ ἀνθρώπων τῷ χρόνῳ ἐξίτηλα γένηται, μήτε ἔργα μεγάλα τε καὶ θαυμαστά, τὰ μὲν ὑπὸ τῶν Ἑλλήνων, τὰ δὲ ὑπὸ τῶν βαρβάρων ἐργασθέντα, ἀκλεᾶ γένηται, τά τε ἄλλα καὶ δι' ἣν αἰτίᾱν ἐπολέμησαν ἀλλήλοις.

[**Ἁλικαρνασσέος** of Halicarnassus   **ἱστορίᾱς** of the inquiry   **ἀπόδειξις** display   **μήτε . . . μήτε** neither . . . nor   **ἐξίτηλα** faded   **θαυμαστά** wondrous   **ἀκλεᾶ** without fame   **δι' ἣν αἰτίᾱν** for what reason]

1. What four words in the sentence above would best serve as a title for Herodotus' book?
2. For what two purposes is Herodotus publishing the results of his investigations?
3. What are at least four of the subjects that Herodotus indicates that he will treat in his work?

Herodotus first gives a semi-mythical account of the origin of the feud between Europe (the Greeks) and Asia (the barbarians, including the Persians). Persian chroniclers, according to Herodotus, said that first some Phoenician traders carried off a Greek princess (Io) to Egypt; in retaliation the Greeks stole a Phoenician princess (Europa); then Greeks, led by Jason, carried off Medea from Colchis. Finally, the Trojan prince Paris stole Helen from Sparta and took her back to Troy; Agamemnon led the Greeks to Troy to recover her.

οὕτω μὲν οἱ Πέρσαι λέγουσι, καὶ διὰ τὴν Ἰλίου ἅλωσιν εὑρίσκουσι σφίσιν οὖσαν   5
τὴν ἀρχὴν τῆς ἔχθρᾱς τῆς ἐς τοὺς Ἕλληνας. ἐγὼ δὲ περὶ μὲν τούτων οὐκ ἔρχομαι ἐρέων ὅτι οὕτως ἢ ἄλλως πως ταῦτα ἐγένετο, ὃν δὲ οἶδα αὐτὸς ἄρξαντα ἀδίκων ἔργων ἐς τοὺς Ἕλληνας, περὶ τούτου ἐξηγησάμενος προβήσομαι ἐς τὸ πρόσω τοῦ λόγου.

[τὴν . . . ἅλωσιν the sack   Ἰλίου of Ilium, Troy   σφίσιν for themselves
τῆς ἔχθρᾱς of the hatred   ἐς (+ acc.) toward   ἔρχομαι ἐρέων I am going to say
ἄλλως πως in some other way   προβήσομαι I will go forward   πρόσω (+ gen.)
further into]

4. What do the Persians say was the origin of their hatred of the Greeks?
5. Does Herodotus commit himself as to the truth of the Persian account?
6. How will Herodotus begin his own account?

Κροῖσος ἦν Λῡδὸς μὲν γένος, παῖς δὲ Ἀλυάττεω, τύραννος δὲ ἐθνῶν τῶν ἐντὸς   10
Ἅλυος ποταμοῦ. οὗτος ὁ Κροῖσος πρῶτος ἐκείνων οὓς ἡμεῖς ἴσμεν τοὺς μὲν Ἑλλήνων
κατεστρέψατο, τοὺς δὲ φίλους ἐποιήσατο. κατεστρέψατο μὲν Ἴωνας τοὺς ἐν Ἀσίᾳ,
φίλους δὲ ἐποιήσατο Λακεδαιμονίους. πρὸ δὲ τῆς Κροίσου ἀρχῆς πάντες Ἕλληνες
ἦσαν ἐλεύθεροι.

[Λῡδός Lydian   γένος by race   Ἀλυάττεω of Alyattes   τύραννος ruler
ἐθνῶν of the peoples   Ἅλυος Halys   ἴσμεν we know   κατεστρέψατο
subdued   ἀρχῆς reign]

7. What four things do we learn about Croesus in the first sentence?
8. What was Croesus the first to do?
9. Whom did Croesus subdue and whom did he make his friends?
10. In what condition were the Greeks before the time of Croesus?

Exercise 24d

Translate into Greek (these sentences are based on Herodotus 1.27):

1. When his father died (*genitive absolute*), Croesus became king, who,
   waging war against (*use στρατεύομαι + ἐπί + acc. throughout this
   exercise*) the Greeks in Asia, subdued (them).
2. When all the Greeks in Asia had been defeated (*use genitive absolute
   with aorist passive participle*), he built (made for himself) very many
   ships and prepared to wage war against (ὡς + *future participle*) the
   islanders (ὁ νησιώτης, τοῦ νησιώτου).
3. But a Greek (man) arriving at Sardis and hearing what Croesus had
   in mind, said, "King, the islanders are gathering many cavalry
   (ἱππέᾱς), intending to wage war against (ὡς + *future participle or
   purpose clause*) you."
4. And Croesus, thinking that the Greek was speaking the truth, said, "I
   hope that the islanders will wage war against me; for they will
   certainly (σαφῶς) be defeated."
5. But the Greek answered, "Don't you think that the islanders hope that
   you will wage war against them (σφᾱς) by sea, believing that they
   will defeat you?"
6. Thus Croesus was persuaded not (μή) to wage war against the
   islanders but to make (them) friends.

25
Ο ΚΡΟΙΣΟΣ ΤΟΝ
ΣΟΛΩΝΑ ΞΕΝΙΖΕΙ (α)

ὁ Σόλων ἀφικόμενος ἐς τὰς Σάρδῑς ἵνα πάντα θεωροίη ἐξενίζετο ὑπὸ τοῦ Κροίσου.

Vocabulary

Verbs

ἀποδημέω I am abroad, go
  abroad

θάπτω, θάψω, ἔθαψα,
  τέθαμμαι, ἐτάφην I bury

καταστρέφω, καταστρέψω,
  κατέστρεψα, κατέστραμ-
  μαι, κατεστράφην I overturn; (*middle*) I subdue

κρῑνω, κρινῶ, ἔκρῑνα,
  κέκρικα, κέκριμαι, ἐκρίθην
  I judge

ξενίζω, ξενιῶ, ἐξένισα,
  ἐξενίσθην I entertain

περιάγω (*see* ἄγω *for principal
  parts*) I lead around

Nouns

ἡ βασιλείᾱ, τῆς βασιλείᾱς
  kingdom

τὰ βασίλεια, τῶν βασιλείων
  palace

ὁ θεράπων, τοῦ θεράποντος
  attendant, servant

ἡ θεωρίᾱ, τῆς θεωρίᾱς
  viewing, sight-seeing

ὁ θησαυρός, τοῦ θησαυροῦ
  treasure, treasury

ὁ ὅρκος, τοῦ ὅρκου oath

ἡ σοφίᾱ, τῆς σοφίᾱς wisdom

ἡ τελευτή, τῆς τελευτῆς end

Preposition

κατά (+ *acc.*) down, on,
  according to, at, through

Adverb

μετά afterward, later

Expressions

οἷός τ' εἰμί I am able

Proper Names

ὁ Ἀλυάττης, τοῦ Ἀλυάττεω
  Alyattes

αἱ Σάρδεις, τῶν Σάρδεων;
  (*Ionic*) αἱ Σάρδιες, τῶν
  Σαρδίων, τὰς Σάρδῑς
  Sardis

τελευτήσαντος δὲ Ἀλυάττεω, ἐδέξατο τὴν βασιλείᾱν Κροῖσος ὁ
Ἀλυάττεω, ἔτη γενόμενος πέντε καὶ τριάκοντα, ὃς δὴ τοῖς ἐν Ἀσίᾳ
Ἕλλησι ἐπιστρατεύων ἐν μέρει κατεστρέψατο. ὡς δὲ τοὺς ἐν Ἀσίᾳ
Ἕλληνας κατεστρέψατο, ἀφικνοῦνται ἐς τὰς Σάρδῑς ἄλλοι τε ἐκ τῆς
Ἑλλάδος σοφισταὶ καὶ δὴ καὶ ὁ Σόλων, ἀνὴρ Ἀθηναῖος, ὃς   5
Ἀθηναίοις νόμους ποιήσᾱς ἀπεδήμησεν ἔτη δέκα, λόγῳ μὲν θεωρίᾱς
ἕνεκα ἐκπλεύσᾱς, ἔργῳ δὲ ἵνα μή τινα τῶν νόμων ἀναγκασθῇ λῦσαι
ὧν ἔθετο. αὐτοὶ γὰρ οὐχ οἷοί τ’ ἦσαν τοῦτο ποιῆσαι Ἀθηναῖοι·
ὅρκοις γὰρ μεγάλοις κατείχοντο δέκα ἔτη χρήσεσθαι νόμοις οὓς ἂν
σφίσι Σόλων θῆται. ἀποδημήσᾱς οὖν ἐς Αἴγυπτον ἀφίκετο καὶ δὴ καὶ   10
ἐς Σάρδῑς παρὰ Κροῖσον. ἀφικόμενος δὲ ἐξενίζετο ἐν τοῖς βασιλείοις
ὑπὸ τοῦ Κροίσου. μετὰ δέ, ἡμέρᾳ τρίτῃ ἢ τετάρτῃ, κελεύσαντος
Κροίσου, τὸν Σόλωνα θεράποντες περιῆγον κατὰ τοὺς θησαυροὺς
καὶ ἐδείκνυσαν πάντα ὄντα μεγάλα καὶ ὄλβια.

[ἐν μέρει in turn   λῦσαι to repeal   ἔθετο (*from* τίθημι) he enacted
κατείχοντο they were constrained   σφίσι for themselves]

θεᾱσάμενον δὲ αὐτὸν τὰ πάντα καὶ σκεψάμενον ἤρετο ὁ Κροῖσος   15
τάδε· "ξένε Ἀθηναῖε, παρὰ ἡμᾶς περὶ σοῦ λόγος ἥκει πολὺς καὶ
σοφίᾱς ἕνεκα σῆς καὶ πλάνης, ὡς θεωρίᾱς ἕνεκα γῆν πολλὴν
ἐπελήλυθας. νῦν οὖν βούλομαι ἐρέσθαι σε τίς ἐστιν ὀλβιώτατος
πάντων ὧν εἶδες;" ὁ μὲν ἐλπίζων αὐτὸς εἶναι ὀλβιώτατος ταῦτα
ἠρώτᾱ, Σόλων δὲ οὐδὲν ὑποθωπεύσᾱς ἀλλὰ τῷ ἀληθεῖ χρησάμενος   20
λέγει· "ὦ βασιλεῦ, Τέλλος Ἀθηναῖος." θαυμάσᾱς δὲ Κροῖσος τὸ
λεχθέν, ἤρετο, "πῶς δὴ κρίνεις Τέλλον εἶναι ὀλβιώτατον;" ὁ δὲ εἶπε·
"Τέλλῳ καὶ παῖδες ἦσαν καλοί τε κἀγαθοὶ καὶ τοῖς παισὶ εἶδε τέκνα
ἐκγενόμενα καὶ πάντα παραμείναντα, καὶ τελευτὴ τοῦ βίου
λαμπροτάτη ἐγένετο· γενομένης γὰρ Ἀθηναίοις μάχης πρὸς γείτονας   25
ἐν Ἐλευσῖνι, βοηθήσᾱς καὶ τροπὴν ποιήσᾱς τῶν πολεμίων ἀπέθανε
κάλλιστα, καὶ αὐτὸν Ἀθηναῖοι δημοσίᾳ τε ἔθαψαν ὅπου ἔπεσε καὶ
ἐτίμησαν μεγάλως.

[πλάνης wandering   ἐπελήλυθας you have passed through   ὑποθωπεύσᾱς
flattering   τὸ λεχθέν what was said   κἀγαθοί = καὶ ἀγαθοί   ἐκγενόμενα
being born (having been born) from/to (+ *dat.*)   παραμείναντα surviving,
remaining alive   γείτονας neighbors   τροπήν rout   δημοσίᾳ publicly]

—adapted from Herodotus 1.26 and 29–30

Principal Parts: Three Deponent Verbs

δύνα-μαι, δυνήσομαι, δεδύνημαι, ἐδυνήθην I am able, can
ἐπίστα-μαι, ἐπιστήσομαι, ἠπιστήθην I understand, know
κεῖ-μαι, κείσομαι I lie, am laid

Word Study

Give the Greek words from which the following English terms used in the study of history are derived:

1. history
2. chronicle
3. chronology
4. genealogy
5. paleography
6. archaeology

Grammar

1. The Optative Mood Used to Express Wishes

The last mood of the Greek verb for you to learn is the *optative*, so called from its use in wishes and named from the Latin word for "to wish," *optāre*. Optative forms of Greek verbs may be immediately identified by the diphthongs οι, αι, or ει, e.g., λύοιμι, λύσαιμι, and λυθείην.

One use of the optative in main clauses is to express wishes for the future (the negative is μή), e.g.:

εὐτυχοῖτε, ὦ φίλοι.
May you be happy, friends. *I hope you may be happy*, friends.

μὴ εἰς κακὰ **πέσοιτε**, ὦ φίλοι.
May you not fall into trouble, friends. *I hope you don't.* . . .

Both the present optative (εὐτυχοῖτε) and the aorist optative (πέσοιτε) refer to the future; they differ in aspect, not time.

The word εἴθε or the words εἰ γάρ "if only," "oh, that" are often used to introduce wishes with the optative, e.g.:

εἴθε/εἰ γὰρ μὴ **ὀργίζοιτο** ἡμῖν ὁ δεσπότης.
If only the master *would* not *be angry* with us!

2. The Optative Mood in Subordinate Clauses

a. In some subordinate clauses, the optative may be used as an alternative to the subjunctive. This option is available only if the verb of the main clause is in the imperfect, aorist, or pluperfect tense. The subordinate clause is then said to be in *secondary* sequence. (If the main verb of the sentence is in the present, future, or perfect tense or in the present or aorist imperative, the subordinate clause is said to be in *primary* sequence.)

In the following examples of sentences with subordinate clauses in secondary sequence, the optional optative verb forms are given after the slash. Note that the translation into English is the same regardless of whether the optative or the subjunctive mood is used in Greek; the Greek authors seem to have used the subjunctive or optative indifferently in secondary sequence, with no difference in meaning.

εἰς τὸ ἄστυ ἐσπεύδομεν ἵνα τῶν ῥητόρων ἀκούωμεν/**ἀκούοιμεν**.
We hurried to the city *to hear* the politicians.

οἱ πολῖται ἐφοβοῦντο μὴ οἱ πολέμιοι εἰς τὴν γῆν εἰσβάλωσιν/
εἰσβάλοιεν.
The citizens were afraid the enemy *would invade* the land.

b. In secondary sequence, indefinite or general clauses regularly have their verbs in the optative without ἄν, e.g.:

οἱ Ἀθηναῖοι αὐτῷ φρουρίῳ ἐχρῶντο, ὁπότε πόλεμος **γένοιτο**.
The Athenians used it as a garrison, whenever war *occurred*.

οἱ Ἀθηναῖοι ἠναγκάζοντο χρῆσθαι νόμοις οὓς σφίσι Σόλων **θεῖτο**.
The Athenians were compelled to use whatever laws Solon *laid down* for them.

In indirect statement, however, or in implied indirect statement, ἄν + the subjunctive of the original words are often retained, e.g.:

ὅρκοις κατείχοντο χρήσεσθαι νόμοις οὓς ἂν σφίσι Σόλων **θῆται**.
They were constrained by oaths to use whatever laws Solon *laid down* for them.
(They swore: χρησόμεθα νόμοις οὓς ἂν ἡμῖν Σόλων **θῆται**.)

3. The Forms of the Optative

The optative, associated with secondary sequence, uses secondary endings in the present middle and passive and in the aorist middle.

Pres. Act.	*Pres. Mid. and Pass.*	*Aor. Act.*	*Aor. Mid.*	*Aor. Pass.*
λύ-οιμι	λῡ-οίμην	λύ-σαιμι	λῡ-σαίμην	λυ-θείην
λύ-οις	λύ-οιο	λύ-σαις (-σειας)	λύ-σαιο	λυ-θείης
λύ-οι	λύ-οιτο	λύ-σαι (-σειε)	λύ-σαιτο	λυ-θείη
λύ-οιμεν	λῡ-οίμεθα	λύ-σαιμεν	λῡ-σαίμεθα	λυ-θεῖμεν
λύ-οιτε	λύ-οισθε	λύ-σαιτε	λύ-σαισθε	λυ-θεῖτε
λύ-οιεν	λύ-οιντο	λύ-σαιεν (-σειαν)	λύ-σαιντο	λυ-θεῖεν
φιλοίην	φιλοίμην	φιλήσαιμι	φιλησαίμην	φιληθείην
φιλοίης	φιλοῖο	φιλήσαις (-σειας)	φιλήσαιο	φιληθείης
φιλοίη	φιλοῖτο	φιλήσαι (-σειε)	φιλήσαιτο	φιληθείη
φιλοῖμεν	φιλοίμεθα	φιλήσαιμεν	φιλησαίμεθα	φιληθεῖμεν
φιλοῖτε	φιλοῖσθε	φιλήσαιτε	φιλήσαισθε	φιληθεῖτε
φιλοῖεν	φιλοῖντο	φιλήσαιεν (-σειαν)	φιλήσαιντο	φιληθεῖεν

Pres. Act.	*Pres. Mid. and Pass.*	*Aor. Act.*	*Aor. Mid.*	*Aor. Pass.*
τῑμῴην τῑμῴης	τῑμῴμην τῑμῷο	τῑμήσαιμι τῑμήσαις (-σειας)	τῑμησαίμην τῑμήσαιο	τῑμηθείην τῑμηθείης
δηλοίην δηλοίης	δηλοίμην δηλοῖο	δηλώσαιμι δηλώσαις	δηλωσαίμην δηλώσαιο	δηλωθείην δηλωθείης
διδοίην διδοίης	διδοίμην διδοῖο	δοίην δοίης	δοίμην δοῖο	δοθείην δοθείης
τιθείην τιθείης	τιθείμην τιθεῖο	θείην θείης	θείμην θεῖο	τεθείην τεθείης
ἱσταίην ἱσταίης	ἱσταίμην ἱσταῖο	σταίην σταίης	στησαίμην στήσαιο	σταθείην σταθείης
ἱείην ἱείης	ἱείμην ἱεῖο	εἵην εἵης	εἵμην εἷο	

The optatives of εἰμί and εἶμι are as follows:

εἴην	ἴοιμι or ἰοίην
εἴης	ἴοις
εἴη	ἴοι
εἶμεν or εἴημεν	ἴοιμεν
εἶτε or εἴητε	ἴοιτε
εἶεν or εἴησαν	ἴοιεν

The future optative is formed from the future indicative stem, and its endings are the same as those for the present optative of λύω, e.g.:

λύσοιμι / λῡσοίμην	δηλώσοιμι / δηλωσοίμην	στήσοιμι / στησοίμην
φιλήσοιμι / φιλησοίμην	δώσοιμι / δωσοίμην	ἥσοιμι / ἡσοίμην
τῑμήσοιμι / τῑμησοίμην	θήσοιμι / θησοίμην	ἐσοίμην

There is no future optative of εἶμι. The use of the future optative is limited (see page 125).

Exercise 25a

Change the following indicative forms first to the subjunctive and then to the optative:

1. λύουσιν	6. νῑκῶμεν	11. ἐθέμην
2. λύεται	7. φιλεῖ	12. ἔλαβον
3. ἐλύσαμεν	8. ἔστη	13. ἐγένετο
4. ἐλύθη	9. ἐστί	14. ἐφιλήσαμεν
5. βούλομαι	10. τῑμᾷ	15. ἴᾱσιν

Exercise 25b

Read aloud and translate:

1. εἴθε ταχέως παραγένοιτο ἡ μήτηρ.
2. μηδέποτε αὖθις ἐς πόλεμον κατάσταιμεν.
3. εἰ γὰρ μὴ ἴδοιμι τοὺς κακοὺς εὖ πράσσοντας.
4. σώφρονες εἶτε, ὦ παῖδες, καὶ αἰεὶ τοὺς τεκόντας φιλοῖτε.
5. κακῶς ἀποθάνοιεν πάντες οἱ τοιαῦτα πράσσοντες.

Exercise 25c

Rewrite the following sentences, changing the main verbs to the designated past tenses and the subjunctives to optatives; then translate the new sentences:

1. οἱ νέοι παιδεύονται (*imperfect*) ἵνα ἀγαθοὶ γένωνται.
2. ὁ Σόλων ἀποδημεῖ (*aorist*) ἵνα μὴ ἀναγκασθῇ τοὺς νόμους λῦσαι.
3. ὁ πατὴρ τοῖς τέκνοις δίδωσιν (*imperfect*) ὅσ' ἂν βούλωνται ἔχειν.
4. οἱ ὁπλῖται φοβοῦνται (*imperfect*) μὴ οὐκ ἀμύνωσι τοὺς πολεμίους.
5. οἱ Ἀθηναῖοι μεγάλοις ὅρκοις κατέχονται (*imperfect*) νόμοις χρήσεσθαι οἷς ἂν θῆται ὁ Σόλων.
6. φοβούμενος τὸν κίνδῦνον, τοὺς φίλους καλῶ (*aorist*) ὅπως ὑμῖν βοηθῶσιν.

Exercise 25d

Translate into Greek:

1. The Greeks sent their children to school to learn writing.
2. The boy was afraid he would never return home.
3. Whenever winter came, the shepherds drove their flocks to the plain.
4. The slaves always did whatever (their) master commanded.

Bust of Herodotus

Herodotus

Herodotus was born at Halicarnassus, on the southern fringe of Ionia, some years before Xerxes' invasion of Greece. As a boy, he must have seen the queen of Halicarnassus, Artemisia, lead her fleet to join the invasion force. As a young man he joined the unsuccessful uprising against the tyrant Lygdamis, Artemisia's grandson, and after its failure went into exile in Samos. From there he embarked on his travels, which eventually took him around most of the known world. He visited Lydia, including Sardis, and Syria, from where he reached the Euphrates and sailed down the river to Babylon. From Babylon he went on to the Persian capital, Susa. In the North he sailed right around the Black Sea (Pontus Euxinus), stayed some time at Olbia at the mouth of the Dnieper (Borysthenes) and traveled up the river into the wild interior of Scythia. In the South, he visited Egypt twice, staying for several months, and sailed up the Nile as far as Elephantine. In the West he knew Sicily and south Italy. Whether he traveled as a merchant or, as Solon, simply for sightseeing (θεωρίας ἕνεκα), he continually amassed information, seeing and listening, gathering oral tradition, and studying records and monuments, all of which he was to use in his history.

During this period he settled in Athens for some time. He became a friend of the tragedian Sophocles, who wrote an ode to him when he left Athens to join the panhellenic colony of Thurii in south Italy (443 B.C.). Thurii became his home thereafter, though he continued to travel and returned to Athens to give recitations of his history in the 430's. He lived through the first years of the Peloponnesian War (he refers to events of 431–430 B.C.), and his history must have been published before 425 B.C., when Aristophanes parodies its introduction in the *Acharnians*.

He has rightly been called the "father of history." He had no predecessor except Hecataeus of Miletus (fl. 500 B.C.), who wrote a description of the earth in two books, one on Asia, the other on Europe. Herodotus knew this work and refers to it twice, when he disagrees with Hecataeus' statements. It is hard for us, with books and libraries at hand, to imagine the difficulties that confronted a man who set out to write a history of events that took place a generation or more earlier. The only written sources he could consult were local records, e.g., temple lists and oracles, and in some cases official documents, e.g., he must have had access to some Persian records, such as the Persian army list. Otherwise he had to rely entirely on what he saw on his travels and what he heard from the people he met. He was a man of infinite curiosity with an unflagging interest in the beliefs and customs of foreign peoples. Free from all racial prejudice, he listened to what strangers had to tell him with an open mind, and he could never resist passing on a good story. Not that he believed all that he was told. He had a healthy scepticism: "I am obliged to report what people say, but I feel no obligation to believe it always; this principle applies to my whole history" (7.152).

He was a deeply religious man, and his interpretation of history is theological. He believed firmly that the gods did intervene in human affairs and that no man could escape his fate. In particular, he believed that human pride (ὕβρις) resulted in divine vengeance (νέμεσις). This is clearly seen in the story of Croesus and on a larger scale in the whole treatment of the pride, defeat, and downfall of Xerxes. Dreams, signs, and oracles play an important part in his narrative. These are the means by which man might know his fate, which could not be changed but which might be postponed. Myth permeates his work. He moves in a world where mythical explanations of phenomena are commonplace; he is not a thoroughgoing sceptic, nor does he swallow the mythical tradition whole.

Before telling the story of Croesus, he goes back to give an account of the kings of Lydia, from whom Croesus was descended, and the whole section ends with the words Λῦδοὶ μὲν δὴ ὑπὸ Πέρσῃσι ἐδεδούλωντο "the Lydians had been enslaved by the Persians." One of the major themes of the history is freedom and slavery.

There follows a description of the rise of Persia, including the subjugation of the Greeks in Asia Minor and the defeat and capture of Babylon, ending with the death of Cyrus. Book 2 opens with the accession of Cyrus' son Cambyses, who invaded and conquered Egypt. The remainder of Book 2 is then taken up with a description and history of Egypt, the longest of Herodotus' digressions from his main theme. Book 3 starts with the conquest of Egypt and Cambyses' subsequent madness and death. After a digression on Polycrates of Samos, we have an account of the accession of Darius and the organization and resources of the Persian Empire. Book 4 is devoted to Darius' invasions of Scythia and Cyrene; Book 5, to the reduction of Thrace and the Ionian revolt. The Persian menace is seen to be looming larger and larger over Greece. Book 6 centers on Darius' expedition to punish the Athenians for helping the Ionians in their revolt, an expedition that culminates in the Marathon campaign. Book 7 opens with the accession of Xerxes and his decision to invade Greece. It ends with the Thermopylae campaign. Books 8 and 9 continue the story of the invasion and end with the battle of Mycale and the revolt of Ionia.

Within this broad framework, Herodotus continually makes digressions wherever a topic that interests him crops up. He is particularly fascinated by the strange customs and beliefs of the remoter peoples he met, but he also tells us a great deal about the earlier history of Greece, as occasion arises. The whole story moves in a leisurely and expansive way, not unlike Homer's *Iliad* in this respect, and like Homer he also continually uses speeches to heighten the drama of events and to illuminate the characters of the leading actors. Despite the poetic qualities of his work, he is usually found to be correct on matters of historical fact where we can check them from any other source.

Ο ΚΡΟΙΣΟΣ ΤΟΝ ΣΟΛΩΝΑ ΞΕΝΙΖΕΙ (β)

Vocabulary

Verbs
ἕλκω, (*imperfect*) **εἷλκον,**
  ἕλξω, εἵλκυσα, εἵλκυσμαι,
  εἱλκύσθην I drag
καταφρονέω (+ *gen*.) I despise
Nouns
ἡ εὐδαιμονίᾱ, τῆς
  εὐδαιμονίᾱς happiness,
  prosperity, good luck
ἡ εὐχή, τῆς εὐχῆς prayer

ὁ πλοῦτος, τοῦ πλούτου
  wealth
ἡ ῥώμη, τῆς ῥώμης strength
Adjectives
ἀμφότερος, -ᾱ, -ον both
ἱκανός, -ή, -όν sufficient,
  capable
Proper Name
οἱ Δελφοί, τῶν Δελφῶν
  Delphi

ὡς δὲ ταῦτα περὶ τοῦ Τέλλου ὁ Σόλων εἶπε, ὁ Κροῖσος ἤρετο τίνα δεύτερον μετ' ἐκεῖνον ὀλβιώτατον ἴδοι, νομίζων πάγχυ δευτερεῖα οἴσεσθαι. ὁ δέ, "Κλέοβίν τε καὶ Βίτωνα. τούτοις γὰρ οὖσι γένος Ἀργείοις πλοῦτός τε ἦν ἱκανὸς καὶ πρὸς τούτῳ ῥώμη σώματος τοιάδε· ἀεθλόφοροί τε ἀμφότεροι ἦσαν, καὶ δὴ καὶ λέγεται ὅδε ὁ λόγος· 5 οὔσης ἑορτῆς τῇ Ἥρᾳ τοῖς Ἀργείοις, ἔδει πάντως τὴν μητέρα αὐτῶν ζεύγει κομισθῆναι ἐς τὸ ἱερόν, οἱ δὲ βόες ἐκ τοῦ ἀγροῦ οὐ παρεγίγνοντο ἐν καιρῷ. οἱ δὲ νεᾱνίαι, ἵνα παραγένοιτο ἡ μήτηρ ἐν καιρῷ, αὐτοὶ εἷλκον τὴν ἅμαξαν, ἐπὶ δὲ τῆς ἁμάξης ἐφέρετο ἡ μήτηρ, σταδίους δὲ πέντε καὶ τεσσαράκοντα κομίσαντες ἀφίκοντο ἐς τὸ 10 ἱερόν.

[**πάγχυ** certainly   **δευτερεῖα** (*neut. pl.*) second prize   **οἴσεσθαι** (*future middle infinitive of* φέρω) he would carry (off)   **γένος** by race   **ἀεθλόφοροι** prize winners (in athletic contests)   **πάντως** absolutely   **ζεύγει** by means of a yoke of oxen **σταδίους . . . πέντε καὶ τεσσαράκοντα** = about five miles]

ταῦτα δὲ αὐτοῖς ποιήσᾱσι καὶ ὀφθεῖσι ὑπὸ τῶν παρόντων, τελευτὴ τοῦ βίου ἀρίστη ἐγένετο, ἔδειξέ τε ἐν τούτοις ὁ θεὸς ὅτι ἄμεινον εἴη ἀνθρώπῳ τεθνάναι μᾶλλον ἢ ζῆν. οἱ μὲν γὰρ Ἀργεῖοι περιστάντες ἐμακάριζον τῶν νεᾱνιῶν τὴν ῥώμην, αἱ δὲ Ἀργεῖαι τὴν μητέρα αὐτῶν 15 ἐμακάριζον, διότι τοιούτων τέκνων ἐκύρησεν. ἡ δὲ μήτηρ στᾶσα ἀντίον τοῦ ἀγάλματος τῆς θεοῦ ηὔχετο Κλεόβει τε καὶ Βίτωνι τοῖς ἑαυτῆς τέκνοις, οἳ αὐτὴν ἐτίμησαν μεγάλως, τὴν θεὸν δοῦναι ὅ τι

ἀνθρώπῳ τυχεῖν ἄριστον εἴη. μετὰ δὲ ταύτην τὴν εὐχήν, ὡς ἔθῡσάν
τε καὶ εὐώχθησαν, κατακοιμηθέντες ἐν αὐτῷ τῷ ἱερῷ οἱ νεᾱνίαι   20
οὐκέτι ἀνέστησαν ἀλλ' οὕτως ἐτελεύτησαν. Ἀργεῖοι δὲ αὐτῶν
εἰκόνας ποιησάμενοι ἀνέθεσαν ἐν Δελφοῖς, ὡς ἀνδρῶν ἀρίστων
γενομένων."

[τεθνάναι to be dead   περιστάντες standing around   ἐμακάριζον called
blessed, praised   ἐκύρησεν (+ *gen*.) obtained, had   ἀντίον τοῦ ἀγάλματος in
front of the statue   εὐώχθησαν (*from* εὐωχέω) had feasted   κατακοιμηθέντες
(*from* κατακοιμάω) having gone to sleep   εἰκόνας statues]

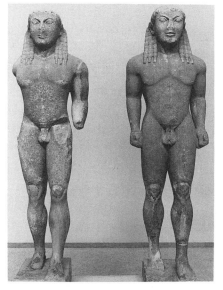

Κλέοβις καὶ Βίτων

Σόλων μὲν οὖν εὐδαιμονίᾱς δευτερεῖα ἔνειμε τούτοις, Κροῖσος δὲ
ὀργισθεὶς εἶπε· "ὦ ξέν' Ἀθηναῖε, τῆς δὲ ἡμετέρᾱς εὐδαιμονίᾱς οὕτω   25
καταφρονεῖς ὥστε οὐδὲ ἰδιωτῶν ἀνδρῶν ἀξίους ἡμᾶς ἐποίησας;"

[ἔνειμε (*aorist of* νέμω) gave   ἰδιωτῶν (*adjective here*) private]

—adapted from Herodotus 1.31–32

Principal Parts: Verbs that Augment to εἰ- *in the Imperfect*

ἐργάζομαι, (*imperfect*) εἰργαζόμην, ἐργάσομαι, εἰργασάμην,
    εἴργασμαι, εἰργάσθην I work, accomplish
ἕπομαι (σεπ-/σπ-), (*imperfect*) εἱπόμην, ἕψομαι, ἑσπόμην (+ *dat*.) I follow
ἔχω (ἐχ-/σχ-/σχε-), (*imperfect*) εἶχον, ἕξω *or* σχήσω, ἔσχον, ἔσχηκα,
    ἔσχημαι I have, hold; (*middle* + *gen*.) I hold onto

Word Building

Nouns formed from the stem of another noun or from an adjective are called denominative nouns.

Give the meanings of the nouns in the following sets:

1. Suffixes -της and -εύς (nominative) denote the person concerned or occupied with anything, e.g.:

    ὁ πολῑ́-της (ἡ πόλι-ς), ὁ ναύ-της (ἡ ναῦ-ς)
    ὁ ἱππ-εύς (ὁ ἵππ-ος), ὁ ἱερ-εύς (ἱερ-ός, -ά, -όν)

2. Abstract nouns denoting qualities are formed by adding suffixes to adjectives, e.g.,

-ίᾱ/-ια (nominative)	φίλος, -η, -ον	ἡ φιλίᾱ
	ἀληθής, -ές	ἡ ἀλήθε-ια
-σύνη (nominative)	δίκαι-ος, -ᾱ, -ον	ἡ δικαιο-σύνη
	σώφρων, σώφρον-ος	ἡ σωφρο(ν)-σύνη
-της (nominative)	ἴσος, -η, -ον	ἡ ἰσό-της, τῆς ἰσότητος
	νέος, -ᾱ, -ον	ἡ νεό-της, τῆς νεότητος

3. Patronymics, i.e., nouns meaning "son of . . . ," "descended from . . . ," are most commonly formed with the suffix -ίδης (nominative), e.g., ὁ Ἀλκμεων-ίδης.

4. Various suffixes are added to nouns to express smallness; the resulting words are called diminutives. The most common are:

-ιον (nominative)	τὸ παιδίον (ὁ παῖς, τοῦ παιδ-ός)
-ίδιον	τὸ οἰκ-ίδιον (ἡ οἰκί-α)
-ίσκος	ὁ παιδ-ίσκος (ὁ παῖς, τοῦ παιδ-ός)
	ὁ νεᾱν-ίσκος (ὁ νεᾱνί-ᾱς)

Diminutives can express affection, e.g., πατρίδιον (daddy dear), or contempt ἀνθρώπιον (wretched little man).

Grammar

4. The Optative Mood in Indirect Speech

In indirect statements and questions the optative may be used as an alternative to the indicative in *secondary sequence*; the tense of the optative is the same as that of the direct statement. Examine the following sentence from reading passage β (lines 1–2):

ὁ Κροῖσος ἤρετο **τίνα δεύτερον μετ' ἐκεῖνον ὀλβιώτατον ἴδοι**. . . .
Croesus asked *what (person) he had seen second most happy after that one (Tellus).* . . .

The direct question would have been τίνα δεύτερον μετ' ἐκεῖνον ὀλβιώτατον εἶδες; "Whom have you seen second most happy after that one?" In the indirect question the aorist tense of the verb is preserved.

The indicative mood could also have been preserved, changing only the person (εἶδες > εἶδε), but here the alternative of the optative was used instead.

Remember that it is only in secondary sequence that indicatives may be changed to optatives.

The only use of the future optative in Greek is as an alternative to the future indicative in indirect statements or indirect questions in secondary sequence.

Exercise 25e

Rewrite the following sentences, making the leading verb aorist and changing the verbs in indirect statements from indicative to optative. Then translate the new sentences:

1. ἡ γυνὴ ἡμᾶς ἐρωτᾷ εἰ τῷ παιδὶ αὐτῆς ἐν τῇ ὁδῷ ἐνετύχομεν.
2. ἀποκρῑνόμεθα ὅτι οὐδένα ἀνθρώπων εἴδομεν ἀλλ' εὐθὺς ἐπάνιμεν ὡς αὐτὸν ζητήσοντες.
3. τῷ παιδὶ ἐντυχόντες λέγομεν ὅτι ἡ μήτηρ αὐτὸν ζητεῖ.
4. ὁ ἄγγελος λέγει ὅτι τῶν πολεμίων ἀπελθόντων τοῖς αὐτουργοῖς ἔξεστιν οἴκαδε ἐπανιέναι.
5. ὁ Πρωταγόρᾱς λέγει ὅτι τοῦτο περὶ πλείστου ποιοῦνται οἱ πατέρες, ὅπως ἀγαθοὶ γενήσονται οἱ παῖδες.
6. ὁ Ἡρόδοτος ἐξηγεῖται ὅπως εἰς πόλεμον κατέστησαν οἵ τε βάρβαροι καὶ οἱ Ἕλληνες.
7. ὁ Σόλων ἐπίσταται ὅτι οἱ Ἀθηναῖοι οὐ λύσουσι τοὺς νόμους.
8. ὁ Κροῖσος τὸν Σόλωνα ἐρωτᾷ τίνα ὀλβιώτατον εἶδεν.
9. ὁ Σόλων λέγει ὅτι οἱ νεᾱνίαι, τὴν μητέρα εἰς τὸ ἱερὸν κομίσαντες, ἀπέθανον.
10. οὕτω δείκνῡσιν ὁ θεὸς ὅτι ἄμεινόν ἐστιν ἀνθρώπῳ τεθνάναι μᾶλλον ἢ ζῆν.

* * *

Ο ΣΟΛΩΝ ΤΟΝ ΚΡΟΙΣΟΝ ΟΡΓΙΖΕΙ

Read the following passages (adapted from Herodotus 1.32–33) and answer the comprehension questions:

Solon explains to Croesus why he does not count him happy:

ὁ δὲ Σόλων εἶπεν· "ὦ Κροῖσε, ἐρωτᾷς με περὶ ἀνθρωπίνων πρᾱγμάτων, ἐγὼ δὲ ἐπίσταμαι πᾶν τὸ θεῖον φθονερὸν ὂν καὶ ταραχῶδες. ἐν μὲν γὰρ τῷ μακρῷ χρόνῳ πολλὰ μέν ἐστιν ἰδεῖν ἃ μή τις ἐθέλει, πολλὰ δὲ καὶ παθεῖν. ἐς γὰρ ἑβδομήκοντα ἔτη ὅρον τῆς ζωῆς ἀνθρώπῳ τίθημι. ταῦτα δὲ ἔτη ἑβδομήκοντα ὄντα παρέχεται ἡμέρᾱς διᾱκοσίᾱς καὶ ἑξακισχῑλίᾱς καὶ δισμῡρίᾱς. ἡ δὲ ἑτέρᾱ αὐτῶν τῇ ἑτέρᾳ   5 οὐδὲν ὅμοιον προσάγει πρᾶγμα.

[ἀνθρωπίνων human	τὸ θεῖον divinity	φθονερόν jealous	ταραχῶδες
troublemaking	ὅρον boundary, limit	τῆς ζωῆς of the life	παρέχεται

offer   ἑξακισχιλίᾱς six thousand   δισμῡρίᾱς twenty thousand   ἡ . . . ἑτέρᾱ
. . . τῇ ἑτέρᾳ the one . . . to the other   προσάγει brings]

1. What two realms does Solon distinguish?
2. How does he characterize divinity?
3. What do men see and experience in the length of their lives?
4. At how many years does Solon set the limit of a man's life? At how many days?
5. What does each day bring?

    ἐμοὶ δὲ σὺ καὶ πλουτεῖν μέγα φαίνῃ καὶ βασιλεὺς εἶναι πολλῶν ἀνθρώπων·
ἐκεῖνο δὲ ὃ ἐρωτᾷς με οὔπω σε λέγω, πρὶν ἄν σε τελευτήσαντα καλῶς βίον μάθω.
οὐ γὰρ ὁ μέγα πλούσιος ὀλβιώτερός ἐστι τοῦ ἐφ' ἡμέρᾱν βίον ἔχοντος, εἰ μὴ αὐτῷ ἡ
τύχη παραμεῖναι, ὥστε εὖ τελευτῆσαι τὸν βίον. πολλοὶ γὰρ πλούσιοι ἀνθρώπων   10
ἄνολβοί εἰσι, πολλοὶ δὲ μέτριον ἔχοντες βίον εὐτυχεῖς. σκοπεῖν δὲ χρὴ παντὸς
χρήματος τὴν τελευτήν, πῶς ἀποβήσεται. πολλοῖς γὰρ δὴ ὑποδείξᾱς ὄλβον ὁ θεὸς
προρρίζους ἀνέτρεψεν."

[πλουτεῖν to be rich   οὔπω not yet   πρὶν ἄν . . . μάθω until I learn
πλούσιος rich   τοῦ ἐφ' ἡμέρᾱν βίον ἔχοντος (gen. of comparison) than the
one having livelihood for a day   εἰ μὴ . . . παραμεῖναι unless . . . should stay
with (+ dat.)   ἄνολβοι unhappy   μέτριον . . . βίον a moderate livelihood
εὐτυχεῖς lucky, happy   παντὸς χρήματος of every event   ἀποβήσεται it will
turn out   ὑποδείξᾱς having shown, having given a glimpse of   ὄλβον happiness
προρρίζους by the roots, root and branch   ἀνέτρεψεν overturns (the aorist is
gnomic here, stating an eternal truth, hence the present tense in the English translation)]

6. How does Croesus appear to Solon?
7. What does Solon need to know before he can answer Croesus' question with certainty?
8. What, according to Solon, does the rich man need in order to be called truly happy?
9. With what Greek words does Solon describe the men whom he contrasts with the πλούσιοι?
10. What Greek word does Solon use as the opposite of ἄνολβοι?
11. When assessing men's lives, what, according to Solon, must be examined in each case?
12. What two things does Solon say that god often does to men?

    ὁ Σόλων ταῦτα λέγων τῷ Κροίσῳ οὐκέτι ἐχαρίζετο, ἀλλὰ ὁ Κροῖσος ἀποπέμπει
αὐτόν, δόξᾱς αὐτὸν ἀμαθῆ εἶναι, ὃς τὰ παρόντα ἀγαθὰ μεθεὶς τὴν τελευτὴν   15
παντὸς χρήματος ὁρᾶν κελεύοι.

[ἐχαρίζετο found favor with (+ dat.)   δόξᾱς thinking   ἀμαθῆ stupid   μεθείς
(aorist participle of μεθίημι) letting go, ignoring]

13. What two things resulted from the "lecture" that Solon gave to Croesus?
14. What opinion of Solon did Croesus have?

15. What did Croesus think should be considered when judging a man's happiness?

Exercise 25f

Translate into Greek:

1. Croesus thought that he was the happiest of men, but Solon said that he had seen others happier.
2. Croesus asked Solon why he judged that the others were happier (*use infinitive*).
3. Solon answered that he called no one happy until he learned that he had ended his life well.
4. Croesus grew angry at Solon and sent him away, thinking that he was stupid.
5. After this Croesus, having suffered terrible things, learned that Solon was right.

26
Ο ΚΡΟΙΣΟΣ ΤΟΝ ΠΑΙΔΑ ΑΠΟΛΛΥΣΙΝ
(α)

ὁ Κροῖσος ἄγεται τῷ παιδὶ γυναῖκα· ἰδού, ὁ Ἄτυς τὴν νύμφην οἴκαδε φέρει ἐν ἁμάξῃ.

Vocabulary

Verbs

ἀπόλλῡμι, ἀπολῶ, ἀπώλεσα
I destroy, ruin, lose
ἀπολώλεκα I have ruined,
ἀπόλωλα I am ruined
ἀπόλλυμαι, ἀπολοῦμαι,
ἀπωλόμην I perish

δέομαι, δεήσομαι, ἐδεήθην
I ask for X (*acc.*) from Y (*gen.*);
I beg (+ *infinitive*); I want (+
gen.)

ἐφίσταμαι, ἐπέστην (+ *dat.*)
I stand near, appear to

καθαίρω, καθαρῶ, ἐκάθηρα,
κεκάθαρμαι, ἐκαθάρθην
I purify

ὀνομάζω, ὀνομάσω, ὠνόμασα,
ὠνόμακα, ὠνόμασμαι,
ὠνομάσθην I name, call

πυνθάνομαι, πεύσομαι,
ἐπυθόμην, πέπυσμαι
I inquire, learn by inquiry,
hear, find out about X (*acc.*)
from Y (*gen.*)

φαίνω, φανῶ, ἔφηνα I show

φονεύω, φονεύσω, ἐφόνευσα,
πεφόνευκα, πεφόνευμαι,
ἐφονεύθην I slay

Nouns

ἡ ἀλήθεια, τῆς ἀληθείᾱς
truth

ὁ γάμος, τοῦ γάμου marriage

τὸ δόρυ, τοῦ δόρατος spear

ἡ νέμεσις, τῆς νεμέσεως
retribution

τὸ οἰκίον, τοῦ οἰκίου house,
palace (*often in plural for a
single house or palace*)

ὁ ὄνειρος, τοῦ ὀνείρου dream

Adjectives

ἄκων, ἄκουσα, ἄκον
unwilling(ly),
involuntary(-ily)

ἕτερος, -ᾱ, -ον one or the other (of two)

ὁ μὲν ἕτερος . . . ὁ δὲ ἕτερος the one . . . the other

Prepositions

ἐπί (+ *gen.*) toward, in the direction of, on; (+ *dat.*) at,

upon, on, for (of price); (+ *acc.*) at, against, onto, to or for (of direction or purpose)

κατά (+ *acc.*) down, on, according to, at, through, with regard to

Adverb

ὁπόθεν from where

ὡς δὲ ἀπῆλθεν ὁ Σόλων, ἔλαβεν ἐκ τοῦ θεοῦ νέμεσις μεγάλη Κροῖσον, διότι ἐνόμισεν ἑαυτὸν εἶναι ἀνθρώπων ἁπάντων ὀλβιώτατον. καθεύδοντι γὰρ αὐτῷ ἐπέστη ὄνειρος, ὃς αὐτῷ τὴν ἀλήθειαν ἔφαινε τῶν μελλόντων γενέσθαι κακῶν κατὰ τὸν παῖδα. ἦσαν δὲ Κροίσῳ δύο παῖδες, ὧν ὁ μὲν ἕτερος κωφὸς ἦν, ὁ δὲ ἕτερος 5 τῶν ἡλίκων πολὺ πρῶτος· ὄνομα δὲ αὐτῷ ἦν Ἄτυς. τοῦτον οὖν τὸν Ἄτυν σημαίνει τῷ Κροίσῳ ὁ ὄνειρος ἀποθανεῖσθαι αἰχμῇ σιδηρέᾳ βληθέντα. ὁ δὲ ἐπεὶ ἐξηγέρθη, φοβούμενος τὸν ὄνειρον, ἄγεται μὲν τῷ παιδὶ γυναῖκα, ἐπὶ πόλεμον δὲ οὐκέτι ἐξέπεμψεν αὐτόν, ἀκόντια δὲ καὶ δόρατα καὶ πάντα οἷς χρῶνται ἐς πόλεμον ἄνθρωποι, ἐκ τῶν 10 ἀνδρεώνων ἐκκομίσας ἐς τοὺς θαλάμους συνένησε, μή τι τῷ παιδὶ ἐμπέσοι.

[κωφός dumb, mute   τῶν ἡλίκων those of the same age   αἰχμῇ σιδηρέᾳ an iron spear-point   ἀκόντια javelins   τῶν ἀνδρεώνων the men's chambers τοὺς θαλάμους the storerooms   συνένησε (*from* συννέω) he piled up]

ἔχοντος δὲ ἐν χερσὶ τοῦ παιδὸς τὸν γάμον, ἀφικνεῖται ἐς τὰς Σάρδῑς ἀνὴρ οὐ καθαρὸς ὢν τὰς χεῖρας. παρελθὼν δὲ οὗτος ἐς τὰ Κροίσου οἰκία καθαρσίου ἐδέετο ἐπικυρῆσαι· ὁ δὲ Κροῖσος αὐτὸν 15 ἐκάθηρεν. ἐπεὶ δὲ τὰ νομιζόμενα ἐποίησεν ὁ Κροῖσος, ἐπυνθάνετο ὁπόθεν τε ἥκοι καὶ τίς εἴη, λέγων τάδε· "ὦ ἄνθρωπε, τίς τ' ὢν καὶ πόθεν ἥκων ἐς τὰ ἐμὰ οἰκία παρεγένου;" ὁ δὲ ἀπεκρίνατο· "ὦ βασιλεῦ, Γορδίου μέν εἰμι παῖς, ὀνομάζομαι δὲ Ἄδρηστος, φονεύσᾱς δὲ τὸν ἐμαυτοῦ ἀδελφὸν ἄκων πάρειμι, ἐξεληλαμένος ὑπὸ τοῦ 20 πατρός." ὁ δὲ Κροῖσος ἀπεκρίνατο· "ἀνδρῶν τε φίλων ἔκγονος εἶ καὶ ἥκεις ἐς φίλους, ὅπου ἀμηχανήσεις οὐδενὸς μένων ἐν τοῖς ἡμετέροις οἰκίοις. συμφορὰν δὲ ταύτην παραινῶ σοι ὡς κουφότατα φέρειν."

[καθαρσίου purification   ἐδέετο = ἐδεῖτο, *from* δέομαι   ἐπικυρῆσαι (+ *gen.*) to obtain   τὰ νομιζόμενα the customary rituals   ἐξεληλαμένος (*perfect passive participle of* ἐξελαύνω) having been driven out   ἔκγονος offspring   ἀμηχανήσεις (+ *gen.*) you will lack   ὡς κουφότατα as lightly as possible]

—adapted from Herodotus 1.34–35

Principal Parts: Verbs with Present Reduplication

γί-γνομαι (γεν-/γενε-/γον-/γν-), γενήσομαι, ἐγενόμην, γέγονα,
    γεγένημαι I become, happen
γι-γνώ-σκω (γνω-/γνο-), γνώσομαι, ἔγνων (I learned, perceived), ἔγνωκα,
    ἔγνωσμαι, ἐγνώσθην I get to know, learn
δι-δά-σκω (διδαχ-), διδάξω, ἐδίδαξα, δεδίδαχα, δεδίδαγμαι,
    ἐδιδάχθην I teach
πί-πτω (πετ-/πτω-/πτ-), πεσοῦμαι, ἔπεσον, πέπτωκα I fall

Word Study

Give the Greek words from which the following English literary terms are derived:

1. epic
2. lyric
3. drama
4. tragedy
5. comedy
6. biography

What genre of modern literature is missing from this list?

Grammar

1. Correlatives

The following table lists interrogative, indefinite, demonstrative, and relative forms, most of which you have met in the readings, vocabulary lists, and discussions of grammar:

Interrogative	Indefinite	Demonstrative	Relative
Personal			
τίς; who?	τις anyone, any, some	οὗτος, ὅδε this	ὅς, ὅσπερ who ὅστις anyone who; (pl.) all who
Explanatory			
πῶς; how?	πως somehow	οὕτω(ς), ὧδε, ὥς thus	ὡς, ὥσπερ, ὅπως as, just as, how
Locational			
ποῦ; where?	που somewhere	ἐνθάδε, ἐνταῦθα here ἐκεῖ there	οὗ, οὗπερ, ὅπου where
ποῖ; to what place?	ποι to some place where to?	δεῦρο to here ἐκεῖσε to there	οἷ, ὅποι to what place, where
πόθεν; from where?	ποθέν from some place	ἐντεῦθεν from this place ἐκεῖθεν from that place	ὅθεν, ὁπόθεν from where

Interrogative	Indefinite	Demonstrative	Relative
Temporal			
πότε; when?	ποτέ at some time, once, ever	τότε then	ὅτε, ὁπότε when
Qualitative			
ποῖος; of what kind?	ποιός of some kind	τοιοῦτος, τοιόσδε such, of this kind	οἷος, ὁποῖος (such) as
Quantitative			
πόσος; how much? (pl.) how many?	ποσός of some size	τοσοῦτος, τοσόσδε so great; (pl.) so many	ὅσος, ὁπόσος as great as, as much as; (pl.) as many as
Alternative			
πότερος; which (of two)?		ἕτερος one or the other (of two)	ὁπότερος which of two

The words ὅστις, ὅπως, ὅπου, and so forth, are often used to introduce indirect questions instead of the ordinary form of the interrogative, e.g.:

εἰπέ μοι **ποῦ/ὅπου** ἐστὶν ὁ πατήρ.
Tell me *where* father is.

Exercise 26a

Read aloud and translate:

1. "πῶς τοῦτο ἐποίησας;" "τοῦτο ὧδε ἐποίησα, ὥσπερ παρήνεσεν ὁ πατήρ."
2. "πόθεν ἥκεις;" "οὐκ οἶδα ὁπόθεν· τῆς γὰρ ὁδοῦ ἥμαρτον."
3. "ποῦ οἰκεῖ ὁ γέρων;" "ἐκεῖ οἰκεῖ ὁ γέρων ἐγγὺς τοῦ ποταμοῦ, ὅπου εἶδον αὐτὸν νεωστί (recently)."
4. "ἐν ποίᾳ νηὶ δεῦρο ἔπλευσας;" "ἐν τοιαύτῃ νηὶ ἔπλευσα οἵα σῖτον ἀπὸ τῆς Αἰγύπτου φέρει."
5. τοσοῦτον χρόνον ἐν τῇ ἀγορᾷ ἐμένομεν ὅσον ἐκέλευσας.
6. ἡ παρθένος τὸν πατέρα ἤρετο ποῖ ἔρχεται· ὁ δὲ οὐκ ἤθελεν ἀποκρίνεσθαι.
7. πότε οἴκαδε ἐπάνεισιν ἡ μήτηρ; ἡ μήτηρ οἴκαδε ἐπάνεισιν ὅταν τὸν πατέρα εὕρῃ.
8. πόσας ναῦς ἔχουσιν οἱ πολέμιοι; οὐκ οἶδα ἔγωγε ὁπόσας ναῦς ἔχουσιν.
9. ὁ ὁπλίτης τῇ μὲν ἑτέρᾳ χερὶ δόρυ ἔφερε, τῇ δὲ ἑτέρᾳ ξίφος (sword).
10. ὁ στρατηγὸς δύο ἀγγέλους ἔπεμψεν, οἱ δὲ οὐ λέγουσι τὰ αὐτά· ποτέρῳ πιστεύωμεν;

Shame and Guilt

When Solon explained to Croesus why he would not call him the happiest man he had seen, he said: "ἐπίσταμαι πᾶν τὸ θεῖον φθονερὸν ὂν καὶ ταραχῶδες. When Solon had left Sardis, ἔλαβεν ἐκ τοῦ θεοῦ νέμεσις μεγάλη Κροῖσον. Shortly after Solon's departure, Adrastus arrived οὐ καθαρὸς ὢν τὰς χεῖρας and καθαρσίου ἐδέετο ἐπικυρῆσαι. The concepts in these passages from Herodotus are quite alien to our modes of thought but are central to the Greek view of man's relation to the gods and his place in the universe.

In the *Iliad*, there is a division between morality (man's relations with his fellow men) and religion (man's relations with the gods). The gods are not usually interested in how men behave toward each other but are very interested in how men behave toward themselves, the gods. They demand from men a proper τῑμή, just as a king demands honor from his nobles. The gods must receive prayer and sacrifice from mortals, accompanied by the appropriate rituals. Provided you fulfill these obligations, you may expect the gods to be well disposed toward you, although, of course, you cannot constrain them by any amount of prayer and sacrifice. The gods are often arbitrary in their behavior, and they, like men, are bound by the dictates of fate (μοῖρα), which even they cannot change. Nevertheless, in the *Iliad* men, though recognizing the power of the gods, do not generally go in fear of them, and religion shows little of the darker side that is prominent in Herodotus and the poets of his time.

Homeric heroes in their relations with their fellow men are motivated not by religious considerations but by what their peers think of them. The mainspring of their action is honor, which is literally dearer than life. Conversely, they avoid certain actions through fear of what others may say or think of them. They are restrained by αἰδώς (sense of shame, self-respect). So the whole plot of the *Iliad* turns on Achilles' refusal to fight when Agamemnon has insulted his honor. Life was a competition in which honor was the prize. Achilles' father told him: αἰὲν ἀριστεύειν καὶ ὑπείροχον ἔμμεναι ἄλλων "always to be the best and to excel over others" (*Iliad* 11.784).

The honor ethic (a shame culture, as the anthropologists call it) persisted throughout Greek history, but in the time of Herodotus there was alongside it a very different ethic, which was based on a different view of the gods and the whole human predicament. According to this view, to court the preeminence that Achilles' father recommended to his son was positively dangerous and wrong. In Herodotus and the poets of his time, Zeus is the agent of justice (δίκη). Man is helpless before the power of the gods and the dictates of μοῖρα (one's allotted portion, fate), and all who offend must suffer. The surest way of offending the gods and bringing down νέμεσις (divine retribution) on yourself is to become too prosperous or too great. Such excess leads to pride (ὕβρις), a condition in which you may think yourself more than mortal and so incur the jealousy (φθόνος) of the gods: φιλέει γὰρ ὁ θεὸς τὰ ὑπερέχοντα πάντα κολούειν "for God is accustomed to cut down everything that excels (overtops others)" (Herodotus 7.10).

What of those who have not offended but still suffer? One answer was inherited or corporate guilt. If a righteous man suffers, he must be paying for the offense of one of his kin (so the family curse is a prominent theme in Greek tragedy, e.g., Aeschylus' *Oresteia* or Sophocles' *Antigone*). Such corporate guilt can infect not just one family but whole societies: "Often a whole city reaps the reward of an evil man who sins and plots wicked deeds" (Hesiod, *Works and Days* 240–241). So man is helpless (ἀμήχανος) in a frightening and unpredictable world, governed by gods who are jealous and troublemaking.

What could man do to avoid disaster (συμφορά)? The only way was to refrain from offending the gods and if offense occurred, to seek purification, a cleansing of guilt. Purification (κάθαρσις) was a ritual washing away of pollution, as Christian baptism is a symbolic washing away of sin, and was regularly performed on all occasions that brought man into contact with the gods, e.g., before sacrifice or feasting (which was a meal shared with the gods). Rituals, of which we know little, were prescribed for various occasions, e.g., after childbirth.

The greatest pollution (μίασμα) was blood-guilt. Adrastus arrived at Croesus' court οὐ καθαρὸς ὢν τὰς χεῖρας. He had involuntarily killed his own brother. Whether the act was voluntary or involuntary was beside the point as far as his family was concerned. He had to go into exile, since otherwise he would have infected the whole family with his μίασμα. He comes to Croesus as a suppliant (ἱκέτης), and Croesus, a god-fearing man, is bound to accept him. Such were the rules of supplication, which had its own ritual. Suppliants were under the protection of Zeus. Croesus, although he does not know Adrastus, at once understands the situation and purifies him, using the customary rites. We do not know precisely what these rites were, but they involved the sacrifice of a suckling pig, in the blood of which the guilty man was cleansed. Pollution could infect a whole people. In the opening scene of Sophocles' *Oedipus the King*, the whole land of Thebes is devastated by plague. Oedipus sends Creon to Delphi to ask Apollo what he should do. Apollo's answer is that they must drive out the pollution of the land (μίασμα χώρας); "By what sort of purification (ποίῳ καθάρμῳ)?" asks Oedipus. The answer is "By driving out (the guilty man), or by exacting blood for blood."

The society that accepted such ideas must have been suffering from a deep sense of guilt, all the more terrifying because one could not always know the cause of one's pollution nor, in the last resort, was there any way of escaping it. When Croesus had been saved by Apollo, he sent messengers to Delphi to ask why Apollo had deceived him. The answer came back: "It is impossible even for a god to escape his destined lot. Croesus has paid for the sin of his ancestor five generations back, who murdered his master and took the honor (i.e., the throne) which was not rightly his" (Herodotus 1.91). Zeus might be just, but it was a harsh justice.

Ο ΚΡΟΙΣΟΣ ΤΟΝ ΠΑΙΔΑ ΑΠΟΛΛΥΣΙΝ (β)

Vocabulary

Verbs

ἀποφαίνω (*see* φαίνω *for principal parts*) I show, reveal, prove

μεθίημι (*see* ἵημι *for principal parts*) I let go

μέλει, μελήσει, ἐμέλησε, μεμέληκε (+ *dat.*) it is a care to, X cares for

μεταπέμπομαι, (*see* πέμπω *for principal parts*) I send for

χαρίζομαι, χαριοῦμαι, ἐχαρισάμην, κεχάρισμαι (+ *dat.*) I show favor to, oblige

Nouns

ἡ ἄγρᾱ, τῆς ἄγρᾱς hunt, hunting

ἡ ἀθῡμίᾱ, τῆς ἀθῡμίᾱς lack of spirit, despair

ἡ δειλίᾱ, τῆς δειλίᾱς cowardice

τὸ θηρίον, τοῦ θηρίου wild beast

ὁ κύκλος, τοῦ κύκλου circle

ἡ φήμη, τῆς φήμης saying, report, voice, message

ὁ φόνος, τοῦ φόνου murder

ὁ φύλαξ, τοῦ φύλακος guard

Preposition

πρός (+ *gen.*) from, at the hand of; (+ *dat.*) at, near, by, in addition to; (+ *acc.*) to, toward, against, upon

Conjunction

ἐπεί when, since

Proper Names

οἱ Μῡσοί, τῶν Μῡσῶν Mysians

ὁ Ὄλυμπος, τοῦ Ὀλύμπου Mount Olympus

ὁ μὲν οὖν Ἄδρηστος δίαιταν εἶχε ἐν Κροίσου, ἐν δὲ τῷ αὐτῷ χρόνῳ ἐν τῷ Ὀλύμπῳ τῷ ὄρει ὗς μέγας γίγνεται· ὁρμώμενος δὲ οὗτος ἐκ τοῦ ὄρους τούτου τὰ τῶν Μῡσῶν ἔργα διέφθειρε, πολλάκις δὲ οἱ Μῡσοὶ ἐπ' αὐτὸν ἐξελθόντες ἐποίουν μὲν κακὸν οὐδέν, ἔπασχον δὲ κακὰ πρὸς αὐτοῦ. τέλος δὲ ἀφικόμενοι παρὰ τὸν Κροῖσον τῶν Μῡσῶν ἄγγελοι ἔλεγον τάδε· "ὦ βασιλεῦ, ὗς μέγιστος ἀνεφάνη ἡμῖν ἐν τῇ χώρᾳ, ὃς τὰ ἔργα διαφθείρει. τοῦτον προθῡμούμενοι ἑλεῖν οὐ δυνάμεθα. νῦν οὖν δεόμεθά σου τὸν παῖδα καὶ λογάδας νεᾱνίᾱς καὶ κύνας πέμψαι ἡμῖν, ἵνα αὐτὸν ἐξέλωμεν ἐκ τῆς χώρας." 5

[**δίαιταν εἶχε** he had a dwelling, he lived   **ἐν Κροίσου** in Croesus' (palace)   **ὗς** a wild boar   **ἀνεφάνη** (*from* ἀναφαίνω) appeared   **προθῡμούμενοι** being very eager   **λογάδας** picked, selected]

Κροῖσος δὲ μεμνημένος τοῦ ὀνείρου τὰ ἔπη ἔλεγε τάδε· "τὸν παῖδα   10
οὐκ ἐθέλω πέμψαι· νεόγαμος γάρ ἐστι καὶ ταῦτα αὐτῷ νῦν μέλει.
Λῡδῶν μέντοι λογάδας καὶ κύνας πέμψω καὶ κελεύσω τοὺς ἰόντας
ἐξελεῖν τὸ θηρίον ἐκ τῆς χώρᾱς."

[μεμνημένος remembering   τὰ ἔπη the words   νεόγαμος newly married]

οἱ Μῡσοὶ ἐπὶ τὸν ὗν ἐξελθόντες ἐποίουν μὲν κακὸν οὐδέν, ἔπασχον δὲ κακὰ πρὸς αὐτοῦ.

ὁ δὲ παῖς ἀκούσᾱς ἃ εἶπεν Κροῖσος τοῖς Μῡσοῖς, πρὸς αὐτὸν
προσῆλθε καί, "ὦ πάτερ," φησίν, "διὰ τί οὐκ ἐθέλεις με πέμψαι ἐς τὴν   15
ἄγρᾱν; ἆρα δειλίᾱν τινὰ ἔν μοι εἶδες ἢ ἀθῡμίᾱν;" ὁ δὲ Κροῖσος
ἀποκρίνεται τοῖσδε· "ὦ παῖ, οὔτε δειλίᾱν οὔτε ἄλλο οὐδὲν ἄχαρι ἰδὼν
ποιῶ ταῦτα, ἀλλά μοι ὄψις ὀνείρου ἐν τῷ ὕπνῳ ἐπιστᾶσα ἔφη σε
ὀλιγοχρόνιον ἔσεσθαι· ὑπὸ γὰρ αἰχμῆς σιδηρέᾱς ἀπολεῖσθαι."
ἀποκρίνεται δὲ ὁ νεᾱνίᾱς τοῖσδε· "συγγνώμη μέν ἐστί σοι, ὦ πάτερ,   20
ἰδόντι ὄψιν τοιαύτην περὶ ἐμὲ φυλακὴν ἔχειν. λέγεις δὲ ὅτι ὁ ὄνειρος
ἔφη ὑπὸ αἰχμῆς σιδηρέᾱς ἐμὲ τελευτήσειν· ὑὸς δὲ ποῖαι μέν εἰσι χεῖρες,
ποῖᾱ δὲ αἰχμὴ σιδηρέᾱ; ἐπεὶ οὖν οὐ πρὸς ἄνδρας ἡμῖν γίγνεται ἡ
μάχη, μέθες με." ἀμείβεται Κροῖσος, "ὦ παῖ, νῑκᾷς με γνώμην
ἀποφαίνων περὶ τοῦ ὀνείρου. μεταγιγνώσκω οὖν καὶ μεθῑημί σε ἰέναι   25
ἐπὶ τὴν ἄγρᾱν."

[ἄχαρι unpleasant, objectionable   ὄψις sight, vision, apparition   ὀλιγοχρόνιον
short-lived   αἰχμῆς σιδηρέᾱς an iron spear-point   συγγνώμη . . . ἐστί σοι you
have an excuse, you may be pardoned   ὑός (gen. of ὗς) of a wild boar   ἀμείβεται
answers   μεταγιγνώσκω I change my mind]

εἰπὼν δὲ ταῦτα ὁ Κροῖσος τὸν Ἄδρηστον μεταπέμπεται καὶ αὐτῷ
λέγει τάδε· ""Ἄδρηστε, ἐγώ σε ἐκάθηρα καὶ ἐν τοῖς οἰκίοις ἐδεξάμην·
νῦν οὖν φύλακα τοῦ παιδὸς ἐμοῦ σε χρῄζω γενέσθαι ἐς ἄγρᾱν
ὁρμωμένου." ὁ δὲ Ἄδρηστος ἀπεκρίνατο· "ἐπεὶ σὺ σπεύδεις καὶ δεῖ   30
μέ σοι χαρίζεσθαι, ἕτοιμός εἰμι ποιεῖν ταῦτα, τόν τε παῖδα σὸν ὃν
κελεύεις φυλάσσειν ἀσφαλῆ τοῦ φυλάσσοντος ἕνεκα προσδόκᾱ σοι
νοστήσειν."

[χρῄζω I want, need   σπεύδεις you are (so) earnest   τοῦ φυλάσσοντος ἕνεκα
as far as his guardian is concerned   προσδόκᾱ (imperative of προσδοκάω) expect]

ἦσαν μετὰ ταῦτα ἐξηρτῦμένοι λογάσι τε νεανίαις καὶ κυσίν.
ἀφικόμενοι δὲ ἐς τὸν Ὄλυμπον τὸ ὄρος ἐζήτουν τὸ θηρίον, εὑρόντες   35
δὲ καὶ περιστάντες αὐτὸ κύκλῳ ἐσηκόντιζον. ἐνταῦθα δὴ ὁ ξένος, ὁ
καθαρθεὶς τὸν φόνον, ἀκοντίζων τὸν ὗν, τοῦ μὲν ἁμαρτάνει,
τυγχάνει δὲ τοῦ Κροίσου παιδός. ὁ μὲν οὖν βληθεὶς τῇ αἰχμῇ
ἐξέπλησε τοῦ ὀνείρου τὴν φήμην, ἔτρεχε δέ τις ὡς ἀγγελῶν τῷ Κροίσῳ
τὸ γενόμενον. ἀφικόμενος δὲ ἐς τὰς Σάρδῑς τήν τε μάχην καὶ τὸν τοῦ   40
παιδὸς μόρον εἶπεν αὐτῷ.

[ἐξηρτῡμένοι (*from* ἐξαρτῦω) equipped   ἐσηκόντιζον they threw their javelins
at (it)   ἀκοντίζων throwing (aiming) his javelin at   ἐξέπλησε (*from* ἐκπίμπλημι)
fulfilled   τὸν . . . μόρον the fate, death]

—adapted from Herodotus 1.36–43

Principal Parts: Verbs with Three Grades of Stem Vowel

γί-γνομαι (γεν-/γενε-/γον-/γν-), γενήσομαι, ἐγενόμην, γέγονα,
    γεγένημαι I become, happen
λείπω (λειπ-/λοιπ-/λιπ-), λείψω, ἔλιπον, λέλοιπα, λέλειμμαι (I am left
    behind, am inferior), ἐλείφθην I leave
πάσχω (πενθ-/πονθ-/παθ-), πείσομαι, ἔπαθον, πέπονθα I suffer, experience

Word Building

*Adjectives are formed by adding suffixes to verb or noun stems. Study the ways
in which the following are formed and give their meanings:*

1. λείπ-ω	λοιπ-ός, -ή, -όν	9. ὁ λίθ-ος	λίθ-ινος, -η, -ον
2. ἥδ-ομαι	ἡδ-ύς, -εῖα, -ύ	10. ἡ μάχ-η	μάχ-ιμος, -η, -ον
3. ψεύδ-ομαι	ψευδ-ής, -ές	11. χρά-ομαι	χρή-σιμος, -η, -ον
4. ὁ πόλεμ-ος	πολέμ-ιος, -ᾱ, -ον	12. λάμπ-ω	λαμπ-ρός, -ά, -όν
5. ἡ δίκ-η	δίκα-ιος, -ᾱ, -ον	13. φοβέ-ομαι	φοβε-ρός, -ά, -όν
6. οἰκέ-ω	οἰκε-ῖος, -ᾱ, -ον	14. ποιέ-ω	ποιη-τός, -ή, -όν
7. ὁ πόλεμ-ος	πολεμ-ικός, -ή, -όν	15. γράφ-ω	γραπ-τός, -ή, -όν
8. πράττω (πρᾱγ-)	πρᾱκ-τικός, -ή, -όν	16. χρά-ομαι	χρη-στός, -ή, -όν

Grammar

2. Some Uses of the Genitive Case

The uses of the genitive, dative, and accusative cases are
summarized in this and the following sections; you have already met
most of them in your reading.

a. The genitive is frequently used to show possession, e.g., ὁ τοῦ παιδὸς
κύων "the *boy's* dog," "the dog *of the boy*." Note that the word in the
genitive case is here in the attributive position between the article and
the noun. It may also be placed after the repeated article, e.g., ὁ κύων ὁ
τοῦ παιδός.

b. The genitive may be used with adjectives, such as αἴτιος and ἄξιος, e.g.:

> δεῖ γάρ σε ἄξιον γίγνεσθαι **τῶν πατέρων.**
> You must become worthy *of your ancestors (fathers).*

c. The genitive of the whole or partitive genitive expresses the whole of which something is a part, e.g., πολλοὶ **τῶν πολῑτῶν** "many *of the citizens.*" Note that this genitive often comes first in its phrase, e.g.:

> **τῶν πολῑτῶν** οἱ μὲν ἔμενον, οἱ δὲ ἀπῆλθον.
> Some *of the citizens* stayed, others went away.

d. The genitive may express time within which, e.g.:

> ὁ δοῦλος ἐξῆλθεν **νυκτός.**
> The slave went out *in the night.*

> **τριῶν ἡμερῶν** οἴκαδε ἐπάνιμεν.
> We will return home *within three days.*

e. After a comparative adjective or adverb the second of the two things compared may be in the genitive, e.g.:

> οἱ ἀθάνατοι οὐδὲν ἄμεινον ἔπρᾱττον **τῶν ἄλλων.**
> The Immortals fared no better *than the others.*

f. The genitive may express separation, e.g.:

> τὸ ἄστυ πολὺ ἀπέχει **τῆς θαλάττης.**
> The city is far *from the sea.*

> οἱ δοῦλοι ἐπαύσαντο **ἔργου.**
> The slaves stopped *working.*

> δύο παῖδες **Κροίσου** ἐγένοντο.
> Two sons were born *from Croesus* (we say *to Croesus*).

g. The genitive is used after verbs that mean *to hold onto* (ἔχομαι, λαμβάνομαι), *to rule* (ἄρχω, κρατέω, βασιλεύω), *to hit* (τυγχάνω), *to miss* (ἁμαρτάνω), *to perceive* (ἀκούω, αἰσθάνομαι), and *to share in* (μετέχω). See list in Reference Grammar, paragraph 30. Verbs of perceiving take the genitive of the person but the accusative of the thing perceived, e.g., **σοῦ** ἀκούω "I hear *you,*" but **ταῦτα** ἀκούω "I hear *these things.*"

3. Some Uses of the Dative Case

The dative has a wide range of uses, the meanings of which may be summarized as "to" (indirect object), "for" (dative of the person concerned or interested), "with" or "by" (dative of means or instrument), "with" (dative of accompaniment), and "on" (dative of time when).

a. The dative is used for the indirect object and with many verbs (see Reference Grammar, paragraph 30 for list), e.g.:

ὁ Κροῖσος οὐκ ἔδωκεν δόρυ **τῷ παιδί**.
Croesus did not give a spear *to the boy*.

ὁ γάμος **αὐτῷ** νῦν μέλει.
Marriage is *his* concern now.

b. The dative of the person concerned or interested is seen in its simplest
    form in sentences such as the following:

    πᾶς ἀνὴρ **ἑαυτῷ** πονεῖ.
    Every man labors *for himself*.

    ὁ Σόλων **Ἀθηναίοις** νόμους ἔθηκεν.
    Solon made laws *for the Athenians*.

The dative of respect, e.g., is seen in the following. Sometimes this use of the dative may be rendered in English by a
possessive adjective, e.g.:

    οὐ πρὸς ἄνδρας **ἡμῖν** γίγνεται ἡ μάχη.
    The battle *for us* (= *our battle*) is not against men.

The dative of possession is a type of the dative of the person concerned
or interested, e.g.:

    ἦσαν **Κροίσῳ** δύο παῖδες.
    There were *for Croesus* two sons. = Croesus had two sons.

    ἄλλοις μὲν χρήματά ἐστι πολλά, **ἡμῖν** δὲ σύμμαχοι ἀγαθοί.
    Others have much money, but *we* have good allies.

c. The dative of respect, e.g., **ὀνόματι** Θησεύς Theseus *by name*.

d. The dative of means or instrument may be translated "with" or "by,"
    e.g.:

    ὀφθαλμοῖς ὁρῶμεν.   **δόρατι** ἐβλήθη.
    We see *with our eyes*.   He was hit *by a spear*.

e. The dative of accompaniment may also be translated "with" or more
    freely, e.g.:

    ταῖς ναυσὶ πλευσόμεθα.
    We will sail *with our ships*.

    ἡ ναῦς διεφθάρη **αὐτοῖς τοῖς ἀνδράσιν**.
    The ship was destroyed, *crew and all*.

f. The dative of time when may be translated "on," e.g.:

    τῇ αὐτῇ ἡμέρᾳ ἀπέθανεν.
    He died *on the same day*.

g. The dative may be used to express the degree of difference with
    comparatives, e.g.:

πολλῷ μείζων
greater *by much* = *much* greater

4. Some Uses of the Accusative Case

a. Many verbs take a direct object in the accusative case, e.g.:

ὁ ἄνθρωπος γεωργεῖ **τὸν κλῆρον.**
The man cultivates *the farm.*

A few verbs can take two accusative objects, e.g.:

τοῦτό σε ἐρωτῶ.	**τοῦτό σε** αἰτῶ.
I ask *you this.*	I ask *you for this.*

b. The neuter accusative of adjectives and of some pronouns is often used *adverbially*, e.g., the comparative adverb is the neuter accusative singular of the comparative adjective; thus, θᾶσσον = "more quickly." The superlative adverb is the neuter accusative plural of the superlative adjective; thus, τάχιστα = "very quickly," "most quickly."

The words μέγα, πολύ, ὀλίγον, οὐδέν, τί (= διὰ τί) are commonly used adverbially, e.g.:

μέγα βοᾷ. He/she shouts *loudly.*
οὐδέν σε φοβεῖται. He/she does *not* fear you *at all.*
τί τοῦτο ποιεῖς; *Why* are you doing this?

c. One kind of adverbial accusative is the accusative of respect, e.g.:

ὁ Κροῖσος Λῦδὸς ἦν **τὸ γένος.**
Croesus was Lydian *with respect to his race*, i.e., *by birth.*

ἀνήρ τις ἀφίκετο οὐ καθαρὸς **τὰς χεῖρας.**
A man arrived impure *in respect to his hands.*

d. Another kind of adverbial accusative is the accusative of duration of time or extent of space, e.g.:

ἐμείναμεν **πέντε ἡμέρᾱς.**
We stayed *five days.*

τὸ ἄστυ **πολλοὺς σταδίους** ἀπέχει.
The city is *many stades* distant.

e. Another adverbial use of the accusative case is the accusative absolute, used with participles of impersonal verbs instead of the genitive absolute, e.g.:

δόξαν τὸν παῖδα ἐς τὴν ἄγρᾱν πέμψαι, ὁ Κροῖσος μάλιστα ἐφοβεῖτο.
When he had decided to send his son to the hunt, Croesus was very afraid.

(The word δόξαν is the accusative neuter of the aorist participle of δοκεῖ = "it having been decided.")

ἔξον ἐς τὴν ἄγραν ἰέναι, ὁ Ἄτυς εὐθὺς ὁρμᾶται.
Being allowed to go to the hunt, Atys sets out at once.
(The word ἔξον is the accusative neuter of the participle of ἔξεστι = "it being possible," "it being allowed.")

δέον τὸ θηρίον αἱρεῖν, ἐς τὸ ὄρος ἔσπευδον.
Since it was necessary to take the beast, they hurried to the mountain.
(The word δέον is the accusative neuter of the participle of δεῖ = "it being necessary.")

f. The accusative is used in oaths after νή (positive) and μά (negative), e.g.:

νὴ τοὺς θεούς. . . .   **μὰ** τὸν Δία. . . .
By the gods, I will. . . .   *By* Zeus, I won't. . . .

Exercise 26b

Translate each sentence and explain the uses of the cases in the underlined phrases.

1. ὁ Κροῖσος φοβούμενος μὴ <u>δόρατι</u> βληθείη ὁ παῖς, ἐκέλευσεν αὐτὸν <u>μάχης</u> ἀπέχειν.
2. ἀνήρ τις, Φρύγιος <u>τὸ γένος</u>, ἐς τὰς Σάρδῑς ἀφικόμενος, τὸν Κροῖσον <u>κάθαρσιν</u> ᾔτησεν.
3. <u>δόξαν</u> καθῆραι αὐτόν, ὁ Κροῖσος ἐπυνθάνετο πόθεν ἥκει καὶ <u>τίνος πατρὸς</u> ἐγένετο.
4. <u>δέον</u> τὸ ἀληθὲς εἰπεῖν, ὁ ξένος ἀπεκρῑνατο· "<u>Γορδίου</u> μὲν ἐγενόμην, ὄνομα δὲ <u>μοί</u> ἐστιν Ἄδρηστος, φονεύσᾱς δὲ τὸν ἐμαυτοῦ ἀδελφὸν ἄκων πάρειμι."
5. ὁ δὲ Κροῖσος δεξάμενος αὐτόν, "ἥκεις ἐς φίλους," ἔφη. "μένε οὖν ἐν τοῖς ἡμετέροις οἰκίοις <u>ὅσον</u> ἂν <u>χρόνον</u> βούλῃ."
6. ἄγγελοί τινες, Μῡσοὶ <u>γένος</u>, ἐς Σάρδῑς ἀφικόμενοι, "πέμψον <u>ἡμῖν</u>, ὦ βασιλεῦ," ἔφασαν, "τὸν σὸν παῖδα ἵνα μέγα θηρίον <u>τῆς χώρᾱς</u> ἐξέλωμεν."
7. ὁ δὲ Κροῖσος, "δύο μὲν παῖδές εἰσί <u>μοι</u>, ὧν οὗτος <u>πολλῷ</u> φιλαίτερός ἐστί μοι <u>τοῦ ἑτέρου</u>."
8. "οὐ μὰ <u>Δία</u> πέμψω αὐτὸν <u>ὑμῖν</u>, τὸν δὲ Ἄδρηστον πέμψω <u>νεᾱνίαις</u> τε καὶ <u>κυσίν</u>."
9. ὁ δὲ παῖς, <u>οὐδὲν</u> φοβούμενος τὴν ἄγρᾱν, τὸν πατέρα ἔπεισεν ἑαυτὸν πέμψαι· "οὐ γάρ," φησίν, "πρὸς ἄνδρας <u>ἡμῖν</u> γίγνεται ἡ μάχη."
10. <u>ἔξον</u> οὖν ἐς τὴν ἄγρᾱν ἰέναι, ὁ Ἄτυς εὐθὺς ὡρμήθη.
11. <u>μακρὰν</u> οὖν <u>ὁδὸν</u> πορευθέντες καὶ τὸ θηρίον εὑρόντες, <u>τῶν νεᾱνιῶν</u> οἱ μὲν αὐτὸ ἐδίωκον, οἱ δὲ περιστάντες κύκλῳ ἐσηκόντιζον.
12. ὁ δὲ Ἄδρηστος ἀκοντίζων <u>τοῦ ὑός</u>, <u>τοῦ</u> μὲν ἁμαρτάνει, τυγχάνει δὲ <u>τοῦ</u> Κροίσου <u>παιδός</u>.

*   *   *

Ο ΑΔΡΗΣΤΟΣ ΕΑΥΤΟΝ ΣΦΑΖΕΙ

Read the following passages (adapted from Herodotus 1.44–45) and answer the comprehension questions:

The story of Croesus and Adrastus concluded:

ὁ δὲ Κροῖσος τῷ μὲν θανάτῳ τοῦ παιδὸς συνεταράχθη, ἔτι δὲ μᾶλλον ὠδύρετο διότι τὸν παῖδα ἀπέκτεινεν ἐκεῖνος ὃν αὐτὸς φόνου ἐκάθηρεν. λῡπούμενος δὲ τῇ συμφορᾷ δεινῶς, ἐκάλει μὲν Δία καθάρσιον, μαρτυρόμενος ἃ ὑπὸ τοῦ ξένου ἔπαθεν, ἐκάλει δὲ Δία ἐφέστιον, διότι ἐν τοῖς οἰκίοις δεξάμενος τὸν ξένον ἐλάνθανε βόσκων τὸν φονέᾱ τοῦ παιδός, ἐκάλει δὲ καὶ Δία ἑταιρεῖον, διότι φύλακα συμπέμψᾱς αὐτὸν 5
ηὗρε πολεμιώτατον.

[συνεταράχθη (*from* συνταράττω) was thrown into confusion, confounded καθάρσιον of purification (a title of Zeus)   μαρτυρόμενος calling (him) to witness   ἐφέστιον who presides over the hearth (ἑστίᾱ) and hospitality (a title of Zeus)   βόσκων feeding, sheltering   τὸν φονέᾱ the murderer   ἑταιρεῖον presiding over companionship (a title of Zeus)]

1. By what was Croesus confounded?
2. Why did he grieve even more?
3. With what three titles did Croesus call upon Zeus?
4. To what irony does Croesus call attention when invoking Zeus as καθάρσιος?
5. To what irony does he call attention when invoking Zeus as ἐφέστιος?
6. To what irony does he call attention when invoking Zeus as ἑταιρεῖος?

παρῆσαν δὲ μετὰ τοῦτο οἱ Λῡδοὶ φέροντες τὸν νεκρόν, ὄπισθε δὲ εἵπετο αὐτῷ ὁ φονεύς. στὰς δὲ οὗτος πρὸ τοῦ νεκροῦ παρεδίδου ἑαυτὸν Κροίσῳ προτείνων τὰς χέρας, ἐπικατασφάξαι ἑαυτὸν κελεύων τῷ νεκρῷ, λέγων ὅτι οὐκέτι χρὴ βιοῦν.

[ὄπισθε behind   παρεδίδου tried to surrender   προτείνων stretching forth χέρας = χεῖρας   ἐπικατασφάξαι to slaughter X (*acc.*) over Y (*dat.*)   βιοῦν to live]

7.   Who follows the corpse of Croesus' son?
8.   With what gesture does Adrastus attempt to surrender to Croesus?
9.   What does Adrastus order Croesus to do?
10. What reason does Adrastus give for ordering Croesus to do this?

Κροῖσος δὲ ταῦτα ἀκούσᾱς τόν τε Ἄδρηστον οἰκτῑρει, καίπερ ὢν ἐν κακῷ 10
οἰκείῳ τοσούτῳ, καὶ λέγει πρὸς αὐτόν· "ἔχω, ὦ ξένε, παρὰ σοῦ πᾶσαν δίκην, ἐπειδὴ σεαυτοῦ καταδικάζεις θάνατον. οὐ σύ μοι τοῦδε τοῦ κακοῦ αἴτιος εἶ, ἀλλὰ θεῶν τις, ὅς μοι πάλαι προεσήμαινε τὰ μέλλοντα ἔσεσθαι." Κροῖσος μὲν οὖν ἔθαψε τὸν ἑαυτοῦ παῖδα, Ἄδρηστος δέ, οὗτος δὴ ὁ φονεὺς μὲν τοῦ ἑαυτοῦ ἀδελφοῦ, φονεὺς δὲ τοῦ καθήραντος, ἐπεὶ οὐδεὶς ἀνθρώπων ἐγένετο περὶ τὸ σῆμα, ἐπικατασφάζει 15
τῷ τύμβῳ ἑαυτόν.

[κακῷ trouble   οἰκείῳ of his own   παρά (+ *gen.*) from   καταδικάζεις you
condemn someone (*gen.*) to some punishment (*acc.*)   προεσήμαινε foretold   τὸ
σῆμα the tomb   ἐπικατασφάζει he slaughters X (*acc.*) over Y (*dat.*)   τῷ τύμβῳ
the tomb]

11.   Why is it surprising that Croesus pities Adrastus?
12.   How does Croesus explain that he has received full justice from
        Adrastus?
13.   Who, in Croesus' view, is responsible for what has happened?
14.   What does Adrastus do at the end of the story?
15.   What hints does Herodotus give in the last sentence as to why Adrastus
        did what he did?
16.   Does Adrastus seem to have been able to accept Croesus' explanation of
        who was responsible for what happened?
17.   Is there any indication in the story of Herodotus' own views as to who
        was responsible for what happened?   Can Croesus himself be held
        responsible in any way?   Look back at the beginning of the story at the
        beginning of this chapter.

Exercise 26c

Translate into Greek:

1.   A foreigner, Phrygian by race, arriving at Sardis with impure hands,
       asked Croesus to purify him.
2.   When the Mysians asked Croesus for help (βοήθεια; *use two
       accusatives*), at first he refused to send his son.
3.   But his son said, "Our (*use dative of possession*) battle is not against
       men; and so fear nothing but send me."
4.   And so Croesus was persuaded by these words, but he sent for (*use
       participle*) the foreigner and told him to guard his son.
5.   Being allowed to go, Atys set out immediately and arrived at the
       mountain on the third day.
6.   When they found the boar, the foreigner threw his spear (ἀκοντίζω)
       and missed the boar but hit Croesus' son.

27
Ο ΚΡΟΙΣΟΣ ΕΠΙ ΤΟΝ ΚΥΡΟΝ ΣΤΡΑΤΕΥΕΤΑΙ
(α)

οἱ τοῦ Κροίσου ἄγγελοι ἐς τοὺς Δελφοὺς ἀφῑγμένοι τῷ θεῷ ἐχρήσαντο.

The Ionic Dialect

Herodotus wrote in the Ionic dialect; in the preceeding chapters we changed most of his Ionic forms to their Attic equivalents, preserving only ἐς (ἐσ-) and -σσ-, but from now on we leave most Ionic forms as Herodotus actually wrote them. Note the following:

1. Ionic has η where Attic has ᾱ, e.g., Ionic ἡμέρη = Attic ἡμέρᾱ; Ionic πρῆξις = Attic πρᾶξις.
2. Contraction does not take place in Ionic with verbs and nouns, the stems of which end in ε, e.g., Ionic has φιλέω, φιλέεις, φιλέει, etc., instead of the Attic φιλῶ, φιλεῖς, φιλεῖ, etc. Note also that Ionic has ἐών, ἐοῦσα, ἐόν for the present participle of the verb εἰμί. As examples of nouns, note that Ionic has γένεος instead of Attic γένους and γένεα instead of Attic γένη, also Περσέων instead of Attic Περσῶν. Note also that νόος does not contract.
3. Dative plurals of the first and second declensions end in -ῃσι and -οισι, e.g., κρήνῃσι and ἀγροῖσι.
4. Occasionally Ionic has ει where Attic has ε and ου where Attic has ο, e.g., Ionic ζεῖνος (Attic ξένος) and Ionic μοῦνος (Attic μόνος).
5. Ionic has some pronouns not common in Attic prose, e.g., οἱ (dative, enclitic) "to him/her/it," and μιν (accusative, enclitic) "him/her."

While we preserve these Ionic forms in the readings, in the exercises we use only those Ionic forms that you have met previously (ἐς, ἐσ-, and -σσ-).

Vocabulary

Verbs

ἀγείρω, ἤγειρα I gather

ἀγωνίζομαι, ἀγωνιοῦμαι, ἠγωνισάμην, ἠγώνισμαι I contend

ἀντιόομαι, ἀντιώσομαι, ἠντιώθην (+ *dat.*) I oppose

διαβαίνω (*see* βαίνω *for principal parts*) I cross

ἐπέρχομαι (*see* ἔρχομαι *for principal parts*) I approach; (+ *dat.*) I attack

καταλύω (*see* λύω *for principal parts*) I dissolve, break up, destroy

μέμφομαι, μέμψομαι, ἐμεμψάμην *or* ἐμέμφθην (+ *dat. or acc.*) I blame, find fault with

παρακαλέω (*see* καλέω *for principal parts*) I summon

φωνέω I speak

Nouns

τὸ ἀνάθημα, τοῦ ἀναθήματος temple offering

ὁ ἀριθμός, τοῦ ἀριθμοῦ number

τὸ δῶρον, τοῦ δώρου gift

τὸ μαντεῖον, τοῦ μαντείου oracle

τὸ μέτρον, τοῦ μέτρου measure

τὸ ὅρκιον, τοῦ ὁρκίου oath; (*plural*) treaty

τὸ στράτευμα, τοῦ στρατεύματος army

ἡ συμμαχίᾱ, τῆς συμμαχίᾱς alliance

ὁ χρησμός, τοῦ χρησμοῦ oracular response

τὸ χρηστήριον, τοῦ χρηστηρίου (*often plural with singular meaning*) oracle (either the seat of the oracle or the oracular response)

Adjectives

καρτερός, -ά, -όν strong, fierce

οὐδέτερος, -ᾱ, -ον neither

Prepositions

ἐπί (+ *gen.*) toward, in the direction of, on; (+ *dat.*) at, upon, on, for (of price or purpose); (+ *acc.*) at, against, onto, to *or* for (of direction or purpose), for (of time)

πρός (+ *gen.*) from; (+ *dat.*) at, near, by, in addition to; (+ *acc.*) to, toward, against, upon, with (i.e., in relation to)

Adverbs

ἄλλοσε to another place, to other places

αὐτίκα straightway

πάνυ altogether, very, exceedingly

Expressions

ἄλλοι ἄλλοσε some to some places, others to other places

Proper Name

ἡ Πῡθίᾱ, τῆς Πῡθίᾱς Pythia, the Delphic priestess of Apollo

Κροῖσος δὲ ἐπὶ δύο ἔτεα ἐν πένθει μεγάλῳ ἐκάθητο τοῦ παιδὸς ἐστερημένος· μετὰ δὲ ταῦτα, ἐπεὶ ὁ Κῦρος βασιλεὺς γενόμενος τῶν Περσέων τούς τε Μήδους ἐνίκησε καὶ τὰ τῶν Περσέων πρήγματα ηὔξανεν, ἤθελεν ὁ Κροῖσος, εἴ πως δύναιτο, τὴν δύναμιν αὐτῶν παῦσαι πρὶν μεγάλους γενέσθαι. ἔδοξεν οὖν αὐτῷ χρῆσθαι τῷ   5 μαντείῳ τῷ ἀρίστῳ, ἵνα μάθοι εἰ δέοι ἐπὶ τοὺς Πέρσᾱς στρατεύεσθαι· πρῶτον μέντοι ἔδει γιγνώσκειν τί μαντεῖόν ἐστι ἄριστον. πάντων οὖν

τῶν μαντείων ἀπεπειρᾶτο, ἀγγέλους πέμψας, τοὺς μὲν ἐς Δωδώνην,
τοὺς δὲ ἐς Δελφούς, ἄλλους δὲ ἄλλοσε. τοὺς δὲ ἀγγέλους ἐκέλευε τῇ
ἑκατοστῇ ἡμέρῃ ἀφ' ἧς ἂν ὁρμηθῶσι ἐκ Σαρδίων χρῆσθαι τοῖς   10
χρηστηρίοις, ἐρωτῶντας τί ποιῶν τυγχάνει ὁ Λυδῶν βασιλεὺς
Κροῖσος, καὶ ὅσ' ἂν λέγῃ τὰ χρηστήρια γράψαντας ἀναφέρειν παρ'
ἑαυτόν.

[πένθει sorrow   ἐστερημένος (from στερέω) (+ gen.) bereft of   χρῆσθαι (+ dat.)
to consult (an oracle)   ἀπεπειρᾶτο (+ gen.) made trial of   ἑκατοστῇ hundredth
ἀναφέρειν to bring back, report]

ὅ τι μὲν τὰ ἄλλα χρηστήρια ἐθέσπισεν, οὐ λέγεται ὑπ' οὐδενός, ἐν
δὲ Δελφοῖσι ἐπεὶ τάχιστα εἰσῆλθον οἱ Λυδοὶ χρησόμενοι τῷ θεῷ, ἡ   15
Πυθίη λέγει τάδε·

οἶδα δ' ἐγὼ ψάμμου τ' ἀριθμὸν καὶ μέτρα θαλάσσης,
καὶ κωφοῦ συνίημι καὶ οὐ φωνεῦντος ἀκούω.
ὀδμή μ' ἐς φρένας ἦλθε κραταιρίνοιο χελώνης
ἑψομένης ἐν χαλκῷ ἅμ' ἀρνείοισι κρέεσσιν.   20

[ἐθέσπισεν prophesied   ἐπεὶ τάχιστα as soon as   ψάμμου of the sand(s)
κωφοῦ (gen. with συνίημι) dumb, mute   φωνεῦντος = Ionic for φωνοῦντος   ὀδμή
smell   μ' = μοι   φρένας mind   κραταιρίνοιο χελώνης ἑψομένης ἐν
χαλκῷ ἅμ' ἀρνείοισι κρέεσσιν of a hard-shelled tortoise being boiled in a bronze
(kettle) along with the flesh of a lamb]

    ταῦτα θεσπισάσης τῆς Πυθίης, οἱ Λυδοὶ γράψαντες ἀπῆλθον ἐς
τὰς Σάρδῑς. ὡς δὲ καὶ οἱ ἄλλοι οἱ περιπεμφθέντες παρῆσαν φέροντες
τοὺς χρησμούς, ὁ Κροῖσος πάντα τὰ γεγραμμένα ἀνεγίγνωσκε. τῶν
μὲν οὖν ἄλλων οὐδὲν ἤρεσκέ οἱ, ὡς δὲ τὸ ἐκ Δελφῶν ἤκουσε, αὐτίκα
ηὔχετο καὶ ἐδέξατο, νομίσας μοῦνον εἶναι μαντεῖον τὸ ἐν Δελφοῖσιν,   25
διότι ἐξηῦρεν ἃ αὐτὸς ἐποίησεν.

[τὰ γεγραμμένα the things that had been written]

    μετὰ δὲ ταῦτα ὁ Κροῖσος τὸν ἐν Δελφοῖσι θεὸν ἐτίμα, Λυδούς τε
πάντας ἐκέλευε θύειν ὅ τι ἔχοι ἕκαστος. καὶ πλεῖστα καὶ κάλλιστα
δῶρα ἔπεμψεν ἐς Δελφοὺς καὶ τοὺς ἄγειν μέλλοντας ἐκέλευεν ἐρωτᾶν
τὰ χρηστήρια εἰ δέοι Κροῖσον στρατεύεσθαι ἐπὶ Πέρσᾱς. ὡς δὲ   30
ἀφικόμενοι οἱ Λυδοὶ ἀνέθεσαν τὰ ἀναθήματα, ἐχρήσαντο τοῖς
χρηστηρίοις. ἡ δὲ Πυθίη τάδε ἀπεκρίνατο, ὅτι ἐὰν στρατεύηται
Κροῖσος ἐπὶ Πέρσᾱς, μεγάλην ἀρχὴν καταλύσει. ἐπεὶ δὲ τὸν
χρησμὸν ἐπύθετο ὁ Κροῖσος, ἥσθη πάνυ ἐλπίσας καταλύσειν τὴν

Κύρου ἀρχήν. οὕτως οὖν ἐλπίσᾱς ἐστρατεύετο ἐς τὴν Περσῶν	35
ἀρχήν. καὶ ὡς ἀφίκετο ἐς τὸν Ἅλυν ποταμὸν διαβὰς σὺν τῷ στρατῷ
τῶν Πτερίων εἷλε τὴν πόλιν.

Κῦρος δὲ ἀγείρᾱς τὸν ἑαυτοῦ στρατὸν ἠντιοῦτο Κροίσῳ. μάχης
δὲ καρτερῆς γενομένης καὶ πεσόντων ἀμφοτέρων πολλῶν, τέλος
οὐδέτεροι νῑκήσαντες διέστησαν νυκτὸς ἐπελθούσης. καὶ τὰ μὲν	40
στρατόπεδα ἀμφότερα οὕτως ἠγωνίσατο. Κροῖσος δὲ μεμφθεὶς κατὰ
τὸ πλῆθος τὸ ἑαυτοῦ στράτευμα (ἦν γὰρ οἱ στρατὸς πολλῷ ἐλάσσων
ἢ ὁ Κύρου), τοῦτο μεμφθείς, ὡς τῇ ὑστεραίῃ οὐκ ἐπειρᾶτο ἐπιὼν ὁ
Κῦρος, ἀπήλαυνε ἐς τὰς Σάρδῑς, ἐν νόῳ ἔχων τούς τε Αἰγυπτίους
παρακαλεῖν κατὰ τὸ ὅρκιον (ἐποιήσατο γὰρ πρὸς Ἄμασιν	45
βασιλεύοντα Αἰγύπτου συμμαχίην) καὶ μεταπέμψασθαι τοὺς
Βαβυλωνίους (καὶ γὰρ πρὸς τούτους αὐτῷ ἐπεποίητο συμμαχίη),
καλέσᾱς τε δὴ τούτους καὶ τὴν ἑαυτοῦ συλλέξᾱς στρατιήν, ἐν νόῳ
εἶχε ἅμα τῷ ἦρι στρατεύειν ἐπὶ τοὺς Πέρσᾱς.

[διέστησαν they parted	τὰ . . . στρατόπεδα (here) the armies	οἱ to/for him,
his	ἐπεποίητο had been made]

—adapted from Herodotus 1.46–50, 53–54, and 76–77

Principal Parts: Verbs from Unrelated Stems

αἱρέω (αἱρε-/ἑλ-), αἱρήσω, εἷλον, ᾕρηκα, ᾕρημαι, ᾑρέθην I take;
   (middle) I choose
ἔρχομαι (ἐρχ-/ἐλθ-/ἐλυθ-), [εἶμι (ἰ-/εἰ-), (infinitive) ἰέναι], ἦλθον, ἐλήλυθα
   I come, go
τρέχω (τρεχ-/δραμ-/δραμε-), δραμοῦμαι, ἔδραμον, δεδράμηκα,
   δεδράμημαι I run, sail

Word Study

From what Greek words are the following English philosophical terms derived:

1. philosophy
2. logic
3. ethics
4. epistemology
5. metaphysics
6. political theory.

Explain the meaning of the terms with reference to their Greek roots.

Grammar

1. Perfect and Pluperfect Middle and Passive

Note the following extracts from the reading passage above:

ὁ Κροῖσος πάντα τὰ γεγραμμένα ἀνεγίγνωσκε.
Croesus read all the things that had been written.

ἀπήλαυνε . . . ἐν νόῳ ἔχων . . . μεταπέμψασθαι τοὺς Βαβυλωνίους (καὶ γὰρ πρὸς τούτους αὐτῷ **ἐπεποίητο** συμμαχίη).

He marched away. . . intending . . . to summon the Babylonians (for an alliance *had* also *been made* by him with these (i.e., the Babylonians).

The words in boldface above are *perfect* (γεγραμμένα) and *pluperfect* (ἐπεποίητο) in tense and *passive* in voice. These tenses indicate states or conditions that existed as a result of actions that were *completed* prior to the action of the main verb in each sentence (the term *perfect* comes from a Latin verb meaning "to complete").

In the first sentence above the participle γεγραμμένα is perfect in tense and indicates a state or condition completed prior to the action of the main verb ἀνεγίγνωσκε, which is in a past tense (imperfect); we thus translate "Croesus read all the things *that had been written*" (prior to his reading them). In the second sentence the pluperfect indicative ἐπεποίητο indicates an action completed prior to the action of the other verb ἀπήλαυνε, which is in a past tense (aorist); we thus translate the pluperfect ἐπεποίητο "*had been made.*"

To form the perfect middle/passive of λύω, reduplicate the stem (i.e., put the first consonant + ε before the stem, which appears here with short υ) and add the primary middle/passive endings:

Indicative	*Imperative*	*Infinitive*	*Participle*
λέ-λυ-μαι		λε-λύ-σθαι	λε-λυ-μένος, -η, -ον
λέ-λυ-σαι	λέλυσο		
λέ-λυ-ται			
λε-λύ-μεθα			
λέ-λυ-σθε	λέλυσθε		
λέ-λυ-νται			

Subjunctive	*Optative*
λελυμένος ὦ	λελυμένος εἴην
λελυμένος ᾖς	λελυμένος εἴης
λελυμένος ᾖ	λελυμένος εἴη
λελυμένοι ὦμεν	λελυμένοι εἶμεν
λελυμένοι ἦτε	λελυμένοι εἶτε
λελυμένοι ὦσι(ν)	λελυμένοι εἶεν

The above forms may be either middle or passive in sense, according to the context, e.g., λέλυμαι may mean either "I have ransomed" (middle sense) or "I have been loosed" (passive sense).

Note (1) that there is no thematic vowel (ο/ε) between the stem and the ending, (2) that the reduplication is retained throughout, and (3) that the accent of the infinitive and participle is not recessive. The perfect middle/passive subjunctive and optative are periphrastic, that is, they are formed from the perfect middle/passive participle plus the subjunctive and optative of the verb εἰμί.

Reduplication in the perfect and the pluperfect is a sign of completed action; the perfect tense denotes or records a state that is the result of an action *completed* in the past, thus, λέλυμαι can most accurately be translated "I was freed (at some moment in the past), and as a consequence I am free now (in the present)." More simply, we can translate "I have been freed," or "I am free"; you will note that when the Greeks used the perfect tense they always had in mind a state that was the result of the completion of an action in the past. It is this *completed aspect* of the action that is of paramount importance.

To form the pluperfect middle/passive indicative, augment the reduplicated stem and add the secondary middle/passive endings, e.g.:

ἐ-λε-λύ-μην
ἐ-λέ-λυ-σο
ἐ-λέ-λυ-το
ἐ-λε-λύ-μεθα
ἐ-λέ-λυ-σθε
ἐ-λέ-λυ-ντο

The augment, as always, indicates past time; the pluperfect therefore records a state that existed in the past as the result of an action completed at some time more remote: "I was free as a consequence of being freed at some earlier time" = "I had been freed." Only indicative forms appear in the pluperfect tense; there are no pluperfect subjunctives, optatives, imperatives, infinitives, or participles.

Most verbs form their perfect and pluperfect by reduplication as described above, but note the following special cases:

a. If the verb starts with θ, φ, or χ, the reduplication uses the unaspirated equivalents of these consonants, namely, τ, π, and κ, e.g.:

θάπτω > τέθαμμαι
φιλέω > πεφίλημαι
χράομαι > κέχρημαι

b. If the verb starts with a vowel or double consonant (ζ, ξ, or ψ), it does not reduplicate but augments, e.g.:

ἀγγέλλω > ἤγγελμαι
οἰκέω > ᾤκημαι
ζητέω > ἐζήτημαι
ξενίζω > ἐξένισμαι
ψεύδομαι > ἔψευσμαι

The augment is retained throughout, e.g.: ἠγγελμένος, ᾠκῆσθαι, ἐψευσμένος.

c. If the verb starts with two consonants, in most cases the first is reduplicated, e.g.:

γράφω > γέγραμμαι
βλάπτω > βέβλαμμαι

In some combinations, there is augment instead of reduplication, e.g.:

σκ- σκοπέω (σκεπ-) > ἔσκεμμαι
γν- γιγνώσκω (γνω-) > ἔγνωσμαι
σπ- σπεύδω > ἔσπευσμαι

Κροῖσος . . . ἐν πένθει μεγάλῳ ἐκάθητο τοῦ παιδὸς **ἐστερημένος**.
Croesus sat in great grief, *bereft* of his son.

Note that contract verbs lengthen the stem vowel, e.g.:

φιλέω > πεφίλημαι
τῑμάω > τετῑμημαι
δηλόω > δεδήλωμαι

When the stem of the verb ends in a consonant, spelling changes take place for the sake of euphony, and the third person plural becomes a periphrastic form consisting of a perfect participle and a form of the verb "to be," e.g.:

Labial Stems (-β, -π, -φ) e.g., λείπ-ω	*Guttural Stems* (-γ, -κ, -χ) e.g., δέχ-ομαι	*Dental Stems* (-δ, -θ -ζ, -τ) e.g., πείθ-ω
Perfect		
λέλειμμαι	δέδεγμαι	πέπεισμαι
λέλειψαι	δέδεξαι	πέπεισαι
λέλειπται	δέδεκται	πέπεισται
λελείμμεθα	δεδέγμεθα	πεπείσμεθα
λέλειφθε	δέδεχθε	πέπεισθε
λελειμμένοι εἰσί(ν)	δεδεγμένοι εἰσί(ν)	πεπεισμένοι εἰσί(ν)
λελεῖφθαι	δεδέχθαι	πεπεῖσθαι
λελειμμένος, -η, -ον	δεδεγμένος, -η, -ον	πεπεισμένος, -η, -ον
Pluperfect		
ἐλελείμμην	ἐδεδέγμην	ἐπεπείσμην
ἐλέλειψο	ἐδέδεξο	ἐπέπεισο
ἐλέλειπτο	ἐδέδεκτο	ἐπέπειστο
ἐλελείμμεθα	ἐδεδέγμεθα	ἐπεπείσμεθα
ἐλέλειφθε	ἐδέδεχθε	ἐπέπεισθε
λελειμμένοι ἦσαν	δεδεγμένοι ἦσαν	πεπεισμένοι ἦσαν

Note that with perfect and pluperfect passive verbs the dative case without a preposition is often used to designate the person or agent by whom the action is carried out, instead of the preposition ὑπό with the genitive case, as is usual with other passive verbs, e.g.:

ἔργα μεγάλα τὰ μὲν τοῖς Ἕλλησι, τὰ δὲ τοῖς βαρβάροις εἰργασμένα ἐστίν. Great deeds have been done, some by the Greeks, others by the barbarians.

Exercise 27a

Locate the following perfect and pluperfect passive forms in the reading at the beginning of this chapter: (1) ἐστερημένος, (2) γεγραμμένα, and (3) ἐπεποίητο. Identify each form; translate the sentence in which each occurs; and explain why the perfect or pluperfect tense was needed in each sentence.

Exercise 27b

Change the following present forms to the corresponding perfect forms:

1. λύονται	5. γράφεται	9. οἰκεῖσθαι
2. λῡόμενος	6. λείπετε	10. ψεύδεσθε
3. ποιεῖται	7. πράττονται	11. πείθομαι
4. νῑκᾶσθαι	8. ἀγγέλλεται	12. πέμπονται

Change the following present forms to the corresponding pluperfect forms:

1. λύεται	3. πείθῃ	5. ἀφικνεῖται
2. δέχονται	4. ἄγομαι	6. ποιοῦνται

Exercise 27c

Read aloud and translate into English:

1. συμμαχίᾱ πρὸς τοὺς Βαβυλωνίους ἐπεποίητο τῷ Κροίσῳ.
2. οἱ ὁπλῖται ἐν τῷ πεδίῳ τεταγμένοι τοὺς πολεμίους ἔμενον.
3. πάντα τῷ στρατηγῷ ἤδη ἐβεβούλευτο.
4. ὁ Κροῖσος τῷ χρησμῷ ἐπέπειστο ἐς τὴν τοῦ Κύρου ἀρχὴν ἐσβαλεῖν.
5. οἱ Λῡδοὶ ἐς μάχην ἐξηγμένοι ἦσαν ἵνα τοὺς πολεμίους ἀμῡνοιεν.
6. αἱ πύλαι ἀνεῳγμέναι εἰσίν· ἐσέλθωμεν οὖν ταχέως.
7. ἆρα πέπεισαι ὑπὸ τοῦ ἰᾱτροῦ τὸν παῖδα ἐς Ἐπίδαυρον κομίζειν;
8. ἆρα συνῆς τὰ γεγραμμένα; ἐγὼ γὰρ δύναμαι αὐτὰ συνιέναι.
9. ὁ ἔμπορος οὐκ ἔφη τὸ ἀργύριον δεδέχθαι.
10. οἱ παῖδες οἱ ἐν τῷ ἄστει τοῖς πατράσι λελειμμένοι ἐς διδασκάλων καθ᾽ ἡμέρᾱν ἐφοίτων.

Exercise 27d

Translate into Greek:

1. Freed (λύω) by (their) master, the slaves were all delighted.
2. The ambassadors had already arrived at the gates.

3. The messenger said that the king had been persuaded to spare (φείδεσθαι + *gen.*) the old man.
4. We have been sent to tell (*use* ὡς + *future participle*) you that the ship has already arrived at the harbor.
5. Have you received the money that I sent you?

Signs, Dreams, and Oracles

The Pythia sits on the sacred tripod, veiled and holding in one hand a bowl of lustral water and in the other a branch of laurel. The suppliant who is consulting Apollo is separated from her by a pillar.

In a world that was dangerous and controlled by gods who were arbitrary, the Greeks needed means of ascertaining the will of the gods. There were several ways of trying to do this. First, the gods were thought to send signs to men, particularly in the behavior of birds and in dreams. Interpretation of these signs was open to anyone, but throughout Greek history there were always prophets who were especially gifted in this sphere. In the second book of the *Odyssey* Telemachus, Odysseus' son, addressed an assembly of the people of Ithaca, complaining of the behavior of Penelope's suitors:

Zeus sent two eagles from the top of the mountain, which flew down close to each other on the breath of the wind. And when they reached the middle of the meeting place, they wheeled around and flapped their wings. They went for the heads of all who were there, and they foreboded death, tearing with their talons at their cheeks and necks; then they flew off on the right over the houses and city. The people were amazed at the birds when they saw them and wondered in their hearts what was destined to happen. The old hero Halitherses spoke to them, for he excelled all his generation in understanding birds and expounding omens: "Listen to me, men of Ithaca, I speak particularly to the suitors. Great trouble is rolling toward you, for Odysseus will not be long away . . . ."

Such prophets were not always believed; on this occasion the leader of the suitors, Eurymachus, replied:

Old man, go home and prophesy to your children, in case they get into trouble. I can make a much better prophecy on this than you; lots of birds fly under the rays of the sun and not all bring omens: Odysseus died far away, and you should have died with him." (*Odyssey* 2.146–184)

Dreams were also thought to be sent by the gods. In the first book of the *Iliad*, when the Greeks are struck by plague, Achilles called a meeting and said: "Let us consult a prophet (μάντις) or a priest (ἱερεύς) or an interpreter of dreams (for dreams also come from Zeus), who may tell us why Apollo is so angry with us" (*Iliad* 1.62–64). In the story of Adrastus Croesus was warned by a dream, which revealed the truth of the disaster that was going to strike his son.

If either states or individuals were in some serious dilemma and needed to know what to do, they had recourse to oracles. There were many oracles in Greece, but by far the most prestigious and wealthy at this time was Apollo's oracle at Delphi. It was consulted by inquirers from all over the Greek world and beyond. Apollo, god of light, music, poetry, healing, and prophecy, was a comparative latecomer to the Greek pantheon. He seems to have arrived at Delphi early in the eighth century, and his oracle rapidly acquired a high reputation. Grateful states and individuals showered gifts upon it, and by the sixth century the sanctuary was an elaborate complex. The Sacred Way wound up the hill toward the great temple. On either side of the way stood treasuries (little temples in which states stored their offerings) and dedications of statues and tripods. Above the temple was the theater, and high above this again was the stadium. Every four years games second in importance only to those of Olympia were held in honor of Apollo. The wealth and beauty of the sanctuary in its remote and awe-inspiring site on the slopes of the foothills of Mount Parnassus must have made a deep impression on all visitors.

There were full-time priests or prophets (προφῆται) at Delphi. The priestess (ἡ Πῡθία) was chosen from an ordinary family, a woman past middle age and of blameless life. She received no special training, since, when she prophesied, she was simply the mouthpiece of Apollo. The procedure for consulting the oracle was elaborate. Consultations were held only nine times a year. There were consequently always many state embassies and individuals waiting for their turn. At dawn the Pythia purified herself in the water of the Castalian spring. The priest then prepared to sacrifice a goat and tested the omens by sprinkling it with water. If the omens were satisfactory, the day was declared auspicious, and the Pythia was admitted to the inner sanctuary of the temple. There she drank sacred water and may have chewed laurel leaves (the laurel was sacred to Apollo) before ascending the sacred tripod.

Inquirers purified themselves in the water of Castalia and offered a sacred cake on the altar outside the temple. On entering the temple they sacrificed a

goat on the inner hearth where burned the eternal fire. They were then conducted to the inner sanctuary. They were told " to think holy thoughts and
speak well-omened words." The priest put the inquirer's question to the
Pythia and brought back the answer, usually in verse form. The Greeks believed that when the Pythia sat on the sacred tripod, after completing the
rituals, she was possessed by Apollo and "filled with god" (ἔνθεος). Descrip-
tions certainly suggest that she fell into some kind of trance, in which her voice
changed, like modern spiritualist mediums.

It is probably true to say that the vast majority of Herodotus' contempo-
raries believed firmly in the Delphic oracle and that in a serious crisis they
would choose to consult it, if they were rich enough to afford the procedure. Individuals went for advice on religious questions, cult and pollution, and on
practical questions, "Should I marry?" "Should I go abroad?" These individuals
must have far outnumbered the deputations from the cities, but it is of the latter that we hear most in our sources. One of the most famous was the depu-
tation sent by the Athenians when Xerxes' invasion was threatening. The
moment the deputies had taken their seat in the inner sanctuary, before their
question had been put, the Pythia exclaimed: "Unhappy men, why do you sit
here? Leave your homes and flee to the ends of the earth. . . . For fire and war
strike you down. . . . Be gone from my shrine, and steep your hearts in woe."
The deputies were aghast, but, on the advice of a prominent Delphian, they
went for a second consultation as suppliants and said: "Lord, give us a better
answer about our country, respecting our suppliant branches." The second reply was ambiguous:

"Pallas Athena cannot propitiate Olympian Zeus, though she prays to him
with many words and all her skill. All else will be taken, . . . but far-see-
ing Zeus grants to Athena that only the wooden wall will be unsacked. Do
not wait for the host of cavalry and infantry that come from the mainland
but turn your backs and flee; yet some day you will face them. O divine
Salamis, you will destroy the sons of women, when the grain is scattered
or gathered in." (Herodotus 7.140–141)

The answer was brought back to Athens, and a debate followed in which
its meaning was discussed. Some of the older men said that the wooden wall
meant the wall with which the Acropolis had once been fortified. Others said
it meant their ships, and this view prevailed when Themistocles argued that
the last two lines foretold the death not of Athenians but of their enemies, for
Salamis is called "divine Salamis." If the oracle foretold their own destruction,
it would have said "unhappy Salamis." This story illustrates the difficulty of
interpreting some of Apollo's oracles correctly and the seriousness with which
the oracles were treated. It is impossible for us to distinguish which oracles
quoted by Herodotus are genuine and which forged later to suit past events
(the first oracle given the Athenians in the case above certainly rings true). In
any case the prestige of Delphi survived, and states and individuals continued
to consult Apollo throughout Greek history until the oracle was closed in A.D.
390 by a Roman emperor in the name of Christianity.

Ο ΚΡΟΙΣΟΣ ΕΠΙ ΤΟΝ ΚΥΡΟΝ ΣΤΡΑΤΕΥΕΤΑΙ (β)

Vocabulary

Verbs

ἀναστρέφω (see στρέφω for principal parts) I turn around

ἀνέχομαι, (imperfect) ἠνειχόμην, ἀνέξομαι, ἠνεσχόμην I endure, am patient

ἱππεύω, ἱππεύσω, ἵππευσα (active or middle) I am a horseman, ride a horse

κτείνω, κτενῶ, ἔκτεινα, ἔκτονα I kill

προστάττω (see τάττω for principal parts) I command

φείδομαι, φείσομαι, ἐφεισάμην (+ gen.) I spare

Nouns

τὸ ἔθνος, τοῦ ἔθνους tribe, people

τὸ ἱππικόν, τοῦ ἱππικοῦ cavalry

ἡ ἵππος, τῆς ἵππου cavalry

ἡ κάμηλος, τῆς καμήλου camel

ὁ πεζός, τοῦ πεζοῦ infantry

Adjectives

ἄχρηστος, -ον useless

δειλός, -ή, -όν cowardly

Preposition and Adverb

ὄπισθε(ν) (adverb or preposition + gen.) behind

ὀπίσω backward

Expression

κατὰ τάχος quickly

Κῦρος δὲ αὐτίκα ἀπελαύνοντος Κροίσου μετὰ τὴν μάχην τὴν γενομένην ἐν τῇ Πτερίῃ, ἐπιστάμενος ὡς ἀπελάσᾱς μέλλοι Κροῖσος διασκεδᾶν τὸν στρατόν, ἐβουλεύσατο ἐλαύνειν ὡς τάχιστα δύναιτο ἐπὶ τὰς Σάρδῑς. ὡς δέ οἱ ταῦτα ἔδοξε, καὶ ἐποίεε κατὰ τάχος· ἐλάσᾱς γὰρ τὸν στρατὸν ἐς τὴν Λῡδίην αὐτὸς ἄγγελος ἦλθε Κροίσῳ. 5 ἐνταῦθα Κροῖσος ἐς ἀπορίην πολλὴν ἀφῑγμένος, ὅμως τοὺς Λῡδοὺς ἐξῆγε ἐς μάχην. ἦν δὲ τοῦτον τὸν χρόνον ἔθνος οὐδὲν ἐν τῇ Ἀσίῃ οὔτε ἀνδρειότερον οὔτε ἀλκιμώτερον τοῦ Λῡδίου. ἡ δὲ μάχη αὐτῶν ἦν ἀφ᾽ ἵππων καὶ αὐτοὶ ἦσαν ἱππεύεσθαι ἀγαθοί.

[διασκεδᾶν (from διασκεδάννῡμι) to disperse   ἐποίεε he did (it)   ἀλκιμώτερον more stalwart]

ἐς δὲ τὸ πεδίον συνελθόντων αὐτῶν τὸ πρὸ τοῦ ἄστεως, ὁ Κῦρος 10 ὡς εἶδε τοὺς Λῡδοὺς ἐς μάχην τασσομένους, φοβούμενος τὴν ἵππον,

ἐποίησε τοιόνδε· πάσᾱς τὰς καμήλους, αἳ τόν τε σῖτον ἔφερον καὶ τὰ
σκεύεα, προσέταξε πρὸ τῆς ἄλλης στρατιῆς προϊέναι πρὸς τὴν
Κροίσου ἵππον, ταῖς δὲ καμήλοις ἕπεσθαι τὸν πεζὸν ἐκέλευε. ὄπισθε
δὲ τοῦ πεζοῦ ἔταξε τὴν πᾶσαν ἵππον. ὡς δὲ πάντες τεταγμένοι ἦσαν,   15
παρήνεσε αὐτοῖς τῶν μὲν ἄλλων Λῡδῶν μὴ φειδομένοις κτείνειν
πάντας, Κροῖσον δὲ αὐτὸν μὴ κτείνειν. τὰς δὲ καμήλους ἔταξε
ἀντίον τῆς ἵππου τῶνδε εἵνεκα· κάμηλον γὰρ ἵππος φοβεῖται καὶ οὐκ
ἀνέχεται οὔτε τὴν ἰδέην αὐτῆς ὁρῶν οὔτε τὴν ὀσμὴν ὀσφραινόμενος.
ταῦτα οὖν ἐσεσόφιστο ἵνα τῷ Κροίσῳ ἄχρηστον ᾖ τὸ ἱππικόν. ὡς δὲ   20
καὶ συνῆσαν ἐς τὴν μάχην, ἐνταῦθα ὡς τάχιστα ὤσφροντο τῶν
καμήλων οἱ ἵπποι καὶ εἶδον αὐτᾱς, ὀπίσω ἀνέστρεφον, διέφθαρτο τε
τῷ Κροίσῳ ἡ ἐλπίς.

[**τὴν ἵππον** i.e., of Croesus   **σκεύεα** baggage   **τῆς ἄλλης στρατιῆς**   the rest
of his army   **ἀντίον** (+ *gen.*) opposite   **τὴν ἰδέην** the form, appearance   **τὴν**
ὀσμὴν ὀσφραινόμενος smelling its smell   **ἐσεσόφιστο** (*from* σοφίζομαι) he had
devised   **ὡς τάχιστα** as soon as   **ὤσφροντο** (*from* ὀσφραίνομαι) they caught the
scent of, smelled (+ *gen.*)]

   οὐ μέντοι οἵ γε Λῡδοὶ δειλοὶ ἦσαν. ἀλλ᾽ ὡς ἔμαθον τὸ γιγνόμενον,
ἀποθορόντες ἀπὸ τῶν ἵππων πεζοὶ τοῖς Πέρσῃσι συνέβαλλον. χρόνῳ   25
δὲ πεσόντων ἀμφοτέρων πολλῶν, ἐτράποντο οἱ Λῡδοὶ καὶ
κατειληθέντες ἐς τὸ τεῖχος ἐπολιορκέοντο ὑπὸ τῶν Περσέων.

[**ἀποθορόντες** (*from* ἀποθρῴσκω)   having leaped off   **ἐτράποντο** (*second aorist*
middle of τρέπω) turned tail   **κατειληθέντες** (*from* κατειλέω) cooped up]

—adapted from Herodotus 1.79–80

Principal Parts: Another Verb from Unrelated Stems

I say, tell, speak:
λέγω (λεγ-)   λέξω   ἔλεξα   λέλεγμαι   ἐλέχθην
[εἴρω (ἐρ-/ῥη-)]   ἐρῶ   εἴρηκα   εἴρημαι   ἐρρήθην
(ἐπ-)   εἶπον

Word Building

If you know the meaning of each part of a compound word, you can usually
deduce the meaning of the word as a whole. Give the meaning of each part of
the following compound words and then the meaning of the whole:

Compound words formed by prefixing an adverb or ἀ-privative:

1. εὐγενής, -ές   3. εὐτυχής, -ές   5. ἀμαθής, -ές
2. δυσγενής, -ές   4. ἀτυχής, -ές   6. ἀείμνηστος, -ον

Note that compound adjectives have the same form for masculine and feminine.

Compound words formed by combining the stem of an adjective with another word:

1. φιλάνθρωπος, -ον   3. φιλότῑμος, -ον   5. μεγαλόψῡχος, -ον
2. φιλόσοφος, -ον   4. ὀλιγοχρόνιος, -ον 6. ὁ ψευδόμαντις

Compound words formed by combining the stem of a noun with another word:

1. ἡ ναυμαχίᾱ   3. ὁ ναυβάτης   5. θαλαττοκρατέω
2. ὁ ναύκληρος   4. ἡ δημοκρατίᾱ   6. ὁ παιδαγωγός

Exercise 27e

In passage β above, locate and identify the form of four verbs or participles in the perfect or pluperfect middle or passive.

Grammar

2. Uses of πρίν

The conjunction πρίν may mean "until" or "before."

a. After a negative main clause πρίν means "until," and the usual rules for temporal conjunctions (see Chapter 22, Grammar 2) apply, i.e., like ἕως it is followed by the indicative in past time and the indefinite construction (ἄν + subjunctive, usually aorist) in future time, e.g.:

> αἱ γυναῖκες οὐκ ἀπῆλθον πρὶν ἀφίκετο ὁ ἱερεύς.
> The women did not go away until the priest arrived.

> αἱ γυναῖκες οὐκ ἀπίᾱσι πρὶν ἂν ἀφίκηται ὁ ἱερεύς.
> The women will not go away until the priest arrives.

b. After a positive main clause πρίν usually means "before," and it is followed by an infinitive. As in indirect statements, if the subject of the infinitive is the same as that of the leading verb, it is not expressed (but may be intensified with αὐτός); if the subject of the infinitive is different from that of the leading verb, it is in the accusative, e.g.:

> ἀποπέμπουσιν αὐτὸν πρὶν ἀκοῦσαι.
> They send him away before they hear him.

> ἐδείπνησα πρὶν ἰέναι εἰς τὴν ἐκκλησίᾱν.
> I dined before going to the Assembly.

> οἱ πολῖται συνῆλθον πρὶν εἰσιέναι τοὺς πρυτάνεις.
> The citizens gathered before the Prytaneis arrived.

Exercise 27f

Translate the following pairs of sentences:

1. ὁ νεᾱνίᾱς ἐς τὸ ἄστυ ἀφίκετο πρὶν γενέσθαι ἡμέρᾱν.
   The farmers returned to the country before evening fell.

2. πρὶν ἀπιέναι ὁ πατὴρ τοὺς παῖδας ἐκέλευσε τῇ μητρὶ πάντα πείθεσθαι.
   Before climbing the hill, the old man rested by the road.

3. μὴ παύετε ἐργαζόμενοι πρὶν ἂν καταδύῃ ὁ ἥλιος.
   Let us not try to board the ship until the captain orders.

4. οἱ ἄγγελοι οὐκ ἀπῆλθον ἀπὸ τῶν Δελφῶν πρὶν ἐθέσπισεν ἡ Πῡθίᾱ.
   Croesus did not wage war against the Persians until he (had) consulted the oracle.

5. πρὶν ἄρξαι τῆς μάχης, ὁ Κῦρος τοὺς στρατιώτᾱς ἐκέλευσε τοῦ Κροίσου φείδεσθαι.
   Cyrus arrived at Sardis before Croesus knew (**ἐπίσταμαι**) what was happening.

3. The Articular Infinitive

The infinitive can be used as a verbal noun in any case, simply by introducing it with the neuter of the definite article (the negative is μή), e.g.:

τοῦτό ἐστι **τὸ ἀδικεῖν, τὸ** πλέον τῶν ἄλλων **ζητεῖν** ἔχειν.
Wrongdoing is this, *seeking* to have more than others. (Plato, *Gorgias* 483e)

> (Here τὸ ἀδικεῖν is nominative, subject of ἐστί, and τὸ ... ζητεῖν is another nominative, in apposition to τοῦτο.)

ὁ Περικλῆς πιστεύει ὀρθῶς γιγνώσκειν περὶ **τοῦ μὴ ἐπεξιέναι**.
Pericles believes that he is right about *not going out to attack*.

τῷ ταχέως ἱππεύειν ἐν καιρῷ ἀφίκοντο.
By riding fast they arrived on time.

ἵνα ... χρήσιμοι ὦσιν εἰς **τὸ λέγειν τε καὶ πράττειν**.
... so that they may be useful in *both speech and action*.

The infinitive may have its own subject in the accusative (see sentence no. 8 in Exercise 27g below) and its own complement (such as a direct object), e.g.:

ὁ Ἄδρηστος διὰ **τὸ ἀδελφὸν φονεῦσαι** ὑπὸ τοῦ πατρὸς ἐξηλάθη.
Adrastus because of *slaying his brother* was driven out by his father.

Exercise 27g

Read aloud and translate:

1. ὁ Θεμιστοκλῆς μάλιστα αἴτιος ἦν τοῦ ἐν τοῖς στενοῖς ναυμαχῆσαι.
2. ὁ Κροῖσος ἐς τὸ ἀπορεῖν ἀφῑκτο.
3. τί ἐστι τὸ δίκαιον; τὸ δίκαιόν ἐστι τὸ τοὺς μὲν φίλους ὠφελεῖν, τοὺς δὲ ἐχθροὺς βλάπτειν.
4. ἆρ’ ἔμπειρος (*skilled at + gen.*) εἶ τοῦ κιθαρίζειν;
5. τῷ ταχέως διώκειν τὸ θηρίον δι’ ὀλίγου καταληψόμεθα.

6. πρὸς τὴν πόλιν προσβαλόντες ἐς ἐλπίδα ἦλθον τοῦ ἑλεῖν. (Thucydides 2.56)

7. τῷ ζῆν ἐστί τι ἐναντίον (*opposite*), ὥσπερ τῷ ἐγρηγορέναι τὸ καθεύδειν; (Plato, *Phaedo* 71c)

8. Περικλῆς δὲ στρατηγὸς ὢν καὶ τότε περὶ μὲν τοῦ μὴ ἐπεξιέναι τοὺς Ἀθηναίους τὴν αὐτὴν γνώμην εἶχεν ὥσπερ καὶ ἐν τῇ προτέρᾳ ἐσβολῇ. (Thucydides 2.55)

*   *   *

Η ΛΑΒΔΑ ΣΩΙΖΕΙ ΤΟ ΠΑΙΔΙΟΝ

Read the following passages (adapted from Herodotus 5.92) and answer the comprehension questions:

The following story from Herodotus is concerned with events a hundred years before the time of Croesus. In the seventh century a family called the Bacchiadae rule Corinth. They received an oracle that the child born to Labda, wife of Eetion, would overthrow them. They decided to kill the child as soon as it was born. The child survived and became tyrant of Corinth about 650 B.C.

ὡς δὲ ἔτεκε ἡ Λάβδα, οἱ Βακχίαδαι πέμπουσι δέκα ἄνδρας ἐς τὸν δῆμον ἐν ᾧ ᾤκεε ὁ Ἡετίων, ὡς ἀποκτενέοντας τὸ παιδίον. ἀφικόμενοι δὲ οὗτοι καὶ παρελθόντες ἐς τὴν αὐλήν, τὴν Λάβδαν ᾔτεον τὸ παιδίον. ἡ δὲ οὐκ ἐπισταμένη διὰ τί ἦλθον καὶ δοκέουσα αὐτοὺς φίλους εἶναι τοῦ ἀνδρός, φέρουσα τὸ παιδίον ἔδωκεν αὐτῶν ἑνί. τοῖσι δὲ ἐβεβούλευτο ἐν τῇ ὁδῷ τὸν πρῶτον αὐτῶν λαβόντα τὸ παιδίον   5
ἀποκτεῖναι. ἡ οὖν Λάβδα φέρουσα ἔδωκε, τὸ δὲ παιδίον θείῃ τύχῃ προσεγέλασε τὸν λαβόντα τῶν ἀνδρῶν· ὁ δὲ οἰκτίρᾱς οὐκ ἐδύνατο αὐτὸ ἀποκτεῖναι ἀλλὰ τῷ δευτέρῳ παρέδωκεν, ὁ δὲ τῷ τρίτῳ· οὕτω τε διεξῆλθε διὰ πάντων παραδιδόμενον, οὐδενὸς βουλομένου τὸ ἔργον ἐργάσασθαι.

[**ἔτεκε** (*from* τίκτω) gave birth   **ἡ Λάβδα** Labda   **οἱ Βακχίαδαι** the Bacchiadae   **ὁ Ἡετίων** Eetion   **τὸ παιδίον** the baby   **τὴν αὐλήν** the courtyard   **δοκέουσα** thinking   **ἐβεβούλευτο** (*from* βουλεύομαι) it had been planned that (+ *acc. and infinitive*)   **θείῃ** divine   **προσεγέλασε** (*from* προσγελάω) smiled at   **διεξῆλθε** passed through]

1. What do the Bacchiadae send men to do?
2. What do the men do when they enter the courtyard of Labda's house?
3. What does Labda know of the men's purpose?
4. What had the men agreed upon among themselves?
5. What did the baby do when one of the men took it?
6. To what does Herodotus attribute the baby's action?
7. Why was the man not able to kill the baby?
8. What did he do with it?

ἀποδόντες οὖν τῇ μητρὶ τὸ παιδίον καὶ ἐξελθόντες, ἑστῶτες ἐπὶ τῇ θύρῃ 10
ἀλλήλους ᾐτιῶντο καὶ μάλιστα τὸν πρῶτον λαβόντα, ὅτι οὐκ ἐποίησε κατὰ τὰ
δεδογμένα, ἕως μετὰ πολύν τινα χρόνον ἔδοξεν αὐτοῖς αὖθις ἐσελθοῦσι πᾶσι
μετέχειν τοῦ φόνου. ἡ δὲ Λάβδα πάντα ταῦτα ἤκουε, ἑστῶσα πρὸς αὐτῇ τῇ θύρῃ·
φοβουμένη δὲ μὴ τὸ δεύτερον λαβόντες τὸ παιδίον ἀποκτείνωσι, φέρουσα ἀποκρύπτει
ἐς κυψέλην, ἐπισταμένη ὡς εἰ ἐπανίοιεν, πάντα ἐρευνήσειν μέλλοιεν· ὃ δὴ καὶ 15
ἐγένετο. ἐσελθοῦσι δὲ καὶ ἐρευνήσασι, ὡς οὐκ ἐφαίνετο τὸ παιδίον, ἔδοξεν ἀπιέναι
καὶ λέγειν πρὸς τοὺς πέμψαντας ὡς πάντα ἐποίησαν ἃ ἐκεῖνοι ἐκέλευσαν. οἱ μὲν
δὴ ἀπελθόντες ταῦτα ἔλεγον. μετὰ δὲ ταῦτα ὁ παῖς ηὐξάνετο καὶ τοῦτον τὸν
κίνδῦνον διαφυγών, Κύψελος ὠνομάσθη ἀπὸ τῆς κυψέλης ἐν ᾗ ἐκρύφθη.

[ἑστῶτες standing   ᾐτιῶντο *(from* αἰτιάομαι) they accused   τὰ δεδογμένα
what had been decided   μετέχειν to share in (+ *gen.*)   ἑστῶσα standing
ἀποκρύπτει hides   κυψέλην chest   ἐρευνήσειν *(from* ἐρευνάω) to search
Κύψελος Cypselus]

9. When they left the house, where did the men stop to talk?
10. Whom did they especially accuse?
11. What did the men decide to do now?
12. What did Labda hear and why was she able to hear it?
13. What did she do with the baby? Why did she do it?
14. What did the men do when they returned into the house?
15. What did they decide to tell those who had sent them?
16. Why was the child named Cypselus?

Exercise 27h

Translate into Greek:

1. Cyrus has already arrived at Sardis. We must prepare to fight (*use* ὡς + *future participle*).
2. The army of the enemy, having been drawn up by Cyrus, is waiting on the plain before the city.
3. The camels have been drawn up before the rest of the army. Why has this been done by the Persians?
4. The horses, afraid of the camels, are fleeing. Although we are skilled (ἔμπειρος + *gen.*) at riding horses, now we must fight on foot.
5. We have fought bravely, but we have been defeated by Cyrus' trick (τὸ σόφισμα).

28

Ο ΑΠΟΛΛΩΝ
ΤΟΝ ΚΡΟΙΣΟΝ ΣΩΙΖΕΙ
(α)

Vocabulary

Verbs

ἁλίσκομαι (ἁλ-/ἁλο-),
ἁλώσομαι, ἑάλων *or* ἥλων,
ἑάλωκα *or* ἥλωκα I am
caught, taken

ἀναιρέομαι (*see* αἱρέω *for
principal parts*) I take up, pick
up

δέω, δήσω, ἔδησα, δέδεκα,
δέδεμαι, ἐδέθην I bind

διαφέρει (*see* φέρω *for principal
parts*) (*impersonal + dat.*) it
makes a difference to

ἐπιβαίνω (*see* βαίνω *for
principal parts*) (+ *gen.*) I get
up on, mount, board

κατακαίω, κατακαύσω,
κατέκαυσα, κατα-
κέκαυκα, κατακέκαυμαι,
κατεκαύθην I burn
completely

καταπαύω (*see* παύω *for
principal parts*) I put an end to

πορθέω I sack

προλέγω (*see* λέγω *for
principal parts*) I proclaim

Nouns

ἡ ἀκρόπολις, τῆς ἀκροπόλεως
citadel

ὁ δαίμων, τοῦ δαίμονος
spirit, god, the power
controlling one's destiny,
fate, lot

τὸ δέος, τοῦ δέους fear

ἡ ζωή, τῆς ζωῆς life

ὁ ἱππεύς, τοῦ ἱππέως
horseman, cavalryman

ἡ πυρά, τῆς πυρᾶς funeral
pyre

Preposition

κατά (+ *acc.*) down, on, along,
according to, at, through, with
regard to, after

αἱ Σάρδιες δὲ ἑάλωσαν ὧδε· ἐπειδὴ τεσσερεσκαιδεκάτη ἐγένετο
ἡμέρη πολιορκεομένῳ Κροίσῳ, Κῦρος τῇ στρατιῇ τῇ ἑαυτοῦ
διαπέμψᾱς ἱππέᾱς προεῖπε τῷ πρώτῳ ἐπιβάντι τοῦ τείχεος δῶρα
δώσειν. μετὰ δὲ τοῦτο πειρησαμένης τῆς στρατιῆς, ὡς οὐ προεχώρεε,
ἐνταῦθα τῶν ἄλλων πεπαυμένων ἀνήρ τις Ὑροιάδης ὀνόματι   5
ἐπειρᾶτο προσβαίνων κατὰ τοῦτο τῆς ἀκροπόλεως μέρος ὅπου
οὐδεὶς ἐτέτακτο φύλαξ· ἀπότομός τε γὰρ ἐστι ταύτῃ ἡ ἀκρόπολις καὶ

ἄμαχος. ὁ δὲ Ὑροιάδης οὗτος, ἰδὼν τῇ προτεραίῃ τινὰ τῶν Λυδῶν
κατὰ τοῦτο τῆς ἀκροπόλεως καταβάντα ἐπὶ κυνέην ἄνωθεν
κατακυλισθεῖσαν καὶ ἀνελόμενον, ἐφράσθη καὶ ἐς θυμὸν ἐβάλετο. 10
τότε δὲ δὴ αὐτός τε ἀνεβεβήκει καὶ κατ᾽ αὐτὸν ἄλλοι Περσέων
ἀνέβαινον. προσβάντων δὲ πολλῶν οὕτω δὴ Σάρδιές τε ἑάλωσαν καὶ
πᾶν τὸ ἄστυ ἐπορθέετο.

[ἑάλωσαν: *this aorist is conjugated like* ἔγνων   **τεσσερεσκαιδεκάτη** fourteenth
διαπέμψας sending X (*acc.*) through Y (*dat.*)   **ὡς οὐ προεχώρεε** when there was
no success   **ἀπότομος** steep, sheer   **ἄμαχος** impregnable   **κυνέην** helmet
ἄνωθεν from above   **κατακυλισθεῖσαν** (*from* κατακυλίνδω) which had rolled
down   **ἐς θυμὸν ἐβάλετο** he laid it to heart, thought about it   **ἀνεβεβήκει** he had
climbed up]

κατ᾽ αὐτὸν δὲ Κροῖσον τάδε ἐγένετο. ἦν οἱ παῖς τὰ μὲν ἄλλα
ἐπιεικής, ἄφωνος δέ. ἁλισκομένου δὴ τοῦ τείχεος ἤιε τῶν Περσέων τις 15
ὡς Κροῖσον ἀποκτενέων· καὶ ὁ μὲν Κροῖσος ὁρέων αὐτὸν ἐπιόντα
ὑπὸ τῆς παρεούσης συμφορῆς παρημελήκει οὐδέ τί οἱ διέφερε
ἀποθανεῖν. ὁ δὲ παῖς οὗτος ὁ ἄφωνος, ὡς εἶδε ἐπιόντα τὸν Πέρσην
ὑπὸ δέους ἔρρηξε φωνήν, εἶπε δέ· "ὦ ἄνθρωπε, μὴ κτεῖνε Κροῖσον."
οὗτος μὲν δὴ τοῦτο πρῶτον ἐφθέγξατο, μετὰ δὲ τοῦτο ἤδη ἐφώνεε τὸν 20
πάντα χρόνον τῆς ζωῆς.

[οἱ = αὐτῷ   τὰ . . . ἄλλα in other respects   **ἐπιεικής** able, capable   **ἄφωνος**
dumb, mute   **ἤιε** = *Ionic for* ἤει "was going" (*imperfect of* εἶμι)   **ὁρέων** = *Ionic for*
ὁρῶν   **ὑπό** (+ *gen.*) because of   **παρημελήκει** (*from* παραμελέω) paid (had paid) no
heed   **ἔρρηξε** (*from* ῥήγνυμι) we say "broke his silence" or "broke into speech"
rather than "broke his voice"   **ἐφθέγξατο** (*from* φθέγγομαι) spoke]

οἱ δὲ Πέρσαι τάς τε Σάρδις ἔσχον καὶ αὐτὸν Κροῖσον ἐζώγρησαν,
ἄρξαντα ἔτεα τεσσερεσκαίδεκα καὶ τεσσερεσκαίδεκα ἡμέρας
πολιορκηθέντα, κατὰ τὸ χρηστήριόν τε καταπαύσαντα τὴν ἑαυτοῦ
μεγάλην ἀρχήν. λαβόντες δὲ αὐτὸν οἱ Πέρσαι ἤγαγον παρὰ Κῦρον. 25
ὁ δὲ ποιήσας μεγάλην πυρὴν ἀνεβίβασε ἐπ᾽ αὐτὴν τόν τε Κροῖσον ἐν
πέδῃσι δεδεμένον καὶ δὶς ἑπτὰ Λυδῶν παῖδας, εἴτε ἐν νόῳ ἔχων αὐτοὺς
θεῶν τινι θύσειν, εἴτε πυθόμενος τὸν Κροῖσον εἶναι θεοσεβέα τοῦδε
εἵνεκα ἀνεβίβασε ἐπὶ τὴν πυρήν, βουλόμενος γιγνώσκειν εἴ τις αὐτὸν
δαιμόνων σώσει ὥστε μὴ ζῶντα κατακαυθῆναι. 30

[ἐζώγρησαν (*from* ζωγρέω) took alive, captured   **τεσσερεσκαίδεκα** fourteen
ἀνεβίβασε (*from* ἀναβιβάζω) put him up on   **πέδῃσι** shackles   **δὶς ἑπτά** twice
seven   **θεοσεβέα** god-fearing, religious]

—adapted from Herodotus 1.84–86.2

Principal Parts: Another Verb from Unrelated Stems

φέρω (φερ-/οἰ-/ἐνεκ-/ἐνεγκ-), οἴσω, ἤνεγκα *or* ἤνεγκον, ἐν-ήνοχ-α, ἐν-ήνεγ-μαι, ἠνέχθην I carry, (of roads) lead

Word Study

In what branches of medicine do the following specialize?

1. gynecologist
2. pharmacologist
3. physiotherapist
4. pediatrician
5. gerontologist
6. anesthetist

Give the Greek roots from which these words are formed.

Grammar

1. First Perfect and Pluperfect Active

For the perfect active, reduplicate or augment the stem, as for the perfect middle. Verbs that reduplicate the stem in the perfect are augmented to form the pluperfect. The forms of the perfect and pluperfect active of λύω are as follows (note the reduplication, the short-vowel stem λυ-, the presence of the letter κ in all forms, and the augment in the pluperfect):

Perfect

Indicative	Imperative	Infinitive	Participle
λέ-λυ-κα		λε-λυ-κέναι	λε-λυ-κώς, -κυῖα,
λέ-λυ-κας	λελυκὼς ἴσθι		-κός
λέ-λυ-κε(ν)			
λε-λύ-καμεν			
λ-λύ-κατε	λελυκότες ἔστε		
λε-λύ-κᾱσι(ν)			

Subjunctive	*or (very rarely)*	Subjunctive
λελυκὼς ὦ		λελύκω
λελυκὼς ᾖς		λελύκῃς
λελυκὼς ᾖ		λελύκῃ
λελυκότες ὦμεν		λελύκωμεν
λελυκότες ἦτε		λελύκητε
λελυκότες ὦσι(ν)		λελύκωσι(ν)

Optative	*or (occasionally)*	Optative
λελυκὼς εἴην		λελύκοιμι
λελυκὼς εἴης		λελύκοις
λελυκὼς εἴη		λελύκοι

λελυκότες εἴημεν *or* εἶμεν   λελύκοιμεν
λελυκότες εἴητε *or* εἶτε   λελύκοιτε
λελυκότες εἴησαν *or* εἶεν   λελύκοιεν

Pluperfect Indicative

ἐ-λε-λύ-κη
ἐ-λε-λύ-κης
ἐ-λε-λύ-κει(ν)
ἐ-λε-λύ-κεμεν
ἐ-λε-λύ-κετε
ἐ-λε-λύ-κεσαν

The declension of the perfect active participle is as follows:

	Masculine	*Feminine*	*Neuter*
Nom.	λελυκώς	λελυκυῖα	λελυκός
Gen.	λελυκότος	λελυκυίᾱς	λελυκότος
Dat.	λελυκότι	λελυκυίᾳ	λελυκότι
Acc.	λελυκότα	λελυκυῖαν	λελυκός
Nom.	λελυκότες	λελυκυῖαι	λελυκότα
Gen.	λελυκότων	λελυκυιῶν	λελυκότων
Dat.	λελυκόσι	λελυκυίαις	λελυκόσι
Acc.	λελυκότας	λελυκυίᾱς	λελυκότα

The same rules apply for reduplication and augment in the perfect and pluperfect active as in the perfect and pluperfect middle and passive (see Chapter 27, Grammar 1), thus, for example, ἀμελέω > ἠμέληκα.

Contract verbs lengthen the stem vowel, e.g.:

φιλέω > πεφίληκα
τῑμάω > τετίμηκα
δηλόω > δεδήλωκα

Consonant stems:

a. Verbs with stems ending in dentals (δ, ζ, θ) drop the final consonant, e.g.:

δείδ-ω > δέ-δοι-κα
νομίζ-ω > νε-νόμι-κα
πείθ-ω > πέ-πει-κα

b. Some verbs with stems ending in liquids (λ, μ, ν, ρ) drop the final consonant of the stem, e.g.:

κρῑ́ν-ω > κέ-κρι-κα

Others extend the stem with an ε, which is lengthened to η in the perfect, e.g.:

μέν-ω (μεν-/μενε-) > με-μένη-κα
μανθάνω (μαθ-/μαθε-) > με-μάθη-κα
εὑρίσκω (εὑρ-/εὑρε-) > ηὕρη-κα
τρέχω (δραμ-/δραμε-) > δε-δράμη-κα

c. A few verbs reverse vowel and consonant in the stem (metathesis), e.g.:

βάλλω (βαλ-/βλη-) > βέ-βλη-κα
ἀπο-θνῄσκω (θαν-/θνη-) > τέ-θνη-κα

2. Second Perfect and Pluperfect Active

Some verbs do not have the κ that appears in all of the forms given above; these are called second perfects and pluperfects, e.g.:

Present: γράφ-ω
Second perfect: γέ-γραφ-α
Second pluperfect: ἐ-γε-γράφ-η

Most verbs with stems in labials (β, π, φ) and gutturals (γ, κ, χ) form second perfects and usually aspirate the final consonant of the stem, e.g.:

ἄγ-ω > ἦχ-α
δείκνῡμι (δεικ-) > δέ-δειχ-α
κρύπ-τ-ω (κρυφ-) > κέ-κρυφ-α
τάττω (ταγ-) > τέ-ταχ-α

Note the change of vowel from ε to o in verbs with second perfects, e.g.:

πέμπ-ω > πέπομφ-α
τρέπ-ω > τέτροφ-α
λείπ-ω > λέλοιπ-α
κτείν-ω > ἔκτον-α

3. Aspect

The perfect tense records the results of an action completed in the past (see Chapter 27, Grammar 1) and thus describes a present state. Many verbs in the perfect tense can therefore best be translated with the present tense in English, e.g.:

ἀπο-θνῄσκω (θαν-/θνη-) > τέθνηκα (no prefix in the perfect) (I have died and therefore) I am dead   οἱ τεθνηκότες = the dead
ἵστημι (στα-/στη-) > ἕστηκα (I have stood up and therefore) I stand
βαίνω (βα-) > βέβηκα (I have taken a step, made a stand and therefore) I stand, stand firm, am set

Note the following sentences with verbs in the pluperfect from the reading passage at the beginning of this chapter:

τότε δὲ δὴ αὐτός τε **ἀνεβεβήκει** καὶ κατ' αὐτὸν ἄλλοι Περσέων ἀνέβαινον.
Next thing, he himself *had climbed up*, and others of the Persians were climbing up after him.
(The action of Hyroides was completed before the others ascended, and hence the pluperfect ἀνεβεβήκει is used in the Greek.)

καὶ ὁ μὲν Κροῖσος ὁρέων αὐτὸν ἐπιόντα ὑπὸ τῆς παρεούσης συμφορῆς **παρημελήκει** οὐδέ τι αὐτῷ διέφερε ἀποθανεῖν.
And Croesus seeing him coming against (him), because of his present misfortune, *paid no heed (had got into a state of heedlessness)*, nor did it make any difference to him at all whether he died (to die).
(The pluperfect παρημελήκει implies that Croesus had gotten into a state of heedlessness by the time he was attacked; therefore at that moment in time he did not care whether he died or not.)

Exercise 28a

Change the following present forms to the corresponding perfect forms:

1. λύουσι
2. λύοντες
3. μανθάνειν
4. πέμπεις

5. ἀποθνῄσκει
6. ἄγετε
7. δηλοῦμεν
8. νῑκῶντες

9. δεικνύᾱσι
10. λείπειν
11. γράφουσα
12. πείθομεν

Change the following present forms to the corresponding pluperfect forms:

1. λύομεν
2. τῑμᾷ

3. ἄγουσι
4. πείθεις

5. πέμπουσι
6. δηλῶ

Exercise 28b

Read aloud and translate:

1. ἆρα πεποίηκας πάνθ' ὅσα κεκέλευκεν ὁ πατήρ;
2. ἆρα πέπεικέ σε ἡ μήτηρ οἴκοι μένειν;
3. οἱ Ἀθηναῖοι ἐς μέγιστον κίνδῡνον καθεστήκασιν.
4. οἵ τε ὁπλῖται ὑπὸ τῶν πολεμίων νενίκηνται καὶ αὐτὸς ὁ στρατηγὸς τέθνηκεν.
5. οἱ ἐν τῇ μάχῃ τεθνηκότες ὑπὸ τοῦ δήμου τετίμηνται.
6. οἱ δοῦλοι τοὺς βοῦς ἐλελύκεσαν πρὶν καταδῦναι (*set*) τὸν ἥλιον.
7. διὰ τί τὸ ἄροτρον ἐν τῷ ἀγρῷ λελοίπατε;
8. ἐγὼ νεᾱνίᾱς τότε ὢν οὔπω ἐμεμαθήκη τὴν γεωμετρίᾱν.
9. νῦν δὲ σοφιστής τις πάντα τὰ μαθηματικά με δεδίδαχεν.
10. ὁ Ἀρχιμήδης ἐν τῷ λουτρῷ (*bath*) καθήμενος, ἐξαίφνης βοήσᾱς, "ηὕρηκα," ἔφη.

Exercise 28c

Translate into Greek:

1. The slaves have loosened the oxen and have led (*use* ἄγω) them home.
2. We have sent the women and children to the islands.
3. The woman is standing by the door, waiting for her husband.
4. Why have you done this? The teacher has shown you what you ought to do.
5. It is better to be dead than to live shamefully.

Rationalism and Mysticism

In the essay on Greek medicine (Chapter 11), we saw that the Ionian cosmologists attempted to explain the world in terms of natural causation. This intellectual revolution involved rejection of the old mythical explanations of phenomena and led inevitably to criticism of the traditional religion, to agnosticism, and to atheism. The criticism was not all destructive. For instance, the poet and philosopher Xenophanes, born ca. 570 B.C., attacked the immorality of the gods as they are portrayed in myth: "Homer and Hesiod attributed to the gods all that is a shame and a rebuke to men, theft, adultery, and deceit" (Kirk and Raven, *The Presocratic Philosophers*, Cambridge, 1964, p. 169). He criticizes anthropomorphism: "The Ethiopians say that their gods are snub-nosed and black, the Thracians that theirs are blue-eyed and red-haired. . . . There is one god, like mortals neither in body nor in thought (*ibid.*, pp. 171 and 173).

An example of the agnostic is provided by Protagoras, the first and greatest of the sophists (see essay, Chapter 24), who begins his work *On the Gods* as follows: "Concerning the gods, I am unable to discover whether they exist or not, or what they are like in form" (*Protagoras*, fragment 4).

The clearest surviving statement of the atheist's position is a fragment from a play by Critias (born ca. 460 B.C.):

> There was a time when the life of men was disorderly and beast-like. . . . Then, as I believe, man laid down laws to chastise, and whoever sinned was punished. Then when the laws prevented men from open deeds of violence but they continued to commit them in secret, I believe that a man of shrewd and subtle mind invented for men the fear of the gods, so that there might be something to frighten the wicked even if they acted, spoke, or thought in secret. From this motive he introduced the conception of divinity. (Translated by Guthrie, *The Sophists*, Cambridge, 1971, pp. 82 and 243)

The sixth century saw the development of religious ideas that were to have profound influence on Western thought, including Christian theology. The central tenet of this new mysticism was the duality of body and soul. The soul was conceived as a spiritual entity that existed before its confinement in the body and that survives the body's dissolution. This teaching was attributed to a poet-prophet named Orpheus, who was said to have lived in Thrace; his followers were called Orphics. Little is known about their beliefs. We are on firmer ground with Pythagoras, who seems to have incorporated Orphic beliefs into his teaching. Born ca. 550 B.C. in Samos, he settled in southern Italy, where he founded a religious community of men and women. He is best remembered today as a mathematician, but he also taught a way of life that was based on the belief that our present life is but a preparation for a further life or lives. The soul is divine and immortal; in successive reincarnations it is imprisoned in the body, and in its lives it must try to rid itself of bodily impurity by living as well as possible. Eventually it may be freed from the cycle of life and death and return to its divine origins.

The beliefs we have outlined were those of a limited circle of intellectuals, but the ordinary Greeks, who adhered to the traditional religion, could also find comfort in mysteries. There were various mystery cults in different parts of Greece, of which the most important were the Eleusinian mysteries. Starting as an ancient agrarian cult in honor of Demeter, goddess of grain, these mysteries by the middle of the seventh century offered initiates a blessed afterlife, from which the uninitiated were excluded: "Blessed is the man among mortals on earth who has seen these things. But he who has not taken part in the rites and has no share in them, he never knows these good things when he is dead beneath the grim darkness" (Homeric Hymn to Demeter, ca. 625 B.C.).

The mysteries were open to all, men and women, Athenians and foreigners, slave and free. On the first day of the festival, the sacred herald made a proclamation, inviting all who wished to be initiated to assemble; they were warned that they must be of pure hands and "have a soul conscious of no evil and have lived well and justly." After three days of sacrifice and preparation, the μύσται, numbering over 10,000, made their pilgrimage of fourteen miles from Athens to Eleusis, led by the officials of the Eleusinian cult. The last day was spent in fasting and sacrifice. In the evening the rites were performed in the Hall of the Mysteries. The rites were secret, and all who participated took a vow of silence, so that we know very little of what happened. At the climax of the ceremony, in the darkness of the night, the ἱεροφάντης (revealer of holy things) appeared in a brilliant light and revealed the holy objects. We are told that these included a sheaf of grain, which may have had symbolical significance, offering the hope of resurrection.

The cult of Eleusis, with its emphasis on moral as well as ritual purity and with the hope it offered the initiates of a blessed life hereafter, answered a deep spiritual need. The mysteries were celebrated with unbroken continuity from the archaic age until the site at Eleusis was finally devastated by Alaric the Goth in A.D. 395. "In a civilization where official religion did little to support the soul, Eleusis provided some comfort to those who faced the anxieties of this world and the next" (Parke, *Festivals of the Athenians*, London, Thames & Hudson, 1977, p. 71).

Ο ΑΠΟΛΛΩΝ
ΤΟΝ ΚΡΟΙΣΟΝ ΣΩΙΖΕΙ
(β)

Vocabulary

Verbs

αἱρέομαι (*see* αἱρέω *for principal parts*) I choose

ἀναμιμνῄσκω, ἀναμνήσω, ἀνέμνησα I remind someone (*acc.*) of something (*acc. or gen.*)

  μέμνημαι (*perfect middle = present*) I have reminded myself, I remember

  ἐμνήσθην (*aorist passive in middle sense*) I remembered

  μνησθήσομαι (*future passive in middle sense*) I will remember

ἀναστενάζω (*see* στενάζω *for principal parts*) I groan

ἐνθῡμέομαι, ἐνθῡμήσομαι, ἐντεθῡμημαι, ἐνεθῡμήθην I take to heart, ponder

ἐπικαλέω (*see* καλέω *for principal parts*) I call upon; (*middle*) I call upon X to help

μεταγιγνώσκω (*see* γιγνώσκω *for principal parts*) I change my mind, repent

παρίσταμαι, παρέστην, παρέστηκα (+ *dat.*) I stand near, stand by, help

Nouns

ἡ ἡσυχίᾱ, τῆς ἡσυχίᾱς quietness

ἡ νεφέλη, τῆς νεφέλης cloud

ὁ ὄλβος, τοῦ ὄλβου happiness, bliss, prosperity

ἡ σῑγή, τῆς σῑγῆς silence

Adjectives

ἀνόητος, -ον foolish

ἔσχατος, -η, -ον furthest, extreme

Preposition

ἀντί (+ *gen.*) instead of, against

Expression

περὶ οὐδενὸς ποιοῦμαι I consider of no importance

ὁ μὲν Κῦρος ἐποίεε ταῦτα, ὁ δὲ Κροῖσος ἑστηκὼς ἐπὶ τῆς πυρῆς, καίπερ ἐν κακῷ ἐὼν τοσούτῳ, ἐμνήσθη τὸν τοῦ Σόλωνος λόγον, ὅτι οὐδεὶς τῶν ζώντων εἴη ὄλβιος. ὡς δὲ τοῦτο ἐμνήσθη ἀναστενάξᾱς ἐκ πολλῆς ἡσυχίης τρὶς ὠνόμασε, "Σόλων." καὶ Κῦρος ἀκούσᾱς ἐκέλευσε τοὺς ἑρμηνέᾱς ἐρέσθαι τὸν Κροῖσον τίνα τοῦτον ἐπικαλέοιτο. Κροῖσος δὲ πρῶτον μὲν σῑγὴν εἶχεν ἐρωτώμενος, τέλος δὲ ὡς ἠναγκάζετο, εἶπε ὅτι ἦλθε παρ' ἑαυτὸν ὁ Σόλων ἐὼν Ἀθηναῖος

καὶ θεησάμενος πάντα τὸν ἑαυτοῦ ὄλβον περὶ οὐδενὸς ἐποιήσατο,
καὶ αὐτῷ πάντα ἀποβεβήκοι ᾗπερ ἐκεῖνος εἶπεν.

[τρίς three times   τοὺς ἑρμηνέας interpreters   ἀποβεβήκοι (perfect optative
of ἀποβαίνω) had turned out]

ὁ μὲν Κροῖσος ταῦτα ἐξηγήσατο, τῆς δὲ πυρῆς ἤδη ἀμμένης   10
ἐκαίετο τὰ ἔσχατα. καὶ ὁ Κῦρος ἀκούσας τῶν ἑρμηνέων ἃ Κροῖσος
εἶπε, μεταγνούς τε καὶ ἐνθυμεόμενος ὅτι καὶ αὐτὸς ἄνθρωπος ἐὼν
ἄλλον ἄνθρωπον, γενόμενον ἑαυτοῦ εὐδαιμονίῃ οὐκ ἐλάσσονα,
ζῶντα πυρῇ διδοίη, καὶ ἐπιστάμενος ὅτι οὐδὲν εἴη τῶν ἐν ἀνθρώποις
ἀσφαλές, ἐκέλευσε σβεννύναι ὡς τάχιστα τὸ καιόμενον πῦρ καὶ   15
καταβιβάζειν Κροῖσόν τε καὶ τοὺς μετὰ Κροίσου. καὶ οἱ πειρώμενοι
οὐκ ἐδύναντο ἔτι τοῦ πυρὸς ἐπικρατῆσαι.

[ἀμμένης (from ἅπτω I touch, set on fire) kindled, lit   σβεννύναι (from σβέννυμι)
(his men) to put out   καταβιβάζειν to bring down   ἐπικρατῆσαι (+ gen.) to
master, get control of]

ἐνταῦθα λέγεται ὑπὸ τῶν Λυδῶν τὸν Κροῖσον, μαθόντα τὴν
Κύρου μετάγνωσιν, βοῆσαι τὸν Ἀπόλλωνα, καλέοντα παραστῆναι
καὶ σῶσαί μιν ἐκ τοῦ παρέοντος κακοῦ· τὸν μὲν δακρύοντα   20
ἐπικαλέεσθαι τὸν θεόν, ἐκ δὲ αἰθρίης καὶ νηνεμίης συνδραμεῖν
ἐξαίφνης νεφέλας, καὶ χειμῶνά τε γενέσθαι καὶ πολὺ ὕδωρ,
σβεσθῆναί τε τὴν πυρήν. οὕτω δὴ μαθόντα τὸν Κῦρον ὡς εἴη ὁ
Κροῖσος καὶ θεοφιλὴς καὶ ἀνὴρ ἀγαθός, ἐρέσθαι τάδε· "Κροῖσε, τίς σε
ἀνθρώπων ἔπεισε ἐπὶ γῆν τὴν ἐμὴν στρατευόμενον πολέμιον ἀντὶ   25
φίλου ἐμοὶ καταστῆναι;" ὁ δὲ εἶπε· "ὦ βασιλεῦ, ἐγὼ ταῦτα ἔπρηξα τῇ
σῇ μὲν εὐδαιμονίῃ, τῇ δὲ ἐμαυτοῦ κακοδαιμονίῃ· αἴτιος δὲ τούτων
ἐγένετο ὁ Ἑλλήνων θεὸς ἐπάρας ἐμὲ στρατεύεσθαι. οὐδεὶς γὰρ οὕτω
ἀνόητός ἐστι ὅστις πόλεμον πρὸ εἰρήνης αἱρέεται· ἐν μὲν γὰρ τῇ
εἰρήνῃ οἱ παῖδες τοὺς πατέρας θάπτουσι, ἐν δὲ τῷ πολέμῳ οἱ πατέρες   30
τοὺς παῖδας. ἀλλὰ ταῦτα δαίμονί που φίλον ἦν οὕτω γενέσθαι." ὁ
μὲν ταῦτα ἔλεγε, Κῦρος δὲ αὐτὸν λύσας καθεῖσέ τε ἐγγὺς ἑαυτοῦ καὶ
μεγάλως ἐτίμα.

[μετάγνωσιν change of mind   μιν him   αἰθρίης . . . νηνεμίης clear sky . . .
windless calm   σβεσθῆναι (from σβέννυμι; aorist passive infinitive in indirect
statement) was put out   θεοφιλής dear to the gods   οὕτω δὴ . . . τὸν
Κῦρον . . . ἐρέσθαι still indirect statement, reporting what was said   καταστῆναι
to become   κακοδαιμονίη bad luck   ἐπάρας (from ἐπαίρω) having raised,
prompted, urged, induced   πρό in preference to   που I suppose   καθεῖσε (aorist
of καθίζω) made X sit down]

—adapted from Herodotus 1.86.3–87

Principal Parts: Verbs Adding ε to Stem

βούλομαι (βουλ-/βουλε-), βουλήσομαι, βεβούλημαι, ἐβουλήθην I want, wish

ἐθέλω (ἐθελ-/ἐθελε-) or θέλω, (imperfect) ἤθελον, ἐθελήσω, ἠθέλησα, ἠθέληκα I wish, am willing

μάχομαι (μαχ-/μαχε-), μαχοῦμαι, ἐμαχεσάμην, μεμάχημαι I fight, fight with (+ dat.)

χαίρω (χαρ-/χαρε-/χαιρε-), χαιρήσω, κεχάρηκα, ἐχάρην (I rejoiced) I rejoice; (+ participle) I am glad to

Word Building

The following verbs have present reduplication, i.e., in the present and imperfect only, the first consonant of the stem + ι are prefixed to the verb stem:

δί-δω-μι	(δω-/δο-)	γί-γν-ομαι	(γεν-/γον-)
τί-θη-μι	(θη-/θε-)	γι-γνώ-σκω	(γνω-/γνο-)
ἵ-στη-μι	(στη-/στα-)	ἀνα-μι-μνή-σκω	(μνη-/μνα-)

Give the meaning of the following sets formed from these verbs. Note that nouns and adjectives formed from such verbs are formed from the verb stem proper, not the reduplicated form:

1. δω-/δο-   ἡ δόσις   τὸ δῶρον   προ-δο- >   ὁ προδότης   ἡ προδοσίᾱ
2. θη-/θε-   ἡ θέσις   ὁ νομο-θέτης   ἡ ὑπό-θεσις
3. στη-/στα-   ἡ στάσις   προ-στα- >   ὁ προστάτης   ἡ προστασίᾱ
4. γεν-/γον-   τὸ γένος   ἡ γένεσις   ὁ πρόγονος
5. γνω-/γνο-   ἡ γνώμη   ἡ γνῶσις   γνωστός, -ή, -όν
6. μνη-/μνα-   ἡ μνήμη   τὸ μνῆμα   τὸ μνημεῖον   ἀεί-μνηστος, -ον

Grammar

4. Verbs Found Most Commonly in the Perfect Tense

The following verbs are found most commonly in the perfect tense with present meanings. The pluperfect of these verbs is translated as imperfect in English. The present forms given below in parentheses do not occur in Attic Greek:

Present	Aorist	Perfect
(δείδω)	ἔδεισα I feared	δέδοικα I am afraid
(ἔθω)		εἴωθα I am acccustomed to
(εἴκω)		ἔοικα I am like, I am likely to; ὡς ἔοικε as it seems
(ἰδ-)		οἶδα I know
φύω I produce	ἔφῡσα I produced	πέφῡκα I am by nature

5. The Uses of ὡς

You have met all the following uses already, but this summary will be helpful.

a. The word ὡς may be used as a conjunction with a verb in the indicative, meaning "as," e.g.:

σώφρων ἐστὶν ὁ νεᾱνίᾱς, **ὡς ἐμοὶ δοκεῖ/ὡς ἔοικε/ὡς λέγεται.**
The young man is sensible, *as it seems to me /as it seems /as it is said.*

b. As a conjunction used with the indicative, ὡς may also mean "when," e.g.:

ὡς ἀφίκοντο, τὸν δοῦλον ἐκάλεσαν.
When they arrived, they called the slave.

c. When introducing an indirect statement, ὡς is a conjunction meaning "that" and is equivalent to ὅτι, e.g.:

εἶπεν ὁ ἄγγελος **ὡς πάρεισιν οἱ πρέσβεις.**
The messenger said *that the ambassadors were present.*

d. As an adverb, ὡς may modify an adjective or another adverb and mean "how," e.g.:

ἐθαύμαζον **ὡς ταχέως** τρέχουσιν οἱ παῖδες.
I was surprised *how quickly* the boys ran.

e. Prepositional phrases may be used with ὡς to express purpose, e.g.:

ὁ Ἀρχίδαμος περὶ τὰς Ἀχαρνὰς **ὡς ἐς μάχην** ταξάμενος ἔμεινε.
Archidamus stayed around Acharnae drawn up *as for battle* (i.e., *for the purpose of fighting*).

f. A future participle may be introduced by ὡς to express purpose, e.g.:

παρεσκευάζοντο **ὡς πολεμήσοντες.**
They were preparing themselves *to make war* (literally, *as being about to make war*).

g. A participle may also be used with ὡς to express alleged cause, e.g.:

τὸν νεᾱνίᾱν ἐκόλασαν **ὡς ἀδικήσαντα.**
They punished the young man *for having done wrong.*

τὸν γέροντα οἰκτῑρουσιν **ὡς μαινόμενον.**
They pity the old man *as being mad.*

h. With a superlative adjective or adverb, ὡς means "as . . . as possible," e.g.:

ὡς πλεῖστοι *as many as possible*
ὡς τάχιστα *as quickly as possible*

The verb δύναμαι is sometimes added, e.g.:

ἤρεσσον ὡς τάχιστα ἐδύναντο.
They rowed *as quickly as they could.*

Exercise 28d

Read aloud and translate:

1. αὕτη ἡ γυνή, ὡς ἔοικε, σωφρονεστάτη πέφῡκεν.
2. οὐκ οἶδα γυναῖκα σωφρονεστέρᾱν· βούλομαι οὖν γαμεῖν (*to marry*) αὐτήν.
3. δέδοικα δὲ μὴ ὁ πατὴρ οὐκ ἐθέλῃ αὐτήν μοι ἐκδοῦναι.
4. οἱ νεᾱνίαι ἀνδρειότατοι πεφῡκότες οὐκ ἐδεδοίκεσαν.
5. οἱ παῖδες εἰώθᾱσιν εἰς διδασκάλων καθ' ἡμέρᾱν φοιτᾶν.
6. ἀλλ' οὐκ αἰεὶ μέμνηνται ὅσα λέγει ὁ διδάσκαλος.
7. ὁ Κροῖσος ἐμνήσθη πάνθ' ὅσα εἶπεν ὁ Σόλων.
8. τῶν Ἀθηναίων οἱ πολλοί (*the majority*) ἐν τοῖς ἀγροῖς οἰκεῖν εἰώθεσαν.
9. ὡς ἐς τὸν Πειραιᾶ ἀφῑκόμεθα, εὐθὺς ἐσπεύσαμεν πρὸς τὴν ἀγορᾱν.
10. ἐκεῖ δὲ ἠκούσαμέν τινος λέγοντος ὡς αἱ νῆες ἤδη ἐς τὸν λιμένα πεπλευ-
    κότες εἴησαν.
11. ἴωμεν οὖν πρὸς τὸν λιμένα ὡς τὰς ναῦς θεᾱσόμενοι.
12. ὡς καλαί εἰσιν αἱ νῆες· ὡς ταχέως ἐσπλέουσιν.
13. οὗτος ὁ ναύτης λέγει ὡς δύο νῆες οὔπω (*not yet*) ἀφῑγμέναι εἰσίν.
14. ἤδη τὰς ναῦς ἔξεστιν ἰδεῖν πρὸς τὴν Σαλαμῖνα ὡς τάχιστα πλεούσᾱς.
15. ἄκουε δή· ἐς ὀργὴν καθέστηκεν ὁ ναύαρχος, ὡς ἔοικε, καὶ τοὺς ἐρέτᾱς
    (*rowers*) μέμφεται ὡς βραδέως ἐρέσσοντας.

Exercise 28e

Translate into Greek:

1. When we returned home, we saw mother standing by the door.
2. Although she is kindly by nature, she became angry and blamed us
    for returning late.
3. "I have waited all day," she said, "and I was afraid that you were
    dead."
4. "We have come as quickly as possible," I said, "and we are not
    usually late (= we are not accustomed to return late)."

*   *   *

Ο ΚΡΟΙΣΟΣ ΓΙΓΝΩΣΚΕΙ ΤΗΝ ΕΑΥΤΟΥ ΑΜΑΡΤΙΑΝ

*Read the following passages (adapted from Herodotus 1.90–91) and answer the
comprehension questions:*

ὁ δὲ Κῦρος τὸν Κροῖσον θαυμάζων τῆς σοφίης εἵνεκα ἐκέλευε αὐτὸν αἰτεῖν
ἥντινα ἂν δόσιν βούληται. ὁ δὲ Κροῖσος εἶπε· "ὦ δέσποτα, χαριῇ μοι μάλιστα, ἐάν
με ἐᾷς τὸν θεὸν τῶν Ἑλλήνων, ὃν ἐγὼ ἐτίμησα μάλιστα, ἐρέσθαι εἰ ἐξαπατᾶν

τοὺς εὖ ποιέοντας νόμος ἐστί οἱ." Κῦρος δὲ ἤρετο διὰ τί τοῦτο αἰτέει. Κροῖσος δὲ
πάντα οἱ ἐξηγέετο, τάς τε ἀποκρίσεις τῶν χρηστηρίων διεξιὼν καὶ τὰ ἀναθήματα   5
ἃ ἐς Δελφοὺς ἔπεμψε καὶ ὅπως ἐπαρθεὶς τῷ μαντείῳ ἐστρατεύσατο ἐπὶ τοὺς
Πέρσας. Κῦρος δὲ γελάσας εἶπε· "καὶ τούτου τεύξεαι παρ' ἐμοῦ καὶ ἄλλου παντὸς
οὗ ἂν δέῃ."

[δόσιν gift   ἐξαπατᾶν to deceive   οἱ (dative of possession) for him, his   τὰς
ἀποκρίσεις the answers   διεξιών (from διεξέρχομαι) going through in detail,
relating   ἐπαρθείς (from ἐπαίρω) having been raised, urged, induced   τεύξεαι =
τεύξῃ (future of τυγχάνω) you will get (+ gen.)]

1. Why does Cyrus admire Croesus?
2. What does Cyrus order Croesus to do?
3. What does Croesus want to ask the Greek god in Delphi?
4. What three things does Croesus recount to Cyrus?
5. What is Cyrus' reaction and response?

ὡς δὲ ταῦτα ἤκουσε ὁ Κροῖσος πέμπων ἀγγέλους ἐς Δελφοὺς ἐκέλευε αὐτοὺς
τιθέντας τὰς πέδας ἐν τῷ ἱερῷ τὸν θεὸν ἐρωτᾶν εἰ οὔ τι ἐπαισχύνεται τοῖσι   10
μαντείοισι ἐπάρας Κροῖσον στρατεύεσθαι ἐπὶ Πέρσας.

[τὰς πέδας the shackles (that Croesus wore when he was bound on the pyre)
ἐπαισχύνεται he is ashamed]

6. What did Croesus order the messengers to do first when they arrived in
    Delphi?
7. What were the messengers to ask the god?

ἀφικομένοισι δὲ τοῖσι Λυδοῖσι καὶ λέγουσι τὰ ἐντεταλμένα ἡ Πυθίη εἶπε τάδε·
"τὴν πεπρωμένην μοῖραν ἀδύνατόν ἐστι ἀποφυγεῖν καὶ θεῷ. κατὰ δὲ τὸ μαντεῖον
τὸ γενόμενον οὐκ ὀρθῶς Κροῖσος μέμφεται· προηγόρευε γὰρ ὁ Ἀπόλλων, ἐὰν
στρατεύηται ἐπὶ Πέρσας, μεγάλην ἀρχὴν καταλύσειν. τὸν δὲ εὖ μέλλοντα   15
βουλεύεσθαι ἔχρην ἐπερέσθαι πότερον τὴν ἑαυτοῦ ἢ τὴν Κύρου λέγοι ἀρχήν." ταῦτα
μὲν ἡ Πυθίη ἀπεκρίνατο τοῖσι Λυδοῖσι, οἱ δὲ ἐπανῆλθον ἐς Σάρδις καὶ ταῦτα
ἀπήγγειλαν Κροίσῳ. ὁ δὲ ἀκούσας συνέγνω ἑαυτοῦ εἶναι τὴν ἁμαρτίᾶν καὶ οὐ τοῦ
θεοῦ.

[τὰ ἐντεταλμένα (from ἐντέλλω) the things that had been commanded = Croesus'
commands   πεπρωμένην (from πόρω I furnish, offer, give) fated   μοῖραν fate (=
portion, allotment, lot)   καί even   προηγόρευε foretold   ἐπερέσθαι to ask in
addition   ἀπήγγειλαν announced   συνέγνω (from συγγιγνώσκω) he
acknowledged, admitted   τὴν ἁμαρτίᾶν the mistake]

8.   What does the Pythia say is impossible?
9.   Does the Pythia agree with Croesus' criticism of the oracle?
10. What, exactly, had the oracle said?
11. What should Croesus have asked in addition?
12. What words suggest that the Pythia thinks that Croesus was not
     sufficiently cautious?
13. Whom does Croesus finally blame?

Exercise 28f

Translate into Greek:

1. Croesus has sent messengers to Delphi to ask the god why he has betrayed (**προδίδωμι**) him (**ἑαυτόν**).
2. The messengers have arrived at Delphi, and, standing in the temple, have consulted the oracle.
3. The Pythia has interpreted (**ἐξηγέομαι**) the oracle of Apollo; the god blames Croesus for not being prudent.
4. Croesus, having heard (**ἀκούω**, *perfect* **ἀκήκοα**) the oracle, knows that he himself was wrong.
5. "Alas, alas," he says, "how foolish (**ἀνόητος, -ον**) I was! I myself, as it seems, have destroyed my own empire."

*   *   *

ΑΛΛΟΣ ΛΟΓΟΣ ΠΕΡΙ ΤΟΥ ΚΡΟΙΣΟΥ

ὁ Κροῖσος τῆς πυρῆς ἐπιβεβηκὼς σπονδὴν ποιεῖται.

Vocabulary

1   ἐπεί "for"   καί "even"
    δαμασίππου "horse-taming"
2   ἀρχᾱγέτᾱν = ἀρχηγέτην "ruler"
3   εὖτε "when"
    τᾱ̀ν πεπρωμένᾱν (= τὴν πεπρωμένην) . . . κρίσιν "the fated judgment"
4   Ζηνὸς τελέσσαντος = Διὸς τελέσαντος "Zeus having brought to pass"
5   Περσᾶν = Περσῶν   ἁλίσκοντο = ἡλίσκοντο
6   ὁ χρῡσάορος . . . Ἀπόλλων "Apollo of the golden sword"
7   φύλαξ' = ἐφύλαξε   ἄελπτον ἆμαρ "the unexpected day"
8   μολών "having come"
    πολυδάκρυον . . . δουλοσύνᾱν "tearful slavery"
9   μίμνειν = μένειν "to wait for"
10   χαλκοτειχέος . . . αὐλᾶς "the bronze-walled courtyard"
    προπάροιθεν (+ *gen.*) "before," "in front of"

The lyric poet Bacchylides was born on the island of Ceos ca. 524 B.C. None of his poetry was known to us until in 1896 a papyrus was found in Egypt containing the remains of fourteen odes in honor of victors in the great games and four odes in honor of Dionysus. All of Bacchylides' poems belong to the genre called "choral lyric," that is to say, poems written for public performance, usually on religious occasions, by a chorus that sang the poem to the accompaniment of flute and lyre and expressed the drama of the poem through dance. Such performances had been a central part of Greek religious festivals since the Bronze Age and took place at every festival in all parts of Greece.

The lines below are part of a poem commissioned to celebrate the victory of Hieron, tyrant of Syracuse, in the chariot race at the Olympic Games of 468 B.C. This was the most prestigious of all victories in the games and would have been celebrated on Hieron's return to Syracuse as a quasi-religious festival.

The dialect of choral lyric by tradition had a Doric coloring, most clearly seen in the predominance of long α, e.g., ἀρχᾱγέτᾱν = ἀρχηγέτην (to make things easier we have given Attic spellings in the facing notes). Other features of the genre are swift changes of direction in thought or scene, the abbreviated form in which mythical examples are given (it is assumed that the story is known to the audience, and the poet concentrates on the dramatic moments), and the free use of colorful compound adjectives, often coined for the particular context.

In choral odes the central feature is often a myth, which is more or less closely connected with the main subject of the poem. Croesus was an historical figure, but his story is here told as a myth. In Bacchylides' version Croesus builds the pyre himself and ascends it with his family in order to commit suicide and so avoid slavery. Apollo rescues him and takes him and his family to live with the Hyperboreans, a legendary people who live in the far North. The connection with Hieron is that both were exceptionally generous to Delphi and both were rewarded for their generosity.

ἐπεί ποτε καὶ δαμασίππου
   Λῡδίᾱς ἀρχᾱγέτᾱν,
εὖτε τὰν πεπρωμένᾱν
   Ζηνὸς τελέσσαντος κρίσιν
5 Σάρδιες Περσᾶν ἁλίσκοντο στρατῷ,
   Κροῖσον ὁ χρῡσάορος

φύλαξ᾽ Ἀπόλλων· ὁ δ᾽ ἐς ἄελπτον ἆμαρ
μολὼν πολυδάκρυον οὐκ ἔμελλε
μίμνειν ἔτι δουλοσύνᾱν· πυρὰν δὲ
10 χαλκοτειχέος προπάροιθεν αὐλᾶς

11 ναῆσατ' = ἐναήσατο (*from* νηέω) "he heaped up"   ἔνθα "where"
    ἀλόχῳ . . . κεδνᾷ "his dear wife"
12 εὐπλοκάμοις (*with* θυγατράσι) "fair-haired"
    ἄλαστον "inconsolably"
13 δῡρομέναις = ὀδῡρομέναις
    χέρας = χεῖρας
14 αἰπὺν αἰθέρα "the high air"
    σφετέρᾱς "his"   ἀείρᾱς = ἄρᾱς
15 γέγωνεν (*perfect with present sense*) "he calls aloud"
    ὑπέρβιε "mighty"
17 Λᾱτοΐδᾱς (= Λητοΐδης) ἄναξ "lord son of Leto" (i.e., Apollo, whose mother
        was Leto)
18 ἔρρουσιν "are gone," "have vanished"
    'Αλυάττᾱ δόμοι = 'Αλυάττεω δόμος "the house of Alyattes"
19 ἀμοιβᾱ (+ *gen*.) "return for"
20 Πῡθωνόθεν "from Delphi" (Pytho was the old name for Delphi)
21 πέρθουσι = πορθοῦσι
    δοριάλωτον "taken by the spear"
22 ἐρεύθεται "is reddened with," "runs red with"
    χρῡσοδίνᾱς Πακτωλός "the Pactolus eddying with gold" (the river Pactolus,
        which ran through Sardis, contained gold)
23 ἀεικελίως "shamefully"
24 ἐΰκτίτων μεγάρων "their well-built palaces"
25 τὰ πρόσθεν ἐχθρὰ φίλα "what was hateful before (is now) dear"
    γλύκιστον "(it is) sweetest"
26 τόσ' = τόσα "so much," "this"
    ἀβροτάτᾱν "delicately-stepping (servant)"
    κέλευσεν = ἐκέλευσεν
27 ἅπτειν ξύλινον δόμον "to light the wooden pyre" (*literally*, structure, house)
    ἔκλαγον "shrieked"
28 ἀνὰ . . . ἔβαλλον = ἀνέβαλλον   φίλᾱς their own   μᾱτρί = μητρί
29 προφανής "clear beforehand," "foreseen"
    θνᾱτοῖσιν = θνητοῖς "for mortals"
32 λαμπρὸν . . . μένος "the bright strength"
    διάϊσσεν "was rushing through (the pyre)"
33 ἐπιστᾱσᾱς = ἐπιστήσᾱς "having set above"
    μελαγκευθὲς νέφος "a black-covering cloud"
34 σβέννυεν = ἐσβέννυεν "quenched"
    ξανθὰν φλόγα "the yellow flame"
35 ἄπιστον "(is) incredible"
    μέριμνα "the care," "providence"
36 τεύχει "brings to pass"
    Δᾱλογενής = Δηλογενής "born in Delos"
37 'Υπερβορέους "the Hyperboreans," a mythical people living in the far North
    γέροντα i.e., Croesus
38 τανισφύροις . . . κούραις "the maidens of the slender ankles"
    κατένασσε "settled"
39 εὐσέβειαν "his piety"   ὅτι "because"
    θνᾱτῶν = θνητῶν "of (all) mortals"
40 ἀγαθέᾱν . . . Πυθώ "holy Pytho" (Delphi)

νᾱήσατ᾽, ἔνθα σὺν ἀλόχῳ τε κεδνᾷ
σὺν εὐπλοκάμοις τ᾽ ἐπέβαιν᾽ ἄλαστον
θῡγατράσι δῡρομέναις· χέρας δ᾽ ἐς
    αἰπὺν αἰθέρα σφετέρᾱς ἀείρᾱς

15 γέγωνεν· "ὑπέρβιε δαῖμον,
    ποῦ θεῶν ἐστιν χάρις;
ποῦ δὲ Λᾱτοίδᾱς ἄναξ;
    ἔρρουσιν Ἀλυάττᾱ δόμοι,
τίς δὲ νῦν δώρων ἀμοιβᾷ μῡρίων
20   φαίνεται Πῡθωνόθεν;

πέρθουσι Μῆδοι δοριάλωτον ἄστυ,
ἐρεύθεται αἵματι χρῡσοδίνᾱς
Πακτωλός· ἀεικελίως γυναῖκες
    ἐξ ἐϋκτίτων μεγάρων ἄγονται·

25 τὰ πρόσθεν ἐχθρὰ φίλα· θανεῖν γλύκιστον."
τόσ᾽ εἶπε, καὶ ἁβροβάτᾱν κέλευσεν
ἅπτειν ξύλινον δόμον. ἔκλαγον δὲ
    παρθένοι, φίλᾱς τ᾽ ἀνὰ μᾱτρὶ χεῖρας

ἔβαλλον· ὁ γὰρ προφανὴς θνᾱ-
30   τοῖσιν ἔχθιστος φόνων·
ἀλλ᾽ ἐπεὶ δεινοῦ πυρὸς
    λαμπρὸν διάϊσσεν μένος,
Ζεύς ἐπιστᾱσᾱς μελαγκευθὲς νέφος
    σβέννυεν ξανθὰν φλόγα.

35 ἄπιστον οὐδέν, ὅ τι θεῶν μέριμνα
τεύχει· τότε Δᾱλογενὴς Ἀπόλλων
φέρων ἐς Ὑπερβορέους γέροντα
    σὺν τανισφύροις κατένασσε κούραις

δι᾽ εὐσέβειαν, ὅτι μέγιστα θνᾱτῶν
40 ἐς ἀγαθέᾱν ἀνέπεμψε Πῡθώ.

Bacchylides 3.23–62

29

ΜΕΓΑ ΤΟ ΤΗΣ
ΘΑΛΑΣΣΗΣ ΚΡΑΤΟΣ
(α)

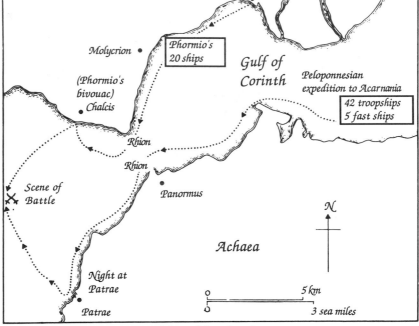

Map of first battle

In this and the next chapter we return to excerpts from Thucydides' account of the Peloponnesian War. That war has been described as a struggle between an elephant and a whale; the Athenians could not face the Peloponnesian army in the field, and the Peloponnesians could not risk a naval battle against the Athenian fleet. In Chapters 29 and 30 we give Thucydides' accounts of two naval victories achieved by the Athenian admiral Phormio against heavy odds in the summer of 429 B.C. These victories were decisive; the Peloponnesians were forced to acknowledge the naval supremacy of the Athenians not only in the Aegean but also in the Gulf of Corinth (Κρισαῖος κόλπος), and they made no attempt to challenge the Athenians by sea throughout the rest of the Archidamian War, i.e., until the truce of 421 B.C.

Vocabulary

Verbs

ἐκπνέω, ἐκπνευσοῦμαι *and*
ἐκπνεύσομαι, ἐξέπνευσα,
ἐκπέπνευκα I blow out, blow
from

ἐπιγίγνομαι (*see* γίγνομαι *for
principal parts*) I come after

ἐπιτίθεμαι, ἐπιθήσομαι,
ἐπεθέμην, ἐπιτέθειμαι
(+ *dat.*) I attack

ἐπιχειρέω (+ *dat.*) I attempt,
attack

παραπλέω (*see* πλέω *for
principal parts*) I sail by, sail
past, sail along

στέλλω, στελῶ, ἔστειλα,
ἔσταλκα, ἔσταλμαι,
ἐστάλην I send, equip

συνάγω (*see* ἄγω *for principal
parts*) I bring together,
compress

φρουρέω I guard

Nouns

ἡ ἕως, τῆς ἕω dawn

ἡ ἤπειρος, τῆς ἠπείρου land,
mainland

ὁ κόλπος, τοῦ κόλπου lap,
gulf

ἡ ναυμαχία, τῆς ναυμαχίας
naval battle

τὸ πλοῖον, τοῦ πλοίου boat

τὸ πνεῦμα, τοῦ πνεύματος
breeze

ἡ πρύμνη, τῆς πρύμνης stern
of a ship

ἡ πρῷρα, τῆς πρῴρας bow of a
ship

ἡ τάξις, τῆς τάξεως rank,
position

ἡ ταραχή, τῆς ταραχῆς
confusion

Adverb

εἴσω (ἔσω) inwards

Conjunction

μήτε and not

μήτε . . . μήτε neither . . .
nor

Expressions

ἐπὶ τὴν ἕω at dawn

κατὰ μέσον . . . in the
middle of . . .

τοῦ δὲ ἐπιγιγνομένου χειμῶνος Ἀθηναῖοι ναῦς ἔστειλαν εἴκοσι μὲν
περὶ Πελοπόννησον καὶ Φορμίωνα στρατηγόν, ὃς ὁρμώμενος ἐκ τοῦ
Ναυπάκτου φυλακὴν εἶχεν ὥστε μήτ' ἐκπλεῖν ἐκ Κορίνθου καὶ τοῦ
Κρισαίου κόλπου μηδένα μήτ' ἐσπλεῖν.

[ὁρμώμενος starting from, based on   τοῦ Κρισαίου κόλπου the Gulf of Corinth]

In the summer of 429 B.C. a Corinthian fleet of forty-seven ships tried to
slip through Phormio's blockade and take reinforcements to their allies
fighting in northwest Greece (Acarnania).

οἱ δὲ Κορίνθιοι καὶ οἱ ἄλλοι ξύμμαχοι ἠναγκάσθησαν περὶ τὰς   5
αὐτὰς ἡμέρας ναυμαχῆσαι πρὸς Φορμίωνα καὶ τὰς εἴκοσι ναῦς τῶν
Ἀθηναίων αἳ ἐφρούρουν ἐν Ναυπάκτῳ. ὁ γὰρ Φορμίων
παραπλέοντας αὐτοὺς ἔξω τοῦ κόλπου ἐτήρει, βουλόμενος ἐν τῇ
εὐρυχωρίᾳ ἐπιθέσθαι.

[ἐτήρει (*from* τηρέω) was watching   τῇ εὐρυχωρίᾳ the broad waters]

οἱ δὲ Κορίνθιοι καὶ οἱ ξύμμαχοι ἔπλεον μὲν οὐχ ὡς ἐπὶ ναυμαχίᾳ   10
ἀλλὰ στρατιωτικώτερον παρεσκευασμένοι ἐς τὴν Ἀκαρνανίᾶν καὶ
οὐκ οἰόμενοι τοὺς Ἀθηναίους ἂν τολμῆσαι ναυμαχίᾶν ποιήσασθαι·
παρὰ γῆν σφῶν μέντοι κομιζόμενοι τοὺς Ἀθηναίους ἀντιπαραπλέοντας ἑώρων καί, ἐπεὶ ἐκ Πατρῶν τῆς Ἀχαίᾶς πρὸς τὴν ἀντιπέρᾶς
ἤπειρον διέβαλλον, εἶδον τοὺς Ἀθηναίους ἀπὸ Χαλκίδος   15
προσπλέοντας σφίσιν· οὕτω δὴ ἀναγκάζονται ναυμαχεῖν κατὰ μέσον
τὸν πορθμόν.

[ἐπί (+ dat.) for (of purpose)   στρατιωτικώτερον more for carrying troops   τὴν
Ἀκαρνανίᾶν Acarnania (an area of northwest Greece, above and to the left of the
area shown in the map on page 178)   ἂν τολμῆσαι would dare   παρὰ γῆν σφῶν
past their own land   κομιζόμενοι being conveyed, sailing along
ἀντιπαραπλέοντας   sailing along opposite   ἑώρων = imperfect of ὁράω
ἀντιπέρᾶς (adverb) opposite   διέβαλλον were crossing   σφίσιν (dative plural
pronoun) (toward) them   Χαλκίδος Chalcis   τὸν πορθμόν straits]

καὶ οἱ μὲν Πελοποννήσιοι ἐτάξαντο κύκλον τῶν νεῶν ὡς μέγιστον
οἷοί τ᾽ ἦσαν, τὰς πρῴρᾶς μὲν ἔξω, ἔσω δὲ τὰς πρύμνᾶς, καὶ τὰ λεπτὰ
πλοῖα ἃ ξυνέπλει ἐντὸς ποιοῦνται. οἱ δὲ Ἀθηναῖοι κατὰ μίαν ναῦν   2
τεταγμένοι περιέπλεον αὐτοὺς κύκλῳ καὶ ξυνῆγον ἐς ὀλίγον, ἐν χρῷ
αἰεὶ παραπλέοντες· προείρητο δ᾽ αὐτοῖς ὑπὸ Φορμίωνος μὴ ἐπιχειρεῖν
πρὶν ἂν αὐτὸς σημήνῃ. ἤλπιζε γὰρ αὐτῶν οὐ μενεῖν τὴν τάξιν ἀλλὰ
τὰς ναῦς ξυμπεσεῖσθαι πρὸς ἀλλήλᾶς καὶ τὰ πλοῖα ταραχὴν
παρέξειν· εἴ τ᾽ ἐκπνεύσειεν ἐκ τοῦ κόλπου τὸ πνεῦμα, ὅπερ εἰώθει
γίγνεσθαι ἐπὶ τὴν ἕω, οὐδένα χρόνον ἡσυχάσειν αὐτούς.

[λεπτά light   κατὰ μίαν ναῦν in single file   ἐς ὀλίγον into a small (space)
ἐν χρῷ (literally) on the skin = within a hair's breadth   προείρητο (from προερέω
I order beforehand) an order had been given   μενεῖν remain, hold (the subject of the
infinitive is αὐτῶν . . . τὴν τάξιν)   ξυμπεσεῖσθαι (future infinitive of συμπίπτω)
would fall together, clash   ἐκπνεύσειε(ν) (alternative aorist optative, third person
singular = ἐκπνεύσαι)]

—adapted from Thucydides 2.69 and 2.83.2–84.2

Principal Parts: ὁράω and οἶδα, Seeing and Knowing

ὁράω (ὁρα-/ὀπ-/ἰδ-), (imperfect) ἑώρων, ὄψομαι, εἶδον, ἑόρᾱκα or
ἑώρᾱκα, ἑώρᾱμαι or ὦμμαι, ὤφθην I see

The stem ἰδ-/εἰδ-/οἰδ- (seen in εἶδον above) also gives οἶδα (perfect with
present meaning) "I know," ἤδη or ᾔδειν (pluperfect with imperfect meaning) "I
knew," and εἴσομαι "I will know." See Grammar 1 on the next page.

Word Study

From what Greek words are the following theological terms derived:

1. theology
2. Bible
3. dogma
4. orthodoxy
5. heresy
6. ecclesiastical

Grammar

1. The Verb οἶδα

The verb οἶδα is an irregular perfect (see Chapter 28, Grammar 4, page 170), formed from the stem ἰδ- (originally ϝιδ-, pronounced *wid*, cf. Latin *videō*, "I see"), which appears also in εἶδον "I saw"; οἶδα means "I have seen (with my mind)" = "I know." As seen in the chart below, the subjunctive, infinitive, and participle are formed regularly from the stem ἰδ , augmented to εἰδ-; the indicative and imperative are irregular and must be very carefully learned.

Indic.	Subj.	Opt.	Imper.	Infin.	Part.

Present

οἶδα	εἰδῶ	εἰδείην		εἰδέναι	εἰδώς,
οἶσθα	εἰδῇς	εἰδείης	ἴσθι		εἰδυῖα,
οἶδε(ν)	εἰδῇ	εἰδείη			εἰδός
ἴσμεν	εἰδῶμεν	εἰδεῖμεν			
ἴστε	εἰδῆτε	εἰδεῖτε	ἴστε		
ἴσᾱσι(ν)	εἰδῶσι	εἰδεῖεν			

Imperfect

ᾔδη	or	ᾔδειν
ᾔδησθα	or	ᾔδεις
ᾔδει		
ᾖσμεν	or	ᾔδεμεν
ᾖστε	or	ᾔδετε
ᾖσαν	or	ᾔδεσαν

The future, εἴσομαι "I will know," is regular (like λύσομαι).

Exercise 29a

Read aloud and translate into English:

1. ἆρ' οἶσθα ὁπόθεν ἐληλύθᾱσιν οἱ ξένοι;
2. οὐδεὶς ᾔδει ὅποι ἔπλευσαν οἱ ἔμποροι.
3. οὐδέποτε ἑώρᾱκα τοσοῦτον θόρυβον. ἆρ' ἴστε τί γέγονεν;
4. ὁ αὐτουργός, οὐκ εἰδὼς τί βούλεται ὁ ξένος, ἠπόρει τί δεῖ ποιῆσαι.
5. οὗτοι οὔτ' ἴσᾱσιν πότε γενήσεται ἡ ἐκκλησίᾱ οὔτε βούλονται εἰδέναι.
6. ὦ κάκιστε, εὖ ἴσθι κακὰ πεισόμενος, οὕτω κακὰ πρᾱξᾱς.

7. οἱ πολῖται οὐκ ᾔδεσαν τὸν ῥήτορα ψευδῆ εἰπόντα.
8. οἱ ἄγγελοι ἀπῆλθον πρὶν εἰδέναι πότερον ἡμεῖς τοὺς λόγους δεξόμεθα ἢ οὔ.
9. μείνατε ἕως ἂν εἰδῆτε τί βουλόμεθα.
10. αἱ γυναῖκες εἰδυῖαι τοὺς ἄνδρας ἐς κίνδῡνον καταστάντας μάλα ἐφοβοῦντο.

Exercise 29b

Translate into Greek:

1. Be assured (= Know well) that the king is becoming angry.
2. Do you know where the children have gone?
3. I wish to know why you did this.
4. Knowing well what had happened, the woman told her husband (*dative*) the truth.
5. Not knowing when the ship would arrive, they waited all day at (**ἐν**) the harbor.
6. Whenever we know who did this, we will tell you immediately.
7. The people soon knew that the speaker was not telling the truth.
8. The old man went away before hearing all we know.
9. We shall soon know why he did not stay.
10. The boy's parents knew that he was telling lies.

2. Clauses of Result with ὥστε

The word ὥστε introduces clauses that express result; the verb in the result clause may be either indicative (negative οὐ) or an infinitive (negative μή). Both constructions have been used freely in the readings, e.g.:

οἱ στρατηγοὶ οὕτως ἐφοβοῦντο **ὥστε** ἀποφυγεῖν **ἐβούλοντο**.
The generals were so afraid *that they wanted* to flee away.

ὁ Ξέρξης τοὺς ναυάρχους ἐκέλευσε φυλάττειν τὰ στενὰ **ὥστε** μηκέτι **ἐξεῖναι** τοῖς Ἕλλησιν ἀποπλεῦσαι.
Xerxes ordered the admirals to guard the straits *so that* the Greeks *could* no longer sail away.

The distinction in meaning is as follows:

a. ὥστε + indicative is used where the result is an actual fact, e.g.:

οὕτως βραδέως ἐπορεύοντο **ὥστε** οὐκ **ἔφυγον** τοὺς διώκοντας.
They traveled so slowly *that they did* not *escape* their pursuers.

b. ὥστε + infinitive is used where the consequence is a tendency or possibility or where there is an expression of purpose as well as result, e.g.:

οὕτως ἀνδρεῖός ἐστιν **ὥστε** μηδὲν **φοβεῖσθαι**.
He is so brave *as not to fear* anything.
He is too brave *to fear* anything.

φυλακὴν εἶχεν **ὥστε** μήτε **ἐκπλεῖν** μήτε **ἐσπλεῖν** μηδένα.
He kept guard *so that* no one *could sail out* or *in*.

Note that if the subject of the infinitive is the same as that of the leading verb it is not expressed or is emphasized with αὐτός in the nominative case. If it is different from that of the main verb, it is in the accusative (in the example just above, the subject is μηδένα).

Exercise 29c

Translate:

1. τοσαῦται νῆες ἦσαν τοῖς Κορινθίοις ὥστε οὐκ ᾤοντο τοὺς ᾿Αθηναίους ναυμαχίᾱν ποιήσεσθαι.
2. ὁ Φορμίων οὕτως ἐθάρρει ὥστε τοῖς Κορινθίοις προσβαλεῖν καίπερ τοσαύτᾱς ναῦς ἔχουσιν.
3. ὁ ἄνεμος τοσοῦτος ἦν ὥστε αἱ νῆες συνέπεσον πρὸς ἀλλήλᾱς.
4. We have waited (*use imperfect with accusative of duration of time*) for father such a long (τοσοῦτος) time in the marketplace that we are very tired.
5. I am willing to do anything (*use neuter plural of* πᾶς) to return home.
6. Look! Father is finally approaching, and so we may hurry home.
7. After returning home (*use participle*), the children were tired enough (so tired as) to sleep.

3. More Pronouns: οὗ and σφῶν

Corresponding to the forms ἐμοῦ, ἐμοί, ἐμέ and σοῦ, σοί and σέ, there is a third person singular pronoun οὗ, οἷ, ἕ, which you have met as part of the reflexive pronoun ἑ-αυτόν "himself." In Attic Greek the most common of these forms is the dative οἷ, and it is used primarily as an alternative to the reflexive ἑαυτῷ in subordinate clauses to refer to the subject of the main verb. It is therefore often called an *indirect reflexive pronoun*, e.g.:

ὁ δοῦλος ἤλπιζε τὸν δεσπότην **οἷ/ἑαυτῷ** μὴ ὀργιεῖσθαι.
The slave hoped the master would not be angry *with him*.

If the pronoun is used emphatically, it has an accent (οὗ, οἷ, ἕ), but if it is not emphatic it is enclitic (οὐ, οἱ, ἑ). There is no nominative form for this pronoun.

The corresponding third person plural pronouon is σφεῖς, σφῶν, σφίσι(ν), and σφᾶς (compare ἡμεῖς, ἡμῶν, ἡμῖν, ἡμᾶς). In this chapter you have met the following:

(οἱ Πελοποννήσιοι) παρὰ γῆν **σφῶν** κομιζόμενοι τοὺς ᾿Αθηναίους ἑώρων καὶ ... εἶδον τοὺς ᾿Αθηναίους προσπλέοντας **σφίσιν**.
(The Peloponnesians) sailing past *their own* land (the land *of themselves*) saw the Athenians . . . and they saw the Athenians sailing toward *them* (i.e., toward *themselves*, the Peloponnesians).

Thucydides is here using these pronouns reflexively; they refer to the nearest subject, the Peloponnesians.

As with οἷ in the example above, σφίσι may be used as an indirect reflexive, but for the genitive and accusative indirect reflexives Attic Greek usually uses ἑαυτοῦ, etc. (rarely οὗ, σφῶν, and σφᾶς), e.g.:

ὁ Κροῖσος ἐρωτᾷ διὰ τί ὁ θεὸς **ἑαυτὸν** προὔδωκεν.
Croesus asks why the god betrayed *him*.

Note also the indirect reflexive adjective σφέτερος, -ᾱ, -ον "their own," e.g.:

ἐνόμιζε τοὺς Ἀχαρνέᾱς οὐ περιόψεσθαι τὰ **σφέτερα** διαφθειρόμενα.
He thought that the Acharnians would not disregard the destruction of *their own* property (*their own* things being destroyed).

Exercise 29d

Read aloud and translate:

1. οἱ δοῦλοι ἐφοβοῦντο μὴ ὁ δεσπότης σφίσιν ὀργίζηται.
2. οὐκ ᾔδεσαν οἱ Κορίνθιοι τοὺς Ἀθηναίους ἑαυτοὺς (σφᾶς) ἰδόντας.
3. ἡ γυνὴ ἤλπιζε τὸν ἄνδρα οἷ βοηθήσειν.
4. οἱ πρέσβεις εἶπον ὡς ἔπεμψεν ἑαυτοὺς (σφᾶς) ὁ βασιλεύς.
5. οἱ Ἀθηναῖοι ὠργίζοντο ὁρῶντες τὰ σφέτερα διαφθειρόμενα.

Thucydides

Thucydides was born about 455 B.C. of a noble Athenian family, probably related to that of the aristocratic Cimon. Little is known about his life. He suffered from the plague (2.49). He was general in 424 B.C. and was exiled for failing to prevent Brasidas from taking the strategic city of Amphipolis (4.105–106). He returned to Athens in 404 B.C. after the end of the war and died there about 400 B.C. In the introduction to his history (1.1), he says that he began writing it as soon as war broke out, feeling certain that it would be the most important war in history up to his time. He died before completing it, breaking off abruptly in his account of 411 B.C.

Unlike Herodotus, Thucydides was writing the history of events through which he had lived and at many of which he had himself been present. Even so, he is well aware of the difficulty of getting the facts right. In his introduction (1.22) he discusses this problem:

With regard to the factual reporting of the events in the war, I did not think it right to give the account of the first man I happened to meet, nor to give my personal impressions, but have examined each question with a view to the greatest possible accuracy both in events at which I was present myself and in those of which I heard from others. But it was a laborious business to find the truth, because eyewitnesses at each event did not give the same report about it, but their reports differed according to their partiality to either side or their powers of memory.

It should be remembered that his sources were not only Athenians. His long exile gave him the chance of making inquiries on the other side. He says (1.22) that the absence of the storytelling element (τὸ μυθῶδες) may make his history less attractive to his audience:

> I shall be satisfied if those who want to examine an accurate account of events that happened in the past and that are likely to be repeated some time in the future in similar form, human nature being what it is, find my history useful. It is composed to be a possession forever (κτῆμα ἐς αἰεί), not a performance to please an immediate public.

So there are lessons to be learned from his history, especially by statesmen. Although Thucydides restricts his history to military and political events, it is human nature, as revealed in both individual and social psychology, that most interests him. When, for instance, he has given a clinical account of the physical symptoms and effects of the plague (2.49–51), he goes on to discuss its psychological effects on the Athenian people (2.52–53).

Such passages of explicit analysis are rare. More often Thucydides uses speeches to show motives, underlying causes of events, and principles at stake. These speeches are placed at key points throughout most of the history. For example, when the Spartans send their final ultimatum, the Athenians debate their reply (see Chapter 21). Of this debate, Thucydides quotes one speech only, that of Pericles (1.140–44). In his speech, which extends to five printed pages, Pericles not only gives reasons for rejecting the Spartan ultimatum but also outlines the military and economic resources of each side and the strategy on which they should conduct the war, which he considered inevitable. The following narrative shows this strategy put into practice. The speech enables the reader to understand why the Athenians acted as they did.

Although less than thirty years separates the publication of Herodotus' history from that of Thucydides, there is a great gulf between them, which is not to be explained simply by the personalities of the authors. Herodotus was a child of the old order, accepting traditional values and beliefs. Thucydides is a product of the sophistic movement. He always searches for rational explanations of events, is sceptical in matters of religion, discounts oracles, and is austerely scientific in intent. Despite the austerity of his narrative, which appears impartial and impersonal even when he is writing of himself, his deep feelings are apparent from the way he tells the story, notably, for instance, in his description of the defeat of the Athenian fleet in the Great Harbor of Syracuse, which sealed the fate of the expedition to Sicily and ultimately led to the downfall of Athens.

ΜΕΓΑ ΤΟ ΤΗΣ
ΘΑΛΑΣΣΗΣ ΚΡΑΤΟΣ
(β)

Vocabulary

Verbs

ἀποστέλλω (*see* στέλλω *for
   principal parts*) I send off
ἐξαρτύω, ἐξαρτύσω,
   ἐξήρτῦσα, ἐξήρτῦκα,
   ἐξήρτῦμαι, ἐξηρτύθην I
   equip
καταδύω, καταδύσω,
   κατέδῦσα, καταδέδυκα,
   καταδέδυμαι, κατεδύθην
   (*transitive*) I sink
      Second aorist κατέδῦν
      (*intransitive*) I sank; (of the
      sun) set

προσπίπτω (*see* πίπτω *for
   principal parts*) (+ *dat.*) I fall
   against, fall on
ταράττω (ταράσσω),
   ταράξω, ἐτάραξα,
   τετάραγμαι, ἐταράχθην I
   confuse
χωρέω I go, come

Nouns

ἡ παρασκευή, τῆς
   παρασκευῆς preparation
τὸ τρόπαιον, τοῦ τροπαίου
   trophy

ὡς δὲ τό τε πνεῦμα κατῄει καὶ αἱ νῆες, ἐν ὀλίγῳ ἤδη οὖσαι, ὑπὸ
τοῦ τ' ἀνέμου καὶ τῶν πλοίων ἅμα ἐταράσσοντο, καὶ ναῦς τε νηὶ
προσέπῑπτε, οἱ δὲ ναῦται βοῇ τε χρώμενοι καὶ λοιδορίᾳ οὐδὲν
ἤκουον τῶν παραγγελλομένων, τότε δὴ σημαίνει ὁ Φορμίων· καὶ οἱ
Ἀθηναῖοι προσπεσόντες πρῶτον μὲν καταδύουσι τῶν στρατηγίδων   5
νεῶν μίαν, ἔπειτα δὲ καὶ τὰς ἄλλᾱς ᾗ χωρήσειαν διέφθειρον, καὶ
κατέστησαν αὐτοὺς ἐς φόβον, ὥστε φεύγουσιν ἐς Πάτρᾱς καὶ Δύμην
τῆς Ἀχαίᾱς. οἱ δὲ Ἀθηναῖοι διώξαντες καὶ ναῦς δώδεκα λαβόντες
τούς τε ἄνδρας ἐξ αὐτῶν τοὺς πλείστους ἀνελόμενοι, ἐς Μολύκρειον
ἀπέπλεον, καὶ τροπαῖον στήσαντες ἐπὶ τῷ Ῥίῳ ἀνεχώρησαν ἐς   10
Ναύπακτον.

[ἐν ὀλίγῳ in a little (space)   λοιδορίᾳ abuse   τῶν παραγγελλομένων of
the orders that were being passed along   τῶν στρατηγίδων νεῶν of the ships of the
generals, the flagships   ᾗ where, wherever   Δύμην three miles southwest of
Patrae   τῷ Ῥίῳ the Headland (Rhion on the north shore of the Gulf of Corinth)]

παρέπλευσαν δὲ καὶ οἱ Πελοποννήσιοι εὐθὺς ταῖς περιλοίποις τῶν
νεῶν ἐκ τῆς Δύμης καὶ Πατρῶν ἐς Κυλλήνην. καὶ ἀπὸ Λευκάδος

Κνημός τε καὶ αἱ ἐκείνων νῆες ἀφικνοῦνται ἐς τὴν Κυλλήνην.
πέμπουσι δὲ καὶ οἱ Λακεδαιμόνιοι τῷ Κνήμῳ ξυμβούλους ἐπὶ τὰς   15
ναῦς, κελεύοντες ἄλλην ναυμαχίᾱν βελτίονα παρασκευάζεσθαι καὶ
μὴ ὑπ' ὀλίγων νεῶν εἴργεσθαι τῆς θαλάσσης. οὐ γὰρ ᾤοντο σφῶν τὸ
ναυτικὸν λείπεσθαι ἀλλὰ γεγενῆσθαί τινα μαλακίᾱν· ὀργῇ οὖν
ἀπέστελλον τοὺς ξυμβούλους. οἱ δὲ μετὰ τοῦ Κνήμου ἀφικόμενοι
ἄλλᾱς τε ναῦς μετεπέμψαντο τοὺς ξυμμάχους παρακαλοῦντες   20
βοηθεῖν καὶ τὰς προϋπαρχούσᾱς ναῦς ἐξηρτύοντο ὡς ἐπὶ μάχην.

[εὐθύς straight (with ἐκ τῆς Δύμης . . . ἐς Κυλλήνην)   ταῖς περιλοίποις with the
rest   Κυλλήνην Cyllene, about fifty-six miles southwest of Patrae   Λευκάδος
Leucas, an island off the coast of Acarnania   ἐκείνων i.e., of the Leucadians
ξυμβούλους advisers   εἴργεσθαι (from εἴργω) to be shut out from (+ gen.)   ᾤοντο
(from οἴομαι) they thought   λείπεσθαι to be deficient   μαλακίᾱν softness,
cowardice   προϋπαρχούσᾱς the (ships) already there]

πέμπει δὲ καὶ ὁ Φορμίων ἐς τὰς Ἀθήνᾱς ἀγγέλους τήν τε
παρασκευὴν αὐτῶν ἀγγελοῦντας καὶ περὶ τῆς ναυμαχίᾱς ἣν
ἐνίκησαν φράσοντας, καὶ κελεύων αὐτοὺς ἑαυτῷ ναῦς ὡς πλείστᾱς
ταχέως ἀποστεῖλαι, ὡς καθ' ἡμέρᾱν ἐλπίδος οὔσης ναυμαχήσειν. οἱ   25
δὲ Ἀθηναῖοι πέμπουσιν εἴκοσι ναῦς αὐτῷ, τῷ δὲ κομίζοντι αὐτὰς
προσεπέστειλαν ἐς Κρήτην πρῶτον ἀφικέσθαι, ἵνα ξυμμάχοις τισὶν
ἐκεῖ βοηθοίη.

[προσεπέστειλαν (from προσεπιστέλλω) (+ dat.)   instructed in addition]

—adapted from Thucydides 2.84.3–85.5

Principal Parts: Verbs with Attic Reduplication

ἀκούω, ἀκούσομαι, ἤκουσα, ἀκ-ήκο-α, ἠκούσθην (+ gen. of person, acc.
    of thing) I listen, listen to, hear
ἐλαύνω (ἐλα-), ἐλάω, ἤλασα, ἐλ-ήλα-κα, ἐλ-ήλα-μαι, ἠλάθην
    (transitive) I drive; (intransitive) I march
ἐσθίω (for ἐδ-θι-ω/φαγ-), ἔδομαι, ἔφαγον, ἐδ-ήδο-κα I eat

Word Building

Give the meanings of the following words:

1. ἡ δίκη   3. δικάζω   5. δικαστικός, -ή, -όν
2. δίκαιος, -ᾱ, -ον   4. ὁ δικαστής   6. ἄδικος, -ον

Grammar

4. Potential Optative

The optative (present or aorist) with the particle ἄν in main clauses
expresses a future possibility or likelihood, sometimes dependent on a

condition, stated or implied. This is called the *potential optative*; compare English statements with "would," "should," and "may," e.g.:

> I would like to see the doctor (if I may).
> βουλοίμην ἄν τὸν ἰᾱτρὸν ἰδεῖν.

There is no one way of translating such clauses; the following examples illustrate some of the uses of the potential optative (the negative is οὐ):

> οὐκ ἄν βοηθοίην σοι. I wouldn't help you.
> ἴσως ἄν ἡμῖν βοηθοίης. Perhaps you would help us.
> οὐκ ἄν δυναίμεθα σοι βοηθεῖν. We couldn't help you.
> χωροῖς ἄν εἴσω; Would you go in? = Please go in.

Exercise 29e

Read aloud and translate:

1. οὐκ ἄν βουλοίμην τὸ παιδίον βλάπτειν.
2. οὐκ ἄν δυναίμην τοῦτο ποιῆσαι.
3. ἡδέως ἄν ἀκούσαιμι τί βούλεται ὁ νεᾱνίᾱς.
4. ἴσως ἄν ἀργύριόν τι ἡμῖν δοίη ὁ βασιλεύς.
5. μόλις ἄν πειθοίμεθα τῷ στρατηγῷ τοιαῦτα κελεύοντι.
6. λέγοιτε ἄν μοι τί γέγονε;
7. τίς ἄν τούτῳ πιστεύοι, ὅσπερ ἡμῖν πολλάκις ἐψεύσατο.
8. οὐκ ἄν λάθοις τοὺς θεοὺς ἀδικῶν.
9. ἐχθροὶ ὄντες οὐκ ἄν βούλοιντο ἡμῖν βοηθεῖν.
10. δὶς εἰς τὸν αὐτὸν ποταμὸν οὐκ ἄν ἐμβαίης (*from* ἐμβαίνω I step into).

Exercise 29f

Translate into Greek:

1. I would like to see the doctor immediately.
2. Perhaps he may not help me.
3. I would gladly go to Epidaurus.
4. The god would be able to cure (ἰᾱτρεύω) me.
5. Would you tell me (*dative*) when the ship is going to sail (*use* μέλλω)?

* * *

ΑΜΦΟΤΕΡΟΙ ΠΑΡΑΣΚΕΥΑΖΟΝΤΑΙ ΩΣ ΑΥΘΙΣ ΝΑΥΜΑΧΗΣΟΝΤΕΣ

Read the following passages (adapted from Thucydides 2.86) and answer the comprehension questions:

οἱ δὲ ἐν Κυλλήνῃ Πελοποννήσιοι, ἐν ᾧ οἱ Ἀθηναῖοι περὶ τὴν Κρήτην κατείχοντο, παρεσκευασμένοι ὡς ἐπὶ ναυμαχίᾱν παρέπλευσαν ἐς Πάνορμον τὸν Ἀχαϊκόν, οὗπερ αὐτοῖς ὁ κατὰ γῆν στρατὸς τῶν Πελοποννησίων προσεβεβοηθήκει. παρέπλευσε δὲ καὶ ὁ Φορμίων ἐπὶ τὸ Ῥίον τὸ Μολυκρικὸν καὶ ὡρμίσατο ἔξω αὐτοῦ ναυσὶν εἴκοσι,

αἷσπερ καὶ ἐναυμάχησεν. ἐπὶ οὖν τῷ Ῥίῳ τῷ Ἀχαϊκῷ οἱ Πελοποννήσιοι, ἀπέχοντι 5
οὐ πολὺ τοῦ Πανόρμου, ὡρμίσαντο καὶ αὐτοὶ ναυσὶν ἑπτὰ καὶ ἑβδομήκοντα, ἐπειδὴ
καὶ τοὺς Ἀθηναίους εἶδον.

[κατείχοντο were held back   Πάνορμον Panormus   Ἀχαϊκόν Achaean
οὖπερ where   προσεβεβοηθήκει (from προσβοηθέω) had come to their aid
Μολυκρικόν Molycrian   ὡρμίσατο (from ὁρμίζω) came to anchor]

1. With what intention did the Peloponnesians sail from Cyllene to
   Achaean Panormus? What was at Panormus?
2. Where did Phormio anchor and with how many and which ships?
3. Where did the Peloponnesians anchor and with how many ships?

καὶ ἐπὶ μὲν ἓξ ἢ ἑπτὰ ἡμέρας ἀνθώρμουν ἀλλήλοις, μελετῶντές τε καὶ
παρασκευαζόμενοι τὴν ναυμαχίαν, γνώμην ἔχοντες οἱ μὲν Πελοποννήσιοι μὴ
ἐκπλεῖν ἔξω τῶν Ῥίων ἐς τὴν εὐρυχωρίαν, φοβούμενοι τὸ πρότερον πάθος, οἱ δὲ 10
Ἀθηναῖοι μὴ ἐσπλεῖν ἐς τὰ στενά, νομίζοντες πρὸς ἐκείνων εἶναι τὴν ἐν ὀλίγῳ
ναυμαχίαν. ἔπειτα ὁ Κνῆμος καὶ οἱ ἄλλοι τῶν Πελοποννησίων στρατηγοί,
βουλόμενοι ταχέως τὴν ναυμαχίαν ποιῆσαι, πρίν τι καὶ ἀπὸ τῶν Ἀθηναίων
ἐπιβοηθῆσαι, ξυνεκάλεσαν τοὺς στρατιώτας καὶ ὁρῶντες αὐτῶν τοὺς πολλοὺς διὰ
τὴν προτέραν ἧσσαν φοβουμένους καὶ οὐ προθύμους ὄντας παρεκελεύσαντο. 15

[ἀνθώρμουν (from ἀνθωρμέω) they were lying at anchor opposite (+ dat.)   τὴν
εὐρυχωρίᾱν broad waters   τὸ . . . πάθος the experience, misfortune   πρὸς
ἐκείνων in their (i.e., the Peloponnesians') favor   τι . . . ἐπιβοηθῆσαι any aid
came   ἧσσαν defeat   προθύμους eager   παρεκελεύσαντο they encouraged,
exhorted]

4. How long did the ships remain anchored opposite one another, and what
   were the sailors doing?
5. What did the Peloponnesians not want to do, and why?
6. What did the Athenians not want to do, and why not?
7. Why did Cnemus and the other Peloponnesian generals want to join
   battle quickly?
8. In what condition were the Peloponnesian soldiers, and why?
9. What did the Peloponnesian generals do?

Exercise 29g

Translate into Greek:

1. The Corinthians had (*use dative of possession*) so many ships that
   they did not fear the Athenians who were (= being) few.
2. For they thought that the Athenians would not dare to attack them.
3. But when they arrived at the broad waters (ἡ εὐρυχωρίᾱ), they saw
   the Athenians sailing toward them.
4. And so they were so frightened that they formed (τάσσω, *use
   participle*) a circle of their ships and prepared to defend themselves.
5. But when the Corinthians were confused by the wind, the Athenians
   fell on them and put them into a panic, so that they fled to Patrae.

30

ΜΕΓΑ ΤΟ ΤΗΣ
ΘΑΛΑΣΣΗΣ ΚΡΑΤΟΣ
(γ)

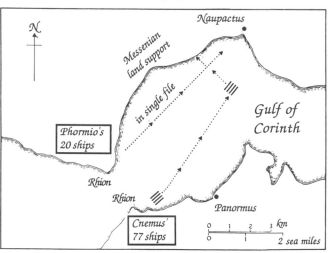

Map of second battle

Vocabulary

Verbs

ἀνάγομαι (*see* ἄγω *for principal parts*) I put out to sea

ἀπολαμβάνω (*see* λαμβάνω *for principal parts*) I cut off, intercept

ἀφαιρέομαι (*see* αἱρέω *for principal parts*) I take away for myself, save

διαφεύγω (*see* φεύγω *for principal parts*) I escape

ἐπεισβαίνω (*see* βαίνω *for principal parts*) I go into

ἐπιβοηθέω (+ *dat.*) I come to aid

ἐπιστρέφω, ἐπιστρέψω, ἐπέστρεψα, ἐπέστραμμαι,

(*second aorist passive, active and intransitive in meaning*)

ἐπεστράφην I turn around

ὁρμέω I lie at anchor

παραβοηθέω (+ *dat.*) I come to aid

ὑπεκφεύγω (*see* φεύγω *for principal parts*) I escape

Nouns

τὸ κέρας, τοῦ κέρως wing

τὰ ὅπλα, τῶν ὅπλων weapons

τὸ σημεῖον, τοῦ σημείου sign

Adjective

κενός, -ή, -όν empty

Prepositions
παρά (+ *dat.*) at the house of;
  (+ *acc.*) to, along, past

περί (+ *gen.*) around, about,
  concerning; (+ *dat.*)
  concerning; (+ *acc.*) around

Expression
ἅμα ἕῳ at dawn

οἱ δὲ Πελοποννήσιοι, ἐπειδὴ αὐτοῖς οἱ Ἀθηναῖοι οὐκ ἐπέπλεον ἐς
τὸν κόλπον, βουλόμενοι ἄκοντας ἔσω προαγαγεῖν αὐτούς,
ἀναγαγόμενοι ἅμα ἕῳ ἔπλεον ἐπὶ τοῦ κόλπου, ἐπὶ τεσσάρων
ταξάμενοι τὰς ναῦς, δεξιῷ κέρᾳ ἡγουμένῳ, ὥσπερ καὶ ὥρμουν· ἐπὶ δὲ
τούτῳ τῷ κέρᾳ εἴκοσι ἔταξαν τὰς ναῦς τὰς ἄριστα πλεούσας, ἵνα, εἰ ὁ   5
Φορμίων νομίσας ἐπὶ τὴν Ναύπακτον αὐτοὺς πλεῖν ἐπιβοηθῶν ἐκεῖσε
παραπλέοι, μὴ διαφύγοιεν τὸν ἐπίπλουν σφῶν οἱ Ἀθηναῖοι ἀλλὰ
αὗται αἱ νῆες περικλήσαιεν.

[ἐπὶ τεσσάρων four deep (they were drawn up at anchor four deep; when they
weighed anchor, they turned right and sailed in column four abreast, with their twenty
fastest ships leading) τὸν ἐπίπλουν the attack περικλήσαιεν (*from* περικλήῄω)
would shut (them) in, trap (them)]

ὁ δὲ Φορμίων, ὅπερ ἐκεῖνοι προσεδέχοντο, φοβηθεὶς περὶ τῷ
χωρίῳ ἐρήμῳ ὄντι, ὡς ἑώρα ἀναγομένους αὐτούς, ἄκων καὶ κατὰ   10
σπουδὴν ἐμβιβάσας ἔπλει παρὰ τὴν γῆν· καὶ ὁ πεζὸς στρατὸς ἅμα
τῶν Μεσσηνίων παρεβοήθει. ἰδόντες δὲ οἱ Πελοποννήσιοι αὐτοὺς
κατὰ μίαν παραπλέοντας καὶ ἤδη ὄντας ἐντὸς τοῦ κόλπου τε καὶ
πρὸς τῇ γῇ, ὅπερ ἐβούλοντο μάλιστα, ἀπὸ σημείου ἑνὸς εὐθὺς
ἐπιστρέψαντες τὰς ναῦς μετωπηδὸν ἔπλεον ὡς τάχιστα ἐπὶ τοὺς   15
Ἀθηναίους, καὶ ἤλπιζον πάσας τὰς ναῦς ἀπολήψεσθαι.

[κατὰ σπουδήν hastily ἐμβιβάσας (*from* ἐμβιβάζω) having embarked ἅμα:
adverbial here τῶν Μεσσηνίων: *genitive with* ὁ πεζὸς στρατός κατὰ μίαν in
single file πρὸς τῇ γῇ close to land μετωπηδόν with their fronts forward, in
close line (i.e., they turned left and advanced four deep toward the north)]

τῶν δὲ Ἀθηναίων νεῶν ἕνδεκα μὲν αἵπερ ἡγοῦντο ὑπεκφεύγουσι
τὸ κέρας τῶν Πελοποννησίων· τὰς δὲ ἄλλας καταλαβόντες οἱ
Πελοποννήσιοι ἐξέωσάν τε πρὸς τὴν γῆν ὑπεκφευγούσας καὶ
διέφθειραν· ἄνδρας τε τῶν Ἀθηναίων ἀπέκτειναν ὅσοι μὴ ἐξένευσαν   20
αὐτῶν. καὶ τῶν νεῶν τινας ἀναδούμενοι εἷλκον κενάς (μίαν δὲ αὐτοῖς
ἀνδράσιν εἷλον ἤδη), τὰς δέ τινας οἱ Μεσσήνιοι, παραβοηθήσαντες
καὶ ἐπεσβαίνοντες ξὺν τοῖς ὅπλοις ἐς τὴν θάλασσαν καὶ ἐπιβάντες
ἀπὸ τῶν καταστρωμάτων μαχόμενοι ἀφείλοντο ἑλκομένας ἤδη.

[ἐξέωσαν (*from* ἐξωθέω) pushed out   ὑπεκφευγούσᾱς as they (tried to) escape
ἐξένευσαν (*from* ἐκνέω) swam out, swam to shore   ἀναδούμενοι (*from*
ἀναδέομαι) fastening with a rope, taking in tow   τῶν καταστρωμάτων the decks
ἀφείλοντο (*from* ἀφαιρέω) took away for themselves, saved]

—adapted from Thucydides 2.90

Principal Parts: ἀναμιμνῄσκω *and* μέμνημαι

ἀναμιμνῄσκω (μνη-/μνα-), ἀναμνήσω, ἀνέμνησα I remind someone
  (*acc.*) of something (*acc. or gen.*)
μέμνημαι (*perfect middle = present*) I have reminded myself, I
  remember
ἐμνήσθην (*aorist passive in middle sense*) I remembered
μνησθήσομαι (*future passive in middle sense*) I will remember

Word Study

*The following passage contains twenty words derived from Greek; list them and
explain their derivation and meaning. Then try to rewrite the passage without
using these Greek derivatives.*

The philosopher in his study can analyze political situations logically; he
can propose hypotheses and produce ideal solutions to problems. The
politician, however, agonizes in the sphere of the practical; he is beset by a
recurring cycle of crises, for which the therapy is empirical. Whatever
his ideology, in the event, he is guided not by dogma or theoretical
analysis but by pragmatic considerations.

Grammar

1. Conditional Sentences

Conditional sentences, in both English and Greek, are of two kinds:

  a. *Open conditions*, in which nothing is implied as to whether the
     condition is fulfilled or not. These may be of two kinds:
     1. *Particular conditions.*
     2. *General conditions.* The conditional clause in sentences of
        this sort is a type of *indefinite* clause (see Chapter 22, Grammar
        2, pages 75–76).
  b. *Contrary to fact* or *remote conditions*, in which it is implied that the
     condition was/is not fulfilled or is not likely to be fulfilled in
     future time.

  a. Open Conditions:

  Past Particular:

     If Philip said this, he was lying.
     εἰ ὁ Φίλιππος τοῦτο εἶπεν, ἐψεύδετο.
       (a past tense, i.e., imperfect, aorist, or pluperfect, of the
       indicative in both clauses)

Past General:

> *If Philip (ever) said this, he was (always) lying.*
> εἰ ὁ Φίλιππος τοῦτο λέγοι, ἐψεύδετο.
> (εἰ + aorist or present optative; imperfect indicative)

Present Particular:

> *If you believe Philip, you are foolish.*
> εἰ τῷ Φιλίππῳ πιστεύεις, μῶρος εἶ.
> (present or perfect indicative in both clauses)

Present General:

> *If you (ever) believe Philip, you are (always) foolish.*
> ἐὰν τῷ Φιλίππῳ πιστεύῃς, μῶρος εἶ.
> (ἐάν + aorist or present subjunctive; present indicative)

Future Particular or Minatory:

> *If you do this, you will die.*
> εἰ τοῦτο ποιήσεις, ἀποθανῇ.
> (εἰ + future indicative; future indicative)
> (Particular future conditions are usually reserved for threats
> and warnings.)

Future More Vivid:

> *If the doctor does this, he will receive (his) pay.*
> ἐὰν ὁ ἰατρὸς τοῦτο ποιήσῃ, τὸν μισθὸν δέξεται.
> (ἐάν + aorist or present subjunctive; future indicative)

The imperative may be used in the main clause, e.g.:

> *If you see father, tell him what happened.*
> ἐὰν τὸν πατέρα ἴδῃς, εἰπὲ αὐτῷ τί ἐγένετο.

b. Contrary to Fact and Remote Conditions:

Past Contrary to Fact:

> *If the doctor had done this, he would have received (his) pay.*
> (It is implied that he did not do this and did not receive his pay.)
> εἰ ὁ ἰατρὸς τοῦτο ἐποίησεν, ἐδέξατο ἂν τὸν μισθόν.
> (aorist indicative; aorist indicative with ἄν)

Present Contrary to Fact:

> *If our father were living, he would be helping us.*
> (It is implied that he is not living and is not helping us.)
> εἰ ἔζη ὁ πατήρ, ἡμῖν ἂν ἐβοήθει.
> (imperfect indicative; imperfect indicative with ἄν)

Future Remote or Future Less Vivid:

> *If the doctor should do this, he would not receive (his) pay.*
> *(If the doctor were to do this, . . .)*
> *(If the doctor did this, . . .)*
> (It is implied that the doctor is not likely to do this.)
> εἰ ὁ ἰᾱτρὸς τοῦτο ποιήσαι, οὐκ ἂν δέξαιτο τὸν μισθόν.
>> (εἰ + aorist or present optative; aorist or present optative with ἄν)

In contrary to fact and future less vivid conditions, the potential particle ἄν always appears near the beginning of the main clause, although not as the first word; it is usually next to the verb. Note that in these clauses the aorist indicative refers to past time, the imperfect indicative to present time, and the optative to future time.

Note that the difference between aorist and present subjunctives and optatives in conditional clauses is in aspect, not time. The aorist subjunctive or optative is used when the action of the verb is looked on as an event, the present, when it is looked on as a process.

In all conditional sentences, the negative is μή in the conditional clause and οὐ in the main clause.

Exercise 30a

Translate the following sentences and identify the type of condition each represents:

1. ἐὰν μὴ περὶ εἰρήνης λέγητε, οὐκ ἀκούσομαι ὑμῶν.
2. εἰ τοὺς βαρβάρους ἐνῑκήσαμεν, πάντες ἂν ἐτίμησαν ἡμᾶς.
3. εἰ οἴκαδε σπεύδοιμεν, ἴσως ἂν ἀφικοίμεθα ἐν καιρῷ.
4. εἰ τῷ βασιλεῖ πάντα εἶπες, μῶρος ἦσθα.
5. εἰ οἴκοι ἐμείνατε, οὐκ ἂν κατέστητε ἐς τοσοῦτον κίνδῡνον.
6. εἰ παρῆσαν οἱ σύμμαχοι, ἡμῖν ἂν ἐβοήθουν.
7. ἐὰν τοὺς συμμάχους παρακαλῶμεν, ἡμῖν βοηθήσουσιν.
8. εἰ τοῦτο ποιήσεις, ἐγώ σε ἀποκτενῶ.
9. εἰ εὐθὺς ὡρμήσαμεν, ἤδη ἀφῑκόμεθα ἂν ἐς τὸ ἄστυ.
10. εἰ τὰ ἀληθῆ λέγοις, πιστεύοιμι ἄν σοι.
11. ἐὰν τοῦτο ποιήσῃς, ἐπαινῶ σε.
12. εἰ οὗτος ὁ κύων λύκον ἴδοι, ἀπέφευγεν.

Exercise 30b

Translate the following pairs of sentences:

1. εἰ εὐθὺς πρὸς τὸ ἄστυ σπεύδοιμεν, ἴσως ἂν ἀφικοίμεθα πρὶν γενέσθαι τὴν ἑσπέρᾱν.
   If you should lead me, I would gladly follow.
2. εἰ μὴ τῷ ποιμένι ἐνετύχομεν, ἡμάρτομεν ἂν τῆς ὁδοῦ.
   If we had not hurried, we would have arrived home late.
3. ἐὰν μου ἀκούητε, πάντα δι’ ὀλίγου γνώσεσθε.
   If you (*pl.*) follow me quickly, we will arrive before night falls.

4. εἰ οἱ παῖδες τῷ πατρὶ ἐπείσθησαν, οὐκ ἂν κατέστησαν ἐς τοσοῦτον κίνδυνον.
   If we had stayed at home, we would not have seen (*use* θεάομαι) the contests.

5. εἰ μή σοι ἐπίστευον, οὐκ ἂν ταῦτά σοι ἔλεγον.
   If father were here, he would be helping us.

6. εἰ μὴ ὁ θεὸς τὸ πῦρ ἔσβεσεν, ὁ Κροῖσος ἂν ζῶν κατεκαύθη.
   If Croesus had not called the god, he would not have been saved.

7. ἐὰν τὴν μητέρα ἐν τῇ ἀγορᾷ ἴδῃς, αἴτησον αὐτὴν οἴκαδε σπεύδειν.
   If mother does not come home soon, I will go myself to look for (*use* ὡς + *future participle*) her.

8. εἰ μὴ ὁ ἀδελφὸς κακὰ ἔπασχεν, οὐκ ἂν οὕτω ἐλυπούμην.
   If mother were here, she would know what we must (*use* δεῖ) do.

9. ἐὰν οἱ πολέμιοι ἐς τὴν γῆν ἐσβάλωσιν, οἱ αὐτουργοὶ ἐς τὸ ἄστυ ἀνίστανται.
   If ever the Corinthians attack Phormio's fleet, they are defeated.

10. εἰ ἐπίοιεν οἱ Ἀθηναῖοι, οἱ πολέμιοι ὑπεχώρουν (*retired*).
    If the Athenians ever retired, the enemy attacked them.

The Downfall of Athens

The essay in Chapter 23 carried the story of the Peloponnesian War as far as the Peace of Nicias, concluded by Sparta and Athens in 421 B.C., when both sides were physically and economically exhausted by the ten years' war. There was little hope of the peace holding. It was not accepted by Corinth and Boeotia, and at Athens a rival to the peace-loving Nicias appeared in the person of Alcibiades, a cousin and ward of Pericles, rich, handsome, unscrupulous, and ambitious. Opposing Nicias, who did all he could to preserve peaceful relations with Sparta, Alcibiades initiated a policy of backing Argos, Sparta's old rival in the Peloponnesus, and forming a coalition of states that were dissatisfied with Spartan leadership. In 419 B.C. a sporadic war broke out, in which Athens was halfheartedly involved as the ally of Argos, but in 418 B.C. Sparta inflicted a crushing defeat on Argos and re-established her hegemony in the Peloponnesus, while the Athenians became interested in other imperial ventures.

In the winter of 416/415 B.C. the Athenians made the fateful decision to add Sicily to their empire. They were given a pretext for intervention by the arrival of ambassadors from a small Sicilian city, which asked for help against a neighboring city, which was backed by the greatest city in the West, Syracuse. When the matter was debated in the Assembly, Nicias advised caution, but Alcibiades argued strongly in favor of the venture. His view prevailed. In a burst of enthusiasm, the people voted for an expedition and for all the resources that the generals in command (Nicias, Alcibiades, and Lamachus) required.

The expedition departed in midsummer 415 B.C.: "It was," says Thucydides, "the most costly and splendid force that ever sailed from one Greek city." It was dogged by disaster. No sooner had it arrived in Sicily than Alcibiades was recalled to stand trial on a charge trumped up by his political enemies, but he jumped ship and fled to Sparta, where he advised the authorities to send help to Syracuse, which the Athenians were by now besieging. Just as the Athenians were about to complete an encircling wall around Syracuse, a Spartan relief force arrived and saved the city (winter 414 B.C.). Nicias decided to lift the siege and retire by sea, but the Syracusans blocked the entrance to the Great Harbor, and in the battle that followed the Athenian fleet suffered a crushing defeat. Nicias decided to destroy what was left of the fleet and retreat over land; his army was split up into two halves. Both were ambushed and annihilated:

> This was the greatest action which took place in this war, . . . the most brilliant for the victors and the most disastrous for the conquered; for they were utterly defeated at all points and after undergoing the extremities of suffering were completely annihilated, infantry, ships, and all. Few of the many returned home.

> (Thucydides 7.87)

Despite this terrible loss, the Athenians immediately began to build a new fleet and fought on for another nine years. This last phase of the war was quite different from what had gone on before. It was a war of movement, fought all over the Aegean. The Spartans, who bartered away the freedom of the Ionian Greeks for Persian gold, built a fleet and roused most of the Athenian Empire to revolt. In 411 B.C. Athens, reduced to desperate straits, underwent an oligarchic revolution. This was fostered by Alcibiades, who had now fled from Sparta to the Persians and undertook to win Persian support for Athens if the Athenians would modify their extreme democracy and recall him. The people agreed that the franchise should be limited to the 5,000 richest citizens and that for the moment there should be a provisional government formed by a council of 400. No sooner were the 400 in power than they tried to make their position permanent and began to negotiate peace terms with Sparta. A counterrevolution followed. The Assembly deposed the 400 and instituted the moderate democracy originally proposed, government by the 5,000. Alcibiades was elected general in his absence and won a brilliant victory at Cyzicus, annihilating the Spartan fleet. This was followed by the restoration of the radical democracy at Athens and a series of operations in which Athens recovered most of her empire in the north Aegean. In 407 B.C. Alcibiades returned to Athens and received a hero's welcome.

A new Spartan commander, Lysander, was soon to change the situation. With Persian support, he rebuilt the Spartan fleet and defeated a squadron of Alcibiades' fleet. Alcibiades, although he was not present at the battle, fearing the volatility of the *demos*, fled to a castle, which he had prepared as a refuge in the Hellespont. The following year (405 B.C.) the Athenians won another major victory at Arginusae, destroying over half the Spartan fleet.

In 405 B.C., however, Lysander, again in command, made a surprise attack on the Athenian fleet when it was beached at Aegospotami and annihilated it.

This was the end for Athens. When the news reached the Piraeus, "A wail of lamentation spread from the Piraeus through the Long Walls to the city; and on that night not a man slept" (Xenophon, *Hellenica* 2.2.3). The Spartans now controlled the seas. They did not attack Athens but proceeded to starve her into submission. At last, when the people were desperate, they sent envoys to Sparta to discuss terms of surrender. The Peloponnesian League was summoned to discuss the issue. The majority voted for the utter destruction of Athens and the enslavement of the whole population, but Sparta resisted these savage terms. Eventually it was settled that Athens should surrender her whole empire; the entire fleet except for twelve triremes was to be handed over; all exiles were to return, and Athens should become an ally of Sparta.

Athena and Hera shake hands.

Hera was the patron goddess of Samos. After the Athenian defeat at Aegospotami, all the subject states of the Athenian Empire except Samos revolted. In gratitude for this loyalty, the Athenians passed a decree praising the Samians and making them Athenian citizens. In 403 B.C. this marble stele was set up on the Acropolis with the decree inscribed below the figures of Hera and Athena.

ΜΕΓΑ ΤΟ ΤΗΣ
ΘΑΛΑΣΣΗΣ ΚΡΑΤΟΣ
(δ)

Vocabulary

Verbs
ἐπιδιώκω (see διώκω for
  principal parts) I pursue
καταφεύγω (see φεύγω for
  principal parts) I flee for
  refuge
περιμένω (see μένω for
  principal parts) I wait for
**σφάζω, σφάξω, ἔσφαξα,
  ἔσφαγμαι, ἐσφάγην** I slay
ὑπομένω (see μένω for principal
  parts) I await (an attack),
  stand firm
φθάνω, φθήσομαι, ἔφθασα or
  ἔφθην (+ acc. and/or
  participle) I anticipate, do
  something before someone
  else
Nouns
  ἡ ἀταξίᾱ, τῆς ἀταξίᾱς
    disorder
  ἡ βοήθεια, τῆς βοηθείᾱς help

ἡ κώπη, τῆς κώπης oar
τὸ ναυάγιον, τοῦ ναυαγίου
  wrecked ship
ἡ ὁλκάς, τῆς ὁλκάδος
  merchant ship
ἡ τροπή, τῆς τροπῆς turn,
  turning, rout (of the enemy)
Adjective
  ἄτακτος, -ον disordered
  ἐναντίος, -ᾱ, -ον opposed,
    opposite, hostile; (as noun) the
    enemy
Prepositions
  πλήν (+ gen.) except, except for
  ὑπό (+ gen.) by (of agent),
    because of; (+ dat.) under; (+
    acc.) at (of time)
Adverbs
  ἀτάκτως in disorder
  ὅθεν from where
    ὅθενπερ (-περ added for
    emphasis)

ταύτῃ μὲν οὖν οἱ Πελοποννήσιοι ἐκράτουν τε καὶ διέφθειραν τὰς
Ἀττικὰς ναῦς· αἱ δὲ εἴκοσι νῆες αὐτῶν αἱ ἀπὸ τοῦ δεξιοῦ κέρως
ἐδίωκον τὰς ἕνδεκα ναῦς τῶν Ἀθηναίων αἵπερ ὑπεξέφυγον τὴν
ἐπιστροφήν. καὶ φθάνουσιν αὐτοὺς πλὴν μιᾶς νεὼς καταφυγοῦσαι ἐς
τὴν Ναύπακτον, καὶ σχοῦσαι ἀντίπρωροι παρεσκευάζοντο   5
ἀμῡνούμενοι, ἐὰν ἐς τὴν γῆν ἐπὶ σφᾶς πλέωσιν οἱ Πελοποννήσιοι. οἱ
δὲ παραγενόμενοι ἐπαιάνιζον ὡς νενῑκηκότες· καὶ τὴν μίαν ναῦν τῶν
Ἀθηναίων τὴν ὑπόλοιπον ἐδίωκε Λευκαδίᾱ ναῦς μία πολὺ πρὸ τῶν
ἄλλων. ἔτυχε δὲ ὁλκὰς ὁρμοῦσα μετέωρος, περὶ ἣν ἡ Ἀττικὴ ναῦς
περιπλεύσᾱσα τῇ Λευκαδίᾳ διωκούσῃ ἐμβάλλει μέσῃ καὶ καταδύ̄ει.   10

[τὴν ἐπιστροφήν the turning movement   φθάνουσιν . . . καταφυγοῦσαι
they (i.e., the eleven Athenian ships) anticipate (them) escaping to safety (i.e., they
escaped before they could be caught)   σχοῦσαι (aorist participle of ἔχω, here
intransitive) facing   ἀντίπρωροι with prows toward the enemy   ἐπαιάνιζον
raised the victory song (παιάν "paean")   ὑπόλοιπον remaining   μετέωρος
raised off the ground, at sea   ἐμβάλλει (+ dat.) strikes with a ram (ἔμβολος)]

τοῖς μὲν οὖν Πελοποννησίοις γενομένου τούτου ἀπροσδοκήτου
φόβος ἐμπίπτει, καὶ ἀτάκτως διώκοντες αἱ μέν τινες τῶν νεῶν
καθεῖσαι τὰς κώπᾱς ἐπέστησαν τοῦ πλοῦ, βουλόμενοι τοὺς ἄλλους
περιμεῖναι, αἱ δὲ ἐς βραχέα ὤκειλαν. οἱ δὲ Ἀθηναῖοι ἰδόντες ταῦτα
γιγνόμενα ἐθάρσουν τε καὶ βοήσαντες ἐπ᾽ αὐτοὺς ὥρμησαν. οἱ δὲ   15
διὰ τὴν παροῦσαν ἀταξίᾱν ὀλίγον μὲν χρόνον ὑπέμειναν, ἔπειτα δὲ
ἐτράποντο ἐς τὸν Πάνορμον ὅθενπερ ἀνηγάγοντο.

[ἀπροσδοκήτου unexpected   καθεῖσαι (aorist participle of καθίημι) dropping
ἐπέστησαν τοῦ πλοῦ they stopped sailing   ἐς βραχέα (from βραχύς, βραχεῖα,
βραχύ "short") onto the shallows   ὤκειλαν (from ὀκέλλω) ran aground]

ἐπιδιώκοντες δὲ οἱ Ἀθηναῖοι τάς τε ἐγγὺς οὔσᾱς ναῦς ἔλαβον ἓξ
καὶ τὰς ἑαυτῶν ἀφείλοντο, ἃς ἐκεῖνοι πρὸς τῇ γῇ διαφθείραντες
ἀνεδήσαντο· ἄνδρας τε τοὺς μὲν ἀπέκτειναν, τινὰς δὲ ἐζώγρησαν. ἐπὶ   20
δὲ τῆς Λευκαδίᾱς νεώς, ἣ περὶ τὴν ὁλκάδα κατέδῡ, Τῑμοκράτης ὁ
Λακεδαιμόνιος πλέων, ὡς ἡ ναῦς διεφθείρετο, ἔσφαξεν ἑαυτόν, καὶ
ἐξέπεσεν ἐς τὸν Ναυπακτίων λιμένα.

[ἀνεδήσαντο (from ἀναδέομαι) they fastened with ropes, took in tow   ἐζώγρησαν
(from ζωγρέω) they took alive, took captive   ἐξέπεσεν fell out (of the sea), was cast
ashore]

ἀναχωρήσαντες δὲ οἱ Ἀθηναῖοι τροπαῖον ἔστησαν καὶ τοὺς
νεκροὺς καὶ τὰ ναυάγια, ὅσα πρὸς τῇ ἑαυτῶν γῇ ἦν, ἀνείλοντο, καὶ   25
τοῖς ἐναντίοις τὰ ἐκείνων ὑπόσπονδα ἀπέδοσαν. ἔστησαν δὲ καὶ οἱ
Πελοποννήσιοι τροπαῖον ὡς νενῑκηκότες τῆς τροπῆς τῶν νεῶν ἃς
πρὸς τῇ γῇ διέφθειραν. μετὰ δὲ ταῦτα φοβούμενοι τὴν ἀπὸ τῶν
Ἀθηναίων βοήθειαν ὑπὸ νύκτα ἐσέπλευσαν ἐς τὸν κόλπον τὸν
Κρῑσαῖον καὶ Κόρινθον ἅπαντες πλὴν Λευκαδίων.   30

[ὑπόσπονδα under truce]

—adapted from Thucydides 2.91–92

Principal Parts: Verbs with -αν-/-ν- That Take Supplementary Participles

λα-ν-θ-άν-ω (λαθ-/ληθ-), **λήσω, ἔλαθον, λέληθα** (+*acc. and/or
   participle*) I escape notice, escape the notice of
τυ-γ-χ-άν-ω (τευχ-/τυχ-/τυχε-), **τεύξομαι, ἔτυχον, τετύχηκα** (+*gen.*)
   I hit, hit upon, get; (+*participle*) I happen to
φθά-ν-ω (φθη-/φθα-), **φθήσομαι, ἔφθασα** or **ἔφθην** (+ *acc. and/or
   participle*) I anticipate, do something before someone else

Word Building

Explain how the words in the following sets are formed and give their meanings:

root: παιδ-

1. ὁ *or* ἡ παῖς
2. τὸ παιδίον
3. παιδικός, -ή, -όν
4. παίζω
5. εὔπαις
6. ἄπαις
7. παιδεύω
8. ἡ παίδευσις
9. ὁ παιδαγωγός
10. παιδαγωγικός, -ή, -όν

root: λεγ-/λογ-

1. λέγω
2. ἡ λέξις
3. λεκτικός, -ή, -όν
4. ὁ λόγος
5. λογικός, -ή, -όν
6. λογίζομαι
7. ὁ λογιστής
8. ἄλογος, -ον
9. ἡ εὐλογίᾱ
10. ὁ λογογράφος

N.B. ὁ λόγος = word, story, speech, account, calculation, reasoning

Grammar

2. Complex Sentences in Indirect Speech

Primary Sequence

When complex sentences (i.e., sentences containing a main clause and a subordinate clause) are stated indirectly after a leading verb in the present, future, or perfect tense (primary sequence), no changes in the tenses or moods of the verbs in the original sentence are made except to substitute an infinitive or participle for the finite verb in the main clause of the original sentence, as required by the introductory verb, e.g.:

a. εἰ ὁ Φίλιππος τοῦτο εἶπεν, ἐψεύδετο.
   If Philip said this, he was lying.   (past particular condition)

   λέγει ὅτι εἰ ὁ Φίλιππος τοῦτο εἶπεν, ἐψεύδετο.
   τὸν Φίλιππόν φησι ψεύδεσθαι, εἰ τοῦτο εἶπεν.
   οἶδε τὸν Φίλιππον ψευδόμενον, εἰ τοῦτο εἶπεν.
   He/she says/knows that if Philip said this, he was lying.
      (Note that the imperfect indicative ἐψεύδετο of the original statement remains unchanged after ὅτι and is replaced by a

present infinitive and a present participle after φησί and οἶδε respectively.)

The particle ἄν must be retained with the infinitive and participle constructions as well as with the indicative construction in indirect speech, e.g.:

b. εἰ ὁ Φίλιππος τοῦτο ἔλεγεν, ἐψεύδετο ἄν.
If Philip said this, he would be lying.   (present contrary to fact condition)

λέγει ὅτι εἰ ὁ Φίλιππος τοῦτο ἔλεγεν, ἐψεύδετο ἄν.
τὸν Φίλιππόν φησι ψεύδεσθαι ἄν, εἰ τοῦτο ἔλεγεν.
οἶδε τὸν Φίλιππον ψευδόμενον ἄν, εἰ τοῦτο ἔλεγεν.
He/she says/knows that if Philip said this, he would be lying.

Secondary Sequence

If the introductory verb is in a past tense (imperfect, aorist, or pluperfect), the following rules for secondary sequence apply:

a. An indicative verb in the <u>main clause</u> of the original sentence *may* be changed to the corresponding tense of the optative when the indirect statement is introduced by ὅτι or ὡς (see Chapter 25, Grammar 4, pages 124–125). Note, however, that an indicative with ἄν in the main clause of contrary to fact conditions is *always* retained.

b. All *primary tenses* of the indicative and all subjunctives (with or without ἄν) in the <u>subordinate clause</u> of the original sentence *may* be changed to the corresponding tenses of the optative (ἐάν becomes εἰ, ὅταν becomes ὅτε, πρὶν ἄν becomes πρίν, etc., i.e., the ἄν drops out when the subjunctive is changed to optative).

c. *Secondary tenses* of the indicative and all optatives in the <u>subordinate clause</u> of the original sentence remain unchanged in mood and tense.

d. Greek writers often chose *not* to make the optional changes to the optative but to retain the original indicatives or subjunctives for the sake of vividness.

The following examples illustrate the rules given above:

i. εἰ ὁ Φίλιππος τοῦτο ἔλεγεν, ἐψεύδετο ἄν.   (see above)

εἶπεν ὅτι εἰ ὁ Φίλιππος τοῦτο ἔλεγεν, ἐψεύδετο ἄν.
ἔφη τὸν Φίλιππόν ψεύδεσθαι ἄν, εἰ τοῦτο ἔλεγεν.
ᾔδει τὸν Φίλιππον ψευδόμενον ἄν, εἰ τοῦτο ἔλεγεν.
He/she said, knew that if Philip said this, he would be lying.
(Note that the indicative with ἄν in the original main clause must be retained after ὅτι and that the secondary tense of the indicative in the original subordinate clause must also be retained. See

rules a and c above. Note that a present infinitive and participle replace the imperfect indicative after ἔφη and ᾔδει.)

ii. εἰ ὁ Φίλιππος τοῦτο εἴποι, ψεύδοιτο ἄν.
If Philip should say this, he would be lying.   (future less vivid condition)

εἶπεν ὅτι εἰ ὁ Φίλιππος τοῦτο εἴποι, ψεύδοιτο ἄν.
ἔφη τὸν Φίλιππόν ψεύδεσθαι ἄν, εἰ τοῦτο εἴποι.
ᾔδει τὸν Φίλιππον ψευδόμενον ἄν, εἰ τοῦτο εἴποι.
He/she said/knew that if Philip should say this, he would be lying.
(The optative with ἄν of the original main clause remains unchanged after ὅτι and changes to the same tense of the infinitive and participle with ἄν retained after ἔφη and ᾔδει. The optative of the original subordinate clause remains unchanged; see rule c.)

iii. μὴ ἐπιχειρεῖτε πρὶν ἄν αὐτὸς σημήνω.
Do not attack until I give the signal.

προείρητο δ᾽ αὐτοῖς ὑπὸ Φορμίωνος μὴ ἐπιχειρεῖν πρὶν ἄν αὐτὸς σημήνῃ.
An order had been given to them by Phormio beforehand   (29α:22–23)
that they were not to attack until he gave the signal.
(The original aorist subjunctive with ἄν is retained for the sake of vividness. See rules b and d above.)

προείρητο δ᾽ αὐτοῖς ὑπὸ Φορμίωνος μὴ ἐπιχειρεῖν πρὶν αὐτὸς σημήνειεν.
(Here the subjunctive is changed to the corresponding tense of the optative, with ἄν dropping out; see rule b above.)

iv. ἐὰν στρατεύηται Κροῖσος ἐπὶ Πέρσας, μεγάλην ἀρχὴν καταλύσει.
If Croesus wages war against the Persians, he will destroy a great empire.   (future more vivid condition)

ἡ δὲ Πυθίη τάδε ἀπεκρίνατο, ὅτι ἐὰν στρατεύηται Κροῖσος ἐπὶ Πέρσας, μεγάλην ἀρχὴν καταλύσει.   (27α:32–33)
And the Pythia answered these things, that if Croesus waged war against the Persians, he would destroy a great empire.
(The original ἐάν + subjunctive and future indicative are retained in the indirect statement. See rules b and d above.)

ἡ δὲ Πυθίη τάδε ἀπεκρίνατο, ὅτι εἰ στρατεύοιτο Κροῖσος ἐπὶ Πέρσας, μεγάλην ἀρχὴν καταλύσοι.
(Optatives are here substituted in both clauses, with ἐάν changing to εἰ; see rules a and b above.)

v. γελοῖόν ἐστιν, εἰ οὕτως ἔχει.
It is ridiculous if this is so.   (present particular condition)

Ἀγασίας εἶπεν ὅτι γελοῖον εἴη, εἰ οὕτως ἔχοι.
Agasias said it was ridiculous if this were so.   (Xenophon, *Anabasis* 5.9.30)
(Both verbs are changed to optative. See rules a and b above.)

Exercise 30c

Rewrite the following conditional sentences as indirect statements introduced by the words in brackets (all secondary sequence); give alternative versions of the moods, where they are permissible:

1. ἐὰν στρατεύηται Κροῖσος ἐπὶ Πέρσᾱς, μεγάλην ἀρχὴν καταλύσει (ἡ Πῡθίη ἔφη . . .).
2. οἱ παῖδες οὐκ ἂν κατέστησαν εἰς κίνδῡνον, εἰ οἴκοι ἔμειναν (ὁ πατὴρ ᾔδει . . .).
3. ὅσ' ἂν λέγῃ τὰ χρηστήρια γράψαντες ἀναφέρετε παρά με (ὁ Κροῖσος τοὺς ἀγγέλους ἐκέλευε . . .).
4. ὁ Κροῖσος πρῶτον μὲν σῑγὴν εἶχε ἐρωτώμενος, τέλος δέ, ὡς ἠναγκάζετο, πάντα εἶπεν (οἱ Λῡδοὶ ἔφασαν . . .).
5. πάντα ἐποιήσαμεν ἃ ἐκελεύσατε (οἱ ἄνδρες πρὸς τοὺς πέμψαντας εἶπον . . .).

*   *   *

ΟΙ ΠΕΛΟΠΟΝΝΗΣΙΟΙ ΒΟΥΛΕΥΟΥΣΙΝ ΑΠΟΠΕΙΡΑΣΑΙ ΤΟΥ ΠΕΙΡΑΙΩΣ

Read the following passages (adapted from Thucydides 2.93–94) and answer the comprehension questions:

Before disbanding their fleet, the Peloponnesians plan a surprise attack on the Piraeus.

πρὶν δὲ διαλῦσαι τὸ ἐς Κόρινθον ἀναχωρῆσαν ναυτικόν, ὁ Κνῆμος καὶ οἱ ἄλλοι στρατηγοὶ τῶν Πελοποννησίων, ἀρχομένου τοῦ χειμῶνος, ἐβούλοντο ἀποπειρᾶσαι τοῦ Πειραιῶς τοῦ λιμένος τῶν Ἀθηναίων· ἀφύλακτος δὲ ἦν ὁ λιμήν. οὐ γὰρ ᾤοντο οἱ Ἀθηναῖοι τοὺς πολεμίους ἂν τολμῆσαι αὐτῷ προσβαλεῖν. ἐδόκει δὲ λαβόντα τῶν ναυτῶν ἕκαστον τὴν κώπην πεζῇ ἰέναι ἐκ Κορίνθου ἐπὶ τὴν πρὸς Ἀθήνᾱς θάλασσαν, καὶ ἀφικομένους ἐς Μέγαρα καὶ καθελκύσαντας τεσσαράκοντα ναῦς, αἳ ἔτυχον ἐκεῖ οὖσαι, πλεῦσαι εὐθὺς ἐπὶ τὸν Πειραιᾶ.   5

[ἀποπειρᾶσαι (*from* ἀποπειράομαι) to make an attempt upon (+ *gen.*)   **ἀφύλακτος** unguarded   **καθελκύσαντας** (*aorist participle of* καθέλκω) having dragged down, launched]

1. At what time of year did the Peloponnesians want to attack the Piraeus?
2. Why was the harbor unprotected?
3. Upon what plan of action did the Peloponnesians decide?

ὡς δὲ ἔδοξεν αὐτοῖς, ἐχώρουν εὐθύς· καὶ ἀφικόμενοι νυκτὸς καὶ καθελκύσαντες τὰς ναῦς ἔπλεον οὐκέτι μὲν ἐπὶ τὸν Πειραιᾶ, φοβούμενοι τὸν κίνδῡνον, ἐπὶ δὲ τῆς Σαλαμῖνος τὸ ἀκρωτήριον τὸ πρὸς Μέγαρα ὁρῶν. καὶ φρούριον   10 τῶν Ἀθηναίων ἐκεῖ ἦν καὶ νεῶν τριῶν φυλακή. οἱ οὖν Πελοποννήσιοι τῷ τε

φρουρίῳ προσέβαλον καὶ τὰς τριήρεις ἀφείλκυσαν κενὰς τήν τε ἄλλην Σαλαμῖνα
ἐπόρθουν.

[ἀκρωτήριον promontory   ἀφείλκυσαν (*aorist of* ἀφέλκω)   dragged away
τήν . . . ἄλλην Σαλαμῖνα the rest of Salamis]

4.   How soon was the action undertaken?
5.   How was the plan changed when the action was undertaken?
6.   Why did the Peloponnesians not do as had been planned?
7.   What did the Athenians have stationed at Salamis?
8.   What three things did the Peloponnesians do there?

ἐς δὲ τὰς ᾿Αθήνᾱς φρυκτοί τε ἤροντο πολέμιοι καὶ μεγίστη ἐγένετο ἔκπληξις· οἱ
γὰρ ἐν τῷ ἄστει ᾤοντο τοὺς πολεμίους ἤδη ἐς τὸν Πειραιᾶ ἐσπεπλευκέναι, οἱ δὲ ἐν   15
τῷ Πειραιεῖ ᾤοντο τήν τε Σαλαμῖνα ᾑρῆσθαι καὶ ἤδη ἐπὶ σφᾶς ἐσπλεῖν αὐτούς.
βοηθήσαντες δὲ ἅμ᾿ ἡμέρᾳ πανδημεὶ οἱ ᾿Αθηναῖοι ἐς τὸν Πειραιᾶ ναῦς τε
καθεῖλκον καὶ ἐσβάντες κατὰ σπουδὴν ταῖς μὲν ναυσὶν ἐπὶ τὴν Σαλαμῖνα
ἔπλεον, τῷ δὲ πεζῷ φυλακὰς τοῦ Πειραιῶς καθίσταντο. οἱ δὲ Πελοποννήσιοι ὡς
ᾔσθοντο τὴν βοήθειαν, κατὰ τάχος ἀπέπλεον.   20

[φρυκτοί . . . πολέμιοι enemy fire signals (i.e., beacons warning of an enemy
attack)   ἔκπληξις a striking out of the wits, consternation   αὐτούς: i.e., the
Peloponnesians   πανδημεῖ altogether, in a mass   καθεῖλκον (*imperfect of*
καθέλκω) they launched   κατὰ σπουδήν hastily   ᾔσθοντο (*from* αἰσθάνομαι)
they perceived]

9.   How were the Athenians alerted to the danger?
10. What was their immediate reaction?
11. What did the Athenians in the city think?
12. What did the Athenians in Salamis think?
13. What two sets of measures did the Athenians take the following day?
14. What indications are there that they took the threat seriously?
15. How did the Peloponnesians react?

Exercise 30d

Translate into Greek:

1.   If the Corinthians had sailed straight against the Piraeus, they would
     easily have taken it.
2.   For there was no fleet guarding the harbor, because the Athenians
     thought that the enemy would never sail against it.
3.   But the Corinthians were so afraid of the danger that they no longer
     sailed against the Piraeus but to Salamis.
4.   There was a garrison there of three triremes, so no one could sail into
     Megara or sail out.
5.   The Corinthians took (*use participle*) these triremes and sacked
     Salamis; but the next day, before the Athenians came to help, they
     quickly sailed away.

31
ΑΧΑΡΝΗΣ
(α)

Aristophanes and Old Comedy

In 486 B.C. a prize was first offered for a comedy in the dramatic competition at the Greater Dionysia, which until then had been for tragedies only. At the time of Aristophanes' first play (427 B.C.), three comedies were put on every year at the Lenaea, a festival of Dionysus held in January, and three at the Greater Dionysia, held in March.

The theater of Dionysus, in which both tragedies and comedies were performed, consisted of a circular ὀρχήστρᾱ, "dancing place," about sixty-six feet in diameter. Behind it was the auditorium, rising in concentric rows up the south slope of the Acropolis. In front of it was the σκηνή, "stage," a permanent set representing a building with two doors. The stage was raised slightly above the level of the orchestra (see illustration, page 11). In both tragedy and comedy the chorus played a leading role. In comedy they numbered twenty-four. Whereas the actors spoke their dialogue, the chorus sang their lyrics to the accompaniment of the lyre and flute.

Aristophanes' first play, the *Banqueters*, was produced in 427 B.C., his last extant play, *Wealth*, in 388 B.C. Eleven of his comedies survive, the earliest being the *Acharnians*, which won first prize at the Lenaea in 425 B.C. When this play was produced, Athens had been at war for more than five years. The people had suffered terribly from the plague, and the war seemed a stalemate. The farmers suffered the most, abandoning their farms every year when the Peloponnesians invaded in late spring, living in the city under appalling conditions during the invasions, and returning home to find their crops destroyed and their vines cut down. The heroes of several of Aristophanes' plays, including Dicaeopolis in the *Acharnians*, are war-weary farmers.

We last saw the family of Dicaeopolis when Philip was left behind in Athens to continue his schooling (Chapter 24). The rest of the family returned to the country when the Peloponnesians withdrew from Attica, only to return to the city every year when the Peloponnesians invaded in late spring. In reading the words of Dicaeopolis in the *Acharnians* you will hear the voice that Aristophanes gave him. He dreams of peace, and after being rebuffed in the normal course of political activity in the Assembly, he makes his own separate peace with Sparta. At the end of the selections from the play that you will read in this chapter, he joyfully assembles his family and celebrates his private peace with a sacred procession and a song in honor of Dionysus.

Vocabulary

Verbs
δάκνω, δήξομαι, ἔδακον,
  δέδηγμαι, ἐδήχθην I bite,
  sting
ἐράω, (*imperfect*) ἤρων,
  ἐρασθήσομαι, ἠράσθην
  (+ *gen.*) I love
λαλέω I talk, chatter
λοιδορέω I abuse
ὀδυνάω, ὀδυνηθήσομαι,
  ὠδυνήθην I cause pain;
  (*passive*) I suffer pain
ποθέω I long for
στυγέω I hate

Nouns
ἡ καρδίᾱ, τῆς καρδίᾱς heart
οἱ πρυτάνεις, τῶν
  πρυτάνεων prytaneis,
  presidents (see essay in
  Chapter 22)
Adjective
κῡριος, -ᾱ, -ον having
  authority, legitimate, regular
Adverbs
ἀτεχνῶς simply, really
εἶτα then, next
οὐδεπώποτε never yet

1 ὅσα δὴ δέδηγμαι "how much I've been stung," literally, "as to how many
    things"; ὅσα, βαιά (2), and ἅ (3) are adverbial accusatives.
2 βαιά "few things" (*accusative with* ἥσθην = "I have had few pleasures")
3 ψαμμακοσιογάργαρα "sand-hundred-heaps," a typical Aristophanic
    coinage
7 ἑωθινῆς "at dawn," the usual time for an Assembly to begin
    αὐτηΐ "this here"; *the suffix* -ΐ *adds demonstrative force and often suggests that
    the actor points with his finger.*
8 οἱ δ' "but they," i.e., the people   κἄνω = καὶ ἄνω
9 τὸ σχοινίον . . . τὸ μεμιλτωμένον "the red rope," i.e., a rope covered
    with red ocherous iron ore used to round up and drive loiterers from the agora
    to the Pnyx for assemblies; those marked with the red would be fined.
10 ἀωρίᾱν (*adverb*) "too late"
11 ὠστιοῦνται . . . ἀλλήλοισι "will jostle each other"
    πῶς δοκεῖς (*literally*) "how do you think?" = "you can't think how,"
    "astonishingly," "like mad"
12 ξύλου "wood" = "bench," "seat"
13 ἀθρόοι "all together"   καταρρέοντες "flowing down," "streaming in"
    εἰρήνη δ' ὅπως . . . οὐδέν = οὐδὲν προτῑμῶσι (= "they don't care a bit")
      ὅπως εἰρήνη ἔσται
15 ἀεί = αἰεί
16 νοστῶν "coming"   κᾆτ' = καὶ εἶτα
17 κέχηνα, σκορδινῶμαι, πέρδομαι "I yawn, stretch, fart"
18 παρατίλλομαι "I pluck out my hairs"
    λογίζομαι "I count," "I make calculations"
21 ἀτεχνῶς *take with* παρεσκευασμένος
22 ὑποκρούειν "to interrupt"
24 ἀλλ' οἱ πρυτάνεις γὰρ οὑτοιΐ "But (look!) for the prytaneis (are) here"
    μεσημβρινοί "at midday"
25 οὐκ ἠγόρευον; "Didn't I tell you?"
    τοῦτ' ἐκεῖν' οὑγὼ 'λεγον = τοῦτό (ἐστιν) ἐκεῖνο ὃ ἐγὼ ἔλεγον
26 τὴν προεδρίᾱν "the front seat"
    ὠστίζεται "pushes and shoves," "jostles"

Speaking Characters

ΔΙΚΑΙΟΠΟΛΙΣ (ΔΙΚ.) Dicaeopolis   ΨΕΥΔΑΡΤΑΒΑΣ (ΨΕΥ.) Pseudartabas
ΚΗΡΥΞ (ΚΥΡ.) Herald   ΧΟΡΟΣ Chorus of Acharnian men
ΑΜΦΙΘΕΟΣ (ΑΜΦ.) Amphitheus   ΘΥΓΑΤΗΡ Daughter of Dicaeopolis
ΠΡΕΣΒΥΣ (ΠΡΕ.) Ambassador

The opening scene is set on the Pnyx where there is to be a meeting of the
Assembly. Dicaeopolis sits alone, waiting for the people to assemble and the
prytaneis to arrive. While waiting, he complains that it has been a terrible year,
in which almost nothing has occurred that gave him any pleasure.

ΔΙΚΑΙΟΠΟΛΙΣ (*soliloquizing*)

1   ὅσα δὴ δέδηγμαι τὴν ἐμαυτοῦ καρδίαν,
2   ἥσθην δὲ βαιά, πάνυ δὲ βαιά, τέτταρα·
3   ἃ δ’ ὠδυνήθην, ψαμμακοσιογάργαρα.
4   ἀλλ’ οὐδεπώποτ’ . . .
5   οὕτως ἐδήχθην . . .
6   ὡς νῦν, ὁπότ’ οὔσης κυρίας ἐκκλησίας
7   ἑωθινῆς ἔρημος ἡ Πνὺξ αὑτηί,
8   οἱ δ’ ἐν ἀγορᾷ λαλοῦσι κἄνω καὶ κάτω
9   τὸ σχοινίον φεύγουσι τὸ μεμιλτωμένον.
10   οὐδ’ οἱ πρυτάνεις ἥκουσιν, ἀλλ’ ἀωρίαν
11   ἥκοντες, εἶτα δ’ ὠστιοῦνται πῶς δοκεῖς
12   ἐλθόντες ἀλλήλοισι περὶ πρώτου ξύλου,
13   ἀθρόοι καταρρέοντες· εἰρήνη δ’ ὅπως
14   ἔσται προτῑμῶσ’ οὐδέν· ὦ πόλις, πόλις.
15   ἐγὼ δ’ ἀεὶ πρώτιστος εἰς ἐκκλησίαν
16   νοστῶν κάθημαι· κᾆτ’ ἐπειδὰν ὦ μόνος,
17   στένω, κέχηνα, σκορδινῶμαι, πέρδομαι,
18   ἀπορῶ, γράφω, παρατίλλομαι, λογίζομαι,
19   ἀποβλέπων ἐς τὸν ἀγρόν, εἰρήνης ἐρῶν,
20   στυγῶν μὲν ἄστυ τὸν δ’ ἐμὸν δῆμον ποθῶν.
21   νῦν οὖν ἀτεχνῶς ἥκω παρεσκευασμένος
22   βοᾶν, ὑποκρούειν, λοιδορεῖν τοὺς ῥήτορας,
23   ἐάν τις ἄλλο πλὴν περὶ εἰρήνης λέγῃ.
24   (*seeing the prytaneis arrive*) ἀλλ’ οἱ πρυτάνεις γὰρ
          οὑτοιὶ μεσημβρινοί.
25   οὐκ ἠγόρευον; τοῦτ’ ἐκεῖν’ οὑγὼ ’λεγον·
26   ἐς τὴν προεδρίαν πᾶς ἀνὴρ ὠστίζεται.

ΑΧΑΡΝΗΣ (β)

Vocabulary

Verbs

ἀδικέω I do wrong; (*transitive*)
I wrong, injure

αἰσθάνομαι, αἰσθήσομαι,
ᾐσθόμην, ᾔσθημαι (+ *gen. or
acc.*) I perceive, learn,
apprehend

ἄχθομαι, ἀχθέσομαι,
ἠχθέσθην (+ *dat.*) I am vexed
(at), grieved (by)

ἡγέομαι I lead (+ *dat.*); I think,
consider

οἴχομαι, ᾤχετο (*present in
perfect sense*) I have gone,
departed; (*imperfect in
pluperfect sense*) I had gone,
departed

προσδοκάω I expect

Nouns

ὁ *or* ἡ ἀλαζών, τοῦ *or* τῆς
ἀλαζόνος imposter,
charlatan, quack

ἡ ἀσπίς, τῆς ἀσπίδος shield

ἡ βίᾱ, τῆς βίᾱς force, violence

ὁ μήν, τοῦ μηνός month

ὁ *or* ἡ ὄρνῑς, τοῦ *or* τῆς ὄρνῑθος
bird

τὸ χρῡσίον, τοῦ χρῡσίου gold
coin, money, jewelry

Adjectives

ἀθάνατος, -ον immortal

κακοδαίμων, κακοδαίμονος
having an evil spirit or bad
luck

ὅλος, -η, -ον whole, entire

χρῡσοῦς, -ῆ, -οῦν golden

Preposition

παρά (+ *gen.*) from; (+ *dat.*) at
the house of; (+ *acc.*) to, along,
past

Adverbs

πρόσθε(ν) before (of time or
place)

πώποτε ever

σαφῶς clearly

Expressions

εἰς τὸ πρόσθεν forward

ναὶ μὰ Δία yes, by Zeus!

οἴμοι κακοδαίμων poor devil!
oh misery!

28 ὡς ἄν = ἵνα
    καθάρματος "the purified area." Before the Assembly began, a suckling pig
    was sacrificed and carried around the boundaries of the meeting place to
    purify the area (on purification, see essay in Chapter 26).
    ΑΜΦΙΘΕΟΣ The name means something like "a god on both sides."
29 τίς ἀγορεύειν βούλεται; the formula for throwing open a motion to debate
    (see essay in Chapter 22)
34 ἐφόδι(α) "journey money," i.e., an allowance paid by the Council for his
    journey to Sparta
35 οἱ τοξόται "archers" Scythian archers (see illustration on page 210) were
    used as police. It was considered improper to use a citizen in this capacity.

Grammar

1. Crasis

A vowel or diphthong at the end of a word sometimes coalesces with a vowel or diphthong at the beginning of the next word. This occurs most frequently with καί, ὦ, ἐγώ, the article, and the relative, e.g.:

καλὸς κᾱγαθός = καλὸς καὶ ἀγαθός   ὦνδρες = ὦ ἄνδρες
ἐγῷδα = ἐγὼ οἶδα   ταὐτά = τὰ αὐτά

Note that the crasis is marked by a breathing and that the vowel is long.

2. Elision

See Book I, Chapter 5, Grammar 4, page 45, e.g.:

πάριτ' ἐς = πάριτε ἐς   πάριθ', ὡς = πάριτε, ὡς

3. Prodelision or Aphaeresis

The vowel ε at the beginning of a word following a word ending in a long vowel or dipthong is sometimes elided. This occurs most frequently with ἐγώ, ἐστί, and augment, e.g.:

ποῦ 'στιν; = ποῦ ἔστιν;   ἐγὼ 'λεγον = ἐγὼ ἔλεγον

*   *   *

27 **ΚΗΡΥΞ** (*addressing the people who are milling around the edge of the area of assembly*) πάριτ' ἐς τὸ πρόσθεν,

28 πάριθ', ὡς ἂν ἐντὸς ἦτε τοῦ καθάρματος.

29 **ΑΜΦΙΘΕΟΣ** (*running in breathless*) ἤδη τις εἶπε; **ΚΗΡ.** (*ignoring Amphitheus and opening the Assembly with a formal question*) τίς ἀγορεύειν βούλεται;

30 **ΑΜΦ.** ἐγώ. **ΚΗΡ.** τίς ὤν; **ΑΜΦ.** Ἀμφίθεος. **ΚΗΡ.** οὐκ ἄνθρωπος; **ΑΜΦ.** οὔ,

31 ἀλλ' ἀθάνατος. . . .

32 . . . ἐμοὶ δ' ἐπέτρεψαν οἱ θεοὶ

33 σπονδὰς ποιεῖσθαι πρὸς Λακεδαιμονίους μόνῳ.

34 ἀλλ' ἀθάνατος ὤν, ὦνδρες, ἐφόδι' οὐκ ἔχω.

35 οὐ γὰρ διδόᾱσιν οἱ πρυτάνεις. **ΚΗΡ.** (*calling for the archers to eject Amphitheus for interrupting the proceedings*) οἱ τοξόται.

ΔΙΚ. (*standing up and shouting an appeal to the prytaneis on Amphitheus' behalf*) ὦνδρες πρυτάνεις, ἀδικεῖτε

36 τὴν ἐκκλησίᾱν

38 κρεμάσαι τὰς ἀσπίδας "to hang up our shields"; shields were usually hung
    on the wall when they were out of use. We see them hanging thus in many
    vase paintings.

39 σῖγα "be quiet," *literally*, "quietly"; σῖγα is an adverb. The imperative of
    σῑγάω is σῑγᾱ, as in line 44.

40 ἢν = ἐάν   ἢν μή "unless"
    πρυτανεύσητέ μοι "prytanize for me" = "introduce a motion for debate for
    me." All motions for debate had to be first discussed by the Council, that was
    presided over by the prytaneis (see essay in Chapter 22). The prytaneis
    introduced the motion to the Assembly as a προβούλευμα.

42 ποίου βασιλέως; Dicaeopolis' indignant question is occasioned by the
    finery of the Persian ambassadors. They are "peacocks" (τοῖς ταῶσι, 43),
    who are likely to prove imposters (τοῖς ἀλαζονεύμασιν, 43, "impostures,"
    abstract noun for concrete).

45 ἐπέμψαθ' = ἐπέμψατε "you (the people) sent us" ὡς (+ *acc.*) "to"

47 ἐπ' Εὐθυμένους ἄρχοντος "in the time of Euthymenes being archon."
    Year dates are given by the name of the eponymous archon. The archon list
    shows that this was the year 437/6.
    οἴμοι τῶν δραχμῶν "oh my, (those) drachmas!" (*genitive of exclamation*)

48 πρὸς βίᾱν "forcibly," "perforce"; the ambassadors *had* to accept the
    entertainment and the drink.

49 ὑαλίνων ἐκπωμάτων "crystal goblets"
    χρῡσίδων "golden vessels"

50 ἄκρᾱτον "unmixed," i.e., undiluted with water. Wine was normally mixed
    with water, unless you intended to get drunk.
    ὦ Κραναὰ πόλις "O Cranian city." Κρανααί was the most ancient name
    for Athens, and the word suggests the adjective κραναός "rocky," "rugged,"
    and the proper noun Κραναός, the name of a mythical king of Athens.
    Dicaeopolis alludes to the good old days, now replaced by the effeminate
    luxury of the ambassadors.

51 τὸν κατάγελων "the mockery," i.e., "how the ambassadors mock you"

53 καταφαγεῖν "to eat" (*second aorist infinitive of* κατεσθίω)

55 ἀπόπατον "latrine"

56 κἄχεζεν = καὶ ἔχεζεν "and he was shitting"

57 τὸν πρωκτόν "his ass"   ξυνήγαγεν "when (within what time) did he
    close his ass?"

58 τῇ πανσελήνῳ "at the full moon" (σελήνη)

60 κρῑβάνου "a ceramic oven" (for baking a loaf of bread)

ὁ τοξότης

37   τὸν ἄνδρ' ἀπάγοντες, ὅστις ἡμῖν ἤθελε
38   σπονδὰς ποιεῖσθαι καὶ κρεμάσαι τὰς ἀσπίδας.
39   ΚΗΡ.   κάθησο, σῖγα. ΔΙΚ. μὰ τὸν Ἀπόλλω, 'γὼ μὲν οὔ,
40   ἢν μὴ περὶ εἰρήνης γε πρυτανεύσητέ μοι. (*Dicaeopolis*
            reluctantly sits down, but far from remaining silent he will keep
            up a running commentary on the proceedings.)

The first item on the agenda of the Assembly is a report from ambassadors who
were sent to Persia to ask the King to help in the war against the Peloponnesians;
in fact both sides were continually sending ambassadors to ask the King for help.
These ambassadors were dispatched from Athens in 437/6 when Euthymenes
was archon, eleven years before this play was staged! They bring with them
envoys from Persia, dressed in Oriental splendor (i.e., as peacocks).

41   ΚΗΡ.   (*formally announcing the arrival of the*
            ambassadors) οἱ πρέσβεις οἱ παρὰ βασιλέως.
42   ΔΙΚ.   ποίου βασιλέως; ἄχθομαι 'γὼ πρέσβεσιν
43   καὶ τοῖς ταῶσι τοῖς τ' ἀλαζονεύμασιν.
44   ΚΗΡ.   σῖγᾱ. . . .
45   ΠΡΕΣΒΥΣ (*addressing the Assembly*) ἐπέμψαθ' ἡμᾶς ὡς βασιλέᾱ
            τὸν μέγαν
46   μισθὸν φέροντας δύο δραχμὰς τῆς ἡμέρᾱς
47   ἐπ' Εὐθυμένους ἄρχοντος. ΔΙΚ. οἴμοι τῶν δραχμῶν.
48   ΠΡΕ.   (*ignoring Dicaeopolis and continuing his speech*)
            ξενιζόμενοι δὲ πρὸς βίαν ἐπίνομεν
49   ἐξ ὑαλίνων ἐκπωμάτων καὶ χρῡσίδων
50   ἄκρᾱτον οἶνον ἡδύν. ΔΙΚ. ὦ Κραναὰ πόλις,
51   ἆρ' αἰσθάνει τὸν κατάγελων τῶν πρέσβεων;
52   ΠΡΕ.   (*continuing to ignore Dicaeopolis*) οἱ βάρβαροι γὰρ ἄνδρας
            ἡγοῦνται μόνους
53   τοὺς πλεῖστα δυναμένους καταφαγεῖν καὶ πιεῖν.
54   ἔτει τετάρτῳ δ' ἐς τὰ βασίλει' ἤλθομεν·
55   ἀλλ' εἰς ἀπόπατον ᾤχετο στρατιὰν λαβών,
56   κἄχεζεν ὀκτὼ μῆνας ἐπὶ χρῡσῶν ὀρῶν.
57   ΔΙΚ.   πόσου δὲ τὸν πρωκτὸν χρόνου ζυνήγαγεν;
58   ΠΡΕ.   (*answering Dicaeopolis and continuing his speech*)
            τῇ πανσελήνῳ· κᾆτ' ἀπῆλθεν οἴκαδε.
59   εἶτ' ἐξένιζε· παρετίθει δ' ἡμῖν ὅλους
60   ἐκ κρῑβάνου βοῦς. ΔΙΚ. καὶ τίς εἶδε πώποτε

61   κρῑβανίτᾱς "baked" (in a κρῑβανος)
     τῶν ἀλαζονευμάτων "what humbug!" (for the genitive, see line 47 above; for
        the word, see line 43)
62   τριπλάσιον Κλεωνύμου "three times as big as Cleonymus." Aristophanes
        frequently poked fun at Cleonymus for having thrown away his shield to
        escape from battle, for being a glutton and a perjurer, and, as here, for the
        huge bulk of his body.
63   φέναξ "cheat," with a pun on the word φοῖνιξ, the fabled Oriental phoenix;
        translate "cheatiebird"
64   ταῦτ᾽ . . . ἐφενάκιζες "this is how you cheated (us)"
     ἄρα "as it seems" (distinguish this from ἆρα, which introduces a question)
65   Ψευδαρτάβᾱν "Falseartabas." The second half of the name rings true.
        Xerxes had an uncle named Artabanes (see Herodotus 7.10).
66   τὸν βασιλέως ὀφθαλμόν "the King's Eye" is the actual title of the Persian
        King's intelligence official (see Herodotus 1.114).
     ἐκκόψειέ γε / κόραξ πατάξᾱς "may a raven (κόραξ) strike (πατάξᾱς) it
        and knock it out (ἐκκόψειε)"
67   τόν τε σὸν τοῦ πρέσβεως "and yours too, the ambassador's"
68   ὦναξ Ἡράκλεις = ὦ ἄναξ Ἡράκλεις "O lord Heracles!"—an exclamation
        expressing disgust
69   σὺ βασιλεὺς . . . Ἀθηναίοισιν = σὺ φράσον ἅττα (= ἅτινα)
     βασιλεὺς ἀπέπεμψέ σε λέξοντα Ἀθηναίοις
71   The words of Pseudartabas are a meaningless jumble.
72   ξυνήκαθ᾽ = ξυνήκατε "Did you understand?" (from συνίημι)
74   μεῖζον "louder"
75   This time Pseudartabas speaks a sort of pidgin Greek, of which sense of a sort
        can be made: "No getty goldy, wide-assed Ioni."
77   λέγει "he calls" (+ two accusatives)
79   ἀχάνᾱς "bushels"; ἡ ἀχάνη can mean either a basket for provisions or the
        Greek name for a Persian measure.
     ὅδε γε the words suggest that the ambassador has hold of the King's Eye and is
        trying to make him say his piece again.
83   ἐς τὸ πρυτανεῖον "to the Prytaneum" (for a public banquet)
     ταῦτα δῆτ᾽ οὐκ ἀγχόνη; "well, isn't this a hanging (matter)?" i.e.,
        enough to make you hang yourself

Principal Parts: Verbs in -μι

δί-δω-μι (δω-/δο-), (imperfect) ἐδίδουν, δώσω, ἔδωκα, (infinitive) δοῦναι,
   (participle) δούς, δέδωκα, δέδομαι, ἐδόθην I give
ἵ-στη-μι (στη-/στα- for σιστα-/σιστη-), (imperfect) ἵστην, στήσω, (first
   aorist) ἔστησα, (second aorist) ἔστην, ἔστηκα, ἐστάθην I make to
   stand, stop, set up; (second aorist, intransitive) I stood, stood still, stopped;
   (perfect, intransitive) I stand
τί-θη-μι (θη-/θε-), (imperfect) ἐτίθην, θήσω, ἔθηκα, (infinitive) θεῖναι,
   (participle) θείς, τέθηκα, τέθειμαι, ἐτέθην I put, place

61		βοῦς κρῑβανίτᾱς; τῶν ἀλαζονευμάτων.
62	ΠΡΕ.	(*ignoring Dicaeopolis*) καὶ ναὶ μὰ Δί' ὄρνῑν τριπλάσιον
		Κλεωνύμου
63		παρέθηκεν ἡμῖν· ὄνομα δ' ἦν αὐτῷ φέναξ.
64	ΔΙΚ.	ταῦτ' ἄρ' ἐφενάκιζες σὺ δύο δραχμὰς φέρων.
65	ΠΡΕ.	(*ignoring Dicaeopolis*) καὶ νῦν ἄγοντες ἥκομεν
		Ψευδαρτάβᾱν,
66		τὸν βασιλέως ὀφθαλμόν. ΔΙΚ. ἐκκόψειέ γε
67		κόραξ πατάξᾱς, τόν τε σὸν τοῦ πρέσβεως.
68	ΚΗΡ.	(*formally presenting Pseudartabas to the Assembly*)
		ὁ βασιλέως ὀφθαλμός. ΔΙΚ. ὦναξ Ἡράκλεις.
69	ΠΡΕ.	(*to Pseudartabas*) ἄγε δὴ σὺ βασιλεὺς ἄττα σ' ἀπέπεμψεν
		φράσον
70		λέξοντ' Ἀθηναίοισιν, ὦ Ψευδαρτάβᾱ.
71	ΨΕΥΔΑΡΤΑΒΑΣ	(*making his announcement to the Assembly*)
		ἰαρταμὰν ἐξάρξαν ἀπισσόνᾱ σάτρα.
72	ΠΡΕ.	(*to the Assembly*) ξυνήκαθ' ὃ λέγει; ΔΙΚ. μὰ τὸν
		Ἀπόλλω 'γὼ μὲν οὔ.
73	ΠΡΕ.	(*to the Assembly*) πέμψειν βασιλέᾱ φησὶν ῡ̔μῖν χρῡσίον.
74		(*to Pseudartabas*) λέγε δὴ σὺ μεῖζον καὶ σαφῶς τὸ
		χρῡσίον.
75	ΨΕΥ.	οὐ λῆψι χρῦσο, χαυνόπρωκτ' Ἰαοναῦ.
76	ΔΙΚ.	οἴμοι κακοδαίμων, ὡς σαφῶς. ΠΡΕ. τί δ' αὖ λέγει;
	ΔΙΚ.	(*standing up and shouting to the ambassador*)
77		ὅ τι; χαυνοπρώκτους τοὺς Ἰάονας λέγει,
78		εἰ προσδοκῶσι χρῡσίον ἐκ τῶν βαρβάρων.
79	ΠΡΕ.	(*answering Dicaeopolis*) οὔκ, ἀλλ' ἀχάνᾱς ὅδε γε χρῡσίου
		λέγει.
80	ΔΙΚ.	(*to the ambassador*) ποίᾱς ἀχάνᾱς; σὺ μὲν ἀλαζὼν εἶ
		μέγας.
81	ΚΗΡ.	(*to Dicaeopolis*) σῖγα, κάθιζε.
82		(*to the Assembly*) τὸν βασιλέως ὀφθαλμὸν ἡ βουλὴ καλεῖ
83		ἐς τὸ πρυτανεῖον. ΔΙΚ. (*refusing to sit down and*
		thoroughly disgusted with the ambassador's announcement)
		ταῦτα δῆτ' οὐκ ἀγχόνη;
84		(*aside*) ἀλλ' ἐργάσομαί τι δεινὸν ἔργον καὶ μέγα.

85 πάρα = πάρειμι
87 μόνῳ *take with* ἐμοί (86)
88 τοῖσι παιδίοισι "for my young children"   τῇ πλάτιδι   "for my wife"
89 πρεσβεύεσθε "be ambassadors!"

κεχήνετε *perfect imperative of* χάσκω "I gape"; the use of the perfect
    suggests that their mouths are always hanging open, either because they are
    naive fools or because they are always half asleep (yawning).

*   *   *

Grammar

4. The Verbal Adjective in -τέος

This suffix, added usually to the verbal stem of the aorist passive,
gives a passive adjective, e.g. λυ-τέος, -ᾱ, -ον = "to be loosened," which
expresses obligation or necessity and is often used with εἰμί, e.g.:

λυτέοι εἰσὶν οἱ βόες.
The oxen *must be loosened.*

The person who must perform the action is in the dative, e.g.:

ὠφελητέᾱ σοι ἡ πόλις ἐστίν. (Xenophon, *Memorabilia* 3.6)
The city *must be helped* by you.   You *must help* the city.

As with δεῖ and other impersonal verbs, the person is often omitted in the
Greek, although we prefer to express it in English, e.g.:

ἄλλαι νῆες ἐκ τῶν ξυμμάχων μεταπεμπτέαι εἰσίν.
Other ships *must be summoned* from the allies.
We *must summon* other ships from the allies.

The verb εἰμί is often omitted, e.g.:

λυτέοι οἱ βόες.
The oxen *must be loosened.*

The neuter of intransitive verbs is used impersonally, e.g.:

ἰτέον ἡμῖν.
It is to be gone by us.   We *must go.*

The neuter plural is often used in this way instead of the singular, e.g.:

καί μοι βαδιστέα ἐστὶν πρὸς τὴν ἀγορᾱν.
And I *must walk* to the agora.

Lastly, although technically passive, the neuter verbal adjective made
from a transitive verb is sometimes used with an accusative object, e.g.:

ἀλήθειάν γε περὶ πολλοῦ ποιητέον. (Plato, *Republic* 389b)
We *must consider the truth* of great importance.

This construction presents little difficulty, provided you recognize the
suffix -τέος. You will find an example in lines 147–148 of the reading.
For exercises, see page 228.

85   (*calling out*) ἀλλ' Ἀμφίθεός μοι ποῦ 'στιν; **ΑΜΦ.**
            οὑτοσὶ πάρα.
86 **ΔΙΚ.** (*to Amphitheus*) ἐμοὶ σὺ ταυτασὶ λαβὼν ὀκτὼ δραχμὰς
87   σπονδὰς ποίησαι πρὸς Λακεδαιμονίους μόνῳ
88   καὶ τοῖσι παιδίοισι καὶ τῇ πλάτιδι.
89   (*to the ambassadors*) ὑμεῖς δὲ πρεσβεύεσθε καὶ κεχήνετε.
            (*Amphitheus rushes off to begin his trip to Sparta.*)

*   *   *

Grammar

5. Summary of the Uses of the Participle

1. Aspect and Time

    The present participle represents the action as a process
    (simultaneous with the time of the main verb), the aorist as an event
    (simultaneous with or prior to the time of the main verb), and the
    perfect as a state; the future participle is used when the action of the
    participle is subsequent to that of the main verb (often expressing
    purpose, with or without ὡς), e.g.:

    ἐξῆλθον **βοῶντες**. (present; simultaneous process)
    They went out *shouting*.

    βοήσας εἶπεν. (aorist; simultaneous event)
    He said *with a shout*.

    τὴν γῆν **καταλιπόντες** ταχέως ἔπλευσαν. (aorist; prior event)
    After leaving the land, they sailed quickly.

    κεῖνται **τεθνηκότες**. (perfect; state)
    They lie *dead*.

    ἥκουσιν ὑμῖν (**ὡς**) **ἀγγελοῦντες**. (future; subsequent)
    They have come *to tell* you.

2. Participles may be used in Greek to represent most of the relation-
   ships between verbs for which English uses clauses, e.g.:

    a. Substantival, i.e., the participle is used as a noun, e.g.:

        οἱ τεθνηκότες = the dead   οἱ θεώμενοι = the spectators
        οἱ τὴν πατρίδα φιλοῦντες = those who love their country

    b. Temporal, e.g.:

        οἴκαδε **ἐπανελθόντες** τὸν πατέρα ἐζήτουν.
        When they had returned home, they looked for their father.

ἐν τοῖς ἀγροῖς **μένοντες** πολλὰ καὶ κακὰ ἔπασχον.
While they stayed in the country, they suffered many terrible things.

c.   Concessive, usually with καί or καίπερ, e.g.:

καὶ/καίπερ πολλὰ καὶ κακὰ **πάσχοντες**, οὐκ ἤθελον εἴκειν.
Although they suffered many hardships, they refused to yield.

d.   Causal, often with ἅτε (real cause) or ὡς (alleged cause), e.g.:

ἅτε πολλὰ καὶ κακὰ **παθόντες**, τοῖς πολεμίοις ἑαυτοὺς παρέδοσαν.
Because they had suffered many hardships, they surrendered to the enemy.

τὸν Περικλέᾱ ἐν αἰτίᾳ εἶχον **ὡς πείσαντα** σφᾶς πολεμεῖν.
They blamed Pericles *on the grounds that he had persuaded* them to go to war.

e.   Purpose, with future participle with or without ὡς, e.g.:

ἥκουσιν (**ὡς**) ῡ̔μῖν τὰ γενόμενα **ἀγγελοῦντες**.
They have come *to tell* you what happened.

f.   With ὥσπερ = as if, e.g.:

ὥσπερ ἤδη σαφῶς **εἰδότες** ὃ δεῖ πρᾱ́ττειν, οὐκ ἐθέλετε ἀκούειν.
You refuse to listen, *as if you* clearly *knew* (*as if* clearly *knowing*) what has to be done.

g.   Conditional, negative μή, e.g.:

οὐδέποτε μαθήσεται κιθαρίζειν **μὴ μελετῶν**.
He will never learn to play the lyre, *if he does not practice.*

h.   Indirect statement after verbs of knowing, seeing, and hearing, e.g.:

οἶδά σε σώφρονα **ὄντα**.
I know that you *are* wise.

ᾐσθόμην ἐς κίνδῡνον **καταστάς**.
I realized *that I had got* into danger.

So also sometimes after other verbs, e.g., ἀγγέλλω:

Κῦρον **ἐπιστρατεύοντα** ἤγγειλεν.
He announced that Cyrus *was marching against* (them).

i.   Supplementary (see Chapter 20, Grammar 3, page 55), e.g.:

λανθάνω   ῥᾷον ἔλαθον εἰσελθόντες.
                    They entered more easily without being seen.

ἔλαθεν ἑαυτὸν τοῦτο ποιήσας.
He did this unawares.

τυγχάνω   ἔτυχον παρόντες οἱ πρέσβεις.
The ambassadors happened to be present.

ἔτυχον ἐπὶ τοὺς Πέρσᾱς στρατευόμενοι.
They were just then campaigning against the
Persians.

φθάνω   ἔφθασαν πολλῷ τοὺς Πέρσᾱς ἀφικόμενοι.
They arrived long before the Persians.
They, arriving, anticipated the Persians by
much.

φαίνομαι   φαίνεται σοφὸς ὤν. He is shown to be wise.
Compare:
φαίνεται σοφὸς εἶναι. He seems to be wise.

δῆλός ἐστιν   δῆλοί εἰσιν ἡμῖν ἐπιβουλεύοντες.
They are clearly plotting against us.
It is clear that they are plotting against us.

Exercise 31a

Read aloud and translate:

1. ὁ Δικαιόπολις πάντας τοὺς πολίτᾱς ἔφθασε ἐς τὴν Πύκνα ἀφικόμενος.
2. μόνος ὤν, στένει, εἰρήνης ἐρῶν, στυγῶν μὲν ἄστυ, τὸν δ' ἑαυτοῦ δῆμον
    ποθῶν.
3. ἥκει παρεσκευασμένος τοὺς ῥήτορας λοιδορεῖν, μὴ λέγοντας περὶ τῆς
    εἰρήνης.
4. ὁ Δικαιόπολις τοὺς πρυτάνεις ἐν ὀργῇ εἶχεν ὡς οὐ τῑμῶντας τὴν εἰρήνην.
5. ἔτυχον παρόντες οἱ παρὰ βασιλέως πρέσβεις, ἀπὸ τῆς Ἀσίᾱς ἀφικόμενοι.
6. ὁ Δικαιόπολις τοὺς τῶν Ἀθηναίων πρέσβεις στυγεῖ, ὡς ἀλάζονας ὄντας.
7. ὠργίζετο αὐτοῖς ἅτε δύο δραχμὰς τῆς ἡμέρᾱς δεξαμένοις.
8. δῆλοί εἰσιν οἱ πρέσβεις ψευδῆ λέγοντες.
9. πάντες ἴσμεν τὸν βασιλέᾱ οὐδὲν χρῡσίον ἡμῖν πέμψοντα.
10. οἱ βάρβαροι ἄνδρας ἡγοῦνται μόνους τοὺς πλεῖστα δυναμένους πιεῖν.
11. ὁ Δικαιόπολις φησὶν ἀνοήτους εἶναι τοὺς Ἀθηναίους, προσδοκῶντας χρῡσίον
    ἐκ τῶν βαρβάρων.
12. ὁ Ἀμφίθεος ἔλαθε τοὺς τοξότᾱς ἐς τὴν ἐκκλησίᾱν ἐσδραμών.
13. καίπερ θεὸς ὤν, οὐ δύναμαι πρὸς τὴν Λακεδαίμονα πορεύεσθαι, μὴ
    διδόντων μοι ἐφόδια τῶν πρυτάνεων.
14. ὁ Δικαιόπολις τὸν Ἀμφίθεον ἔπεμψεν ὡς σπονδὰς ποιησόμενον πρὸς τοὺς
    Λακεδαιμονίους.
15. χαίρει ὥσπερ ἤδη πεποιημένων τῶν σπονδῶν.

ΑΧΑΡΝΗΣ (γ)

Vocabulary

Verbs

ἀνακράζω, ἀνέκραγον,
  ἀνακέκρᾱγα I shout
σπένδω, σπείσω, ἔσπεισα,
  ἔσπεισμαι I pour a libation;
  (*middle*) I make a treaty,
  make peace (by pouring a
  libation with the other party)

Nouns

ἡ ἄμπελος, τῆς ἀμπέλου
  grapevine
τὸ στόμα, τοῦ στόματος
  mouth

Adjective

μιαρός, -ᾱ́, -όν defiled, foul,
  villainous

90 ἀλλ᾽ . . . γάρ "but (look), for . . . "
    ὁδί "this here," i.e., "here he is"
91 μήπω γε "don't (greet me) yet. . . ."
94 ὠσφροντο "smelled" (them i.e., the truces)   πρεσβῦται old men
95 στιπτοί "trodden down," (of old men) "tough," "sturdy"
    πρίνινοι "oaken"
96 ἀτεράμονες "unsoftened," "hard," "tough"
    Μαραθωνομάχαι "fighters at the Battle of Marathon"
    σφενδάμνινοι "made of maple wood"
97 ἀνέκραγον "began to shout"; sometimes the aorist (as here) and the
    imperfect (see lines 99–100) are used to indicate the beginning of an action.
    This is called the *inchoative imperfect* and the *ingressive aorist* (*inchoative*
    and *ingressive* are from Latin verbs that mean "I begin").
99 τρίβωνας "cloaks," usually old and threadbare
    ξυνελέγοντο (+ *partitive gen. here*) "they began gathering (some of the)
    stones"
101 βοώντων "let them shout"; 3rd person plural imperative (see Grammar 6,
    page 223)
102 γεύματα "tastes," "samples"
103 πεντέτεις "for five years"
    γεῦσαι "taste" (*aorist imperative of* γεύομαι)
104 αἰβοῖ "ugh" (an expression of disgust)   ὅτι because
105 ὄζουσι "they smell of" (+ *gen.*)
    πίττης "pitch"; pitch or resin was used both to caulk ships and to line wine
    jars (it is still used in making some Greek wine today, called retsina).
    There is a *double entendre* here; both meanings are intended.
106 δεκέτεις "for ten years"
107 χαὖται = καὶ αὖται "this too"; if a truce were made for only ten years, both
    sides would be sending ambassadors to other cities to gain allies, preparing
    for the next war.
108 ὀξύτατον "very sharply"
109 τριᾱκοντούτιδες "for thirty years"
110 ὦ Διονύσια "O festival of Dionysus!"
111 ἀμβροσίᾱς καὶ νέκταρος ambrosia was the food of the gods, and nectar was
    their drink.

The Assembly continues, with more interruptions from Dicaeopolis. Just as proceedings are coming to an end, Dicaeopolis sees Amphitheus rushing in breathless, having returned from Sparta. He brings with him three specimen truces, which are in the form of wine contained in wine skins.

90	ΔΙΚ.	ἀλλ' ἐκ Λακεδαίμονος γὰρ 'Αμφίθεος ὁδί.
91		χαῖρ', 'Αμφίθεε. **ΑΜΦ.** (*still running*) μήπω γε, πρίν γ' ἂν στῶ τρέχων.
		(*looking behind himself with trepidation*)
92		δεῖ γάρ με φεύγοντ' ἐκφυγεῖν 'Αχαρνέας.
93	ΔΙΚ.	τί δ' ἔστι; **ΑΜΦ.** ἐγὼ μὲν δεῦρό σοι σπονδὰς φέρων
94		ἔσπευδον· οἱ δ' ὤσφροντο πρεσβῦταί τινες
95		'Αχαρνικοί, στιπτοὶ γέροντες πρίνινοι
96		ἀτεράμονες Μαραθωνομάχαι σφενδάμνινοι.
97		ἔπειτ' ἀνέκραγον πάντες, "ὦ μιαρώτατε,
98		σπονδὰς φέρεις τῶν ἀμπέλων τετμημένων;"
99		κᾆς τοὺς τρίβωνας ξυνελέγοντο τῶν λίθων·
100		ἐγὼ δ' ἔφευγον· οἱ δ' ἐδίωκον κᾀβόων.
101	ΔΙΚ.	(*reassuring Amphitheus*) οἱ δ' οὖν βοώντων. ἀλλὰ τὰς σπονδὰς φέρεις;
102	ΑΜΦ.	(*holding up the wine skins for Dicaeopolis to see*) ἔγωγέ φημι, τρία γε ταυτὶ γεύματα.
103		(*holding out one of the wine skins*) αὗται μέν εἰσι πεντέτεις. γεῦσαι λαβών.
104	ΔΙΚ.	(*taking the skin and smelling the wine*) αἰβοῖ. **ΑΜΦ.** τί ἔστιν; **ΔΙΚ.** οὐκ ἀρέσκουσίν μ' ὅτι
105		ὄζουσι πίττης καὶ παρασκευῆς νεῶν.
106	ΑΜΦ.	(*offering another wine skin*) σὺ δ' ἀλλὰ τασδὶ τὰς δεκέτεις γεῦσαι λαβών.
	ΔΙΚ.	(*taking the second wine skin and smelling the wine*)
107		ὄζουσι χαὗται πρέσβεων ἐς τὰς πόλεις
108		ὀξύτατον. . . .
109	ΑΜΦ.	(*offering the third wine skin*) ἀλλ' αὑταιὶ σπονδαὶ τριακοντούτιδες
110		κατὰ γῆν τε καὶ θάλατταν. **ΔΙΚ.** (*taking the third wine skin and smelling the wine*) ὦ Διονύσια,
111		αὗται μὲν ὄζουσ' ἀμβροσίας καὶ νέκταρος.

112 ὅπῃ "where"
113 κᾆκπίομαι = καὶ ἐκπίομαι "and I will drink it off"
114 χαίρειν κελεύων πολλά "bidding a long farewell to," i.e., wishing to have
     nothing to do with
115 ἀπαλλαγείς (*aorist passive participle of* ἀπαλλάσσω) "rid of " (+ *gen.*)
116 τὰ κατ' ἀγροὺς . . . Διονύσια "the Rural Dionysia"
     εἰσιών "going into (my house)"; we are no longer on the Pnyx but outside
     Dicaeopolis's house in the country. Such changes of scene, indicated only by
     the actors' words, are common in comedy.

                        *   *   *

Grammar

6. Summary of the Uses of the Negative

The negative οὐ is used:

a.   in all independent clauses with the indicative and with the potential
     optative
b.   in indirect statements and questions, where the negatives of the
     direct words are retained
c.   in causal clauses, definite relative and temporal clauses, and in ὥστε
     clauses with the indicative

The negative μή is used:

a.   with imperatives and with subjunctives (hortatory, deliberative,
     prohibitions) in independent clauses
b.   in wishes for the future with the optative
c.   With the infinitive in *all* constructions *except* indirect statement
     (where the negatives of the direct words are used)
d.   in purpose clauses (ἵνα, ὅπως, ὡς + subjunctive or optative), in
     conditional clauses, in indefinite (or general) clauses (relative and
     temporal), with generic relative clauses or participles (i.e., relative
     clauses or participles describing not particular persons or things but
     types), and in relative clauses with future indicative expressing
     purpose

N.B. 1. The negative with the participle is οὐ unless the participle has
          a conditional force (e.g., οὐ μαθήσῃ κιθαρίζειν μὴ μελετῶν = you
          won't learn to play the lyre, unless you practice), or the phrase
          is generic (e.g., οἱ μὴ τὴν πόλιν φιλοῦντες οὐκ ἄξιοί εἰσι τιμῆς = the
          sort of people who do not love the city are not worthy of honor).
      2. Verbs expressing hope or threat or promise sometimes have μή
          with the future infinitive (e.g., οἱ Ἀθηναῖοι ἤλπιζον τοὺς
          Πελοποννησίους μὴ ἐς τὸ ἐγγυτέρω προιέναι = The Athenians
          hoped the Peloponnesians would not advance nearer).
      3. In indirect questions μή is sometimes found instead of the
          usual οὐ.

112   (*tasting the wine*) κἂν τῷ στόματι λέγουσι, βαῖν’ ὅπῃ
            θέλεις.

            (*clutching the wine skin, pouring a libation, and drinking deeply*
113   *of the wine*) ταύτᾱς δέχομαι καὶ σπένδομαι κἀκπίομαι,
114   χαίρειν κελεύων πολλὰ τοὺς Ἀχαρνέᾱς.
115   ἐγὼ δὲ πολέμου καὶ κακῶν ἀπαλλαγεὶς
116   ἄξω τὰ κατ’ ἀγροὺς εἰσιὼν Διονύσια.

                                        (*Exit into the house.*)

117   ΑΜΦ.   ἐγὼ δὲ φεύξομαί γε τοὺς Ἀχαρνέᾱς.

                                        (*Runs off stage.*)

                        *   *   *

4.   Note the following compound negatives:

     οὐδέ nor, and not, not even   μηδέ
     οὔτε . . . οὔτε neither . . . nor   μήτε . . . μήτε
     οὐδείς, οὐδεμία, οὐδέν no one, nothing   μηδείς, μηδεμία, μηδέν
     οὐδέποτε never   μηδέποτε
     οὐκέτι no longer   μηκέτι
     οὔπω not yet   μήπω
     οὐδέτερος, -ᾱ, -ον neither (of two)   μηδέτερος, -ᾱ, -ον

5.   Repeated negatives normally reinforce each other, e.g.,

     οὐκ ἔπρᾱξε τοιοῦτο οὐδεὶς οὐδέποτε.
     No one ever did such a thing.

But if the compound negative precedes the simple negative,
they cancel each other, making an emphatic positive, e.g.,

     οὐδεὶς οὐχ ὁρᾷ τὴν ναῦν.
     No one doesn't see (= everyone sees) the ship.

Exercise 31b

Read aloud and translate:

1. οὐδέποτε οὕτως ἐδήχθην ὡς νῦν, ἅτε τῶν πολῑτῶν οὐ παρόντων ἐς τὴν
    ἐκκλησίᾱν.
2. μηκέτι ἐν Πυκνὶ μένωμεν· οὐ γὰρ ἥκουσιν οὐδὲ οἱ πρυτάνεις.
3. ἐὰν μὴ δι’ ὀλίγου ἀφίκωνται οἱ πρυτάνεις, οἱ πολῖται οὐκέτι μενοῦσιν.
4. εἰ μὴ περὶ εἰρήνης λέγοιτε, οὐκ ἂν σῑγῴην ἐγώ.
5. ὁ κῆρυξ τὸν Δικαιόπολιν ἐκέλευσε μὴ λοιδορεῖν τοὺς ῥήτορας μηδὲ
    ὑποκρούειν.

6. οἱ βάρβαροι ἄνδρας οὐχ ἡγοῦνται τοὺς μὴ δυναμένους πλεῖστα πιεῖν.

7. ὁ Δικαιόπολις σαφῶς ᾔδει τὸν βασιλέα οὐκ οὐδέποτε χρῡσίον πέμψοντα.

8. εἴθε μηκέτι ψεύδοιντο οἱ πρέσβεις.

9. οὐ γὰρ οἷός τ' ἐστὶν οὐδέτερος τὸν δῆμον ἐξαπατᾶν (to deceive).

10. οὐδεὶς γὰρ οὐκ οἶδεν αὐτοὺς οὐδὲν ἀληθῆ λέγοντας.

11. οὐκ ἐθελόντων οὔτε τῶν πρυτανέων οὔτε τοῦ δήμου σπονδὰς ποιεῖσθαι, τῷ Δικαιοπόλει ἔδοξε μὴ ἀθῡμεῖν (to despair) ἀλλὰ ἔργον μέγα ἐργάσασθαι.

12. φοβούμενος γὰρ μὴ ἄλλως (any other way) οὐδέποτε γένοιτο εἰρήνη, τὸν Ἀμφίθεον ἐς Λακεδαίμονα ἔπεμψεν.

13. ἤλπιζε γὰρ τοὺς Λακεδαιμονίους μὴ ἐκβαλεῖν τὸν Ἀμφίθεον, ἀθάνατον ὄντα, ἀλλὰ σπονδὰς ποιήσειν.

14. ὅστις γὰρ ἂν ἀθανάτου μὴ ἀκούῃ, δι' ὀλίγου κακῶς πράττει.

15. καίπερ οὔπω ἐπανελθόντος τοῦ Ἀμφιθέου, ὁ Δικαιόπολις χαίρει ὥσπερ οὐκέτι πολέμῳ χρώμενος.

*   *   *

ΑΧΑΡΝΗΣ (δ)

Vocabulary

Verbs

ᾄδω, ᾄσομαι, ᾖσα, ᾖσμαι, ᾔσθην I sing

ἀκολουθέω (+ *dat.*) I follow

ἀπάρχομαι (*see* ἄρχω *for principal parts*) I begin

εὐφημέω I keep holy silence

καταχέω, καταχέω, κατέχεα, κατακέχυκα, κατακέχυμαι, κατεχύθην I pour X (*acc.*) over Y (*gen.*)

μηνύω, μηνύσω, ἐμήνῡσα, μεμήνῡκα, μεμήνῡμαι, ἐμηνύθην I inform

Nouns

ἡ εὐφημίᾱ, τῆς εὐφημίᾱς call for holy silence

οἱ οἰκέται, τῶν οἰκετῶν household

Adjective

μακάριος, -ᾱ, -ον blessed, happy

Adverb or Preposition

ἐξόπισθε(ν) (+ *gen.*) behind

Adverbs

μήν *or* **καὶ μήν** truly, indeed

σφόδρα very much

119 **ὁδοιπόρων** "wayfarers," "passers-by"
ἄξιόν (ἐστι) (+ *dat. and infinitive*) "it is fit," i.e., it is worth while for X to do Y

121 **ὅποι . . . γῆς** "where in the world"

122 **φροῦδος** "gone," "fled," "vanished"

123 **Βαλληνάδε** a comic coinage punning on the verb βάλλω "I pelt" and the name of an Attic deme, Παλλήνη, + suffix -δε = "toward"; translate "toward Pelting," "Peltingward."

Grammar

7. Third Person Imperatives

Greek verbs have third person imperatives, e.g.:

οἱ δ' οὖν βοώντων.
Well, let them shout!

The complete sets of present and aorist imperatives of λύω are:

	Active		*Middle*	*Passive*
Present	2 λῦ-ε	loosen! (*sing.*)	λύ-ου	same as
	3 λῦ-έτω	let him loosen!	λῦ-έσθω	for the middle
	2 λύ-ετε	loosen! (*pl.*)	λύ-εσθε	
	3 λῦ-όντων	let them loosen	λῦ-έσθων	
Aorist				
	2 λῦ-σον		λῦ-σαι	λύ-θητι
	3 λῦ-σάτω		λῦ-σάσθω	λυ-θήτω
	2 λύ-σατε		λύ-σασθε	λύ-θητε
	3 λῦ-σάντων		λῦ-σάσθων	λυ-θέντων

Exercise 31c

Read aloud and translate:

1. οἱ μὲν δοῦλοι τοὺς βοῦς λῡσάντων καὶ οἴκαδε ἐπανελθόντων, ὁ δὲ παῖς μετ' ἐμοῦ σπευδέτω.
2. μὴ φοβείσθων αἱ παρθένοι ἀλλ' ἐν τῇ οἰκίᾳ ἥσυχοι (*quietly*) μενόντων.
3. πάντες οἱ παρόντες σῑγώντων καὶ τὴν πομπὴν θεάσθων.
4. μὴ ὀργισθήτω ὁ δεσπότης ἀλλὰ τοὺς τοῦ δούλου λόγους ἀκουσάτω.
5. μὴ μαχέσθων οἱ νεᾱνίαι ἀλλὰ καθήσθων ἐν τῇ ἀγορᾷ.

* * *

The chorus of old Acharnian men rush in, armed with stones, in pursuit of Amphitheus.

118	ΧΟΡΟΣ	τῇδε πᾶς ἕπου, δίωκε, καὶ τὸν ἄνδρα πυνθάνου
119		τῶν ὁδοιπόρων ἁπάντων· τῇ πόλει γὰρ ἄξιον
120		ξυλλαβεῖν τὸν ἄνδρα τοῦτον. (*to the audience*) ἀλλά μοι μηνύσατε,
121		εἴ τις οἶδ' ὅποι τέτραπται γῆς ὁ τὰς σπονδὰς φέρων.
122		ἐκπέφευγ', οἴχεται φροῦδος.
123		ἀλλὰ δεῖ ζητεῖν τὸν ἄνδρα καὶ βλέπειν Βαλληνάδε
124		καὶ διώκειν γῆν πρὸ γῆς, ἕως ἂν εὑρεθῇ ποτέ·

125 ἐμπλήμην (*second aorist passive optative of* ἐμπίμπλημι "I fill full," *passive,*
      "I sate myself") *potential optative,* "I could never have my fill of "
      λίθοις *take with* βάλλων

128 δεῦρο πᾶς / ἐκποδών "everyone (come) here, out of the way"

129 ἀνήρ = ὁ ἀνήρ

131 ἡ κανηφόρος "basket-bearer"; the daughter carries the basket on her head.

132 τὸν φαλλόν "phallus-pole," an image carried in Dionysiac processions

133 τὸ κανοῦν "basket"; the daughter sets the basket down near the altar.

134 τὴν ἐτνήρυσιν "soup-ladle"

135 ἔτνος "soup," made of peas or beans and contained in the pot that Dicaeopolis
      carries
      τοὐλατῆρος = τοῦ ἐλατῆρος "broad, flat cake"; the daughter takes one of
      these cakes from the basket, places it on the altar, and pours the soup over it.

136 καὶ μὴν . . . γ(ε) "and indeed. . . . "

137 κεχαρισμένως (*adverb formed from the perfect participle of* χαρίζομαι)
      "acceptably," "in a manner pleasing to" (+ *dat.*)
      ἐμὲ . . . (139) ἀγαγεῖν . . . (140) τὰς σπονδὰς . . . ξυνενεγκεῖν *the
      infinitives express prayers*: "(grant) that I may conduct the Rural Dionysia . .
      . and (grant) that this truce may turn out well. . . . "

139 τυχηρῶς "with good fortune," "with good luck"

140 ἀπαλλαχθέντα (+ *gen.*) (*see line 115 above*) "rid of"

141 ξυνενεγκεῖν (*aorist infinitive of* συμφέρει "it is useful," "it is profitable")
      with καλῶς "may turn out well"
      τριᾱκοντούτιδας "for thirty years"

142 ὅπως "(see to it) that. . . . "

143 βλέπουσα θυμβροφάγον "looking as if you have eaten savory" ("The
      eating of the bitter herb 'savory' would pucker the lips up, and give a prim,
      demure look to the girl's face"–W. W. Merry)

144 ὀπύσει "will marry" (the Greek verb is from a root meaning "to nourish/
      maintain")

145 τὤχλῳ = τῷ ὄχλῳ "the crowd"
      φυλάττεσθαι (*infinitive for
      imperative*) "watch out!"

146 περιτράγη "nibble at," i.e.,
      steal
      χρῡσία "your golden
      jewelry"

Dionysus with a panther at his altar

125   ὡς ἐγὼ βάλλων ἐκεῖνον οὐκ ἂν ἐμπλήμην λίθοις.

As the chorus search fruitlessly for Amphitheus, Dicaeopolis is heard from within the house calling for holy silence.

126   ΔΙΚ.   εὐφημεῖτε, εὐφημεῖτε.

127   ΧΟΡ.   (addressing its own members) σῖγα πᾶς. ἠκούσατ᾽, ἄνδρες,
     ἆρα τῆς εὐφημίας;

128   οὗτος αὐτός ἐστιν ὃν ζητοῦμεν. (retiring to one side of the
     stage) ἀλλὰ δεῦρο πᾶς

129   ἐκποδών· θύσων γὰρ ἀνήρ, ὡς ἔοικ᾽, ἐξέρχεται.

As the members of the chorus withdraw, Dicaeopolis, carrying a pot, leads his family out of his house—his wife, his daughter, who carries a sacred basket, and Xanthias and a second slave, who carry a phallus-pole.

130   ΔΙΚ.   εὐφημεῖτε, εὐφημεῖτε.

131   (referring to his daughter) προΐτω ᾽ς τὸ πρόσθεν ὀλίγον ἡ
     κανηφόρος·

132   (referring to his slave Xanthias) ὁ Ξανθίᾱς τὸν φαλλὸν
     ὀρθὸν στησάτω.

133   (to his daughter) κατάθου τὸ κανοῦν, ὦ θύγατερ, ἵν᾽
     ἀπαρξώμεθα.

134   ΘΥΓΑΤΗΡ   ὦ μῆτερ, ἀνάδος δεῦρο τὴν ἐτνήρυσιν,

135   ἵν᾽ ἔτνος καταχέω τοὐλατῆρος τουτουΐ.

   ΔΙΚ.   (addressing Dionysus, at his altar on the stage)

136   καὶ μὴν καλόν γ᾽ ἔστ᾽· ὦ Διόνῡσε δέσποτα,

137   κεχαρισμένως σοι τήνδε τὴν πομπὴν ἐμὲ

138   πέμψαντα καὶ θύσαντα μετὰ τῶν οἰκετῶν

139   ἀγαγεῖν τυχηρῶς τὰ κατ᾽ ἀγροὺς Διονύσια,

140   στρατιᾶς ἀπαλλαχθέντα· τὰς σπονδὰς δέ μοι

141   καλῶς ξυνενεγκεῖν τὰς τριᾱκοντούτιδας.

142   (addressing his daughter and arranging the sacred procession)
     ἄγ᾽, ὦ θύγατερ, ὅπως τὸ κανοῦν καλὴ καλῶς

143   οἴσεις βλέπουσα θυμβροφάγον. ὡς μακάριος

144   ὅστις σ᾽ ὀπύσει. . . .

   (urging his daughter to advance in among the audience, leading

145   the procession) πρόβαινε, κἂν τὤχλῳ φυλάττεσθαι
     σφόδρα

146   μή τις λαθὼν σου περιτράγῃ τὰ χρῡσία.

147 σφῷν "by the two of you"   ἐστὶν . . . ἐκτέος/ὁ φαλλός "the phallus-
pole must be held" (see Grammar 4, page 214)
150 τοῦ τέγους "the roof"
πρόβᾱ = πρόβηθι
151 Βακχίου "of Bacchus"
152 ἕκτῳ "sixth"
προσεῖπον "I address"
156 ἀπαλλαγείς see lines 115 and 140.
158 ξυμπίῃς "drink with"
ἐκ κραιπάλης "in (literally, from) a drinking-bout"
159 ἕωθεν "from earliest dawn"
ῥοφήσῃ τρύβλιον "you will drain the cup dry"
160 φεψάλῳ "chimney"
κρεμήσεται "will be hung"

The fertile valley of the river Eurotas, in which Sparta lay, with the Taygetus range of
mountains behind

147   (*urging Xanthias and the second slave to perform their duty*
          properly) ὦ Ξανθίᾱ, σφῷν δ' ἐστὶν ὀρθὸς ἑκτέος

148   ὁ φαλλὸς ἐξόπισθε τῆς κανηφόρου·

149   ἐγὼ δ' ἀκολουθῶν ᾄσομαι τὸ φαλλικόν·

150   (*sending his wife to watch from the roof*) σὺ δ', ὦ γύναι, θεῶ
          μ' ἀπὸ τοῦ τέγους. (*urging on his daughter*) πρόβᾱ.

*Dicaeopolis celebrates his own Rural Dionysia by singing the following joyous
song to Phales, Dionysiac god of the phallus, in honor of the peace he has made:*

151   Φαλῆς ἑταῖρε Βακχίου,

152   ἕκτῳ σ' ἔτει προσεῖπον ἐς

153   τὸν δῆμον ἐλθὼν ἄσμενος,

154   σπονδὰς ποιησάμενος ἐμαυ-

155   τῷ, πρᾱγμάτων τε καὶ μαχῶν

156   ἀπαλλαγείς.

157   ὦ Φαλῆς Φαλῆς,

158   ἐὰν μεθ' ἡμῶν ξυμπίῃς, ἐκ κραιπάλης

159   ἕωθεν εἰρήνης ῥοφήσῃ τρύβλιον·

160   ἡ δ' ἀσπὶς ἐν τῷ φεψάλῳ κρεμήσεται.

* * *

Corinth: the site of the ancient city, dominated by the remains of the temple of Apollo

εἰρήνης ῥοφήσῃ τρύβλιον.

Exercise 31d

The following examples are all taken from Plato Republic Books 2–5, in which Plato is discussing (a) the education of the guardians of his ideal state (1–3), (b) the selection of the rulers from the guardian class (4), and (c) the education of women (5). Translate the sentences and see how far you can reconstruct Plato's views on the education of his "guardians":

1. ἆρ' οὖν μουσικῇ πρότερον ἀρξόμεθα παιδεύοντες ἢ γυμναστικῇ; λόγων (*of stories*) δὲ διττὸν εἶδος (*two sorts*), τὸ μὲν ἀληθές, ψεῦδος (*falsehood*) δ' ἕτερον. παιδευτέον δ' ἐν ἀμφοτέροις; (376e).

2. οὗτοι οἱ λόγοι οὐ λεκτέοι ἐν τῇ ἡμετέρᾳ πόλει. (378b)

3. μετὰ δὲ τὴν μουσικὴν γυμναστικῇ θρεπτέοι (*from* τρέφω = *I rear, train*) οἱ νεᾱνίαι. (403c)

4. ἐκλεκτέον (ἐκλέγω = *I select*) ἐκ τῶν ἄλλων φυλάκων τοιούτους ἄνδρας, οἳ ἂν μάλιστα φαίνωνται, ὃ ἂν τῇ πόλει ἡγήσωνται συμφέρειν (= *to benefit* + *dat.*), πάσῃ προθῡμίᾳ (*eagerness*) ποιεῖν. (412d)

5. εἰ ταῖς γυναιξὶν ἐπὶ ταὐτὰ (*for the same purpose, i.e. for acting as guardians*) χρησόμεθα καὶ (*as*) τοῖς ἀνδράσι, ταὐτὰ διδακτέον αὐτᾱς. (451e)

REFERENCE GRAMMAR

1. THE DEFINITE ARTICLE

	Singular			*Plural*		
	M.	**F.**	**N.**	**M.**	**F.**	**N.**
Nom.	ὁ	ἡ	τό	οἱ	αἱ	τά
Gen.	τοῦ	τῆς	τοῦ	τῶν	τῶν	τῶν
Dat.	τῷ	τῇ	τῷ	τοῖς	ταῖς	τοῖς
Acc.	τόν	τήν	τό	τούς	τάς	τά

2. NOUNS OF THE FIRST DECLENSION

Feminine

	Sing.		*Pl.*		*Sing.*		*Pl.*	
Nom.	ἡ	κρήνη	αἱ	κρῆναι	ἡ	οἰκίᾱ	αἱ	οἰκίαι
Gen.	τῆς	κρήνης	τῶν	κρηνῶν	τῆς	οἰκίᾱς	τῶν	οἰκιῶν
Dat.	τῇ	κρήνῃ	ταῖς	κρήναις	τῇ	οἰκίᾳ	ταῖς	οἰκίαις
Acc.	τὴν	κρήνην	τᾱ̀ς	κρήνᾱς	τὴν	οἰκίᾱν	τᾱ̀ς	οἰκίᾱς
Voc.	ὦ	κρήνη	ὦ	κρῆναι	τῶ	οἰκίᾱ	ὦ	οἰκίαι

	Sing.		*Pl.*		*Sing.*		*Pl.*	
Nom.	ἡ	θάλαττᾰ	αἱ	θάλατται	ἡ	μάχαιρᾰ	αἱ	μάχαιραι
Gen.	τῆς	θαλάττης	τῶν	θαλαττῶν	τῆς	μαχαίρᾱς	τῶν	μαχαιρῶν
Dat.	τῇ	θαλάττῃ	ταῖς	θαλάτταις	τῇ	μαχαίρᾳ	ταῖς	μαχαίραις
Acc.	τὴν	θάλατταν	τᾱ̀ς	θαλάττᾱς	τὴν	μάχαιρᾰν	τᾱ̀ς	μαχαίρᾱς
Voc.	ὦ	θάλαττᾰ	ὦ	θάλατται	ὦ	μάχαιρᾰ	ὦ	μάχαιραι

Masculine

	Sing.		*Pl.*		*Sing.*		*Pl.*	
Nom.	ὁ	δεσπότης	οἱ	δεσπόται	ὁ	νεᾱνίᾱς	οἱ	νεᾱνίαι
Gen.	τοῦ	δεσπότου	τῶν	δεσποτῶν	τοῦ	νεᾱνίου	τῶν	νεᾱνιῶν
Dat.	τῷ	δεσπότῃ	τοῖς	δεσπόταις	τῷ	νεᾱνίᾳ	τοῖς	νεᾱνίαις
Acc.	τὸν	δεσπότην	τοὺς	δεσπότᾱς	τὸν	νεᾱνίᾱν	τοὺς	νεᾱνίᾱς
Voc.	ὦ	δέσποτα	ὦ	δεσπόται	ὦ	νεᾱνίᾱ	ὦ	νεᾱνίαι

3. NOUNS OF THE SECOND DECLENSION

	M.				**F.**			
Nom.	ὁ	ἀγρός	οἱ	ἀγροί	ἡ	ὁδός	αἱ	ὁδοί
Gen.	τοῦ	ἀγροῦ	τῶν	ἀγρῶν	τῆς	ὁδοῦ	τῶν	ὁδῶν
Dat.	τῷ	ἀγρῷ	τοῖς	ἀγροῖς	τῇ	ὁδῷ	ταῖς	ὁδοῖς
Acc.	τὸν	ἀγρόν	τοὺς	ἀγρούς	τὴν	ὁδόν	τᾱ̀ς	ὁδούς
Voc.	ὦ	ἀγρέ	ὦ	ἀγροί	ὦ	ὁδέ	ὦ	ὁδοί

	N.				Contract		
Nom.	τὸ	δένδρον	τὰ	δένδρα	ὁ	νοῦς	οἱ	νοῖ
Gen.	τοῦ	δένδρου	τῶν	δένδρων	τοῦ	νοῦ	τῶν	νῶν
Dat.	τῷ	δένδρῳ	τοῖς	δένδροις	τῷ	νῷ	τοῖς	νοῖς
Acc.	τὸ	δένδρον	τὰ	δένδρα	τὸν	νοῦν	τοὺς	νοῦς
Voc.	ὦ	δένδρον	ὦ	δένδρα	ὦ	νοῦ	ὦ	νοῖ

4. NOUNS OF THE THIRD DECLENSION

Type 1: Consonant Stems:

	Sing.		Pl.			Sing.		Pl.	

Stem: παιδ-   Stem: ὀνοματ-

Nom.	ὁ	παῖς	οἱ	παῖδες		τὸ	ὄνομα	τὰ	ὀνόματα
Gen.	τοῦ	παιδός	τῶν	παίδων		τοῦ	ὀνόματος	τῶν	ὀνομάτων
Dat.	τῷ	παιδί	τοῖς	παισί(ν)		τῷ	ὀνόματι	τοῖς	ὀνόμασι(ν)
Acc.	τὸν	παῖδα	τοὺς	παῖδας		τὸ	ὄνομα	τὰ	ὀνόματα
Voc.	ὦ	παῖ	ὦ	παῖδες		ὦ	ὄνομα	ὦ	ὀνόματα

Type 2: Stems in -εσ-:

Stem: τειχεσ-   Stem: τριηρες-

Nom.	τὸ	τεῖχος	τὰ	τείχη		ἡ	τριήρης	αἱ	τριήρεις
Gen.	τοῦ	τείχους	τῶν	τειχῶν		τῆς	τριήρους	τῶν	τριήρων
Dat.	τῷ	τείχει	τοῖς	τείχεσι(ν)		τῇ	τριήρει	ταῖς	τριήρεσι.
Acc.	τὸ	τεῖχος	τὰ	τείχη		τὴν	τριήρεις	τὰς	τριήρεις
Voc.	ὦ	τεῖχος	ὦ	τείχη		ὦ	τριήρης	ὦ	τριήρεις

Type 3: Stems Ending in Vowels:

Stem: πολι-   Stem: ἀστυ-

Nom.	ἡ	πόλις	αἱ	πόλεις		τὸ	ἄστυ	τὰ	ἄστη
Gen.	τῆς	πόλεως	τῶν	πόλεων		τοῦ	ἄστεως	τῶν	ἄστεων
Dat.	τῇ	πόλει	ταῖς	πόλεσι(ν)		τῷ	ἄστει	τοῖς	ἄστεσι(ν)
Acc.	τὴν	πόλιν	τὰς	πόλεις		τὸ	ἄστυ	τὰ	ἄστη
Voc.	ὦ	πόλι	ὦ	πόλεις		ὦ	ἄστυ	ὦ	ἄστη

Stem: βασιλευ-

Nom.	ὁ	βασιλεύς	οἱ	βασιλῆς
Gen.	τοῦ	βασιλέως	τῶν	βασιλέων
Dat.	τῷ	βασιλεῖ	τοῖς	βασιλεῦσι(ν)
Acc.	τὸν	βασιλέ-ᾱ	τοὺς	βασιλέᾱς
Voc.	ὦ	βασιλεῦ	ὦ	βασιλῆς

Stem: ναυ-   Stem: βου-

Nom.	ἡ	ναῦς	αἱ	νῆες		ὁ	βοῦς	οἱ	βόες
Gen.	τῆς	νεώς	τῶν	νεῶν		τοῦ	βοός	τῶν	βοῶν
Dat.	τῇ	νηΐ	ταῖς	ναυσίν		τῷ	βοΐ	τοῖς	βουσί(ν)
Acc.	τὴν	ναῦν	τὰς	ναῦς		τὸν	βοῦν	τοὺς	βοῦς
Voc.	ὦ	ναῦ	ὦ	νῆες		ὦ	βοῦ	ὦ	βόες

Type 4: Stems with Three Forms of Gradation (ηρ, ερ, and ρ)

ὁ	ἀνήρ	ὁ	πατήρ	ἡ	μήτηρ	ἡ	θυγάτηρ
τοῦ	ἀνδρός	τοῦ	πατρός	τῆς	μητρός	τῆς	θυγατρός
τῷ	ἀνδρί	τῷ	πατρί	τῇ	μητρί	τῇ	θυγατρί
τὸν	ἄνδρα	τὸν	πατέρα	τὴν	μητέρα	τὴν	θυγατέρα
ὦ	ἄνερ	ὦ	πάτερ	ὦ	μῆτερ	ὦ	θύγατερ
οἱ	ἄνδρες	οἱ	πατέρες	αἱ	μητέρες	αἱ	θυγατέρες
τῶν	ἀνδρῶν	τῶν	πατέρων	τῶν	μητέρων	τῶν	θυγατέρων
τοῖς	ἀνδράσι(ν)	τοῖς	πατράσι(ν)	ταῖς	μητράσι(ν)	ταῖς	θυγατράσι(ν)
τοὺς	ἄνδρας	τοὺς	πατέρας	τὰς	μητέρας	τὰς	θυγατέρας
ὦ	ἄνδρες	ὦ	πατέρες	ὦ	μητέρες	ὦ	θυγατέρες

5. ADJECTIVES AND PARTICIPLES OF THE FIRST AND SECOND DECLENSIONS

	Singular			*Plural*		
	M.	*F.*	*N.*	*M.*	*F.*	*N.*
Nom.	καλός	καλή	καλόν	καλοί	καλαί	καλά
Gen.	καλοῦ	καλῆς	καλοῦ	καλῶν	καλῶν	καλῶν
Dat.	καλῷ	καλῇ	καλῷ	καλοῖς	καλαῖς	καλοῖς
Acc.	καλόν	καλήν	καλόν	καλούς	καλάς	καλά
Voc.	καλέ	καλή	καλόν	καλοί	καλαί	καλά
Nom.	ῥᾴδιος	ῥᾳδίᾱ	ῥᾴδιον	ῥᾴδιοι	ῥᾴδιαι	ῥᾴδια
Gen.	ῥᾳδίου	ῥᾳδίᾱς	ῥᾳδίου	ῥᾳδίων	ῥᾳδίων	ῥᾳδίων
Dat.	ῥᾳδίῳ	ῥᾳδίᾳ	ῥᾳδίῳ	ῥᾳδίοις	ῥᾳδίαις	ῥᾳδίοις
Acc.	ῥᾴδιον	ῥᾳδίᾱν	ῥᾴδιον	ῥᾳδίους	ῥᾳδίᾱς	ῥᾴδια
Voc.	ῥᾴδιε	ῥᾳδίᾱ	ῥᾴδιον	ῥᾴδιοι	ῥᾴδιαι	ῥᾴδια

	M.	*F.*	*N.*

Present Middle and Passive Participles

Nom.	λῡόμενος	λῡομένη	λῡόμενον
Gen.	λῡομένου	λῡομένης	λῡομένου
Dat.	λῡομένῳ	λῡομένῃ	λῡομένῳ
Acc.	λῡόμενον	λῡομένην	λῡόμενον
Nom.	λῡόμενοι	λῡόμεναι	λῡόμενα
Gen.	λῡομένων	λῡομένων	λῡομένων
Dat.	λῡομένοις	λῡομέναις	λῡομένοις
Acc.	λῡομένους	λῡομένᾱς	λῡόμενα
Nom.	φιλούμενος	φιλουμένη	φιλούμενον
Gen.	φιλουμένου	φιλουμένης	φιλουμένου
Dat.	φιλουμένῳ	φιλουμένῃ	φιλουμένῳ
Acc.	φιλούμενον	φιλουμένην	φιλούμενον
Nom.	φιλούμενοι	φιλούμεναι	φιλούμενα
Gen.	φιλουμένων	φιλουμένων	φιλουμένων
Dat.	φιλουμένοις	φιλουμέναις	φιλουμένοις
Acc.	φιλουμένους	φιλουμένᾱς	φιλούμενα

Nom.	τῑμώμενος	τῑμωμένη	τῑμώμενον, etc.
Nom.	δηλούμενος	δηλουμένη	δηλούμενον, etc.

Aorist Middle Participles

Nom.	λῡσάμενος	λῡσαμένη	λῡσάμενον, etc.
Nom.	γενόμενος	γενομένη	γενόμενον, etc.

6. ADJECTIVES OF IRREGULAR DECLENSION

	M.	*F.*	*N.*	*M.*	*F.*	*N.*
Nom.	μέγας	μεγάλη	μέγα	μεγάλοι	μεγάλαι	μεγάλα
Gen.	μεγάλου	μεγάλης	μεγάλου	μεγάλων	μεγάλων	μεγάλων
Dat.	μεγάλῳ	μεγάλῃ	μεγάλῳ	μεγάλοις	μεγάλαις	μεγάλοις
Acc.	μέγαν	μεγάλην	μέγα	μεγάλους	μεγάλᾱς	μεγάλα
Voc.	μέγας	μεγάλη	μέγα	μεγάλοι	μεγάλαι	μεγάλα

Nom.	πολύς	πολλή	πολύ	πολλοί	πολλαί	πολλά
Gen.	πολλοῦ	πολλῆς	πολλοῦ	πολλῶν	πολλῶν	πολλῶν
Dat.	πολλῷ	πολλῇ	πολλῷ	πολλοῖς	πολλαῖς	πολλοῖς
Acc.	πολύν	πολλήν	πολύ	πολλούς	πολλάς	πολλά
Voc.	none					

7. ADJECTIVES OF THE THIRD DECLENSION

Adjectives with stems in -ον

	Singular		*Plural*	
	M. & F.	*N.*	*M. & F.*	*N.*
Nom.	σώφρων	σῶφρον	σώφρονες	σώφρονα
Gen.	σώφρονος	σώφρονος	σωφρόνων	σωφρόνων
Dat.	σώφρονι	σώφρονι	σώφροσι(ν)	σώφροσι(ν)
Acc.	σώφρονα	σῶφρον	σώφρονας	σώφρονα
Voc.	σῶφρον	σῶφρον	σώφρονες	σώφρονα

Irregular Comparative Adjectives:

Nom.	βελτῑων	βέλτῑον	βελτῑονες (βελτῑους)	βελτῑονα (βελτῑω)
Gen.	βελτῑονος	βελτῑονος	βελτῑόνων	βελτῑόνων
Dat.	βελτῑονι	βελτῑονι	βελτῑοσι(ν)	βελτῑοσι(ν)
Acc.	βελτῑονα (βελτῑω)	βέλτῑον	βελτῑονας (βελτῑους)	βελτῑονα (βελτῑω)
Voc.	βέλτῑον	βέλτῑον	βελτῑονες	βελτῑονα

Adjectives with stems in -εσ-:

Nom.	ἀληθής	ἀληθές	ἀληθεῖς	ἀληθῆ
Gen.	ἀληθοῦς	ἀληθοῦς	ἀληθῶν	ἀληθῶν
Dat.	ἀληθεῖ	ἀληθεῖ	ἀληθέσι(ν)	ἀληθέσι(ν)
Acc.	ἀληθῆ	ἀληθές	ἀληθεῖς	ἀληθῆ

8. ADJECTIVES AND PARTICIPLES OF MIXED DECLENSION

Adjectives

	M.	F.	N.
Nom.	πᾶς	πᾶσα	πᾶν
Gen.	παντός	πάσης	παντός
Dat.	παντί	πάσῃ	παντί
Acc.	πάντα	πᾶσαν	πᾶν
Nom.	πάντες	πᾶσαι	πάντα
Gen.	πάντων	πασῶν	πάντων
Dat.	πᾶσι(ν)	πάσαις	πᾶσι(ν)
Acc.	πάντας	πάσᾱς	πάντα

	M.	F.	N.
Nom.	ταχύς	ταχεῖα	ταχύ
Gen.	ταχέος	ταχείᾱς	ταχέος
Dat.	ταχεῖ	ταχείᾳ	ταχεῖ
Acc.	ταχύν	ταχεῖαν	ταχύ
Nom.	ταχεῖς	ταχεῖαι	ταχέα
Gen.	ταχέων	ταχειῶν	ταχέων
Dat.	ταχέσι(ν)	ταχείαις	ταχέσι(ν)
Acc.	ταχεῖς	ταχείᾱς	ταχέα

Participles: Present Active

	M.	F.	N.
Nom.	ὤν	οὖσα	ὄν
Gen.	ὄντος	οὔσης	ὄντος
Dat.	ὄντι	οὔσῃ	ὄντι
Acc.	ὄντα	οὖσαν	ὄν
Nom.	ὄντες	οὖσαι	ὄντα
Gen.	ὄντων	οὐσῶν	ὄντων
Dat.	οὖσι(ν)	οὔσαις	οὖσι(ν)
Acc.	ὄντας	οὔσᾱς	ὄντα

	M.	F.	N.
Nom.	λύων	λύουσα	λῦον
Gen.	λύοντος	λῡούσης	λύοντος
Dat.	λύοντι	λῡούσῃ	λύοντι
Acc.	λύοντα	λύουσαν	λῦον
Nom.	λύοντες	λύουσαι	λύοντα
Gen.	λῡόντων	λῡουσῶν	λῡόντων
Dat.	λύουσι(ν)	λῡούσαις	λύουσι(ν)
Acc.	λύοντας	λῡούσᾱς	λύοντα

	M.	F.	N.
Nom.	φιλῶν	φιλοῦσα	φιλοῦν
Gen.	φιλοῦντος	φιλούσης	φιλοῦντος
Dat.	φιλοῦντι	φιλούσῃ	φιλοῦντι
Acc.	φιλοῦντα	φιλοῦσαν	φιλοῦν
Nom.	φιλοῦντες	φιλοῦσαι	φιλοῦντα
Gen.	φιλούντων	φιλουσῶν	φιλούντων
Dat.	φιλοῦσι	φιλούσαις	φιλοῦσι
Acc.	φιλοῦντας	φιλούσᾱς	φιλοῦντα

Nom.	τῑμῶν	τῑμῶσα	τῑμῶν
Gen.	τῑμῶντος	τῑμώσης	τῑμῶντος
Dat.	τῑμῶντι	τῑμώσῃ	τῑμῶντι
Acc.	τῑμῶντα	τῑμῶσαν	τῑμῶν

Nom.	τῑμῶντες	τῑμῶσαι	τῑμῶντα
Gen.	τῑμώντων	τῑμωσῶν	τῑμώντων
Dat.	τῑμῶσι	τῑμώσαις	τῑμῶσι
Acc.	τῑμῶντας	τῑμώσᾱς	τῑμῶντα

| Nom. | δηλῶν | δηλοῦσα | δηλοῦν, etc. |

First Aorist Active

Nom.	λῦσᾱς	λῦσᾱσα	λῦσαν
Gen.	λῦσαντος	λῦσάσης	λῦσαντος
Dat.	λῦσαντι	λῦσάσῃ	λῦσαντι
Acc.	λῦσαντα	λῦσᾱσαν	λῦσαν

Nom.	λῦσαντες	λῦσᾱσαι	λῦσαντα
Gen.	λῡσάντων	λῡσᾱσῶν	λῡσάντων
Dat.	λῦσᾱσι(ν)	λῡσάσαις	λῦσᾱσι(ν)
Acc.	λῦσαντας	λῡσάσᾱς	λῦσαντα

First Aorist Passive (see Book II, Chapter 24, Grammar 1):

Nom.	λυθείς	λυθεῖσα	λυθέν
Gen.	λυθέντος	λυθείσης	λυθέντος
Dat.	λυθέντι	λυθείσῃ	λυθέντι
Acc.	λυθέντα	λυθεῖσαν	λυθέν

Nom.	λυθέντες	λυθεῖσαι	λυθέντα
Gen.	λυθέντων	λυθεισῶν	λυθέντων
Dat.	λυθεῖσι	λυθείσαις	λυθεῖσι
Acc.	λυθέντας	λυθείσᾱς	λυθέντα

Second Aorist Active

Nom.	λαβών	λαβοῦσα	λαβόν
Gen.	λαβόντος	λαβούσης	λαβόντος
Dat.	λαβόντι	λαβούσῃ	λαβόντι
Acc.	λαβόντα	λαβοῦσαν	λαβόν

Nom.	λαβόντες	λαβοῦσαι	λαβόντα
Gen.	λαβόντων	λαβουσῶν	λαβόντων
Dat.	λαβοῦσι(ν)	λαβούσαις	λαβοῦσι(ν)
Acc.	λαβόντας	λαβούσᾱς	λαβόντα

Perfect Active (see Book II, Chapter 28, Grammar 1):

Nom.	λελυκώς	λελυκυῖα	λελυκός
Gen.	λελυκότος	λελυκυίας	λελυκότος
Dat.	λελυκότι	λελυκυίᾳ	λελυκότι
Acc.	λελυκότα	λελυκυῖαν	λελυκός

Nom.	λελυκότες	λελυκυῖαι	λελυκότα
Gen.	λελυκότων	λελυκυιῶν	λελυκότων
Dat.	λελυκόσι	λελυκυίαις	λελυκόσι
Acc.	λελυκότας	λελυκυίᾱς	λελυκότα

9. COMPARISON OF ADJECTIVES

Positive	*Comparative*	*Superlative*
Regular		
ἀνδρεῖος	ἀνδρειότερος	ἀνδρειότατος
χαλεπός	χαλεπώτερος	χαλεπώτατος
ἀληθής	ἀληθέστερος	ἀληθέστατος
σώφρων	σωφρονέστερος	σωφρονέστατος

Irregular (see Book II, Chapter 24, Grammar 5)

ἀγαθός, -ή, -όν	ἀμείνων, ἄμεινον	ἄριστος, -η, -ον
	βελτΐων	βέλτιστος
	κρείσσων	κράτιστος
κακός, -ή, -όν	κακΐων, κάκῑον	κάκιστος, -η, -ον
	χείρων	χείριστος
αἰσχρός	αἰσχΐων	αἴσχιστος
καλός, -ή, -όν	καλλΐων, κάλλῑον	κάλλιστος, -η, -ον
μέγας, μεγάλη, μέγα	μείζων, μεῖζον	μέγιστος, -η, -ον
ὀλίγος, -η, -ον	ἐλάττων, ἔλαττον	ὀλίγιστος, -η, -ον
		ἐλάχιστος
πολύς, πολλή, πολύ	πλείων/πλέων, πλεῖον, πλέον	πλεῖστος, -η, -ον
ἐχθρός	ἐχθΐων	ἔχθιστος
ἡδύς	ἡδΐων	ἥδιστος
ῥᾴδιος	ῥᾴων	ῥᾷστος
ταχύς	θάσσων	τάχιστος

For the use of comparative and superlative adjectives, see Book I, page 172.

For the declension of the irregular comparative adjectives, see Book II, Chapter 24, Grammar 5, and above, paragraph 7.

10. DEMONSTRATIVE ADJECTIVES

	Singular			*Plural*		
	M.	*F.*	*N.*	*M.*	*F.*	*N.*
Nom.	οὗτος	αὕτη	τοῦτο	οὗτοι	αὗται	ταῦτα
Gen.	τούτου	ταύτης	τούτου	τούτων	τούτων	τούτων
Dat.	τούτῳ	ταύτῃ	τούτῳ	τούτοις	ταύταις	τούτοις
Acc.	τοῦτον	ταύτην	τοῦτο	τούτους	ταύτᾱς	ταῦτα
Nom.	ἐκεῖνος	ἐκείνη	ἐκεῖνο	ἐκεῖνοι	ἐκεῖναι	ἐκεῖνα
Gen.	ἐκείνου	ἐκείνης	ἐκείνου	ἐκείνων	ἐκείνων	ἐκείνων
Dat.	ἐκείνῳ	ἐκείνῃ	ἐκείνῳ	ἐκείνοις	ἐκείναις	ἐκείνοις
Acc.	ἐκεῖνον	ἐκείνην	ἐκεῖνο	ἐκείνους	ἐκείνᾱς	ἐκεῖνα
Nom.	ὅδε	ἥδε	τόδε	οἵδε	αἵδε	τάδε
Gen.	τοῦδε	τῆσδε	τοῦδε	τῶνδε	τῶνδε	τῶνδε
Dat.	τῷδε	τῇδε	τῷδε	τοῖσδε	ταῖσδε	τοῖσδε
Acc.	τόνδε	τήνδε	τόδε	τούσδε	τάσδε	τάδε

11. THE ADJECTIVE αὐτός

	M.	*F.*	*N.*
Nom.	αὐτός	αὐτή	αὐτό
Gen.	αὐτοῦ	αὐτῆς	αὐτοῦ
Dat.	αὐτῷ	αὐτῇ	αὐτῷ
Acc.	αὐτόν	αὐτήν	αὐτό

Nom.	αὐτοί	αὐταί	αὐτά
Gen.	αὐτῶν	αὐτῶν	αὐτῶν
Dat.	αὐτοῖς	αὐταῖς	αὐτοῖς
Acc.	αὐτούς	αὐτάς	αὐτά

For the uses of αὐτός, αὐτή, αὐτό, see Book II, Chapter 18, Grammar 2.

12. THE INTERROGATIVE ADJECTIVE

	Singular		**Plural**	
	M. & F.	**N.**	**M. & F.**	**N.**
Nom.	τίς	τί	τίν-ες	τίν-α
Gen.	τίν-ος	τίν-ος	τίν-ων	τίν-ων
Dat.	τίν-ι	τίν-ι	τίν-σι > τίσι	τίν-σι > τίσι
Acc.	τίν-α	τί	τίν-ας	τίν-α

13. THE INDEFINITE ADJECTIVE

	Singular		**Plural**	
	M. & F.	**N.**	**M. & F.**	**N.**
Nom.	τις	τι	τιν-ές	τιν-ά
Gen.	τιν-ός	τιν-ός	τιν-ῶν	τιν-ῶν
Dat.	τιν-ί	τιν-ί	τιν-σί > τισί	τιν-σί > τισί
Acc.	τιν-ά	τι	τιν-άς	τιν-ά

14. THE VERBAL ADJECTIVE IN -τέος (see Book II, Chapter 31, Grammar 4)

15. PERSONAL PRONOUNS

	1st Person Singular			**1st Person Plural**	
Nom.	ἐγώ		I	ἡμεῖς	we
Gen.	ἐμοῦ	μου	of me	ἡμῶν	of us
Dat.	ἐμοί	μοι	to or for me	ἡμῖν	to or for us
Acc.	ἐμέ	με	me	ἡμᾶς	us

	2nd Person Singular			**2nd Person Plural**	
Nom.	σύ		you	ὑμεῖς	you
Gen.	σοῦ	σου	of you	ὑμῶν	of you
Dat.	σοί	σοι	to or for you	ὑμῖν	to or for you
Acc.	σέ	σε	you	ὑμᾶς	you

There is no 3rd person pronoun; in the genitive, dative, and accusative cases, forms of αὐτός "self" are used in its place (see Book I, pages 50–51):

	M.			**F.**			**N.**	
G.	αὐτοῦ	of him or it	αὐτῆς	of her or it	αὐτοῦ	of it
D.	αὐτῷ	to or for him or it	αὐτῇ	to or for her or it	αὐτῷ	to it
A.	αὐτόν	him or it	αὐτήν	her or it	αὐτό	it
G.	αὐτῶν	of them	αὐτῶν	of them	αὐτῶν	of them
D.	αὐτοῖς	to or for them	αὐταῖς	to or for them	αὐτοῖς	to or for them
A.	αὐτούς	them	αὐτάς	them	αὐτά	them

16. REFLEXIVE PRONOUNS

	First Person		**Second Person**	
	M.	**F.**	**M.**	**F.**
G.	ἐμαυτοῦ	ἐμαυτῆς	σεαυτοῦ	σεαυτῆς
D.	ἐμαυτῷ	ἐμαυτῇ	σεαυτῷ	σεαυτῇ
A.	ἐμαυτόν	ἐμαυτήν	σεαυτόν	σεαυτήν
G.	ἡμῶν αὐτῶν	ἡμῶν αὐτῶν	ὑμῶν αὐτῶν	ὑμῶν αὐτῶν
D.	ἡμῖν αὐτοῖς	ἡμῖν αὐταῖς	ὑμῖν αὐτοῖς	ὑμῖν αὐταῖς
A.	ἡμᾶς αὐτούς	ἡμᾶς αὐτάς	ὑμᾶς αὐτούς	ὑμᾶς αὐτάς

	Third Person			
	M.	**F.**	**N.**	
G.	ἑαυτοῦ	ἑαυτῆς	ἑαυτοῦ	For the
D.	ἑαυτῷ	ἑαυτῇ	ἑαυτῷ	indirect
A.	ἑαυτόν	ἑαυτήν	ἑαυτό	reflexives,
G.	ἑαυτῶν	ἑαυτῶν	ἑαυτῶν	see Chapter 29
D.	ἑαυτοῖς	ἑαυταῖς	ἑαυτοῖς	Grammar 3.
A.	ἑαυτούς	ἑαυτάς	ἑαυτά	

17. THE RECIPROCAL PRONOUN

	M.	**F.**	**N.**
G.	ἀλλήλων	ἀλλήλων	ἀλλήλων
D.	ἀλλήλοις	ἀλλήλαις	ἀλλήλοις
A.	ἀλλήλους	ἀλλήλᾱς	ἄλληλα

18. THE PRONOUNS οὗ and σφῶν (see Book II, Chapter 29, Grammar 3)

19. POSSESSIVES

Possessive Adjectives:

	Singular	*Plural*
First Person	ἐμός, -ή, -όν my, mine	ἡμέτερος, -ᾱ, -ον our
Second Person	σός, -ή, -όν your	ὑμέτερος, -ᾱ, -ον your

Possessive Pronouns:

Third Person		
αὐτοῦ his *or* its	αὐτῶν their
αὐτῆς her *or* hers *or* its	αὐτῶν their
αὐτοῦ its	αὐτῶν their

20. THE INTERROGATIVE PRONOUN

For the interrogative pronoun τίς, τί "who?" "what?" see Book I, page 79. Its forms are the same as those of the interrogative adjective (see above, paragraph 12) and are not repeated here; it always has an acute accent on the first syllable.

21. THE INDEFINITE PRONOUN

For the indefinite pronoun τις, τι "someone," "something," "anyone," "anything," see Book I, page 79. This pronoun is enclitic, and it has the same forms as the indefinite adjective (see above, paragraph 13).

22. THE RELATIVE PRONOUN

	Singular			**Plural**		
	M.	**F.**	**N.**	**M.**	**F.**	**N.**
Nom.	ὅς	ἥ	ὅ	οἵ	αἵ	ἅ
Gen.	οὖ	ἧς	οὖ	ὧν	ὧν	ὧν
Dat.	ᾧ	ᾗ	ᾧ	οἷς	αἷς	οἷς
Acc.	ὅν	ἥν	ὅ	οὕς	ἅς	ἅ

Relative pronouns introduce relative clauses, and the pronouns agree with their antecedents in gender and number and take their case from their use in their own clause. For the indefinite ὅστις, see Book II, Chapter 22, Grammar 2.

23. FORMATION OF ADVERBS

Adverbs regularly have the same spelling and accent as the genitive plural of the corresponding adjective, but with the final ν changed to ς (see Book I, page 39):

Adjective καλός (genitive plural καλῶν) > adverb καλῶς
Adjective σώφρων (genitive plural σωφρόνων) > adverb σωφρόνως
Adjective ἀληθής (genitive plural ἀληθῶν) > adverb ἀληθῶς
Adjective ταχύς (genitive plural ταχέων) > adverb ταχέως

24. COMPARISON OF ADVERBS

For the comparative adverb the neuter singular of the comparative adjective is used, and for the superlative the neuter plural of the superlative adjective (see Book I, pages 171–172), e.g.:

ἀνδρείως	ἀνδρειότερον	ἀνδρειότατα
χαλεπῶς	χαλεπώτερον	χαλεπώτατα
ἀληθῶς	ἀληθέστερον	ἀληθέστατα
σωφρόνως	σωφρονέστερον	σωφρονέστατα

Irrregular:

εὖ	ἄμεινον	ἄριστα
κακῶς	κάκῑον	κάκιστα
πόλυ	πλέον	πλεῖστα
μάλα	μᾶλλον	μάλιστα

25. CORRELATIVES

See Book II, Chapter 26, Grammar 1.

26. THE NEGATIVE

See Book II, Chapter 31, Grammar 6.

27. NUMBERS

For the cardinal and ordinal numbers from one to ten, see Book I, page 93. For more numbers, see Book I, page 205.

The Greek numbers from one to twenty are:

1	εἷς, μία, ἕν	11	ἕνδεκα
2	δύο	12	δώδεκα
3	τρεῖς, τρία	13	τρεῖς (τρία) καὶ δέκα or τρεισκαίδεκα
4	τέτταρες, τέτταρα	14	τέτταρες (τέτταρα) καὶ δέκα
5	πέντε	15	πεντεκαίδεκα
6	ἕξ	16	ἑκκαίδεκα
7	ἑπτά	17	ἑπτακαίδεκα
8	ὀκτώ	18	ὀκτωκαίδεκα
9	ἐννέα	19	ἐννεακαίδεκα
10	δέκα	20	εἴκοσι(ν)

Other numbers

21	εἷς καὶ εἴκοσι
100	ἑκατόν
1,000	χίλιωι, -αι, -α
10,000	μύριοι, -αι, -α

Forms:

	M.	F.	N.
Nom.	εἷς	μία	ἕν
Gen.	ἑν-ός	μιᾶς	ἑν-ός
Dat.	ἑν-ί	μιᾷ	ἑν-ί
Acc.	ἕν-α	μίαν	ἕν

The word οὐδείς, οὐδεμία, οὐδέν (*pronoun/adjective*) "no one," "no," is declined exactly like εἷς, μία, ἕν.

	M. F. N.	M. F.	N.	M. F.	N.
Nom.	δύο	τρεῖς	τρία	τέτταρες	τέτταρα
Gen.	δυοῖν	τριῶν	τριῶν	τεττάρων	τεττάρων
Dat.	δυοῖν	τρισί(ν)	τρισί(ν)	τέτταρσι(ν)	τέτταρσι(ν)
Acc.	δύο	τρεῖς	τρία	τέτταρας	τέτταρα

The ordinals ("first," "second," "third," etc.) are as follows:

1st	πρῶτος, -η, -ον	9th	ἔνατος, -η, -ον
2nd	δεύτερος, -ᾱ, -ον	10th	δέκατος, -η, -ον
3rd	τρίτος, -η, -ον	11th	ἑνδέκατος, -η, -ον
4th	τέταρτος, -η, -ον	12th	δωδέκατος, -η, -ον
5th	πέμπτος, -η, -ον	20th	εἰκοστός, -ή, -όν
6th	ἕκτος, -η, -ον	100th	ἑκατοστός
7th	ἕβδομος, -η, -ον	1,000th	χῑλιοστός, -ή, -όν
8th	ὄγδοος, -η, -ον	10,000th	μῡριοστός, -ή, -όν

The ordinals are declined as first and second declension adjectives.

28. PREPOSITIONS

ἅμα (+ dat.)
    together with, with: ἅμα τῷ παιδί
    (5α:22)

ἀνά (+ acc.)
    up: ἀνὰ τὴν ὁδόν (5α:4)

ἀντί (+ gen.)
    instead of, against: ἀντὶ φίλου
    (28β:25–26)

ἀντίον (+ gen.)
    opposite: ἀντίον τῆς ἵππου
    (27β:18)

ἀπό (+ gen.)
    from: ἀπὸ τοῦ ἄστεως (4α:20)

διά (+ gen.)
    through: δι' ὀλίγου (= "soon,"
    5α:8)

διά (+ acc.)
    because of: διὰ τί (3α:5)

ἐγγύς (+ gen.)
    near: ἐγγὺς τῆς οἰκίας (9 tail
    reading:8)

εἰς (+ acc.)
    into: εἰς τὸν ἀγρόν (2β:3)
    to: εἰς τὴν κρήνην (4 tail
    reading:1)
    at (with verbs such as
    ἀφικνέομαι): εἰς τὴν νῆσον
    (6α:14)
    onto: εἰς τὴν γῆν (16β:33–34)
    for: εἰς πολλὰς ἡμέρας (6β:5–6)
    for (of purpose): εἰς τὸ λέγειν τε
    καὶ πράττειν (24β:16)
    against: ἐς αὐτόν (23 tail
    reading:1)

ἐκ, ἐξ (+ gen.)
    out of: ἐκ τοῦ ἀγροῦ (1β:2), ἐξ
    ἔργων (8α:16)

ἐκτός (+ gen.)
    outside: ἐκτὸς ὁρίων (22β:30)

ἐν (+ dat.)
    in: ἐν ταῖς Ἀθήναις (1α:1–2)
    on: ἐν τῇ ὁδῷ (4β:9)
    among: ἐν τοῖς δούλοις (11 tail
    reading: 5)

ἕνεκα (+ preceding gen.)
    for the sake of, because of: τίνος
    ἕνεκα (21α:5–6)

ἐντός (adverb or preposition + gen.)
    within: λιμένος πολυβενθέος
    ἐντός (16β:30)

ἐξόπισθε(ν) (adverb or preposition
    +gen.)
    behind: ἐξόπισθε τῆς κανηφόρου
    (31δ:149)

ἔξω (adverb or preposition + gen.)]
    outside: ἔξω τῶν τειχῶν (20δ:31)

ἐπί (+ gen.)
    toward, in the direction of: ἐπὶ τῆς
    Κορίνθου (20δ:12)
    on: ἐπὶ τῶν βάθρων (24β:6)

ἐπί (+ dat.)
    upon, on: ἐπὶ τῇ γῇ (5β:15)
    at: ἐπὶ τῇ θύρᾳ (9 tail reading:10)
    for (of price): ἐπὶ μιᾷ δραχμῇ
    (18β:13)
    for (of purpose): ἐπὶ ναυμαχίᾳ
    (29α:10)

ἐπί (+ acc.)
    at, against: ἐπ' αὐτόν (5β:7–8)
    onto (with ἀναβαίνω): ἐπὶ ἄκραν
    τὴν ἀκτήν (7 tail reading:4)
    upon: ἐπὶ τὸν ὄχθον (15 tail
    reading:3)
    to or for (of direction or purpose):
    ἐπὶ πόλεμον (26α:9)
    for (of time): ἐπὶ δύο ἔτεα (27α:1)

κατά (+ acc.)
    down: κατὰ τὴν ὁδόν (5 tail
    reading:5)
    distributive: κατ' ἔτος (= "each
    year," 6α:5) and καθ' ἡμέραν
    (="every day," 24α:2)
    by: κατὰ θάλατταν (11α:38)
    on: κατὰ τοῦτο τοῦ ὄρους (14 tail
    reading:6)
    at (of place): κατ' οἶκον (16a:30)
    according to: κατὰ νόμον
    (17β:45–46)
    at (of time): κατ' ἐκεῖνον τὸν
    χρόνον (21β:1–2)
    through: κατὰ τοὺς θησαυρούς
    (25α:13)
    with regard to: κατὰ τὸν παῖδα
    (26α:4)
    after: κατ' αὐτόν (28α:11)

μετά (+ gen.)
 with: μετὰ τῶν ἑταίρων (6α:11)
μετά (+ acc.) (of time and place)
 after (of time): μετὰ τὸ δεῖπνον
  (3β:7)
 after (of place): μετὰ αὐτούς
  (5α:10)
ὄπισθε(ν) (adverb or preposition +
 gen.)
 behind: ὄπισθεν τοῦ ἱεροῦ (9α:35)
παρά (+ gen.)
 from: παρὰ σοῦ (26 tail
  reading:11)
παρά (+ dat.)
 at the house of: παρ' ἑαυτῷ (24α:9)
παρά (+ acc.)
 along, past: παρὰ τὴν Σικελίαν (10
  tail reading: 2)
 to (of persons only): παρὰ ἰατρόν
  τινα (11α:3–4)
 in (respect of each) = distributive:
  παρ' ἕκαστον ἔργον (24α:21–22)
περί (+ gen.)
 around: περὶ οὗ (18α:3)
 about, concerning: περὶ τοῦ
  πολέμου (21α:16)
περί (+ dat.)
 concerning: περὶ τῷ χωρίῳ
  (30γ:9–10)
περί (+ acc.)
 around: περὶ Τροίαν (7α:8)
πλήν (+ acc.)
 except, except for : πλὴν ἑνός (8
  tail reading:7)
πρό (+ gen.)
 before (of time or place): πρὸ τῆς
  νυκτός (10β:3)
 in preference to: πρὸ εἰρήνης
  (28β:29)

πρός (+ gen.)
 from, at the hand of: πρὸς αὐτοῦ
  (26β:5)
πρός (+ dat.)
 on: πρὸς τῇ γῇ (7β:12)
 at, near: πρὸς τῷ ᾽Αρτεμισίῳ
  (14β:23)
 in addition to: πρὸς . . . τούτοις
  (24β:11)
πρός (+ acc.)
 to, toward: πρὸς τὸ ἕρμα (1β:3)
 upon: πρὸς τὸν τοῦ Δικαιοπόλεως
  πόδα (3α:17)
 against: πρὸς τοὺς λίθους (11β:3–
  4)
 toward (of time): πρὸς ἑσπέραν
  (17α:22)
 with (i.e., in relation to): πρὸς
  ῎Αμασιν (27α:45)
σύν (+ dat.)
 with: σὺν θεῷ (12β:31)
ὑπέρ (+ gen.)
 on behalf of, for: ὑπὲρ σοῦ (7 tail
  reading:2)
 over, above: ὑπὲρ Θερμοπυλῶν (14
  tail reading, title)
ὑπέρ (+ acc.)
 over, above: ὑπὲρ τὸ ὄρος (14 tail
  reading:1)
ὑπό (+ gen.)
 under: ὑπὸ τῶν οἰῶν (7β:31–32)
 by (of agent): ὑπὸ τῶν πολεμίων
  (22α:23)
 because of: ὑπὸ τῆς παρεούσης
  συμφορῆς (28α:17)
ὑπό (+ dat.)
 under: ὑπὸ τῷ δένδρῳ (1β:5)
ὑπό (+ acc.)
 under (with verbs of motion): ὑπὸ
  τὸ ζυγόν (2β:8)
 at (of time): ὑπὸ νύκτα (30δ:29)

29. USES OF THE ARTICLE

a. Greek sometimes uses the definite article where we would not use an article
  in English (see Book I, page 5), e.g.:
   ὁ Δικαιόπολις αὐτουργός ἐστιν.
   Dicaeopolis is a farmer.

b. The neuter of the adjective + the article is often used as an abstract noun (see
  Book II, Chapter 19, Grammar 4), e.g.:
   τὸ καλόν = beauty

c. Article + Adjective = Noun Phrase (see Book II, Chapter 19, Grammar 4). Note the following:

αἱ σώφρονες = sensible women

d. The article + a participle form a noun phrase that may be translated by a noun or a relative clause in English (see Book I, page 110), e.g.:

ὁ ἱερεὺς ὁ τὴν θυσίαν ποιούμενος   οἱ τρέχοντες
the priest who is making the sacrifice   the runners

e. Genitives, prepositional phrases, and adverbs may be attached to the article as attributives without a noun (see Book II, Chapter 19, Grammar 4), e.g.:

οἱ ἐν τῇ ἀγορᾷ = the men in the market place

f. The article + δέ is often used at the beginning of a clause to indicate a change of subject (see Book I, pages 44 and 109–110), e.g.:

ὁ δεσπότης τὸν δοῦλον καλεῖ· ὁ δὲ οὐ πάρεστιν.
The master calls the slave, *but he* is not present.

g. The Articular Infinitive (see Book II, Chapter 27, Grammar 3)

τοῦτό ἐστι **τὸ ἀδικεῖν**, τὸ πλέον τῶν ἄλλων **ζητεῖν** ἔχειν.
Wrongdoing is this, *to seek* to have more than others. (Plato, *Gorgias* 483e)

ὁ Περικλῆς πιστεύει ὀρθῶς γιγνώσκειν περὶ **τοῦ μὴ ἐπεξιέναι**.
Pericles believes that he is right about *not going out to attack*. (Chapter 23β)

τῷ ταχέως **ἱππεύειν** ἐν καιρῷ ἀφίκοντο.
By riding fast they arrived on time.

ἵνα . . . χρήσιμοι ὦσιν **εἰς τὸ λέγειν** τε καὶ **πράττειν**.
. . . so that they may be useful *in both speech and action*. (Chapter 24β)

30. USES OF THE CASES

See summaries in Book 2, Chapter 26, Grammar 2, 3, and 4.
The following verbs that have appeared in the vocabulary lists are used with the genitive case:

αἰσθάνομαι (+ *gen. or acc.*) I perceive

ἀκούω I hear (a person talking; the accusative is used for the thing heard)

ἁμαρτάνω I miss

ἀπέχω I am distant from

ἀποπειράω I attempt, test

ἄρχω I begin, rule

ἀφίσταμαι I revolt from

δέομαι I ask X (*acc.*) from Y (*gen.*)

ἐπιβαίνω I set foot on, mount

ἐπιμελέομαι I care for

ἐράω I love

ἔχομαι I hold onto

καταφρονέω I despise

κρατέω I have power over, rule

λαμβάνομαι I seize, take hold of

μέμνημαι (+ *gen. or acc.*) I remember

πυνθάνομαι I learn X (*acc.*) from Y (*gen.*)

συνίημι (+ *gen. of person, acc. of thing*) I understand

τυγχάνω I hit, get

φείδομαι I spare

The following verbs in the vocabulary lists are used with the dative case:

ἀκολουθέω I follow, accompany
ἀμύνομαι I defend myself against
ἀντέχω I resist
ἀντιόομαι I oppose
ἀρέσκει It pleases
βοηθέω I help
διαλέγομαι I talk to, converse with
εἴκω I yield
εἰσηγέομαι I lead into
ἐμβάλλω I strike
ἐμπῑ́πτω I fall into, fall on
ἐντυγχάνω I meet
ἐπέρχομαι I go against, attack
ἐπιπλέω I sail against
ἐπιστρατεύω I campaign against, attack
ἐπιτίθεμαι I attack

ἕπομαι I follow
εὔχομαι I pray to
ἡγέομαι I lead
ἥδομαι I enjoy
μάχομαι I fight with
ὀργίζομαι I grow angry at
παραινέω I advise
παρίσταμαι I stand by (to help)
πείθομαι I obey
πιστεύω I trust, am confident in
προσβάλλω I attack
προσέρχομαι I approach
προσχωρέω I go toward, approach
συμβάλλω I join battle with
συμπῑ́πτω I clash with
τέρπομαι I enjoy
χαρίζομαι I show favor to, oblige
χράομαι I use, enjoy

31. AGREEMENT

Definite articles and adjectives agree with the nouns they go with in gender, number, and case (see Book I, page 5), e.g.:

ὁ καλὸς ἀγρός   ὁ ἀληθὴς μῦθος   ἡ ἀληθὴς γνώμη

The definite article will indicate the gender, number, and case of the noun with which it goes; this helps identify the forms of unfamiliar nouns (see Book I, page 40).

Normally subjects and verbs agree in number (i.e., a singular subject takes a singular verb, and a plural subject, a plural verb), but in Greek neuter plural subjects regularly take singular verbs (see Book I, page 44), e.g.:

τὰ μῆλα ἐν τῷ ἀγρῷ μένει.   The flocks remain in the field.

32. WORD ORDER

It is the endings of words and not the order in which they are placed that builds the meaning of a Greek sentence. Word order in Greek is therefore more flexible than in English and can be manipulated to convey emphasis. See Book I, page 5.

Attributive and Predicate Position

For the attributive and predicate position of adjectives, see Book I, page 52, and Book II, Chapter 19, Grammar 2. For the predicate position of possessive genitives of αὐτός, see Book I, page 52, and Book II, Chapter 19, Grammar 3. For the predicate position of demonstrative adjectives, see Book I, page 179, and Book II, Chapter 19, Grammar 2. For the attributive position of the possessive genitive of nouns, prepositional phrases, and adverbs, see Book I, page 109, and Book II, Chapter 19, Grammar 3.

33. USES OF PARTICIPLES

See summary in Chapter 31, Grammar 5.

34. INFORMATION ABOUT VERB FORMS IN BOOK II

The future tense, pages 8–10
The irregular verb εἰμί, page 17
The verbs δίδωμι and τίθημι, pages 22–24
The verb ἵστημι, pages 48–50
The subjunctive mood, pages 60–62
The verb ἵημι, pages 69–70
The verb δείκνυμι, pages 82–83
The passive voice: present and imperfect tenses, page 88
The verb φημί, page 96
The passive voice: first aorist and first future passive, pages 102–103

Second aorist passive and second future passive, page 104
Aorist of deponent verbs, page 104
The forms of the optative, pages 117–118
Perfect and pluperfect middle and passive, pages 146–149
First perfect and pluperfect active, pages 162–164
Second perfect and pluperfect active, page 164
Verbs found mostly in the perfect tense, page 170
The verb οἶδα, page 181
Third person imperatives, page 223

35. PRINCIPAL PARTS OF VERBS

The principal parts of verbs, knowledge of which enables you to recognize or construct all other forms of any given verb are:

present active	future active	aorist active
λύω	λύσω	ἔλῡσα
perfect active	perfect middle/passive	aorist passive
λέλυκα	λέλυμαι	ἐλύθην

The other forms are constructed as follows:

The imperfect is constructed from the present stem: ἔ-λῡ-ον.
The present, future, and aorist middle are constructed from the corresponding active stems: λύ-ομαι, λύσ-ομαι, ἐ-λῡσ-άμην.
The future passive is constructed from the aorist passive stem: λυθή-σομαι

The principal parts of compound verbs are the same as those of simple verbs, with the prepositional prefix (see paragraph 58, Euphony), e.g.:

καταλύω, καταλύσω, κατέλῡσα, καταλέλυκα, καταλέλυμαι, κατελύθην

The principal parts of most verbs follow simple patterns, so that if you know the first principal part (the present active indicative) you can construct the remaining principal parts according to the rules for the tenses and voices that you have learned.

The verbs that are given in the lists after the reading passages have been arranged in groups of verbs with similar patterns. The following is a summary showing some of the patterns visible in these groupings. The numbers and letters in brackets refer to the lists after the reading passages.

a. Verbs with stems in -υ-, -αυ-, -ευ-, and -ου- [17α, 17β], e.g., λύω, λύσω, ἔλῡσα, λέλυκα, λέλυμαι, ἐλύθην.

Similarly (apart from differences in the length of the stem vowel, -υ-/-ῡ-, and some aorist passives that insert σ before θ): **(-υ-):** δακρύω, ἐξαρτύω, θύω, μηνύω; **(-αυ-):** παύω (ἐπαύθην *or* ἐπαύσθην); **(-ευ-):** ἀγορεύω, ἀροτρεύω, βασιλεύω, βουλεύω, γεύομαι, ἱππεύω, κελεύω (ἐκελεύσθην), κινδυνεύω, νυκτερεύω, παιδεύω, πιστεύω, πορεύομαι, στρατεύω, φονεύω.

Irregular: **(-υ-)** καταδύω, φύω; **(-ου-):** ἀκούω, λούω.

b. Contract verbs with stems in -ε- [18α], e.g., φιλέω, φιλήσω, ἐφίλησα, πεφίληκα, πεφίλημαι, ἐφιλήθην.

Similarly: ἀγνοέω, ἀδικέω, αἰτέω, ἀκολουθέω, ἀποδημέω, ἀπορέω, αὐλέω, βοηθέω, δειπνέω, ἐνθῡμέομαι (*aorist* ἐνεθῡμήθην), ἐπιμελέομαι (*aorist* ἐπεμελήθην), ἐπιχειρέω, εὐφημέω, ἡγέομαι, ζητέω, θαρρέω, θεωρέω, κῑνέω, κρατέω, λαλέω, λοιδορέω, λῡπέω, ναυμαχέω, νοσέω, νοστέω, οἰκέω, ὁρμέω, ποθέω, ποιέω, πολεμέω, πολιορκέω, πονέω, πορθέω, στυγέω, φοβέομαι, φρονέω, φρουρέω, φωνέω, χωρέω, ὠφελέω.

Irregular verbs with stems in -ε- are: αἱρέω, ἀκέομαι, δέομαι, δέω, καλέω, παραινέω, πνέω. For δοκέω (δοκεῖ), see e.ii. below; for πλέω, see Greek to English Vocabulary; and for σκοπέω, see e.i. below.

c. Contract verbs with stems in -α- [18α, 18β], e.g., τῑμάω, τῑμήσω, ἐτίμησα, τετίμηκα, τετίμημαι, ἐτῑμήθην.

Similarly: βοάω, μελετάω, νῑκάω, ὁρμάω, σῑγάω, τελευτάω, τολμάω, φοιτάω.

But if ε, ι, or ρ precedes the final α of the stem, the principal parts are: πειράω, πειράσω, ἐπείρᾱσα, πεπείρᾱκα, πεπείρᾱμαι, ἐπειρᾱθην.

Similarly: θεάομαι (χράομαι is an exception to this rule).

Irregular verbs with stems in -α- are: γελάω, ἐάω, ἐράω, ἐρωτάω, ζάω, ὁράω.

d. Contract verbs with stems in -ο- [18β], e.g., δηλόω, δηλώσω, ἐδώλωσα, δεδήλωκα, δεδήλωμαι, ἐδηλώθην.

Similarly: ἀντιόομαι (*aorist* ἠντιώθην), δουλόω, ἐλευθερόω, πληρόω.

e. Verbs with stems ending in consonants:

   i. Labials (β, π, and φ) [19α, 19β], e.g., γράφω, γράψω, ἔγραψα, γέγραφα, γέγραμμαι, ἐγράφην.

   Similarly (stems and aorist passives are given in parentheses): **(-β-):** βλάπτω (βλαβ-) (ἐβλάφθην *or* ἐβλάβην); **(-π-):** βλέπω (future βλέψομαι), κόπτω (κοπ-) (-εκόπην), τέρπομαι; **(-φ-):** θάπτω (θαφ-) (ἐτάφην), κρύπτω (κρυφ-) (ἐκρύφθην), μέμφομαι (ἐμέμφθην).

   For λείπω, πέμπω, σκοπέω (stem σκεπ-), στρέφω, and τύπτω (τυπ-/τυπτε-), see Greek to English Vocabulary.

   ii. Gutturals (γ, κ, and χ) [20γ, 20δ], e.g., διώκω, διώξομαι *or* διώξω, ἐδίωξα, δεδίωχα, ἐδιώχθην.

   Similarly: **(-γ-):** ἀμέλγω, ζεύγνῡμι (ζευγ-), πράττω (πρᾱγ-), στενάζω (στεναγ-), σφάζω (σφαγ-), τάττω (ταγ-); **(-κ-):** δείκνῡμι (δεικ-), εἴκω, φυλάττω (φυλακ-); **(-χ-):** ἄρχω, δέχομαι, εὔχομαι, ταράττω (ταραχ-).

Irregular: (-γ-): ἄγω, διαλέγομαι, λέγω, συλλέγω, φεύγω; (-κ-): δοκέω (δοκ-/δοκε-), ἕλκω; (-χ-): τρέχω. Note that μάχομαι has stem μαχε- in all but the present and imperfect.

Most verbs with suffix -νῡμι added to the stem in the present and imperfect have guttural stems and regular principal parts:

ζεύγ-νῡμι (ζευγ-), ζεύξω, ἔζευξα, ἔζευγμαι, ἐζεύχθην.
For the principal parts of ἀνοίγ-νῡμι and ῥήγ-νῡμι (ῥηγ-/ῥωγ-/ ῥαγ-), see Greek to English Vocabulary.
But σβέ-ν-νῡμι has stem σβε- with ν added (original stem σβεσ-), σβέσω, ἔσβεσα, ἔσβηκα (has gone out), ἐσβέσθην.

For verbs ending -(ί)σκω, see 2 below.

iii. Dentals (δ, ζ, θ, and τ) [21α, 21β], e.g., ὀνομάζω, ὀνομάσω, ὠνόμασα, ὠνόμακα, ὠνόμασμαι, ὠνομάσθην.

Similarly: (-δ-): σπεύδω, φείδομαι, ψεύδομαι; (-ζ-): ἀναγκάζω, ἐργάζομαι (εἰργασάμην, εἴργασμαι), θαυμάζω (future θαυμάσομαι), ὀνομάζω, σῴζω (σώσω, ἔσωσα, σέσωκα, σέσωσμαι, ἐσώθην), φράζω; (-τ-): ἐρέσσω (ἐρετ-).

But: (-ίζω): κομίζω, κομιῶ, ἐκόμισα, κεκόμικα, κεκόμισμαι, ἐκομίσθην.

Similarly: ἀγωνίζομαι, ἀκοντίζω, βαδίζω, ἐλπίζω, θεσπίζω, κιθαρίζω, νομίζω, ξενίζω, ὀργίζομαι, φροντίζω, ψηφίζομαι, χαρίζομαι.

Irregular: ᾄδω, ἥδομαι, καθέζομαι, καθίζω, καθίζομαι, πείθω, πίπτω (πετ-), σπένδομαι.

iv. Liquids (λ, μ, ν, and ρ) [22α, 22β, 23α]; these are all regarded as irregular, and their principal parts will be found in the Greek to English Vocabulary.

(-λ-): ἀγγέλλω, βάλλω, στέλλω; (-μ-): νέμω I distribute; (-ν-): ἀμ́νω, ἀποκρίνομαι, ἀποκτείνω, μένω, σημαίνω, φαίνω; (-ρ-): ἀγείρω, αἴρω, διαφθείρω, ἐγείρω, οἰκτίρω, σπείρω.

Many of the so-called irregular verbs in fact follow quite simple rules in the formation of their principal parts, which can be easily recognized if the verb stems are known.

1. Nasal Infixes. Some verbs insert infixes containing -ν- in the present and imperfect only [23β, 24α], e.g., αὐξ-άν-ω.
2. Inceptive -(ί)σκω. Some verbs add -σκω (after a vowel) or -ίσκω (after a consonant), which appear only in the present and imperfect tenses [24β], e.g., ἀποθνῄ-σκω.
3. Irregular Augment. A few verbs starting with ε or ι augment to ει in the imperfect, and this augment sometimes shows up in other tenses as well [25β], e.g., ἐργάζομαι, (imperfect) εἰργαζόμην, (aorist) εἰργασάμην, etc.
4. Present Reduplication. A few verbs reduplicate their stems in the present and imperfect by repeating first consonant of the stem + ι [26α], e.g., γί-γνομαι.
5. A number of verbs show two or three grades of stem vowel (see paragraph 59 on page 262) [26β], e.g., in γίγνομαι, γενήσομαι, ἐγενόμην, γέγονα, γεγένημαι,

there are three grades of stem vowel, namely, γεν-, γον-, and γν-. Change of ε to ο in the second perfect is common, e.g., (γεν-) γέγονα and (λειπ-) λέλοιπα. Verbs with stems ending in liquids (λ, μ, ν, ρ) often change ε to α in the first perfect, perfect middle, and second aorist passive, e.g., στέλλω (στελ-/σταλ-), στελῶ, ἔστειλα, ἔσταλκα, ἔσταλμαι, ἐστάλην.

6. Metathesis. A few verbs transpose vowel and consonant of the stem, most commonly in the perfects and aorist passive, e.g., βάλλω (βαλ-/βλη-), βαλῶ, ἔβαλον, βέβληκα, βέβλημαι, ἐβλήθην.

7. Composite Verbs. The parts of some common verbs are formed from two or more unrelated stems [27α, 27β, 28α, 29α], e.g., αἱρέω (αἱρε-/ἑλ-), αἱρήσω, εἷλον, ᾕρηκα, ᾕρημαι, ᾑρέθην.

8. Irregular Second Aorists. Some verbs form their principal parts regularly except for the second aorist, e.g., ἄγω, ἄξω, ἤγαγον, ἦχα, ἦγμαι, ἤχθην (regular guttural formations except for the second aorist).

9. Verbs Adding ε to Stem. Many verbs insert ε after the present stem in the formation of the other tenses (except the second aorist); the ε usually lengthens to η [28β], e.g., βούλομαι (βουλ-/βουλε-), βουλήσομαι, βεβούλημαι, ἐβουλήθην.

10. Attic Reduplication. A few verbs starting in α, ε, or ο reduplicate in the perfect by repeating the initial vowel and consonant of the stem and lengthening α or ε to η and ο to ω [29β], e.g., ἀκούω, (*perfect*) ἀκ-ήκο-α.

11. Irregular Perfect. The verbs λαμβάνω, διαλέγομαι, and συλλέγω have the prefix εἰ- instead of perfect reduplication: λαμβάνω (λαβ-/ληβ-), εἴ-ληφα; διαλέγομαι, δι-εί-λεγμαι; and συλλέγω (λεγ-/λοχ-), συν-εί-λοχα.

36. ASPECT

Apart from the future tense, which presents no difficulty, Greek tenses function rather differently from ours. There are three tense systems, differentiated by how the action of the verb is viewed (*aspect*).

1. The imperfective, i.e., the present and imperfect tenses; the action is viewed as a process or a continuous state, e.g.:
   οἱ φύλακες τὰς πύλᾱς κλείουσιν.
   The guards are shutting the gates.
   οἱ φύλακες τὰς πύλᾱς ἔκλειον.
   The guards were shutting the gates.
   The action viewed as a process is often continuous or incomplete.

2. The aorist ; the action is viewed as a simple event or fact, e.g.:
   ὡς ἀφῑκόμεθα, οἱ φύλακες τὰς πύλᾱς ἔκλεισαν.
   When we arrived, the guards shut the gates.

3. The perfective, i.e., the perfect and pluperfect tenses; the action is viewed as a state, e.g.:

   αἱ πύλαι κέκλεινται. The gates are (have been) shut.
   αἱ πύλαι ἐκέκλειντο. The gates were (had been) shut.

Greek perfects consequently are often translated by English presents, e.g., δέδοικα I am afraid, πέφῡκα I am by nature, and τέθνηκε he/she is dead.

These distinctions apply to imperatives, subjunctives, optatives, infinitives, and participles as well as to the indicative, e.g.:

Imperative:

μηκέτι μένε, ὦ παῖ. Don't go on waiting, boy. (process)

στῆθι, ὦ παῖ, καὶ μεῖνον. Stop, boy, and wait. (event)

ἀκούετέ μου λέγοντος. Listen to what I say. (process)

σίγησον καὶ ἄκουσον. Shut up and listen. (event)

τεθνήκετε. Die (be dead). (state)

Infinitive:

παρήνεσεν ἡμῖν βραδέως πορεύεσθαι. He advised us to travel slowly. (process)

ἐκέλευσεν ἡμᾶς στῆναι. He told us to stand still. (event)

ἔπειθεν ἡμᾶς μὴ δεδοικέναι. He urged us not to be afraid (to be in a state of fear).

Participle:

ταχέως πορευόμενοι δι' ὀλίγου ἀφῑκόμεθα. Traveling quickly we soon arrived. (process)

εἰς τὴν πόλιν εἰσελθόντες πρὸς τὴν ἀγορὰν ἔσπευδον. Entering the city they hurried to the agora. (event)

ἀποκρῑνάμενος εἶπεν. He said in answer (clearly not "having answered, he said") (event, simultaneous with the action of the main verb)

ἡ γυνὴ δακρύσᾱσα ἀπῄει. The woman burst into tears and left. (event, prior to the action of the main verb)

δακρύουσα ἀπῄει. She went away crying. (process)

The following extract from the story of Croesus and Atys (Herodotus 1.43–45) illustrates the use of tenses and aspect:

ὁ μὲν δὴ ['Ἄτῡς] βληθεὶς τῇ αἰχμῇ ἐξέπλησε τοῦ ὀνείρου τὴν φήμην, ἔθεε δέ τις ἀγγελέων τῷ Κροίσῳ τὸ γεγονός, ἀφικόμενος δὲ ἐς τὰς Σάρδῑς τήν τε μάχην καὶ τὸν τοῦ παιδὸς μόρον ἐσήμηνέ οἱ. ὁ δὲ Κροῖσος τῷ θανάτῳ τοῦ παιδὸς συντεταραγμένος μᾶλλόν τι ἐδεινολογέετο ὅτι μιν ἀπέκτεινε τὸν (= ὃν) αὐτὸς φόνου ἐκάθηρε. περιημεκτέων δὲ τῇ συμφορῇ δεινῶς ἐκάλεε μὲν Δία καθάρσιον, μαρτυρόμενος τὰ ὑπὸ τοῦ ξείνου πεπονθὼς εἴη. . . . παρῆσαν δὲ μετὰ τοῦτο οἱ Λῡδοὶ φέροντες τὸν νεκρόν, ὄπισθε δὲ εἵπετο οἱ ὁ φονεύς. στὰς δὲ οὗτος πρὸ τοῦ νεκροῦ παρεδίδου ἑωυτὸν Κροίσῳ προτείνων τὰς χεῖρας, ἐπικατασφάξαι μιν κελεύων τῷ νεκρῷ, λέγων τήν τε προτέρην ἑωυτοῦ συμφορήν, καὶ ὡς ἐπ' ἐκείνῃ τὸν καθήραντα ἀπολωλεκὼς εἴη . . . Κροῖσος δὲ τούτων ἀκούσᾱς τόν τε Ἄδρηστον κατοικτῑρει. . . καὶ λέγει πρὸς αὐτόν. . . .

So Atys, struck (βληθείς–aorist participle–event) by the spear point, fulfilled (ἐξέπλησε–aorist–event) the warning of the dream, and someone ran (ἔθεε–imperfect–process) to tell (ἀγγελέων–future participle–purpose) what had happened (τὸ γεγονός–perfect participle–state–the event was fixed and irrevocable), and arriving (ἀφικόμενος–event) at Sardis he reported (ἐσήμηνε–aorist–event) to him the battle and the fate of his son. And Croesus, confounded (συντεταραγμένος–perfect participle; he was in a state of confusion) by the death of his son, lamented (ἐδεινολογέετο–imperfect; his lamentation was a continuous process) all the more because the man had killed (ἀπέκτεινε–aorist–event) him whom he himself had purified (ἐκάθηρε–aorist–event) of murder, and grieving (περιημεκτέων–present participle–process) terribly at the disaster, he called (ἐκάλεε–imperfect–process) on Zeus of purification, protesting (μαρτυρόμενος–

present participle–process) what he had suffered (πεπονθὼς εἴη–perfect optative in indirect statement–his suffering was a state) at the hands of the stranger. . . . After this, the Lydians arrived (παρῆσαν–"were present"), carrying (φέροντες–present participle–process) the corpse, and behind followed the murderer (εἵπετο–imperfect–process). And he stopped (στάς– aorist participle–event; it does not mean "standing," which would be perfect participle) and tried to hand himself (παρεδίδου–imperfect– process, incomplete, since Croesus would not accept his surrender) over to Croesus, stretching out (προτείνων–present participle–process) his hands, telling him (κελεύων–present participle–process) to slaughter (ἐπικατασφάξαι–aorist infinitive–event) himself on top of the corpse, telling (λέγων–present participle–process) of his former disaster and (saying) that on top of that he had destroyed (ἀπολωλεκὼς εἴη–perfect optative in indirect statement–the destruction was complete and irrevocable) the man who had purified him (τὸν καθήραντα–aorist participle–event). . . . But Croesus hearing (ἀκούσας–aorist participle– event) pitied (literally, pities) Adrastus and said (literally, says) (κατοικτίρει . . . λέγει–historic presents) to him . . .

37. USES OF THE SUBJUNCTIVE AND OPTATIVE IN MAIN CLAUSES

   a. Subjunctive
     1. Hortatory subjunctive: see Book II, Chapter 21, Grammar 3.
     2. Subjunctive in deliberative questions: see Book II, Chapter 21, Grammar 3.
     3. Subjunctive in prohibitions (negative commands): see Book II, Chapter 21, Grammar 3.
   b. Optative
     1. The optative used to express wishes: see Book II, Chapter 25, Grammar 1.
     2. Potential optative: see Book II, Chapter 29, Grammar 4.
     3. Future less vivid conditions: see Book II, Chapter 30, Grammar 1.

38. USES OF THE SUBJUNCTIVE AND OPTATIVE IN SUBORDINATE CLAUSES

   a. Purpose clauses: see Book II, Chapter 21, Grammar 3.
   b. Clauses of fearing: see Book II, Chapter 22, Grammar 1.
   c. Indefinite or general clauses: see Book II, Chapter 22, Grammar 2.
   d. For the use of the optative in subordinate clauses, see Book II, Chapter 25, Grammar 2 and 4, and Book II, Chapter 30, Grammar 1 and 2.
   e. For the use of ἕως and πρίν in temporal clauses, see Book II, Chapter 22, Grammar 2, and Book II, Chapter 27, Grammar 2.
   f. For the use of the subjunctive and optative in conditional clauses, see Book II, Chapter 30, Grammar 1 and 2.

39. SUBORDINATE CLAUSES

See paragraph 38 above and the following:
   a. For indirect statements and questions: see Book II, Chapter 22, Grammar 4; Book II, Chapter 23, Grammar 3 and 4; and Book II, Chapter 30, Grammar 2.
   b. For ὅπως + future indicative after verbs expressing care or effort, see Book II, Chapter 24, Grammar 4.
   c. For subordinate clauses introduced by πρίν, see Book II, Chapter 27, Grammar 2.
   d. For clauses of result with ὥστε, see Book II, Chapter 29, Grammar 2.

40. The Conjugation of λύω, I loosen

ACTIVE VOICE

	PRESENT	IMPERFECT	FUTURE	AORIST	PERFECT	PLUPERFECT
Indicative	λύω, λύομεν	ἔλυον, ἐλύομεν	λύσω, λύσομεν	ἔλῡσα, ἐλύσαμεν	λέλυκα, λελύκαμεν	ἐλελύκη, ἐλελύκεμεν
	λύεις, λύετε	ἔλυες, ἐλύετε	λύσεις, λύσετε	ἔλῡσας, ἐλύσατε	λέλυκας, λελύκατε	ἐλελύκης, ἐλελύκετε
	λύει, λύουσι	ἔλυε, ἔλυον	λύσει, λύσουσι	ἔλῡσε, ἔλῡσαν	λέλυκε, λελύκᾱσι	ἐλελύκει, ἐλελύκεσαν
Subjunctive	λύω, λύωμεν			λύσω, λύσωμεν	λελυκὼς ὦ*, λελυκότες ὦμεν	
	λύῃς, λύητε			λύσῃς, λύσητε	λελυκὼς ᾖς, λελυκότες ἦτε	
	λύῃ, λύωσι			λύσῃ, λύσωσι	λελυκὼς ᾖ, λελυκότες ὦσι	
Optative	λύοιμι, λύοιμεν		λύσοιμι, λύσοιμεν	λύσαιμι, λύσαιμεν	λελυκὼς εἴην*, λελυκότες εἴημεν	
	λύοις, λύοιτε		λύσοις, λύσοιτε	λύσαις*, λύσαιτε	λελυκὼς εἴης, λελυκότες εἴητε	
	λύοι, λύοιεν		λύσοι, λύσοιεν	λύσαι*, λύσαιεν*	λελυκὼς εἴη, λελυκότες εἴησαν	
Imperative	λῦε, λύετε			λῦσον, λύσατε	λελυκὼς ἴσθι, λελυκότες ἔστε	
	λυέτω, λυόντων			λῡσάτω, λῡσάντων	λελυκὼς ἔστω, λελυκότες ὄντων	
Infinitive	λύειν		λύσειν	λῦσαι	λελυκέναι	
Participle	λύων, λύουσα, λῦον		λύσων, λύσουσα, λῦσον	λύσᾱς, λύσᾱσα, λῦσαν	λελυκώς, -υῖα, -ός	
Indicative	λύομαι, λῡόμεθα	ἐλῡόμην, ἐλῡόμεθα	λύσομαι, λῡσόμεθα	ἐλῡσάμην, ἐλῡσάμεθα	λέλυμαι, λελύμεθα	ἐλελύμην, ἐλελύμεθα
	λύῃ*, λύεσθε	ἐλύου, ἐλύεσθε	λύσῃ*, λύσεσθε	ἐλύσω, ἐλύσασθε	λέλυσαι, λέλυσθε	ἐλέλυσο, ἐλέλυσθε
	λύεται, λύονται	ἐλύετο, ἐλύοντο	λύσεται, λύσονται	ἐλύσατο, ἐλύσαντο	λέλυται, λέλυνται	ἐλέλυτο, ἐλέλυντο
Subjunctive	λύωμαι, λῡώμεθα			λύσωμαι, λῡσώμεθα	λελυμένος ὦ, λελυμένοι ὦμεν	
	λύῃ, λύησθε			λύσῃ, λύσησθε	λελυμένος ᾖς, λελυμένοι ἦτε	
	λύηται, λύωνται			λύσηται, λύσωνται	λελυμένος ᾖ, λελυμένοι ὦσι	

*or λύει   *or λύσει   *See page 117.   *See pages 162–163.

MIDDLE VOICE

Present (middle)

Optative
λῡοίμην λῡοίμεθα
λῡοιο λῡοισθε
λῡοιτο λῡοιντο

Imperative
λῡου λῡεσθε
λῡέσθω λῡέσθων

Infinitive
λῡεσθαι

Participle
λῡόμενος, -η, -ον

Future (middle)

Optative
λῡσοίμην λῡσοίμεθα
λῡσοιο λῡσοισθε
λῡσοιτο λῡσοιντο

Infinitive
λῡσεσθαι

Participle
λῡσόμενος, -η, -ον

Aorist (middle)

Optative
λῡσαίμην λῡσαίμεθα
λῡσαιο λῡσαισθε
λῡσαιτο λῡσαιντο

Imperative
λῦσαι λῦσασθε
λῡσάσθω λῡσάσθων

Infinitive
λῡσασθαι

Participle
λῡσάμενος, -η, -ον

Perfect (middle)

Optative
λελυμένος εἴην λελυμένοι εἶμεν
λελυμένος εἴης λελυμένοι εἶτε
λελυμένος εἴη λελυμένοι εἶησαν

Imperative
λέλυσο λέλυσθε
λελύσθω λελύσθων

Infinitive
λελύσθαι

Participle
λελυμένος, -η, -ον

PASSIVE VOICE

Present passive same as middle above

Imperfect passive same as middle above

Perfect passive same as middle above

Pluperfect passive same as middle above

Aorist passive

ἐλύθην ἐλύθημεν
ἐλύθης ἐλύθητε
ἐλύθη ἐλύθησαν

Subjunctive
λυθῶ λυθῶμεν
λυθῇς λυθῆτε
λυθῇ λυθῶσι

Optative
λυθείην λυθεῖμεν
λυθείης λυθεῖτε
λυθείη λυθεῖεν

Imperative
λύθητι λύθητε
λυθήτω λυθέντων

Infinitive
λυθῆναι

Participle
λυθείς, λυθεῖσα, λυθέν

Future passive

Indicative
λυθήσομαι λυθησόμεθα
λυθήσῃ λυθήσεσθε
λυθήσεται λυθήσονται

Optative
λυθησοίμην λυθησοίμεθα
λυθήσοιο λυθήσοισθε
λυθήσοιτο λυθήσοιντο

Infinitive
λυθήσεσθαι

Participle
λυθησόμενος, -η, -ον

41. Second Aorist, Second Perfect, and Second Pluperfect of λείπω

	SECOND AORIST	SECOND PERFECT	SECOND PLUPERFECT
ACTIVE VOICE	**Indicative** ἔλιπον ἐλίπομεν ἔλιπες ἐλίπετε ἔλιπε ἔλιπον	λέλοιπα λελοίπαμεν λέλοιπας λελοίπατε λέλοιπε λελοίπᾱσι	ἐλελοίπη ἐλελοίπεμεν ἐλελοίπης ἐλελοίπετε ἐλελοίπει(ν) ἐλελοίπεσαν
	Subjunctive λίπω λίπωμεν λίπῃς λίπητε λίπῃ λίπωσι	λελοιπὼς ὦ λελοιπότες ὦμεν λελοιπὼς ᾖς λελοιπότες ἦτε λελοιπὼς ᾖ λελοιπότες ὦσι	
	Optative λίποιμι λίποιμεν λίποις λίποιτε λίποι λίποιεν	λελοιπὼς εἴην λελοιπότες εἴημεν λελοιπὼς εἴης λελοιπότες εἴητε λελοιπὼς εἴη λελοιπότες εἴησαν	
	Imperative λίπε λίπετε λιπέτω λιπόντων		
	Infinitive λιπεῖν	λελοιπέναι	
	Participle λιπών, λιποῦσα, λιπόν	λελοιπώς, -υῖα, -ός	
MIDDLE AND PASSIVE VOICE	**Indicative** ἐλιπόμην ἐλιπόμεθα ἐλίπου ἐλίπεσθε ἐλίπετο ἐλίποντο	For the perfect and pluperfect middle and passive, see page 149.	
	Subjunctive λίπωμαι λιπώμεθα λίπῃ λίπησθε λίπηται λίπωνται		
	Optative λιποίμην λιποίμεθα λίποιο λίποισθε λίποιτο λίποιντο		
	Imperative λιποῦ λίπεσθε λιπέσθω λιπέσθων		
	Infinitive λιπέσθαι		
	Participle λιπόμενος, -η, -ον		

42. The Liquid-stem Verb φαίνω, I show

	PRESENT AND IMPERF.	FUTURE	FIRST AORIST	SECOND PERFECT AND PLUPERFECT
ACTIVE VOICE	φαίνω φανεῖς φανεῖ	φανῶ φανοῦμεν φανεῖς φανεῖτε φανεῖ φανοῦσι	ἔφηνα ἐφήναμεν ἔφηνας ἐφήνατε ἔφηνε ἔφηναν	πέφηνα πεφήναμεν πέφηνας πεφήνατε πέφηνε πεφήνασι
	ἔφαινον			*ἐπεφήνη*
	φαίνω		φήνω	πεφηνὼς ὦ
	φαίνοιμι	φανοίην φανοῖμεν φανοίης φανοῖτε φανοίη φανοῖεν	φήναιμι	πεφηνὼς εἴην
	φαῖνε		φῆνον	
	φαίνειν	φανεῖν	φῆναι	πεφηνέναι
	φαίνων	φανῶν, -οῦσα, -οῦν	φήνας	πεφηνώς
MIDDLE VOICE	φαίνομαι	φανοῦμαι	ἐφηνάμην	πέφασμαι πεφάσμεθα πεφασμένος πέφανθε εἶ πέφανται πεφασμένοι εἰσί
	ἐφαινόμην			*ἐπεφάσμην ἐπεφάσμεθα πεφασμένος ἐπέφανθε ἦσθα ἐπέφαντο πεφασμένοι ἦσαν*
	φαίνωμαι		φήνωμαι	πεφασμένος ὦ
	φαινοίμην	φανοίμην	φηναίμην	πεφασμένος εἴην
	φαίνου		φῆναι	πεφασμένος ἴσθι
	φαίνεσθαι	φανεῖσθαι	φήνασθαι	πεφάνθαι
	φαινόμενος	φανούμενος	φηνάμενος	πεφασμένος
PASSIVE VOICE	Passive same as middle above	SECOND FUTURE PASSIVE φανήσομαι	SECOND AORIST PASSIVE ἐφάνην	Passive same as middle above
			φανῶ, -ῇς, -ῇ	
		φανησοίμην	φανείην	
			φάνηθι	
		φανήσεσθαι	φανῆναι	
		φανησόμενος	φανείς	

43. Present and Imperfect of φιλέω, I love, τῑμάω, I honor, and δηλόω, I show

<table>
<tr><td rowspan="9">A C T I V E   V O I C E</td>
<td>φιλῶ φιλοῦμεν
φιλεῖς φιλεῖτε
φιλεῖ φιλοῦσι</td>
<td>τῑμῶ τῑμῶμεν
τῑμᾷς τῑμᾶτε
τῑμᾷ τῑμῶσι</td>
<td>δηλῶ δηλοῦμεν
δηλοῖς δηλοῦτε
δηλοῖ δηλοῦσι</td></tr>
<tr>
<td>ἐφίλουν ἐφιλοῦμεν
ἐφίλεις ἐφιλεῖτε
ἐφίλει ἐφίλουν</td>
<td>ἐτίμων ἐτῑμῶμεν
ἐτίμας ἐτῑμᾶτε
ἐτίμα ἐτίμων</td>
<td>ἐδήλουν ἐδηλοῦμεν
ἐδήλους ἐδηλοῦτε
ἐδήλου ἐδήλουν</td></tr>
<tr>
<td>φιλῶ φιλῶμεν
φιλῇς φιλῆτε
φιλῇ φιλῶσι</td>
<td>τῑμῶ τῑμῶμεν
τῑμᾷς τῑμᾶτε
τῑμᾷ τῑμῶσι</td>
<td>δηλῶ δηλῶμεν
δηλοῖς δηλῶτε
δηλοῖ δηλῶσι</td></tr>
<tr>
<td>φιλοίην φιλοῖμεν
φιλοίης φιλοῖτε
φιλοίη φιλοῖεν</td>
<td>τῑμῴην τῑμῷμεν
τῑμῴης τῑμῷτε
τῑμῴη τῑμῷεν</td>
<td>δηλοίην δηλοῖμεν
δηλοίης δηλοῖτε
δηλοίη δηλοῖεν</td></tr>
<tr>
<td>φίλει φιλεῖτε
φιλείτω φιλούντων</td>
<td>τίμᾱ τῑμᾶτε
τῑμάτω τῑμώντων</td>
<td>δήλου δηλοῦτε
δηλούτω δηλούντων</td></tr>
<tr>
<td>φιλεῖν</td>
<td>τῑμᾶν</td>
<td>δηλοῦν</td></tr>
<tr>
<td>φιλῶν, -οῦσα, -οῦν</td>
<td>τῑμῶν, τῑμῶσα, τῑμῶν</td>
<td>δηλῶν, -οῦσα, -οῦν</td></tr>
<tr><td rowspan="9">M I D D L E   V O I C E</td>
<td>φιλοῦμαι φιλούμεθα
φιλῇ (-εῖ) φιλεῖσθε
φιλεῖται φιλοῦνται</td>
<td>τῑμῶμαι τῑμώμεθα
τῑμᾷ τῑμᾶσθε
τῑμᾶται τῑμῶνται</td>
<td>δηλοῦμαι δηλούμεθα
δηλοῖ δηλοῦσθε
δηλοῦται δηλοῦνται</td></tr>
<tr>
<td>ἐφιλούμην ἐφιλούμεθα
ἐφιλοῦ ἐφιλεῖσθε
ἐφιλεῖτο ἐφιλοῦντο</td>
<td>ἐτῑμώμην ἐτῑμώμεθα
ἐτῑμῶ ἐτῑμᾶσθε
ἐτῑμᾶτο ἐτῑμῶντο</td>
<td>ἐδηλούμην ἐδηλούμεθα
ἐδηλοῦ ἐδηλοῦσθε
ἐδηλοῦτο ἐδηλοῦντο</td></tr>
<tr>
<td>φιλῶμαι φιλώμεθα
φιλῇ φιλῆσθε
φιλῆται φιλῶνται</td>
<td>τῑμῶμαι τῑμώμεθα
τῑμᾷ τῑμᾶσθε
τῑμᾶται τῑμῶνται</td>
<td>δηλῶμαι δηλώμεθα
δηλοῖ δηλῶσθε
δηλῶται δηλῶνται</td></tr>
<tr>
<td>φιλοίμην φιλοίμεθα
φιλοῖο φιλοῖσθε
φιλοῖτο φιλοῖντο</td>
<td>τῑμῴμην τῑμῴμεθα
τῑμῷο τῑμῷσθε
τῑμῷτο τῑμῷντο</td>
<td>δηλοίμην δηλοίμεθα
δηλοῖο δηλοῖσθε
δηλοῖτο δηλοῖντο</td></tr>
<tr>
<td>φιλοῦ φιλεῖσθε
φιλείσθω φιλείσθων</td>
<td>τῑμῶ τῑμᾶσθε
τῑμάσθω τῑμάσθων</td>
<td>δηλοῦ δηλοῦσθε
δηλούσθω δηλούσθων</td></tr>
<tr>
<td>φιλεῖσθαι</td>
<td>τῑμᾶσθαι</td>
<td>δηλοῦσθαι</td></tr>
<tr>
<td>φιλούμενος, -η, -ον</td>
<td>τῑμώμενος, -η, -ον</td>
<td>δηλούμενος, -η, -ον</td></tr>
<tr><td>P. V.</td>
<td colspan="3" align="center">Passive same as middle above</td></tr>
</table>

Note: in this and the following charts the imperfect and pluperfect indicative are given indented and in italics immediately under the present and perfect indicative respectively. The imperfect uses the same stem as the present, and the pluperfect uses the same stem as the perfect.

44. The Verb δίδωμι, δώσω, ἔδωκα, δέδωκα, δέδομαι, ἐδόθην, I give

	PRESENT AND IMPERFECT		FUTURE	SECOND AORIST		PERFECT AND PLUPERFECT
ACTIVE VOICE	δίδωμι δίδως δίδωσι	δίδομεν δίδοτε διδόασι	δώσω	ἔδωκα ἔδωκας ἔδωκε	ἔδομεν ἔδοτε ἔδοσαν	δέδωκα
	ἐδίδουν *ἐδίδους* *ἐδίδου*	*ἐδίδομεν* *ἐδίδοτε* *ἐδίδοσαν*				*ἐδεδώκη*
	διδῶ διδῷς διδῷ	διδῶμεν διδῶτε διδῶσι		δῶ δῷς δῷ	δῶμεν δῶτε δῶσι	δεδωκὼς ὦ
	διδοίην διδοίης διδοίη	διδοῖμεν διδοῖτε διδοῖεν	δώσοιμι	δοίην δοίης δοίη	δοῖμεν δοῖτε δοῖεν	δεδωκὼς εἴην
	δίδου διδότω	δίδοτε διδόντων		δός δότω	δότε δόντων	No imperative
	διδόναι		δώσειν	δοῦναι		δεδωκέναι
	διδούς, -οῦσα, -όν		δώσων	δούς, δοῦσα, δόν		δεδωκώς
MIDDLE VOICE	δίδομαι δίδοσαι δίδοται	διδόμεθα δίδοσθε δίδονται	δώσομαι	ἐδόμην ἔδου ἔδοτο	ἐδόμεθα ἔδοσθε ἔδοντο	δέδομαι
	ἐδιδόμην *ἐδίδοσο* *ἐδίδοτο*	*ἐδιδόμεθα* *ἐδίδοσθε* *ἐδίδοντο*				*ἐδεδόμην*
	διδῶμαι διδῷ διδῶται	διδώμεθα διδῶσθε διδῶνται		δῶμαι δῷ δῶται	δώμεθα δῶσθε δῶνται	δεδομένος ὦ
	διδοίμην διδοῖο διδοῖτο	διδοίμεθα διδοῖσθε διδοῖντο	δωσοίμην	δοίμην δοῖο δοῖτο	δοίμεθα δοῖσθε δοῖντο	δεδομένος εἴην
	δίδοσο διδόσθω	δίδοσθε διδόσθων		δοῦ δόσθω	δόσθε δόσθων	δέδοσο
	δίδοσθαι		δώσεσθαι	δόσθαι		δεδόσθαι
	διδόμενος, -η, -ον		δωσόμενος	δόμενος, -η, -ον		δεδομένος
P. V.	Passive same as middle above		δοθήσομαι	ἐδόθην		Passive same as middle above

256 Athenaze: Book II

45. The Verb τίθημι, θήσω, ἔθηκα, τέθηκα, τέθειμαι, ἐτέθην, I put

		PRESENT AND IMPERFECT		FUTURE	SECOND AORIST		PERFECT AND PLUPERFECT
ACTIVE VOICE		τίθημι	τίθεμεν	θήσω	ἔθηκα	ἔθεμεν	τέθηκα
		τίθης	τίθετε		ἔθηκας	ἔθετε	
		τίθησι	τιθέᾱσι		ἔθηκε	ἔθεσαν	
		ἐτίθην	*ἐτίθεμεν*				*ἐτεθήκη*
		ἐτίθεις	*ἐτίθετε*				
		ἐτίθει	*ἐτίθεσαν*				
		τιθῶ	τιθῶμεν		θῶ	θῶμεν	τεθηκὼς ὦ
		τιθῇς	τιθῆτε		θῇς	θῆτε	
		τιθῇ	τιθῶσι		θῇ	θῶσι	
		τιθείην	τιθεῖμεν	θήσοιμι	θείην	θεῖμεν	τεθηκὼς εἴην
		τιθείης	τιθεῖτε		θείης	θεῖτε	
		τιθείη	τιθεῖεν		θείη	θεῖεν	
		τίθει	τίθετε		θές	θέτε	No imperative
		τιθέτω	τιθέντων		θέτω	θέντων	
		τιθέναι		θήσειν	θεῖναι		τεθηκέναι
		τιθείς, -εῖσα, -έν		θήσων	θείς, θεῖσα, θέν		τεθηκώς, -κυῖα, -κός
MIDDLE VOICE		τίθεμαι	τιθέμεθα	θήσομαι	ἐθέμην	ἐθέμεθα	τέθειμαι
		τίθεσαι	τίθεσθε		ἔθου	ἔθεσθε	
		τίθεται	τίθενται		ἔθετο	ἔθεντο	
		ἐτιθέμην	*ἐτιθέμεθα*				*ἐτεθείμην*
		ἐτίθεσο	*ἐτίθεσθε*				
		ἐτίθετο	*ἐτίθεντο*				
		τιθῶμαι	τιθώμεθα		θῶμαι	θώμεθα	τεθειμένος ὦ
		τιθῇ	τιθῆσθε		θῇ	θῆσθε	
		τιθῆται	τιθῶνται		θῆται	θῶνται	
		τιθείμην	τιθείμεθα	θησοίμην	θείμην	θείμεθα	τεθειμένος εἴην
		τιθεῖο	τιθεῖσθε		θεῖο	θεῖσθε	
		τιθεῖτο	τιθεῖντο		θεῖτο	θεῖντο	
		τίθεσο	τίθεσθε		θοῦ	θέσθε	τέθεισο
		τιθέσθω	τιθέσθων		θέσθω	θέσθων	
		τίθεσθαι		θήσεσθαι	θέσθαι		τεθεῖσθαι
		τιθέμενος, -η, -ον		θησόμενος	θέμενος		τεθειμένος, -η, -ον
P. V.		Passive same as middle above		τεθήσομαι	ἐτέθην		Passive same as middle above

46. The Verb ἵστημι, στήσω, ἔστησα, ἔστην, ἔστηκα, ἐστάθην, I set up, etc.

	PRESENT AND IMPERFECT		FUTURE	SECOND AORIST		FIRST AND SECOND PERFECT AND PLUPERFECT	
ACTIVE VOICE	ἵστημι	ἵσταμεν	στήσω	ἔστην	ἔστημεν	ἔστηκα	ἔσταμεν
	ἵστης	ἵστατε		ἔστης	ἔστητε	ἔστηκας	ἔστατε
	ἵστησι	ἱστᾶσι		ἔστη	ἔστησαν	ἔστηκε	ἑστᾶσι
	ἵστην	ἵσταμεν				εἱστήκη	ἔσταμεν
	ἵστης	ἵστατε				εἱστήκης	ἔστατε
	ἵστη	ἵστασαν				εἱστήκει	ἔστασαν
	ἱστῶ	ἱστῶμεν		στῶ	στῶμεν	ἑστῶ	ἑστῶμεν
	ἱστῇς	ἱστῆτε		στῇς	στῆτε	ἑστῇς	ἑστῆτε
	ἱστῇ	ἱστῶσι		στῇ	στῶσι	ἑστῇ	ἑστῶσι
	ἱσταίην	ἱσταῖμεν	στήσοιμι	σταίην	σταῖμεν	ἑσταίην	ἑσταῖμεν
	ἱσταίης	ἱσταῖτε		σταίης	σταῖτε	ἑσταίης	ἑσταῖτε
	ἱσταίη	ἱσταῖεν		σταίη	σταῖεν	ἑσταίη	ἑσταῖεν
	ἵστη	ἵστατε		στῆθι	στῆτε	ἔσταθι	ἔστατε
	ἱστάτω	ἱστάντων		στήτω	στάντων	ἑστάτω	ἑστάντων
	ἱστάναι		στήσειν	στῆναι		ἑστηκέναι/ἑστάναι	
	ἱστάς, -ᾶσα, -άν		στήσων	στάς, στᾶσα, στάν		ἑστηκώς, ἑστηκυῖα, ἑστηκός	
MIDDLE VOICE	ἵσταμαι	ἱστάμεθα	στήσομαι			or ἑστώς, ἑστῶσα, ἑστός	
	ἵστασαι	ἵστασθε					
	ἵσταται	ἵστανται					
	ἱστάμην	ἱστάμεθα					
	ἵστασο	ἵστασθε					
	ἵστατο	ἵσταντο					
	ἱστῶμαι	ἱστώμεθα					
	ἱστῇ	ἱστῆσθε					
	ἱστῆται	ἱστῶνται					
	ἱσταίμην	ἱσταίμεθα	στησοίμην				
	ἱσταῖο	ἱσταῖσθε					
	ἱσταῖτο	ἱσταῖντο					
	ἵστασο	ἵστασθε					
	ἱστάσθω	ἱστάσθων					
	ἵστασθαι		στήσεσθαι				
	ἱστάμενος		στησόμενος				
P.	Passive same as middle above		σταθήσομαι	ἐστάθην			

There is no second aorist middle; forms of the perfect and pluperfect middle are rare and not included in the chart.

47. The Verb εἰμί, ἔσομαι, I am

PRESENT AND IMPERFECT		FUTURE	
εἰμί	ἐσμέν	ἔσομαι	ἐσόμεθα
εἶ	ἐστέ	ἔσῃ/ἔσει	ἔσεσθε
ἐστί	εἰσί	ἔσται	ἔσονται
ἦν	ἦμεν		
ἦσθα	ἦτε		
ἦν	ἦσαν		
ὦ	ὦμεν		
ᾖς	ἦτε		
ᾖ	ὦσι		
εἴην	εἶμεν*	ἐσοίμην	ἐσοίμεθα
εἴης	εἶτε*	ἔσοιο	ἔσοισθε
εἴη	εἶεν*	ἔσοιτο	ἔσοιντο
ἴσθι	ἔστε		
ἔστω	ἔστων		
εἶναι		ἔσεσθαι	
ὤν, οὖσα, ὄν		ἐσόμενος, -η, -ον	

*See page 118.

---

48. The Verb εἶμι, I will go		**49. The Verb φημί, I say**	
		PRESENT AND IMPERFECT	
εἶμι	ἴμεν	φημί	φαμέν
εἶ	ἴτε	φῄς	φατέ
εἶσι	ἴασι	φησί	φασί
ᾖα/ᾔειν	ᾖμεν	ἔφην	ἔφαμεν
ᾔεις	ᾖτε	ἔφησθα/ἔφης	ἔφατε
ᾔει	ᾖσαν/ᾔεσαν	ἔφη	ἔφασαν
ἴω	ἴωμεν	φῶ	φῶμεν
ἴῃς	ἴητε	φῇς	φῆτε
ἴῃ	ἴωσι	φῇ	φῶσι
ἴοιμι/ἰοίην	ἴοιμεν	φαίην	φαῖμεν
ἴοις	ἴοιτε	φαίης	φαῖτε
ἴοι	ἴοιεν	φαίη	φαῖεν
ἴθι	ἴτε	φαθί/φάθι	φάτε
ἴτω	ἰόντων	φάτω	φάντων
ἰέναι		φάναι	
ἰών, ἰοῦσα, ἰόν		φάς, φᾶσα, φάν	

---

50. The Verb δείκνῡμι, δείξω, ἔδειξα, δέδειχα, δέδειγμαι, ἐδείχθην, I show

	PRESENT AND IMPERFECT	
	δείκνῡμι	δείκνυμεν
	δείκνῡς	δείκνυτε
	δείκνῡσι	δεικνύᾱσι
A C T I V E V O I C E	ἐδείκνῡν	ἐδείκνυμεν
	ἐδείκνῡς	ἐδείκνυτε
	ἐδείκνῡ	ἐδείκνυσαν
	δεικνύω	δεικνύωμεν
	δεικνύῃς	δεικνύητε
	δεικνύῃ	δεικνύωσι
	δεικνύοιμι	δεικνύοιμεν
	δεικνύοις	δεικνύοιτε
	δεικνύοι	δεικνύοιεν
	δείκνῡ	δείκνυτε
	δεικνύτω	δεικνύντων
	δεικνύναι	
	δεικνύς, δεικνῦσα, δεικνύν	
M I D D L E V O I C E	δείκνυμαι	δεικνύμεθα
	δείκνυσαι	δείκνυσθε
	δείκνυται	δείκνυνται
	ἐδεικνύμην	ἐδεικνύμεθα
	ἐδείκνυσο	ἐδείκνυσθε
	ἐδείκνυτο	ἐδείκνυντο
	δεικνύωμαι	δεικνυώμεθα
	δεικνύῃ	δεικνύησθε
	δεικνύηται	δεικνύωνται
	δεικνυοίμην	δεικνυοίμεθα
	δεικνύοιο	δεικνύοισθε
	δεικνύοιτο	δεικνύοιντο
	δείκνυσο	δείκνυσθε
	δεικνύσθω	δεικνύσθων
	δείκνυσθαι	
	δεικνύμενος, -η, -ον	
P.	Passive same as middle above	

51. The Verb ἵημι, ἥσω, ἧκα, εἷκα, εἷμαι, εἵθην, I send
52. The Verb δύναμαι, δυνήσομαι, δεδύνημαι, ἐδυνήθην, I am able
53. The Verb κεῖμαι, κείσομαι, I lie

	PRESENT AND IMPERFECT		SECOND AORIST			PRESENT AND IMPERFECT	
ACTIVE VOICE	ἵημι	ἵεμεν	ἧκα	εἷμεν		δύναμαι	δυνάμεθα
	ἵης	ἵετε	ἧκας	εἷτε		δύνασαι	δύνασθε
	ἵησι	ἵᾶσι	ἧκε	εἷσαν		δύναται	δύνανται
	ἵην	ἵεμεν				ἐδυνάμην	ἐδυνάμεθα
	ἵεις	ἵετε				ἐδύνασο*	ἐδύνασθε
	ἵει	ἵεσαν				ἐδύνατο	ἐδύναντο
	ἱῶ	ἱῶμεν	ὧ	ὧμεν		δύνωμαι	δυνώμεθα
	ἱῆς	ἱῆτε	ἧς	ἧτε		δύνῃ	δύνησθε
	ἱῇ	ἱῶσι	ἧ	ὧσι		δύνηται	δύνωνται
	ἱείην	ἱεῖμεν	εἵην	εἷμεν/εἵημεν		δυναίμην	δυναίμεθα
	ἱείης	ἱεῖτε	εἵης	εἷτε/εἵητε		δύναιο	δύναισθε
	ἱείη	ἱεῖεν	εἵη	εἷεν/εἵησαν		δύναιτο	δύναιντο
	ἵει	ἵετε	ἕς	ἕτε		δύνασο	δύνασθε
	ἱέτω	ἱέντων	ἕτω	ἕντων		δυνάσθω	δυνάσθων
	ἱέναι		εἷναι			δύνασθαι	
	ἱείς, ἱεῖσα, ἱέν		εἵς, εἷσα, ἕν			δυνάμενος, -η, -ον	
MIDDLE VOICE	ἵεμαι	ἱέμεθα	εἵμην	εἵμεθα		κεῖμαι	κείμεθα
	ἵεσαι	ἵεσθε	εἷσο	εἷσθε		κεῖσαι	κεῖσθε
	ἵεται	ἵενται	εἷτο	εἵντο		κεῖται	κεῖνται
	ἱέμην	ἱέμεθα				ἐκείμην	ἐκείμεθα
	ἵεσο	ἵεσθε				ἔκεισο	ἔκεισθε
	ἵετο	ἵεντο				ἔκειτο	ἔκειντο
	ἱῶμαι	ἱώμεθα	ὧμαι	ὥμεθα		κέωμαι	κεώμεθα
	ἱῇ	ἱῆσθε	ἧ	ἧσθε		κέῃ	κέησθε
	ἱῆται	ἱῶνται	ἧται	ὧνται		κέηται	κέωνται
	ἱείμην	ἱείμεθα	εἵμην	εἵμεθα		κεοίμην	κεοίμεθα
	ἱεῖσο	ἱεῖσθε	εἷο	εἷσθε		κέοιο	κέοισθε
	ἱεῖτο	ἱεῖντο	εἷτο	εἵντο		κέοιτο	κέοιντο
	ἵεσο	ἵεσθε	οὗ	ἔσθε		κεῖσο	κεῖσθε
	ἱέσθω	ἱέσθων	ἔσθω	ἔσθων		κείσθω	κείσθων
	ἵεσθαι		ἔσθαι			κεῖσθαι	
	ἱέμενος, -η, -ον		ἕμενος, -η, -ον			κείμενος, -η, -ον	
P.	Passive same as middle above					*or ἐδύνω	

54. The Verb βαίνω, βήσομαι, ἔβην, βέβηκα, I step, walk, go
55. The Second Aorist of γιγνώσκω, γνώσομαι, ἔγνων, ἔγνωκα, ἔγνωσμαι, ἐγνώσθην, I get to know, learn

PRESENT AND IMPERFECT	FUTURE	SECOND AORIST		PERFECT ACTIVE
βαίνω	βήσομαι	ἔβην	ἔβημεν	βέβηκα
		ἔβης	ἔβητε	
		ἔβη	ἔβησαν	
ἔβαινον				*ἐβεβήκη*
βαίνω		βῶ	βῶμεν	βεβήκω
		βῇς	βῆτε	
		βῇ	βῶσι	
βαίνοιμι	βησοίμην	βαίην	βαῖμεν	βεβήκοιμι
		βαίης	βαῖτε	
		βαίη	βαῖεν	
βαῖνε		βῆθι	βῆτε	βεβηκὼς ἴσθι
		βήτω	βάντων	
βαίνειν	βήσεσθαι	βῆναι		βεβηκέναι
βαίνων	βησόμενος	βάς, βᾶσα, βάν		βεβηκώς

ἔγνων	ἔγνωμεν
ἔγνως	ἔγνωτε
ἔγνω	ἔγνωσαν
γνῶ	γνῶμεν
γνῷς	γνῶτε
γνῷ	γνῶσι
γνοίην	γνοῖμεν
γνοίης	γνοῖτε
γνοίη	γνοῖεν
γνῶθι	γνῶτε
γνώτω	γνόντων
γνῶναι	
γνούς, γνοῦσα, γνόν	

56. The Verb οἶδα, εἴσομαι, I know	
PERFECT = PRESENT PLUPERFECT = IMPERFECT	
οἶδα	ἴσμεν
οἶσθα	ἴστε
οἶδε	ἴσασι
ᾔδη/ᾔδειν ᾔδησθα/ᾔδεις ᾔδει(ν)	ᾖσμεν/ᾔδεμεν ᾖστε/ᾔδετε ᾖσαν/ᾔδεσαν
εἰδῶ	εἰδῶμεν
εἰδῇς	εἰδῆτε
εἰδῇ	εἰδῶσι
εἰδείην	εἰδεῖμεν/εἰδείημεν
εἰδείης	εἰδεῖτε/εἰδείητε
εἰδείη	εἰδεῖεν/εἰδείησαν
ἴσθι	ἴστε
ἴστω	ἴστων
εἰδέναι	
εἰδώς, εἰδυῖα, εἰδός	

The future, εἴσομαι, is regular (like λύσομαι).

57. IMPERSONAL VERBS

Impersonal verbs are used in the third person singular with an implied impersonal "it" as subject, see Book I, page 118.

Impersonal verb plus accusative and infinitive:

δεῖ ἡμᾶς πρὸ τῆς νυκτὸς ἐκεῖσε παρεῖναι.
It is necessary for us to be there before night.
We must be there before night.

Impersonal verb plus dative and infinitive:

ἆρ' ἔξεστιν ἡμῖν αὔριον ἐπανιέναι;
Is it possible for us to return tomorrow?
May we return tomorrow?   Can we return tomorrow?

58. EUPHONY

Certain changes in spelling take place when consonants are combined, e.g., labial + σ becomes ψ (πέμπ-σω > πέμψω) and guttural + σ becomes ξ (ἄγ-σω > ἄξω, διώκ-σω > διώξω, and δέχ-σομαι > δέξομαι). Other changes are seen taking place in the forms of the perfect passive (see Book II, Chapter 27, Grammar 1).

The following rules should be noted:

a.   Where a labial (β, π) or guttural (κ, γ) is followed by an aspirated consonant (θ, φ, χ), it is itself aspirated, e.g., ἐπέμπ-θην > ἐπέμφθην and ἐπράγ-θην > ἐπράχθην.

b.   ν before consonants:
    ν before β, π, φ, and ψ becomes μ, e.g., ἐν- + πίπτω > ἐμπίπτω (ἐνέπεσον, ἐμπεσών).

ν before γ, κ, ξ, and χ becomes γ, e.g., ἐν- + καλέω > ἐγκαλέω
(ἐνεκάλεσα, ἐγκαλέσᾱς) and συν- + γράφω > συγγράφω (συνέγραψα,
συγγράψᾱς).

ν before μ becomes μ, e.g., ἐν- + μένω > ἐμμένω (ἐνέμεινα, ἐμμείνᾱς).

ν before λ or ρ is fully assimilated, e.g., συν- + λέγω > συλλέγω
(συνέλεξα, συλλέξᾱς).

c.   Verbs beginning with ρ double the ρ when they are augmented, e.g.,
ῥήγνῡμι > ἔρρηξα (ῥήξᾱς).

d.   All prepositional prefixes ending in a vowel elide when followed by another
vowel, except for πρό and περί, e.g., ἀνα- + ἔρχομαι > ἀνέρχομαι; ἀπο- +
ἔρχομαι > ἀπέρχομαι; ἐπι- + ἔρχομαι > ἐπέρχομαι; but προέρχομαι and
περιέρχομαι.

e.   Prepositional prefixes compounded with a verb beginning with an aspirated
vowel aspirate their final consonant if it is π or τ, e.g., ἀπο- + ὁρμάω >
ἀφορμάω; ἐπι- + ἵστημι > ἐφίστημι; κατα- + ὁράω > καθοράω; μετα- +
ἵημι > μεθίημι; ἀντι- + ἵστημι > ἀνθίστημι; and ὑπο- + αἱρέω > ὑφαιρέω.

f.   When verbs compounded with πρό are augmented, contraction is optional,
e.g., προχωρέω, προεχώρουν, προὐχώρουν.

59. VOWEL GRADATION

Many Greek verbs show three grades of stem vowel (see principal parts,
Chapter 26β, page 136), similar to the pattern *sing, sang, sung* in English. One such
gradation of vowels in Greek consists of the following:

Strong grade 1: ε
Strong grade 2: ο
Weak grade: either no vowel or α

The three grades of stem vowel for φθείρω are: φθερ-, φθορ-, and φθαρ-.
The three grades of stem vowel for ἐγείρω are: ἐγερ-, ἐγορ-, and ἐγρ-.

Some linguists refer to the three grades of stem vowel as *e-grade*, *o-grade* and
zero-grade. The term zero grade covers both possibilities for weak grade given
above, namely no vowel or α (i.e., neither ε nor ο).

60. THE USES OF ὡς

See summary in Book II, Chapter 28, Grammar 5.

GREEK TO ENGLISH VOCABULARY

Note: the numbers in parentheses indicate the chapters in which words appear in the vocabulary lists, lists of principal parts, and grammar sections. Chapter numbers are given for the first occurrence of proper names. Nouns are listed with the nominative case first, then the genitive, and then the definite article.

The principal parts of all verbs are given with the exception of (1) contract verbs that follow the regular patterns of φιλέω, τῑμάω, and δηλόω (the principal parts of these three verbs are given as models) and (2) most compound verbs, for which the principal parts are the same as for the uncompounded forms that are given in full.

For numbers above ten, see Reference Grammar, paragraph 27.

A

ἀγαθός, ἀγαθή, ἀγαθόν good (5, 14, 24)

'Αγαμέμνων, 'Αγαμέμνονος, ὁ Agamemnon (7)

ἀγγέλλω, ἀγγελῶ, ἤγγειλα, ἤγγελκα, ἤγγελμαι, ἠγγέλθην I announce (14, 22)

ἄγγελος, ἀγγέλου, ὁ messenger (4)

ἄγε, (*plural*) ἄγετε come on! (9)

ἀγείρω, ἤγειρα I gather (27)

ἀγνοέω I do not know (19)

ἄγομαι γυναῖκα (+ *dat.*) I bring home a wife for

ἀγορά, ἀγορᾶς, ἡ agora, city center, marketplace (8)

ἀγορεύω, ἀγορεύσω, ἠγόρευσα, ἠγόρευκα, ἠγόρευμαι, ἠγορεύθην (*only present and imperfect found in uncompounded forms in Attic*) I speak in the Assembly; (*more generally*) I speak, say (21)

ἄγρᾱ, ἄγρᾱς, ἡ hunt, hunting (26)

ἄγριος, ἀγρίᾱ, ἄγριον savage, wild, fierce (5)

ἀγρός, ἀγροῦ, ὁ field (1)
ἀγροί, ἀγρῶν, οἱ the country
ἐν τοῖς ἀγροῖς in the country

ἄγω, ἄξω, ἤγαγον, ἦχα, ἦγμαι, ἤχθην I lead, take (2, 13, 20)

ἀγών, ἀγῶνος, ὁ struggle, contest (15)

ἀγωνίζομαι, ἀγωνιοῦμαι, ἠγωνισάμην, ἠγώνισμαι I contend (27)

ἀδελφός, ἀδελφοῦ, ὁ brother (11)

ἀδικέω I do wrong; (*transitive*) I wrong, injure (31)

ἄδικος, ἄδικον unjust (24)

"Αδρηστος, 'Αδρήστου, ὁ Adrastus (26)

ἀδύνατος, ἀδύνατον impossible, incapable (21)

ᾄδω, ᾄσομαι, ᾖσα, ᾖσμαι, ᾔσθην I sing (31)

ἀεί = αἰεί

ἀθάνατος, ἀθάνατον immortal (31)

'Αθήναζε to Athens (12)

'Αθῆναι, 'Αθηνῶν, αἱ Athens (6)

'Αθηναῖος, 'Αθηναίᾱ, 'Αθηναῖον Athenian (1)
οἱ 'Αθηναῖοι the Athenians

'Αθήνη, 'Αθήνης, ἡ Athena, daughter of Zeus (9)

ἀθῡμίᾱ, ἀθῡμίᾱς ἡ lack of spirit, despair (26)

Αἰγαῖος πόντος, Αἰγαίου πόντου, ὁ Aegean Sea (16)

Αἰγεύς, Αἰγέως, ὁ Aegeus, king of Athens (6)

Αἰγύπτιοι, Αἰγυπτίων, οἱ Egyptians (16)

Αἴγυπτος, Αἰγύπτου, ἡ Egypt (16)

αἰεί always (4)

αἷμα, αἵματος, τό blood (20)

αἱρέω, αἱρήσω, εἷλον, ᾕρηκα, ᾕρημαι, ᾑρέθην I take; (*middle*) I choose (7, 11, 27, 28)

αἴρω, ἀρῶ, ἦρα, ἦρκα, ἦρμαι, ἤρθην I lift, raise up; (*with reflexive pronoun*) I get up; (*intransitive*) I get under way, set out (1, 23)

αἰσθάνομαι, αἰσθήσομαι, ᾐσθόμην, ᾔσθημαι (+ *gen. or acc.*) I perceive, learn, apprehend (31)

αἴσχιστος, αἰσχίστη, αἴσχιστον most shameful (24)

αἰσχίων, αἴσχιον more shameful (24)

αἰσχρός, αἰσχρά, αἰσχρόν shameful (24)

Αἰσχύλος, Αἰσχύλου, ὁ Aeschylus
(15)
αἰτέω I ask, ask for (11)
αἰτίᾱ, αἰτίᾱς, ἡ blame, responsibility,
cause (23)
αἴτιος, αἰτίᾱ, αἴτιον responsible, to
blame, responsible for (+ gen.) (3)
Αἰτναῖον ὄρος, Αἰτναίου ὄρους, τό
Mount Etna (16)
αἰχμή, αἰχμῆς, ἡ spear point
Ἀκαρνᾱνίᾱ, Ἀκαρνᾱνίᾱς, ἡ
Acarnania (29)
ἀκέομαι, ἀκοῦμαι, ἠκεσάμην I heal
(17)
ἀκολουθέω (+ dat.) I follow (31)
ἀκοντίζω, ἀκοντιῶ, ἠκόντισα (+ gen.)
I throw a javelin at
ἀκούω, ἀκούσομαι, ἤκουσα,
ἀκήκοα, ἠκούσθην (+ gen. of person,
acc. of thing) I listen, listen to, hear (4,
29)
ἀκρόπολις, ἀκροπόλεως, ἡ citadel
(28)
Ἀκρόπολις, Ἀκροπόλεως, ἡ
Acropolis, the citadel of Athens (8)
ἄκρος, ἄκρᾱ, ἄκρον top (of) (5)
ἄκρον τὸ ὄρος the top of the
mountain/hill (5)
ἄκων, ἄκουσα, ἄκον unwilling(ly),
involuntary(-ily) (26)
ἀλαζών, ἀλαζόνος, ὁ or ἡ imposter,
charlatan, quack (31)
ἀλήθεια, ἀληθείᾱς, ἡ truth (26)
ἀληθής, ἀληθές true (13)
ἀληθές, ἀληθοῦς, τό the truth
ἀληθῆ, ἀληθῶν, τά the truth (13)
ἀλίσκομαι, ἀλώσομαι, ἑάλων or
ἥλων, ἑάλωκα or ἥλωκα I am
caught, taken (28)
ἀλλά but (1)
οὐ μόνον . . . ἀλλὰ καί not
only . . . but also (15)
ἀλλήλων of one another (13)
ἄλλος, ἄλλη, ἄλλο other, another, rest
(of) (4)
ἄλλοι ἄλλοσε some to some places,
others to other places (27)
ἄλλοσε to another place, to other
places (27)
Ἀλυάττης, Ἀλυάττεω, ὁ Alyattes
(25)
Ἅλυς, Ἅλεως, ὁ Halys River (27)
ἁλῶναι (aorist infinitive of ἁλίσκομαι)
ἅμα together, at the same time (with + dat.)
(13)
ἅμα ἔῳ at dawn (30)
ἀμαθής, ἀμαθές stupid
ἅμαξα, ἁμάξης, ἡ wagon (22)
ἁμαρτάνω, ἁμαρτήσομαι, ἥμαρτον,
ἡμάρτηκα, ἡμάρτημαι,
ἡμαρτήθην I miss (+ gen.); I make a

mistake, am mistaken (18)
ἁμαρτίᾱ, ἁμαρτίᾱς, ἡ mistake
Ἄμασις, Ἀμάσεως, ὁ Amasis (27)
ἀμείνων, ἄμεινον better (14, 24)
ἀμέλγω, ἀμέλξω, ἤμελξα I milk
ἄμπελος, ἀμπέλου, ἡ grapevine (31)
ἀμύνω, ἀμυνῶ, ἤμῡνα (active) I ward
off X (acc.) from Y (dat.); (middle) I
ward off, defend myself (against + acc.)
(13)
ἀμφότερος, ἀμφοτέρᾱ, ἀμφότερον
both (25)
ἄν (potential particle) (30)
ἄν (used with subjunctive) (22)
ἀνά (+ acc.) up (5)
ἀναβαίνω I go up, get up; I climb, go up
onto (+ ἐπί "onto" + acc.) (9)
ἀναβλέπω I look up
ἀναγιγνώσκω I read (21)
ἀναγκάζω, ἀναγκάσω, ἠνάγκασα,
ἠνάγκακα, ἠνάγκασμαι,
ἠναγκάσθην I compel (15)
ἀνάγκη, ἀνάγκης, ἡ necessity (21)
ἀνάγκη ἐστί(ν) it is necessary (21)
ἀνάγομαι I put out to sea (30)
ἀνάθημα, ἀναθήματος, τό temple
offering (27)
ἀναιρέομαι I take up, pick up (28)
ἀνακράζω, ἀνέκραγον, ἀνακέκρᾱγα
I shout (31)
ἀναμιμνήσκω, ἀναμνήσω, ἀνέμνησα
I remind someone (acc.) of something
(acc. or gen.) (28, 30)
μέμνημαι (perfect middle = present) I
have reminded myself, I remember
(28, 30)
ἐμνήσθην (aorist passive in middle
sense) I remembered (28, 30)
μνησθήσομαι (future passive in
middle sense) I will remember (28,
30)
ἀναπαύομαι, ἀναπαύσομαι,
ἀνεπαυσάμην, ἀναπέπαυμαι I rest
(19)
ἀνάστασις, ἀναστάσεως, ἡ removal
(22)
ἀναστενάζω I groan (28)
ἀνάστηθι stand up!
ἀναστρέφω I turn around (27)
ἀνατίθημι I set up, dedicate (18)
ἀναχωρέω I retreat, withdraw (14)
ἀνδρεῖος, ἀνδρείᾱ, ἀνδρεῖον brave
(3)
ἀνδρείως bravely
ἄνεμος, ἀνέμου, ὁ wind (13)
ἀνέστην I stood up (15)
ἀνέρχομαι I go up
ἀνέχομαι, (imperfect) ἀνειχόμην or
ἠνειχόμην, ἀνέξομαι, ἀνεσχόμην
or ἠνεσχόμην or ἠνσχόμην I endure,
am patient (27)

ἀνήρ, ἀνδρός, ὁ man, husband (4)
ἀνθίσταμαι, ἀντιστήσομαι,
  ἀντέστην, ἀνθέστηκα (+ dat.) I
  stand up against, withstand (22)
ἄνθρωπος, ἀνθρώπου, ὁ man, human
  being, person (1)
ἀνίστημι I stand or set (something) up;
  (second aorist, intransitive) I stood up;
  (second aorist participle, intransitive)
  having stood up (15)
    ἀνίσταμαι, ἀναστήσομαι,
    ἀνέστην, ἀνέστηκα I stand up,
    am forced to move, remove (22)
ἀνόητος, ἀνόητον foolish (28)
ἀνοίγνῡμι, (imperfect) ἀνέῳγον,
  ἀνοίξω, ἀνέῳξα, ἀνέῳχα,
  ἀνέῳγμαι (I stand open),
  ἀνεῴχθην I open (22)
ἀντέχω, ἀνθέξω, ἀντέσχον I resist (+
  dat.); I hold out against (+ πρός + acc.)
  (14)
ἀντί (+ gen.) instead of, against (28)
ἀντιόομαι, ἀντιώσομαι, ἠντιώθην (+
  dat.) I oppose (27)
ἄνω up, above (20)
ἄξιος, ἀξίᾱ, ἄξιον (+ gen.) worthy of
  (16)
ἀπάγω I lead away
ἀπάρχομαι I begin (31)
ἅπᾱς, ἅπᾱσα, ἅπαν all, every, whole
  (14)
ἄπειμι I am away; (+ gen.) I am away from
  (5)
ἀπελαύνω (transitive) I drive away;
  (intransitive) I march away
ἀπέρχομαι I go away (6, 17)
ἀπέχω, (imperfect) ἀπεῖχον, ἀφέξω,
  ἀπέσχον, ἀπέσχηκα, ἀπέσχημαι I
  am distant (from + gen.); (middle) I
  abstain from (+ gen.) (17)
ἀπό (+ gen.) from (4)
ἀποβαίνω I go away (6)
ἀποβλέπω I look away
ἀποδημέω I am abroad, go abroad (25)
ἀποδίδωμι I give back, return, pay (18)
  χάριν ἀποδίδωμι (+ dat.) I render
  thanks, thank (18)
ἀποθνῄσκω, ἀποθανοῦμαι,
  ἀπέθανον, τέθνηκα I die; (perfect) I
  am dead (11, 24)
ἀποκρῑνομαι, ἀποκρινοῦμαι,
  ἀπεκρῑνάμην, ἀποκέκριμαι
  I answer (7, 22)
ἀποκτείνω, ἀποκτενῶ, ἀπέκτεινα,
  ἀπέκτονα I kill (6, 22)
ἀπολαμβάνω I cut off, intercept (30)
ἀπόλλῡμι, ἀπολῶ, ἀπώλεσα,
  ἀπολώλεκα (I have ruined), ἀπόλωλα
  (I am ruined) I destroy, ruin, lose;
  (middle) I perish (26)
Ἀπόλλων, Ἀπόλλωνος, ὁ Apollo (31)

ἀποπέμπω I send away
ἀποπλέω I sail away
ἀπορέω I am at a loss (12)
ἀπορίᾱ, ἀπορίᾱς, ἡ perplexity,
  difficulty, the state of being at a loss (15)
ἀποστέλλω I send off (29)
ἀποφαίνω I show, reveal, prove (26)
ἀποφεύγω I flee (away) (6)
ἀποχωρέω I go away
ἆρα (introduces a question) (4)
Ἀργεῖος, Ἀργείᾱ, Ἀργεῖον Argive
  (25)
Ἄργη, Ἄργης, ἡ Arge (name of a
  dog) (19)
Ἄργος, Ἄργου, ὁ Argus (name of a
  dog) (5)
ἀργύριον, ἀργυρίου, τό silver, money
  (11)
ἀρέσκει, ἀρέσει, ἤρεσε (+ dat.) it is
  pleasing (20)
ἀρετή, ἀρετῆς, ἡ excellence, virtue,
  courage (15)
Ἀριάδνη, Ἀριάδνης, ἡ Ariadne,
  daughter of King Minos (6)
ἀριθμός, ἀριθμοῦ, ὁ number (27)
ἀριστερά, ἀριστερᾶς, ἡ left hand (9)
ἄριστος, ἀρίστη, ἄριστον best, very
  good, noble (9, 14, 24)
ἁρμονίᾱ, ἁρμονίᾱς, ἡ harmony (24)
ἀροτρεύω, ἀροτρεύσω, ἠρότρευσα,
  ἠρότρευκα, ἠρότρευμαι,
  ἠροτρεύθην I plow (3)
ἄροτρον, ἀρότρου, τό plow (2)
Ἀρτεμίσιον, Ἀρτεμισίου, τό
  Artemisium (14)
ἀρχή, ἀρχῆς, ἡ beginning, rule,
  empire (13, 21)
Ἀρχίδᾱμος, Ἀρχιδάμου, ὁ
  Archidamus (22)
Ἀρχιμήδης, Ἀρχιμήδου, ὁ
  Archimedes (28)
ἄρχω, ἄρξω, ἦρξα, ἦργμαι, ἤρχθην
  (+ gen.) (active or middle) I begin; (active)
  I rule (21)
Ἀσίᾱ, Ἀσίᾱς, ἡ Asia (Minor) (15)
Ἀσκληπιεῖον, Ἀσκληπιείου, τό the
  sanctuary of Asclepius (17)
Ἀσκλήπιος, Ἀσκληπίου, ὁ
  Asclepius, the Greek god of healing (11)
ἄσμενος, ἀσμένη, ἄσμενον glad(ly)
  (24)
ἀσπίς, ἀσπίδος, ἡ shield (31)
ἄστυ, ἄστεως, τό city (8)
ἀσφαλής, ἀσφαλές safe (20)
ἄτακτος, ἄτακτον disordered (30)
  ἀτάκτως in disorder (30)
ἀταξίᾱ, ἀταξίᾱς, ἡ disorder (30)
ἄτε (+ participle) since (31)
ἀτεχνῶς simply, really (31)
Ἀττική, Ἀττικῆς, ἡ Attica (14)

Ἀττικός, Ἀττική, Ἀττικόν Attic
(30)
Ἄτυς, ὁ Atys (26)
αὖ again (24)
αὖθις, again (3)
αὐξάνω, αὐξήσω, ηὔξησα, ηὔξηκα,
ηὔξημαι, ηὐξήθην I increase (9, 23)
αὔριον tomorrow (11)
αὐτήν her, it
αὐτίκα straightway (27)
αὐτό it (3)
αὐτόν him, it (1, 3)
αὐτός, αὐτή, αὐτό (intensive adjective)
-self, -selves; (pronoun) him her, it, them
(5, 18)
αὐτουργός, αὐτουργοῦ, ὁ farmer (1)
ἀφαιρέομαι I take away for myself, save
(30)
ἀφῑημι I send away, let go, give up (21)
ἀφικνέομαι, ἀφίξομαι, ἀφῑκόμην,
ἀφῑγμαι I arrive, arrive at (+ εἰς + acc.)
(6, 11, 17, 24)
ἀφίσταμαι, ἀπέστην I revolt from (16)
Ἀχαιοί, Ἀχαιῶν, οἱ Achaeans,
Greeks (7)
Ἀχαίᾱ, Ἀχαίᾱς, ἡ Achaea (29)
Ἀχαρναί, Ἀχαρνῶν, αἱ Acharnae
(23)
Ἀχαρνῆς, Ἀχαρνῶν, οἱ inhabitants
of Acharnae, the Acharnians (23)
Ἀχαρνικός, Ἀχαρνική, Ἀχαρνικόν
Acharnian (31)
ἄχθομαι, ἀχθέσομαι, ἠχθέσθην (+
dat.) I am vexed (at), grieved (by) (31)
ἄχρηστος, ἄχρηστον useless (27)

B
Βαβυλώνιοι, Βαβυλωνίων, οἱ
Babylonians (27)
βαδίζω, βαδιοῦμαι, ἐβάδισα,
βεβάδικα I walk, go (1)
βαθύς, βαθεῖα, βαθύ deep (18, 19)
βαίνω, βήσομαι, ἔβην, βέβηκα I
step, walk, go (2, 15, 24)
βάλλω, βαλῶ, ἔβαλον, βέβληκα,
βέβλημαι, ἐβλήθην I throw, put, pelt,
strike (7, 22)
βάρβαρος, βαρβάρου, ὁ barbarian
(13)
βασιλείᾱ, βασιλείᾱς, ἡ kingdom (25)
βασίλεια, βασιλείων, τά palace (25)
βασιλεύς, βασιλέως, ὁ king (6)
βασιλεύω (used primarily in present tense)
I rule, rule over (+ gen.) (6)
βέβαιος, βεβαίᾱ, βέβαιον firm (13)
βέλτιστος, βελτίστη, βέλτιστον best
(24)
βελτῑων, βέλτῑον better (24)
βίᾱ, βίᾱς, ἡ force, violence (31)
βιβλίον, βιβλίου, τό book (24)
βίος, βίου, ὁ life (16)
Βίτων, Βίτωνος, ὁ Biton (25)

βλάπτω, βλάψω, ἔβλαψα, βέβλαφα,
βέβλαμμαι, ἐβλάφθην or ἐβλάβην
I harm (15, 19)
βλέπω, βλέψομαι, ἔβλεψα I look, see
(2)
βοάω I shout (5)
βοή, βοῆς, ἡ shout (10)
βοήθεια, βοηθείᾱς, ἡ help (30)
βοηθέω (+ dat.) I help, come to help (2, 6)
Βοιωτίᾱ, Βοιωτίᾱς, ἡ Boeotia (14)
Βοιωτοί, Βοιωτῶν, οἱ Boeotians (23)
βουλεύω, βουλεύσω, ἐβούλευσα,
βεβούλευκα, βεβούλευμαι,
ἐβουλεύθην (active or middle) I
deliberate, plan (21)
βουλή, βουλῆς, ἡ plan, advice,
Council (22)
βούλομαι, βουλήσομαι, βεβούλημαι,
ἐβουλήθην I want, wish (6, 28)
βοῦς, βοός, ὁ ox (2)
βραδύς, βραδεῖα, βραδύ slow (18)
βραδέως slowly (2)
Βρόμιος, Βρομίου, ὁ Thunderer (an
epithet of Dionysus) (9)
Βυζάντιον, Βυζαντίου, τό
Byzantium
βωμός, βωμοῦ, ὁ altar (8)

Γ
γάμος, γάμου, ὁ marriage (26)
γάρ (postpositive) for (1)
γε (postpositive enclitic) at least, indeed
(restrictive or intensive) (6)
γέγονε he/she/it has become, is
γελάω, γελάσομαι, ἐγέλασα,
ἐγελάσθην I laugh (18)
γένος, γένους, τό race
γεραιός, γεραιά, γεραιόν old (12)
γέρων, γέροντος, ὁ old man (9)
γεύομαι, γεύσομαι, ἐγευσάμην,
γέγευμαι I taste
γεωμετρίᾱ, γεωμετρίᾱς, ἡ geometry
γῆ, γῆς, ἡ land, earth, ground (4)
κατὰ γῆν on, by land (14)
ποῦ γῆς; where (in the world)? (16)
γίγνομαι, γενήσομαι, ἐγενόμην,
γέγονα, γεγένημαι I become, happen
(6, 26)
γιγνώσκω, γνώσομαι, ἔγνων (I
learned, perceived), ἔγνωκα,
ἔγνωσμαι, ἐγνώσθην I get to know,
learn (5, 15, 17, 24, 26)
ὀρθῶς γιγνώσκω I am right (18)
γνώμη, γνώμης, ἡ opinion, judgment,
intention (18)
τίνα γνώμην ἔχεις; What do you
think? (18)
Γορδίης, Γορδίου, ὁ Gordias (26)
γράμμα, γράμματος, τό letter (of the
alphabet); (plural) writing (24)
γραμματιστής, γραμματιστοῦ, ὁ
schoolmaster (24)

γράφω, γράψω, ἔγραψα, γέγραφα, γέγραμμαι, ἐγράφην I write (14, 19)

γυμναστική, γυμναστικῆς, ἡ gymnastics (24)

γυνή, γυναικός, ἡ woman, wife (4)

Δ

δαίμων, δαίμονος, ὁ spirit, god, the power controlling one's destiny, fate, lot (28)

δάκνω, δήξομαι, ἔδακον, δέδηγμαι, ἐδήχθην I bite, sting (31)

δακρύω, δακρύσω, ἐδάκρυσα, δεδάκρῡκα, δεδάκρῡμαι (I am in tears) I cry, weep (11, 17)

δέ (postpositive) and, but (1)

    μέν . . . δέ . . . on the one hand . . . on the other hand . . . (2)

δέδοικα (perfect with present meaning) I am afraid (28)

δεῖ, (subjunctive) δέῃ, (optative) δέοι, (imperfect) ἔδει, δεήσει, ἐδέησε (+ acc. and infinitive) it is necessary, he/she ought, must (10)

δείκνῡμι, δείξω, ἔδειξα, δέδειχα, δέδειγμαι, ἐδείχθην I show (22, 24)

δειλίᾱ, δειλίᾱς, ἡ cowardice (26)

δειλός, δειλή, δειλόν cowardly (27)

δεινός, δεινή, δεινόν terrible, skilled (6)

    δεινά terrible things
    δεινῶς terribly, frightfully

δειπνέω, I eat

δεῖπνον, δείπνου, τό dinner (3)

δέκα ten (8)

    δέκατος, δεκάτη, δέκατον tenth (8)

Δελφοί, Δελφῶν, οἱ Delphi (25)

δένδρον, δένδρου, τό tree (2)

δεξιά, δεξιᾶς, ἡ right hand (9)

δεξιός, δεξιά, δεξιόν right (i.e., on the right hand) (15)

δέομαι, δεήσομαι, ἐδεήθην I ask for X (acc.) from Y (gen.); I beg (+ infinitive); I want (+ gen.) (26)

δέος, δέους, τό fear (28)

δεσπότης, δεσπότου, ὁ master (2)

δεῦρο here, to here (3, 26)

δευτερεῖα, δευτερείων, τά second prize

δεύτερος, δευτέρᾱ, δεύτερον second (8)

    δεύτερον or τὸ δεύτερον a second time

δέχομαι, δέξομαι, ἐδεξάμην, δέδεγμαι I receive, accept (6)

δέω, δήσω, ἔδησα, δέδεκα, δέδεμαι, ἐδέθην I bind (28)

δή (postpositive) indeed, in fact (emphasizes that what is said is obvious or true) (6)

δῆλος, δήλη, δῆλον clear (18)

δῆλόν ἐστι(ν) it is clear (18)

δηλόω, δηλώσω, ἐδήλωσα, δεδήλωκα, δεδήλωμαι, ἐδηλώθην I show (15, 18)

δημοκρατίᾱ, δημοκρατίᾱς, ἡ democracy

δῆμος, δήμου, ὁ the people, township, deme (9, 23)

δήπου I suppose (20)

διά (+ gen.) through; (+ acc.) because of (9, 18)

    διὰ πολλοῦ after a long time (19)
    διὰ τί; why? (2)

διαβαίνω I cross (27)

διαβάλλω I pass over, cross (29)

διακομίζω I bring, take over or across (25)

διακόσιοι, διακόσιαι, διακόσια two hundred (16)

διαλέγομαι, διαλέξομαι or διαλεχθήσομαι, διείλεγμαι, διελέχθην (+ dat.) I talk to, converse with (8)

διαλύω I disband (an army), disperse (a fleet) (23)

διάνοια, διανοίᾱς, ἡ intention, intellect (24)

διαπέμπω I send X (acc.) through Y (dat.) (28)

διὰ πολλοῦ after a long time (19)

διὰ τί; why? (2)

διαφέρει (impersonal + dat.) it makes a difference to (28)

διαφεύγω I escape (30)

διαφθείρω, διαφθερῶ, διέφθειρα, διέφθαρκα, διέφθορα (I am ruined), διέφθαρμαι, διεφθάρην I destroy (15, 23)

διδάσκαλος, διδασκάλου, ὁ teacher (24)

    ἐν διδασκάλων (οἰκίᾳ) at school
    εἰς διδασκάλων (οἰκίᾱν) to school

διδάσκω, διδάξω, ἐδίδαξα, δεδίδαχα, δεδίδαγμαι, ἐδιδάχθην I teach (24, 26)

δίδωμι, (imperfect) ἐδίδουν, δώσω, ἔδωκα, (infinitive) δοῦναι, (participle) δούς, δέδωκα, δέδομαι, ἐδόθην I give (18, 31)

διέρχομαι I come through, go through (14)

διίσταμαι, διαστήσομαι, διέστην, διέστηκα (intransitive) I separate, part

Δικαιόπολις, Δικαιοπόλεως, Δικαιοπόλει, Δικαιόπολιν, ὁ Dicaeopolis (1)

δίκαιος, δικαίᾱ, δίκαιον just (24)

δίκη, δίκης, ἡ custom, justice, right, lawsuit, penalty (21)

δι' ὀλίγου soon (5)

Διόνῡσος, Διονύσου, ὁ Dionysus (8)

διότι because (18)
διώκω, διώξομαι or διώξω, ἐδίωξα,
  δεδίωχα, ἐδιώχθην I pursue (5, 20)
δοκεῖ, ἔδοξε (+ dat. and infinitive) it
  seems (good) (11)
    δοκεῖ μοι it seems good to me, I
      decide, I think it best (11)
    ἔδοξεν αὐτῷ he decided
    ὡς δοκεῖ as it seems (13)
δοκέω, δόξω, ἔδοξα, δέδογμαι,
  ἐδόχθην I seem, think (17, 20)
δόρυ, δόρατος, τό spear (26)
δοῦλος, δούλου, ὁ slave (2)
δουλόω I enslave
δραμεῖν (aorist infinitive of τρέχω)
δραχμή, δραχμῆς, ἡ drachma (11)
Δύμη, Δύμης, ἡ Dyme (29)
δύναμαι, (imperfect) ἐδυνάμην,
  δυνήσομαι, δεδύνημαι ἐδυνήθην
  I am able, can (12, 25)
δύναμις, δυνάμεως, ἡ power, strength,
  (military) forces (21)
δυνατός, δυνατή, δυνατόν possible,
  capable, powerful (3, 21)
δύο two (7)
δώδεκα twelve
δωδέκατος, δωδεκάτη, δωδέκατον
  twelfth
Δωδώνη, Δωδώνης, ἡ Dodona (27)
δώματα, δωμάτων, τά (Homeric word)
  palace
δῶρον, δώρου, τό gift (27)

E

ἐάν (+ subjunctive) if (21)
ἔαρ, ἦρος, τό spring (22)
ἑαυτόν himself (10)
ἐάω, ἐάσω, εἴασα, εἴακα, εἴαμαι,
  εἰάθην I allow, let be (23)
ἑβδομήκοντα seventy
ἕβδομος, ἑβδόμη, ἕβδομον seventh
  (8)
ἐγγύς (adverb or preposition + gen.) near
  (13)
ἐγείρω, ἐγερῶ, ἤγειρα ἐγρήγορα (I
  am awake), ἐγήγερμαι, ἠγέρθην I
  wake (someone) up; (middle and passive,
  intransitive) I wake up (8, 23)
ἐγώ I (2)
  ἔγωγε (an emphatic ἐγώ) I (17)
ἐθέλω or θέλω, (imperfect) ἤθελον,
  ἐθελήσω, ἠθέλησα, ἠθέληκα I
  wish, am willing (4, 28)
  οὐκ ἐθέλω I refuse (4)
ἔθνος, ἔθνους, τό tribe, people (27)
εἰ if (11)
  εἰ γάρ if only; oh, that (25)
  εἰ μή unless, except
εἴθε if only; oh, that (25)
εἴκοσι twenty
εἴκω, εἴξω, εἶξα (+ dat.) I yield (15)
εἷλον (aorist indicative of αἱρέω)

εἰμί, (imperfect) ἦν, ἔσομαι I am (1)
  οἷός τ᾽ εἰμί I am able (25)
εἶμι I will go (17)
εἵνεκα (Ionic for ἕνεκα)
εἰπέ, (plural) εἴπετε tell! (7)
εἰπεῖν (aorist infinitive of λέγω) (7)
εἰρήνη, εἰρήνης, ἡ peace (16)
εἷς, μία, ἕν one (7)
εἰς (+ acc.) into, to, at, onto, for (2)
εἰσάγω I lead in, take in (2, 11)
εἰσβαίνω I go in, come in
  εἰς ναῦν εἰσβαίνω I go on board ship,
    board the ship, embark
εἰσβάλλω (+ εἰς + acc.) I invade (22)
εἰσβολή, εἰσβολῆς, ἡ invasion (23)
εἰς διδασκάλων (οἰκίᾱν) to school
εἰσελαύνω I drive in (6)
εἰσέρχομαι (+ εἰς + acc.) I go in, come in
  (17)
εἰσηγέομαι (+ dat.) I lead in (11)
εἰς καιρόν at just the right time (12)
εἰσκομίζω I bring in
εἰσπίπτω I fall upon
εἰσπλέω I sail into
εἰσρέω I flow in (16)
εἰστίθημι I put in
εἰς τὸ πρόσθεν forward (31)
εἰσφέρω I bring in (12)
εἴσω inwards (29)
εἶτα then, next (31)
εἴωθα (perfect with present meaning) I am
  accustomed to (28)
ἐκ (+ gen.) out of (3)
ἕκαστος, ἑκάστη, ἕκαστον each (23)
ἑκάτερος, ἑκατέρᾱ, ἑκάτερον each (of
  two) (21)
ἑκατόν (indeclinable) a hundred (16)
ἐκβαίνω I step out, come out (2)
  ἐκβαίνω ἐκ τῆς νεώς I disembark
ἐκβάλλω I throw out (16)
ἐκδίδωμι I give (in marriage)
ἐκεῖ there (6, 26)
ἐκεῖθεν from that place (26)
ἐκεῖνος, ἐκείνη, ἐκεῖνο that; (plural)
  those (13)
ἐκεῖσε to there (8, 26)
ἐκκλησίᾱ, ἐκκλησίᾱς, ἡ assembly (21)
ἐκκομίζω I bring, carry out
ἐκπέμπω I send out
ἐκπίπτω I fall out
ἐκπνέω, ἐκπνευσοῦμαι and
  ἐκπνεύσομαι, ἐξέπνευσα,
  ἐκπέπνευκα I blow out, blow from (29)
ἐκτός (+ gen.) outside (22)
ἕκτος, ἕκτη, ἕκτον sixth (8)
ἐκφέρω I carry out (3)
ἐκφεύγω I flee (out) (6)
ἐλάᾱ, ἐλάᾱς, ἡ olive, olive tree (19)
ἐλάττων, ἔλαττον smaller, rather
  small; (plural) fewer, rather few (14, 24)

ἐλαύνω, ἐλάω, ἤλασα, ἐλήλακα, ἐλήλαμαι, ἠλάθην (transitive) I drive; (intransitive) I march (2, 29)

ἐλάχιστος, ἐλαχίστη, ἐλάχιστον smallest; (plural) fewest (24)

ἐλεῖν (aorist infinitive of αἱρέω)

ἐλευθερίᾱ, ἐλευθερίᾱς, ἡ freedom (8)

ἐλεύθερος, ἐλευθέρᾱ, ἐλεύθερον free (16)

ἐλευθερόω I set free, free (15)

Ἐλευσίς, Ἐλευσῖνος, ἡ Eleusis (20)

ἐλθέ, (plural) ἐλθέτε come! (2)

ἐλθεῖν (aorist infinitive of ἔρχομαι)

ἕλκω, (imperfect) εἷλκον, ἕλξω, εἵλκυσα, εἵλκυσμαι, εἱλκύσθην I drag (25)

Ἑλλάς, Ἑλλάδος, ἡ Hellas, Greece (13)

Ἕλλην, Ἕλληνος, ὁ Greek; (plural) the Greeks (14)

ἐλπίζω, ἐλπιῶ, ἤλπισα I hope, expect, suppose (14)

ἐλπίς, ἐλπίδος, ἡ hope, expectation (23)

ἐμαυτοῦ, σεαυτοῦ, ἑαυτοῦ of myself, of yourself, of him-, her-, itself, etc. (7)

ἐμβάλλω (+ dat.) I strike with a ram (ἔμβολος)

ἐμμένω I remain in (23)

ἐμνήσθην (aorist passive in middle sense) I remembered (28, 30)

ἐμός, ἐμή, ἐμόν my, mine (5)

ἔμπειρος, ἔμπειρον (+ gen.) skilled in or at

ἐμπῑπτω (+ dat.) I fall into, fall upon, attack (15)

ἔμπορος, ἐμπόρου, ὁ merchant (12)

ἐν (+ dat.) in, on, among (3)

ἐν ταῖς Ἀθήναις, in Athens (1)

ἐν ... τούτῳ meanwhile (8)

ἐναντίος, ἐναντίᾱ, ἐναντίον opposed, opposite, hostile; (as noun) the enemy (30)

ἔνατος, ἐνάτη, ἔνατον ninth (8)

ἕνδεκα eleven

ἐν διδασκάλων (οἰκίᾳ) at school

ἐνδίδωμι I give in, yield (22)

ἔνεγκαι (aorist infinitive of φέρω)

ἔνειμι, ἐνέσομαι, ἐνῆν I am in (12)

ἕνεκα (+ preceding gen.) for the sake of, because of (21)

ἐνθάδε here, to this place (7, 26)

ἐνθῡμέομαι, ἐνθῡμήσομαι, ἐντεθῡμημαι, ἐνεθῡμήθην I take to heart, ponder (28)

ἔνιοι, ἔνιαι, ἔνια some (20)

ἐν μέσῳ (+ gen.) between (14)

ἐννέα nine (8)

ἐν νῷ ἔχω (+ infinitive) I have in mind, intend (4)

ἔνοικος, ἐνοίκου, ὁ inhabitant (16)

ἐνταῦθα then, there, here (5, 26)

ἐνταῦθα δή at that very moment, then (5)

ἐντεῦθεν from this place (26)

ἐντός (adverb or preposition + gen.) within (20)

ἐν τούτῳ meanwhile (8)

ἐντυγχάνω (+ dat.) I meet (19)

ἐν ᾧ while (8)

ἐξ (before words beginning with vowels) = ἐκ (8)

ἕξ six (8)

ἐξάγω I lead out

ἐξαιρέω I take out, remove

ἐξαίφνης suddenly (20)

ἐξαμαρτάνω I miss, fail, make a mistake (23)

ἐξαρτῡω, ἐξαρτῡσω, ἐξήρτῡσα, ἐξήρτῡκα, ἐξήρτῡμαι, ἐξηρτῡθην I equip (29)

ἐξελαύνω I drive out (16)

ἐξέρχομαι (+ ἐκ + gen.) I go out of, come out of (6, 17)

ἔξεστι(ν) (+ dat. and infinitive) it is allowed, possible (10)
    ἔξεστί μοι I am allowed, I may, I can

ἐξευρίσκω I find out

ἐξηγέομαι I relate (12)

ἐξήκοντα sixty

ἔξοδος, ἐξόδου, ἡ going out, marching forth, military expedition (23)

ἐξόπισθε(ν) (adverb or preposition + gen.) behind (31)

ἔξω (adverb or preposition + gen.) outside (20)

ἔοικα (perfect with present meaning) I am like, I am likely to (28)
    ὡς ἔοικε as it seems (28)

ἑορτή, ἑορτῆς, ἡ festival (4)
    ἑορτὴν ποιοῦμαι I hold a festival

ἔπαινος, ἐπαίνου, ὁ praise (24)

ἐπαίρω I raise up, lift up, urge, induce; (with reflexive pronoun) I get up

ἐπανέρχομαι I come back, return, return to (+ εἰς or πρός + acc.) (9, 17)

ἐπεί when, since (3, 26)

ἐπειδάν (+ subjunctive) when(ever) (22)

ἐπειδή when, since (22)

ἐπεισβαίνω I go into (30)

ἔπειτα, then (2)

ἐπεξέρχομαι (+ dat.) I go out against, attack (23)

ἐπέρχομαι I approach; (+ dat.) I attack (27)

ἐπί (+ gen.) toward, in the direction of, on; (+ dat.) at, upon, on, for (of price or purpose); (+ acc.) at, against, onto, to or for (of direction or purpose), for (of time) (5, 9, 18, 20, 24, 26, 27)

ἐπιβαίνω (+ gen.) I get up on, mount, board (28)

ἐπιβοηθέω (+ *dat.*) I come to aid (30)
ἐπιβουλεύω (+ *dat.*) I plot against (21)
ἐπιγίγνομαι I come after (29)
Ἐπίδαυρος, Ἐπιδαύρου, ἡ
  Epidaurus (11)
ἐπιδιώκω I pursue (30)
ἐπικαλέω I call upon; (*middle*) I call upon
  X to help (28)
ἐπιμελέομαι, ἐπιμελήσομαι,
  ἐπιμεμέλημαι, ἐπεμελήθην
  (+ *gen.*) I take care for; (+ ὅπως + *future
  indicative*) I take care that (24)
ἐπιπέμπω I send against, send in (14)
ἐπιπλέω (+ *dat.*) I sail against (15)
ἐπίσταμαι, ἐπιστήσομαι, ἠπιστήθην
  I understand, know (16, 25)
ἐπιστρατεύω (+ *dat.* or ἐπί + *acc.*) I
  march against, attack (18)
ἐπιστρέφω, ἐπιστρέψω, ἐπέστρεψα,
  ἐπέστραμμαι, (*second aorist passive,
  active and intransitive in meaning*)
  ἐπεστράφην I turn around (30)
ἐπιτήδειος, ἐπιτηδείᾱ, ἐπιτήδειον
  friendly, suitable for (+ *infinitive*) (23)
ἐπιτίθημι I put X (*acc.*) on Y (*dat.*) (18)
  ἐπιτίθεμαι, ἐπιθήσομαι, ἐπεθέμην,
  ἐπιτέθειμαι (+ *dat.*) I attack (29)
ἐπὶ τὴν ἕω at dawn (29)
ἐπιτρέπω (+ *dat.*) I entrust (17)
ἐπιχειρέω (+ *dat.*) I attempt, attack (29)
ἕπομαι, (*imperfect*) εἱπόμην, ἕψομαι,
  ἑσπόμην (+ *dat.*) I follow (8, 17, 25)
ἑπτά seven (8)
ἐράω, (*imperfect*) ἤρων, ἐρασθήσομαι,
  ἠράσθην (+ *gen.*) I love (31)
ἐργάζομαι, (*imperfect*) εἰργαζόμην,
  ἐργάσομαι, εἰργασάμην,
  εἴργασμαι, εἰργάσθην I work,
  accomplish (8, 25)
ἔργον, ἔργου, τό work, deed; (*plural*)
  tilled fields (8)
ἔργῳ in fact
ἐρέσσω, ἤρεσα I row (13)
ἔρημος, ἔρημον deserted (19)
Ἐρῑνύες, Ἐρῑνυῶν, αἱ the Furies,
  avenging spirits (20)
ἑρμηνεύς, ἑρμηνέως, ὁ interpreter
ἔρχομαι, εἶμι, (*infinitive*) ἰέναι, ἦλθον,
  ἐλήλυθα I come, go (6, 11, 17, 27)
ἐρωτάω, ἐρωτήσω, ἠρόμην, ἠρώτηκα
  I ask (12)
ἐς = εἰς
ἐσβάλλω = εἰσβάλλω
ἐσθίω, ἔδομαι, ἔφαγον, ἐδήδοκα I
  eat (9, 19, 29)
ἐσηκοντίζω I throw a javeline at
ἐσκομίζω (εἰσ-) I bring in, take in
ἑσπέρᾱ, ἑσπέρᾱς, ἡ evening (8)
ἔστην I stood
ἐστί(ν) he/she/it is (1)
ἔστω let it be so! all right!

ἔσχατος, ἐσχάτη, ἔσχατον furthest,
  extreme (28)
ἑταῖρος, ἑταίρου, ὁ comrade,
  companion (6)
ἕτερος, ἑτέρᾱ, ἕτερον one or the other
  (of two) (26)
  ὁ μὲν ἕτερος . . . ὁ δὲ ἕτερος
    the one . . . the other (26)
ἔτι still (3)
ἕτοιμος, ἑτοίμη, ἕτοιμον ready (9)
ἔτος, ἔτους, τό year (16)
εὖ well (12, 14)
Εὔβοια, Εὐβοίᾱς, ἡ Euboea (14)
εὖ γε good! well done! (8)
εὐδαιμονίᾱ, εὐδαιμονίᾱς, ἡ
  happiness, prosperity, good luck (25)
εὐθύς immediately, straight (10)
εὐμενής, εὐμενές kindly (18)
εὑρίσκω, εὑρήσω, ηὗρον *or* εὗρον,
  ηὕρηκα *or* εὕρηκα, ηὕρημαι *or*
  εὕρημαι, ηὑρέθην *or* εὑρέθην I
  find (7, 24)
Εὐρυμέδων ποταμός, Εὐρυμέδοντος
  ποταμοῦ, ὁ the Eurymedon River (16)
εὐφημέω I keep holy silence (31)
εὐφημίᾱ, εὐφημίᾱς, ἡ call for holy
  silence (31)
εὐχή, εὐχῆς, ἡ prayer (25)
εὔχομαι, εὔξομαι, ηὐξάμην, ηὖγμαι
  I pray, pray to (+ *dat.*) (8, 20)
ἔφη he/she said (11)
  ἔφασαν they said
Ἐφιάλτης, Ἐφιάλτου, ὁ Ephialtes
  (14)
ἐφίσταμαι, ἐπέστην (+ *dat.*) I stand
  near, appear to (26)
ἔχθιστος, ἐχθίστη, ἔχθιστον most
  hostile (24)
ἐχθίων, ἔχθῑον more hostile (24)
ἐχθρός, ἐχθρά, ἐχθρόν hostile (18, 24)
  ἐχθρός, ἐχθροῦ, ὁ enemy (18)
ἔχω, (*imperfect*) εἶχον, ἕξω *or* σχήσω,
  ἔσχον, ἔσχηκα, ἔσχημαι I have,
  hold; (*middle* + *gen.*) I hold onto (4, 25)
ἕως until, while (14)
  ἕως ἄν (+ *subjunctive*) until (22)
ἕως, ἕω, ἡ dawn (29)
  ἅμα ἕῳ at dawn (30)
  ἐπὶ τὴν ἕω at dawn (29)

Z

ζάω (*infinitive*) ζῆν, (*imperfect*) ἔζων,
  ζήσω *or* βιώσομαι (*from* βιόω),
  (*second aorist*) ἐβίων, βεβίωκα I live
  (24)
ζεύγνῡμι, ζεύξω, ἔζευξα, ἔζευγμαι,
  ἐζεύχθην I yoke (22)
Ζεύς, ὁ, τοῦ Διός, τῷ Διί, τὸν Δία,
  ὦ Ζεῦ Zeus, king of the gods (3, 8)
  μὰ Δία by Zeus (19)
ζητέω I seek, look for (5)
ζωή, ζωῆς, ἡ life (28)

ζῷον, ζῴου, τό animal

Η

ἤ or; (with comparatives) than (12, 14)
ἤ . . . ἤ either . . . or (12)
ἡγέομαι I lead (+ dat.); I think, consider (6, 31)
ἡδέως sweetly, pleasantly, gladly (18)
ἤδη already, now (2)
ἤδιστα (superlative of ἡδέως) most sweetly, most pleasantly, most gladly (19)
ἤδιστος, ἡδίστη, ἤδιστον sweetest (24)
ἡδίων, ἤδιον sweeter (24)
ἤδομαι, ἡσθήσομαι, ἤσθην (+ participle or dat.) I enjoy, am glad, delighted (24)
ἡδύς, ἡδεῖα, ἡδύ sweet (18, 24)
ἤκιστά γε (the opposite of μάλιστά γε) least of all, not at all (16)
ἥκω I have come, (imperfect) ἧκον I had come, (future) ἥξω I will have come (5)
ἥλιος, ἡλίου, ὁ sun (1)
ἡμεῖς we (5)
ἡμέρᾱ, ἡμέρᾱς, ἡ day (6)
καθ᾽ ἡμέρᾱν every day (24)
ἡμέτερος, ἡμετέρᾱ, ἡμέτερον our (5)
ἡμίονος, ἡμιόνου, ὁ mule (12)
ἤπειρος, ἠπείρου, ἡ land, mainland (29)
ᾗπερ where (23)
Ἥρᾱ, Ἥρᾱς, ἡ Hera, wife of Zeus and principal deity of Argos (25)
Ἡρόδοτος, Ἡροδότου, ὁ Herodotus (24)
ἡσυχάζω, ἡσυχάσω, ἡσύχασα I keep quiet (13)
ἡσυχίᾱ, ἡσυχίᾱς, ἡ quietness (28)
ἥττων, ἧττον inferior, weaker, less (24)

Θ

θάλαττα, θαλάττης, ἡ sea (7)
κατὰ θάλατταν by sea (14)
θάνατος, θανάτου, ὁ death (16)
θάπτω, θάψω, ἔθαψα, τέθαμμαι, ἐτάφην I bury (25)
θαρρέω I am confident (17)
θάρρει. Cheer up! Don't be afraid! (17)
θάττων, θᾶττον quicker, swifter (24)
θαυμάζω, θαυμάσομαι, ἐθαύμασα, τεθαύμακα, τεθαύμασμαι, ἐθαυμάσθην I wonder at, am amazed, admire (5, 21)
θεάομαι, θεάσομαι, ἐθεᾱσάμην, τεθέᾱμαι I see, watch, look at (8)
Θεμιστοκλῆς, Θεμιστοκλέους, ὁ Themistocles (15)
θεός, θεοῦ, ἡ goddess (9)
θεός, θεοῦ, ὁ god (8)
σὺν θεοῖς God willing, with luck (17)
θεράπων, θεράποντος, ὁ attendant,

servant (25)
Θερμοπύλαι, Θερμοπυλῶν, αἱ Thermopylae (14)
θεσπίζω I prophesy
θεωρέω I watch, see (16)
θεωρίᾱ, θεωρίᾱς, ἡ viewing, sightseeing (25)
θηρίον, θηρίου, τό wild beast (26)
θησαυρός, θησαυροῦ, ὁ treasure, treasury (25)
Θησεύς, Θησέως, ὁ Theseus, son of King Aegeus (6)
θνῄσκω, θανοῦμαι, ἔθανον, τέθνηκα I die; (perfect) I am dead
θόρυβος, θορύβου, ὁ uproar, din (15)
Θριάσιος, Θριᾱσίᾱ, Θριάσιον Thriasian (23)
θυγάτηρ, θυγατρός, ἡ daughter (4)
θῡμός, θῡμοῦ, ὁ spirit (16)
θύρᾱ, θύρᾱς, ἡ door (8)
θυσίᾱ, θυσίᾱς, ἡ sacrifice (18)
θύω, θύσω, ἔθυσα, τέθυκα, τέθυμαι, ἐτύθην I sacrifice (21)

Ι

ἰᾱτρός, ἰᾱτροῦ, ὁ doctor (11)
ἰδεῖν (aorist infinitive of ὁράω)
ἰδίᾳ privately (21)
ἰδιώτης, ἰδιώτου, ὁ private person (21)
ἰδού look! (4)
ἰέναι to go (7)
ἱερεῖον, ἱερείου, τό sacrificial victim (9)
ἱερεύς, ἱερέως, ὁ priest (9)
ἱερόν, ἱεροῦ, τό temple (9)
ἱερός, ἱερά, ἱερόν holy, sacred (17)
ἴθι, (plural) ἴτε go! (5)
ἵημι, (infinitive) ἱέναι, (participle) ἱείς, ἥσω, ἧκα, (infinitive) εἶναι, (participle) εἵς, εἷκα, εἷμαι, εἵθην I send, release, let go; (middle) I hasten, go (21)
ἱκανός, ἱκανή, ἱκανόν sufficient, capable (25)
ἱκέτης, ἱκέτου, ὁ suppliant (17)
ἵλαος, ἵλαον propitious (9)
ἵνα (+ subjunctive or optative) so that, in order to (expressing purpose) (21)
ἵνα μή so that . . . not
ἱππεύς, ἱππέως, ὁ horseman, cavalryman (28)
ἱππεύω, ἱππεύσω, ἵππευσα (active or middle) I am a horseman, ride a horse (27)
ἱππικόν, ἱππικοῦ, τό cavalry (27)
ἵππος, ἵππου, ἡ cavalry (27)
ἵππος, ἵππου, ὁ horse (16)
ἴσθι, (plural) ἔστε be!
Ἴσθμος, Ἴσθμου, ὁ the Isthmus of Corinth
ἵστημι, (imperfect) ἵστην, στήσω, (first aorist) ἔστησα, (second aorist) ἔστην, ἔστηκα, ἐστάθην I make to stand,

stop, set up; (*second aorist, intransitive*) I stood, stood still, stopped; (*perfect, intransitive*) I stand (20, 31)
ἱστία, ἱστίων, τά sails (13)
ἰσχῡρός, ἰσχῡρά, ἰσχῡρόν strong (1)
ἴσως perhaps (17)
Ἴωνες, Ἰώνων, οἱ Ionians (16)
Ἰωνίᾱ, Ἰωνίᾱς, ἡ Ionia (16)

K
καθαίρω, καθαρῶ, ἐκάθηρα, κεκάθαρμαι, ἐκαθάρθην I purify (26)
καθαρός, καθαρά, καθαρόν clean, pure (17)
κάθαρσις, καθάρσεως, ἡ purification
καθέζομαι, καθεδοῦμαι I sit down, encamp (23)
καθέλκω I drag down, launch (a ship)
καθεύδω, (*imperfect*) ἐκάθευδον *or* καθηῦδον, καθευδήσω I sleep (2)
κάθημαι I sit (18)
καθ’ ἡμέρᾱν every day (24)
καθίζω, (*imperfect*) ἐκάθιζον, καθιῶ, ἐκάθισα I sit (1)
καθίζομαι, (*imperfect*) ἐκαθιζόμην, καθιζήσομαι, ἐκαθισάμην I sit down (8)
καθίστημι I set up, appoint, put into a certain state; (*middle and intransitive tenses of active*) I am appointed, established, get into a certain state (+ εἰς + *acc.*), become (20)
καθοράω I look down on (20)
καί, and, also, too (1)
  καί (+ *participle*) although (31)
  καί . . . καί both . . . and (5)
  καὶ δὴ καί and in particular, and what is more (16)
  καὶ μήν truly, indeed (31)
καίπερ (+ *participle*) although (12, 31)
καιρός, καιροῦ, ὁ time, right time (4)
καίω, καύσω, ἔκαυσα, κέκαυκα, κέκαυμαι, ἐκαύθην I kindle, burn; (*middle, intransitive*) I burn, am on fire (9)
κάκιστος, κακίστη, κάκιστον worst (14, 24)
κακῑ́ων, κάκῑον worse (14, 24)
κακοδαίμων, κακοδαίμονος having an evil spirit or bad luck (31)
κακός, κακή, κακόν bad (12, 14, 24)
  κακά, τά evils
  κακόν τι something bad
  κακῶς badly (14)
καλέω, καλῶ, ἐκάλεσα, κέκληκα, κέκλημαι (I am called), ἐκλήθην I call (2, 18)
κάλλιστος, καλλίστη, κάλλιστον most beautiful, very beautiful (9, 14, 24)
καλλῑ́ων, κάλλῑον more beautiful (14, 24)

καλός, καλή, καλόν beautiful (1, 14, 24)
  καλῶς well (10)
  καλῶς ἔχω I am well (11)
κάμηλος, καμήλου, ἡ camel (27)
κάμνω, καμοῦμαι, ἔκαμον, κέκμηκα I am sick, tired (9, 24)
καρδίᾱ, καρδίᾱς, ἡ heart (31)
καρτερός, καρτερά, καρτερόν strong, fierce (27)
κατά (+ *acc.*), down, on, along, according to, at (of time), through, with regard to, after (5, 17, 21, 25, 26, 28)
καταβαίνω I come down, go down (5)
κατὰ γῆν on land (14)
καταγώγιον, καταγωγίου, τό inn
καταδύω, καταδύσω, κατέδῡσα, καταδέδῡκα, καταδέδυμαι, κατεδύθην (*transitive*) I sink (29)
  Second aorist κατέδῡν (*intransitive*) I sank; (of the sun) set (29)
κατὰ θάλατταν by sea (11)
κατακαίω I burn completely (28)
κατάκειμαι I lie down (16)
καταλαμβάνω I overtake, catch (16)
καταλείπω I leave behind, desert (12)
καταλύω I dissolve, break up, destroy (27)
κατὰ μέσον . . . in the middle of . . . (29)
καταπαύω I put an end to (28)
καταπίπτω I fall down
καταστρέφω I overturn; (*middle*) I subdue (25)
κατὰ τάχος quickly (27)
κατατίθημι I set down
καταφεύγω I flee for refuge (30)
καταφρονέω (+ *gen.*) I despise (25)
καταχέω, καταχέω, κατέχεα, κατακέχυκα, κατακέχυμαι, κατεχύθην I pour X (*acc.*) over Y (*gen.*) (31)
κατ’ εἰκός probably (10)
κατέρχομαι I come down
κατέστην I got into
κατ’ οἶκον at home (16)
κάτω down, below (20)
κεῖμαι, κείσομαι I lie, am laid (16, 25)
κελεύω, κελεύσω, ἐκέλευσα, κεκέλευκα, κεκέλευσμαι, ἐκελεύσθην I order, tell (someone to do something) (7, 17)
κενός, κενή, κενόν empty (30)
κέρας, κέρως, τό wing (30)
κεφαλή, κεφαλῆς, ἡ head (10)
κῆρυξ, κήρῡκος, ὁ herald (9)
κιθαρίζω, κιθαριῶ, ἐκιθάρισα I play the lyre (24)
κιθαριστής, κιθαριστοῦ, ὁ lyre player (24)
Κίμων, Κίμονος, ὁ Cimon (16)

κινδῡνεύω, κινδῡνεύσω,
ἐκινδῡνευσα, κεκινδῡνευκα I run
risks
κίνδῡνος, κινδῡνου, ὁ danger (9)
κῑνέω I move (18)
Κλέοβις, Κλεόβεως, ὁ Cleobis (25)
κλῆρος, κλήρου, ὁ farm
Κνῆμος, Κνήμου, ὁ Cnemus (29)
Κνωσσός, Κνωσσοῦ, ἡ Knossos (6)
κοινός, κοινή, κοινόν common
κόλπος, κόλπου, ὁ lap, gulf (29)
κομίζω, κομιῶ, ἐκόμισα, κεκόμικα,
κεκόμισμαι, ἐκομίσθην I bring,
take (11, 21)
κόπτω, κόψω, ἔκοψα, κέκοφα,
κέκομμαι, ἐκόπην I strike, knock on
(a door) (11, 19)
κόρη, κόρης, ἡ girl
Κορίνθιοι, Κορινθίων, οἱ
Corinthians (18)
Κόρινθος, Κορίνθου, ἡ Corinth (14)
κόσμος, κόσμου, ὁ good order (15)
κόσμῳ in order (15)
κρατέω (+ gen.) I rule, have power over,
control, prevail (18)
κράτιστος, κρατίστη, κράτιστον best
(24)
κράτος, κράτους, τό power (18)
κρείττων, κρεῖττον better, stronger (24)
κρήνη, κρήνης, ἡ spring (4)
Κρήτη, Κρήτης, ἡ Crete (6)
κρῑνω, κρινῶ, ἔκρῑνα, κέκρικα,
κέκριμαι, ἐκρίθην I judge (25)
Κρισαῖος, Κρισαίᾱ, Κρισαῖον
Crisean (Crisa was a city in Phocis near
Delphi) (29)
Κροῖσος, Κροίσου, ὁ Croesus (24)
κρύπτω, κρύψω, ἔκρυψα, κέκρυμμαι,
ἐκρύφθην I hide (20)
κτείνω, κτενῶ, ἔκτεινα, ἔκτονα I kill
(27)
κύκλος, κύκλου, ὁ circle (26)
Κύκλωπες, Κυκλώπων, οἱ the Cyclopes
(20)
Κύκλωψ, Κύκλωπος, ὁ Cyclops (one-
eyed monster) (7)
Κυλλήνη, Κυλλήνης, ἡ Cyllene (29)
κῦμα, κύματος, τό wave (13)
κυνηγέτης, κυνηγέτου, ὁ hunter
Κύπρος, Κύπρου, ἡ Cyprus (16)
Κυρήνη, Κυρήνης, ἡ Cyrene (16)
κύριος, κῡρίᾱ, κύριον having authority,
legitimate, regular (31)
Κῦρος, Κύρου, ὁ Cyrus (24)
κύων, κυνός, ὁ or ἡ dog (5)
κώπη, κώπης, ἡ oar (30)

Λ

λαβύρινθος, λαβυρίνθου, ὁ labyrinth
(6)
λαγώς, λαγώ, ὁ hare
Λακεδαιμόνιοι, Λακεδαιμονίων, οἱ

the Lacedaemonians, Spartans (14)
λαλέω I talk, chatter (31)
λαμβάνω, λήψομαι, ἔλαβον, εἴληφα,
εἴλημμαι, ἐλήφθην I take; (middle +
gen.) I seize, take hold of (2, 11, 23)
λαμπρός, λαμπρά, λαμπρόν bright,
brilliant (13)
λανθάνω, λήσω, ἔλαθον, λέληθα
(+ acc. and / or participle) I escape notice,
escape the notice of (20, 30)
λέγω, λέξω or ἐρῶ, εἶπον or ἔλεξα,
εἴρηκα, εἴρημαι, ἐλέχθην or
ἐρρήθην I say, tell, speak (1, 11, 27)
λείπω, λείψω, ἔλιπον, λέλοιπα,
λέλειμμαι (I am left behind, am
inferior), ἐλείφθην I leave (3, 19, 26)
Λευκάδιος, Λευκαδίᾱ, Λευκάδιον
Leucadian (30)
Λευκάς, Λευκάδος, ἡ Leucas (29)
λέων, λέοντος, ὁ lion (20)
Λεωνίδης, Λεωνίδου, ὁ Leonidas (14)
λίθινος, λιθίνη, λίθινον made of
stone (20)
λίθος, λίθου, ὁ stone (3)
λιμήν, λιμένος, ὁ harbor (12)
λογάδες, λογάδων, οἱ picked, selected
men
λόγος, λόγου, ὁ word, story (11)
λόγῳ in word, ostensibly
λοιδορέω I abuse (31)
λούω, (imperfect) ἔλουν, λούσομαι,
ἔλουσα, λέλουμαι I wash; (middle,
reflexive) I wash myself, bathe (22)
λόφος, λόφου, ὁ hill (5)
Λῡδίᾱ, Λῡδίᾱς, ἡ Lydia (27)
Λῡδοί, Λῡδῶν, οἱ Lydians (24)
Λῡδιος, Λῡδίᾱ, Λῡδιον Lydian (27)
λύκος, λύκου, ὁ wolf (5)
λῡπέω I grieve, pain, give someone grief
or pain; (middle) I am sad, sorrowful,
depressed; (middle / passive) I am grieved
(16)
λῡ́ω, λῡ́σω, ἔλῡσα, λέλυκα, λέλυμαι,
ἐλύθην I loosen (3, 17)

M

μὰ Δία by Zeus (19)
μαθηματικά, μαθηματικῶν, τά
mathematics
μαθητής, μαθητοῦ, ὁ pupil (24)
μακάριος, μακαρίᾱ, μακάριον blessed,
happy (31)
μακρός, μακρά, μακρόν long, large
(1)
μάλα very (4, 14)
μάλιστα very much, especially (4)
μάλιστά γε certainly, indeed (12)
μᾶλλον more, rather (18)
μᾶλλον ἤ rather than (18)
μανθάνω, μαθήσομαι, ἔμαθον,
μεμάθηκα I learn, understand (11, 23)
μαντεῖον, μαντείου, τό oracle (27)

μάχη, μάχης, ἡ battle (13)
μάχομαι, μαχοῦμαι, ἐμαχεσάμην,
  μεμάχημαι I fight, fight with (+ dat.)
  (6, 28)
μέγα greatly, loudly (12)
μεγάλως greatly
Μέγαρα, Μεγάρων, τά Megara (20)
μέγας, μεγάλη, μέγα big (3, 14, 24)
μέγεθος, μεγέθους, τό size (20)
μέγιστος, μεγίστη, μέγιστον very big,
  biggest (7, 14, 24)
μεθίημι I let go (26)
μείζων, μεῖζον bigger (14, 24)
μέλει, μελήσει, ἐμέλησε, μεμέληκε
  (+ dat.) it is a care to, X cares for (26)
μελετάω I study, practice (24)
Μέλιττα, Μελίττης, ἡ Melissa,
  daughter of Dicaeopolis and Myrrhine
  (4)
μέλλω, μελλήσω, ἐμέλλησα (+ present
  or future infinitive) I am about to, am
  destined to, intend to; (without infinitive
  or with present infinitive) I delay (7)
μέμνημαι (perfect middle = present) I
  have reminded myself, I remember (28,
  30)
Μέμφις, Μέμφεως, ἡ Memphis (16)
μέμφομαι, μέμψομαι, ἐμεμψάμην or
  ἐμέμφθην (+ dat. or acc.) I find fault
  with, blame (27)
μέν . . . δέ . . . on the one hand . . . on
  the other hand . . . (2)
μέντοι however (18)
μένω, μενῶ, ἔμεινα, μεμένηκα I stay,
  wait; (transitive) I wait for (3, 22)
μέρος, μέρους, τό part (15)
μέσος, μέση, μέσον middle (of) (9)
  ἐν μέσῳ (+ gen.) between
  κατὰ μέσον . . . in the middle of . . .
  (29)
Μεσσήνιοι, Μεσσηνίων, οἱ
  Messenians (30)
μετά (+ gen.) with; (+ acc.) after (6, 14)
  μετά (adverb) afterward, later (25)
μεταγιγνώσκω I change my mind, repent
  (28)
μεταξύ between
μεταπέμπομαι I send for (26)
μέτρον, μέτρου, τό measure (27)
μέχρι οὗ as long as
μή (with infinitive) not; (with imperative)
  don't ; (with aorist subjunctive) don't; (in
  negative purposes clauses) lest; (in clauses
  of fearing) that (2, 20, 21, 22, 31)
  εἰ μή unless
μηδέ and . . . not, nor, not even (31)
μηδείς, μηδεμία, μηδέν (used instead
  of οὐδείς with subjunctives, imperatives,
  and infinitives) no one, nothing, no (13,
  31)
μηδέποτε never (31)

μηδέτερος, μηδετέρᾱ, μηδέτερον
  neither (of two) (31)
Μηδικός, Μηδική, Μηδικόν Median
  (24)
Μῆδοι, Μήδων, οἱ Medes (Persians)
  (24)
μηκέτι (+ imperative) don't . . . any
  longer; (+ infinitive) no longer (3, 15, 31)
μῆλα, μήλων, τά (plural) flocks (5)
μήν or καὶ μήν truly, indeed (31)
μήν, μηνός, ὁ month (31)
μηνύω, μηνύσω, ἐμήνῡσα, μεμήνῡκα,
  μεμήνῡμαι, ἐμηνύθην I inform (31)
μήπω not yet (31)
μήτε and not (29)
μήτε . . . μήτε neither . . . nor (29,
  31)
μήτηρ, μητρός, ἡ mother (4)
μιαρός, μιαρά, μιαρόν defiled, foul,
  villainous (31)
μῑκρός, μῑκρά, μῑκρόν small (1)
Μῑνόταυρος, Μῑνοταύρου, ὁ
  Minotaur (6)
Μίνως, Μίνωος, ὁ Minos, king of Crete
  (6)
μισθός, μισθοῦ, ὁ reward, pay (11)
μνῆμα, μνήματος, τό monument
μνησθήσομαι (future passive in middle
  sense) I will remember (28, 30)
μόλις with difficulty, scarcely, reluctantly
  (4)
Μολύκρειον, Μολυκρείου, τό
  Molycreon (29)
μόνος, μόνη, μόνον alone, only (15)
  μόνον only (15)
  οὐ μόνον . . . ἀλλὰ καί not
    only . . . but also (15)
μουσική, μουσικῆς, ἡ music (24)
μῦθος, μύθου, ὁ story (5)
Μυκάλη, Μυκάλης, ἡ Mycale
Μυκῆναι, Μυκηνῶν, αἱ Mycenae (20)
μύριοι, μύριαι, μύρια ten thousand,
  numberless (21)
Μυρρίνη, Μυρρίνης, ἡ Myrrhine,
  wife of Dicaeopolis (4)
Μῡσοί, Μῡσῶν, οἱ Mysians (26)
μῶρος, μώρᾱ, μῶρον foolish

N
ναὶ μὰ Δία yes, by Zeus! (31)
ναυάγιον, ναυᾱγίου, τό wrecked ship
  (30)
ναύαρχος, ναυάρχου, ὁ admiral (15)
ναύκληρος, ναυκλήρου, ὁ ship's
  captain (12)
ναυμαχέω I fight by sea (15)
ναυμαχίᾱ, ναυμαχίᾱς, ἡ naval battle
  (29)
Ναυπάκτιοι, Ναυπακτίων, οἱ
  inhabitants of Naupactus
Ναύπακτος, Ναυπάκτου, ὁ Naupactus
ναῦς, νεώς, ἡ ship (6)

ναύτης, ναύτου, ὁ sailor (12)
ναυτικόν, ναυτικοῦ, τό fleet (13)
νεᾱνίᾱς, νεᾱνίου, ὁ young man (8)
Νεῖλος, Νείλου, ὁ Nile
νεκρός, νεκροῦ, ὁ corpse (15)
νέμεσις, νεμέσεως, ἡ retribution (26)
νέμω, νεμῶ, ἔνειμα, νενέμηκα,
  νενέμημαι, ἐνεμήθην I distribute
νέος, νέᾱ, νέον young, new (21)
νεφέλη, νεφέλης, ἡ cloud (28)
νῆσος, νήσου, ἡ island (6)
νῑκάω I defeat, win (10)
νίκη, νίκης, ἡ victory (15)
  Νίκη, Νίκης, ἡ Nike, the goddess of
    victory (9)
νομίζω, νομιῶ, ἐνόμισα, νενόμικα,
  νενόμισμαι, ἐνομίσθην I think (21)
νόμος, νόμου, ὁ law, custom (17)
νοσέω I am sick, ill (11)
νόσος, νόσου, ἡ sickness, plague
νοστέω I return home (19)
νόστος, νόστου, ὁ return (home) (19)
νοῦς, νοῦ, ὁ mind (15)
  ἐν νῷ ἔχω I have in mind, intend (4)
νυκτερεύω, νυκτερεύσω,
  ἐνυκτέρευσα I spend the night
νύμφη, νύμφης, ἡ bride, nymph
νύξ, νυκτός, ἡ night (6)
νῦν now (5)

Ξ
Ξανθίᾱς, Ξανθίου, ὁ Xanthias (2)
Ξανθίππος, Ξανθίππου, ὁ Xanthippus
ξενίζω, ξενιῶ, ἐξένισα, ἐξενίσθην I
  entertain (25)
ξένος, ξένου, ὁ guest-friend (guest or
  host), stranger, foreigner (7)
  ξεῖνος = ξένος
Ξέρξης, Ξέρξου, ὁ Xerxes (14)
ξίφος, ξίφους, τό sword

Ο
ὀβολός, ὀβολοῦ, ὁ obol (11)
ὄγδοος, ὀγδόη, ὄγδοον eighth (8)
ὅδε, ἥδε, τόδε this; (plural) these (14,
  26)
ὁ δέ and he
ὁδός, ὁδοῦ, ἡ road, way, journey (4)
ὀδυνάω, ὀδυνηθήσομαι, ὠδυνήθην
  I cause pain; (passive) I suffer pain (31)
ὀδύρομαι (rare in tenses other than
  present) I grieve (22)
Ὀδυσσεύς, Ὀδυσσέως, ὁ Odysseus
  (7)
ὄζω, ὀζήσω, ὤζησα (+ gen.) I smell of
ὅθεν from where (26, 30)
  ὅθενπερ (-περ added for emphasis) (30)
οἱ to what place, where (26)
οἶδα (perfect with present meaning) I
  know (17, 28, 29)
οἴκαδε homeward, to home (4)
οἰκέω I live, dwell, inhabit (1)

οἰκεῖοι, οἰκείων, οἱ the members of the
  house, family, relations (22)
οἰκεῖος, οἰκείᾱ, οἰκεῖον of one's own
οἰκέται, οἰκετῶν, οἱ household (31)
οἴκησις, οἰκήσεως, ἡ dwelling (22)
οἰκίᾱ, οἰκίᾱς, ἡ house, home, dwelling
  (5)
οἰκίον, οἰκίου, τό house, palace (often
  in plural for a single house or palace) (26)
οἴκοι at home (8)
οἶκος, οἴκου, ὁ house, home, dwelling
  (1)
  κατ' οἶκον at home (16)
οἰκτίρω, οἰκτιρῶ, ᾤκτῑρα I pity (20)
οἴμοι alas! (11)
  οἴμοι κακοδαίμων poor devil! oh
    misery! (31)
Οἰνόη, Οἰνόης, ἡ Oinoe
οἰνοπώλιον, οἰνοπωλίου, τό wine-
  shop, inn (12)
οἶνος, οἴνου, ὁ wine (7)
οἴομαι or οἶμαι, (imperfect) ᾤμην or
  ᾠόμην, οἰήσομαι, ᾠήθην I think
  (23)
οἷος, οἵᾱ, οἷον (such) as (26)
οἷός τ' εἰμί I am able (25)
οἷς, οἰός, ὁ or ἡ sheep
οἴχομαι, ᾤχετο (present in perfect sense)
  I have gone, departed; (imperfect in
  pluperfect sense) I had gone, departed (31)
ὀκτώ eight (8)
ὄλβιος, ὀλβίᾱ, ὄλβιον happy, blest,
  prosperous (24)
ὄλβος, ὄλβου, ὁ happiness, bliss,
  prosperity (28)
ὀλίγιστος, ὀλιγίστη, ὀλίγιστον
  smallest; (plural) fewest (14, 24)
ὀλίγος, ὀλίγη, ὀλίγον small; (plural)
  few (14, 24)
ὁλκάς, ὁλκάδος, ἡ merchant ship (30)
ὅλος, ὅλη, ὅλον whole, entire (31)
Ὄλυμπος, Ὀλύμπου, ὁ Mount
  Olympus (26)
ὅμῑλος, ὁμίλου, ὁ crowd (12)
ὅμοιος, ὁμοίᾱ, ὅμοιον (+ dat.) like (21)
ὅμως nevertheless (8)
ὄνειρος, ὀνείρου, ὁ dream (26)
ὄνομα, ὀνόματος, τό name (7)
  ὀνόματι by name, called (7)
ὀνομάζω, ὀνομάσω, ὠνόμασα,
  ὠνόμακα, ὠνόμασμαι, ὠνομάσθην
  I name, call (26)
ὄπισθε(ν) (adverb or preposition + gen.)
  behind (27)
ὀπίσω backward (27)
ὁπλίτης, ὁπλίτου, ὁ hoplite (14)
ὅπλα, ὅπλων, τά (plural) weapons (30)
ὁπόθεν from where (26)
ὅποι to what place, where (26)
ὁποῖος, ὁποίᾱ, ὁποῖον (such) as (26)
ὁπόσος, ὁπόση, ὁπόσον as great as, as

much as, how much; (*plural*) as many as, how many (16, 26)

ὁπόταν (+ *subjunctive*) when(ever) (22, 23)

ὁπότε when (23, 26)

ὁπότερος, ὁποτέρᾱ, ὁπότερον which of two (26)

ὅπου where (14, 26)

ὅπως as, just as, how; (+ *subjunctive*) so that, in order to; (+ *future indicative*) that (22, 24, 26)

ὁράω, (*imperfect*) ἑώρων, ὄψομαι, εἶδον, ἑόρᾱκα *or* ἑώρᾱκα, ἑώρᾱμαι *or* ὦμμαι, ὤφθην I see (5, 11, 29)

ὀργή, ὀργῆς, ἡ anger (20)

ὀργίζομαι, ὀργιοῦμαι *or* ὀργισθήσομαι, ὤργισμαι, ὠργίσθην I grow angry (at + *dat.*), am angry (13, 21)

ὀργίζω, ὤργισα I make someone angry

ὀρθός, ὀρθή, ὀρθόν straight, right, correct (12)

     ὀρθῶς γιγνώσκω I am right (18)

ὅρκιον, ὁρκίου, τό oath; (*plural*) treaty (27)

ὅρια, ὁρίων, τά boundaries

ὅρκος, ὅρκου, ὁ oath (25)

ὁρμάω I set in motion, set out, start, rush; (*middle and passive, intransitive*) I set out, start, rush (7)

ὁρμέω I lie at anchor (30)

ὄρνῑς, τῆς ὄρνῑθος, ὁ *or* ἡ bird (31)

ὄρος, ὄρους, τό mountain, hill (5)

ὅς, ἥ, ὅ who, whose, whom, which, that (13, 26)

ὅσιος, ὁσίᾱ, ὅσιον holy, pious (17)

ὅσος, ὅση, ὅσον as great as, as much as, how much; (*plural*) as many as, how many (22, 26)

     ὅσοι, ὅσαι, ὅσα whoever, whatever

     πάντα ὅσα all that, whatever (22)

ὅσπερ, ἥπερ, ὅπερ (*emphatic forms of the relative pronoun* ὅς, ἥ, ὅ) who, whose, whom, which, that (13, 26)

ὅστις, ἥτις, ὅ τι anyone who, whoever, anything that, whatever; (*plural*) all who, all that (22, 26)

ὅταν (+ *subjunctive*) when(ever) (22)

ὅτε when (13, 26)

ὅτι that, because (5)

ὅτι τάχιστα as quickly as possible (12)

οὐ, οὐκ, οὐχ not (1)

     οὐ διὰ πολλοῦ not much later, soon (17)

     οὐ μόνον . . . ἀλλὰ καί not only . . . but also (15)

     οὐχί not, no! (7)

οὗ where (26)

οὗ (*pronoun*) (29)

οὐδαμοῦ nowhere (16)

οὐδέ and . . . not, nor, not even (5, 31)

οὐδείς, οὐδεμία, οὐδέν (*pronoun*) no

one, nothing; (*adjective*) no (7, 31)

     περὶ οὐδενὸς ποιοῦμαι I consider of no importance (28)

οὐδέν nothing, no (10)

οὐδέποτε never (22, 31)

οὐδεπώποτε never yet (31)

οὐδέτερος, οὐδετέρᾱ, οὐδέτερον neither (27, 31)

οὐκέτι no longer (3, 31)

οὔκουν and so . . . not (18)

οὖν (*postpositive*) and so (1)

οὗπερ where (26)

οὔπω not yet (31)

οὐρανός, οὐρανοῦ, ὁ sky, heaven (9)

οὔτε . . . οὔτε neither . . . nor (5, 31)

οὗτος, αὕτη, τοῦτο this; (*plural*) these (14, 26)

οὕτω(ς) so, thus (2, 6, 26)

οὐχί (*an emphatic form of* οὐ, οὐκ, οὐχ) not, no (6)

ὀφθαλμός, ὀφθαλμοῦ, ὁ eye (7)

ὀψέ late (17)

Π

παιδαγωγός, παιδαγωγοῦ, ὁ slave who accompanied a boy to school and back home as a tutor

παίδευσις, παιδεύσεως, ἡ education (24)

παιδεύω, παιδεύσω, ἐπαίδευσα, πεπαίδευκα, πεπαίδευμαι, ἐπαιδεύθην I educate (24)

παθεῖν (*aorist infinitive of* πάσχω)

παῖς, παιδός, ὁ *or* ἡ boy, girl, child (3)

πάλαι long ago (18)

     πάλαι εἰσίν they have been for a long time now (18)

παλαιός, παλαιά, παλαιόν old, of old (24)

Πάνορμος, Πανόρμου, ὁ Panormus (30)

πανταχοῦ everywhere (15)

πάνυ altogether, very, exceedingly (27)

πάππας, πάππου, ὁ father, papa (6)

πάππος, πάππου, ὁ grandfather (5)

παρά (+ *gen.*) from; (+ *dat.*) at the house of; (+ *acc.*) to, along, past (11, 24, 30, 31)

παραβοηθέω (+ *dat.*) I come to aid (30)

παραγίγνομαι I arrive (14)

παραδίδωμι I hand over, give (18)

παραινέω, παραινέσω, παρήνεσα, παρήνεκα, παρήνημαι, παρηνέθην (+ *dat. and infinitive*) I advise (someone to do something) (19)

παρακαλέω I summon (27)

παραπλέω I sail by, sail past, sail along (29)

παρασκευάζω, παρασκευάσω, παρεσκεύασα, παρεσκεύασμαι (I am ready) I prepare; (*middle*) I prepare myself, get ready (*often followed by* ὡς + *future participle*) (7)

παρασκευή, παρασκευῆς, ἡ
preparation (29)
παρατίθημι I put beside, serve
πάρειμι, (imperfect) παρῆν I am
present, am here, am there; (+ dat.) I am
present at, am present with (2)
παρέρχομαι I go past, come forward (to
speak) (17)
παρέχω I provide, give (6)
παρθένος, παρθένον virgin, chaste (9)
παρθένος, παρθένου, ἡ maiden,
girl (6)
Παρθένος, Παρθένου, ἡ the
Maiden, the goddess Athena (9)
Παρθενών, Παρθενῶνος, ὁ the
Parthenon, temple of Athena on the
Acropolis in Athens (8)
παρίσταμαι, παρέστην, παρέστηκα
(+ dat.) I stand near, stand by, help (28)
πᾶς, πᾶσα, πᾶν all, every (7)
πάσχω, πείσομαι, ἔπαθον, πέπονθα I
suffer, experience (5, 11, 26)
πατήρ, πατρός, ὁ father (3)
Πάτραι, Πατρῶν, αἱ Patrae (29)
πατρίς, πατρίδος, ἡ fatherland (15)
Παυσανίᾱς, Παυσανίου, ὁ Pausanias
παύω, παύσω, ἔπαυσα, πέπαυκα,
πέπαυμαι, ἐπαύθην I stop; (middle,
intransitive) I stop (+ participle), cease
from (+ gen.) (7, 17)
πεδίον, πεδίου, τό plain (19)
πεζῇ on foot (21)
πεζός, πεζοῦ, ὁ infantry (27)
πείθω, πείσω, ἔπεισα, πέπεικα (I have
persuaded) or πέποιθα (I trust + dat.),
πέπεισμαι, ἐπείσθην I persuade;
(middle, present and future + dat.) I obey
(4, 6, 21)
πεῖρα, πείρᾱς, ἡ trial, attempt (23)
Πειραιεύς, Πειραιῶς, ὁ Piraeus, the
port of Athens (11)
πειράω, πειράσω, ἐπείρᾱσα,
πεπείρᾱκα, πεπείρᾱμαι, ἐπειρ ἅθην
(active or middle) I attempt, try (14, 18)
Πελοποννήσιοι, Πελοποννησίων, οἱ
Peloponnesians (21)
Πελοπόννησος, Πελοποννήσου, ἡ
the Peloponnesus (14)
πέμπτος, πέμπτη, πέμπτον fifth (8)
πέμπω, πέμψω, ἔπεμψα, πέπομφα,
πέπεμμαι, ἐπέμφθην I send (6, 19)
πέντε five (8)
πεζός, πεζή, πεζόν on foot (15)
πέπλος, πέπλου, ὁ robe, cloth (15)
περί (+ gen.) around, about, concerning;
(+ dat.) concerning; (+ acc.) around (7,
18, 21, 30)
περιάγω I lead around (25)
περιίσταμαι, περιστήσομαι,
περιέστην I stand around
Περικλῆς, Περικλέους, ὁ Pericles

περιμένω I wait for (30)
περιοράω I overlook, disregard (23)
περὶ οὐδενὸς ποιοῦμαι I consider of no
importance (28)
περιπέμπω I send around
περιπλέω I sail around
περὶ πολλοῦ ποιοῦμαι I consider of
great importance (24)
  περὶ πλείστου ποιοῦμαι I
  consider of greatest importance (24)
Πέρσαι, Περσῶν, οἱ the Persians (14)
Πέρσης, Πέρσου, ὁ Persian
Περσικός, Περσική, Περσικόν
Persian (15)
πεσεῖν (aorist infinitive of πίπτω)
πέφῡκα (perfect with present meaning) I
am by nature (28)
πίνω, πίομαι, ἔπιον, πέπωκα,
πέπομαι, ἐπόθην I drink (9)
πίπτω, πεσοῦμαι, ἔπεσον, πέπτωκα I
fall (3, 26)
πιστεύω, πιστεύσω, ἐπίστευσα,
πεπίστευκα, πεπίστευμαι,
ἐπιστεύθην (+ dat.) I trust, am
confident (in), believe (15, 17)
Πλάτων, Πλάτωνος, ὁ Plato (24)
πλεῖστος, πλείστη, πλεῖστον most,
very great; (plural) very many (12, 14,
24)
πλείων/πλέων (alternative forms for
either masculine or feminine), πλέον
(neuter) more (12, 14, 24)
πλέω, πλεύσομαι or πλευσοῦμαι,
ἔπλευσα, πέπλευκα I sail (6, 17)
πλῆθος, πλήθους, τό number,
multitude (14)
πλήν (+ gen.) except, except for (30)
πληρόω I fill (21)
πλοῖον, πλοίου, τό boat (29)
πλούσιος, πλουσίᾱ, πλούσιον rich
πλοῦτος, πλούτου, ὁ wealth (25)
πνεῦμα, πνεύματος, τό breeze (29)
Πνύξ, Πυκνός, ἡ the Pnyx, the hill in
Athens on which the Assemblies were
held (21)
ποθέν (enclitic) from some place (14, 26)
πόθεν; from where? (7, 14, 26)
ποθέω I long for (31)
ποι (enclitic) to some place (26)
ποῖ; to what place? where to? (14, 17, 26)
ποιέω I make, do (4)
  περὶ οὐδενὸς ποιοῦμαι I consider of
  no importance (28)
  περὶ πολλοῦ ποιοῦμαι I consider of
  great importance (24)
  περὶ πλείστου ποιοῦμαι I consider
  of greatest importance (24)
ποίημα, ποιήματος, τό poem
ποιητής, ποιητοῦ, ὁ poet (8)
ποιμήν, ποιμένος, ὁ shepherd (19)
ποῖος, ποίᾱ, ποῖον; of what kind? (26)

ποιός, ποιά, ποιόν (*enclitic*) of some kind (26)

πολεμέω I make war, go to war (21)

πολέμιος, πολεμία, πολέμιον hostile, enemy (14)

πολέμιοι, πολεμίων, οἱ the enemy (14)

πόλεμος, πολέμου, ὁ war (14)

πολιορκέω I besiege (16)

πόλις, πόλεως, ἡ city (7)

πολίτης, πολίτου, ὁ citizen (8)

πολλάκις many times, often (6)

πολλοί, πολλαί, πολλά many (3)

πολύς, πολλή, πολύ much; (*plural*) many (1, 3, 14, 24)

     διὰ πολλοῦ after a long time (19)

     περὶ πολλοῦ ποιοῦμαι I consider of great importance (24)

     πολύ far, by far (20)

πομπή, πομπῆς, ἡ procession (9)

πονέω I work (1)

πονηρίᾱ, πονηρίᾱς, ἡ fault, wickedness (24)

πόνος, πόνου, ὁ toil, work (1)

Πόντος, Πόντου, ὁ Pontus, the Black Sea

πορεύομαι, πορεύσομαι, πεπόρευμαι, ἐπορεύθην I go, walk, march, journey (6, 17)

πορθέω I sack (28)

πόσος, πόση, πόσον; how much? how big? (*plural*) how many? (16, 26)

ποσός, ποσή, ποσόν (*enclitic*) of some size (26)

ποταμός, ποταμοῦ, ὁ river (16)

πότε; when? (9, 14, 26)

ποτέ (*enclitic*) at some time, once, ever (10, 14, 26)

πότερον . . . ἤ (whether . . .) or (17)

πότερος, ποτέρᾱ, πότερον; which (of two)? (26)

που (*enclitic*) somewhere, anywhere (26)

ποῦ; where? (5, 14, 26)

ποῦ γῆς; where (in the world)? (16)

πούς, ποδός, ὁ foot

πρᾶγμα, πρᾱγματος, τό matter, trouble (18)

     πῶς ἔχει τὰ πράγματα; How are things? (18)

πρᾶξις, πρᾱξεως, ἡ deed (24)

πρᾱττω, πρᾱξω, ἔπρᾱξα, πέπρᾱγα, πέπρᾱγμαι, ἐπρᾱχθην I do, fare (14, 20)

     εὖ πρᾱττω I fare well, succeed

πρέσβυς, πρέσβεως, ὁ old man, ambassador; (*usually plural*) πρέσβεις, πρέσβεων, οἱ ambassadors (21)

πρίν (+ *infinitive*) before; (+ ἄν + *subjunctive*) until; (+ *indicative*) until (22, 27)

πρό (+ *gen.*) before (of time or place) (10)

προάγω I lead forward (21)

προβαίνω, (*imperfect*) προὔβαινον,

προβήσομαι, προὔβην I go forward

πρόγονος, προγόνου, ὁ ancestor (15)

προέρχομαι I go forward, advance (20)

προθῡμίᾱ, προθῡμίᾱς, ἡ eagerness

πρόκειμαι, προκείσομαι (+ *dat.*) I lie before (21)

προλέγω I proclaim (28)

πρός (+ *gen*) from, at the hand of; (+ *dat.*) at, near, by, in addition to; (+ *acc.*) to, toward, against, upon, with (i.e., in relation to) (1, 4, 11, 24, 26, 27)

προσβαίνω I approach (16)

προσβάλλω (+ *dat.* or + πρός + *acc.*) I attack (14)

προσβολή, προσβολῆς, ἡ attack (23)

προσδέχομαι I receive, admit, await, expect (22)

προσδοκάω I expect (31)

προσέρχομαι (+ *dat.* or πρός + *acc.*) I approach (11, 17)

πρόσθε(ν) before (of time or place) (31)

     εἰς τὸ πρόσθεν forward (31)

προσπίπτω (+ *dat.*) I fall against, fall on (29)

προσπλέω (+ *dat.*) I sail toward (15)

προστάττω I command (27)

προστρέχω I run toward (18)

προσχωρέω (+ *dat.*) I go toward, approach (3)

τῇ προτεραίᾳ on the day before (14)

πρότερος, προτέρᾱ, πρότερον former πρότερον formerly, before, earlier, first (17)

προχωρέω, προχωρήσω, προεχώρησα (*or* προὐχώρησα) I go forward, come forward, advance (6)

πρύμνη, πρύμνης, ἡ stern of a ship (29)

πρυτάνεις, πρυτάνεων, οἱ prytaneis, presidents (31)

πρῷρα, πρῷρᾱς, ἡ bow of a ship (29)

Πρωταγόρᾱς, Πρωταγόρου, ὁ Protagoras (24)

πρῶτος, πρώτη, πρῶτον first; (*as noun in plural*) leaders (5)

     πρῶτον first (4)

     τὸ πρῶτον at first

Πτερίᾱ, Πτερίᾱς, ἡ Pteria (27)

Πτέριοι, Πτερίων, οἱ Pterians (27)

Πῡθίᾱ, Πῡθίᾱς, ἡ the Pythia, the Delphic priestess of Apollo (27)

πύλη, πύλης, ἡ gate; (*plural*) double gates, pass (through the mountains) (6, 14)

πυνθάνομαι, πεύσομαι, ἐπυθόμην, πέπυσμαι I inquire, learn by inquiry, hear, find out about X (*acc.*) from Y (*gen.*) (26)

πῦρ, πυρός, τό fire (7)

πύργος, πύργου, ὁ tower (22)

πυρά, πυρᾱς, ἡ funeral pyre (28)

πώποτε ever (31)

πως (enclitic) somehow, in any way (14, 17, 26)

πῶς; how? (7, 14, 26)
πῶς ἔχετε τοῦ σίτου; How are you off for food? (19)
πῶς ἔχεις; How are you? (11)
πῶς ἔχει τὰ πράγματα; How are things? (18)

P

ῥᾴδιος, ῥᾳδίᾱ, ῥᾴδιον easy (4, 24)
ῥᾴθῡμος, ῥᾴθῡμον lazy (4)
ῥᾷστος, ῥᾴστη, ῥᾷστον easiest (24)
ῥᾴων, ῥᾷον easier (24)
ῥήγνῡμι, ῥήξω, ἔρρηξα, ἔρρωγα (I am broken), ἐρράγην I break (22)
ῥήτωρ, ῥήτορος, ὁ speaker, politician (21)
Ῥίον, Ῥίου, τό Rhion (Rhium), Headland
ῥυθμός, ῥυθμοῦ, ὁ rhythm (24)
ῥώμη, ῥώμης, ἡ strength (25)

Σ

Σαλαμίς, Σαλαμῖνος, ἡ Salamis (13)
Σάμος, Σάμου, ἡ Samos
Σάρδεις, Σάρδεων, αἱ; (Ionic) Σάρδιες, Σαρδίων, (acc.) Σάρδῑς, αἱ Sardis (25)
σαφῶς clearly (31)
σβέννῡμι, σβέσω, ἔσβεσα, ἔσβηκα (I have gone out), ἐσβέσθην I put out, extinguish
σεμνός, σεμνή, σεμνόν holy, august (18)
σημαίνω, σημανῶ, ἐσήμηνα, σεσήμασμαι, ἐσημάνθην I signal, sign, show (19)
σημεῖον, σημείου, τό sign (30)
σῑγάω I am silent (9)
σῑγή, σῑγῆς, ἡ silence (28)
Σικελίᾱ, Σικελίᾱς, ἡ Sicily
Σιμωνίδης, Σιμωνίδου, ὁ Simonides (15)
σῖτος, σίτου, ὁ grain, food, bread (1)
σκοπέω, σκέψομαι, ἐσκεψάμην ἔσκεμμαι I look at, examine, consider (11)
Σκυθίᾱ, Σκυθίᾱς, ἡ Scythia (16)
σμῑκρός, σμῑκρά, σμῑκρόν small (24)
Σόλων, Σόλωνος, ὁ Solon (25)
σός, σή, σόν your (singular) (5, 11)
σοφίᾱ, σοφίᾱς, ἡ wisdom (25)
σοφιστής, σοφιστοῦ, ὁ wise man, sophist (24)
σοφός, σοφή, σοφόν skilled, wise, clever (11)
Σπαρτιάτης, Σπαρτιάτου, ὁ Spartan (14)
σπείρω, σπερῶ, ἔσπειρα, ἔσπαρμαι, ἐσπάρην I sow (3)
σπένδω, σπείσω, ἔσπεισα, ἔσπεισμαι

I pour a libation; (middle) I make a treaty, make peace (by pouring a libation with the other party) (31)
σπεύδω, σπεύσω, ἔσπευσα, ἔσπευκα, ἔσπευσμαι I hurry (2, 21).
σπονδή, σπονδῆς, ἡ libation (10)
σπονδὴν ποιοῦμαι I make a libation
σπονδαί, σπονδῶν, αἱ (plural) peace treaty, truce (16)
σπονδὰς ποιοῦμαι I make a peace treaty, make a truce
σπουδή, σπουδῆς, ἡ haste, eagerness (15)
στάδιον, σταδίου, τό; (plural) τὰ στάδια or οἱ στάδιοι stade (8.7 stades = 1 mile) (23)
στέλλω, στελῶ, ἔστειλα, ἔσταλκα, ἔσταλμαι, ἐστάλην I send, equip, take down (sails) (29)
στενά, στενῶν, τά (plural) narrows, straits, mountain pass (13)
στενάζω, στενάξω, ἐστέναξα I groan (4)
στενός, στενή, στενόν narrow (14)
στόλος, στόλου, ὁ expedition, army, fleet (14)
στόμα, στόματος, τό mouth (31)
στράτευμα, στρατεύματος, τό army (27)
στρατεύω, στρατεύσω, ἐστράτευσα, ἐστράτευκα, ἐστράτευμαι (active or more frequently middle) I wage war, campaign (against + ἐπί + acc.) (16)
στρατηγός, στρατηγοῦ, ὁ general (15)
στρατιά, στρατιᾶς, ἡ army (21)
στρατιώτης, στρατιώτου, ὁ soldier (14)
στρατόπεδον, στρατοπέδου τό camp, army (22)
στρατός, στρατοῦ, ὁ army (14)
στρέφω, στρέψω, ἔστρεψα, ἔστραμμαι, (second aorist passive, intransitive and active in meaning) ἐστράφην I turn
στυγέω I hate (31)
σύ you (singular) (3)
συγκαλέω I call together
συλλαμβάνω I catch, arrest
συλλέγω, συλλέξω, συνέλεξα, συνείλοχα, συνείλεγμαι, συνελέγην I collect, gather (19)
συμβάλλω (+ dat.) I join battle with (14)
σύμβουλος, συμβούλου, ὁ adviser
συμμαχίᾱ, συμμαχίᾱς, ἡ alliance (27)
σύμμαχος, συμμάχου, ὁ ally (16)
συμπέμπω I send with
συμπίπτω (+ dat.) I clash with (15)
συμπλέω I sail with
συμφορά, συμφορᾶς, ἡ misfortune, disaster (16)

σύν (+ dat.) with (17)
συναγείρω (transitive) I gather; (middle, intransitive) I gather together (16)
συνάγω I bring together, compress (29)
συνέρχομαι I come together (14)
σὺν θεοῖς God willing, with luck (17)
συνθήκη, συνθήκης, ἡ compact
συνίημι (+ gen. of person, acc. of thing) I understand (24)
συντρέχω I run together
σφάζω, σφάξω, ἔσφαξα, ἔσφαγμαι, ἐσφάγην I slay (30)
Σφίγξ, Σφιγγός, ἡ Sphinx
σφόδρα very much (31)
σφῶν (pronoun) (29)
σῴζω, σώσω, ἔσωσα, σέσωκα, σέσωσμαι, ἐσώθην I save (6)
σῶμα, σώματος, τό body (24)
σωφροσύνη, σωφροσύνης, ἡ moderation, self-discipline, good sense (24)
σώφρων, σῶφρον wise, prudent, well-behaved (7)

T

τάξις, τάξεως, ἡ rank, position (29)
ταράττω, ταράξω, ἐτάραξα, τετάραγμαι, ἐταράχθην I confuse (29)
ταραχή, ταραχῆς, ἡ confusion (29)
τάττω, τάξω, ἔταξα, τέταχα, τέταγμαι, ἐτάχθην I marshal, draw up in battle array (23)
τάφρος, τάφρου, ἡ ditch
ταχέως quickly (4)
  τάχιστα very quickly, most quickly (12)
  ὡς τάχιστα as quickly as possible (12)
τάχιστος, ταχίστη, τάχιστον quickest, swiftest (24)
τάχος, τάχους, τό speed
  κατὰ τάχος quickly (27)
ταχύς, ταχεῖα, ταχύ quick, swift (13, 18, 24)
τε and (5)
  τε . . . καί or τε καί both . . . and (3)
τείχισμα, τειχίσματος, τό wall, fort
τεῖχος, τείχους, τό wall (12)
τέκνον, τέκνου, τό child (20)
τεκών, τεκόντος, ὁ parent (24)
  τεκόντες, τεκόντων, οἱ (plural) parents (10)
τελευταῖος, τελευταίᾱ, τελευταῖον last (21)
τελευτάω I end, bring to an end, come to an end, die (16)
τελευτή, τελευτῆς, ἡ end (25)
Τέλλος, Τέλλου, ὁ Tellus (25)
τέλος in the end, finally (8)
τέμενος, τεμένους, τό sacred precinct (17)
τέμνω, τεμῶ, ἔτεμον, τέτμηκα,

τέτμημαι, ἐτμήθην I cut, ravage (23)
τέρπομαι, τέρψομαι, ἐτερψάμην I enjoy myself; (+ dat. or participle) I enjoy (9)
τέταρτος, τετάρτη, τέταρτον fourth (8)
τετταράκοντα forty
τέτταρες, τέτταρα four (8)
τῇδε here
τήμερον today (20)
τῇ ὑστεραίᾳ on the next day (8)
τῇ προτεραίᾳ on the day before (14)
τί; what? (4)
τίθημι, (imperfect) ἐτίθην, θήσω, ἔθηκα (infinitive) θεῖναι, (participle) θείς, τέθηκα, τέθειμαι, ἐτέθην I put, place (18, 31)
τῑμάω, τῑμήσω, ἐτίμησα, τετίμηκα, τετίμημαι, ἐτῑμήθην I honor (6, 18)
τῑμή, τῑμῆς, ἡ honor (21)
Τῑμοκράτης, Τῑμοκράτου, ὁ Timocrates (30)
τίνα γνώμην ἔχεις; What do you think? (18)
τις (indefinite pronoun, enclitic) someone, something, anyone, anything; (indefinite adjective, enclitic) a certain, a, some, any (7, 26)
τίς; (interrogative pronoun) who? (interrogative adjective) which . . . ? what . . . ? (7, 26)
τοιόσδε, τοιάδε, τοιόνδε such, of this kind, such as the following (21, 26)
τοιοῦτος, τοιαύτη, τοιοῦτο such, of this kind (21, 26)
τολμάω I dare (18)
τοξότης, τοξότου, ὁ archer (31)
τόπος, τόπου, ὁ place (20)
τοσόσδε, τοσήδε, τοσόνδε so great; (plural) so many (22, 26)
τοσοῦτος, τοσαύτη, τοσοῦτο so great; (plural) so many, so great (3, 26)
τότε then (12, 26)
τραχύς, τραχεῖα, τραχύ rough (18, 19)
τρεῖς, τρία three (8)
τρέπω, τρέψω, ἔτρεψα, τέτροφα, τέτραμμαι, ἐτράπην I turn, put to flight; (middle, intransitive) I turn myself, turn, flee; (second aorist passive) I turned, fled (10)
τρέχω, δραμοῦμαι, ἔδραμον, δεδράμηκα, δεδράμημαι I run, sail (5, 27)
τριάκοντα thirty (16)
τριᾱκόσιοι, τριᾱκόσιαι, τριᾱκόσια three hundred
τριήρης, τριήρους, ἡ trireme (13)
τρίτος, τρίτη, τρίτον third (8)
Τροίᾱ, Τροίᾱς, ἡ Troy (7)
τρόπαιον, τροπαίου, τό trophy (29)
τροπή, τροπῆς, ἡ turn, turning, rout (of

the enemy) (30)

τρόπος, τρόπου, ὁ manner, way (21)

τυγχάνω, τεύξομαι, ἔτυχον, τετύχηκα (+ gen.) I hit, hit upon, get; (+ participle) I happen to (17, 30)

τύπτω, τυπτήσω I strike (6, 19)

τυφλός, τυφλή, τυφλόν blind (11)

τύχη, τύχης, ἡ chance, luck, fortune (15)

τῷ ὄντι in truth (13)

Υ

ὕδωρ, ὕδατος, τό water (10)

ὑγιής, ὑγιές healthy (18)

υἱός, υἱοῦ, ὁ son (24)

ὕλη, ὕλης, ἡ woods, forest (19)

ὑμεῖς you (plural)

ὑμέτερος, ὑμετέρᾱ, ὑμέτερον your (plural)

ὑπάρχω I am, exist, am ready (22)

ὑπεκφεύγω I escape (30)

ὑπέρ (+ gen.) on behalf of, for, above; (+ acc.) over, above (8, 18)

ὑπηρέτης, ὑπηρέτου, ὁ servant, attendant (17)

ὕπνος, ὕπνου, ὁ sleep (18)

ὑπό (+ gen.) by (of agent), because of; (+ dat.), under; (+ acc.) at (of time) (5, 22, 30)

ὑποκρούω I interrupt

ὑπομένω I await (an attack), stand firm (30)

ὑποχωρέω I retire

Ὑροιάδης, Ὑροιάδου, ὁ Hyroeades

ὗς, ὑός, ὁ wild boar

ὑστεραίᾳ (see τῇ ὑστεραίᾳ)

ὕστερον later (16)

Φ

φαγεῖν (aorist infinitive of ἐσθίω)

φαίνω, φανῶ, ἔφηνα I show (22, 26)

φαίνομαι, φανήσομαι or φανοῦμαι, πέφηνα, ἐφάνην (+ infinitive) I appear, seem; (+ participle) I am shown to be, proved to be, am clearly (12, 20, 22, 31)

Φάληρον, Φαλήρου, τό Phalerum, the old harbor of Athens (14)

φᾱσί(ν) (postpositive enclitic) they say (6)

Φειδίᾱς, Φειδίου, ὁ Pheidias, the great Athenian sculptor (9)

φείδομαι, φείσομαι, ἐφεισάμην (+ gen.) I spare (27)

φέρω, οἴσω, ἤνεγκα or ἤνεγκον, ἐνήνοχα, ἐνήνεγμαι, ἠνέχθην I carry, (of roads) lead (1, 28)

φεῦ (often used with gen. of cause) alas! (10)

φεύγω, φεύξομαι, ἔφυγον, πέφευγα I flee, escape (5, 20)

φήμη, φήμης, ἡ saying, report, voice, message (26)

φημί (postpositive enclitic), φήσω, ἔφησα I say (3, 23)

οὐ φημί I deny

φᾱσί(ν) (postpositive enclitic) they say (6)

φησί(ν) (postpositive enclitic) he/she says (3)

φθάνω, φθήσομαι, ἔφθασα or ἔφθην (+ acc. and/or participle) I anticipate, do something before someone else (20, 30)

φιλαίτερος, φιλαιτέρᾱ, φιλαίτερον (irregular comparative of φίλος) dearer (18, 24)

φιλέω, φιλήσω, ἐφίλησα, πεφίληκα, πεφίλημαι, ἐφιλήθην I love (1, 18)

Φίλιππος, Φιλίππου, ὁ Philip (3)

φίλος, φίλη, φίλον dear, friendly; (as noun) friend (4, 24)

φίλτατος, φιλτάτη, φίλτατον or φιλαίτατος, φιλαιτάτη, φιλαίτατον (irregular superlatives of φίλος) dearest (18, 24)

φοβέομαι, (imperfect; usually used for fearing in past time) ἐφοβούμην, φοβήσομαι, πεφόβημαι, ἐφοβήθην I fear, am afraid of (something or someone), am frightened, am afraid (6)

φόβος, φόβου, ὁ fear, panic (19)

φοιτάω I go, visit (24)

φονεύς, φονέως, ὁ murderer

φονεύω, φονεύσω, ἐφόνευσα, πεφόνευκα, πεφόνευμαι, ἐφονεύθην I slay (26)

φόνος, φόνου, ὁ murder (26)

Φορμίων, Φορμίονος, ὁ Phormio (29)

φράζω, φράσω, ἔφρασα, πέφρακα, πέφρασμαι, ἐφράσθην I tell of, show, explain; (middle and aorist passive in middle sense) I think about, consider (14, 21)

φρονέω I think, am minded (17)

φροντίζω, φροντιῶ, ἐφρόντισα, πεφρόντικα I worry, care (12)

φρουρέω I guard (29)

φρούριον, φρουρίου, τό garrison (23)

Φρύγιος, Φρυγίᾱ, Φρύγιον Phrygian

φυγή, φυγῆς, ἡ flight (15)

φυλακή, φυλακῆς, ἡ guard, garrison (22)

φύλαξ, φύλακος, ὁ guard (26)

φυλάττω, φυλάξω, ἐφύλαξα, πεφύλαχα, πεφύλαγμαι (I am on my guard), ἐφυλάχθην I guard (5, 20)

φύσις, φύσεως, ἡ nature

φύω, φύσω, ἔφῡσα, ἔφῡν (I grew), πέφῡκα (I am by nature, am) I produce (28)

φωνέω I speak (27)

φωνή, φωνῆς, ἡ voice, speech (24)

X

χαῖρε, (*plural*) χαίρετε greetings! (4)

χαίρω, χαιρήσω, κεχάρηκα, ἐχάρην (I rejoiced) I rejoice; (+ *participle*) I am glad to (1, 28)

   χαίρειν κελεύω I bid farewell (12)

χαλεπός, χαλεπή, χαλεπόν difficult (1)

Χαλκίς, Χαλκίδος, ἡ Chalcis (29)

χαρίζομαι, χαριοῦμαι, ἐχαρισάμην, κεχάρισμαι (+ *dat.*) I show favor to, oblige (26)

χάρις, χάριτος, ἡ thanks, gratitude (18)

   χάριν ἀποδίδωμι (+ *dat.*) I render thanks, thank (18)

χειμών, χειμῶνος, ὁ storm, winter (7)

χείρ, χειρός, ἡ hand (8)

χείριστος, χειρίστη, χείριστον worst (24)

χείρων, χεῖρον worse (24)

χορός, χοροῦ, ὁ dance, chorus (4)

χράομαι, χρήσομαι, ἐχρησάμην, κέχρημαι, ἐχρήσθην (+ *dat.*) I use, enjoy, consult (an oracle) (14, 18)

χρή, (*imperfect*) ἔχρην it is necessary, one ought, must (+ *infinitive or acc. and infinitive*) (17)

χρήματα, χρημάτων, τά money (18)

χρήσιμος, χρησίμη, χρήσιμον useful (24)

χρησμός, χρησμοῦ, ὁ oracular response (27)

χρηστήριον, χρηστηρίου, τό (*often plural with singular meaning*) oracle (either the seat of the oracle or the oracular response) (27)

χρηστός, χρηστή, χρηστόν useful, good (24)

χρόνιος, χρονίᾱ, χρόνιον lengthy (21)

χρόνος, χρόνου, ὁ time (1)

χρῡσίον, χρῡσίου, τό gold coin, money, jewelry (31)

χρῡσοῦς, χρῡσῆ, χρῡσοῦν golden (31)

χώρᾱ, χώρᾱς, ἡ land (21)

χωρέω I go, come (29)

χωρίον, χωρίου, τό place, district (23)

χῶρος, χώρου, ὁ place (23)

Ψ

ψευδής, ψευδές false (13)

   ψευδῆ, ψευδῶν, τά lies (13)

ψεύδομαι, ψεύσομαι, ἐψευσάμην, ἔψευσμαι I lie

ψηφίζομαι, ψηφιοῦμαι, ἐψηφισάμην, ἐψήφισμαι I vote (21)

ψῡχή, ψῡχῆς, ἡ soul (17)

Ω

ὦ Ζεῦ O Zeus (3)

ὧδε thus (26)

ὦμος, ὤμου, ὁ shoulder (19)

ὡς (*adverb*) how; (*conjunction*) as, when, just as, that; (+ *future participle expressing purpose*) to ... (6, 13, 14, 17, 23, 26, 28)

   ὡς δοκεῖ as it seems (13)

ὥς thus (26)

ὥσπερ as, just as, how, as if (+ *participle*) (8, 26, 31)

ὡς τάχιστα as quickly as possible (12)

ὥστε (+ *infinitive or indicative*) so that, that (5, 29)

ὠφελέω I help, benefit (11)

ENGLISH TO GREEK VOCABULARY

Note: This English to Greek vocabulary is provided merely as a reminder of approximate Greek equivalents of English words. For further information about the Greek words, you must consult the Greek to English vocabulary and the readings and grammar sections in the various chapters of this book.

This list contains all words needed for the English to Greek exercises.

A

a τις
able, I am δύναμαι, οἷός τ᾽ εἰμί
about περί
above ὑπέρ
abroad, I am ἀποδημέω
Acarnania Ἀκαρνᾱνίᾱ
according to κατά
Achaea Ἀχαίᾱ
Achaeans Ἀχαιοί
Acharnae Ἀχαρναί
Acharnians Ἀχαρνῆς
admiral ναύαρχος
admire, I θαυμάζω
Adrastus Ἄδρηστος
advance, I προέρχομαι, προχωρέω
advice βουλή
advise (someone to do something), I παραινέω
Aegean Sea Αἰγαῖος πόντος
Aegeus Αἰγεύς
Aeschylus Αἰσχύλος
afraid, don't be θάρρει
afraid (of), I am φοβέομαι
after a long time διὰ πολλοῦ
after κατά, μετά
afterwards μετά
again αὖ, αὖθις
against ἐπί, πρός
Agamemnon Ἀγαμέμνων
agora ἀγορά
alas! οἴμοι, φεῦ
all ἅπᾱς, πᾶς
all that ὅσος (plural)
alliance συμμαχίᾱ
allow, I ἐάω
allowed, being ἔξον
allowed, I am ἔξεστί μοι
allowed, it is ἔξεστι(ν)
ally σύμμαχος

alone μόνος
along κατά, παρά
already ἤδη
also καί
altar βωμός
although καίπερ
altogether πάνυ
always αἰεί
Alyattes Ἀλυάττης
am, I εἰμί
Amasis Ἄμασις
ambassadors πρέσβεις
among ἐν
ancestor of πρόγονος
and δέ, καί, τε
and not μηδέ
and so οὖν
and so . . . not οὔκουν
anger ὀργή
angry (at), I grow ὀργίζομαι
announce, I ἀγγέλλω
another ἄλλος
another, of one ἀλλήλων
answer, I ἀποκρῑνομαι
appear, I φαίνομαι
appoint, I καθίστημι
approach, I προσβαίνω, προσέρχομαι, προσχωρέω
Archidamus Ἀρχίδᾱμος
Arge (name of a dog) Ἀργή
Argive Ἀργεῖος
Argus (name of a dog) Ἄργος
Ariadne Ἀριάδνη
army στόλος, στρατός, στρατιά
around περί
arrive (at), I ἀφικνέομαι, παραγίγνομαι
Artemisium Ἀρτεμίσιον
as great as ὅσος
as many as ὅσοι

as much as ὅσος
as quickly as possible ὡς τάχιστα
as ὡς
Asclepius Ἀσκλήπιος
Asia (Minor) Ἀσίᾱ
ask for X from Y, I δέομαι
ask, I αἰτέω, ἐρωτάω
assembly ἐκκλησίᾱ
at εἰς, ἐπί, κατά, ὑπό, πρός
at a loss, I am ἀπορέω
Athena Ἀθήνη, Παρθένος
Athenian Ἀθηναῖος
Athenians Ἀθηναῖοι
Athens Ἀθῆναι
Athens, in ἐν ταῖς Ἀθήναις
Athens, to Ἀθήναζε
at some time ποτέ
attack προσβολή
attack, I ἐμπῑπτω, ἐπεξέρχομαι, ἐπέρχομαι, ἐπιτίθεμαι, ἐπιχειρέω, προσβάλλω
attempt πεῖρα
attempt, I ἐπιχειρέω, πειράω, πειράομαι
attendant θεράπων, ὑπηρέτης
at the hand of πρός
Attic Ἀττικός
Attica Ἀττική
Atys Ἄτυς
await, I προσδέχομαι
away (from), I am ἄπειμι

B

Babylonians Βαβυλώνιοι
badly κακῶς
barbarian βάρβαρος
bathe, I λούομαι
battle μάχη

be so!, let it ἔστω
beautiful καλός
beautiful, most/very
  κάλλιστος
because διότι
because of διά, ἕνεκα
become, I γίγνομαι
before πρίν, πρό,
  πρότερον
begin, I ἄρχομαι, ἄρχω
beginning ἀρχή
behind ὄπισθε
benefit, I ὠφελέω
besiege, I πολιορκέω
best ἄριστος, βέλτιστος
better ἀμείνων, βελτίων,
  κρείττων
between ἐν μέσῳ
bid farewell, I χαίρειν
  κελεύω
big μέγας
big, very/biggest μέγιστος
bind, I δέω
Biton Βίτων
blame αἰτίᾱ
blame, I μέμφομαι
blame, to (adj.) αἴτιος
blest ὄλβιος
blind τυφλός
blood αἷμα
blow from, I ἐκπνέω
blow out, I ἐκπνέω
boar ὗς
board, I εἰσβαίνω,
  ἐπεισβαίνω, ἐπιβαίνω
boat πλοῖον
body σῶμα
Boeotia Βοιωτίᾱ
Boeotians Βοιωτοί
book βιβλίον
both . . . and καί . . . καί,
  τε . . . καί
both ἀμφότερος
bow of a ship πρῷρα
boy παῖς
brave ἀνδρεῖος
bravely ἀνδρείως
bread σῖτος
bright λαμπρός
brilliant λαμπρός
bring in, I εἰσφέρω,
  εἰσκομίζω
bring out, I ἐκκομίζω
bring to an end, I τελευτάω
bring together, I συνάγω
bring, I διακομίζω,
  κομίζω
brother ἀδελφός
burn, I καίω
bury, I θάπτω
but ἀλλά, δέ

by ὑπό, πρός
by far πολύ
by land κατὰ γῆν
by night νυκτός
by sea κατὰ θάλατταν
Byzantium Βυζάντιον

C

call upon, I ἐπικαλέομαι
call, I καλέω, ὀνομάζω
called ὀνόματι
camel κάμηλος
camp στρατόπεδον
campaign against, I
  στρατεύω
campaign, I στρατεύομαι
can, I δύναμαι, ἔξεστί
  μοι
capable δυνατός, ἱκανός
captain: see ship's captain
care for, it is a μέλει
care, I φροντίζω
carry out, I ἐκφέρω,
  ἐκκομίζω
carry, I φέρω
catch, I καταλαμβάνω
caught, I am ἁλίσκομαι
cause αἰτίᾱ
cavalry ἱππικόν, ἵππος
cavalryman ἱππεύς
cease from, I παύομαι
certain, a τις
certainly μάλιστά γε
Chalcis Χαλκίς
chance τύχη
chance, I τυγχάνω
change my mind, I
  μεταγιγνώσκω
chase, I διώκω
child παῖς, τέκνον
chorus χορός
Cimon Κίμων
circle κύκλος
citadel ἀκρόπολις
citizen πολίτης
city center ἀγορά
city ἄστυ, πόλις
clash with, I συμπίπτω
clean καθαρός
clear δῆλος
clear, it is δῆλόν ἐστι(ν)
Cleobis Κλέοβις
climb, I ἀναβαίνω
cloth πέπλος
cloud νεφέλη
Cnemus Κνῆμος
collect, I συλλέγω
come, I ἔρχομαι
come after, I ἐπιγίγνομαι
come down, I καταβαίνω,
  κατέρχομαι

come forward (to speak), I
  παρέρχομαι
come forward, I προχωρέω
come in, I εἰσβαίνω,
  εἰσέρχομαι
come on! ἄγε
come out (of), I ἐκβαίνω
come out, I ἐξέρχομαι
come to aid, I ἐπιβοηθέω,
  παραβοηθέω
come to an end, I τελευτάω
come together, I
  συνέρχομαι
come to help, I βοηθέω
come upon, I ἐπέρχομαι
come! ἐλθέ
come, I have ἥκω
compel, I ἀναγκάζω
comrade ἑταῖρος
concerning περί
confident, I am θαρρέω,
  πιστεύω
confuse, I ταράττω
confusion ταραχή
consider of great
  importance, I περὶ
  πολλοῦ ποιοῦμαι
consider of no importance, I
  περὶ οὐδενὸς ποιοῦμαι
consider, I σκοπέω
consult (an oracle)
  χράομαι
contend, I ἀγωνίζομαι
contest ἀγών
control, I κρατέω
converse with, I
  διαλέγομαι
Corinth Κόρινθος
Corinthians Κορίνθιοι
corpse νεκρός
correct ὀρθός
Council βουλή
country, in the ἐν τοῖς
  ἀγροῖς
country, to the εἰς τοὺς
  ἀγρούς
courage ἀρετή
cowardice δειλίᾱ
cowardly δειλός
Crete Κρήτη
Crisean Κρισαῖος
Croesus Κροῖσος
cross, I διαβαίνω,
  διαβάλλω
crowd ὅμιλος
cry, I δακρύω
custom νόμος
cut off, I ἀπολαμβάνω
cut, I τέμνω
Cyclopes, the Κύκλωπες

Cyclops Κύκλωψ
Cyllene Κυλλήνη
Cyprus Κύπρος
Cyrus Κῦρος

D

dance χορός
danger κίνδυνος
dare, I τολμάω
daughter θυγάτηρ
dawn ἕως
dawn, at ἅμα ἕῳ, ἐπὶ τὴν ἕω
day ἡμέρᾱ
day before, on the τῇ προτεραίᾳ
day, on the next τῇ ὑστεραίᾳ
dear φίλος
death θάνατος
decide, if you εἴ σοι δοκεῖ
decided, he ἔδοξεν αὐτῷ
dedicate, I ἀνατίθημι
deed ἔργον, πρᾶξις
deep βαθύς
defeat, I νῑκάω
defend myself, I ἀμύνομαι
deliberate, I βουλεύομαι
delighted, I am ἥδομαι
Delphi Δελφοί
deme δῆμος
deny, I οὐ φημί
deserted ἔρημος
despair ἀθῡμίᾱ
despise, I καταφρονέω
destroy, I διαφθείρω, καταλύω
Dicaeopolis Δικαιόπολις
die, I ἀποθνῄσκω, τελευτάω
difference, it makes a διαφέρει
difficult χαλεπός
difficulty ἀπορίᾱ
difficulty, with μόλις
din θόρυβος
dinner δεῖπνον
Dionysus Διόνῡσος
direction of, in the ἐπί
disaster συμφορά
disband (an army), I διαλύω
disembark, I ἐκβαίνω
disorder ἀταξίᾱ
disorder, in οὐδενὶ κόσμῳ
disordered ἄτακτος
distant (from), I am ἀπέχω
distressed, I am βαρύνομαι
do, I ἐργάζομαι, ποιέω, πράττω
doctor ἰᾱτρός

Dodona Δωδώνη
dog κύων
don't . . . any longer μηκέτι
don't μή
door θύρᾱ
double gates πύλαι
down κατά, κάτω
drachma δραχμή
drag, I ἕλκω
draw up in battle array, I τάττω
draw up, I τάττω
dream ὄνειρος
drink, I πίνω
drive, I ἐλαύνω
drive away, I ἀπελαύνω
drive in, I εἰσελαύνω
drive out, I ἐξελαύνω

dwelling οἴκησις
Dyme Δύμη

E

each ἕκαστος
each of two ἑκάτερος
eath other ἀλλήλων
eagerness σπουδή
earth γῆ
easily ῥᾳδίως
easy ῥᾴδιος
eat, I δειπνέω, ἐσθίω
educate, I παιδεύω
education παίδευσις
Egypt Αἴγυπτος
Egyptians Αἰγύπτιοι
eight ὀκτώ
either . . . or ἤ . . . ἤ
Eleusis Ἐλευσίς
empire ἀρχή
empty κενός
encamp, I καθέζομαι, στρατοπεδεύω
end τελευτή
end to, I put an καταπαύω
end, I τελευτάω
end, in the τέλος
endure, I ἀνέχομαι
enemy ἐχθρός, πολέμιος
enemy, the πολέμιοι
enjoy (myself), I τέρπομαι
enjoy, I ἥδομαι
entertain, I ξενίζω
entrust, I ἐπιτρέπω
Ephialtes Ἐφιάλτης
Epidaurus Ἐπίδαυρος
equip, I ἐξαρτύω, στέλλω
err, I ἁμαρτάνω, ἐξαμαρτάνω
escape the notice of, I λανθάνω
escape, I διαφεύγω,

ὑπεκφεύγω, φεύγω
especially μάλιστα
Euboea Εὔβοια
Eurymedon River, the Εὐρυμέδων
evening ἑσπέρᾱ
ever ποτέ
every day καθ' ἡμέραν
every ἅπᾱς, πᾶς
everywhere πανταχοῦ
examine, I σκοπέω
exceedingly πάνυ
excellence ἀρετή
except for πλήν
exist, I ὑπάρχω
expect, I ἐλπίζω, προσδέχομαι
expectation ἐλπίς
expedition στόλος
experience, I πάσχω
explain, I φράζω
extreme ἔσχατος
eye ὀφθαλμός

F

fail, I ἐξαμαρτάνω
fall, I πίπτω
fall against, I προσπίπτω
fall down, I καταπίπτω
fall into, I ἐμπίπτω
fall (of night, etc.) γίγνεται
fall on, I ἐμπίπτω, προσπίπτω
fall out, I ἐκπίπτω
false ψευδής
family, of the οἰκεῖος
fare, I πράττω
farmer αὐτουργός
father πάππας, πατήρ
fatherland πατρίς
fault πονηρίᾱ
fear δέος, φόβος
fear, I φοβέομαι
festival ἑορτή
few (plural of ὀλίγος)
field ἀγρός
fierce καρτερός
fight (with), I μάχομαι
fight by sea, I ναυμαχέω
fill, I πληρόω
finally τέλος
find out, I ἐξευρίσκω
find, I εὑρίσκω
fire πῦρ
firm βέβαιος
first πρῶτος
first πρότερον, πρῶτον
five πέντε
flee (away), I ἀποφεύγω
flee (out), I ἐκφεύγω

flee, I καταφεύγω, φεύγω
fleet ναυτικόν, στόλος
flight φυγή
flocks μῆλα (plural)
flow in, I εἰσρέω
follow, I ἕπομαι
food σῖτος
foolish ἀνόητος
foot, on πεζῇ, πεζός
for γάρ, εἰς, ἐπί, ὑπέρ
for the sake of ἕνεκα
foreigner ξένος
forest ὕλη
formerly πρότερον
fortune τύχη
forty τετταράκοντα
four τέτταρες
fourth τέταρτος
free ἐλεύθερος
free, I ἐλευθερόω
freedom ἐλευθερίᾱ
friend φίλη, φίλος
frightfully δεινῶς
from ἀπό, πρός
from where ὅθεν, ὁπόθεν
funeral pyre πυρή
Furies, the Ἐρῑνύες
furthest ἔσχατος

G
garrison φρούριον
gather, I ἀγείρω, συλλέγω
gather (together), I
   συναγείρω
general στρατηγός
get into, I καθίσταμαι
get under way, I αἴρομαι
get up on, I ἐπιβαίνω
gift δῶρον
girl παρθένος
give back, I ἀποδίδωμι
give in, I ἐνδίδωμι
give, I δίδωμι,
   παραδίδωμι, παρέχω
glad, I am ἥδομαι
gladly ἀσμενῶς, ἡδέως
go, I βαίνω, εἰσβαίνω,
   ἔρχομαι, πορεύομαι,
   φοιτάω
go, I will εἶμι
go away, I ἀπέρχομαι,
   ἀποχωρέω
go forward, I προβαίνω,
   προχωρέω
go in, I εἰσέρχομαι
go out against, I
   ἐπεξέρχομαι
go out of, I ἐκβαίνω
go out, I ἐξέρχομαι
go over, I ἐπέρχομαι
go through, I διέρχομαι

go to war, I πολεμέω
go toward, I προσχωρέω
go up (onto), I ἀναβαίνω
go up on, I ἐπεισβαίνω
go up, I ἀνέρχομαι
go, to ἰέναι
God willing σὺν θεοῖς
god δαίμων, θεός
goddess θεός
going out ἔξοδος
going to, I am μέλλω
good ἀγαθός, χρηστός
good luck εὐδαιμονίᾱ
good order κόσμος
good! εὖ γε
Gordias Γορδίης
grain σῖτος
grandfather πάππος
gratitude χάρις
Greece Ἑλλάς
Greek(s) Ἕλλην(ες)
Greeks Ἀχαιοί
greetings! χαῖρε
grieve, I λῡπέω, ὀδύρομαι
groan, I ἀναστενάζω,
   στενάζω
ground γῆ
grow angry, I ὀργίζομαι
guard φυλακή, φύλαξ
guard, I φρουρέω,
   φυλάττω
gulf κόλπος
gymnastics γυμναστική

H
Halys River Ἅλυς
hand χείρ
happen, I γίγνομαι,
   τυγχάνω
happiness εὐδαιμονίᾱ
happy ὄλβιος
harbor λιμήν
harm, I βλάπτω
harmony ἀρμονίᾱ
haste σπουδή
have, I ἔχω
he, and ὁ δέ
head κεφαλή
heal, I ἀκέομαι
healthy ὑγιής
hear, I ἀκούω,
   πυνθάνομαι
heaven οὐρανός
Hellas Ἑλλάς
help βοήθεια
help, I βοηθέω, ὠφελέω
Hera Ἥρᾱ
herald κῆρυξ
here, to δεῦρο, ἐνταῦθα
here, I am πάρειμι
Herodotus Ἡρόδοτος

hide, I κρύπτω
hill λόφος, ὄρος
him αὐτόν
himself (see ἐμαυτοῦ)
hit upon, I τυγχάνω
hit, I τυγχάνω
hold out against, I ἀντέχω
hold, I ἔχω
hold a festival, I ἑορτὴν
   ποιοῦμαι
holy ἱερός, ὅσιος
home οἰκίᾱ, οἶκος
home, at κατ' οἶκον,
   οἴκοι
home, to, for οἴκαδε
homeward οἴκαδε
honor, I τῑμάω
honor τῑμή
hope ἐλπίς
hope, I ἐλπίζω
hoplite ὁπλίτης
horse ἵππος
horseman ἱππεύς
hostile ἐχθρός, πολέμιος
house οἰκίᾱ, οἶκος,
   οἰκίον
house, of the οἰκεῖος
How are things? πῶς ἔχει
   τὰ πράγματα;
How are you off for food?
   πῶς ἔχετε τοῦ σίτου;
How are you? πῶς ἔχεις;
how many (plural of πόσος)
how much πόσος
how ὡς
how? πῶς;
however μέντοι
hundred, a ἑκατόν
hunt ἄγρᾱ
hunting ἄγρᾱ
hurry, I σπεύδω
husband ἀνήρ
Hyroeades Ὑροιάδης

I
I ἐγώ; (emphatic) ἔγωγε
idle ῥᾴθυμος
if εἰ, ἐάν
ill, I am νοσέω
immediately εὐθύς
impossible ἀδύνατος
in addition to πρός
in ἐν
in, I am ἔνειμι
incapable ἀδύνατος
increase, I αὐξάνω
indeed γε, δή, μάλιστά
   γε
infantry πεζός
inhabit, I οἰκέω
inhabitant ἔνοικος

inn οἰνοπώλιον
in order to ἵνα, ὅπως, ὡς
instead of ἀντί
intellect διάνοια
intend, I ἐν νῷ ἔχω,
μέλλω
intention γνώμη, διάνοια
in time ἐν καιρῷ
into εἰς
invade, I εἰσβάλλω
invasion εἰσβολή
inwards εἴσω (ἔσω)
Ionia Ἰωνίᾱ
Ionians Ἴωνες
is, he/she/it ἐστί(ν)
island νῆσος
Isthmus of Corinth Ἴσθμος
it αὐτόν, αὐτήν, αὐτό

J

join battle with, I
συμβάλλω
journey ὁδός
journey, I πορεύομαι
judge, I κρίνω
judgment γνώμη
just as ὥσπερ
just δίκαιος
justice δίκη

K

kill, I ἀποκτείνω,
κτείνω,
kindle, I καίω
kindly εὐμενής
king βασιλεύς
kingdom βασιλείᾱ
knock on (a door), I κόπτω
Knossos Κνωσσός
know, get to, I γιγνώσκω
know, I do not ἀγνοέω
know, I ἐπίσταμαι, οἶδα

L

labyrinth λαβύρινθος
Lacedaemonians, the
Λακεδαιμόνιοι
Laconian Λάκαινος
land γῆ, ἤπειρος, χώρᾱ
land, on or by κατὰ γῆν
large μακρός
last τελευταῖος
late ὀψέ
later μετά, ὕστερον
later, not much οὐ διὰ
πολλοῦ
laugh I γελάω
law νόμος
lazy ῥᾴθυμος
lead around, I περιάγω
lead forward, I προάγω
lead in, I εἰσηγέομαι

lead out, I ἐξάγω
lead, I ἄγω, ἡγέομαι; (of
roads) φέρω
leaders (plural of πρῶτος)
learn by inquiry, I
πυνθάνομαι
learn, I γιγνώσκω,
μανθάνω
leave behind, I καταλείπω
leave, I λείπω
left hand ἀριστερά
lengthy χρόνιος
Leonidas Λεωνίδης
let be, I ἐάω
let go, I ἀφίημι, μεθίημι
Leucadian Λευκάδιος
Leucas Λευκάς
libation σπονδή
lie at anchor, I ὁρμέω
lie before, I πρόκειμαι
lie down, I κατάκειμαι
lie, I κεῖμαι
lies ψευδῆ
life βίος, ζωή
lift, I αἴρω
light, I καίω
like ὅμοιος
lion λέων
listen (to), I ἀκούω
live, I οἰκέω, ζάω
long ago πάλαι
long μακρός, (of time)
τοσοῦτος
long time, after a διὰ
πολλοῦ
look down on, I καθοράω
look for, I ζητέω
look up, I ἀναβλέπω
look! ἰδού
look, I βλέπω
loosen, I λύω
loss, I am at a ἀπορέω
loss, state of being at a
ἀπορίᾱ
loudly μέγα
love, I φιλέω
luck τύχη
luck, with σὺν θεοῖς
Lydia Λῡδίᾱ
Lydian Λῡδιος
Lydians Λῡδοί
lyre player κιθαριστής

M

maiden παρθένος
mainland ἤπειρος
make, I ποιέω
make war, I πολεμέω,
πόλεμον ποιοῦμαι
man ἀνήρ, ἄνθρωπος
manner τρόπος
many πολλοί

many times πολλάκις
march away, I ἀπελαύνω
march, I ἐλαύνω,
πορεύομαι
marching forth ἔξοδος
marriage γάμος
marshal, I τάττω
master δεσπότης
matter πρᾶγμα
may, I ἔξεστί μοι
meanwhile ἐν τούτῳ
measure μέτρον
Medes Μῆδοι
Median Μηδικός
meet, I ἐντυγχάνω
Megara Μέγαρα
Melissa Μέλιττα
Memphis Μέμφις
merchant ἔμπορος
message φήμη
messenger ἄγγελος
Messenians Μεσσήνιοι
middle (of) μέσος
middle of, in the κατὰ
μέσον
military expedition ἔξοδος
mind νοῦς
minded, I am φρονέω
mine ἐμός
Minos Μῑνως
Minotaur Μῑνόταυρος
misfortune συμφορά
miss, I ἁμαρτάνω,
ἐξαμαρτάνω
mistake, I make a
ἁμαρτάνω
mistaken, I am ἁμαρτάνω
moderation σωφροσύνη
Molycrian Μολύκρειος
money ἀργύριον,
χρήματα
more μᾶλλον,
πλείων/πλέων
more, and what is καὶ δὴ
καί
most pleasantly ἥδιστα
most pleasurably ἥδιστα
most πλεῖστος
most sweetly ἥδιστα
mother μήτηρ
mount, I ἐπιβαίνω
Mount Etna Αἰτναῖον
ὄρος
Mount Olympus Ὄλυμπος
mountain ὄρος
move ἀνάστασις
move, I ἀνίσταμαι, κῑνέω
much πολύς
mule ἡμίονος
multitude πλῆθος
music μουσική

must δεῖ, χρή
my ἐμός
Mycale Μυκαλή
Mycenae Μυκῆναι
Myrrhine Μυρρίνη
Mysians Μῦσοί

N

name ὄνομα
name, by ὀνόματι
name, I ὀνομάζω
narrow στενός
nature, I am by πέφῡκα
Naupactus Ναύπακτος
near ἐγγύς, πρός
necessary, it is ἀνάγκη
  ἐστί(ν), δεῖ, χρή
necessity ἀνάγκη
neither . . . nor
  οὔτε . . . οὔτε
neither οὐδέτερος
never οὐδέποτε
nevertheless ὅμως
new νέος
night νύξ
Nike Νίκη
Nile Νεῖλος
nine ἐννέα
no longer μηκέτι, οὐκέτι
no μηδείς, οὐδείς,
  οὐδέν, οὐχί
no one μηδείς, οὐδείς
noble ἄριστος
nor μηδέ, μήτε, οὐδέ
not at all ἥκιστά γε
not only . . . but also οὐ
  μόνον . . . ἀλλὰ καί
not μή, οὐ, οὐκ, οὐχ,
  οὐχί
not, and μηδέ, οὐδέ
nothing μηδέν, οὐδέν
now ἤδη, νῦν
nowhere οὐδαμοῦ
number ἀριθμός, πλῆθος
numberless μῡρίοι

O

oar κώπη
oath ὅρκιον, ὅρκος
obey πείθομαι
obol ὀβολός
Odysseus Ὀδυσσεύς
offering, temple ἀνάθημα
often πολλάκις
Oinoe Ὀινόη
old γεραιός
old man γέρων
old, (of) παλαιός
olive tree ἐλάᾱ
olive ἐλάᾱ
on behalf of ὑπέρ
on foot πεζός

on the one hand . . . on the
  other hand . . . μέν . . . δέ
  . . .
on ἐν, ἐπί, πρός
one . . . the other, the ὁ μὲν
  ἕτερος . . . ὁ δὲ
  ἕτερος
one εἷς
one or the other (of two)
  ἕτερος
only μόνον, μόνος
onto εἰς, ἐπί
opinion γνώμη
oppose, I ἀντιόομαι
opposed ἐνάντιος
opposite ἐνάντιος
or ἤ
oracle μαντεῖον,
  χρηστήριον
oracular response χρησμός
order, I κελεύω
other ἄλλος
ought δεῖ, χρή
our ἡμέτερος
out of ἐκ
outside of ἐκτός, ἔξω
overlook, I περιοράω
overtake, I καταλαμβάνω
ox βοῦς

P

pain, cause, I λῡπέω
palace βασίλεια, οἰκίον
Panormus Πάνορμος
papa πάππας
parent τεκών
part μέρος
part, I διΐσταμαι
Parthenon Παρθενών
particular, and in καὶ δὴ
  καί
pass (through the
  mountains) πύλαι
pass over διαβάλλω
past παρά
patient, I am ἀνέχομαι
Patrae Πάτραι
Pausanias Παυσανίᾱς
pay μισθός
peace εἰρήνη
peace treaty σπονδαί
Peloponnesians
  Πελοποννήσιοι
Peloponnesus, the
  Πελοπόννησος
pelt, I βάλλω
penalty δίκη
people ἔθνος
people, the δῆμος
perhaps ἴσως
Pericles Περικλῆς

perplexity ἀπορίᾱ
Persian Περσικός
Persians, the Πέρσαι
persuade, I πείθω
Phalerum Φάληρον
Pheidias Φειδίᾱς
Philip Φίλιππος
Phormio Φορμίων
Phrygian Φρύγιος
Piraeus Πειραιεύς
pity, I οἰκτίρω
place τόπος, χώριον,
  χῶρος
place, I τίθημι
place, to another ἄλλοσε
place, to this ἐνθάδε
plague νόσος
plain πεδίον
plan βουλή
plan, I βουλεύομαι
Plato Πλάτων
play the lyre, I κιθαρίζω
pleasantly ἡδέως
pleasing, it is ἀρέσκει
plot against, I ἐπιβουλεύω
plow ἄροτρον
plow, I ἀροτρεύω
Pnyx, the Πνύξ
poet ποιητής
politician ῥήτωρ
ponder, I ἐνθῡμέομαι
Pontus Πόντος
position τάξις
possible δυνατός
possible, it is ἔξεστι(ν)
power δύναμις, κράτος
power over, I have κρατέω
powerful δυνατός
practice, I μελετάω
praise ἔπαινος
pray (to), I εὔχομαι
prayer εὐχή
preparation παρασκευή
prepare, I παρασκευάζω
present (at), I am πάρειμι
priest ἱερεύς
private person ἰδιώτης
privately ἰδίᾳ
probably κατ' εἰκός
procession πομπή
proclaim, I προλέγω
propitious ἵλαος
prosperity εὐδαιμονίᾱ
prosperous ὄλβιος
Protagoras Πρωταγόρᾱς
prove, I ἀποφαίνω
provide, I παρέχω
Pteria Πτερίᾱ
Pterians Πτέριοι
pupil μαθητής

pure καθαρός
purify, I καθαίρω
pursue, I διώκω, ἐπιδιώκω
put in, I εἰστίθημι
put out to sea, I ἀνάγομαι
put X upon Y, I ἐπιτίθημι
put, I τίθημι
Pythia, the Πῡθίᾱ

Q

quick ταχύς
quickly κατὰ τάχος,
  ταχέως
quickly, very/most
  τάχιστα
quiet, keep, I ἡσυχάζω
quietness ἡσυχίᾱ

R

race γένος
raise up, I αἴρω
rank τάξις
rather than μᾶλλον ἤ
ravage, I τέμνω
read, I ἀναγιγνώσκω
ready ἑτοῖμος
ready, I am ὑπάρχω
receive, I δέχομαι
refuse, I οὐκ ἐθέλω
regard to, with κατά
rejoice, I τέρπομαι,
  χαίρω
relate, I ἐξηγέομαι
reluctantly μόλις
remain in, I ἐμμένω
remain, I παραμένω
remember, I
  ἀναμιμνήσκομαι,
  μέμνημαι,
  μιμνήσκομαι
removal ἀνάστασις
repent, I μεταγιγνώσκω
report φήμη
resist, I ἀντέχω
responsibility αἰτίᾱ
responsible (for) αἴτιος
rest (of) ἄλλος
rest, I ἀναπαύομαι
retire, I ὑποχωρέω
retribution νέμεσις
return, I ἀναχωρέω,
  ἀποδίδωμι,
  ἐπανέρχομαι
revolt from, I ἀφίσταμαι
reward μισθός
rhythm ῥυθμός
ride horses, I ἱππεύω
right, I am ὀρθῶς
  γιγνώσκω
right δεξιός, ὀρθός
right hand δεξιά
right time, just at the εἰς

καιρόν
river ποταμός
road ὁδός
robe πέπλος
rough τραχύς
row, I ἐρέσσω
rule (over), I βασιλεύω
rule, I ἄρχω, κρατέω
run, I τρέχω
run together, I συντρέχω
run toward, I προστρέχω
rush, I ὁρμάομαι, ὁρμάω

S

sack, I πορθέω
sacred precinct τέμενος
sacrifice θυσίᾱ
sacrifice, I θύω
sad, I am λῡπέομαι
safe ἀσφαλής
said, he/she ἔφη
said, they ἔφασαν
sail, I πλέω, τρέχω
sail against, I ἐπιπλέω
sail around, I περιπλέω
sail away, I ἀποπλέω,
  ἐκπλέω
sail by, I παραπλέω
sail into, I εἰσπλέω
sail out, I ἐκπλέω
sail past, I παραπλέω
sail toward, I προσπλέω
sail with, I συμπλέω
sailor ναύτης
sails ἱστία
Salamis Σαλαμίς
same αὐτός
same time, at the ἅμα
Samos Σάμος
sanctuary of Asclepius
  Ἀσκληπιεῖον
Sardis Σάρδεις
savage ἄγριος
save, I σῴζω
say, I λέγω
say, they φᾱσί(ν)
saying φήμη
says, he/she φησί(ν)
scarcely μόλις
schoolmaster
  γραμματιστής
Scythia Σκυθίᾱ
sea battle ναυμαχίᾱ
sea θάλαττα
sea, by κατὰ θάλατταν
second δεύτερος
see, I βλέπω, θεάομαι,
  θεωρέω, ὁράω
seek, I ζητέω
seems (good), it δοκεῖ

seems good to you, if it εἴ
  σοι δοκεῖ
seems, as it ὡς δοκεῖ
self-discipline σωφροσύνη
send, I πέμπω, στέλλω
send around, I περιπέμπω
send away, I ἀποπέμπω,
  ἀφίημι
send for, I μεταπέμπομαι
send in, I ἐπιπέμπω
send off, I ἀποστέλλω
send out, I ἐκπέμπω
send X through Y, I
  διαπέμπω
separate, I διίσταμαι
servant θεράπων,
  ὑπηρέτης
set (something) up, I
  ἀνίστημι
set down, I κατατίθημι
set out, I αἴρομαι,
  ὁρμάομαι, ὁρμάω
set up, I ἀνατίθημι,
  ἵστημι
set up house, I
  κατασκευάζομαι
seven ἑπτά
shameful αἰσχρός
shepherd ποιμήν
ship ναῦς
ship's captain ναύκληρος
shoulder ὦμος
shout βοή
shout, I βοάω
show favor to, I χαρίζομαι
show, I ἀποφαίνω,
  δείκνυμι, δηλόω,
  φαίνω, φράζω
Sicily Σικελίᾱ
sick, I am κάμνω, νοσέω
sight-seeing θεωρίᾱ
sign σημεῖον
sign, I σημαίνω
signal, I σημαίνω
silence σῑγή
silent, I am σῑγάω
silver ἀργύριον
Simonides Σιμωνίδης
since ἐπεί, ἐπειδή
sink, I καταδύω
sit down, I καθέζομαι,
  καθίζομαι
sit, I κάθημαι
six ἕξ
size μέγεθος
skilled δεινός
sky οὐρανός
slave δοῦλος
slay, I σφάζω, φονεύω
sleep ὕπνος

sleep, I καθεύδω
slow βραδύς
slowly βραδέως
small μῑκρός, ὀλίγος,
σμικρός
so great τοσόσδε,
τοσοῦτος
so many (plural of)
τοσόσδε, τοσοῦτος
so οὕτω(ς)
so that . . . not ἵνα μή
so that ἵνα, ὅπως, ὥστε
soldier στρατιώτης
Solon Σόλων
some to some places, others to
other places ἄλλοι
ἄλλοσε
some ἔνιοι
somehow πως
sometime ποτέ
son υἱός (and see Chapter
19, Grammar 4)
soon δι᾽ ὀλίγου, οὐ διὰ
πολλοῦ
sophist σοφιστής
sorrowful, I am λῡπέομαι
soul ψῡχή
sow, I σπείρω
spare, I φείδομαι
Spartan Σπαρτιάτης
Spartans, the
Λακεδαιμόνιοι
speak, I ἀγορεύω, λέγω,
φωνέω
speaker ῥήτωρ
spear δόρυ
speech φωνή
Sphinx Σφίγξ
spirit δαίμων, θῡμός
spring ἔαρ, κρήνη
stade στάδιον
stand (something) up, I
ἀνίστημι
stand around, I
περιίσταμαι
stand near, I παρίσταμαι
stand over, I ἐφίσταμαι
stand up! ἀνάστηθι
stand up, I ἀνίσταμαι
start, I ὁρμάω
stay, I μένω
stern of a ship πρύμνη
still ἔτι
stone λίθος
stone, made of λίθινος
stood up, having ἀναστάς
stood up, I ἀνέστην
stop, I παύω
storm χειμών
story λόγος, μῦθος
straight εὐθύς, ὀρθός

straightway αὐτίκα
straits στενά
strength δύναμις, ῥώμη
strike with a ram, I
ἐμβάλλω
strike, I κόπτω, τύπτω
strong καρτερός, ἰσχῡρός
struggle ἀγών
study, I μελετάω
stupid ἀμαθής
subdue, I καταστρέφω
such as the following
τοιόσδε
such τοιοῦτος, τοιόσδε
suddenly ἐξαίφνης
suffer, I πάσχω
sufficient ἱκανός
suitable for ἐπιτήδειος
summon, I παρακαλέω
sun ἥλιος
suppliant ἱκέτης
suppose, I δήπου
survive, I παραμένω
sweetly ἡδέως
swift ταχύς

T

take, I ἄγω, αἱρέω,
κομίζω, λαμβάνω
take care for, I
ἐπιμελέομαι
take in, I ἐσκομίζω
take over or across
διακομίζω
take to heart ἐνθῡμέομαι
take to the field, I στρατεύω
taken, I am ἁλίσκομαι
talk to, I διαλέγομαι
teach, I διδάσκω
teacher διδάσκαλος
tell, I λέγω
tell (of), I φράζω
tell (someone to do
something), I κελεύω
tell! εἰπέ
Tellus Τέλλος
temple ἱερόν
ten δέκα
ten thousand μύριοι
terrible δεινός
terribly δεινῶς
than ἤ
thank, I χάριν ἀποδίδωμι
that ἐκεῖνος, ὅπως, ὅς,
ὅσπερ, ὅτι, ὥστε
Themistocles
Θεμιστοκλῆς
then ἐνταῦθα, ἔπειτα,
τότε
there ἐνταῦθα
there, to ἐκεῖσε
Thermopylae Θερμοπύλαι

Theseus Θησεύς
think it best, if you εἴ σοι
δοκεῖ
think, I γιγνώσκω,
νομίζω, οἴομαι,
φρονέω
think?, What do you τίνα
γνώμην ἔχεις;
third τρίτος
thirty τριάκοντα
this, these ὅδε, οὗτος
those (plural of) ἐκεῖνος
three τρεῖς
Thriasian Θριάσιος
through διά, κατά
throw, I βάλλω
throw out, I ἐκβάλλω
Thunderer Βρόμιος
thus οὕτω(ς)
tilled fields τὰ ἔργα
time χρόνος
time, (right) καιρός
Timocrates Τῑμοκράτης
tired, I am κάμνω
to εἰς, παρά, πρός
to blame (adj.) αἴτιος
to what place? ποῖ;
today τήμερον
together ἅμα
toil πόνος
tomorrow αὔριον
too καί
top (of) ἄκρος
to school εἰς διδασκάλων
toward ἐπί, πρός
tower πύργος
township δῆμος
treasure θησαυρός
tribe ἔθνος
trireme τριήρης
trophy τροπαῖον
trouble πρᾶγμα
Troy Τροίᾱ
true ἀληθής
trust, I πιστεύω
truth ἀλήθεια, ἀληθές,
ἀληθῆ
truth, in τῷ ὄντι
try, I πειράω, πειράομαι
turn around, I ἀναστρέφω,
ἐπιστρέφω
turn myself, I τρέπομαι
turn, I τρέπω
twelve δώδεκα
twenty εἴκοσι
two δύο
two hundred διακόσιοι

U

under ὑπό
understand, I συνίημι,
ἐπίσταμαι

unjust ἄδικος
unless εἰ μή
until ἔως, ἔως ἄν, πρίν,
πρὶν ἄν
unwilling(ly) ἄκων
up ἀνά, ἄνω
use, I χράομαι
useful χρήσιμος,
χρηστός
useless ἄχρηστος

V

very good ἄριστος
very many (plural of)
πλεῖστος
very μάλα, πάνυ
very much μάλιστα,
πλεῖστος
victim, sacrificial ἱερεῖον
victory νίκη
viewing θεωρίᾱ
virtue ἀρετή
visit, I φοιτάω
voice φωνή
vote, I ψηφίζομαι

W

wage war, I στρατεύω,
στρατεύομαι
wagon ἄμαξα
wait (for), I μένω
wait, I ὑπομένω
wake (someone) up, I
ἐγείρω
walk, I βαδίζω,
πορεύομαι
wall τεῖχος
want, I βούλομαι, δέομαι
war πόλεμος
war, I go to πολεμέω
war, I make πολεμέω
ward off from myself, I
ἀμύνομαι
ward off, I ἀμύνω
watch, I θεάομαι, θεωρέω

water ὕδωρ
wave κῦμα
way ὁδός, τρόπος
way, in any πως
wealth πλοῦτος
weapon ὅπλον
weep, I δακρύω
well done! εὖ γε
well εὖ, καλῶς
well, I am καλῶς ἔχω
What do you think? τίνα
γνώμην ἔχεις;
what? τί; τίς;
whatever (πάντα) ὅσα ἄν
when ἐπεί, ἐπειδή, ὅτε,
πότε, ὡς
whenever ἐπειδάν,
ὁπόταν
where (in the world)? ποῦ
γῆς;
where ᾗπερ, ὅπου, ποῖ,
ποῦ
where?, from πόθεν;
whether ... or
πότερον ... ἤ
which ὅς
while ἐν ᾧ, ἔως
who, whose, whom, which,
that ὅς, ὅσπερ
who? τίς;
whoever ὅστις ἄν, ὅσοι
ἄν
whole ἄπᾱς, πᾶς
why? διὰ τί;
wickedness πονηρίᾱ
wife γυνή
wild beast θήριον
wild ἄγριος
willing, I am ἐθέλω
win, I νῑκάω
wind ἄνεμος, πνεῦμα
wine οἶνος
wine-shop οἰνοπώλιον
wing κέρας
winter χειμών

wisdom σοφίᾱ,
σωφροσύνη
wise man σοφιστής
wish, I βούλομαι, ἐθέλω
with luck σὺν θεοῖς
with μετά, σύν
withdraw, I ἀναχωρέω,
χωρέω
within ἐντός
withstand, I ἀνθίσταμαι
wolf λύκος
woman γυνή
wonder (at), I θαυμάζω
woods ὕλη
word λόγος
work ἔργον, πόνος
work, I ἐργάζομαι, πονέω
worry, I φροντίζω
worthy (of) ἄξιος
wrecked ship ναυάγιον
write, I γράφω
writing γράμματα
wronged by you (pl.)
ἀδικούμενοι ὑφ' ὑμῶν

X

Xanthias Ξανθίᾱς
Xanthippus Ξανθίππος
Xerxes Ξέρξης

Y

year ἔτος
yield, I εἴκω, ἐνδίδωμι
yoke, I ζεύγνῡμι
you (singular) σύ
young man νεᾱνίᾱς
young νέος
your (singular) σός, (plural)
ὑμέτερος

Z

Zeus Ζεύς
Zeus, by μὰ Δία
Zeus, O ὦ Ζεῦ

INDEX

This index is selective; it usually does not include proper names in Greek passages (see the Greek to English Vocabulary for the first occurrences of proper names.) Numbers in boldface refer to illustrations. At the end of the Index is a separate listing of Greek words and terms for grammatical and cultural reference.

Greek Words

CREDITS

Front cover and pages 37, 39, 58, 64, 123, 143, 226, 227: Alison Frantz, Princeton. Frontispiece: Drawing by Catherine Balme. Page 6: Deutsches Archäologisches Institut, Athens. Page 11: T.A.P. Service, Athens. Page 13, 34, 72, 105, 114, 210, 228: Reproduced by courtesy of the Trustees of the British Museum. Page 20: Epidaurus Museum (photo Museum). Page 21: Drawing by John Cavacco Page 46: Photograph by Gilbert Lawall. Page 86: Map by Catherine Balme. Pages 100, 107, 151: Antikenmuseum Berlin, Staatliche Museen Preußischer Kulturbesitz. Page 119, 128: All rights reserved, The Metropolitan Museum of Art. Page 135: Hirmer Fotoarchiv, Hirmer Verlag, München. Page 174: Louvre, © Photo R.M.N. Pages 178, 190: Based on maps in *The Athenian Trireme* by J. S. Morrison and J. F. Coates, © 1986 by Cambridge University Press. Page 197: Acropolis Museum (photo Museum). Page 224: Catherine Page Perkins Fund, Courtesy, Museum of Fine Arts, Boston.

ACKNOWLEDGMENTS

We wish to thank the following for reading Book II of this course in its final stages of preparation and for help with the macrons, innumerable constructive suggestions, and corrections of errors: Stephen G. Daitz of The City University of New York; Douglas Domingo-Forasté of California State University, Long Beach; Cynthia King of Wright State University, Dayton, Ohio; and Z. Philip Ambrose of the University of Vermont. We wish to thank Marjorie Dearworth Keeley, Quirk Middle School, Hartford, Connecticut, for typing the greater part of these books into the computer, preparation of the end vocabularies and indexes, proofreading, and innumerable suggestions for improvement of layout and format. The authors themselves bear responsibility for any errors remaining.

Maurice Balme
Gilbert Lawall